HUMAN SEXUALITY 95/96

Twentieth Edition

Editor

Susan J. Bunting
Lincoln College

Susan Bunting is an adolescent therapist at Chestnut Health Systems, and she is an instructor of sociology and psychology at Lincoln College. She received her B.S. and M.S. in sociology and Ed.D. in curriculum and instruction from Illinois State University. She has taught, counseled, trained, and developed curriculum in human sexuality, sexual abuse, substance abuse, self-esteem, child and human development, learning disabilities, marriage, family, and intimate relationships. She publishes pamphlets, instructional materials, articles, and books in these areas.

A Library of Information from the Public Press

Cover illustration by Mike Eagle

The Dushkin Publishing Group, Inc.
Sluice Dock, Guilford, Connecticut 06437

The Annual Editions Series

Annual Editions is a series of over 65 volumes designed to provide the reader with convenient, low-cost access to a wide range of current, carefully selected articles from some of the most important magazines, newspapers, and journals published today. Annual Editions are updated on an annual basis through a continuous monitoring of over 300 periodical sources. All Annual Editions have a number of features designed to make them particularly useful, including topic guides, annotated tables of contents, unit overviews, and indexes. For the teacher using Annual Editions in the classroom, an Instructor's Resource Guide with test questions is available for each volume.

VOLUMES AVAILABLE

Africa
Aging
American Foreign Policy
American Government
American History, Pre-Civil War
American History, Post-Civil War
Anthropology
Archaeology
Biology
Biopsychology
Business Ethics
Canadian Politics
Child Growth and Development
China
Comparative Politics
Computers in Education
Computers in Business
Computers in Society
Criminal Justice
Developing World
Drugs, Society, and Behavior
Dying, Death, and Bereavement
Early Childhood Education
Economics
Educating Exceptional Children
Education
Educational Psychology
Environment
Geography
Global Issues
Health
Human Development
Human Resources
Human Sexuality
India and South Asia

International Business
Japan and the Pacific Rim
Latin America
Life Management
Macroeconomics
Management
Marketing
Marriage and Family
Mass Media
Microeconomics
Middle East and the Islamic World
Money and Banking
Multicultural Education
Nutrition
Personal Growth and Behavior
Physical Anthropology
Psychology
Public Administration
Race and Ethnic Relations
Russia, the Eurasian Republics, and Central/Eastern Europe
Social Problems
Sociology
State and Local Government
Urban Society
Violence and Terrorism
Western Civilization, Pre-Reformation
Western Civilization, Post-Reformation
Western Europe
World History, Pre-Modern
World History, Modern
World Politics

Cataloging in Publication Data
Main entry under title: Annual Editions: Human sexuality. 1995/96.
    1. Sexual behavior—Periodicals. 2. Sexual hygiene—Periodicals. 3. Sex education—Periodicals. 4. Human relations—Periodicals. I. Bunting, Susan J., comp.
II. Title: Human sexuality.
ISBN 1–56134–360–9   155.3'05   75–20756

Twentieth Edition

Printed in the United States of America

Editors/ Advisory Board

To the Reader

In publishing ANNUAL EDITIONS we recognize the enormous role played by the magazines, newspapers, and journals of the *public press* in providing current, first-rate educational information in a broad spectrum of interest areas. Within the articles, the best scientists, practitioners, researchers, and commentators draw issues into new perspective as accepted theories and viewpoints are called into account by new events, recent discoveries change old facts, and fresh debate breaks out over important controversies.

Many of the articles resulting from this enormous editorial effort are appropriate for students, researchers, and professionals seeking accurate, current material to help bridge the gap between principles and theories and the real world. These articles, however, become more useful for study when those of lasting value are carefully *collected, organized, indexed,* and *reproduced* in a *low-cost format,* which provides easy and permanent access when the material is needed. That is the role played by *Annual Editions.* Under the direction of each volume's *Editor,* who is an expert in the subject area, and with the guidance of an *Advisory Board,* we seek each year to provide in each *ANNUAL EDITION* a current, well-balanced, carefully selected collection of the best of the public press for your study and enjoyment. We think you'll find this volume useful, and we hope you'll take a moment to let us know what you think.

> Sex lies at the root of life, and we can never learn to reverence life until we know how to understand sex.
> —Havelock Ellis

The above observation by one of the first sexologists highlights the objective of this book. Learning about sex is a lifelong process that can occur informally and formally. With knowledge comes the understanding that we are all born sexual, and that sex, per se, is neither good nor bad, beautiful nor ugly, moral nor immoral.

While we are all born with basic sexual interests, drives, and desires, human sexuality is a dynamic and complex force that involves psychological and sociocultural dimensions in addition to the physiological ones. Sexuality includes an individual's whole body and personality. We are not born with a fully developed body or mind, but instead we grow and learn; so it is with respect to our sexuality. A great deal of our sexuality is learned. We learn what "appropriate" sexual behavior is, how to express it, when to do so, and under what circumstances. We also learn sexual feelings—positive feelings such as joy and the acceptance of sexuality, or negative and repressive feelings such as guilt and shame.

Sexuality, which affects human life so basically and powerfully, has, until recently, received little attention in scientific research, and even less attention within higher education communities. Yet our contemporary social environment is expanding its sexual and social horizons toward greater freedom for the individual, especially for women and for people who deviate from societal norms—those who are somehow handicapped and those who make less common sexual or relationship choices. Without proper understanding, this expansion in sexual freedom can lead to new forms of sexual bondage as easily as to increased joy and pleasure. The celebration of sexuality today is most likely found somewhere between the traditional, rigid, repressive morality that is our sociosexual heritage and a new performance-oriented, irresponsible, self-seeking mentality. However, there are many signs of growing public disagreement and controversy as to where that appropriate balance exists.

In trying to understand sexuality, our goal is to seek a joyful acceptance of being sexual and to express this awareness in the most considerate way for ourselves and our sexual partners, while at the same time taking personal and social consequences into account. This anthology is aimed at helping all of us achieve this goal.

The articles selected for this edition cover a wide range of important topics and were written primarily by professionals for a nonprofessional audience. In them, health educators, psychologists, sociologists, sexologists, and sex therapists writing for professional journals and popular magazines present their views on how and why sexual attitudes and behaviors are developed, maintained, and changed. This edition of *Annual Editions: Human Sexuality 95/96* is organized into six sections. *Sexuality and Society* notes historical and cross-cultural views and analyzes our constantly changing society and sexuality. *Sexual Biology, Behavior, and Orientation* explains the functioning and responses of the human body and a range of common, and not-so-common, sexual behaviors and practices. *Interpersonal Relationships* provides suggestions for establishing and maintaining intimate, responsible, quality relationships. *Reproduction* discusses some recent trends related to pregnancy and childbearing and deals with reproductive topics, including conception, contraception, and abortion. *Sexuality through the Life Cycle* looks at what happens sexually throughout one's lifetime—from childhood to the later years. Finally, *Old/New Sexual Concerns* deals with such topics as violence and rape and issues and dynamics of males, females, and their relationships with each other.

The articles in this anthology have been carefully reviewed and selected for their quality, currency, and interest. They present a variety of viewpoints. Some you will agree with, some you will not, but you will learn from all of them.

Appreciation and thanks go to Loree Adams for her suggestions and expertise and Cynthia James for her organization and assistance. We feel that *Annual Editions: Human Sexuality 95/96* is one of the most useful and up-to-date books available. Please let us know what you think. Return the article rating form on the last page of this book with your suggestions and comments. Any book can be improved. This one will continue to be—annually.

Susan J. Bunting
Editor

Contents

Unit 1

Sexuality and Society

Eleven selections consider sexuality from historical and cross-cultural perspectives and examine today's changing attitudes toward human sexual interaction.

A. HISTORICAL AND CROSS-CULTURAL PERSPECTIVES

B. CHANGING SOCIETY/CHANGING SEXUALITY

The concepts in bold italics are developed in the article. For further expansion please refer to the Topic Guide, the Index, and the Glossary.

Unit 2

Sexual Biology, Behavior, and Orientation

Eleven selections examine the biological aspects of human sexuality, sexual attitudes, and sexual orientation.

The concepts in bold italics are developed in the article. For further expansion please refer to the Topic Guide, the Index, and the Glossary.

Unit 3

Interpersonal Relationships

Five selections examine the dynamics of establishing sexual relationships and the need to make these relationships responsible and effective.

The concepts in bold italics are developed in the article. For further expansion please refer to the Topic Guide, the Index, and the Glossary.

Unit 4

Reproduction

Seven articles discuss the roles of both males and females in pregnancy and childbirth and consider the influences of the latest birth control methods and practices on individuals and society as a whole.

Unit 5

Sexuality through the Life Cycle

Nine articles consider human sexuality as an important element throughout the life cycle. Topics include responsible adolescent sexuality, sex in and out of marriage, and sex in old age.

Unit 6

Old/New Sexual Concerns

Sixteen selections discuss ongoing sexual concerns of sexual hygiene, sexual harassment and violence, and gender roles.

The concepts in bold italics are developed in the article. For further expansion please refer to the Topic Guide, the Index, and the Glossary.

ARTICLE LIST

The following list of article titles, article numbers (in parenthesis), and page numbers are listed alphabetically for convenience and easy reference:

The concepts in bold italics are developed in the article. For further expansion please refer to the Topic Guide, the Index, and the Glossary.

Topic Guide

This topic guide suggests how the selections in this book relate to topics of traditional concern to students and professionals involved with the study of human sexuality. It is useful for locating articles that relate to each other for reading and research. The guide is arranged alphabetically according to topic. Articles may, of course, treat topics that do not appear in the topic guide. In turn, entries in the topic guide do not necessarily constitute a comprehensive listing of all the contents of each selection.

TOPIC AREA	TREATED IN:	TOPIC AREA	TREATED IN:
Abortion	9. Feminism at the Crossroads 17. Psychotrends 30. Philosopher's Stone 31. Men, Sex, and Parenthood 34. Abortion, Adoption, or a Baby?	**Attitudes/Values (cont'd)**	31. Men, Sex, and Parenthood 34. Abortion, Adoption, or a Baby? 35. How Should We Teach Our Children? 36. What Do Girls See? 37. Coming Out in Care 38. Let the Games Begin 42. Doctors and Others Need to Know 44. Future of AIDS 45. Campuses Confront AIDS 54. Why Don't We Act Like the Opposite Sex? 55. Men, Women, and Computers 56. Women and Men 57. It's a Jungle Out There 58. Blame Game 59. Ending the Battle between the Sexes
Abuse	7. Fine Line 36. What Do Girls See? 49. Breaking the Silence 50. Is *This* Sexual Harassment? 51. Pain of Sexual Harassment 52. When "No" Isn't Enough 53. Sexual Correctness 56. Women and Men 57. It's a Jungle Out There 58. Blame Game 59. Ending the Battle between the Sexes		
Aging	10. Sex in America 12. Male Hormone Molds Women, Too 33. How Far Should We Push Mother Nature? 38. Let the Games Begin 41. Do Men Go Through Menopause? 42. Doctors and Others Need to Know 43. Sexuality and Aging	**Birth Control/ Contraception**	1. Closer Look at Sexuality Education 2. New Generation 28. Choosing a Contraceptive 29. Female Condom 30. Philosopher's Stone 31. Men, Sex, and Parenthood 33. How Far Should We Push Mother Nature? 34. Abortion, Adoption, or a Baby? 35. How Should We Teach Our Children? 36. What Do Girls See? 48. Preventing STDs
AIDS	1. Closer Look at Sexuality Education 2. New Generation 10. Sex in America 11. New Sexual Revolution 20. Sex and the Brain 29. Female Condom 31. Men, Sex, and Parenthood 35. How Should We Teach Our Children? 36. What Do Girls See? 37. Coming Out in Care 44. Future of AIDS 45. Campuses Confront AIDS 46. HIV Dating Game 47. AIDS Update	**Females/Female Sexuality**	4. Who Should Wear the Apron? 6. When Is a Woman Not a Woman? 7. Fine Line 9. Feminism at the Crossroads 11. New Sexual Revolution 12. Male Hormone Molds Women, Too 15. Truth about Women and Sex 16. Sexual Arousal of College Students 19. Power and the Pride 20. Sex and the Brain 24. Motivating the Opposite Sex 36. What Do Girls See? 42. Doctors and Others Need to Know 43. Sexuality and Aging 54. Why Don't We Act Like the Opposite Sex? 56. Women and Men
Attitudes/Values	1. Closer Look at Sexuality Education 2. New Generation 3. Late-Night Talk Show 4. Who Should Wear the Apron? 5. Family, Work, and Gender Equality 6. When Is a Woman Not a Woman? 7. Fine Line 8. Man Troubles 9. Feminism at the Crossroads 10. Sex in America 11. New Sexual Revolution 17. Psychotrends 18. Born Gay? 19. Power and the Pride 20. Sex and the Brain 21. Hearts and Minefields 22. Lifting the Gay Ban 23. Lessons of Love 24. Motivating the Opposite Sex 26. Adultery of the Heart 28. Choosing a Contraceptive 30. Philosopher's Stone	**Gender Equality/ Sex Roles**	2. New Generation 4. Who Should Wear the Apron? 5. Family, Work, and Gender Equality 6. When Is a Woman Not a Woman? 8. Man Troubles 9. Feminism at the Crossroads 11. New Sexual Revolution 17. Psychotrends 18. Born Gay? 19. Power and the Pride 20. Sex and the Brain 24. Motivating the Opposite Sex 27. Forecast for Couples 31. Men, Sex, and Parenthood 36. What Do Girls See?

TOPIC AREA	TREATED IN:	TOPIC AREA	TREATED IN:
Gender Equality/ Sex Roles (cont'd)	51. Pain of Sexual Harassment 55. Men, Women, and Computers 56. Women and Men 57. It's a Jungle Out There 58. Blame Game 59. Ending the Battle between the Sexes	**Pregnancy (cont'd)**	35. How Should We Teach Our Children? 40. Sex 42. Doctors and Others Need to Know
Homosexuality	9. Feminism at the Crossroads 11. New Sexual Revolution 18. Born Gay? 19. Power and the Pride 20. Sex and the Brain 21. Hearts and Minefields 35. How Should We Teach Our Children? 36. What Do Girls See? 37. Coming Out in Care 44. Future of AIDS 45. Campuses Confront AIDS 46. HIV Dating Game 47. AIDS Update	**Sex Education**	1. Closer Look at Sexuality Education 2. New Generation 3. Late-Night Talk Show 15. Truth about Women and Sex 28. Choosing a Contraceptive 30. Philosopher's Stone 35. How Should We Teach Our Children? 36. What Do Girls See? 42. Doctors and Others Need to Know 43. Sexuality and Aging 44. Future of AIDS 45. Campuses Confront AIDS 48. Preventing STDs 59. Ending the Battle between the Sexes
Males/Male Sexuality	4. Who Should Wear the Apron? 8. Man Troubles 11. New Sexual Revolution 12. Male Hormone Molds Women, Too 13. Premature Ejaculation 14. Etiology and Treatment of Early Ejaculation 16. Sexual Arousal of College Students 18. Born Gay? 20. Sex and the Brain 21. Hearts and Minefields 24. Motivating the Opposite Sex 31. Men, Sex, and Parenthood 42. Doctors and Others Need to Know 43. Sexuality and Aging 54. Why Don't We Act Like the Opposite Sex? 56. Women & Men	**Sexual Dysfunction**	7. Fine Line 10. Sex in America 12. Male Hormone Molds Women, Too 13. Premature Ejaculation 14. Etiology and Treatment of Early Ejaculation 15. Truth about Women and Sex 27. Forecast for Couples 40. Sex 41. Do Men Go Through Menopause? 42. Doctors and Others Need to Know 43. Sexuality and Aging 46. HIV Dating Game 56. Women and Men 57. It's a Jungle Out There
Media	3. Late-Night Talk Show 4. Who Should Wear the Apron? 5. Family, Work, and Gender Equality 6. When Is a Woman Not a Woman? 8. Man Troubles 9. Feminism at the Crossroads 11. New Sexual Revolution 17. Psychotrends 19. Power and the Pride 23. Lessons of Love 27. Forecast for Couples 31. Men, Sex, and Parenthood 35. How Should We Teach Our Children? 36. What Do Girls See? 53. Sexual Correctness 55. Men, Women, and Computers 56. Women and Men 58. Blame Game 59. Ending the Battle between the Sexes	**STDs (Sexually Transmitted Diseases)**	1. Closer Look at Sexuality Education 2. New Generation 10. Sex in America 11. New Sexual Revolution 17. Psychotrends 28. Choosing a Contraceptive 30. Philosopher's Stone 31. Men, Sex, and Parenthood 35. How Should We Teach Our Children? 48. Preventing STDs
Pregnancy	5. Family, Work, and Gender Equality 17. Psychotrends 19. Power and the Pride 30. Philosopher's Stone 31. Men, Sex, and Parenthood 32. Reproductive Revolution 33. How Far Should We Push Mother Nature? 34. Abortion, Adoption, or Baby?	**Therapy/Counseling**	3. Late-Night Talk Show 4. Who Should Wear the Apron? 8. Man Troubles 9. Feminism at the Crossroads 11. New Sexual Revolution 13. Premature Ejaculation 14. Etiology and Treatment of Early Ejaculation 15. Truth about Women and Sex 24. Motivating the Opposite Sex 25. Soul Mates 27. Forecast for Couples 36. What Do Girls See? 37. Coming Out in Care 39. Ways to Make Your Marriage Sexier 40. Sex 41. Do Men Go Through Menopause? 43. Sexuality and Aging 45. Campuses Confront AIDS 49. Breaking the Silence 51. The Pain of Sexual Harassment

Sexuality and Society

- Historical and Cross-Cultural Perspectives (Articles 1–7)

- Changing Society/Changing Sexuality (Articles 8–11)

People of different civilizations in different historical periods have engaged in a variety of modes of sexual expression and behavior. Despite this cultural and historical diversity, one important principle should be kept in mind: Sexual awareness, attitudes, and behaviors are learned within sociocultural contexts that define appropriate sexuality for society's members. Our sexual attitudes and behaviors are in large measure social and cultural phenomena.

For several centuries, Western civilization has been characterized by an "antisex ethic" that encompasses a norm of denial and beliefs that sex is bad unless it is controlled or proscribed in certain ways. These certain ways have usually meant that sexual behavior should be confined to monogamous heterosexual pair bonds (marriages) for the sole purpose of procreation. Fear, myth, and lack of factual information or dialogue have maintained antisex and, many say, harmful beliefs, customs, and behaviors. Today, changes in our social environment—widespread availability of effective contraception, the liberation of women from the kitchen, the reconsideration of democratic values of individual freedom and the pursuit of happiness, and increasingly open dialogue about sex and sexuality—are strengthening our concept of ourselves as sexual beings and posing a challenge to the antisex ethic that has traditionally served to orient sexuality.

As a rule, social change is not easily accomplished. Sociologists generally acknowledge that changes in the social environment are accompanied by the presences of interest groups that confront and question existing beliefs, norms, and behavior. The contemporary sociocultural changes with respect to sexuality are highly illustrative of such social dynamics. Many of the articles in this section document changes in the social environment while highlighting the questions, confrontations, and beliefs of different groups about what are or should be our social policies regarding sexuality. The articles also illustrate the diversity of beliefs regarding what was beneficial or detrimental about the past, and what needs to be preserved or changed for a better future.

The fact that human sexuality is primarily a learned behavior can be both a blessing and a curse. The learning process enables humans to achieve a range of sexual expression and meaning that far exceeds their biological programming. Unfortunately, however, our society's lingering antisex ethic tends to foreclose constructive learning experiences and contexts, often driving learning underground. What is needed for the future is high-quality pervasive sex education to counteract the locker room, commercial sex, and the trial-and-error contexts in which most individuals in our society acquire misinformation, anxiety, and fear—as opposed to knowledge, reassurance, and comfort—about themselves as sexual people.

A view of the past illustrates the connectedness of our values and perceptions of sexuality with other sociopolitical events and beliefs. Cross-cultural perspectives provide common human patterns and needs with respect to sexuality and other interpersonal issues. Several of the articles in this section describe and examine patterns of change in political, economic, medical, and educational spheres as they relate to sexuality, while exploring and challenging present sociocultural, educational, medical, and legal practices in controversial areas. These areas include education in school and public media, sex roles and expectations, AIDS, family planning, contraception, homosexuality, censorship, and what constitutes appropriate vs. abusive sexual interaction. Although the authors may not agree on the desirability of the changes they describe or advocate the same future directions, they do emphasize the necessity for people to have information and awareness about a wide range of sexual topics. They also share another belief: We as individuals and as a world society have a vital interest in the translation of social consciousness and sexuality into a meaningful and rewarding awareness and expression for all of society's members.

The first subsection, *Historical and Cross-Cultural Perspectives*, contains seven articles on sexuality-related issues in settings as varied as China, India, the former Soviet Union, Denmark, Sweden, Finland, Japan, Africa, and the United States. Each article challenges the reader to question why cultures dictate and/or proscribe certain beliefs, values, or practices. They also link misinformation about sexuality to problematic personal, interpersonal, and societal consequences. Each article connects each country's sociocultural beliefs to its sex education, sex

roles, and prescribed and proscribed sexual behaviors. Each article calls for increased awareness, understanding, and acceptance as avenues for more positive sexual experiences for individuals and improved sexual health.

The four articles that make up the second subsection, *Changing Society/Changing Sexuality*, illustrate the varied, even conflicting, nature of the changes occurring in the sexual arena. The first two articles appear at first glance to be about two opposing positions: the women's and men's movements. However, upon closer examination, many of the same issues are raised calling for common ground. The next two articles look at changes in American attitudes and sexual behaviors. "Sex in America: Faithfulness in Marriage Is Overwhelming" compares a variety of behaviors of people in different age brackets. The final article looks at sexuality issues of the 1970s, 1980s, and 1990s.

Looking Ahead: Challenge Questions

What kind of sex education did you have in elementary school? Do you think fifth grade (10- to 11-year-olds) is too early, too late, or about the right time for education about anatomy, physiology, and reproduction? Explain your answer.

Have you ever spoken to a young person from another culture/country about sexuality regarding ideas, norms, education, or behavior? If so, what surprised you? What did you think about their perspective or ways?

Have you ever called into a radio (or television) show dealing with sexuality questions or issues? Do you think they help people and society? Why, or why not?

What are your impressions of the women's and men's movements? What role, if any, do you see them playing as we approach the twenty-first century?

What beliefs, interests, or behaviors, if any, do you consider unmanly or unwomanly? How do you feel about the current overlap of gender roles?

Do you think people are more sexually active today than they were five years ago? How much do you think fear of STDs/HIV affects sexual changes and behavior? Why?

A CLOSER LOOK AT SEXUALITY EDUCATION AND JAPANESE YOUTH

Tsuguo Shimazaki

Secretary General and Director,
The Japanese Association for Sex Education
Tokyo, Japan

Translated by Yoshimi Kaji,
Graduate Student, New York University, New York

In April 1992, the Japanese Ministry of Education revised its "Course of Study," the public school curiculum which is generally renewed once every decade. This is the fifth revision of the curriculum since the Japanese Democratic Educational Reformation in 1945. Among the changes, the following items have received a particularly sensationalized media response:

1) The secondary sexual characteristics (such as voice changes, growth of hair, menstruation, maturation of the reproductive organs, etc.) for both females and males will be taught in co-educational health classes for fifth graders; and

2) The development of the fetus in the mother's uterus will be taught in the curriculum called "Continuity of Life" in science classes for fifth graders.

Until recently, no education about sexuality has been included in elementary school, save for an hour lecture from the school nurse to girls in the fifth or sixth grade concerning menstruation and female hygiene. The secondary sexual characteristics have only been taught in junior high schools in health education classes. The additional information listed above added to elementary school health and science classes is ground-breaking.

Initial reactions to the Ministry of Education's changes in the curriculum were favorable. Japanese television and newspapers, for instance, reported with enthusiasm. Many reporters wrote, "We finally started sexuality education for elementary school children!" However, it is my opinion that these changes are far from the launching of true sexuality education in Japan. The Japanese Ministry of Education also feels adamantly that sexuality education has not been instituted. A letter from the Ministry states, "The new content is to be part of health education and science classes. This is not the establishment of sexuality classes." For the institution of sexuality education in Japan, the curriculum would also need to include information about responsible relationships and respect for other people's sexual existence, not simply the mechanism of menstruation and ejaculation.

Most Japanese teachers — especially fifth grade teachers — have received the addition of sexuality information to science and health curricula rather negatively. They have found the new material quite troublesome to teach, since many elementary level teachers find talking about menstruation in front of male students and ejaculation in front of female students very difficult. Most of them wish to keep the old way of teaching and would like to avoid talking about sexuality.

What Keeps Japan from Sexuality Education

The sensationalism of the mass media and the drastic reactions from the general public demonstrate quite clearly the need for human sexuality education in Japan. The Japanese Association for Sexuality Education (JASE) is a private advocacy organization, which was founded in 1974 to establish comprehensive sexuality education in the schools. The task has been difficult, since most Japanese teachers are not in favor of sexuality education, and, therefore, most schools have generally failed to include sexuality in the curricula. Traditional Japanese culture and the lack of sexuality training for teachers have contributed to the problem. In fact, in Japanese culture there is no such concept as human sexuality. For the most part, teachers who were raised in traditional Japanese culture find it difficult to establish their own sexuality, and even more difficult to teach the concept to young people. In Japan, to be a teacher, one must graduate from a teacher's college or must attend a regular university and earn credits to become certified. In these colleges and universities, there are very few chances to receive sexuality information. When offered at all, these instructions are buried in courses such as health education, biology, psychology, and philosophy of education. In short, there is no such thing as sexuality education in teacher's colleges.

Another factor blocking sexuality education in Japan is an uncooperative Japanese school administration system. It is not an overstatement to assert that the Japanese Ministry of Education controls everything related to the educational system, especially in the elementary and junior high schools. The school superintendent and the individual teachers do not have control over what is taught in the classroom. The Japanese Ministry of Education establishes the course of study and defines the overriding framework. This happens through an executive body called the Municipal Board of Education. If a group of teachers in a school were to try to develop a human sexuality curriculum, they would first have to consult with the chief teacher in the school, bring up the subject at a teachers' conference in order to get feedback and cooperation, and then obtain approval from the school superintendent. The school superintendent would then informally ask the Municipal Board of Education for approval. If the changes were acceptable and stay within the frame work of the Course of Study, they would be instituted. The Japanese way for decision-making is indeed very democratic. However, it can be cumbersome and work against the institution of new subjects in the classroom, especially controversial ones like human sexuality education.

A third and more specific problem is the issue of authorization concerning textbooks and teaching material. All textbooks used in the Japanese public school system must be screened and authorized by the Ministry of Education according to the Course of Study guidelines. Moreover, individual teachers have no freedom to choose which textbooks will be used in their classrooms. All textbooks are selected by the Municipal Board members with input from representatives from each school. There are no exceptions to this screening process, and textbooks selected are used throughout the entire district. In private schools — which make up 1% of all Japanese elementary schools and 6% of junior high schools — the situation is a little better, since teachers are freer to choose their own texts. Whether the authorization of textbooks is in direct violation of an individual's right to education is a critical issue up for debate in Japanese education today. In fact, a lawsuit has been filed to protest the Ministry's screening and authorization of textbooks as unconstitutional.

Finally, the problem which is commonly referred to as "examination hell" is an important issue to explore. Japanese people are famous for their enthusiasm for having their children work hard, achieve high grades, and continue on with higher education, which in Japan includes high school, junior colleges, and universities. The Japanese school enrollment rate for elementary and junior high school levels is extremely high at 99.99%. High school, even though technically attendance is not required, enrolls 98.5% of all eligible Japanese young adults. The rate of enrollment for junior colleges and other means of higher education is 37.5%.

Children in elementary school often have no time for play, since they often attend daily preparatory sessions after regular schools hours. This is so they may prepare for the entrance examinations of the higher schools. This philosophy of education affects not only children but teachers. What most parents perceive as a good teacher is one who pushes as many students as possible into better and higher schools. Since Japanese entrance examinations require an enormous amount of memorization, "good teachers" concentrate only on subjects such as Japanese, Mathematics, Science and Foreign Language (English). Of course, human sexuality education falls outside of the rubric of "examination hell" study subjects, and it tends to be ignored by both parents and teachers.

From Sex Education into Sexuality Education

Thus far, I have focused on Japanese sexuality education in a rather pessimistic way, since regretfully educators for the most part do not favor sexuality education. However, I can proudly assert that Japanese sexuality education is well on its way, thanks to the efforts of enthusiastic individual teachers and the organizations that support them.

In June, 1980, the Japanese Association for Sexuality Education (JASE) published sexuality guidelines for teaching in elementary grades through high school. Although the guidelines are published by JASE, a private organization without official sanction, the guidelines are highly regarded, especially by teachers interested and willing to start sexuality education in their classrooms. In JASE's *Sexuality Education Course of Study*, the same themes are repeated several times in each grade level with increasing age-appropriate depth and content. Each unit explores the psychological, physical, and sociological aspects involved with every sexuality topic. These guidelines are systematically structured to include a wide range of aspects covering human sexuality. Not only was JASE's *Sexuality Education Course of Study* ground-breaking in 1980 when it was first published, but today, after three revisions, the guidelines are still viewed as a dependable sexuality education guide. The Municipal Board of Education in each district has its own guidelines for sexuality education. These were mostly written in 1960 to reinforce "morality and chastity education," rather than human sexuality education. It has been a recent trend to revise these old guidelines into new and more appropriate ones by introducing the concept of healthy sexuality. In order to do so, many Municipal Boards have followed JASE guidelines.

Many teachers have long considered education concerning sexuality to be merely a lesson in biology or so called "sex ed." Today, however, some teachers are beginning to have a fuller conceptualization of the meaning of teaching sexuality and are actually calling such programs "sexuality education." The number of teachers who are interested in human sexuality education is increasing. Every year, during summer vacation, many private seminars, conferences, and study meetings concerning the topic are being held all across Japan.

This summer, there were about 20 such major seminars with more than 20,000 teachers in attendance. These 20,000 teachers are willing to initiate human sexuality education in their own schools, and such are the seeds of sexually education, which we hope will grow influentially to power in the near future. For now, human sexuality education is usually taught during homeroom with the assistance of the school nurses. The nurses — responsible for the school clinics — are also expected to counsel students and guide teachers concerning matters of sexual health and sexual problems. This is so because in Japan there are no school counselors.

Although the press erred in its announcement that a new era of sexuality education is upon us, there is an exciting opportunity for teachers to begin to institute human sexuality under the new guidelines calling for sexuality information to be added to health education and the science curricula. Not all fifth-grade teachers are feeling troubled by the idea of discussing sexuality with their students, and there are those teachers who have been looking forward to this opportunity for a long time. These teachers must be encouraged and supported, since sexuality education in Japan has a long way to go before it will be fully accepted by educators and the general society.

HIV/AIDS Education in Japanese Schools

HIV/AIDS education in Japanese schools has been intimately associated with sexuality education. Japanese society did not pay any attention to AIDS when it was first discovered in New York and Los Angeles in 1981. The announcement of Rock Hudson's AIDS-related death and the report of the first HIV-positive Japanese people, infected by imported tainted blood products in 1985, received a small amount of attention by some Japanese people. In 1987, reports of the first Japanese woman with AIDS were greatly sensationalized by the media, which allowed people to begin to realize the significance of AIDS in the world and at home. Nonetheless, the initial Japanese response HIV/AIDS was very modest.

The Japanese Ministry of Education was also quite sluggish in responding to the epidemic. In February 1987, the Ministry sent out an official letter for the "distribution of the knowledge of AIDS prevention." The letter was sent to all the boards of education calling for HIV/AIDS education in each of the individual schools. In March 1988, the Ministry of Education published the official teaching manual entitled *Guidelines For A Curriculum on AIDS* for all schools in the public system. For the most part, these guidelines were ignored. In fact, they were mostly routed to the school clinic library without ever being opened. After 1990, more AIDS cases through heterosexual sexual contact were publicized in Japan. The misunderstanding that AIDS was only a threat for homosexual men began to be diminished.

Finally, education professionals took HIV education more seriously.

The Japanese Ministry of Education recently published a pamphlet called *AIDS: A Correct Understanding* which was distributed to 500,000 high school students. Because the pamphlet recommended the use condoms for HIV/AIDS prevention, many high schools refused to distribute it to students. The Ministry of Education has begun to take positive actions to resolve these problems by revising teaching guidelines and providing seminars for the supervisors of school health departments and for the Municipal Boards. Various seminars are being held all over Japan for health education teachers and for school supervisors concerning HIV/AIDS education. However, there needs to be still more education for teachers about AIDS.

Informal Sexuality Education and Japanese Youth

It is difficult to evaluate the effectiveness of informal education on young people today, but it is perhaps the most influential educational system concerning sexuality. Traditionally, for Japanese children, peer education was an important factor contributing to socialization and education. Children learned how to play, how to fight, and how to relate to children of the other gender, through contact with older children in their same peer group. Male Youth Groups and Female Youth Groups once played an important part in the coming-of-age for each member of a traditional Japanese village, especially where sexuality was concerned. Today, however, these community groups have been lost due to rapid changes in the social environment, such as urbanization, the decrease in number of children born to each family, the decrease in space for playgrounds, and an emphasis on intellectual and formal educational systems to the exclusion of other systems. Without the guidance of such groups, children are surrounded by a flood of confusing sexual messages and information.

In the summer of 1990, a movement to ban comic books was started by the mother of an elementary school girl who wrote a letter to a national newspaper, complaining that the comic books her daughter was reading were overtly sexual. The "Porno-Comic Persecution" movement urged its members to try to stop the publishing and selling of such magazines to children. Others suggested that the police regulate over-the-counter sales of these kinds of comic books. Naturally, this became a political issue concerning freedom of expression vs. the appropriate environment for children. Regulations were tightened in the name of maintaining an environment suitable for young people. Publishers and book stores publicly announced that they would regulate themselves, and the maelstrom died down. However, the public opinion resulting from this movement was that sexual information in comic books directly affects children's sexual behaviors and are therefore harmful.

In objection to the idea that comic books with sexual content directly threaten young people and should be regulated by law the JASE conducted a survey in 1991 called "Youth and Comics." The survey showed that junior and senior high school students enjoyed comics that were "funny," "action-packed," or "scary," but the respondents reported that they were not so interested in comics with "overt sexual messages." Respondents also reported that they received most of their sexual information from "friends and seniors of the same gender," "magazines," and "television." Very few pointed to comic books as an influential source for sexual information. The survey report concluded that blaming comic books for children's behavior is short-sighted.

Compared to the sexual behavior of American young adults, Japanese youth are more moderate, according to nationwide survey of sexual behavior in Japanese youth conducted by JASE in 1987. This survey shows that only 19% of males and 14% of females have experienced sexual intercourse by the age of 18. The survey was given again in 1992 with a slight increase in these rates. This time 22% of males and 16% of females had experienced sexual intercourse by the age of 18. The traditional value system still binding Japanese youth may explain their moderate sexual behavior. For example, the virginity of young females is considered very important to the maintenance of the traditional male-centered family system. Even as we near the 21st century, the Japanese people still hold on to the old non-democratic male-cen-

tered system. Additionally, Japanese people tend to worry about appearances a great deal. It is difficult for a Japanese person to establish an individual identity, especially one that might be negatively perceived by family, peers, and co-workers. This tendency keeps Japanese youth from actively engaging in premarital sexual activities and other unsanctioned sexual behaviors. Further, the preoccupation with passing examinations may keep young people too busy to engage in such recreational activities. In fact, JASE's youth survey showed an increase in sexual activities after the age of 18, which coincides with the end of examination hell, when university entrance exams are over.

Conclusion
With the defeat of Japanese nationalism and militarism after the Second World War, the democratic educational system emerged with emphasis on individualism. However, traditional value systems are not easily overcome. Sexuality education helps students be responsible for their own individual sexual choices, a result which may appear to oppose Japanese traditionalism. No one knows how long it will take before Japanese sexuality education is firmly rooted and viewed as a positive force in society. But a long fight against cultural values will most probably ensue. Facing these difficult odds, Japanese teachers who are aware of the importance of the struggle work daily to make real a new era of sexuality education.

College students . . . today are decisive, highly competitive, street smart and materialistic. They hate politics and drugs, love discos and flings, but no commitments please says . . .

THE NEW GENERATION

Rahul Pathak

He is as smooth as the gel on his hair. As cool as his deep-grey sunglasses. As rushed as the beat on his raunchy rap disc. He scratches a moustache, just starting to sprout, and says life is a bitch. Tame it or get bitten on the seat of your bell-bottoms. The new generation is playing by a fresh set of rules, OK?

Rule 1: *It's a war out there. Choose your weapons and make sure you are quick on the draw. If all you have got is a degree, you are dead.*

Rule 2: *You've got only yourself to bank on, so watch your back. Friends are potential rivals.*

Rule 3: *Idealism is a drag. Rebellion is a bum trip and no one has time for losers. Work the system.*

Rule 4: *If you've got it, flaunt it. Date in style, splurge like there is no tomorrow, pamper yourself.*

Rule 5: *Rules 1–4 are confidential. Mention them and they'll say you're hyper. Break them and they'll know you're totally bonkers.*

Through the '70s, they burned flags and smoked pot and launched their class struggle by boycotting classes. Rebellion was hip. The '80s were a hangover, in which the vastly unpopular 'library types' were hooted and jeered by the 'canteen types' who thought the system was screwed up, the job market dicey and sex far out but far away. But these discussions only served to kill time and cigarettes when campuses had plenty of both. There was a languor to college life that cushioned immediacy. Tomorrow was distant and dim. Anyone half-way bright could sail through it, because others were too busy learning to spell 'disestablishmentarianism' or drooling over possible dates.

Being carefree and irreverent was the done thing.

Suddenly someone put the evolutionary cycle on fast forward. Before the old-timers could say 'Fresher!' they saw their diffident, tangle-haired, *hawai-chappaled* colleagues transformed into stylish, no-nonsense youngsters who proffered business cards by way of introduction. An INDIA TODAY-MARG poll, conducted last month among a representative sample of 1,365 undergraduates across eight cities, including four metropolitan ones, shows that a whole new species now populates the colleges. It is 4.5 million strong, knows the landscape and has a stomach for battle.

Do you go on dates regularly? YES: 35.5% (Male) 15% (Female)

There has rarely been a generation so competitive across the board. The poll shows that as many as 68 per cent of them have their eyes already set on a zooming career and outrageous wealth. Pragmatism, that once-shameful word, is a conviction more than a slogan. Nearly 89 per cent believe that the job market opens its gates only when you exert 'influence', while merit bleats unattended. And 63 per cent say they will play the game and network to get ahead. Many of them are already on the job, and for nearly a third of college students, the most important aspect of university life is to make useful future contacts.

The romantics seem to have died unwept. Two-thirds of the undergraduates surveyed would settle for an arranged marriage and a third of them will pack their dowry, even as they rush into pre-

marital sex and casual affairs. They do not confuse raging hormones with the financially correct. While in the '70s, universities were founts of political ferment, today's generation doesn't want to buck the system. It is content with getting around it to get ahead. And politics is a real no-no: half said they would never be interested in getting involved in politics.

Bombay psychologist A. K. Srivastava terms it the 'Me-only' generation which only dreams of "my life, my money, my success, any which way". This is just the kind of attitude that university lecturers find easy to trash and difficult to understand. All they admit is that they have never seen a set like this.

For Indrani Majumdar, who teaches at Delhi University's Miranda House, this is a Rajiv-ite generation. "When Rajiv Gandhi first talked of liberalisation and computers these were the children listening to him," she says. They lapped up the consumerist ad spiel, imbibed a taste for life on the fast track and strived to achieve Yuppiedom. The poll, in fact, indicates that Rajiv remains their ultimate role model, years after his death.

Would you bribe someone if necessary? YES: 43% (Male) 34% (Female)

The new teenagers are also growing up in an era when socialist ideals are in the process of being ejected. Profit is no longer a bad word. And a new breed of unknown entrepreneurs are the engines of this radical change. People like Dhirubhai Ambani showed that you did not need an inheritance to create more wealth. You only needed street savvy.

INDIA TODAY-MARG Opinion Poll

INDIA TODAY commissioned MARG to conduct a survey among undergraduates in Bombay, Delhi, Madras, Calcutta, Mysore, Nasik, Allahabad and Cuttack. The sample of 1,365 students, equally split between the sexes and income groups, was weighted to match the population profile.

- My priorities in life: Good career 60%; Social service 18%; Happy marriage 13%, Fame: 8%

- Degree is of no use: YES 60%

- We are competitive: YES 75%

- My parents influenced my course choice: YES 69%

- Girls should not work after marriage: YES 34% (M), 17% (F)

- I will accept dowry: YES 31%

Nor do the means seem to matter. One indicator: in Delhi and Bombay campuses a surprise runner-up for the role model slot was stockbroker Harshad Mehta. Dr. Avdesh Sharma, vice-president of the Indian Psychiatrists' Association, has an explanation: "When no one appears clean, the message going down is that one should at least be successful."

The new generation's views are also being shaped by the turbulent political events that have marred the nation in the past 10 years. The Mandal firestorm crystallised a growing belief that in the new system merit was the first casualty. And that opportunities were shrinking and had to be grabbed.

Nor did teenagers have time for the inverse snobbery of the *jholawallahs*, whose wrinkled kurtas and dishevelled beards had taunted generations of ladder-climbers. "Students do not want to change the world any more. They just want to manipulate it," says Manish Tiwari, president of the Congress(I)-affiliated National Students Union of India (NSUI). The worldwide decline of communism seems to have had its effect too.

For the '90s generation, being Left was hardly the right thing to do. Marxists insist that reactionary is too good a word for this generation. "They should save their breath. They don't have much left," says Calcutta teenager Sourav Das, who plans to conquer the corporate world.

The life-style of the new brat-pack reflects the change. They date with a gusto that leaves orthodox campuses such as Ahmedabad's strewn with embracing couples and discotheques in Bombay throbbing through the night. In the survey more than a third of the boys say they date regularly. But they don't have time for the attendant niceties. Many romances start two hours after couples have met and can end the same evening. "They have wise heads. You can trust them to draw the line," says Anil Wilson, principal of St Stephens College in New Delhi.

Part of the reason is that parents have changed too. The dad of the '90s is perfectly willing to split a beer with his teenager and wink at his escapades. Mom drives her daughter to the harried career counsellor who would then be badgered by both. This is a generation in a hurry. It works hard, plays hard. It is not willing to lose out on anything except perhaps sleep.

Late-Night Talk Show: Giving Listeners What They Want

When it comes to the question of sex, ignorance is no longer bliss as far as many Chinese are concerned. The best source of information, they have found, is the radio.

SHAN QUANFENG

Shan Quanfeng is a lecturer at Beijing University.

IT'S 11:10 p.m., and the great, bustling metropolis of Shanghai has finally quietened down for the night. But not everyone is asleep, Thousands of people are glued to their radios, eagerly listening to the Shanghai People's Broadcasting Station, which has just gone on the air with its most popular program, "Night Talk on Sex."

In the not-so-distant past sex was a subject so embarrassing, even husbands and wives rarely spoke about it. Famous scholar Pan Guangdan described the situation at the time: "Adolescents are supposed to ask neither their parents nor teachers about sex. They find very few books on this subject and must read them in secret." A public airing of the topic — a radio talk, for instance — would have sent people into a state of shock.

But in the last 10 years or so, the Chinese attitude toward the subject has changed tremendously. Many parents are now paying closer attention to their children's sexual problems, schools have put sex education on the curriculum, and books dealing with the topic are appearing more and more often on the market.

Scientific studies and the dissemination of information on sex are growing as well. In 1986 the Sex Education Research Institute was established in Shanghai, the first in China. Around that time also, a number of magazines came out for public education on the topic. *Science of Sex*, *Sex Knowledge Handbook* and *Private Doctor* were among the more popular publications.

Local schools have put on special sex-education exhibitions. In 1988 the Shanghai municipal government held the Science Exhibition on Adolescence and Puberty, an event that drew tens of thousands of visitors. Similar shows were held in Beijing in 1990 and in Guangzhou in 1993. The latter drew 180,000 visitors over a period of 15 days. Radio stations got into the act fairly recently. Shanghai's "Night-Talk on Sex" was the first, starting up in October 1992, and the Guangzhou People's Broadcasting Station began broadcasting "Midnight 1 + 1" in June 1993. The most recent one to go on the air has been the educational program, "Health Teacher," put out by the Central People's Broadcasting Station in Beijing. All three programs have set up special post-office boxes and telephone hotlines to answer questions on sex.

Beijing's Adam and Eve Shop, which opened in February last year, is even bolder than the radio stations in dealing with the subject. Located on Zhaodengyu Road in the capital, this is the first shop in China to sell products related to sex. At the same time it does research and provides outpatient services to those in need, giving advice on such matters as the use of contraceptives, the prevention of venereal disease, and ways to overcome problems with the sex drive. Business was so brisk right from the start, the store opened a branch last June.

The new store is situated beside the Beijing People's Hospital (attached to the Beijing Medical Sciences University) and is named Adam and Eve Sex Goods. The typical customer at the shop is usually quite cool and unembarrassed about being there, and the sales assistants are amazed at how well the store is doing. The fact that the first Chinese sex shop came into being with so little fuss indicates that Beijing residents are psychologically ready for such a place. According to the manager, the main reason he opened this shop was to help wipe out people's ignorance about sex so that they could find their own way to better sexual health.

The 1990s are also witnessing the arrival of the sex-change operation in China. In July 1990 Professor He Qinglian, of the Shanghai Long March Hospital, completed the first successful sex-change operation, turning a man into a woman. In October of the following year he repeated the process, this time changing a woman into a man. In July 1992 Professor Xia Zhaoji of the Third Beijing Hospital (attached to the Beijing Medical Sciences University) exchanged the sexual organs of two patients, male and female, in one operation.

One must remember, however, that sexual enlightenment in China is still quite new and recent, and that all kinds of difficulties will continue to exist. Su Muhan, a research fellow at the Guangdong Provincial Birth Control and Sex Research Institute, claims the enlightenment hasn't gone far enough: Family and school, the main channels for spreading knowledge about sex, have done very little, he says, and government is paying scant attention to either doing research on or spreading public information about the subject. He adds that schools

need to set up formal, systematic sex-education courses, and that more parents need to overcome their reluctance to talk of sex in front of their children. He suggests that a special research institute be set up to study and spread greater knowledge about human sexuality.

A somewhat opposing view comes in an article by Xia Guomei in *Social Sciences* (second issue, 1993), which argues that people in our country have too suddenly been inundated with Western ideas on sex and sexual freedom and that as a result, a whole new set of sexual problems has sprung up. He thinks that to get research on sexual problems onto the right track, we should enhance studies on sexual dysfunction and establish a research institute devoted to studying and restoring psychological and sexual balance.

No matter how many different views there may be, you can't beat statistics, and a survey done by the Shanghai People's Broadcasting Station shows just how great people's interest is in this topic. Sixty percent

of Shanghai's senior-citizen couples tune in to "Night Talk on Sex," as do 80 percent of middle-aged cou-

---

The fact that the first Chinese sex shop came into being with so little fuss indicates that Beijing residents are psychologically ready for such a place.

---

ples and 90 percent of young couples. At least 60 percent of the city's high school students stay up late enough to listen and learn, and the most avid listeners of all are university students, 95 percent of whom never miss a show. There's no denying that in China, as in the rest of the world, sex is an important and fascinating topic to young and old alike.

Who Should Wear the Apron?

Editor's Note: As the pace of life speeds up in China, one of the most controversial topics in the country today is male-female relationships—especially the division of labor between the sexes in the workplace and between husband and wife at home. To show you the kind of discussions going on in China today, we bring you some excerpts from a running column on the topic in Chinese Youth News.

A Case of Incompatibility

YI DA

THE YOUNG man and woman were bitter. They were a well-educated couple — he held a university degree, she was a graduate from senior high school who had taken a college-level TV course in Chinese — but their marriage hadn't lasted. In some ways it was the question of education that had driven them apart.

When she finished her TV course and got a diploma, her work unit refused to promote her because, they said, her study-major had not been what they needed. She then started taking accounting, with the result that most of the housework responsibility fell on the husband's shoulders. Tensions mounted, tempers flared and serious quarrels broke out, often over such trivial matters as to who should do the cooking. The marriage ended in divorce.

"I *had* to get a diploma," the woman explained. "If you don't have a diploma, you don't get promoted — you don't even get housing. In all those years I spent on my education, I didn't have time to even do the shopping, never mind have a child. I would have loved to look after our home and do housework, it would have been much easier and more enjoyable than competing in society. But a voice inside me kept warning me that I had to have my own career, realize my own potential. Even if I lost my husband, I would still have my self-esteem."

"Well, who was it that put this great load on your shoulders?" her former husband wanted to know. "Why do you place such a high value on burdens generally regarded as belonging to men? If you had given half the time and energy you spent on yourself to us as a couple, I would have been 10 times more

---

It's a great, fascinating world out there. When you've spent the day staring at the four walls of your home, what have you got to talk about when your husband comes home?

---

effective at my job and we would have had a much easier life. How can you talk of increasing women's inner strength when you are always so worried about what would hap-

pen to you if you lived alone? Don't forget, half of men's achievements are made with the support of women."

Father as Baby-sitter

MENG CHUNMING

IN MY family the old formula that the man works outside the house and the woman works inside no longer holds true. My wife has gone to southern China to make money, while I'm back home, taking care of my son and at the same time slaving away at a full-time job. Life is pretty hard. As far as I'm concerned, every day is a Xeroxed copy of the one before: In the morning I hurry my son to kindergarten, then dash to the office to face the daily routine of poring over a pile of insipid documents. Back home from the office, I bolt down a mixture of instant noodles, sausage and vegetables. Then I go get my son and spend most of the evening being his playmate and reader, so he doesn't have time to think of his mother. Only when he's gone to bed and I've finished my housework can I actually sit down and read, write or relax.

I'm so tired all the time, I sometimes want to let go and curse. But I know it won't help me, so I keep myself under control.

My wife used to work in a foreign trade company. One day she came up to me with the idea of going to the south to see if she could make a success of herself. I had always wanted to try this myself, but she was ahead of me, so I agreed and stayed behind with our son.

Friends ask me why I gave my wife the freedom to go gallivanting around the country. I tell them, I understand and trust her. And this is true — but no one knows how much it costs me.

One night, while looking at my son fast asleep in his bed, I said to him silently, "Hurry up and grow so your father can get a chance to make something of himself!" By the time he's reached adulthood, though, I'll probably be too old.

We Don't Have Any Choice

XIAO JIN

WE'RE LIVING in a new era, an era of revolution, competition and struggle. Life is demanding, and we're constantly nagged by uncertainty. This holds true for both men and women, but while men see themselves as free to choose between family and career, too many of them ask women to forget the career and concentrate on family alone. Is this fair, or even reasonable?

Sure, it's an easy, comfortable life, staying home, doing housework, taking care of kids, shopping — but where does it get you? You can become dull, insipid, old, even ugly, and your husband may leave you for someone more interesting. If husband, family and home are all you've been used to, then without these you have nothing left, nothing to hold on to.

Women today have learned that devoting all their energies to the family unit does not necessarily help protect or strengthen it. They have to be independent economically and intellectually. The more you understand the society around you, the better you function as a person and the more useful you can be. Women have to improve themselves constantly so as to be able to understand men — also so that they themselves are interesting enough for men to care about understanding them. Being lovable is just as important as loving.

The problem is that many men can't take the idea of a "strong" woman. They say they want a woman to be tender, gentle and submissive, a person who is willing to devote herself entirely to taking care of house and home. Why? Because they're afraid — afraid to lose their so-called dignity and power, both of which are based on the concept of the weakness of women. With a nice, obedient wife at home this kind of man feels proud of his "strength" as the sole breadwinner and backbone of the family. But this kind of strength is like that of a paper tiger — it can't take a direct hit.

We women want to be both friends with men and human beings in our own right. To protect the family, a bastion of warmth and security in this competitive era, we have no choice, we *have* to play an active role in the affairs of society.

A Wife's Fear: I Might Be Sacrificing My Husband

ER NIU

WITH INCREASING workloads becoming the norm in the business world today, the load of housework at home seems to be getting heavier as well. There's a great deal of talk about proper home atmosphere, quality of life, relations between husbands and

Husband doing his share of the housework.

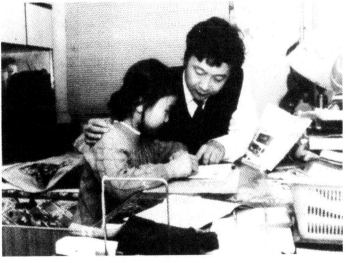

Father helping his little girl.

15

Wife and mother in her role as business executive.

wives, and so on, but where does a wife find the time to deal with it all? And the husband? I can just imagine what must go through my husband's mind as he sits at one of his interminable evening business meetings: "How am I going to find the time to fit in my poor kid's bedtime story tonight?"

When God made men and women, He gave them different characteristics and talents, so the old adage that women can do anything men can may not be true — and vice versa. Men are better than women at some things, women are better than men in others, and this holds true at home as well as in the workplace.

Personally, I love cooking, doing housework, decorating our home, and telling our child stories, yet I don't dare admit any of this to others. Why? I'm afraid they'll sneer and wonder why I bothered going through all those years of education, just to end up wishing I were a homemaker. Also, I often feel guilty because I suspect I'm sacrificing my

husband — I mean in the sense of dragging him into activities I like and am good at and in trying to make him constantly see things from a woman's point of view.

Is this wrong? Isn't a "model" husband supposed to be open-minded and flexible? I just don't know.

What's a Home All About?

PAN SUIMING

LET'S SUPPOSE a woman gives up her job and career in order to be a wife and mother, what kind of life will she lead? What is there at home for her to do that might make her feel like a useful member of society?

Housework: In Beijing, the average living space per citizen is no more than six square meters. Middle-aged couples might get as much as a two-room apartment. They don't have to worry about mowing a lawn or working on their

car or giving parties — they don't have enough space for any of these things. But pretty well every household has a washing machine and other labor-saving devices. So that, exhausting though it might be to spend eight hours on the job, two hours going back and forth to work, and two hours doing housework, staying home is worse because you might die of boredom.

Looking after children: The rule now is one child per couple. Even if the couple is rich enough for the mother to stay home all day, she won't see much of her child if it's old enough to go to school or be outside playing with other kids.

Devoting oneself to family relationships: It's a great, fascinating world out there. When you've spent the day staring at the four walls of your home, what have you got to talk about when your husband comes home? He might appreciate your services, but he won't feel any real interest in you. It's a dangerous thing to base a marriage on a husband's gratitude to his wife.

Improving yourself: This takes you back to those four walls again. If you're stuck inside all day, you can't catch up with what's going on outside in society. And if you don't have even the simplest kind of job or outside interest, how can you really improve yourself? One thinks of the aristocrats in the past who became mindless, loose-living dilettantes because they existed only inside their own little world.

We're told now that in the wealthy Zhu River delta area many wives are opting to stay home, and that this is a sign of social progress. Really? Then why did so many of the wives in this area join forces to sign an appeal for a crackdown on prostitution? Apparently it is not rare for their men to visit "ladies of the night" despite their progressive homes.... In other words, happiness in the family depends on many different factors; it doesn't necessarily depend on a stay-at-home wife.

FAMILY, WORK, AND GENDER EQUALITY
A Policy Comparison of Scandinavia, the United States, and the Former Soviet Union

Elina Haavio-Mannila, Ph.D.
Department of Sociology, University of Helsinki, Finland

The workplace is not separate from other human institutions. Workers bring into the workplace their values and expectations from home, from the community and from the larger society that bear on their relationships and aspirations at work. They also take home from the workplace feelings of frustration or worth that affect their roles as parents, community members, and citizens. To view work in isolation from other role relationships is to remove it from the normative context that sustains it and gives it meaning.[1]

The sociology of family and gender roles has long tended to link work, the family, and even the community and state. As early as 1956 social scientists presented strategies by which women could combine their traditional family obligations with paid work. Today we recognize that women have many more than two roles, and the contemporary interface of family and work produces many a dilemma. Most women now see the challenge they face not in terms of becoming exactly like men in their work lives or returning to the domestic hearth but in terms of restructuring the family and work roles both for themselves and for men as well.[2]

This article will first compare public work policy among Scandinavia, the U.S., and the former Soviet Union. Traditional work policies focus on norms and standards for safety, occupational health, and working conditions. Labor-market policy also includes workers' participation in management and ownership, as well as rules for collective bargaining. Family policies are a part of all developed nations, designed to give economic support to families. Some countries emphasize cash child allowances, others emphasize tax reductions. Family support -- with the exception of maternity insurance -- does not affect the labor market or the bargaining power of workers.

Background: Comparison of Work Policies
In the United States, large firms provide services that mirror those of government services. For instance, businesses have a social service component to deal with issues of alcoholism, drug abuse, and family needs; a justice component to address issues of equal opportunity; and an educational component to provide training.[3] Nevertheless, only a minuscule proportion of even the large firms have made determined efforts to reform their internal structure to better accommodate workers' needs. Rosabeth Moss Kanter suggests that the "new workplace" is less hierarchical, more egalitarian, and more conducive to the freedom that the new work force seeks.[4] This means bureaucratic control: a system of labor control that weakens bonds of solidarity among workers. In the U.S. auto industry, for instance, men and women who run the factories and staff the offices are said to do surprisingly well in the global competitiveness race — but only when managers give them a chance.[5] At General Motors and Ford, the companies for which we conducted research in 1988, the organization is said to be more authoritarian and patriarchal than in some newer branches of U.S. industry, like computer manufacturing, for example.

Scandinavia has been a forerunner in industrial democracy, management-worker cooperation, and work-safety research and policy. Discussions of the democratization of work life entered the political arena in Scandinavian countries around 1960, and since then many changes have been made.[6] Many Scandinavian organizations assumed new experimental forms with researchers, trade unions, and cooperative employers' organizations working together to bring about change. The Scandinavian countries revised work-safety laws in the 1970s, allowing the state to establish norms, supervise and sanction employer compliance through, for example, occupational inspections. Those inspections rely heavily on medical, chemical, and technical expertise. Since the 1980s, laws dealing with worker/management cooperation and workers' influence on decision making have guaranteed a degree of industrial democracy in all Nordic countries. Dialogue among partners in the labor market is encouraged, even to the point that the state intervenes as a third party in wage and fringe-benefit negotiations. It is considered important for work policy to encourage innovative organizational arrangements and to avoid polarization of work conditions and tasks.

Occupational health -- the prevention and treatment of occupational diseases and accidents -- is a major work-policy issue in Nordic countries. Recently, quality of work, the environment at work, and human relations in the work community have also become concerns of workers' health policy.[7] Work is an important part of the quality of life. A healthy, safe, and comfortable work environment which promotes motivating, meaningful work is believed to promote the health of workers, better productivity, and a higher quality product.

In the Nordic countries, there is at present a trend toward less governmental control of work life. This means that both public and private employers have an increasing "freedom of responsibility" in the development of working conditions. An additional goal of recent Finnish work policy is to increase self-initiation in work organizations.[8]

In the former Soviet Union, state control of individuals was strict. During the politically shaky, economically difficult, and inflationary last years of Communist rule, social policy could not guarantee reasonable welfare to pensioners, the ill, the handicapped, and many other groups in need of social services.

Family Policy in the United States

The United States is unique in its reluctance to address the issues of family roles and women's and men's work in the policy arena. European countries provide support to families, parents, and women in the form of children's allowances, paid parental leaves of absence, and maternity benefits. The United States, while paying lip service to the importance of families and children, has no comprehensive family policy and has been notably disinclined to pay the costs of government benefits and services for families, for working parents, and for women.[9]

Child allowances and tax reductions, which exist in the United States, are only a small part of family policy. Otherwise, the official infrastructure of the country does not encourage people to have and rear children.[10] Working hours are long;[11] paid parental leave is short, if paid at all. Only a portion of employers offer job guarantees for parents staying home without pay to care for a baby, the quality of municipal day-care centers varies (when such facilities are available), and high-quality private child care is expensive.

Some employers have privately developed measures to make the workplace more responsible to the needs of employees. Major companies are providing modest paid disability benefits at the time of pregnancy and childbirth, and some allow female employees brief additional unpaid but job-protected leaves. The 1970s saw a rapid expansion in the establishment of flex-time policies, but the trend has since slowed. Part-time work, in contrast, is growing, as is temporary work. The number of counseling services in the workplace has increased, and that expansion seems likely to continue. Childcare remains the family-related service most discussed in the workplace in the United States.

For years, a dramatic difference in vacation time between many European countries and the United States has existed. In Scandinavia, for instance, most employees have an annual paid vacation of five to six weeks. Further, daily work hours are considerably shorter than in the United States.

It is puzzling that, in the United States, women have high labor-force participation rates despite no benefit legislation, highly uneven coverage through collective bargaining, and modest benefits for sickness or maternity and parental leave. At the end of the 1980s, the proportion of women in the labor force was similar in the United States (45%) and Scandinavia (45%-48%). In the former Soviet Union, the proportion of women in the labor force at that time was over 50%. It is generally agreed that changes in the relationship between men and women and transformations in family life have had profound social repercussions. As the rate of divorces climbed and the ranks of women in the labor force has grown, a whole new set of issues relating to child support and the problems involved in mixing work and family have been raised in all income ranges in all countries.

Family Policy in Scandinavia

Gender equality is one of the main goals of Scandinavia's social democracies. Actual policy, however, has been developed according to conflicting views about the extent to which public policy should support family functions or substitute for the family through public-service arrangements.[12] According to detailed studies by Kamerman and Kahn, Sweden has the most comprehensive family policy of all capitalist countries. Finland and Denmark also have explicit policies, but they are focused more narrowly.

Policy in the Scandinavian countries supports employed parents in their attempts to cope with both work and family demands. Women, who have carried the main responsibility for care in the family circle and in the multigenerational chain, now receive help from public services in fulfilling the tasks of everyday life. Day care for children, elder care, home health services, and so on, have begun to liberate women from both family and intergenerational dependency.[13] The municipal day-care system covers a large proportion of children under school age (which is seven years).

Parental leave with 80% - 90% compensation for lost salary extends for 15 months in Sweden, 12 months in Finland, and about half a year in Denmark. Fathers as well as mothers are eligible for this leave. In the early 1990s, practically every eligible Swedish father used "daddy days" immediately after the birth of a child, and 34% of Finnish fathers took advantage of "daddy days" in 1989.[14] In addition, parents have their jobs guaranteed by law for several years if they choose to stay at home to care for their children. It is still predominantly mothers who take this longer period of parental leave.

The Nordic countries represent a special tradition of women's economic activity: early integration into the labor market, high labor-force participation rates, high rates of union organization, low unemployment, high segregation, frequent but "safe" atypical employment (part-time and temporary work), and relatively small wage differentials. Most of the stability of women's employment in Scandinavia was achieved by means of general economic policy, not so much by policies targeting gender equality in pay or employment opportunities.[15]

The Nordic countries have laws guaranteeing equality between men and women in society generally and at work. There are also state gender-equality councils and ombudsmen for coordinating public equality policy. Shortcomings and backlashes concerning gender equality still exist in the Nordic countries, however. The Nordic model has supported, perhaps even strengthened, segregation and gender division in the workplace. It has made women increasingly dependent on the state instead of on husbands: the private patriarchy has merely become public.[16]

From the point of view of gender equality in the labor market, Scandinavia and the United States show different developmental tendencies. The Swedish employment structure was, in the 1970s and 1980s, evolving toward two economies: one, a heavily male private sector; the other, a female-dominated public sector. Although there was a small increase in "female" job concentration, women were also moving into traditional male jobs. The share of women in privileged "male" occupations in the United States was twice that in Sweden.[17]

The present cuts in social services in Scandinavia due to economic recession will mean a reduction in employment opportunities for women.[18] Since 1970, women have composed almost two-thirds of the public employees in the Nordic Countries.[19] In 1985, the public sector employed almost every second working woman. In Denmark 45%, in Finland 39%, and in Sweden 55% of employed women were public employees.

Family Policy in the Former Soviet Union

A socialist vision of the future emphasized the importance of public life. Women's drudgery in the home would be replaced by public, collective arrangements in which men and women would participate freely and symmetrically. But the introduction of women into the labor force is not enough to produce change in the gender system. The traditional attitudes of male superiority in the former Soviet Union outweighed the pronouncements of official egalitarian ideology. No real change occurred in the roles of men; they merely looked on while women took more jobs. The main goal of recent Soviet social policy, according to Narusk,[20] was to reconcile the woman's duties in society and at home, to facilitate her ability to perform her dual role, and to lessen the differences in material welfare existing among families based on number of children.

As of the latter half of the 1980s, it was obligatory for both men (aged 16 - 59) and women (aged 18 - 54) to work or study outside the home. Free education (with grants to students in secondary and vocational schools and universities), free medical care (with payments for being on the sick list and also for time spent in the hospital), almost-free day-care centers, cash child allowances, and other social services helped families. There were practically no housewives who stayed at home, and women were supposed to take an active role in social life and politics.

A new stage in Estonian family policy began in the early 1980s, when the rights of state enterprises and collective farms were broadened to include the use of company social funds for the help of workers' families. Working mothers became entitled to paid maternity leave until their child was one year old and to additional unpaid leave until the child was 18 months old. A state grant was established for the birth of a first child, and a double sum for the birth of a second or third.[21] Mothers of small children were entitled to shorter working days or were given the opportunity to work at home, if their managers deemed this possible. The use of these measures depended on the good will of the managers and on the real amount of social funds at their disposal. There were great differences in benefits from enterprise to enterprise.

Lapidus identifies three features of the Soviet system that impede women's work freedom and choices.[22] First, sexual stereotyping of occupations was not eliminated. Second, female occupational choices were profoundly influenced by the continuing identification of both creativity and authority with men. Third, culturally and in legislation, household and family responsibilities were explicitly treated as the primary and proper domain of women. At the same time, shortages of consumer goods and everyday services made household responsibilities especially onerous.

The social policy system was supposed to satisfy the basic needs for food and housing, as well as for health, education, cultural and social services for all citizens without separate charge. However, the continuing lack of consumer goods and housing have made daily life difficult, and the quality of state services has been poor. For example, day-care facilities were often understaffed; children disliked them and got sick, adding to parental stress. In addition, the hours were too long for children, often nine hours a day, since most women worked, and full-time and flex-time did not exist.[23]

Nevertheless, the official Soviet ideology of gender equality was successful in some respects. For example, female-male gaps in the number of third-level science students, in the labor force, and in parliament, were smaller in the Soviet Union than in the capitalist countries studied. After the fall of the Soviet Union, however, women criticized the official gender-equality ideology for its lip-service. They questioned the value of gender equality in science, the labor force, and politics. For example, surveys of Estonian high school students in 1979 and 1990 showed that the value girls assigned to education, particularly technical studies, had diminished in the 1980s. The few girls who were interested in technology had low self-esteem.[24] According to a survey of 921 adult women in 1990, women valued family and children more than economic welfare. They also valued love, hobbies, friends, and relationships with their parents more than their jobs or studies.[25]

In 1990, Estonian women were relatively unconscious of inequality between men and women. More than half of the 921 respondents in the survey could not point out gender inequalities, a situation related to the fact that "'feminist' in Estonia is a word of abuse."[26] Opposition to forced equality during the Communist period resulted in a strengthening of traditional attitudes with regard to the position of women. In 1988-90, the Estonian women's movement proposed that women should concentrate on giving birth to many (Estonian) children and care for them at home.

The high number of women in the Supreme Soviets (parliaments) in the former Soviet Union was achieved by applying a 30% quota for women members in elected bodies at the national, regional, and local levels.[27] After the breakdown of the Soviet Union, the proportion of women sank in the representative political bodies of the Soviet republics. The legislature elected in independent Estonia in 1991, for example, included only seven women among 105 members. Women were simply not interested in running as candidates. Their attitude toward politics was negative and based on frustration and alienation. In the prior Communist period, women legislators were like toys in the hands of their male counterparts, even though some of the women were quite competent.[28] The Soviet Women's Committees were the only officially accepted women's organizations functioning on both the national and local levels during the period from 1940 to 1991, and they were not allowed to discuss women's social, economic, and political inequality, the existence of which was denied.

Summary

In the mid-1980s, the five countries we studied were ranked according to gender equality as measured by a combined index.[29] The comparison included 99 countries, representing 92% of the world's female population, and the index was based on 20 indicators, including health, marriage and children, education, employment, and social equality. The status of the women in the five countries in this study declined in the following order:

Sweden	(with a score of 87)
Finland	(85)
U.S.	(82.5)
Denmark	(80)
USSR	(70)

This comparison indicates that, in practice, there was more gender equality in Scandinavia and the U.S. than in the former Soviet Union.

Gender equality seems to be especially high in Scandinavia, according to another international comparison. The Human Development Index combined indices of longevity (life expectancy at birth); knowledge (adult literacy rate and years of schooling); and decent living standards (adjusted real gross domestic product). In 1990, the overall Human Development Index was on the same level for the U.S. (.976) and Scandinavia (Denmark .967, Finland .963, and Sweden .982), but lower in the USSR (.908). When the male-female disparities were taken into account, Scandinavian countries turned out to have higher scores (.878 for Denmark, .902 for Finland, and .886 for Sweden) than the United States (.809). Finland ranked highest among the countries of the world on this gender-sensitive index.[30]

The high level of social development in Scandinavia is reflected in people's satisfaction with life. At the beginning of 1980s, life satisfaction was higher in Scandinavia than in the U.S.[31] (Life satisfaction is part of a syndrome of positive attitudes toward the world in which one lives.)

Nowhere, however, has equality of economic opportunity for women followed automatically from their higher levels of educational attainment and labor force participation. The basic problem is still lower pay for women's work than for men's work. Men derive greater benefits from educational and occupational attainments, even when women's work ex-

perience and levels of current labor-force participation are comparable. The gender gap in wages is larger in the United States, where female wages are 69% of male wages, as compared to Scandinavia, where female wages vary between 76% and 84% of male wages.[32] In 1989, the average full-time earnings of women in the Soviet Union ranged from 65% to 75% of those of men.[33] Scandinavian countries have relatively high economic equality between men and women, but a gender gap in earnings remains.

We found by conducting social research and other comparative work among the three regions that type of society and type of workplace (with its specific gender composition) have strong connections with the organization of work, with the social relations at work and in the family, and with the well-being of women.[34]

Elina Haavio-Mannila is a professor of sociology at the University of Helsinki. She has published nearly 200 sociological books and articles in her main field of interest which is gender roles in the family, at work, and in politics. Haavio-Mannila has also conducted studies on medical sociology and sexual behavior. She has been a visiting scholar at the Center for the Education of Women at the University of Michigan and a visiting professor at the University of Minnesota, among others. Presently she is conducting a large study of sexual behavior in Finland with Osmo Kontula.

Author's References

[1] Epstein, C. The Cultural perspective and the study of work. In Kai Erikson & Steven Peter Vallas (eds.), The Nature of Work: Sociological Perspectives (New Haven and London: American Sociological Association Presidential Series and Yale University Press, 1990).
[2] Moen P. Women's Two Roles — A Contemporary Dilemma (New York: Auburn House, 1992).
[3] Vallas SP. The future of work. In Kai Erikson and Steven Peter Vallas (eds.), The Nature of Work: Sociological Perspectives. (New Haven and London: American Sociological Association Presidential Series and Yale University, 1990).
[4] Kanter, RM Men and Women of the Corporation. (New York: Basic Books, 1990.)
[5] Magnet M. The truth about the American worker. *Fortune Magazine*, May 4, 1992, pp. 48-65.
[6] Gustavsen B. Reforms on the place of work and democratic dialogue. In Jan Odhnoff and Casten von Otter (eds.), Rationalities of Work: On Working Life of the Future (Stockholm: Arbetslivscentrum, 1987).
[7] Komiteanmietinto. Report on the Committee on Working Conditions. (Helsinki: Valtion Painatuskeskus, 1991).
[8] Komiteanmietinto. Report on the Committee on Working Conditions. (Helsinki: Valtion Painatuskeskus, 1991).
[9] Moen P. Op. cit.
[10] Kamerman SB and Kahn AJ. Family Policy: Government and Families in Fourteen Countries (New York: Columbia University Press, 1978); Kamerman SB and Kahn AJ. Child Care, Family Benefits and Working Parents: A study in Comparative Policy (New York: Columbia University Press, 1981); and Kamerman SB and Kahn AJ. The Responsive Workplace (New York: Columbia University Press, 1987).
[11] Schor J. The Overworked American: The Unexpected Decline of Leisure (New York: Basic Books, 1991).
[12] Dahlstrom E. Theories and ideologies of family ideologies, gender relations and human reproduction. In Katja Boh et al

(eds.) Changing Patterns of European Family Life: A Comparative Analysis of 14 European Countries. (London and New York: Routledge, 1989).

[13] Simonen L. Change of Women's Caring Work at the Turning Point of the Welfare State — A Nordic Perspective. Paper Presented at the Fourth Annual International Conference of the Society for the Advancement of Socio-Economics, Graduate School of Management, University of California, Irvine, March 27-29, 1992.

[14] Haavio-Mannila E, Kauppinen, K. Women and the welfare state in Nordic countries. In Hilda Kahne and Janet Z. Giele (eds.) Women's Work and and Women's Lives: The Continuing Struggle Worldwide (Boulder: Westview Press, 1992).

[15] Allen T. The Nordic Model of Gender Equality and the Labour Market. Paper presented at the Fourth Annual International Conference of the Society for the Advancement of Socio-Economics, Graduate School of Management, University of California, Irvine, March 27-29, 1992.

[16] Ibid.

[17] Esping-Andersen, G. The Three Worlds of Welfare Capitalism (Cambridge: Polity Press, 1990).

[18] Julkunen R. The Welfare State at a Turning Point (Tampere: Vastapaino, 1992).

[19] Marklund S. Paradise Lost? The Nordic Welfare States and the Recession, 1975-1985. (Lund: Lund Studies in Social Welfare II, 1988 and Alestalo M. The Expansion of the Public Sector (Vammala: Sosiaalipolitiikka, 1991).

[20] Narusk A. Parenthood, partnership and family in Estonia. In Ulla Bjornberg (ed.) European Parents in the 1990s: Contradictions and Comparisons (London: Transaction Publishers, 1991).

[21] Ibid.

[22] Lapidus GW. Gender and restructuring: The impact of perestroika on soviet women. In Valentine M. Mogdaham (ed.) Gender and Restructuring (Oxford: Clarendon Press 1993).

[23] Laas A. The future for Estonian women: Real women are mothers. Family Research Institute of Tartu University, Estonia. (Stencil) 1992.

[24] Hansen H. Attitudes of Girls to Future Occupations. Paper presented at Finnish-Estonian Seminar on the position of women at work and in society, Tallinn, May 14-15, 1992.

[25] Narusk A. Satisfaction of women with work and family life. Paper presented at Finnish-Estonian Seminar on the position of women at work and in Society, Tallinn, May 14-15, 1992.

[26] Meri T. Feminist on Eestis soimusona (feminist is in Estonia a word of abuse) Naised Eestis 2(32), 28 February, 8, 1992

[27] Laas A. The future for Estonian women: Real women are mothers. Family Research Institute of Tartu University, Estonia. (Stencil) 1992.

[28] Kilvet K. Interview of Krista Kilvet, president of the Estonian Women's Union, Finnish Radio, July 1, 1992).

[29] Population Crisis Committee. Country rankings of the status of women: Poor, powerless and pregnant. Population Briefing Paper No. 20, June, 1988 (Washington: Population Crisis Committee).

[30] Human Development Report. Published for the United Nations Development Programme. (New York and Oxford: Oxford University Press, 1991).

[31] Inglehart R. Culture Shift in Advanced Industrial Society (Princeton: Princeton University Press, 1990).

[32] Human Development Report. Op. cit.

[33] Lapidus G. Op. cit.

[34] Haavio-Mannila E. Work, Family and Well-Being in Five North and East-European Capitals. (Helsinki: The Finish Academy of Science and Letters B:255, 1992); Haavio-Mannila E. Women's Work in Three Types of Societies (Ann Arbor, Michigan: University of Michigan, Center for the Education of Women, 1993).

When Is a Woman Not a Woman?

Olga Linde

Women are venturing into new sports. They take up karate and kick-boxing, self defence and judo, weight-lifting and body-building, football and water polo. Up to recently, men reigned supreme in these sports. Today, women are squeezing them out of their positions and have won a place for themselves in the sports Olympus. They seek new sensations, new adventures, fame, success and awards. They fiercely attack in the ring, tackle weights with veins swelling on their brows, train their belly muscles till they become hard as rock and in soccer adroitly tackle the ball taking it away from a rival.

Fans watching these matches from the stands experience conflicting feelings. On the one hand, one cannot but give due credit to the superb play of women soccer players or the bulging muscles of body-building women. On the other hand, what one sees strikes one with horror. What is all this for? I saw the amazement of the audience when Polish catch sportswomen clutched at each other's hair in a Moscow gym. Some faces expressed bestial delight, while others squeamish surprise, disgust and pity. What has a woman dragging another woman face down to the mat got to do with sport and beauty? Thoughts of perversion insinuated their way into my mind. But when the catch wrestlers washed the make-up off their faces and combed their hair, changed their clothes, they turned out to be quite ordinary, pleasant girls. Although perhaps rather jubilant and loud.

Who are those "new women"—goddesses or furies, latter-day eccentrics or forerunners of the future? What do they,

these tough karate fighters and kick-boxers think about the mission of the woman in our world, about the qualities seen by tradition as purely feminine? Of kindness? Tolerance? Beauty? I, for one, would like to pose just one question: what is beauty?

Is it beauty when a woman has shoulders and thighs like those of Muhammed Ali? Or Schwarzenegger's biceps? Or tackles with such dexterity that male hockey players may envy them? What do they dream about? A steel pole with iron weights on each end? Or an effete, flabby, languorous beau who likes to sit before a mirror or take a bath with fragrant additives and to spend lots of time combing his hair? For if a woman becomes a man, what should a man be like?

"I do not believe that such dreams haunt women," says Yelena Vaitsekhovskaya, Olympic champion in diving. "I know from my own experience, though I have done a lot of weight-lifting. I have particularly unpleasant memories of those training sessions. And I do not like women weight-lifting. Also I do not like water polo. You know, when a woman goalie leaps up in the water and the ball hurtles into her breast like a cannon ball, this is not a sight for those with weak nerves. Nor does a woman's head in a snuggly fitting rubber cap make an aesthetic sight.

"I am more inclined to accept women's football. Because it is more customary. And also, it is a game after all. You always watch it from a distance, as if it were shown on the TV screen. And you cannot hear what football players shout on the pitch. You can only guess."

"I think I should not even mention boxing and catch wrestling."

"Of course. In my view, a girl demonstrating karate or catch-wrestling holds with great pleasure will never be gentle and gracious. Sport in general (and not only those particular types), apart from everything else, fosters aggressiveness. It is easier for a man to cope with it: life offers him ample chances to display it and not to store it up. And what about a woman? Who would fancy living with a Rambo in a skirt? You have to conceal your aggressiveness, to give vent to it in sport. You no longer restrain yourself. You get accustomed to being equal to man in sport. For the aim is the same and the same means are used to attain it.

"But this is my personal opinion. I may be wrong."

It seems to me that each woman is free to be what she wants to be. Each affirms herself in her own way. Some women try on a flounced skirt before the mirror, others handle weights, some go to a tennis court and others get into the ring where no punches are faked and falls are hard. But whether you come into the ring, or stand on the tatami mat attempting to acquire male characteristics, a woman remains a woman, even against her own will, against her resolve to be tough, strong in our world based on power. She cannot get away from her own self, especially in moments of defeat. When she loses, she drops her head and weeps. Then her eternal, weak, female soul comes to the fore and words of consolation come to your lips . . . "Stop crying! Whatever you are—a goddess or a fury, a karate wrestler or football player, do not cry! Everything will come out alright!"

Abridged from the magazine SPORT IN THE USSR AND IN THE WORLD, No 10, 1991

A Fine Line

The complex issue of female genital mutilation sees social workers torn between interfering with cultural beliefs and protecting girls from abuse.

Lynn Eaton

Social workers are still struggling to come to terms with one of the most horrific forms of child abuse: female genital mutilation. Mixed up as it is with issues of race, culture and sex, many see it as one of the more complex areas of abuse they have to face.

The Department of Health made it clear under the Children Act and related *Working Together* guidelines that social services should take action if a case of potential mutilation came to light. But the Act emphasises working with parents, so how can social workers do so while taking account of the family's race and culture?

Social workers in Cardiff, which has a large Somali community, are struggling to deal with the issue, which they argue has been made even more problematic by the Children Act.

It is perhaps indicative of their sensitivity on the subject that South Glamorgan social services assistant director Bryan Hartley refuses to discuss the issue, although he recently wrote in a medical journal[1] that his department had had several referrals in the past two years but insufficient evidence to take legal action. Any social worker involved in a case of female genital mutilation is challenging a deep-seated cultural belief. For some social workers that in itself is a problem: are they being racist in trying to impose a western view on an African family?

Efua Dorkenoo, director of Forward, the foundation for women's health research and development, has no doubts about where professionals should stand. 'It is racism not to protect a child because they are of a different colour. If you were walking down the street and saw all the girls with one ear off do you think British society would sit there and say "It's their culture"?' She agrees the issues are complex, but adds: 'All child abuse cases are complex. This is no different.'

Inderjeet Wilkhu, a social worker in Hounslow who also works closely with Forward, has first-hand experience of dealing with African families which planned to have their daughters infibulated, the most severe form of mutilation (see box). Workers have to clarify their own thinking before tackling a family direct, she advises. 'You need to be very clear in your belief that this is abuse.'

Wilkhu carefully plans every session with families, mustering arguments about malpractices in other cultures, such as Chinese foot-binding or Hindu women who committed suicide on their husbands' funeral pyres, which have since died out.

She believes working with these families is a real test of all social work skills, and she argues that it is possible to change attitudes without resorting to the law. Often the mere threat of it is enough, just suggesting what would happen to a woman's children if she were found guilty under the Prohibition Act 1985.

Many of the families, who are often recently arrived refugees, have no idea about the role of social services, or even that any form of female circumcision is illegal here. The social worker must explain why they are there, what their legal powers are, and that female genital mutilation is legally prohibited.

They should also make clear their duty applies to all children in Britain, so the family does not feel it is being targeted because of its race or culture, she says.

But she also advises being positive. 'You should explain that you are required to work in partnership with them. You also have to provide them with positive feedback on other aspects of their child care.'

Many refugee families will have undergone traumatic experiences. Social workers should offer a sympathetic approach, fighting to improve other things in their lives such as benefits, housing or general health entitlement. Wilkhu says it is vital to gain the confidence of the family if it is to respond to any messages about mutilation.

Although the practice of mutilation is in itself an abuse, it often takes place within loving families which see it as being the best thing they can do for their daughters to improve their marriageable status. The mere fact that such abuse might take place does not mean the girl should be removed from the home.

As the school holidays loom the chances of a child being taken away for an operation grow. Sometimes the girl will have told someone at school she will return from the operation 'with a sore bottom'. In that case, a conference should be called to decide

From *Community Care*, July 21-27, 1994, pp. 16-17. Reprinted by permission of the editor of *Community Care*.

23

Female Genital Mutilation—The Facts

There are three types of female genital mutilation:

- circumcision, or sunna, is the least severe and involves removing the hood of the clitoris, but not the clitoris itself;
- excision is the partial or total removal of the clitoris with part of the small lips covering the opening of the vagina;
- infibulation, the most severe of all, is the removal of the clitoris, outer and inner lips of the skin around the vagina, and stitching the two sides of the remaining vulva together, leaving a small hole, the size of a small finger, for blood and urine to pass.

- Infibulation is widely practiced in Somalia, Djibouti, north and central Sudan. Other forms of mutilation are widespread in Ethiopia, Eritrea, Mali, and Sierra Leone
- Forward estimates 10,000 girls are at risk in Britain of having the operation, either here or abroad, each year

- The British government outlawed mutilation in 1985 under the Prohibition of Female Circumcision Act. The penalty is a fine or imprisonment for up to five years. But illegal operations are still taking place in Britain, particularly in east London. Many children go back to Africa for the operation
- The United Nations calls on all signatory nations to take measures to abolish such practices because of the effect on the child's health
- In *Working Together,* the Department of Health says Section 47 of the Children Act can be used to investigate if social workers have a reasonable case to suspect mutilation might be about to take place.
- Girls who have been infibulated can take as long as 20 minutes to urinate. Menstrual blood cannot easily escape. There is a high risk of infection, both urinary and of the womb itself, which can lead to infertility

- Sexual intercourse is impossible, which can lead to both sexual frustration and frigidity, and an alarmingly high marital breakdown rate, according to a recent survey of the Somali community in London, carried out by the NSPCC and London Black Women's Health Action Project. Fourteen per cent of the women surveyed had been married twice, 8.5 per cent three times, and some even four or five times
- Infibulated women in this country do not know where to go to be 'opened' before marriage, which would happen in their countries of origin. They often get pregnant without full intercourse and turn up at antenatal clinics, still infibulated, where doctors have no idea how to deal with them
- An ante-natal clinic at Northwick Park Hospital in Harrow, north west London, is the only one in the country offering a specialist service for women wanting to have their operation 'reversed'

who should meet the family, either a health visitor or social worker. Usually the police would not become involved at this stage.

Wilkhu says it is vital that any interpreter knows the legal framework. She knows of one social worker who visited a family with a male interpreter who took the family's side, completely undermining any work the social services might do.

Even though the child may be placed on the child protection register, it may not be necessary to take any formal action under the Children Act, she believes.

Some social workers will make an informal agreement with the parents for the girl to be medically examined on return from the holiday, or to be seen by the school nurse.

'The last resort is the legal framework,' says Wilkhu. The social worker can get an assessment order requiring the parents to take the girl to the doctor for medical examination or apply for a prohibited steps order, which would prevent the parents taking the child out of the country. But it should not be the responsibility of social workers to tackle the problem single-handed.

'Social workers should be the last line of intervention,' says Dorkenoo. 'The main intervention has to start with education. The local authority needs to start with a planned programme, acknowledging this as a child protection issue. Social services should co-ordinate this and the first thing they have to do is develop a policy.'

---

[1]Bryan Hartley, *Archives of Disease in Childhood,* BMJ Publishing Group, 1994

Man Troubles

Making sense of the men's movement

Cathy Young

Contributing Editor Cathy Young is a writer in Middletown, New Jersey. She is the author of Gender Wars, The Free Press.

Mas·cu·lism (mas'kyə liz'əm), n. 1. the belief that equality between the sexes requires the recognition and redress of prejudice and discrimination against men as well as women. 2. the movement organized around this belief.

Not to worry: This word is not in the dictionary. But it would be if the decision were up to Warren Farrell, Jack Kammer, and others activists in the men's movement.

The men's movement? Even the term evokes ambivalent feelings. Whenever, while working on this article, I mentioned that I was writing about the men's movement and added, "but not the guys who go into the woods and beat drums," the typical response from both women and men was, "Is there any other kind?"

In fact, there are hundreds of men's groups in the United States and Canada. Some are mainly "mythopoetic," geared to "healing" and rediscovering masculine archetypes (typified by Robert Bly's retreats for men). Most, however, emphasize social and political issues, protesting what they see as unfair treatment of men in areas ranging from divorce to health care.

Is sexism against men an oxymoron? A few points to ponder:

• Despite gender-neutral laws in many jurisdictions, pro-maternal bias in custody cases remains widespread. In a Georgia court recently, a father who stated at a hearing on support payments that the child was with him nearly half the time was told, "It's admirable that you want to spend time and actually do spend time with your child, but the *mother* has the responsibility for nurturing, parenting, and raising this child. Your responsibility is to provide child support."

• Alleged bias against girls in schools has been the focus of great concern even though boys are more likely than girls to drop out of school and less likely to go to college. Studies indicating that boys get more teacher attention in the classroom have been widely discussed, while findings that boys are punished much more often and more harshly than girls *for the same misbehavior* are ignored.

• The judicial system tends to treat female defendants more leniently than males. When a man and a woman are accomplices in a crime, the woman is more likely to be offered a plea bargain. And violence against women is singled out for media attention and legislative action. The Violence Against Women Act, passed by Congress this year as part of the crime bill, defines many crimes against women as federal civil-rights offenses and allocates federal funds to areas with the highest rates of crime against women. Yet nearly 65 percent of violent-crime victims and 75 percent of homicide victims are male.

• While 35,000 American men a year die of prostate cancer and 43,000 women die of breast cancer (at a somewhat earlier age), breast-cancer research gets six times as much federal money as prostate-cancer research.

• Abortion is widely available without the father's consent, but men can be forced by the courts to provide financial support for children they never wanted in the first place. Does this mean that only women have reproductive rights and that only men can be forced into parenthood?

The question is how to confront the real biases affecting men without lapsing into the whining and gender warfare that permeate modern feminism—and also show up in some masculist publications, where men said to be unjustly convicted of sexual assault are described as "political prisoners" and the status of

American males under feminist rule is compared to that of Jews in Nazi Germany. Men's advocates have had, at best, limited success in reaching the public. Whatever people may think of the National Organization for Women, they know about it; very few have heard of the National Coalition of Free Men (NCFM) or Men's Rights Inc. Representatives of these organizations are rarely asked for their opinions by the media, let alone by legislatures.

"We must disabuse ourselves of the notion that women are the only gender with valid items for the agenda, and that men constitute the only sex that has advantages to share," writes Baltimore journalist and activist Jack Kammer in the introduction to *Good Will Toward Men* (St. Martin's, 1994). The book consists of conversations with 22 women, including me, who speak of cultural norms and biases that are hurting men today—from the tendency to view sexual miscommunication as unilateral male victimization of women to the devaluation of fatherhood by both the welfare system and the treatment of divorced parents.

The interest in men's issues is a much-needed corrective to the increasingly obsessive tendency to focus on real or fictitious disadvantages affecting females and ignore those affecting males. Moreover, by encouraging more role flexibility for men as well as women, and in particular greater male involvement in home life, the men's movement may be an essential step in achieving the work/family balance often described as the key issue on the "women's agenda." Most men's activists see their cause as the other, neglected half of the feminist enterprise of gender-role transition. "The best, constructive message of feminism," Kammer says, "was to ask men to examine whether they believe that they are inherently superior to women in any important ways. That's very good, but that's only half the problem."

Unfortunately, masculism also has a tendency to adopt the less constructive traits and tactics of modern feminism, including polarizing rhetoric, exaggerated claims of victimization as the basis of political demands, and the tailoring of facts to fit ideology. If the movement becomes simply feminism with a scratchy face, it will be rightly derided as an attempt to convince the world that white heterosexual men are victims, too. But if men's advocates are consistent in applying principles of fairness and equality, they

> The interest in men's issues is a much-needed corrective to the increasingly obsessive tendency to focus on real or fictitious disadvantages affecting females and ignore those affecting males. Moreover, by encouraging more role flexibility for men as well as women, and in particular greater male involvement in home life, the men's movement may be an essential step in achieving the work/family balance often described as the key issue on the "women's agenda." Most men's activists see their cause as the other, neglected half of the feminist enterprise of gender-role transition.

will have much to say of value to women as well as men.

Perhaps the main reason that male claims of gender-based inequities are not taken seriously is that, in the minds of most people, gender oppression is synonymous with oppression of women. In their effort to counter this perception, some men's advocates are challenging not only the view that women are oppressed today but the assumption that women were historically the oppressed sex.

The strongest attack on this assumption comes from an unlikely source: Warren Farrell, formerly an activist in the women's movement and the only man elected three times to the board of the National Organization for Women. Farrell is the author of *The Myth of Male Power* (Simon & Schuster, 1993), which Barbara Dority, co-chair of the Northwest Feminist Anti-Censorship Taskforce, says has the "potential for being *The Feminine Mystique* of the men's movement." Farrell writes: "Feminism justified female 'victim power' by convincing the world that we lived in a sexist, male-dominated, and patriarchal world. *The Myth of Male Power* explains why the world was *bisexist*, both male *and* female-dominated, both patriarchal and matriarchal—each in different ways."

Farrell's book is filled with startling challenges to the standard view of gender inequity. Why, he asks, do we hear about the clustering of women in low-paid jobs but not about the clustering of men in dirty, physically demanding, hazardous jobs, or about the fact that 94 percent of workplace fatalities are male? Why is it that the higher mortality rates of blacks compared to whites are seen as clear evidence of racial disadvantage but the higher mortality rates of men compared to women are overlooked? If women killed themselves four times as often as men, rather than the reverse, wouldn't we be hearing about it from NOW and from Pat Schroeder? How were men empowered by the fact that they were the ones who got killed in wars?

In short, Farrell wants us to see the sacrifices often involved in the male role, from risking one's life in battle to breaking one's back in a factory. (The traditional husband who wanted his wife at home also made himself work harder to support her and the kids.) According to this view, both sexes were equally enslaved by a division of labor that was historically necessary to ensure survival: Men provided and protected so that women could bear and nurse children—and, since the survival of the species required more females, males were more "disposable."

Technological progress, Farrell says, eliminated most of the need for the old division of labor, enabling people to seek personal fulfillment. But because men were seen as the powerful sex, the reexamination of gender roles focused solely on female disadvantage. So role restrictions that oppressed women were largely eliminated, but those affecting men, such as the male-only draft, remained.

This version of history is surely more accurate than, say, Marilyn French's *The War Against Women* (Summit, 1992), according to which the human male is always in search of ever more ingenious ways to abuse and degrade the human female. Traditional sexual arrangements always had elements of social contract, not merely subjugation.

And yet it is far too simplistic to say that men's dominance in the outside world was balanced by women's dominance in the family. "Doesn't Farrell understand that economic power outside the home translates into power within the home?" says feminist writer Wendy Kaminer. "Of course, if the man loves the woman more than the woman loves the man, she has a certain power, and that's a real power. But it's so difficult to generalize. We can find five relationships in which the woman has more power emotionally and five relationships in which the man does."

Even many of Farrell's admirers, such as Barbara Dority, have doubts about the lengths to which he takes the "equal oppression" argument—particularly when it is not limited to recent Western history. On the status of women in Islam, Farrell comments, "If women had to promise to provide for a man for a lifetime before he removed his veil and showed her his smile, would we think of this as a system of female privilege?" He forgets that men in Muslim societies generally have had the power not only to restrict their wives' movements, and in many cases to kill them, but also to divorce them at will.

"If we can make meaningful comparisons," says Ferrell Christensen, a philosophy professor at the University of Alberta in Canada and co-founder of MERGE, the Movement for the Establishment of Real Gender Equality, "I'm inclined to say that in this culture and in this century men and women have been pretty equal. I would not say that this is true historically and at all times." It is more accurate to say, he writes in the pamphlet *The Other Side of Sexism*, that women often received compensations for their subordinate state (such as greater protection) and that men's dominant role often carried a high price.

One of the key issues that animated earlier feminists, from Mary Wollstonecraft to Simone de Beauvoir, was that the human condition was seen as embodied in men, and the activities that defined what it meant to be human were defined as male. "It is [the] unique human capacity…to live one's life by purposes stretching into the future—to live not at the mercy of the world, but as builder and designer of that world—that is the distinction between animal and human behavior," wrote Betty Friedan in 1963. "[M]an has always searched for knowledge and truth." Friedan knew that this destiny was not an easy one, and she even suggested that "men may live longer…when women carry more of the burden of the battle with the world" (anticipating the men's movement's concern with the longevity gap). But she clearly felt that women were hurt more by being left out.

If masculists often seem oblivious to this historical male advantage, it is in part because participation in the human enterprise no longer ranks high on the feminist agenda. In most universities today, the above passages from *The Feminine Mystique* would be branded as conservative. "Battle with the world" reeks of militarism; to speak of the search for knowledge and truth is to accept the patriarchal model of knowledge as possession; to exalt the capacity for building and designing one's world is to glorify white male rape of the earth; to elevate humans above animals is specieist. We are now supposed to see male "separateness" rather than female dependency as the problem, and to scoff at "male" notions of unique genius rather than lament the absence of a female Shakespeare.

The irony is that when "male" civilization and its accomplishments are devalued, the notion of male privilege is much easier to question. If traditionally masculine qualities turn from virtues

> Masculists are oblivious to the historical male advantage because participation in the human enterprise is no longer high on the feminist agenda. Today, many passages from *The Feminine Mystique* would be branded as conservative. To speak of the search for knowledge and truth is to accept the patriarchal model of knowledge as possession; to exalt the capacity for building one's world is to glorify white male rape of the earth; to elevate humans above animals is specieist. We are now supposed to scoff at "male" notions of unique genius rather than lament the absence of a female Shakespeare.

to defects, some men will say that gender oppression made them that way. And if individual liberty is declared to be a (white and bourgeois) male prejudice, the distinction between the burden of oppression and the burden of risk as the price to be paid for freedom will be blurred. Thus radical feminists undermine their own critique of patriarchy.

Similar contradictions can be observed within the men's movement. Many masculists seem to be saying simultaneously that the works of men have been a boon for humanity and should be admired *and* that the roles which enabled and sometimes pushed men to do those things were oppressive and bleak. Although Warren Farrell writes that the socialization of both sexes should combine the best of the "male" and "female" heritage, the overall sense one gets from *The Myth of Male Power* is that being expected to strive is a dismal fate ("Men are not human beings, they are human doings") and that to admire a man for his achievements is as sexist as it is to admire a woman for her large breasts.

Thus, although masculism challenges the politically correct view of women as an oppressed class, it often shares some key elements of P.C.: the "politics of identity," which eclipse the notion of a universal human condition; an antipathy to such Western values as rationality, competitiveness, and individual achievement; the tendency to view human experience as shaped primarily by restrictive social forces rather than individual will and action. Even Kammer, who generally urges both women and men to embrace self-reliance and optimism, echoes academic radicals with their theories of subtly enforced self-policing in liberal societies. He writes, "Men...are in the most maximum security prison of all, the prison that convinces its inmates that they are right where they want to be...and that if they ever begin to think otherwise, they must have a 'personal' problem."

Kammer says the prison metaphor is simply a dramatic way to make a valid point: Men often fail to see their problems as related to gender bias because they have been taught that they are the powerful sex. Yet the result rings uncannily similar to the radical feminist position caustically summed up by Christina Sommers in *Who Stole Feminism* (Simon & Schuster, 1994): "If...some women point out that *they* are not oppressed, they only confirm the existence of a system of oppression, for they 'show'

> Although masculism challenges the politically correct view of women as an oppressed class, it often shares some key elements of P.C.: the "politics of identity," which eclipse the notion of a universal human condition; an antipathy to such Western values as rationality, competitiveness, and individual achievement; the tendency to view human experience as shaped primarily by restrictive social forces rather than individual will and action. At its worst, masculism can sound like the <u>ne plus ultra</u> of political correctness: The pantheon of the oppressed is completed by the admission of straight white guys.

how the system dupes women by socializing them to *believe* they are free, thereby keeping them docile and cooperative."

At its worst, masculism can sound like the *ne plus ultra* of political correctness: The pantheon of the oppressed is completed by the admission of straight white guys. (That leaves us with no oppressor, but an impersonal entity like "the sex/gender system" might do.) Men's advocates often rail against the victim mentality, but they are hardly immune to its temptations: High-school football is "male child abuse"; circumcision is socially sanctioned violence against infant boys comparable to female genital mutilation; women who walk around looking sexy yet remaining unavailable are abusing men; and anyway, men's higher mortality rates are unassailable proof of victimhood.

Barbara Dority has often joined men's groups in opposing pro-censorship feminists. "As long as we're talking simple egalitarianism, we're delighted to work together," she says. "But I refused to participate in anything in the feminist movement that went under the banner of victimhood, and I don't think the mantle of victimhood looks much better on men than on women." The tendency to adopt "the politics of victimization" also disturbs Asa Baber, who has written *Playboy*'s "Men" column since 1982 and is a strong advocate of men's issues. "The focus on the male as victim," he says, "is simply going to deepen this culture of victimhood."

An ex-Marine, Baber has written about the damaging effects of the "masculine mystique," but he bristles at Farrell's description of the soldier as "war slave." He believes that the men's movement, including "mythopoetic" groups, can play an important role in countering negative cultural messages about men. But he does not like to see the movement collude in attacks on traditional masculinity—"the trashing of things like courage and fortitude is just absurd," he says—or try to "get men into therapy." In a speech at the Chicago Men's Conference last February, Baber noted, "It turns out that the men of this culture have been told by *both* the men's and the women's movement that they are not OK."

Baber warns, too, that the strident, chip-on-the-shoulder, Us-vs.-Them mentality that has made much modern feminism a caricature of itself has a mirror image on the men's side. As an example, he cites the angry mail he got from some regular readers after a column that advised men to be aware of the ways in which women often feel uniquely vulnerable in public places.

Other men sympathetic to the movement share these concerns. Mike Arst, a former photographer and typesetter in Seattle who became involved in men's groups a decade ago, moderates the men's issues forum on the Fidonet electronic bulletin board. Many of the complaints aired on such networks are understandable. A common theme is the perception that women want to have it both ways: to be equal in the workplace but to be protected from rough talk; to have the same opportunity to work in trades that require stamina, yet to enjoy special protection from violence. But Arst finds himself put off by "angry men" in search of causes. He recalls the activist who tried to draw him into an anti-circumcision crusade, demanding, among other things, the right for "mutilated" men to sue the hospital for trauma 20 years later.

"I agree with much of what Warren Farrell says about men and power," says Arst, 43. "But if I think of the men of my father's generation, the bottom line for them was *support*: They worked their asses off to support their families. It was something of which they were proud, and rightly so; they were *not* in a gulag."

It is easy to poke fun at male victimism, a stance likely to be dismissed as misogynist by the left and unmanly by the right. Yet it is ultimately a male response to the "culture of complaint" in which, with major help from feminists, we are now enmeshed. If victimization is the way to gain status—"authenticity," as Arst puts it, or "innocence," as Shelby Steele has written—one can hardly blame men for figuring out what works and trying to claim their share of the moral high ground.

One reason that laughable tit-for-tat arguments about which sex was more oppressed 500 years ago continue is that many feminists still use the "centuries of oppression" as a stick to beat men. It is hard to argue with Farrell's remark that the perception of men as having all the power and women as powerless (which was never quite true, and is plainly ludicrous when applied to American women in the 1990s) makes us reluctant to question

> Feminism not only displaced men from their traditional ground as the human norm but often depicted them as less than human. While 19th-century notions of male superiority in intellect and leadership are now taboo, Victorian views of female superiority in compassion, morals, and parental love are very much alive. Male putdowns of women are relegated to the lowbrow culture of Andrew Dice Clay; female putdowns of men are found on greeting cards and in the halls of Congress. Many men drawn to the men's movement are reacting at least as much to male bashing as to a frustration with male roles.

any expansion of female power. Increasingly, people are coming to see that here and now, biases against men are as harmful as biases against women (even Naomi Wolf teeters on the brink of this idea in her latest opus, *Fire With Fire*).

After all, feminism has not only displaced men from their traditional ground as the human norm but has often depicted them as *less* than human. While 19th-century notions of male superiority in intellect, creativity, and leadership are now taboo, Victorian views of female superiority in compassion, morals, and parental love are very much alive. Male putdowns of women are relegated to the lowbrow culture of Andrew Dice Clay; female putdowns of men ("What is the difference between bonds and men? Bonds mature.") are found on greeting cards and in the halls of Congress. Recently at the publishing house HarperCollins, a woman editor irked by a male colleague's behavior designed a "stamp out HarperCollins men" button (the male symbol and the letters "HC" in a red circle with a slash) that was spotted on quite a few female staffers.

Mike Arst speculates that most of the men drawn to the men's movement are reacting at least as much to male bashing as to a frustration with male roles. Some, like Warren Farrell and Ferrell Christensen, started out as champions of women's liberation but were repelled by the rise of anti-male feminism. Christensen says that he sought out men's groups such as the National Coalition of Free Men and Men's Rights Inc. because he was "more and more distressed at the hate movement that feminism was becoming."

The roles have changed as well as the images. One of Farrell's strongest points is that this century's social developments have reduced women's burdens far more than men's burdens. Childbirth became much safer and warfare became much deadlier. The notion that a husband owed protection to his wife outlasted the notion that a wife owed obedience to her husband. And since the advent of feminism, women have gained much greater role flexibility and much more choice between traditional and non-traditional lifestyles.

Accordingly, some activists see the "men's agenda" as a matter of truly equalizing the options available to both sexes. While young women today rarely see full-time homemaking as a viable long-term prospect (even if that is the way of life they would prefer), working part-time or taking a few years off to raise children is something many expect to do. Farrell's assertion that 90 percent of the men he has spoken to would like to do the same sounds a bit dubious. But even if it's only 33 percent, as a 1990 *Time* survey of college men showed, these men are likely to find that they have fewer opportunities than their female peers to exercise such a choice: For all the paeans to the new fatherhood, a great many people still look down on Mr. Moms.

"When [women] call and say, 'I have a family situation,' managers or employers think, 'Oh God, those women with their children,' but they think it comes with the territory," says Karen DeCrow, a feminist attorney in Syracuse, New York, and a former president of the National Organization for Women who works with men's activists on fatherhood and custody issues. "When men do it, they're considered somewhat weird, or not really interested in their jobs." Many masculists also complain that while women want equality in the "male" sphere of careers and achievement, they often want, at the same time, to preserve the superiority of motherhood.

This complaint has some validity. On a radio show I did with Jack Kammer, the host, Ann Devlin, chided us for our lack of outrage at the fact that women still earn less than men. When I suggested that the way to gain parity in the workplace was to encourage male participation in child rearing, Devlin huffily replied that I obviously didn't understand the "mystical bond" between mother and child that no other relationship could replicate.

> The outcry over battered women is leading to a situation in which men in some jurisdictions are virtually helpless against the flimsiest charges of abuse. Massachusetts Bar Association President Elaine Epstein recently wrote in the bar association newsletter: "The recent media frenzy surrounding domestic violence has paralyzed us all....The truth is that it has become impossible to effectively represent a man against whom any allegation of domestic violence has been made....In many [divorce] cases, allegations of abuse are now used for tactical advantage."

In its attempt to change attitudes, the men's movement deals with some explosive issues, including false accusations of rape and alleged bias against men in the treatment of family violence. When men's activists insist that husband beating is as big a problem as wife beating, it seems a sure way to make most feminists see red. Even Wendy Kaminer, who is highly critical of the "woman as victim" party line, comments that "it's like saying the moon is made out of green cheese." But while the claim is undoubtedly exaggerated, a body of solid research—from the 1985

National Family Violence Survey sponsored by the National Institute for Mental Health to a number of studies conducted in communities and in marital therapy clinics—supports the view that female violence is a major part of the problem.

Most of the evidence indicates that spousal assault is usually mutual, initiated in equal numbers by men and women. (When only one partner is physically abusive, it is as often the woman as the man.) True, in those domestic violence cases in which one partner is completely controlled and terrorized by the other, most of the victims are female; but such cases make up a tiny percentage of abusive couples. And while women obviously are at far higher risk of bodily damage in domestic fights, up to 15 percent of the serious injuries are to men. Researchers such as Anson Shupe, chair of sociology and anthropology at Indiana University/Purdue University in Fort Wayne, Indiana, and co-author of *The Violent Couple* (Praeger, 1994), confirm that male victims of even severe violence by female partners encounter widespread bias if they try to get the authorities involved. This side of the story, men's advocates say, is ignored by the media and by government, which see domestic violence as synonymous with woman abuse.

Meanwhile, the outcry over battered women is increasingly leading to a situation in which men in some jurisdictions are virtually helpless against the flimsiest charges of abuse. This claim is made not just by men's advocates but by Massachusetts Bar Association President Elaine Epstein, who recently wrote in the bar association newsletter: "The recent media frenzy surrounding domestic violence has paralyzed us all....The truth is that it has become impossible to effectively represent a man against whom any allegation of domestic violence has been made....In many [divorce] cases, allegations of abuse are now used for tactical advantage."

The men's advocates clearly have issues, but do they have a movement? Many men and women who are sympathetic to men's issues don't think so. It is difficult for most men, especially if they are not in the midst of a custody battle, to see any of their problems as gender issues. The movement's image can also be a handicap. Armin Brott, a Berkeley marketing consultant and writer who got involved in men's issues after becoming a father four years ago, says, "If you get labeled as being part of the men's movement, you're either out there dancing with wolves, or you're a woman hater. There's really no place to go if you're a progressive-thinking man."

One way to escape what can become a vicious cycle of masculism and feminism trying to outshout and out-whine each other is for men's activists to focus on specific issues, particularly disparities in the legal or social treatment of women and men. Divorce is a good example. The traditional paternal role may not have been such a bad deal in the past, with unique satisfactions that were not necessarily inferior to those of maternal nurturing. But high divorce rates mean that many men bear the burden of providing without the rewards of any kind of real fatherhood—old or new.

Whether or not pro-maternal bias exists in the courts is the subject of intense debate, with men's advocates (and many divorce lawyers of both sexes) on one side and many feminists on the other (claiming that, on the contrary, men with more money to pay for legal services can ride roughshod over their ex-wives). But it seems that many judges still take the view that the father's main post-divorce function is to provide financial support—what Al Lebow, founder of Fathers for Equal Rights of America, sums up as the "men as wallets" attitude. To many, the fact that non-custodial fathers' child-support obligations are enforced far more vigorously than are their visitation rights is a bitter symbol of the low regard in which fatherhood is held.

"The availability of the father is a crucial issue, and it's also one of the key issues around which a political men's movement can organize," says Laurie Ingraham, a family therapist in Milwaukee who was drawn to men's activism as a result of her relationship work, in which she "noticed that men were always being painted as the bad guys." And indeed, disenfranchised fathers are the political vanguard of the men's movement. Lebow, a Michigan salesman who lost custody of his two daughters and spent six years in courts battling for visitation enforcement, started his organization in 1979. Today, he says, there are about 275 fathers' rights groups in 47 states.

These groups have been pushing for joint custody laws, with varying degrees of success, and for better treatment of non-cus-

> One way to escape what can become a vicious cycle of masculism and feminism trying to outshout and out-whine each other is for men's activists to focus on specific issues, particularly disparities in the legal or social treatment of women and men. Divorce is a good example. The traditional paternal role may not have been such a bad deal in the past, with unique satisfactions that were not necessarily inferior to those of maternal nurturing. But high divorce rates mean that many men bear the burden of providing without the rewards of any kind of real fatherhood—old or new.

todial parents. They complain that divorced fathers are unfairly stigmatized as "deadbeat dads" and viewed as targets for punitive action, even though studies find that support non-compliance is related to many factors, from insolvency to denial of contact with children.

As the example of Ingraham shows, the issue of how parents are treated after divorce has attracted interest from women as well as men. The Children's Rights Council, founded by David Levy in 1985, advocates shared custody and has often addressed fathers' concerns. But it is also affiliated with Mothers Without Custody and Grandparents United for Children's Rights. About 40 percent of its members and state chapter coordinators are women. Palo Alto, California, attorney Anne Mitchell is the founder and executive director of the Fathers' Rights and Equality Exchange (FREE) electronic net; in Michigan, lawyer Kay Schwarzberg works with Fathers for Equal Rights of America.

Basic fairness is not the only reason for women to work on behalf of men's issues. Perhaps the ultimate lesson we have still to learn is that most gender issues are women's *and* men's issues. As Brott says, "You can't achieve the goals of sexual equality without getting men involved." The most obvious example of this is the issue of parenthood: Greater male involvement in child rearing is essential if women's opportunities in the workplace are to be expanded.

Men and women of good will working together is a theme *Playboy*'s Asa Baber frequently emphasizes. "What is needed is an equal rights movement, not a men's movement and a women's movement," he told the Chicago Men's Conference, which had a record number of women this year (about 30 out of 200 attendees). "Not men's rights, not women's rights—equal rights. That should be our goal."

Baber is encouraged by signs that "victim feminism" is waning, and he is confident that "victim masculism" will not prevail either: "As the complaints build, we're going to get tired of it, both sides, and then both men and women are going to ask, OK, now what are we gonna do? And so the culture of complaint will eventually burn itself out."

FEMINISM AT THE CROSSROADS

Katha Pollitt

Feminism, like Broadway, the novel, and God, has been declared dead many times. Indeed, unlike those other items, it has been declared dead almost since its birth—by which I mean its modern rebirth in the 1960s. Feminism has also, as Susan Faludi demonstrated so cleverly in *Backlash*, been blamed for making women miserable, for causing everything from infertility—see? you waited too long to get pregnant because you were hell-bent on a fancy career and didn't settle for that nice boy next door twenty years ago, and now look—to poverty and divorce, which in this version of life is always initiated by men. And if that line doesn't work, there are always children, as in: feminism is all right for *women*, but what about the kids, foisted off on day-care centers run by child molesters and deprived of paternal authority by divorce, which in this version of life is always initiated by women.

So it's with great pleasure and some relief that I observe that we are not gathered here tonight to debate whether feminism is actively bad or just irrelevant, but to discuss its future direction. "Feminism at the Crossroads"—that sounds dramatic, doesn't it, full of promise, or is it threat?—of challenge at any rate, opportunities to be seized or missed, of signposts that if rightly read will send women onto the broad main highway of civic life and personal happiness but if misread or wrongly chosen will send them down some ill-lit alley, or even

up the proverbial garden path. I will quarrel a bit with that metaphor later, but first I'd like to observe that a crossroads is a much more exciting place to be than a graveyard, so clearly we are making progress!

What are the street signs on the feminist crossroads? Women today are enjoying a lively debate on a number of issues, although perhaps "enjoying" is not the *mot juste* here, given how acrimonious these debates can become. There's a debate around sexuality issues, which tends to be played out over pornography. And there's a debate about gender roles in marriage, which is expressed around issues of, say, the "mommy track" at work, whereby women would trade professional advancement for a schedule that would make it easier for them to fulfill a modified version of traditional domestic roles at home: you'll notice that nobody calls it the "parent track." There's a debate about work itself: should women enter the male-dominated professions on terms already laid down, or change them? Or fight for the upward valuation of the traditional female jobs? Grade-school teacher or college professor? Nurse or doctor? Fight for the right of women soldiers to enter combat, or fight the military itself?

What all these debates have in common is that they tend to divide into two broad camps: In one fall those who would shore up and protect some notion of women as different than men—whether by nature, nurture, or more or less immutable social function—who, because of that difference, need special protections in

---

This article is taken from a talk given at the New School for Social Research in New York City in the fall of 1993.

order not to be disadvantaged by a male-dominant social order. And in the other, we find those who see gender as a more fluid social construction, with the sexes sharing a broad range of traits and ways of life, and who see their feminist task as opening every social possibility/opportunity to women. To oversimplify greatly, one can pose the question as, which do women need, more freedom or more protection? More respect for individual variations among women or more respect for traditional feminine traits and roles?

But if one street sign reads freedom and another protection, we can see that there are problems with our crossroads metaphor. In the first place, if standing at the crossroads means having to choose a direction, it will immediately become apparent that American feminism has been divided over which path to take for over a century. Although I'm sure Andrea Dworkin would take issue with me here, I see important continuities between the antipornography movement and, say, the Women's Christian Temperance Union (WCTU): both use powerful Puritan energies already present in American society in order to mount a challenge to male domestic irresponsibility and violence: men will be tamed by being deprived of their evil pleasures (rather than: women will be empowered by confronting inequality head-on); both mistake a symbol for a cause; both share a certain sense of women as pure and nonsexual and better than men: Frances Willard, the head of the WCTU, even espoused the ideal of marriage without sex entirely. And today's pro-sex feminists can trace their lineage back to Frances Wright, Victoria Woodhull, the Utopian feminists of the Oneida community, and other early nineteenth-century social experiments. Similarly, the debate over whether women need more protection or more equality at work has a long history, with surprising people lining up on both sides of the issue: Eleanor Roosevelt, for example, opposed the Equal Rights Amendment because she believed it would expose women to increased exploitation in the workplace, and supported so-called protective legislation that limited the hours of working women.

A second problem with our crossroads metaphor is that it assumes that, along the special/equal or protection/freedom divide women will line up on one side or the other. As Ann Snitow suggested in "Pages from a Gender Diary" (*Dissent*, Spring 1989) this is a misleading picture, which better fits hardened crusaders of the movement than it does most women. It may be true that at some deep philosophical level there is a contradiction between wanting more sexual freedom and wanting less pornography, or wanting to see women's experience reflected across the academic board and wanting independent women's studies departments, or wanting to break down the gender-segregated workforce and wanting comparable worth for the historically underpaid jobs in which women predominate. But at the practical level of lived daily life, one finds surprisingly few women who feel compelled to take a hard and consistent line. In her interesting book, *Feminism Without Illusions*, Elizabeth Fox-Genovese argues that there is a contradiction between the individualism at the heart of the modern American women's movement and the demands it also makes, or ought to make, for more collective responsibility for the disadvantaged. But many women, including myself, don't see it as an either/or situation. Last year, to give an example from my own work, I wrote an article attacking the wing of feminism I called "difference feminism," that is, the notion that women are more or less immutably different than men in ways that have important moral consequences. For example, that women are kinder, gentler, more harmonious, and less competitive than men. I argued that the different social styles of the two sexes are more apparent than real and do not, in any case, translate into moral and political differences in the public realm, and that it was a great mistake to base claims to political power on, for example, the supposed superior altruism and honesty of female politicians. I still think I was right, despite the suspicious fact that of all the essays I've written for the *Nation*, this was the one that got the most favorable comment from men. But the fact is, many women have no trouble at all believing simultaneously that women are morally superior to men and that they are also equal to men. In the same way, women can both admire Hillary Rodham Clinton because she is a smart, powerful working mother, and live with the unfortunate fact that her current political position was achieved through marriage.

A very good example of how close the two different strains of feminism can be is the response to Anita Hill. Now there's certainly a way to read Hill's charges that fits in with protectionist, women-are-better feminism: as many pointed out at the time of the Thomas hearings, not every woman would be disgusted, bowled over and physically upset by off-color remarks of the sort she claimed

Thomas made to her—plenty of women, indeed, have been known to make such remarks themselves. Her ten-year silence also fits a certain vision of women as unable to defend themselves, thus needing lots of extra help from the law and the state. But the political effect of Hill's testimony could not have been more activist: women, the lesson was, must win political power in order for their concerns to be addressed.

It should not, perhaps, surprise us that in daily life, and in the political realm as well, feminists, and many women who resist the label too, should find themselves traveling all roads at once rather than marching firmly down one path or the other. This reflects women's real condition: most women work *and* have children; are married *and* know that marriage these days may well not be for life. Women who have abortions also have babies; women who resent men's interest in pornography *also* have forced Harlequin romances to include semi-explicit sex scenes. They want to have sexual adventures *and* not to be raped or abused. To be both women *and* human beings. It's not so surprising, then, that we find women who consider themselves to be feminists shifting back and forth between these two camps. And historically, indeed, both have achieved some success.

On the whole, however, I would say that feminism's best hope lies with equality, because although equality has the defect of sometimes seeming rather counter-intuitive—why legally treat pregnancy like an illness when we all know very well it *isn't* an illness—it has the great advantage of being open-ended. Protectionist or difference feminism says, in effect: this is what women are like, this is the kind of life they lead, so let's shape social policy and the law to acknowledge and reflect it. For example, the "mommy track" says, look, we all know women do most of the child care and most of the housework, so let's make it easier for them to get through the double day of paid employment and domestic responsibilities. In the short run, this might even genuinely help women—but it also assumes that gender roles in the family aren't going to change, even though they are rapidly doing so, even as we speak, and throws its weight behind keeping those roles the same. Protectionist policies of the past have a way of outdating themselves. When the Soviet Union, in its early days, instituted a policy whereby women could take off from work while they had their menstrual periods, that probably seemed the height of compassion, common sense, and enlightened social policy. But what it really did was ensure that women would do all the domestic labor—after all, they had those days off, free for the asking—

and enshrine in law ideas about menstruation that seem fairly fantastic today.

If I had to predict which road feminism will take, I would have to say that the material conditions for protectionist or "difference" feminism seem to be steadily eroding. Fewer and fewer women can afford to make stay-at-home motherhood the basis for a full identity; you will notice that stay-at-home childless wifehood, once also a common lifestyle, is no longer even discussed as a rational choice. Families are small and not very stable; that seems likely to remain the case, even if the family-values crowd succeeds in making abortion harder to achieve or divorce more difficult to obtain. In the workplace, gender barriers are slowly breaking down: that women are naturally more caring than men may suit the self-image of nurses and social workers, but doesn't really do much for, say, bartenders and marines. Little by little, the genders are converging: they are educated more alike and raised more alike than ever before, and out of economic necessity as much as anything else, their roles within marriage are converging too. Consider the recent census report that 20 percent of fathers care for children while their wives are working.

The idea that men and women are radically different species of being, which not so long ago struck so many as an indisputable fact of nature, is more and more coming to be revealed as a historical construct, connected to the rise of the bourgeois industrial household, a social form whose end we are living through. In that sense, then, protectionist or difference feminism is at bottom a nostalgic project, which I think today appeals to women at least partly because it seems to protect them against new and uncertain social forms and understandings—the sexually predatory behavior, for example, of many male college students, which in previous situations was directed toward women of inferior social class rather than those of their own. The truth is, though, that it can't protect them, it can only make them feel better for a little while, like praying in a foxhole.

So perhaps the real way feminism will resolve its indecisiveness at the crossroads is that it will continue to debate and hesitate and try both roads at once until one day it sees that in fact the crossroads has disappeared. And then, of course, being feminists, we'll all congratulate ourselves over how right we were to choose what was, in fact, the only possible path—equality, which will at that point be understood to mean not women being the same as men, but both sexes sharing a more or less common life.

Sex in America: Faithfulness in Marriage Is Overwhelming

Tamar Lewin

While several previous studies of sex in America have created a popular image of extramarital affairs, casual sex and rampant experimentation, an authoritative new study of American sexual practices—widely described as the most definitive ever—paints a much more subdued picture of marital fidelity, few partners and less exotic sexual practices.

In the new study, based on surveys of 3,432 men and women 18 to 59 years of age, 85 percent of married women and more than 75 percent of married men said they are faithful to their spouses. And married people have more sex than their single counterparts: 41 percent of all married couples have sex twice a week or more, compared with 23 percent of the singles.

But cohabiting singles have the most sex of all, with 56 percent reporting that they had sex twice a week or more.

"We have had the myth that everybody was out there having lots of sex of all kinds," said John H. Gagnon, a co-author of the study. "That's had two consequences. It has enraged the conservatives. And it has created anxiety and unhappiness among those who weren't having it, who thought, 'If I'm not getting any, I must be a defective person.'

"Good sense should have told us that most people don't have the time and energy to manage an affair, a job, a family and the Long Island Rail Road," said Mr. Gagnon, a sociology professor at the State University of New York at Stony Brook.

The study is considered important because it is one of the first to rely on a randomly selected nationally representative sample. Most previous sex studies—from the Kinsey reports in the 1940's and the Masters and Johnson study in the 1960's to more recent popularized studies—by, for example, Playboy magazine, the researcher Shere Hite and Redbook magazine—relied on information from volunteers, a method that may seriously skew the results, experts say, because those who are interested in sex and are most sexually active tend to participate.

"A lot of the people we approached initially said, 'Oh, you don't want to talk to me, I haven't had a partner in three years,' and those people wouldn't have taken part in previous studies, where self-selection decided who would fill out the questionnaires," said Edward O. Laumann, a sociology professor at the University of Chicago who is one of the coauthors of the study.

For an American man, the median number of sexual partners over a lifetime is six; for a woman, the median is two. But the range in the number of lifetime sexual partners varied enormously, with 26 percent reporting only one lifetime partner, while one man in the study reported 1,016 partners and one woman reported 1,009.

To one of the most politicized questions in human sexuality—how common is homosexuality—the study offers a fuzzy answer: It depends.

A subdued picture of few partners and less exotic sexual practices.

For many years, the conventional wisdom was that 1 in 10 Americans was homosexual, a number that came from a 1948 Kinsey report that 10 percent of the men surveyed had had exclusively homosexual relations for at least three years between the ages of 16 and 55. Many recent studies have debunked that figure, including a study last year finding that only 1 percent of the male population was homosexual.

In the new study, 2.8 percent of the men and 1.4 percent of the women identified themselves as homosexual or bisexual. But when the question is asked differently the numbers change.

About 9 percent of the men and 5 percent of the women reported having had at least one homosexual experience since puberty. Forty percent of the men who had a homosexual experience sometime in their life did so before they were 18, and not since. Most women, though, were 18 or older when they had their first homosexual experience.

And when asked whether having sex with someone of the same sex seemed appealing, 5.5 percent of the women said the idea was somewhat or very appealing. About 6 percent of the men said they were attracted to other men.

The survey also found that homosexuals cluster in large cities. More than 9 percent of the men in the 12 largest cities identified themselves as homosexual, compared with less than 4 percent of the men in the suburbs of those cities and only about 1 percent of the men in rural areas. Lesbians also tend to cluster in cities, but not to the same extent as gay men.

The study asked about many different sexual practices, but found that only three were appealing to more than a small fraction of heterosexual Americans.

The vast majority of heterosexual Americans said they included vaginal intercourse in almost every sexual encounter. Many people said that oral sex and watching a partner undress were also appealing, but men were substantially more likely to enjoy both practices than women.

Most men and women said they did not find such practices as anal intercourse, group sex or sex with strangers very appealing, but again, the men were more interested than the women.

Among the other findings were these:

• More than half the men said they thought about sex every day, or several times a day, compared with only 19 percent of the women.

• More than four in five Americans had only one sexual partner, or no partner, in the past year. Generally, blacks reported the most sexual partners, Asians the least.

• Three-quarters of the married women said they usually or always had an orgasm during sexual intercourse, compared with 62 percent of the single women. Among men, 95 percent said they usually or always had an orgasm, married or single.

• Less than 8 percent of the participants reported having sex more than four times a week. About two-thirds said they have sex "a few times a month" or less, and about 3 in 10 have sex a few times a year or less.

• Both men and women who, as children, had been sexually touched by an adult were more likely, as adults, to have more than 10 sex partners, to engage in group sex, to report a homosexual or bisexual identification and to be unhappy.

• About one man in four and one woman in 10 masturbates at least once a week, and masturbation is less common among those 18 to 24 years of age than among those who are 24 to 34.

• Among marriage partners, 93 percent are of the same race, 82 percent are of similar educational level, 78 percent are within five years of each other's age and 72 percent are the same religion.

To gather data for the study, conducted by the National Opinion Research Center at the University of Chicago, 220 researchers spent several months in 1992 conducting face-to-face interviews. Those who agreed to participate—almost four out of five of those contacted—were also given written forms to place in a sealed envelope, so that the oral answers to some of the most intrusive, potentially embarrassing questions could be checked against what they wrote privately.

"There were some differences, but it never amounted to much, percentage-wise," Professor Laumann said. "Of course, you can't be sure that everyone told the truth all the time, but most of the time our interviewers had the sense that people were being extremely candid."

The sex survey grew out of a 1987 attempt by the Federal Government to develop data on sexual practices that would help in the fight against AIDS. The authors got money from the Government to develop a methodology for such a survey, but Senator Jesse Helms, a North Carolina Republican, persuaded the Senate in 1991 to block the financing to carry out the survey. The authors then got money to continue their work from several private foundations.

Among the survey's important implications was the finding that more than a third of the younger women said that peer pressure had made them have sex for the first time, compared with only 13 percent of those from previous generations. The authors suggest, therefore, that one important part of preventing teen-age pregnancy is helping young women learn to resist peer pressure.

The survey results are being published in two forms, one a paperback book, "The Social Organization of Sexuality" (University of Chicago Press), written by Mr. Gagnon, Mr. Laumann, Robert T. Michael, dean of the graduate school of public policy studies at the University of Chicago, and Stuart Michaels, a researcher at the University of Chicago.

The other version is a general-interest hard cover book, "Sex in America: A Definitive Survey" (Little, Brown and Company), by Mr. Gagnon, Mr. Laumann, Mr. Michael and Gina Kolata, a science reporter for The New York Times.

THE NEW SEXUAL REVOLUTION

Liberation at last? Or the same old mess?

Jim Walsh

Special to Utne Reader
Jim Walsh is a writer living in Minneapolis, Minnesota.

Five years ago in a cover section entitled "Remember sex? Are you too tired, too bored, too mad, too scared to enjoy sex these days?" Utne Reader *concluded that sex for pleasure was about as popular as a spring vacation in Antarctica. Well, as the saying goes, time is a great healer. Mindful of—but undaunted by—AIDS and the increase in other sexually transmitted diseases, today's sexual revolutionaries have pioneered new philosophies, techniques, political movements, and equipment to restore our battered sense of eros. To hear the writers in the following section tell it, the new sexual revolution is primarily about appreciating an imaginative range of options. So relax, and get as lusty as you want. As long as nobody gets hurt, whatever gets you through the night really is all right.*

New Year's Even, 1973–74. People are running naked through the streets, stadiums, and shopping centers of America; tonight the streakers take Times Square. *Roe v. Wade*'s first anniversary is three weeks away. A New York judge has deemed *Deep Throat* "indisputably and irredeemably obscene," though even as he speaks, people are lining up to see *Last Tango in Paris*. In San Francisco, the burgeoning new homosexual capital of the world, a camera shop owner by the name of Harvey Milk has just failed in his first bid to become the city's first openly gay city council member. The number one song in the country is Marvin Gaye's "Let's Get It On."

Me, I'm 13 years old. I'm at my first make-out party, and I'm not making out. I've got braces and zits and already I've been turned down by two girls. The first I want because she's a total fox, the second because she's carrying a copy of Alice Cooper's *Billion Dollar Babies*. I don't know who Alice Cooper is, but I know I love records; therefore, I love this girl. The feeling isn't mutual.

It's winter and freezing outside. Inside, a five-alarm fire of teenage hormones is raging. We're in a guy named Jerry's basement; his parents are gone for the evening, and he's got full access to the liquor cabinet and his dad's collection of dirty magazines. I'm on the floor with a girl by the name of Lynne, though I don't discover this bit of trivia until we've been locking lips for over an hour. There are no first or last names here, no rules, no commitment. Just warm bodies, getting warmer by the minute.

Suddenly, a noise comes from upstairs and the basement lights go on. Parents. A collective. "Oh . . . !" goes up, and kids are jumping up, buttoning shirts, zipping up zippers. Then, just as suddenly, the lights go down again and laughter from a couple of bored partnerless partiers tumbles down the stairs. False alarm. The making out resumes. With the threat of getting caught now in the mix, the hots get hotter. Lynne and I lay back down on the floor and . . .

Today it's sex with machines, sex with cathode rays, sex with latex gloves.

Whoa. Zipping up zippers? This is a *make-out* party. I get up from the floor and tell Lynne I'm going to the bathroom, which is true. But I'm also ducking for cover from the ton of bricks that's just fallen on my head. On my way, I run into Jerry. "I . . . mine," he says in a tone that suggests he's already bored with girls, 1974, and adolescence in general. "Are you gonna . . . yours?" I close the door and lock it carefully. He giggles a venomous, singsongy giggle that oozes its way under the bathroom door. "Hey Waaalsh—*are you gonna go all the waaay?*"

Happy new year. I come out of the bathroom and find Lynne on the couch, the same couch where Jerry and little Alice Cooper just had their magic moment. At 1:15, Jerry unpuckers from Alice long enough to announce that his folks are gonna be home soon. Lynne and I are off and smooching again. She's fast, I'm slow, but the ride's been fun: First base. Lovely. Second base. Fabulous. Third base, my first time. Pow! Like going to the moon. And hey, I'm more than happy to stop there. Mission accomplished. Curiosity sated. Lust abated.

Next to me, Jerry's overcome his boredom and he and Alice are doing it for the second time. On the floor, the total fox and a guy I went to grade school with are doing it. I know this because the guy tells me he's doing it while he's doing it. Everyone, it seems, is doing it. Everyone but Lynne, and she knows it. Time's running out. She unzips my jeans, presses up next to me, and coos, "C'mon . . ."

It's the chance of a lifetime. Opportunity knocking. I don't know what to do, so I keep my lips pressed hard on hers. A minute goes by. I kiss her on the neck and run my hand through her hair. Three minutes later—an eternity—I glide my lips across her cheek and put my mouth to her ear. I don't know what I'm going to say, but when I say it, it . . . squeaks.

"We *can't.*"

What I mean to say was *I* can't. What I wanted to say was, I'm not ready I'm sorry I don't know you I like you well enough but, but . . . But what? But like I said, I'm not ready. I'm saving it, that's what. Not for marriage or because I think I'll go to hell or because I think I'll get a disease. I'm saving it for some other time. For someone else. Someone I don't know yet.

The next Monday in school, thanks to Jerry and a kiss-and-tell chat with Lynne, the word is out: Walsh had a chance to go all the way with a superfox and he blew it. In gym, a guy I barely know comes up to me and asks, "Why?" like I'd just won the lottery and thrown all the money off a bridge. Then there's the guys who simply cluck and flap their arms as they pass me in the hall. It lasts about a week.

It was no big deal, really. This isn't a scar. I don't sit around preoccupied with how I was tormented by those kids that first week of 1974. But just as I felt I was on the outside looking in then, I find myself 20 years later sitting on the very same sidelines of the so-called new sexual revolution. I don't have toys or tapes or even anything all that out of the ordinary when it comes to a fantasy life.

What I've got is a wife, the same woman I've been with for 14 years. Mind you, I didn't trot this fact out with any holier-than-thou vanity; fact is, sometimes I'm almost embarrassed to admit it. See, I write about rock and roll for a living, and I spend a lot of time in bars with people who've been through the sex wringer. And while we're able to see eye to eye on any number of artistic and political levels, when they discover I've been happily married for so long, a certain wall goes up. They can't relate to my monogamous existence, just as I can't connect emotionally with their dating war stories.

But I digress. The memory of that New Year's Eve make-out party came rushing back to me when I read an item about this Spur Posse thing. Have you heard about it? Named after the San Antonio Spurs basketball team, a group of California high schoolboys have been keeping a running tally of their sexual conquests, à la ex-basketball star Wilt Chamberlain (over 20,000 served!) and KISS guitarist Paul Stanley (30,000 and more on the way!).

For sure, the members of the Spur Posse never say "I *can't.*" For these punks, "going to the hole" ("driving to the basket" in playground basketball parlance) has undoubtedly taken on a new meaning. Cute, huh? But I've always had an almost sociological curiosity about guys like the Spur Posse, because ever since that night I was made to feel like the wimpiest 13-year-old on the planet, sex with a partner and without love has pretty much been foreign turf for me.

In my worst moments, the Spur Posse makes me feel like an uptight, hyper-cautious square. In my best, I'm happy to simply not be them. Suffice it to say that those pseudostuds and I part ways when it comes to the definition of sex. In fact, I part ways with the rest of the world when it comes to the definition of sex, and that's the way it should be. Personal. My sex life is just that—my sex life—and yours is yours.

Although sex-as-sport escapades (not to mention rape) are nothing new, maybe the sheer excess of the Spur Posse is a reaction—albeit an extreme one—to sexuality during the AIDS era. After surviving a decade of paranoia and arts censorship that cast a chill over the nation's collective sexual identity, folks everywhere are now making up for lost time. Swinging and partner swapping are back. Unsafe hetero and homo sex is on the rise. Sex clubs are all the rage in New York. And alternative arrangements like polyfidelist households are becoming more common.

Part of this mass reframing—indeed, this coming-out party— is the sex positive movement, which embraces various manifestations of sexuality and sensuality from massage and holistic healing to pornography and technosex. It's all part of the healing process, and one of sex positive's most eloquent healers has been Susie Bright (a.k.a. "Susie Sexpert"), the founder of the lesbian erotica magazine *On Our Backs*.

"We live in a 'just say no' culture," says Bright. " 'Sex positive' was a reaction to Nancy Reagan and the work of Andrea Dworkin in fundamentalist feminism. It was saying, 'Look, we believe sex is integral to our well-being and our progressive politics.' And now, as it becomes more widely used, 'sex positive'—I don't even like to use the term anymore—is in danger of becoming another piece of useless rhetoric. Nevertheless, a younger generation has embraced this as their sexual identity and it explains something fundamental about who they are. So sometimes it's a term, sometimes it's a movement, sometimes it's a generation, and now it's about to become a cliché."

But before it does, it serves the crucial purpose of rehabilitation. Writing about Joe Kramer's New York sexual healing school in the *Village Voice* (April 21, 1992), Don Shewey asks, "What is 'sexual healing,' anyway, besides the name of Marvin Gaye's last great record? Partly it has to do with healing the wounds to the spirit and the flesh caused by sexual abuse, addiction, and AIDS. It also has a lot to do with acknowledging that the fun and the pleasure, the vitality and the divine mystery of sex have nourishing properties in and of themselves—a message that can easily get overwhelmed in a culture where 'sex appeal' is routinely exploited to sell products, but sexuality (read: actual . . .) is usually discussed *only* in the context of abuse, addiction, or AIDS transmission."

As a result, there now exists a burgeoning cottage industry of highly hygienic flesh options: computer sex (software that produces erotic on-screen images); computer bulletin board sex (in which subscribers trade fantasies through the magic of E-mail); and our old friend phone sex and our new friend virtual reality sex, which have recently been wed on the new *Cyberorgasm* CD. Produced by the editor of *Future Sex* magazine, Lisa Palac, the "3-D sound" of *Cyberorgasm* is so in-your-libido vivid, it's like being a fly on the wall of some of your best friends' bedrooms, bathrooms, or backseats. An extremely aroused fly, I might add.

As Bright, Palac, and others contend, at the heart of all this technology is sexuality's single most important tool: the human imagination. But is automated sex getting in the way of the real thing? The phenomenon prompted this comment from comedian Jerry Seinfeld in a recent episode of *Seinfeld*: "This whole talking during sex business—I mean, what are we doing here? The question is, does the talking really improve the sex, or is the sex act now there just to spice up the conversation? Of course, eventually I'm sure people will get too lazy even for phone sex, and they'll just have phone machine sex: 'Yeah, yeah, I want you really bad, just leave it on the tape.' And then the phone company will come out with 'sex waiting.' "

It's a joke, but it's a really smart joke. I mean, what *are* we doing here? The great sex *explosion* of the '60s has turned into the great sex *implosion* of the '90s. That is, free love had its obvious failings, but at least the hippies were doing it with human beings. Today it's sex with machines, sex with cathode rays, sex with latex gloves, sex with vibrators, sex with floppy disks, and, coming soon, thanks to the wonder of "tele-dildonics," sex with robots, which begs the question: Is it live or is it memo-sex? Better still, is it even sex? Absolutely yes, says Bright.

"The fear that people have about phone sex or virtual reality sex is the same fear they had about vibrators and masturbating," she says. "The fear is that if you have too much sex—once sex is easily available and you don't have to suffer for it and your fantasy becomes easy for you—you will be sucked into this whirlpool of sexual excess and go straight to hell.

"Incorporating technology into people's sex lives may seem strange at first, but once you pick up the phone and dial, or get on E-mail or whatever, once you plug it in, it's a very intuitive, physical process. It doesn't have anything to do with communicating with a machine. I was on *The Joan Rivers Show,* and that

was her problem. She's like, "My God, we're going to stay home, hooked up to a helmet in some sort of addictive frenzy and not have any need for personal communication anymore.' That's like saying, 'What if the music or a record player ruins [live] music?' "

It's worth repeating: If there is one, the new sexual revolution is about celebrating difference. For me, the sexiest scenario imaginable is Jerry's apartment on *Seinfeld*—a co-op where neighbors drop by spontaneously, flirt with each other, borrow money and clothes and just . . . hang. It's what everyone is ultimately searching for: human contact and a few laughs. In the fast-paced, fragmented '90s, where neighborhoods and families have become ancient history and/or idealized myth, people have an innate need to connect with each other. And the surest, quickest way to feel good about yourself and your species is by having sex. Real or unreal. Slow or fast, careful or careless.

And if none of the above describes your sexual persona, don't worry about it. Bright says she's sick to death of being called a "lesbian" because of all the baggage that goes with it. Likewise, I'm not down with the "straight male" label, which lumps me in with everybody from Jesse Helms to the Spur Posse. The fact of the matter is, it only says what I've *been,* and then only partially so; it doesn't begin to scratch the surface of my sexuality at any given moment.

The point is, the wimpiest 13-year-old on the planet still has more options than he probably has ever imagined. And more than a few questions. Such as: Does the fact that I have occasional soft crushes on my colleague Andrew (who is gay) and the ultra-dishy male owner of the French deli up the street (who is not) mean I'm gay? To some degree, yeah. Does the fact that I get a hard-on when I'm doing a phone interview with Susie Bright mean I'm a lesbian? One can only hope. Finally, does the fact that I put most of my sexual energy into my marriage mean that I bomb abortion clinics in my spare time, or that because I'm monogamous, I'm a dud when it comes to doing the wild thing?

For more on that last one, you'll have to ask my wife. I mean, there are reasons why it's been 14 years—but who's counting?

Sexual Biology, Behavior, and Orientation

- **The Body and Its Responses (Articles 12–15)**

- **Sexual Attitudes and Practices (Articles 16 and 17)**

- **Sexual Orientation (Articles 18–22)**

Human bodies are miraculous things. Most of us, however, have less than a complete understanding of how they work. This is especially true of our bodily responses and functioning during sexual activity. Efforts to develop a healthy sexual awareness are severely hindered by misconceptions and lack of quality information about physiology. The first portion of this unit directs attention to the development of a clearer understanding and appreciation of the workings of the human body.

As you read through the articles in this section, you will be able to see more clearly that matters of sexual biology and behavior are not merely physiological in origin. The articles included clearly demonstrate the psychological, social, and cultural origins of sexual behavior as well. Why we humans feel, react, respond, and behave sexually can be quite complex.

This is especially true regarding the issue of sexual orientation. Perhaps no other area of sexual behavior is as misunderstood as this one. Although experts do not agree about what causes our sexual orientation—homosexual, heterosexual, or bisexual—growing evidence suggests a complex interaction of biological or genetic determination, environmental or sociocultural influence, and free choice. In the early years of this century, sexologist Alfred Kinsey's seven-point continuum of sexual orientation was introduced. It placed exclusive heterosexual orientation at one end, exclusive monosexual orientation at the other, and identified the middle range as where most people would fall if society and culture were unprejudiced. Since Kinsey, many others have added their research findings and theories to what is known about sexual orientation. However, the case remains that more is not known than is known, and the subject is no less controversial.

That the previous paragraph may have been upsetting, even distasteful, to some readers emphasizes the connectedness of psychological, social, and cultural issues with those of sexuality. Human sexual behavior, from arousal through response and interaction, is biology and far more. What behaviors and choices are socially and culturally prescribed and proscribed are also part of human sexuality. This section attempts to address all of these issues.

The subsection *The Body and Its Responses* contains four informative and thought-provoking articles that illuminate the interplay of biological (especially hormonal), psychological, cultural, and interpersonal factors that affect sexual functioning. The articles illustrate the contributions of testosterone to *both* male and female functioning. This dispute between the relative roles of physical and nonphysical factors in male premature ejaculation and orgasm in females is not attributable to any individual cause.

Sexual Attitudes and Practices, the next subsection, opens with an interesting report on research involving over 300 male and female college undergraduate students that explores their attitudes, sexual arousability, and history of sexual activity. Closing the subsection, "Psychotrends: Taking Stock of Tomorrow's Family and Sexuality" discusses and assesses today's sexual attitudes and practices in areas as far reaching as AIDS, cohabitation, contraception, adultery, communication, and gender roles.

The *Sexual Orientation* subsection includes articles that dramatically demonstrate the changes that have occurred during the last decade with respect to homosexuality in the United States. In the past few years, growing numbers of scientific findings have identified biological, genetic, and hormonal differences between heterosexual and homosexual people. In addition, more gay, lesbian, and bisexual people have publicly acknowledged their orientation. Both of these dynamics have challenged a culture that has often been called fundamentally homophobic (or homosexual-fearing). The articles also present the dilemma felt by many people between tolerance for diversity and individual freedoms, and American norms for a married, heterosexual, procreating lifestyle. What impact the new research findings, more visible diversity in sexual orientation, and more public discussion of human sexual orientation (some call human sexualities) issues will have is uncertain, but they suggest a new phase in understanding human sexuality and ourselves.

Looking Ahead: Challenge Questions

How do you react to discoveries about the nondichotomy of sex hormones? Does knowing that both men and women have and are affected by testosterone and estrogen change any of the ways you think about yourself and others? Why, or why not?

If you or your sexual partner were experiencing a sexual problem, would you prefer it have a physical, an emotional, or an interactional cause? Why?

What are the prerequisites for your sexual arousability? What proportions are physical? Do they seem to have changed in the last few years? If so, how? To what do you attribute this change?

How do you feel about the Madison Avenue images of male and female sexiness? What impact do you think they have on real people and intimacy?

It is rare for people to wonder why someone is heterosexual in the same ways that they wonder why someone is homosexual. What do you think has contributed to your sexual orientation?

How do you respond when people around you talk about homosexuality and/or gay rights? What do you do when family, friends, or coworkers make jokes about gays and lesbians? Have you observed or taken part in a discussion of gays in the military, the gay ban, or gay rights? What comments or stances elicited the strongest emotional reactions in you and others you observed? Explain your answers.

Male Hormone Molds Women, Too, in Mind and Body

Natalie Angier

Try as humans may to appreciate life's complexities and half-tones, we often resort to good old-fashioned dualism, dividing the world into conservatives and liberals, rich and poor, straights and gays, somebodies and nobodies, and, of course, men and women, with their complementary genitalia and their characteristic hormones. Men have androgens, most notably testosterone, while women have estrogens.

Even the words have a binary spin: "androgen" comes from the Greek "maker of males," and "estrogen" signifies the maker of the estrus cycle, the boss of ovulation and menstruation, the essence of womanhood.

But nature abhors absolutes, and it turns out that men and women each have a fair amount of the opposite sex's hormones coursing through their blood. Scientists have known this for years, yet they have long played down the implications of that hormonal kinship, particularly when it came to studying how testosterone and other androgens work in a woman's body.

They knew estrogen to be indispensable to the growth of all embryos, regardless of sex. By contrast, testosterone has been viewed as a luxury, needed mainly to shape a male's form and sexual function, and

only vestigially and irrelevantly present in women. But these dismissive assumptions were made in the absence of any research or evidence.

Now, with the explosion of interest in women's health issues generally, physicians and scientists from a broad cross section of disciplines at last have begun to consider the role of so-called male hormones on the making of a female. They are trying to determine how closely testosterone is linked to a woman's sex drive, and whether the hormone is necessary to maintain female muscle mass and bone density into old age.

Debate rages over the wisdom of replacing male hormones.

These preliminary and often conflicting investigations already have physicians sharply divided over the wisdom of giving post-menopausal women small doses of testosterone along with the estrogen-replacement therapy they may receive. Doctors in Britain and Australia are much more likely to prescribe low-dose testosterone pellets or injections for women complaining of flagging libido and depression than are their colleagues in the United States, who are hesitant to begin treating women

with a potent hormone that is linked to men's comparatively early death.

With even greater trepidation, some scientists are seeking to learn the extent to which androgens influence a woman's personality, energy levels, relative aggressiveness or assertiveness, and any other traits commonly described as masculine.

"The borders between classic maleness and femaleness are much grayer than people realized," said Dr. Robert A. Wild, professor and chief of the section on research and education in women's health at the University of Oklahoma Health Sciences Center, in Oklahoma City. "We're mixed bags, all of us."

The Rise and Fall Of Testosterone

One reason researchers have neglected the study of androgens in women is a simple matter of quantity: women have, on average, much less of them than men do. There are many androgens, but the major hormone circulating freely is testosterone.

Men have between 300 and 900 nanograms of testosterone for every deciliter of blood, much of it generated by the testes, but some originating in the adrenals, the little hat-shaped glands abutting the kidneys. (A nanogram is a billionth of a gram.) In women, a high measurement of testosterone is 100 nanograms, but the average is around 40, said Dr. Geoffrey P. Redmond, president of the Foundation for Developmental Endocrinology and a physician at Mount Sinai Hospital in Cleveland.

But the testosterone level varies significantly with the menstrual cycle, as do the more stereotypically female hormones, estrogen and progesterone. That is because a woman's testosterone comes not only from her adrenal glands (which are fairly steady from week to week in their hormonal productivity), but also from her ovaries, with each organ contributing about half. And as the estrogen production in the ovaries falls and soars, so, too, does testosterone output, meaning that a woman's maximum androgen secretion corresponds with her estrogen spike and hence with her ovulation.

Thus, in women with normally high testosterone levels, the ovulatory spike may bring them into androgen ranges approaching those of a low-testosterone male.

The impact of that fluctuating testosterone on the body is not clear. Researchers have a good idea of what testosterone does to males. During fetal development, it shapes the growth of the male genitals and possibly influences brain circuitry. When a boy reaches puberty, androgen production in the testes swings into gear to sculpt the secondary sexual characteristics: the thickening of muscles and vocal cords, the widening of the shoulders, the growth of the penis and the beard and the sudden obsession with sex.

In girls? Well, scientists know testosterone contributes to their adolescent development as well. It makes pubic and underarm hair grow. It could help their muscles and bones develop, although how it interacts with estrogen—which is known to be necessary for calcium absorption and bone strength—is unclear. "I wouldn't be surprised if female athletes have higher testosterone levels than nonathletes, although that's not well defined," said Dr. Roger S. Rittmaster, an associate professor of medicine at Dalhousie University in Halifax, Nova Scotia.

Girls with high androgen levels may also end up with comparatively small breasts, he added, for in males the presence of testosterone is known to prevent a man's circulating estrogen from prompting the breast tissue to swell. Androgens can also cause a teen-age girl's skin to become oily and break out, just as the hormones do to luckless boys.

A Debate Over Treatment

The question would be merely of titillating interest were it not for a fierce debate over the use of testosterone replacement therapy in post-menopausal women. Dr. John Studd of the department of obstetrics and gynecology at Chelsea and Westminster Hospital in London said that besides estrogen-replacement therapy, about 25 percent of his post-menopausal patients receive testosterone pellets inserted under the skin. Among those recipients are women who have had their ovaries removed, as well as non-ovariectimized women who complain that their sex drive and energy levels are not what they used to be.

The degree to which testosterone levels ordinarily decline with age in either women or men is not known, but the atrophying of the ovaries post-menopausally can, in some cases, cut down a woman's testosterone production. Dr. Studd says the pellets clearly help his patients.

"They may have their lives transformed," he said. "Their energy, their sexual interest, the intensity and frequency of orgasm, their wish to be touched and have sexual contact—all improve."

Dr. Studd insisted that the doses used in his patients are so low that they have no adverse health affects. But many American physicians remain reluctant to prescribe the testosterone therapy for women.

"I have not seen women who need testosterone, except those who have had their ovaries removed," Dr. Redmond said. Other American scientists said there was a strong need to do a solid clinical trial of testosterone therapy in women.

Dr. Redmond and others believe that excess androgens are a far more pressing health problem than their diminution. By far, the bulk of the new research is focused on disorders that arise when a woman's body generates too much testosterone, resulting in everything from cosmetic problems like acne, balding and the growth of facial hair so abundant that the woman must shave twice a day to more severe complications like infertility, diabetes, high blood pressure, heart disease and cancer of the uterus. Even some cases of breast cancer, a disease normally associated with too much estrogen, may in fact be the result of excess testosterone, several experts said, although the data on this remain sketchy.

Researchers said the incidence of androgen disorders in women has been grossly underestimated, and that as many as 15 to 30 percent of all women may have problems caused by the overproduction of testosterone, an excessive sensitivity to the influence of circulating androgens, or both. They suggest that doctors should be on the lookout for women—and even young girls—who may be suffering from excess androgen secretion, so that the patients can be treated early enough to prevent the onset of serious and possibly fatal complications of a lifetime of androgen overdosing.

The signs of high androgen output sometimes are obvious: a tendency to put on weight in the upper body, particularly the stomach, rather than on the thighs and buttocks, as most women do; irregular periods; and hair sprouting in great abundance on the face, the thighs, in a woolly stripe from pelvis to belly button. Doctors can also perform blood tests to check for anomalous hormone secretions.

"It's not healthy for women to have abnormalities of androgen production, and these patients ought to be identified and treated as early as possible," said Dr. Philip D. Darney, a professor of obstetrics, gynecology and reproductive medicine at the University of California at San Francisco. "We've got a lot of work ahead of us educating physicians and patients on how to identify these states."

Among the treatments used to suppress or counteract androgen production are birth control pills; spironolactone, an anti-androgen drug, and dexamethasone, a synthetic steroid hormone that suppresses adrenal activity.

So, What Level Is Abnormal?

But scientists concede that the line between normal and abnormal levels of androgens in women is blurry and somewhat arbitrarily assigned. The dark mustache that may be considered unacceptable on women in this country—and thus a symptom of a hormone imbalance—is often viewed as ordinary and even sexy on women in Mediterranean countries. Some critics argue that the new emphasis on androgen excess is just another attempt to pathologize variations on a theme, turning traits once considered relatively normal into diseases that must be treated with potent medications taken over a lifetime.

"What society says is normal and what is normal for women can be very different," said Dr. Rittmaster. "Women can have a full beard and still be breast-feeding."

Many of the issues surrounding androgen disorders in women were discussed at a recent conference in

Rockville, Md., sponsored by the National Institute of Child Health and Human Development. The meeting was organized by Dr. Florence Haseltine, a surgeon, gynecologist and firebrand for the study of women's health.

Dr. Haseltine said she has been shown to have elevated levels of androstenedione, a precursor to testosterone. And though she admits she has no proof for her assumptions, she believes this hormonal excess explains why she becomes quite aggressive when under stress.

One common androgenic disorder in women is polycystic ovarian syndrome, when, for reasons that remain mysterious, the ovaries produce excess testosterone, resulting in infertility and problems with insulin that can prompt the onset of diabetes. Women with the disorder often are very hair on the face and body but balding, and on an ultrasound test their ovaries may appear to be bulging in the middle, in the stromal tissue that produces androgens. The disease sometimes can be treated with anti-androgen drugs, but it must be caught early if diabetes is to be averted.

Other scientists are fascinated by a hereditary disorder called congenital adrenal hyperplasia, in which a person lacks one of the five enzymes needed to produce cortisol, an important hormone in responding to stress. As a result of the defect, precursors to cortisol released by the adrenal glands build up in a budding fetus and act like male hormones.

Girls with congenital adrenal hyperplasia may emerge from the womb looking like boys, with an enlarged clitoris and even a scrotal sac, although they have fully formed ovaries and uterus. In the worst cases, the girls may need genital surgery to give them a more characteristically female appearance.

In other instances of the disorder, said Dr. Maria I. New, chairman of pediatrics at New York Hospital-Cornell Medical Center in Manhattan, girls are born with normal genitals but masculinize later in life, becoming hairy, acned and suffering from reduced fertility. For both severe and mild cases of hyperplasia, patients are given dexamethasone to inhibit adrenal overactivity.

Dr. New and her colleagues are completing a study of the psychology, sexuality and gender identity of women who have congenital adrenal hyperplasia, to see whether the high androgen levels in the womb influenced in any measurable way the women's neurological development. Dr. New will not yet say what their results are, other than to hint that "there are definitely effects of androgens on the brain."

But whether the women are said to be more mathematical, more aggressive, more sexually active, more enamored of guns and computers, or any number of traits commonly attributed to men, the results are sure to arouse the perennial quarrel over the nature of human nature: how much is head, how much hearth and how much a few simple hormones.

Premature Ejaculation: Is It Really Psychogenic?

Pierre Assalian, M.D.

McGill University

Although a number of etiologies have been proposed to explain premature ejaculation, few have been adequately investigated and none have been able to explain satisfactorily the phenomena. A discussion of the different theories is included. A physical etiology in premature ejaculation is proposed.

Despite the prevalence of premature ejaculation (being the most common male sexual dysfunction) and the success reported in its treatment, research has yet to offer convincing, empirically based theory regarding its nature or etiology. Although a number of etiologies have been proposed, few have been adequately investigated and none have been able to explain satisfactorily the phenomena.

Psychoanalytic theory advocates that the premature ejaculator harbors intense, unconscious, sadistic feelings towards women. Recent clinical experiences have failed to support that the premature ejaculator is universally hostile to females. Some couples who seek help for premature ejaculation appear to have a loving relationship. Furthermore, Kaplan (1989) suggests that most men who experience premature ejaculation do not have discernible neuroses.

Clinical evidence, according to Masters and Johnson (1970), indicates that there is a strong learned component to the process (conditioning model), common historical patterns have been found in men suffering PE, with the central feature being early coital experience in which the men ejaculated rapidly. Typical histories include first coital experience with a prostitute, who encouraged rapid ejaculation for quick turnover of customers, or the young male's first sexual experience with girls in his peer group which frequently took place in the back seats of cars, lover's lane parking spots, drive-in movies, or brief visits to the by-the-hour motels or fear of being discovered, the practice of pantomime intercourse and coitus interruptus for prevention of pregnancy.

In effect the man becomes conditioned to fast ejaculation, and in subsequent (more relaxed) sexual experiences he is unable to alter the pattern that has been established. This "conditioning" theory is open to criticism on conceptual grounds. It leaves unanswered the important question of why only a small percentage of married men whose initial experience has occurred under hurried conditions become PE; furthermore its statistical validity has not been established. This supposedly attests to the validity of the dyadic position. No one contests the supposition that premature ejaculation may be an expression of a couple's interpersonal difficulties, but on the other hand the resolution of these difficulties will not per se alter ejaculation prematurity. Marital therapy, in itself, even when it improves the couple's relationship, usually has no effect on premature ejaculation unless this condition is treated specifically at the same time (Masters & Johnson 1970, Kaplan 1974, 1989, Zilbergeld 1978, 1992).

Another theory is that anxiety is the basic problem in PE. According to this formulation, the man experiences anxiety just as he reaches high levels of erotic arousal, and it is this anxiety which triggers the involuntary orgasm. The fact that some studies have indicated that few men respond to systematic desensitization, a technique of reducing anxiety, has been cited in support of this theory.

But the fact that this treatment technique is effective only occasionally, there is a common clinical observation that argues against this hypothesis. After the PE has been "cured," the male often reports feelings of anticipatory anxiety as he reaches high level of excitement and he begins to wonder if his cure is permanent.

Address correspondence to the author at Human Sexuality Unit, Montreal General Hospital, 1650 Cedar Avenue, Montreal, Quebec, Canada H3G 1A4.

Once ejaculatory control has been firmly established, it is not impaired by this kind of anxiety. Strassberg et al (1987) found that PE and NPEs were not different on measures of frequency of intercourse or masturbation. However, they were substantially and significantly different in their estimates of how long it would take them to reach orgasm both in intercourse (as expected) add masturbation, with the PEs reporting shorter orgasmic latencies in both instances. The pattern of their findings led Strassberg et al (1987), to propose that premature ejaculation may be, at least in part, the result of a physiologically determined hypersensitivity to sexual stimulation.

Strassberg et al. (1990) reported that PEs and NPEs manifested very low levels of anxiety during the self-stimulation in the laboratory, and there was no significant difference between the two groups regarding the anxiety they reported typically experienced during sexual intercourse. Their conclusion is that anxiety may not be a necessary etiological element in PE because if it did one would have expected to see greater anxiety in the PE group. They postulated a somatic vulnerability.

Spiers, Geer and O'Donahue (1984) maintained that premature ejaculation is caused by excessive sensitivity to erotic sensation, therefore they advocate the use of tactics which are designed to diminish sexual sensations and delay the onset of high levels of excitement during lovemaking; some of these measures are, use of condoms, application of anaesthetic ointments to the penis, self-inflicted pain, tensing anal muscles, cold showers, use of alcohol and repeated intercourse.

Assalian (1988) reported on 5 men with PE and later on 15 (1991), who had an unsuccessful outcome with conventional treatments. He advocated that these men suffer from a constitutionally hypersensitive sympathetic nervous system which prevents them from differentiating between ejaculation and its inevitability and/or once the sympathetic nervous system is triggered it has to discharge. This constitutional vulnerability would be the same as Strassberg described later as somatic vulnerability. Assalian further stated that the anxiety that is felt by PE is only another manifestation of a hyperactive sympathetic system. Another theory has to be considered, and the role of brain neurotransmitters have to be evaluated in PE. McIntosh and Barfield (1984) reported that serotonergic systems exert an inhibitory effect on male rats copulatory behaviour, including the post-ejaculatory refractory period. Consistent with this finding is the increase in orgasmic latencies in PE by certain medications.

Interference with ejaculation has been reported with a number of drugs: thioridazine, chlorpromazine, chlordiazepoxide, perphenazine, trifluoperazine, reserpine, butyrophenones, monoamine oxidase inhibitors, guanethidine, phenoxybenzamine, clomipramine, and more recently with fluoxetine.

Ejaculatory disturbances appear to be dose related, delay occurring at low doses, failure occurring at a relatively higher dose. Serotonergic antidepressants' effect on ejaculation is through their effect on the sympathetic system, possibly by delaying its discharge and/or on the serotonin neurotransmitter system. Assalian (1988) has treated PE with Clomipramine Anafranil—a selective serotonergic antidepressant. He proposed some guidelines for the pharmacological treatment of PE that includes: Primary PE with no background history of first sexual intercourse under hurried conditions, failure of sex therapy to improve PE and as a life saving measure in cases of pending divorce if PE is considered a major problem and if the PE is suicidal. Segraves (1989) speculated that serotonergic neurotransmission may play a role in inhibiting reflexive ejaculatory neurotransmission, but acknowledged that the process through which this occurs has yet to be identified.

In summary, because PE has been considered primarily a psychogenic disorder, physical etiologies have generally been ignored. Further research is needed in the area of physiological processes of ejaculation and the role of brain neurotransmitters in Human Sexual response.

Who knows, maybe in the future we'll discover that PE has a physical etiology?

REFERENCES

Assalian, P. (1988) Clomipramine in the treatment of premature ejaculation. *The Journal of Sex Research, 24,* 213–215.

Assalian, P. (1991, November). *Premature ejaculation: Is it really psychogenic?* Paper presented at the Annual Meeting of the Society for the Scientific Study of Sex, New Orleans, LA.

Kaplan, H. S. (1974). *The new sex therapy.* New York: Brunner/ Mazel.

Kaplan, H. S. (1989). PE: *How to overcome premature ejaculation.* New York: Brunner / Mazel.

Masters, W. H., & Johnson, V. E. (1970). *Human sexual inadequacy.* Boston: Little Brown and Co.

McIntosh & Garfield (1984). Brain monaminergic control of male reproductive behavior. *Behavioral Brain Research, 12,* 255–265.

Strassberg, D. S., Kelly, M. P., Caroll, C., and Kircher, J. C. (1987). The psychophysiological nature of premature ejaculation. *Archives of Sexual Behavior, 16,* 327–336.

Strassberg, D. S., Mahoney, J. M., Schaugaard, M., & Hale V.E. (1990). The role of anxiety in premature ejaculation: A psychophysiological model. *Archives of Sexual Behavior 19,* 251–258.

Zilbergeld, B. (1978). *The male sexuality.* New York: Bantam.

Zilbergeld, B. (1992). *The new male sexuality.* Toronto: Bantam

Zilbergeld, B. and Evans, M. (August 1980). The inadequacy of Masters and Johnson. *Psychology Today, 14,* 29–43.

Etiology and Treatment of Early Ejaculation

Barry W. McCarthy, Ph.D.

Washington Psychological Center/American University

Human behavior is multi-causal and multi-dimensional. This is especially true of sexual behavior, including early ejaculation. Dr. Assalian raises the hypothesis that early (premature) ejaculation has a physiological etiology and is best treated with medication. Is this part of the trend to medicalize human sexuality, especially male sexuality? LoPiccolo (1992) has convincingly argued that the medical vs. psychological approach to assessment and treatment of erectile dysfunction is a false dichotomy which generates much heat but little light.

Research and clinical studies have reported excellent results in the treatment of early ejaculation (Kaplan, 1989; DeAmicis, Goldberg, LoPiccolo, Friedman, & Davies, 1985; Hawton, Catalan, Martin, & Fagg, 1986). This is especially true when the couple view ejaculatory control as a joint responsibility (McCarthy, 1989). Ejaculatory control can be learned via masturbation and imagery techniques by males without partners (Zilbergeld, 1992). Successful sex therapy involves changing attitudes, behavior, and emotions, and is more than mechanical practice of the stop-start procedure.

There is a need for further research into the etiology of early ejaculation and to increase the efficacy of therapeutic interventions. Studying generalization and relapse prevention procedures should be a priority. The research of Strassberg (Strassberg, Kelly, Carroll, and Kircher, 1987) demonstrated that early ejaculation is a more complex phenomena than originally believed. The concept of a physiological predisposition to early ejaculation is not only possible, but can provide a helpful intervention for the male who engages in self-blame. However, saying to males that taking a pill or using two or three condoms is the way to remedy the problem without assessing and addressing attitudinal, behavioral, emotional, and relationship factors could be iatrogenic.

Crenshaw (1992) reported that when he asked 46 young males whether they preferred therapy for early ejaculation or taking Prozac, all 46 chose Prozac. "Men do not want therapy, they want a pill." Although medication can be helpful, is it really the most appropriate, efficacious intervention? Does medication reinforce myths about sex as a male performance for the woman (McCarthy, 1988)? Is sexuality more than the penis, intercourse, and the perfectly timed orgasm? Offering medical solutions to multi-dimensional problems involving attitudinal, behavioral, emotional, and relationship issues runs the risk of over-promising a quick, effortless cure without addressing important psychological and relational issues. Cognitive-behavioral concepts and exercises (McCarthy and McCarthy, 1993) for ejaculatory control emphasize cognitions of "pleasure, not performance," behavioral skills of identifying the point of ejaculatory inevitability, utilizing the stop-start technique, experimenting with intercourse positions, movements and rhythms; and building comfort, warmth and intimacy. This approach to ejaculatory control can enhance sexuality as an intimate, sharing couple process.

REFERENCES

Crenshaw, R. (1992). *Prozac and premature ejaculation*. Paper presented at the annual meeting of the American Association of Sex Educators, Counselors and Therapists, Orlando, FL.

DeAmicis, L., Goldberg, D., LoPiccolo, J., Friedman, T., & Davies, L. (1985). Clinical follow-up couples treated for sexual dysfunction. *Archives of Sexual Behavior, 14*, 467–489.

Hawton, K., Catalan, J., Martin, P., & Fagg, J. (1986). Long-term outcome of sex therapy. *Behavior Research and Therapy, 24*, 665–675.

Kaplan, H. *How to overcome premature ejaculation*. New York: Brunner/Mazel.

LoPiccolo, J. (1992). Postmodern sex therapy for erectile failure. In R. C. Rosen & S. R. Leiblum (Eds.), *Erectile disorders: Assessment and treatment* (pp. 172–197). New York: Guilford.

McCarthy, B. (1989). Cognitive-behavioral strategies and techniques in the treatment of early ejaculation. In S. R. Leiblum & R. C. Rosen (Eds.), *Principles and practice of sex therapy: Update for the 1990's* (pp. 142–167). New York: Guilford.

McCarthy, B. (1988). *Male sexual awareness*. New York: Carroll and Graf.

McCarthy, B., & McCarthy, E. (1993). *Sexual awareness*. New York: Carroll and Graf.

Strassberg, D., Kelly, M., Carroll, C., & Kircher, J. (1987). The psychophysiological nature of premature ejaculation. *Archives of Sexual Behavior, 16*, 327–336.

Zilbergeld, B. (1992). *The new male sexuality*. New York: Bantam.

Address correspondence to the author at Washington Psychological Center, American University, 4400 Massachusetts Avenue, NW, Washington, DC 20016-8027.

From the *Journal of Sex Education & Therapy*, Vol. 20, No. 1, 1994, pp. 5-6. © 1994 by the American Association of Sex Educators, Counselors, and Therapists. Reprinted by permission.

THE TRUTH ABOUT WOMEN AND SEX

New research shows that women have erotic potential from head to toe. So why are so many women sexually frustrated?

Emily Yoffe

Emily Yoffe is a Los Angeles–based writer whose work appears in The New York Times Magazine, Texas Monthly, Details, *and* Esquire.

A woman I'll call Lisa, because she is a friend of mine and I promised I'd change her name, is telling me about how she uses nothing but her imagination to bring herself to orgasm. She first discovered this ability when she was a teenager. As an adult, it has been enormously handy on business trips. "I found that if I was on an airplane, and sick of reading and bored, I could lose myself in a fantasy, start thinking about sexual things, and work myself up into an orgasm."

Doesn't she move, isn't it obvious?

"I lie still. There are other people around. I don't want to make a spectacle of myself."

Lisa is, to quote the name of a new book by sex therapist Gina Ogden, one of the Women Who Love Sex. It is a title that seems almost comic, or incomplete, as if she forgot the obligatory, Too Much. But the discomfort her title provokes is part of Ogden's point that we have few comfortable words for women with lusty, exuberant desire. Ogden, a sex therapist for more than 20 years, would like to see that change. She also wants to expand our definition of female sexuality beyond a few magic inches of mucus membranes.

Certainly the women she writes about have done that. Ogden has interviewed scores of women who describe themselves as easily orgasmic. More than half of them say they can reach orgasm by touching parts of their bodies other than their genitals. They come to orgasm by having their toes sucked or their back rubbed or the skin inside their elbow stroked. One has such erogenously sensitive ears that she had an orgasm at the doctor's office when he was flushing wax out of her ear canal. And get this: More than 60 percent of them, like Lisa, report reaching states of sexual ecstasy merely by lying back, closing their eyes, and thinking.

Ogden, 58, declines to talk about her own sexual experiences in detail. But these women, she says, did inspire her to find out if she had erotic capacities she hadn't explored. "I found, yes, indeed, it was true, true for me, too. At that time I was in my forties, so maybe part of it was living long enough to explore the boundaries." Which is exactly what Ogden believes more women need to do. She's not alone. Virtually every researcher interviewed for this article talked wistfully about the untapped sexual potential that resides in a woman's body, like a genie waiting to be released. They want to get the word out. "A lot of what women can do, can feel, can sexually is a great big secret," Ogden says. "But it doesn't have to be. Let's be women who love sex. Let's decide we can say that and not get laughed at. Or raped."

Beverly Whipple is a woman who loves sex research. It was Whipple who suggested that Ogden verify in the laboratory that women are able to experience orgasms without touching themselves. In her physiology lab at Rutgers University, Whipple tracked the blood pressure, heart rate, and pupil dilation of ten such women. Sure enough, seven were able to reach orgasm by fantasy alone, and their physiological measurements matched those they reached when they masturbated in the more traditional hands-on style.

Whipple is among the few researchers in this country still investigating female sexuality in the laboratory. The kind of pioneering, large-scale lab work done by William Masters and Virginia Johnson in the sixties went into decline when funding for sex research became scare during the Reagan years.

Whipple is undeterred. Her work is well-respected—she takes pains to conduct her studies with care and decorum—but she is also something of a proselytizer, preaching a gospel of pleasure. She's been criticized over the years, especially after the publication in 1982 of *The G-Spot,* the best-seller in which she and her coauthors argued that many women have a sensitive area inside the vagina capable of bringing them to orgasm. Whipple says she intended the book to broaden women's awareness of their sexual potential. But it was seen by some as a regression to the narrow—and phallocentric—model of sex as intercourse culminating in orgasm. Rather than alerting women to more possibilities, her detractors said, the book sent women off on a scavenger hunt for the right place to find ecstasy.

Whipple, while mentioning with some pride that her book has just been published in China, says she's tired of being the G-spot lady. "I just wanted to show that there is more than one way for women to respond sexually. I wanted to validate the women who had this. I didn't want people to go out searching for this thing."

Today, in the windowless, cinder block basement that serves as her laboratory, Whipple is at it again. This time, her goal is to see whether a 38-year-old woman can come to orgasm by deep stimulation of her vagina alone. One purpose of this ongoing study is to find ways for women with spinal cord injuries to enhance their sexual response. Fifteen of the 20 women being studied have suffered paralyzing injuries that have damaged the nerve pathways between their clitoris and their spinal cord.

The candles, orange velour pillows, and a poster of the volcano Popocatepetl are well-meaning attempts to bring a touch of warmth, even sensuality, to the setting. But nothing can defuse the strangeness of what's about to happen in this room. Whipple, a trim 52-year-old with frosted blond hair and the soothing yet no-nonsense manner of the nurse she used to be, asks the woman to put on a hospital gown and tells her exactly how and where she is allowed to touch. The idea is for the woman to sexually excite herself, using a flexible rod-shaped instrument and whatever fantasies she can muster, without—and here's the catch—stimulating her clitoris, the easy route to female orgasm.

It's an awkward assignment. Lying atop a hospital bed, the woman uses the flexible instrument to rhythmically massage her cervix—the cap-shaped spot at the back of her vagina—for 12 minutes. Then comes a break followed by 12 minutes stimulating the front upper wall of her vagina, the twelve o'clock position that Whipple identifies as the G-spot. During each session, Whipple sits calmly by the rows of equipment and, at regular intervals, asks the woman to assess her level of arousal.

It's a tall order to expect a woman to experience uninhibited ecstasy while wired to monitors betraying her bodily changes and having a weight pressed on her fingertips to measure her pain threshold. It's a whole lot harder than expecting a man to have great sex with his raincoat on. But science requires it, so the woman gives it her best shot. At the height of her arousal, her blood pressure and heart rate double and her pain threshold increases by 60 percent. Whipple and her colleague neurophysiologist

With the soothing yet no-nonsense manner of the nurse she used to be, Whipple asks the woman to put on a hospital gown and tells her exactly how and where she is allowed to touch herself.

Barry Komisaruk were the first to document the extraordinary pain blocking effect of sexual stimulation in women.

While the study may seem esoteric, Whipple hopes it will provide the scientific backbone for the growing anecdotal evidence—including Ogden's—that a woman's whole body is erotic, that sexual response does not reside in the genitals alone.

Ever since Masters and Johnson proclaimed that the clitoris is the source of female orgasm, the rest of the body has been written off—especially the vagina. No wonder. Since the upper two thirds of the vagina has been reported to have few nerve endings, and minor surgery can be performed on the cervix without anesthesia, it was logical to assume that the deep recesses of a woman's vagina played no role in sexual pleasure either.

But Whipple is finding that some women are able to have orgasms when only these innermost organs are stimulated. The study offers a possible explanation for why some women report a decrease in sexual response after hysterectomy, which sometimes involves removal of the cervix. But perhaps most importantly, it suggests that normally insensate nerve endings can be "woken up" during arousal. "This shows that sex is more than just a reflex," says Whipple. "It's a total body experience."

Okay, so women can have orgasms after the connection between their genitals and their spinal cord has been severed. They can find ecstasy simply through the power of sexual thinking. But if they are so erotically charged, why then is sexual fulfillment elusive for so many women?

If it's so easy, why is it so hard?

FOR STARTERS, you have to want sex. And lack of desire is the number one sexual complaint that women bring to therapists. What makes it so difficult to treat is that the cause is rarely limited to the events in the bedroom. Sometimes, hormones are to blame. "What's very exciting is that it's an absolute fact that testosterone is as important to women as it is to men in order to have full libido," says psychiatrist Helen Singer Kaplan, director of the human sexuality program at New York Hospital's Cornell Medical Center.

That's good news for some older women. "Many menopausal women complain that their libido, their responsiveness, is gone, and doctors think it's psychological," says Kaplan. But after menopause a woman's levels of both estrogen *and* testosterone drop. Studies by psychologist Barbara Sherwin at McGill University in Montreal have shown that giving small doses of testosterone to postmenopausal women dramatically increased their sexual desire and energy levels, while estrogen replacement had virtually no effect. Sherwin reports that the return of libido had a few husbands complaining about their wives' overly frisky sex drive.

Kaplan warns that a woman asking for testosterone will likely get some resistance. The word is just filtering out to the medical community. "Your

Are the Sexes Out of Synch?

A HEALTH/GALLUP POLL

IDWAY through Woody Allen's film *Annie Hall,* the camera switches back and forth between two telling scenes: Allen and Diane Keaton are in separate psychiatrists' offices, each being asked how often they make love.

"Hardly ever," Allen whines. "Maybe three times a week."

"Constantly," complains Keaton. "I'd say three times a week."

When it comes to sex, it seems, the sexes are in different time zones. In hopes of better understanding American men's and women's views of their sex lives, HEALTH decided to ask them some personal questions.

Do you, or does your partner, have the stronger sex drive?

	men	women
SELF	44	15
PARTNER	12	30
ABOUT EQUAL	24	20
HAVE NO PARTNER	10	16
DON'T KNOW/REFUSED	10	19

Maybe the stereotype is true. Though the trend among researchers has been to minimize gender differences when it comes to sexual desire, studies consistently find that most men experience an incessant and unvarying appetite for sex, while women's libido varies more from person to person and throughout the month. Our poll found that those who believed their partner's sex drive was stronger than their own tended to be less sexually satisfied.

Do you think you have sex more or less often than the average person?

	men	women
LESS OFTEN	36	36
ABOUT AS OFTEN	24	21
MORE OFTEN	22	14
DON'T KNOW/REFUSED	18	29

Here's one case in which men and women agree. More than a third of each gender believe they have sex less frequently than the average. How much is that? The National Opinion Research Center at the University of Chicago reports that the average married adult had sex 67 times during the last year. Among baby boomers, the rate is 78 times a year. That works out to about six times a month. *The Janus Report on Sexual Behavior* found that 58 percent of married adults say they have sex daily or a few times weekly.

Whom do you talk to explicitly about your sexual desires?

	men	women
PARTNER OR SPOUSE	57	46
NO ONE	24	33
A FRIEND	10	7
SOMEONE ELSE	4	3
DON'T KNOW/REFUSED	5	11

Here's a surprise: Men were *more* likely to confide their sexual wishes to their partners than were women. In fact, one in three women said they didn't discuss their sexual preferences with *anyone.* That's too bad. Our poll found that those who talk explicitly with their partner about their desires were more than twice as likely to enjoy satisfying sex lives.

Have you been satisfied with your sex life during the past month?

	men	women
YES	71	57
NO	16	12
HAVE NO SEX LIFE	7	20
DON'T KNOW/REFUSED	6	11

The good news is that most Americans are happy with their sex lives, although women are less delighted than men. It's not so much that women are dissatisfied with their sex lives, it's that one out of every five aren't having any sex at all. As for those adults who *were* dissatisfied, not having sex often enough might be to blame. The majority of those who said they hadn't been happy with their sex lives believed they had sex less often than the average person. Single and married people were about equally satisfied.

Do you enjoy sex more or less now than you did when you were younger?

	men	women
MORE	45	39
LESS	22	21
NO CHANGE	23	12
DON'T KNOW/REFUSED	10	27

Experience seems to pay off. Both men and women were about twice as likely to enjoy sex more as they get older than to enjoy it less. And that makes sense, especially for women: *The Janus Report* found that the percentage of women who achieved orgasm during lovemaking "always, often, or sometimes" increased as a woman approached middle age, from a low of 79 percent among twentysomethings to a high of 88 percent among those in their forties. Men remained fairly constant in their experience of orgasm during lovemaking, from 96 percent in their twenties to 98 percent in their forties. Apparently, women have more of a "learning curve" when it comes to enjoying sex.

From a telephone poll of 1,002 adults taken for HEALTH *from April 18 to April 24 by Gallup. Sampling error is ±3 percent.*

male doctor will laugh at you and say you'll get a mustache. I prescribe it widely. You need to find a doctor who is enlightened." Though the treatment remains controversial, Kaplan says the doses are so small they should have no masculinizing influence.

The effect of testosterone on younger women's libido is less clear. One intriguing study by Patricia Schreiner-Engel, a therapist at Mount Sinai Hospital School of Medicine in New York, found that women with higher levels of testosterone do seem to become aroused more easily and for longer periods than women with lower but normal levels. Despite their greater responsiveness, however, the "high-T" women were having less sex, and not enjoying it as much, as the "low-T" women. Schreiner-Engel speculates that high-T women, who tend to be more career-oriented, might be more demanding or have higher expectations of their sex lives.

Most often, however, low sexual desire results from a mix of psychological factors—the kinds of things you don't need any expert to tell you about. Too much stress. An unfulfilling relationship. Unhappiness with your body.

"I see sexual dysfunction as a social disease," says Gina Ogden. Women in this culture are bombarded with negative messages about their bodies and their sexuality, she says. As girls, they're taught that their genitals are "dirty" and that girls who like sex are "sluts." As women, they learn that sexy women are considered weak, compliant bimbos. It's easy to become convinced that a woman who loves sex won't be taken seriously. For all these reasons, Ogden believes that most women learn early on to shut down their sexuality.

But it isn't foreordained to be that way. Evidence of just how enduring is the power of female sexuality in the face of overwhelming repression and trauma can be found in the work of Hanny Lightfoot-Klein, a researcher whose book, *Prisoners of Ritual*, documents the lives of circumcised women in the Sudan. As young girls, their clitoris and labia were surgically removed, often without anesthesia. It would seem that a total aversion to sex would be a given for women who have experienced such terrible trauma. Yet in interviews with more than 300 circumcised Sudanese women, Lightfoot-Klein found that almost all of them said they had strong sexual desire and that they experienced orgasm during intercourse. "I asked women what areas were most sensitive to sexual stimulation, and they would say anywhere. Some said inside their vaginas, some still had sensation outside. Some said the breast, neck, knee, back of the hand, lips."

Closer to home, many of Ogden's highly orgasmic women were hardly raised in homes with an open, embracing attitude toward sex. Like many of us, some were told not to touch themselves "down there." Some had histories of childhood sexual abuse. One woman even reported that her strongest arousing fantasy was a painful memory of watching her mother being raped by her stepfather.

"Some women have an incredibly adaptive way of

While growing up, women are taught that girls who like sex are "sluts" and that sexy women are weak and compliant bimbos. It's easy to become convinced that a woman who loves sex won't be taken seriously.

dealing with negative sexual experiences. Women who feel at home with their sexual performance report the same kinds of negative memories routinely reported by clients with sexual complaints," Ogden says. "But their reponse is different. They've somehow learned to change the program in their heads."

In other words, for some women the problem isn't *what* they feel during sex, but the *way* they feel about it. "You can learn how to press these three buttons and produce an anatomic reaction," says Ogden. "That's fine, but there's got to be more. We need a notion of sex that makes it a part of the rest of your life."

THAT SOUNDS wonderful. But many women still want to know which buttons to press. The fact is, an inability to have orgasm during intercourse is the second most common sexual complaint of women. And infrequent orgasm most certainly plays a role in many cases of low sexual desire.

Why is satisfaction during sex so elusive? At the risk of stating the obvious, intercourse does not directly stimulate a woman's most sensitive organ—her clitoris. Therapist Lonnie Barbach points out that if we redefined the sex act as a man rubbing his scrotum against a woman's clitoris, with the expectation he would climax, it would be men who would be seen as sexually dysfunctional.

Going strictly by the physical evidence, women *are* innately more sexual than men. At least, they possess the sole organ in the human species whose raison d'être is sexual pleasure. The clitoris is a tiny bundle, about four millimeters in size, of exquisitely sensitive nerve endings. The penis, derived from the same tissue in the male, is burdened with carrying out the additional tasks of urination and reproduction. It's the latter that puts a crimp on the penis's orgasmic potential. Although it's possible for some men to learn to separate orgasm from ejaculation, for most the two are as inseparable as football and beer. This means that men have a relatively long waiting period between orgasms, while the tank is refilling, so to speak.

No such mechanism need deter a woman from experiencing numerous climaxes during a sexual encounter. In one researcher's laboratory, the most orgasms recorded in an hour by a male was 17; the most prolific female subject had 134.

So why have millions of women never had one sole moment of release? From Kinsey onward, surveys have found that the percentage of women who report never having an orgasm hovers around the 10 percent mark. The numbers are even more depressing when you look at that Holy Grail of sexual functioning—orgasm through intercourse. Helen Singer Kaplan estimates that as many as three in four women rarely or never experience orgasm through penile thrusting alone. "These sexually healthy women can climax only if they receive direct clitoral stimulation before, after, or during intercourse," she says.

One of the most common barriers to pleasure is that many women are simply unfamiliar with their

Rate Your Level of Desire

A MASTERS & JOHNSON TEST

Decide how well each of the following statements applies to your life on a scale of 1 to 9, where 1 = doesn't apply at all, 5 = somewhat or sometimes applies, and 9 = strongly or always applies.

1. I think about sex on a daily basis 1 2 3 4 5 6 7 8 9

2. Sex is very satisfying for me 1 2 3 4 5 6 7 8 9

3. I initiate lovemaking 1 2 3 4 5 6 7 8 9

4. I am receptive to my partner's overtures to make love 1 2 3 4 5 6 7 8 9

5. I feel attractive and desirable 1 2 3 4 5 6 7 8 9

6. I masturbate on a regular basis 1 2 3 4 5 6 7 8 9

7. I find it easy to block out mental distractions when making love 1 2 3 4 5 6 7 8 9

8. I'm a very passionate person 1 2 3 4 5 6 7 8 9

9. My sex drive is as strong as my partner's 1 2 3 4 5 6 7 8 9

10. I would be very unhappy if sex wasn't a part of our relationship 1 2 3 4 5 6 7 8 9

11. I have sexual fantasies 1 2 3 4 5 6 7 8 9

12. I don't pretend to be asleep when my partner wants to make love 1 2 3 4 5 6 7 8 9

A TOTAL SCORE ABOVE 75 means your sexual desire—and, hopefully, your satisfaction—is at a high boil.

A SCORE FROM 60 TO 74 means your desire for sex is simmering. While it's not occupying your every thought, sex is obviously an important part of your life.

A SCORE FROM 40 TO 59 raises the possibility that you may have inhibited sexual desire. But that could have more to do with your lifestyle than any real sexual problem. Since it's difficult to go from ice cold to passionate at a moment's notice, Masters and Johnson suggest scheduling "sex dates," so you can look forward to a romantic interlude all day long. Another way to rev things up is to get some exercise. One study found that men and women who work out regularly had a stronger sex drive and had sex more often than non-exercisers.

TOTAL SCORES BELOW 40 indicate that you probably have inhibited sexual desire, although a diagnosis can't be made from a paper-and-pencil test. There are numerous causes for low sexual desire: Depression, stress, anemia, and certain drugs—such as medications for high blood pressure or anxiety—can interfere with libido. Don't be shy about discussing such concerns with your doctor. Obviously, problems in a relationship can also take a toll on desire. In those cases, therapy can help—but only if both partners really want to change the situation. If a lack of sexual desire is a problem for you, you might consider seeing a sex therapist. For a list of qualified therapists in your area, contact the American Association of Sex Educators, Counselors, and Therapists at 435 N. Michigan Ave., Suite 1717, Chicago, IL 60611; 312/644-0828.

Adapted from the book Heterosexuality, *by William H. Masters, M.D., Virginia E. Johnson, and Robert C. Kolodny, M.D. Copyright © 1994 by Masters, Johnson, and Kolodny. Reprinted by arrangement with HarperCollins Publishers.*

bodies. "Men have this thing hanging out. They touch it when they urinate. Women aren't given permission to touch themselves and explore their bodies," says Whipple.

And most women don't. *The Janus Report on Sexual Behavior* found that 62 percent of women rarely or never masturbate. Yet studies show that women who do have a much easier time reaching climax during intercourse. It makes sense: You've got to know what you're looking for. Research also confirms the flip side of the equation. Women who don't reach orgasm have more negative attitudes toward masturbation and greater discomfort in telling a sexual partner they'd like clitoral stimulation.

But as Whipple and Ogden keep telling us, there isn't only one road to satisfaction. "There is a wide variation in the way women like to be sexually stimulated. It's much more variable than in males," agrees Kaplan. "Some women have a lower threshold for orgasm. For some, mild penetration is enough; some can have orgasm just from kissing or having their breasts touched. And while clitoral sensitivity in women is universal, many women also have erotic sensitivity in their vaginas." Which brings us back to the G-spot.

Lots of women never did find their G-spot. Some sexologists completely accept its existence ("I have one," said one expert by way of proof), some dismiss it as a sort of phantom, others say not enough evidence is in. One of the problems was that Whipple's book so hyped the spot's powers to produce ecstasy that almost anyone's real life experience was bound to fall short. Another was that the authors may have used the wrong culinary metaphor—"a small bean"—to describe it.

"If you touch it, it feels like pushing against a large marshmallow. And a woman can't even feel the area until she becomes aroused," says J. Kenneth Davidson, Sr., a sociologist who with his partner, Carol A. Darling, has done surveys on female sexual experience. Without using the term G-spot, they found that 66 percent of their respondents said they had a sensitive area in the vagina that produces pleasurable feelings. "I'm totally convinced it exists," Davidson says. "That many women can't be wrong."

To Kaplan, the whole controversy—is there a G-spot, are there clitoral or vaginal orgasms?—is idiotic. "I know there is such a thing as a vaginal orgasm. I respond that way. So do some of my friends. But we didn't do it until we got much older. In younger women it's rare. But who cares? You're looking at the toenails of elephants. You just have to find out what you like."

SO HOW DO YOU DO THAT? As with any skill, it takes practice. Lots and lots of practice, says Marilyn Fithian, who along with her partner, William Hartman, worked as a sex therapist and researcher for 30 years before retiring in 1985. Fithian, a small, round, grandmotherly woman, has decorated her office in Long Beach, California, with erotic sculptures from around the world, demonstrating the gymnastic ability involved in the joining of two bodies and the universal fascination with huge phalluses. She points to a small black ottoman. "That's our masturbation machine," she says, flipping open the top to reveal an ocher-colored dildo for women and a suction device for men. She laments that they are no longer manufactured.

Fithian retrieves a sheaf of graph paper documenting the orgasms of some of the 750 people who have been through her laboratory. The Richter scale–like marks are a dead giveaway. Fithian says that while an orgasm is clearly identifiable on the chart, each person's chart is a kind of sexual fingerprint. Presented with a dozen, she could identify the two that were made by the same person.

And therein lies the wonder, and difficulty, of female sexuality: No two orgasms are alike. There are certain physiological changes that signal female arousal—the skin flushes, tissues fill with blood, breasts enlarge by as much as 25 percent. As arousal moves on to orgasm there are the clear signals of spiking blood pressure, pulse, and anal and vaginal contractions.

Ultimately, however, the old canard that sex is in the brain is right. The main event of orgasm—supreme pleasure followed by a feeling of well-being and satiation—occurs in the brain's limbic system, or pleasure center. And you can't measure the pleasure. Its intensity varies from woman to woman and from each encounter to the next. Orgasm can be perceived as mild stimulation or a sensation of ecstasy so overwhelming that a woman momentarily loses consciousness.

This explains why some women are disappointed with their orgasms. They expect fireworks and get a sneeze instead. Fithian did a study of 20 women who said they were not orgasmic. Yet 15 showed clear physical signs of orgasm when they masturbated. "It's always said you'll know when you have it. But that's not true," Fithian says. "Female orgasm is often not easily recognizable. Typically, these women said, 'It wasn't what I expected' or 'It wasn't what my sister said happens.'"

Just as there is no one orgasm, there is no piece of advice—or button to push—that will work for everyone. Learning to become sufficiently aroused to have an orgasm during intercourse is a bit like developing a discerning taste for fine wine. That is, it's not something that is going to happen with the first few sips, or even the first few bottles. There are, of course, always exceptions. A lucky minority of women do experience intense orgasms during intercourse when they first become sexually active. Ironically, Fithian says, some of them would seem to be the least likely. That is, they did not masturbate growing up, so they didn't develop habits of sexual response that rely on clitoral stimulation. Women who masturbate with their legs crossed, for instance, have a harder time adapting their style of feeling pleasure to intercourse.

Some women are disappointed with their orgasms. They expect fireworks and get a sneeze instead. "Typically, women say, 'It wasn't what I expected' or 'It wasn't what my sister said happens.'"

Couples must take the time to simply investigate each other's bodies, fully and slowly. It seems like an obvious starting point, but it is one that many people never get to. Time seems to be the key. When masturbating, women do not linger any longer than men: Kinsey reported that it takes an average of about three minutes for both to come to orgasm. But the deep, "bearing down" sensation that some women describe experiencing during intercourse can take those same women more than 20 minutes to reach. "We tell couples they need two hours minimum to build up the intense levels of response that they dream about," Fithian says. "We have them do a whole body caress, then spend at least fifteen to twenty minutes in intercourse."

Certain angles of entry also seem more likely to produce intensely pleasurable orgasms than others. One Danish study, for instance, compared the intensity of women's orgasms during intercourse in positions ranging from the most popular "missionary" style to the less popular rear-entry or sideways positions. The rear and sideways positions resulted in the maximum penetration by the male and the most satisfying orgasm for the female.

Fithian says the reason many women never experience a vaginal orgasm is that they simply don't experience enough vaginal stimulation to achieve it. "The vagina is unconditioned," she says. "Most women haven't had anything in there long enough to feel anything. People who have orgasm with intercourse have lots of sex. The more you have it, the easier it is."

And that's the catch-22 of sexual satisfaction. Women who have lots of sex are sexually fulfilled, and women who are sexually fulfilled have lots of sex. The first step to entering the circle is to overcome the obstacles that prevent sex from happening spontaneously.

Masters and Johnson offer some suggestions for how a woman can foster sexual arousal. It's important, they say, for a woman not to shut off erotic potential and simply accept that she's not in the mood at any given moment. They point out that many problems with sexual arousal are a result of thinking too much (Did I shave my legs today? Am I getting excited yet?) and not touching enough. They advise using your imagination to jump-start arousal. Finally, a couple must learn how to talk about sex, to tell each other, perhaps for the first time, what they like, don't like, and would like to try. It's amazing how something new can produce different feelings.

As for Gina Ogden, she says it's time women started talking among themselves as a way of finding out what others have discovered—so sex isn't something every woman has to reinvent for herself. "Let's make a sexual revolution, and we don't have to do it on the barricades. We can do it simply by talking together. That's one thing women have done all through history—pounded the corn, done the sewing, and talked."

Sexual Arousal of College Students in Relation to Sex Experiences

Peter R. Kilmann, Ph.D., M.P.H., Joseph P. Boland, Ph.D., Melissa O. West, Ph.D., C. Jean Jonet, Ph.D., and Ryan E. Ramsey, M.A.

University of South Carolina

This study explored whether casual sexual intercourse experiences would be associated with sexual arousability. Three hundred and sixty-two never-married undergraduates were divided into four subgroups based on their history of sexual activity: virgins, sexual intercourse with affection only, relatively less casual sex experiences (1–5), and relatively more casual sex experiences (6 or more). While males rated themselves more easily aroused than females, subjects with casual sex experience did not rate themselves more easily aroused than subjects without that experience. Increasing the frequency of casual sex increased the likelihood that an individual perceived him or herself as "different" from others of the same gender. Males and nonreligious subjects were more likely to engage in intercourse without affection than females and religious subjects. Future research should explore the correlates of casual sexual behavior in married and divorced individuals of different ages.

Numerous studies have explored gender differences in the incidence and prevalence of premarital sexual intercourse. Among the findings, men are more likely than women to have a greater number of premarital sexual partners (Simon, 1989), and to report a more permissive sexual standard (Sprecher, 1989).

Personality attributes are related to more frequent intercourse experiences for single college students (e.g., Keller, Elliot, & Gunberg, 1982; Leary & Snell, 1988). However, the relationship context of intercourse experi-

ences was not clearly defined in these studies. In this regard, intercourse may occur in an "emotionally-committed" relationship versus on a "casual basis" without any emotional commitment given or expected.

Prior research suggests a positive association between the frequency of sexual intercourse and the variable "sexual arousability" (Hoon, Hoon, & Wincze, 1976) for *both* males and females (e.g., Harris, Yulis, & Lacoste, 1980); yet, no differentiation was made between the frequency of intercourse occurring within the context of an ongoing "emotionally-committed" relationship versus the frequency of intercourse in noncommitted relationships. Because sexual arousal at least partially influences the decision to engage in intercourse for sexually experienced individuals (Christopher & Cate, 1984), we predicted a positive association between "sexual arousability" and casual sexual behavior. We differentiated individuals on their intercourse experiences by defining "casual sexual intercourse" as "having sexual intercourse with a person on one occasion only." The subject may have known the partner for a period of time or may have just met the partner prior to having sex. "Afterwards, the partner may never have been seen again, or the person may have maintained a platonic relationship with the partner, but sexual intercourse occurred on that one occasion only." An additional focus was to identify variables associated with sexual activity.

METHOD

Subjects

The subjects were 362 (159 males, 203 females) never-married individuals recruited from three undergraduate human sexuality courses at the University of South Carolina. The subjects' mean age was 20, ranging from 18 to 43. Eighty-five percent of the subjects reported having had at least one sexual intercourse experience. The virgins (never experienced sexual intercourse) consisted of

Address correspondence to Peter R. Kilmann, Ph.D., M.P.H., Department of Psychology, University of South Carolina, Columbia, SC 29208.

From the *Journal of Sex Education & Therapy*, Vol. 19, No. 3, Fall 1993, pp. 157-164. © 1993 by the American Association of Sex Educators, Counselors, and Therapists. Reprinted by permission.

14 males and 33 females. Twenty males and 77 females reported no casual sex experiences and only had sex with affection. Eighty-six males and 76 females reported one to five casual sex experiences. Thirty-nine males and 17 females had six or more casual sex experiences. In essence, 60% of the subjects had experienced casual sex at least once.

Measures

Sexual Behavior and Attitudes Questionnaire. This questionnaire, developed by the experimenters, consisted of 148 multiple choice and Likert scale items designed to elicit information about: (a) demographic variables (e.g., sex, race, marital status, religion); (b) various personality characteristics; (c) descriptions of partners and ratings of satisfaction in casual sex experiences as compared with steady love relationships and partners; and (d) extent of agreement or disagreement with various statements about casual sex.

The Sexual Arousability Inventory (SAI). This inventory was developed by Hoon, Hoon, and Wincze (1976) to measure subjective sexual arousability in women. Anderson, Broffit, Karlson, and Turnquist (1989) found this instrument to be an internally consistent and stable measure of female sexual arousability. The questionnaire items also seem pertinent to the assessment of male sexual arousability.

Procedure

All subjects responded to the measures anonymously. Care was taken to insure privacy by leaving a space of at least one seat between subjects.

RESULTS

A 2 × 2 analysis of variance was conducted on the SAI scores finding that males scored significantly higher than females, $F(1, 336) = 5.40$, $p < .05$. The mean SAI score for males was 90.6 with a standard deviation of 16.9, and for females, 85.4 with a standard deviation of 22.3. Neither the main effect nor the interaction for a single casual intercourse experience were significant. Thus, subjects with casual sex experience did not rate themselves as more easily aroused.

For the statistical analyses, the subjects were divided by gender into four categories: virgins (never had intercourse); sex with affection only (only had intercourse with affection within a steady love relationship); one to five (one to five casual sex experiences); six or more (six or more casual sex experiences).

Descriptive Information

The virgins' beliefs about casual sex were very similar to the subjects who had few such experiences. Most of the

"Sex with affection only" subgroup had between one to five sexual partners. These subjects predicted that they would feel empty, guilty, and remorseful if they engaged in casual sex. They predicted that there would be a better chance for a continuing relationship if one got to know the person before having sex. They considered it wrong to have casual sex while married or in an exclusive relationship. Compared to persons having casual sex, they rated themselves as much more mature and responsible, and much higher on the dimensions of attractiveness, intelligence, friendliness, popularity, sexual experience, and knowledge.

Most of the "one to five" subjects were single, white Protestants, and over half reported not actively practicing their religion. These subjects considered themselves to be more attractive, intelligent, friendly, mature, and sexually knowledgeable than their peers. They estimated that more than half of their peers had casual sex. Many reported that casual sex experiences had become less attractive because of a concern about herpes. It is interesting that almost 11% of these subjects had herpes.

Most of the "one to five" subjects reported feeling lonely and/or in need of affection prior to their casual sex experience. Typically, these subjects did not initiate the encounter, and they did not want to continue the relationship. The experience "just happened" and was less emotionally satisfying than sex in a steady relationship. Their last casual sex partner tended to be over 21 years old (50% were 21–30; 30% were over 30). Most would not engage in casual sex again with the same person but perhaps with someone else. Some felt they should not have engaged in casual sex and most preferred steady love relationships. Most believed that casual sex would not lead to a continuing relationship. Most strongly believed it was wrong to have casual sex while involved in marriage or within the context of an exclusive relationship.

The majority of the "six or more" subjects were single, white Protestants who did not actively practice their religion. Nearly all perceived themselves as having average or more sexual experience than their peers. They also estimated that less than half of their peers had experienced even a single casual sex experience. During their most recent experience, these subjects generally were not involved in another relationship, although those who were reported being satisfied with it. Most of these subjects met their casual sex partners either in a bar or in their neighborhood. Like the "one to five" group, they reported that the experience "just happened," and was less emotionally satisfying than sex within the context of a steady relationship. Typically, these subjects went back to their own home to have sexual intercourse within 24 hours of meeting their partner. Casual sex experiences more often than not occurred after drinking, or after smoking "grass," and these participants typically reported that it "just happened" without much planning. Alcohol was usually consumed and frequently involved more than five drinks. Their partners also had been drinking, and about a third of the subjects used drugs. Casual sex was rated as very enjoyable and these subjects were eager to have another experience with the same partner or with a new one.

The "six or more" subjects used more alcohol and drugs, considered casual sex to be more satisfying, and reported less guilt about it than the "one to five" subjects. They generally chose partners who were between 19–21 years old, single, white, less attractive, less interesting, and average or less mature than the subjects' steady lovers. Further, their steady lovers were perceived as having more sexual knowledge and experience than their casual sex partners. The subjects' rated their casual sex experiences as involving less responsibility, satisfaction, and intimacy than sex with a regular partner.

Although most believed that it was wrong to have casual sex while married or in an exclusive relationship, many had experienced casual sex while dating someone exclusively. Casual sex experiences were considered opportunities to test out different partners with varying techniques, and the spontaneity and unpredictability of the situation. Casual sex made them feel attractive and wanted. Although casual sex was intense and passionate, sex in a steady love relationship was seen as more emotionally satisfying.

In comparison with their peers, the "six or more" women perceived themselves as average or less attractive, while the men thought they were more attractive. Both males and females perceived themselves as average or less responsible, but more friendly, mature, and sexually knowledgeable, and as average or more intelligent, popular, sexually active, and sexually experienced.

Discriminant Function Analyses

In order to further contrast the subjects within the four groupings, we performed a discriminant function analysis separately for males and females on a subset of the questionnaire items. Some items were not responded to by the entire sample, (i.e., subjects who had never had casual sexual intercourse according to our definition responded to 100 of the 148 items), and some items were not appropriate for use as discriminators. Eighteen items were chosen for the analysis; three of the items were the demographic variables for age, race, and year in college, while 15 items were the respondents' self-ratings of personal characteristics such as intelligence, friendliness, likeability, and attitudes about sex.

Similar to the procedure used above, the entire sample was partitioned by gender into four subgroups based on their sexual intercourse experience level; Group 1 consisted of virgins; Group 2 of respondents who had not had a casual sex experience but who had had intercourse with affection only, and the subjects in the remaining two groups were classified as either having experienced relatively few (1-5) or many (6 or more) casual sex experiences (Groups 3 and 4 respectively). The Wilks' method, which determines the appropriate number of functions that used the overall multivariate F-ratio for the test of differences of group centroids, was employed in the analyses.

Analysis of Males. Two significant functions of a possible three existed among the data. The first function, which accounted for approximately 53% of the between group variance that was accountable for by all functions ($X(54) = 103.62$, $p < .001$), primarily utilized the self-rating items for conventionality, responsibleness, and age of partner in their last steady relationship. The males in Group 4 (6 or more casual sex experiences) rated themselves as being relatively less responsible, less conventional, and had older partners in their last relationships. To a lesser extent, the self-rating items for extroversion, age, and a belief about what percentage of the population engages in casual sex, were used in the first discriminant function. The subjects in Group 4 made the highest estimation of all the groups as to how many people engage in casual sex. The males in this group were slightly older and perceived themselves as more outgoing than did the males in the other three groups.

The second function, which accounted for 28% of the between group variance overall ($X(34) = 51.70$, $p < .05$), discriminated Groups 1 and 4 from Groups 2 and 3. That is, the male virgins and males who experienced casual sex six or more times were similar along this second dimension, and yet distinct from the males in the sex-with-affection group (Group 2), and also from the males who reported one to five casual sex experiences (Group 3). Groups 1 and 4 were distinct from Groups 2 and 3 in that their last steady partner was either younger (Group 1) or older (Group 4) than the partners of their peers in groups 2 and 3. The male virgins and the males with frequent casual sex experiences considered themselves more attractive than their counterparts and made higher estimations about how many people engage in casual sex. The male virgins and the males with many casual sex experiences similarly reported higher sexual arousability; they also shared the same belief that casual sex involves the woman being seductive and the man being conquering.

Analysis of Females. One significant function (of a possible three) accounted for approximately 60% of the overall between group variance, ($X(54) = 86.63$, $p < .01$). This function discriminated Groups 1 and 2 (the female virgins and sex with affection females) from Groups 3 and 4 (1–5 casual sex experiences, 6 or more casual sex experiences).

The first function primarily used the self-rating items for conventionality and arousability, and the endorsement of two beliefs about casual sex. The females in Groups 1 and 2 considered themselves more conventional than others, strongly believed that casual sex was both an opportunity to test out different partners without making a commitment, and considered casual sex to involve the woman being seductive and the man being conquering. To a lesser extent, the females in Groups 3 and 4 reported a higher sexual arousability than the females in Groups 1 and 2.

DISCUSSION

We did not find a relationship between the frequency of casual sexual intercourse and level of "sexual arousability" for either gender, suggesting that these two variables are unrelated. Garcia, Brenner, DeCarlo, McGlennan, and Tate (1984) found that females rated erotic stories just as arousing as males when the most active character was also female. From an erotic guided imagery procedure, female subjects experienced a commensurate level of sexual arousal to both committed and casual relationship contexts (Harrell & Stolp, 1985). More evidence is needed using varied measures of subjective sexual arousability (e.g., Mosher, Barton-Henry, Green, 1988) to determine whether the factors contributing to sexual arousal are gender-specific.

As the frequency of casual intercourse experiences increased, males perceived themselves as less conventional, less responsible, more outgoing, and had older partners in their last casual intercourse interaction than did males who had not done so. Females who had not had casual intercourse perceived themselves as more conventional, and believed that casual intercourse was just an opportunity to test out different partners without making a commitment.

The "sex with commitment only" group predicted that casual intercourse would leave them feeling empty, guilty, and remorseful. These subjects may have been reluctant to engage in casual intercourse because of these negative emotions and the lack of expected fulfillment (Keller, Elliott, & Gunberg, 1982). Persons with a "sex with commitment only" philosophy may be more likely to find themselves disagreeing with their partners about the level of desired sexual intimacy in dating (Byers & Lewis, 1988).

The subjects in the "one to five group" reported some negative effects from casual intercourse. Their last casual sex experience was less satisfying, more guilt-producing; these subjects indicated that they would not do it again with the same person. They also reported a greater prevalence of herpes, and a greater reluctance to have casual intercourse due to a fear of contacting a sexually transmitted disease. The partners of these subjects also tended to be much older, and were not perceived to offer a future relationship.

Future research should determine whether there are different intrapersonal and interpersonal variables associated with casual sexual contacts, either as separate from an ongoing relationship or as a lifestyle. Future research also should explore the variables associated with the casual intercourse frequency in married and divorced individuals of different ages using more restrictive definitions of "casual intercourse" (e.g., "intercourse occurring only one time with a 'stranger'; i.e., a person who was not known before the encounter nor ever seen again").

REFERENCES

Anderson, B. L., Broffit, B., Karlson, J. A., & Turnquist, D. C. (1989). A psychometric analysis of the Sexual Arousability Index. *Journal of Consulting and Clinical Psychology, 57,* 123–130.

Byers, E. S., & Lewis, K. (1988). Dating couples' disagreements over the desired level of sexual activity. *Journal of Sex Research, 24,* 15–29.

Christopher, F. S., & Cate, R. M. (1984). Factors involved in premarital decision-making. *Journal of Sex Research, 20,* 363–376.

Garcia, L. T., Brenner, K., DeCarlo, M., McGlennan, R., & Tait, S. (1984). Sex differences in sexual arousal to different erotic stories. *Journal of Sex Research, 20,* 391–402.

Harrell, T. H., & Stolp, R. D. (1985). Effects of erotic guided imagery on female sexual arousal and emotional response. *Journal of Sex Research, 21,* 292–304.

Harris, R., Yulis, S., & LaCoste, D. (1980). Relationships among sexual arousability, imagery ability, and introversion-extraversion. *Journal of Sex Research, 16,* 72–86.

Hoon, E. F., Hoon, P. W., & Wincze, J. P. (1976). An inventory for the measurement of female arousability: The SAI. *Archives of Sexual Behavior, 5,* 291–300.

Keller, J. F., Elliott, S. S., & Gunberg, E. (1982). Premarital sexual intercourse among single college students: A discriminant analysis. *Sex Roles, 8,* 21–32.

Leary, M. R., & Snell, W. E., Jr. (1988). The relationship of instrumentality and expressiveness to sexual behavior in males and females. *Sex Roles, 18,* 509–522.

Mosher, D. L., Barton-Henry, M., Green, S. E. (1988). Subjective sexual arousal and involvement: Development of multiple indicators. *Journal of Sex Research, 25,* 412–425.

Simon, A. (1989). Promiscuity as sex difference. *Psychological Reports, 64,* 802.

Sprecher, S. (1989). Premarital sexual standards for different categories of individuals. *The Journal of Sex Research, 26,* 232–248.

PSYCHOTRENDS

Taking Stock of Tomorrow's Family and Sexuality

Where are we going and what kind of people are we becoming? Herewith, a road map to the defining trends in sexuality, family, and relationships for the coming millenium as charted by the former chair of Harvard's psychiatry department. From the still-rollicking sexual revolution to the painful battle for sexual equality to the reorganization of the family, America is in for some rather interesting times ahead.

Shervert H. Frazier, M.D.

Has the sexual revolution been sidetracked by AIDS, and the return to traditional values we keep hearing about? In a word, no. The forces that originally fueled the revolution are all still in place and, if anything, are intensifying: mobility, democratization, urbanization, women in the workplace, birth control, abortion and other reproductive interventions, and media proliferation of sexual images, ideas, and variation.

Sexuality has moved for many citizens from church- and state-regulated behavior to a medical and self-regulated behavior. Population pressures and other economic factors continue to diminish the size of the American family. Marriage is in sharp decline, cohabitation is growing, traditional families are on the endangered list, and the single-person household is a wave of the future.

AIDS has generated a great deal of heat in the media but appears to have done little, so far, to turn down the heat in the bedroom. It is true that in some surveys people *claimed* to have made drastic changes in behavior—but most telling are the statistics relating to marriage, divorce, cohabitation, teen sex, out-of-wedlock births, sexually transmitted diseases (STDs), contraception,

and adultery. These are far more revealing of what we *do* than what we *say* we do. And those tell a tale of what has been called a "postmarital society" in continued pursuit of sexual individuality and freedom.

Studies reveal women are more sexual now than at any time in the century.

Arguably there are, due to AIDS, fewer visible sexual "excesses" today than there were in the late 1960s and into the 1970s, but those excesses (such as sex clubs, bathhouses, backrooms, swinging singles, group sex, public sex acts, etc.) were never truly reflective of norms and were, in any case, greatly inflated in the media. Meanwhile, quietly and without fanfare, the public, even in the face of the AIDS threat, has continued to expand its interest in sex and in *increased,* rather than decreased, sexual expression.

Numerous studies reveal that women are more sexual now than at any time in the century. Whereas sex counselors used to deal with men's complaints about their wives' lack of "receptivity," it is now more often the women complaining about the men. And women, in this "postfeminist"

era, are doing things they never used to believe were "proper." Fellatio, for example, was seldom practiced (or admitted to) when Kinsey conducted his famous sex research several decades ago. Since that time, according to studies at UCLA and elsewhere, this activity has gained acceptance among women, with some researchers reporting that nearly all young women now practice fellatio.

Women's images of themselves have also changed dramatically in the past two decades, due, in large part, to their movement into the workplace and roles previously filled exclusively by men. As Lilian Rubin, psychologist at the University of California Institute for the Study of Social Change and author of *Intimate Strangers,* puts it, "Women feel empowered sexually in a way they never did in the past."

Meanwhile, the singles scene, far from fading away (the media just lost its fixation on this subject), continues to grow. James Bennett, writing in *The New Republic,* characterizes this growing population of no-reproducers thusly: "Single adults in America display a remarkable tendency to multiply without being fruitful."

Their libidos are the target of million-dollar advertising budgets and entrepreneurial pursuits that seek to put those sex drives on line in the information age. From video dating to computer coupling to erotic faxing, it's now "love at first byte," as one commentator put it. One thing is certain: the computer is doing as much today to promote the sexual revolution as the automobile did at the dawn of that revolution.

Political ideologies, buttressed by economic adversities, *can* temporarily retard the sexual revolution, as can sexually transmitted diseases. But ultimately the forces propelling this revolution are unstoppable. And ironically, AIDS itself is probably doing more to promote than impede this movement. It has forced the nation to confront a number of sexual issues with greater frankness than ever before. While some conservatives and many religious groups have argued for abstinence as the only moral response to AIDS, others have lobbied for wider dissemination of sexual information, beginning in grade schools. A number of school districts are now making condoms available to students—a development that would have been unthinkable before the outbreak of AIDS.

Despite all these gains (or losses, depending upon your outlook) the revolution is far from over. The openness that it has fostered is healthy, but Americans are still ignorant about many aspects of human sexuality. Sexual research is needed to help us deal with teen sexuality and pregnancies, AIDS, and a number of emotional issues related to sexuality. Suffice it to say for now that there is still plenty of room for the sexual revolution to proceed—and its greatest benefits have yet to be realized.

THE REVOLUTION AND RELATIONSHIPS

The idea that the Sexual Revolution is at odds with romance (not to mention tradition) is one that is widely held, even by some of those who endorse many of the revolution's apparent objectives. But there is nothing in our findings to indicate that romance and the sexual revolution are inimical—unless one's defense of romance disguises an agenda of traditional male dominance and the courtly illusion of intimacy and communication between the sexes.

The trend now, as we shall see, is away from illusion and toward—in transition, at least—a sometimes painful reality in which the sexes are finally making an honest effort to *understand* one another.

But to some, it may seem that the sexes are farther apart today than they ever have been. The real gender gap, they say, is a communications gap so cavernous that only the most intrepid or foolhardy dare try to bridge it. Many look back at the Anita Hill affair and say that was the open declaration of war between the sexes.

The mistake many make, however, is saying that there has been a *recent* breakdown in those communications, hence all this new discontent. This conclusion usually goes unchallenged, but there is nothing in the data we have seen from past decades to indicate that sexual- and gender-related communication were ever better than they are today. On the contrary, a more thoughtful analysis makes it very clear they have always been *worse*.

What has changed is our *consciousness* about this issue. Problems in communication between the sexes have been masked for decades by a rigid social code that strictly prescribes other behavior. Communication between the sexes has long been preprogrammed by this code to produce an exchange that has been as superficial as it is oppressive. As this process begins to be exposed by its own inadequacies in a rapidly changing world, we suddenly discover that we have a problem. But, of course, that problem was there for a long time, and the discovery does not mean a decline in communication between the sexes but, rather, provides us with the potential for better relationships in the long run.

Thus what we call a "breakdown" in communications might more aptly be called a *breakthrough*.

Seymour Parker, of the University of Utah, demonstrated that men who are the most mannerly with women, those who adhere most strictly to the "code" discussed above, are those who most firmly believe, consciously or unconsciously, that women are "both physically and psychologically weaker (i.e., less capable) than men." What has long passed for male "respect" toward women in our society is, arguably, *disrespect*.

Yet what has been learned can be unlearned—especially if women force the issue, which is precisely what is happening now. Women's views of themselves are changing and that, more than anything, is working to eliminate many of the stereotypes that supported the image of women as weak and inferior. Women, far from letting men continue to dictate to them, are making it clear they want more *real* respect from men and will accept nothing less. They want a genuine dialogue; they want men to recognize that they speak with a distinct and equal voice, not one that is merely ancillary to the male voice.

The sexual revolution made possible a serious inquiry into the ways that men and women are alike and the ways that each is unique. This revolutionary development promises to narrow the gender gap as nothing else can, for only by understanding the differences that make communication so complex do we stand any chance of mastering those complexities.

SUBTRENDS

Greater Equality Between the Sexes

Despite talk in the late 1980s and early 1990s of the decline of feminism and declarations that women, as a social and political force, are waning, equality between the sexes is closer to becoming a reality than ever before. Women command a greater workforce and wield greater political power than they have ever done. They are assuming positions in both public and private sectors that their mothers and grandmothers believed were unattainable (and their fathers and grandfathers thought were inappropriate) for women. Nonetheless, much remains to be achieved before women attain complete equality—but movement in that direction will continue at a pace that will surprise many over the next two decades.

Women voters, for example, who have long outnumbered male voters, are collectively a sleeping giant whose slumber many say was abruptly interrupted during the Clarence Thomas–Anita Hill hearings in 1991. The spectacle of a political "boy's club" raking the dignified Hill over the coals of sexual harassment galvanized the entire nation for days.

On another front, even though women have a long way to go to match men in terms of equal pay for equal work, as well as in equal opportunity, there is a definite *research* trend that shows women can match men in the skills needed to succeed in business. This growing body of data will make it more difficult for businesses to check the rise of women into the upper echelons of management and gradually help to change the corporate consciousness that still heavily favors male employees.

As for feminism, many a conservative wrote its obituary in the 1980s, only to find it risen from the dead in the 1990s. Actually, its demise was always imaginary. Movements make headway only in a context of dissatisfaction. And, clearly, there is still plenty for women to be dissatisfied about, particularly in the wake of a decade that tried to stifle meaningful change.

The "new feminism," as some call it, is less doctrinaire than the old, less extreme in the sense that it no longer has to be outrageous in order to call attention to itself. The movement today is less introspective, more goal oriented and pragmatic. Demands for liberation are superseded—and subsumed—by a well-organized quest for power. Women no longer want to burn bras, they want to manufacture and market them.

The New Masculinity

To say that the men's movement today is confused is to understate mercifully. Many men say they want to be more "sensitive" but also "less emasculated," "more open," yet "less vulnerable." While the early flux of this movement is often so extreme that it cannot but evoke guffaws, there is, nonetheless, something in it that commands some respect—for, in contrast with earlier generations of males, this one is making a real effort to examine and redefine itself. The movement, in a word, is *real.*

Innumerable studies and surveys find men dissatisfied with themselves and their roles in society. Part of this, undoubtedly, is the result of the displacement men are experiencing in a culture where *women* are so successfully transforming themselves. There is evidence, too, that men are dissatisfied because their own fathers were so unsuccessful in their emotional lives and were thus unable to impart to their sons a sense of love, belonging, and security that an increasing number of men say they sorely miss.

The trend has nothing to do with beating drums or becoming a "warrior." It relates to the human desire for connection, and this, in the long run, can only bode well for communications between humans in general and between the sexes in particular. Many psychologists believe men, in the next two decades, will be less emotionally closed than at any time in American history.

More (and Better) Senior Sex

People used to talk about sex after 40 as if it were some kind of novelty. Now it's sex after 60 and it's considered not only commonplace but healthy.

Some fear that expectations among the aged may outrun physiological ability and that exaggerated hopes, in some cases, will lead to new frustrations—or that improved health into old age will put pressure on seniors to remain sexually active beyond any "decent" desire to do so.

But most seem to welcome the trend toward extended sexuality. In fact, the desire for sex in later decades of life is *heightened,* studies suggest, by society's growing awareness and acceptance of sexual activity in later life.

Diversity of Sexual Expression

As sex shifts from its traditional reproductive role to one that is psychological, it increasingly serves the needs of the individual. In this context, forms of sexual expression that were previously proscribed are now tolerated and are, in some cases increasingly viewed as no more nor less healthy than long-accepted forms of sexual behavior. Homosexuality, for example, has attained a level of acceptance unprecedented in our national history.

More Contraception, Less Abortion

Though abortion will remain legal under varying conditions in most, if not all, states, its use will continue to decline over the next two decades as more—and better-contraceptives become available. After a period of more than two decades in which drug companies shied away from contraceptive research, interest in this field is again growing. AIDS, a changed political climate, and renewed fears about the population explosion are all contributing to this change.

Additionally, scientific advances now point the way to safer, more effective, more convenient contraceptives. A male contraceptive that will be relatively side-effect free is finally within reach and should be achieved within the next decade, certainly the next two decades. Even more revolutionary in concept and probable impact is a vaccine, already tested in animals, that some predict will be available within 10 years—a vaccine that safely stops ovum maturation and thus makes conception impossible.

Religion and Sex: A More
Forgiving Attitude

Just a couple of decades ago mainstream religion was monolithic in its condemnation of sex outside of marriage. Today the situation is quite different as major denominations across the land struggle with issues they previously wouldn't have touched, issues related to

adultery, premarital sex, homosexuality, and so on.

A Special Committee on Human Sexuality, convened by the General Assembly of the Presbyterian Church (USA), for example, surprised many when it issued a report highly critical of the traditional "patriarchal structure of sexual relations," a structure the committee believes contributes, because of its repressiveness, to the proliferation of pornography and sexual violence.

All this will surely pale alongside the brave new world of virtual reality.

The same sort of thing has been happening in most other major denominations. It is safe to say that major changes are coming. Mainstream religion is beginning to perceive that the sexual revolution must be acknowledged and, to a significant degree, accommodated with new policies if these denominations are to remain in touch with present-day realities.

Expanding Sexual Entertainment

The use of sex to sell products, as well as to entertain, is increasing and can be expected to do so. The concept that "sex sells" is so well established that we need not belabor the point here. The explicitness of sexual advertising, however, may be curbed by recent research finding that highly explicit sexual content is so diverting that the viewer or reader tends to overlook the product entirely.

Sexual stereotyping will also be less prevalent in advertising in years to come. All this means, however, is that women will not be singled out as sex objects; they'll have plenty of male company, as is already the case. The female "bimbo" is now joined by the male "himbo" in ever-increasing numbers. Sexist advertising is still prevalent (e.g., male-oriented beer commercials) but should diminish as women gain in social and political power.

There's no doubt that films and TV have become more sexually permissive in the last two decades and are likely to continue in that direction for some time to come. But all this will surely pale alongside the brave (or brazen) new world of "cybersex" and virtual reality, the first erotic emanations of which may well be experienced by Americans in the coming two decades. Virtual reality aims to be just that—artificial, electronically induced experiences that are virtually indistinguishable from the real thing.

The sexual revolution, far from over, is in for some new, high-tech curves.

FROM BIOLOGY TO PSYCHOLOGY: THE NEW FAMILY OF THE MIND

Despite recent pronouncements that the traditional family is making a comeback, the evidence suggests that over the next two decades the nuclear family will share the same future as nuclear arms: there will be fewer of them, but those that remain will be better cared for.

Our longing for sources of nurturance has led us to redefine the family.

Demographers now believe that the number of families consisting of married couples with children will dwindle by yet another 12 percent by the year 2000. Meanwhile, single-parent households will continue to increase (up 41 percent over the past decade.) And household size will continue to decline (2.63 people in 1990 versus 3.14 in 1970). The number of households maintained by women, with no males present, has increased 300 percent since 1950 and will continue to rise into the 21st century.

Particularly alarming to some is the fact that an increasing number of people are choosing *never* to marry. And, throughout the developed world, the one-person household is now the fastest growing household category. To the traditionalists, this trend seems insidious—more than 25 percent of all households in the United States now consist of just one person.

There can be no doubt: the nuclear family has been vastly diminished, and it will continue to decline for some years, but at a more gradual pace. Indeed, there is a good chance that it will enjoy more stability in the next two decades than it did in the last two. Many of the very forces that were said to be weakening the traditional family may now make it stronger, though not more prevalent. Developing social changes have made traditional marriage more elective today, so that those who choose it may, increasingly, some psychologists believe, represent a subpopulation better suited to the situa-

tion and thus more likely to make a go of it.

As we try to understand new forms of family, we need to realize that the "traditional" family is not particularly traditional. Neither is it necessarily the healthiest form of family. The nuclear family has existed for only a brief moment in human history. Moreover, most people don't realize that no sooner had the nuclear family form peaked around the turn of the last century than erosion set in, which has continued ever since. For the past hundred years, reality has chipped away at this social icon, with increasing divorce and the movement of more women into the labor force. Yet our need for nurturance, security, and connectedness continues and, if anything, grows more acute as our illusions about the traditional family dissipate.

Our longing for more satisfying sources of nurturance has led us to virtually redefine the family, in terms of behavior, language, and law. These dramatic changes will intensify over the next two decades. The politics of family will be entirely transformed in that period. The process will not be without interruptions or setbacks. Some lower-court rulings may be overturned by a conservative U.S. Supreme Court, the traditional family will be revived in the headline from time to time, but the economic and psychological forces that for decades have been shaping these changes toward a more diverse family will continue to do so.

SUBTRENDS

Deceptively Declining Divorce Rate

The "good news" is largely illusory. Our prodigious national divorce rate, which more than doubled in one recent 10-year period, now shows signs of stabilization or even decline. Still, 50 percent of all marriages will break up in the next several years. And the leveling of the divorce rate is not due to stronger marriage but to *less* marriage. More people are skipping marriage altogether and are cohabiting instead.

The slight dip in the divorce rate in recent years has caused some prognosticators to predict that younger people, particularly those who've experienced the pain of growing up in broken homes, are increasingly committed to making marriage stick. Others, more persuasively, predict the opposite, that the present lull precedes a storm in which the divorce rate will soar to 60 percent or higher.

Increasing Cohabitation

The rate of cohabitation—living together without legal marriage—has been growing since 1970 and will accelerate in the next two decades. There were under half a million cohabiting couples in 1970; today there are more than 2.5. The trend for the postindustrial world is very clear: less marriage, more cohabitation, easier and—if Sweden is any indication—less stressful separation. Those who divorce will be less likely to remarry, more likely to cohabit. And in the United States, cohabitation will increasingly gather about it both the cultural acceptance and the legal protection now afforded marriage.

We need to realize the "traditional family" is not particularly traditional.

More Single-Parent Families and Planned Single Parenthood

The United States has one of the highest proportions of children growing up in single-parent families. More than one in five births in the United States is outside of marriage—and three quarters of those births are to women who are not in consensual unions.

What is significant about the single-parent trend is the finding that many single women with children now *prefer* to remain single. The rush to the altar of unwed mothers, so much a part of American life in earlier decades, is now, if anything, a slow and grudging shuffle. The stigma of single parenthood is largely a thing of the past—and the economic realities, unsatisfactory though they are, sometimes favor single parenthood. In any case, women have more choices today than they had even 10 years ago; they are choosing the psychological freedom of single parenthood over the financial security (increasingly illusory, in any event) of marriage.

More Couples Childless by Choice

In the topsy-turvy 1990s, with more single people wanting children, it shouldn't surprise us that more married couples *don't* want children. What the trend really comes down to is increased freedom of choice. One reason for increasing childlessness among couples has to do with the aging of the population, but many of the reasons are more purely psychological.

With a strong trend toward later marriage, many couples feel they are "too old" to have children. Others admit they like the economic advantages and relative freedom of being childless. Often both have careers they do not want to jeopardize by having children. In addition, a growing number of couples cite the need for lower population density, crime rates, and environmental concerns as reasons for not wanting children. The old idea that "there must be something wrong with them" if a couple does not reproduce is fast waning.

The One-Person Household

This is the fastest growing household category in the Western world. It has grown in the United States from about 10 percent in the 1950s to more than 25 percent of all households today. This is a trend that still has a long way to go. In Sweden, nearly *40 percent* of all households are now single person.

"Mr. Mom" a Reality at Last?

When women began pouring into the work force in the late 1970s, expectations were high that a real equality of the sexes was at hand and that men, at last, would begin to shoulder more of the household duties, including spending more time at home taking care of the kids. Many women now regard the concept of "Mr. Mom" as a cruel hoax; but, in fact, Mr. Mom *is* slowly emerging.

Men *are* showing more interest in the home and in parenting. Surveys make clear there is a continuing trend in that direction. Granted, part of the impetus for this is not so much a love of domestic work as it is a distaste for work outside the home. But there is also, among many men, a genuine desire to play a larger role in the lives of their children. These men say they feel "cheated" by having to work outside the home so much, cheated of the experience of seeing their children grow up.

As the trend toward more equal pay for women creeps along, gender roles in the home can be expected to undergo further change. Men will feel less pressure to take on more work and will feel more freedom to spend increased time with their families.

More Interracial Families

There are now about 600,000 interracial marriages annually in the United States, a third of these are black-white, nearly triple the number in 1970, when 40 percent of the white population was of the opinion that such marriages should be illegal. Today 20 percent hold that belief. There is every reason to expect that both the acceptance of and the number of interracial unions will continue to increase into the foreseeable future.

Recognition of Same-Sex Families

Family formation by gay and lesbian couples, with or without children, is often referenced by the media as a leading-edge signifier of just how far society has moved in the direction of diversity and individual choice in the family realm. The number of same-sex couples has steadily increased and now stands at 1.6 million such couples. There are an estimated 2 million gay parents in the United States.

And while most of these children were had in heterosexual relationships or marriages prior to "coming out," a significant number of gay and lesbian couples are having children through adoption, cooperative parenting arrangements, and artificial insemination. Within the next two decades, gays and lesbians will not only win the right to marry but will, like newly arrived immigrants, be some of the strongest proponents of traditional family values.

The Rise of Fictive Kinships

Multiadult households, typically consisting of unrelated singles, have been increasing in number for some years and are expected to continue to do so in coming years. For many, "roommates" are increasingly permanent fixtures in daily life.

In fact housemates are becoming what some sociologists and psychologists call "fictive kin." Whole "fictive families" are being generated in many of these situations, with some housemates even assigning roles ("brother," "sister," "cousin," "aunt," "mom," "dad," and so on) to one another. Fictive families are springing up among young people, old people, disabled people, homeless people, and may well define one of the ultimate evolutions of the family concept, maximizing, as they do, the opportunities for fulfillment of specific social and economic needs outside the constraints of biological relatedness.

THE BREAKUP OF THE NUCLEAR FAMILY

It's hard to tell how many times we've heard even well-informed health professionals blithely opine that "the breakup of the family is at the root of most of our problems." The *facts* disagree with this conclusion. Most of the social problems attributed to the dissolution of the "traditional" family (which, in reality, is *not* so traditional) are the product of other forces. Indeed, as we have seen, the nuclear family has itself created a number of economic, social, and psychological problems. To try to perpetuate a manifestly transient social institution beyond its usefulness is folly.

What *can* we do to save the nuclear family? Very little.

What *should* we do? Very little. Our concern should not be the maintenance of the nuclear family as a *moral* unit (which seems to be one of the priorities of the more ardent conservative "family values" forces), encompassing the special interests and values of a minority, but, rather, the strengthening of those social contracts that ensure the health, well-being, and freedom of individuals.

BORN GAY?

**Studies of family trees
and DNA make the case
that male homosexuality
is in the genes**

WILLIAM A. HENRY III

WHAT MAKES PEOPLE GAY? TO conservative moralists, homosexuality is a sin, a willful choice of godless evil. To many orthodox behaviorists, homosexuality is a result of a misguided upbringing, a detour from a straight path to marital adulthood; indeed, until 1974 the American Psychiatric Association listed it as a mental disorder. To gays themselves, homosexuality is neither a choice nor a disease but an identity, deeply felt for as far back as their memory can reach. To them, it is not just behavior, not merely what they do in lovemaking, but who they are as people, pervading every moment of their perception, every aspect of their character.

The origins of homosexuality may never be fully understood, and the phenomenon is so complex and varied—as is every other kind of love—that no single neat explanation is likely to suffice to explain any one man or woman, let alone multitudes. But the search for understanding advanced considerably last week with the release of new studies that make the most compelling case yet that homosexual orientation is at least partly genetic.

A team at the National Cancer Institute's Laboratory of Biochemistry reported in the journal *Science* that families of 76 gay men included a much higher proportion of homosexual male relatives than found in the general population. Intriguingly, almost all the disproportion was on the mother's side of the family. That prompted the researchers to look at the chromosomes that determine gender, known as X and Y. Men get an X from

their mother and a Y from their father; women get two X's, one from each parent. Inasmuch as the family trees suggested that male homosexuality may be inherited from mothers, the scientists zeroed in on the X chromosome.

Sure enough, a separate study of the DNA from 40 pairs of homosexual brothers found that 33 pairs shared five different patches of genetic material grouped around a particular area on the X chromosome. Why is that unusual? Because the genes on a son's X chromosome are a highly variable combination of the genes on the mother's two X's, and thus the sequence of genes varies greatly from one brother to another. Statistically, so much overlap between brothers who also share a sexual orientation is unlikely to be just coincidence. The fact that 33 out of 40 pairs of gay brothers were found to share the same sequences of DNA in a particular part of the chromosome suggests that at least one gene related to homosexuality is located in that region. Homosexuality was the only trait that all 33 pairs shared; the brothers didn't all share the same eye color or shoe size or any other obvious characteristic. Nor, according to the study's principal author, Dean Hamer, were they all identifiably effeminate or, for that matter, all macho. They were diverse except for sexual orientation. Says Hamer: "This is by far the strongest evidence to date that there is a genetic component to sexual orientation. We've identified a portion of the genome associated with it."

The link to mothers may help explain a conundrum: If homosexuality is hereditary, why doesn't the trait gradually disappear, as

gays and lesbians are probably less likely than others to have children? The answer suggested by the new research is that genes for male homosexuality can be carried and passed to children by heterosexual women, and those genes do not cause the women to be homosexual. A similar study of lesbians by Hamer's team is taking longer to complete because the existence and chromosomal location of responsible genes is not as obvious as it is in men. But preliminary results from the lesbian study do suggest that female sexual orientation is genetically influenced.

In a related, unpublished study, Hamer added to growing evidence that male homosexuality may be rarer than was long thought—about 2% of the population, vs. the 4% to 10% found by Kinsey and others. Hamer notes, however, that he defined homosexuality very narrowly. "People had to be exclusively or predominantly gay, and had to be out to family members and an outside investigator like me. If we had used a less stringent definition, we would probably have found more gay men."

BEFORE THE NCI, RESEARCH IS ACcepted as definitive, it will have to be validated by repetition. Moreover, the tight focus on pairs of openly homosexual brothers, who are only a subset of the total gay population, leaves many questions about other categories of gay men, lesbians and bisexuals. The NCI researchers concede that their discovery cannot account for all male homosexuality and may be just associated with gayness rather than be a direct cause.

But authors of other studies indicating a biological basis for homosexuality saluted it as a major advance.

Simon LeVay, who won wide publicity for an analysis of differences in brain anatomies between straight and gay men, acknowledges that the brains he studied were of AIDS victims, and thus he cannot be sure that what he saw was genetic rather than the result of disease or some aspect of gay life. Says LeVay: "This new work and the studies of twins are two lines of evidence pointing in the same direction. But the DNA evidence is much stronger than the twin studies." Dr. Richard Pillard, professor of psychiatry at Boston University School of Medicine—and co-author of some twin studies—showing that identical twins of gay men have a 50% chance of being gay—is almost as laudatory. Says he: "If the new study holds up, it would be the first example of a higher-order behavior that has been found to be linked to a particular gene."

Whatever its ultimate scientific significance, however, the study's social and political impact is potentially even greater. If homosexuals are deemed to have a fore-ordained nature, many of the arguments now used to block equal rights would lose force. Opponents of such changes as ending the ban on gays in uniform argue that homosexuality is voluntary behavior, legitimately subject to regulation. Gays counter that they are acting as God or nature—in other words, their genes—intended. Says spokesman Gregory J. King of the Human Rights Campaign Fund, one of the largest gay-rights lobbying groups: "This is a landmark study that can be very helpful in increasing public support for civil rights for lesbian and gay Americans." Some legal scholars think that if gays can establish a genetic basis for sexual preference, like skin color or gender, they may persuade judges that discrimination is unconstitutional.

In addition, genetic evidence would probably affect many private relationships. Parents might be more relaxed about allowing children to have gay teachers, Boy Scout leaders and other role models, on the assumption that the child's future is written in his or her genetic makeup. Those parents whose offspring do turn out gay might be less apt to condemn themselves. Says Cherie Garland of Ashland, Oregon, mother of a 41-year-old gay son: "The first thing any parent of a gay child goes through is guilt. If homosexuality is shown to be genetic, maybe parents and children can get on with learning to accept it." Catherine Tuerk, a nurse psychotherapist who is Washington chapter president of Parents and Friends of Lesbians and Gays, regrets sending her son Joshua into therapy from ages eight to 12 for an "aggression problem"—preference for games involving

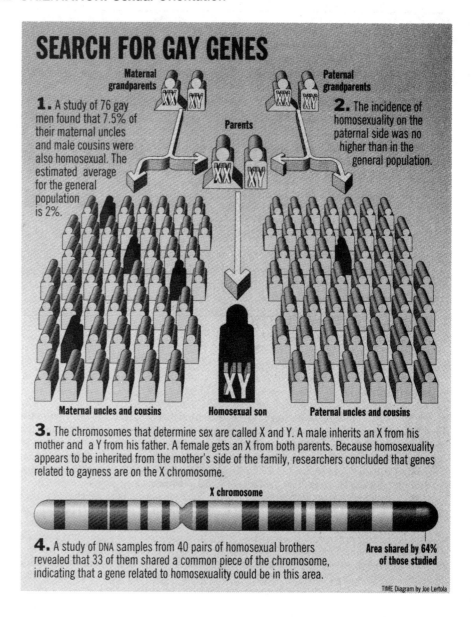

SEARCH FOR GAY GENES

Maternal grandparents

Paternal grandparents

Parents

1. A study of 76 gay men found that 7.5% of their maternal uncles and male cousins were also homosexual. The estimated average for the general population is 2%.

2. The incidence of homosexuality on the paternal side was no higher than in the general population.

Maternal uncles and cousins   Homosexual son   Paternal uncles and cousins

3. The chromosomes that determine sex are called X and Y. A male inherits an X from his mother and a Y from his father. A female gets an X from both parents. Because homosexuality appears to be inherited from the mother's side of the family, researchers concluded that genes related to gayness are on the X chromosome.

X chromosome

4. A study of DNA samples from 40 pairs of homosexual brothers revealed that 33 of them shared a common piece of the chromosome, indicating that a gene related to homosexuality could be in this area.

Area shared by 64% of those studied

TIME Diagram by Joe Lertola

relationships instead of macho play with, say, toy trucks. Says she: "We were trying to cure him of something that doesn't need to be cured. There was nothing wrong with him." On the other hand, mothers who used to blame themselves for faulty upbringing may start blaming themselves for passing on the wrong genes.

Gay brothers surveyed for the study welcome its findings. Rick and Randy Gordon, twins from Orlando, Florida, never felt being gay was a matter of free will. Rick, who works in a law firm, says, "I don't honestly think I chose to be gay." Randy, a supervisor at a bed-and-breakfast, agrees: "I always believed that homosexuality was something I was born with. If homosexuality is genetic, there is nothing you can do about it. If there is more research like this in years to come, hopefully homosexuality will be accepted rather than treated as an abnormality."

Ralph White, 36, an attorney with the General Accounting Office, says he was fired from a senatorial staff in 1982 after admitting he was gay. He foresees abiding significance in the study: "I don't expect people to suddenly change their minds. But the long-term impact will be profound. I can't imagine that rational people, presented with evidence that homosexuality is biological and not a choice, would continue to discriminate." His brother David, 32, a public relations officer, wishes he had had a basis for believing in a genetic cause during his turbulent adolescence: "I was defiant, and to this day I'm probably still that way, because when you're gay in this society you almost have to be."

While many gay leaders welcomed the study, some are queasy. Its very existence, they fret, implies that homosexuality is wrong and defective. Says Donald Suggs of the New York chapter of the Gay & Lesbian Alliance Against Defamation: "Homosexuality is not something to justify and explain, but something that should be accepted. Until people accept us, all the scientific evidence in the world will not do anything to change homophobia." Moreover, gays are worried that precise identification of a "gayness gene" might prompt efforts to tinker with the genetic code of gay adults or to test during pregnancy and abort potentially gay fetuses. Says Thomas Stoddard, director of the Campaign for Military Service: "One can imagine the science of the future manipulating information of this kind to reduce the number of gay people being born."

WARNS ERIC JUENGST OF THE National Center for Human Genome Research: "This is a two-edged sword. It can be used to benefit gays by allowing them to make the case that the trait for which they're being discriminated against is no worse than skin color. On the other hand, it could get interpreted to mean that different is pathological."

Anti-gay activists took up that cry immediately, saying that a genetic basis for homosexuality does not make it any more acceptable. They noted that genetic links are known or suspected for other traits that society judges "undesirable," such as mental and physical illness. Said the Rev. Louis Sheldon, chairman of the Traditional Values Coalition: "The fact that homosexuality may be genetically based will not make much difference for us from a public policy perspective." Reed Irvine, whose watchdog group, Accuracy in Media, increasingly criticizes favorable reportage about gays and gay rights, called for more coverage of studies that he claims show homosexuality can be "cured"—an assertion that both gays and health professionals widely dispute. Says Irvine: "It's a little more complicated than just saying you can prove there's a hereditary factor. The media have given zero attention to the many, many homosexuals who have gone straight. I think it's sending gays the wrong message to say you cannot change because it's something your genes have determined."

Even gays admit that Irvine is partly right. Homosexuality is not simply programmed but is a complex expression of values and personality. As researcher Hamer says, "Genes are part of the story, and this gene region is a part of the genetic story, but it's not all of the story." We may never know all of the story. But to have even part of it can bring light where of late there has been mostly a searing heat. —*Reported by Ellen Germain/Washington and Alice Park/New York*

THE POWER AND THE PRIDE

Lesbians have long been the invisible homosexuals, but now they're coming out strong. What are the limits of tolerance?

Two, four, six, eight, how do you know your grandma's straight?" the women chanted, many thousands strong, on the eve of the recent gay-lesbian-rights march in Washington. There were, in fact, lots of grandmotherly types proceeding down Connecticut Avenue that spring evening, along with bare-breasted teenagers in overalls, aging baby boomers in Birkenstocks and bald biker dykes in from the Coast. Advertising execs strode arm in arm with electricians, architects with politicians. As onlookers pondered the stereotype-defying scene, the demonstrators reveled in their sheer numbers. It was, for once, an unabashed display of lesbian clout.

Lesbians have always been the invisible homosexuals. There are an estimated 2 million to 3 million of them in the United States—far fewer than the approximately 5 percent of the population represented by gay men. Activists believe that most lesbians haven't come out. But now during the dawning of the "Gay '90s," these women are stepping front and center. From the studios of Hollywood to the hearing rooms of the Capitol, lesbians suddenly seem to be out of the closet and in your face. Last June, country singer k.d. lang came out to The Advocate, a biweekly gay magazine, giving new meaning to her hit "Constant Craving." Avowed bisexual Sandra Bernhard took her place in the "Roseanne" lineup, playing the lesbian co-owner of a sandwich shop opposite actress Morgan Fairchild. "We're like the Evian water of the '90s," stand-up comic Suzanne Westenhoefer says wryly. "Everybody wants to know a lesbian or to be with a lesbian or just to dress like one."

Why now? As conservatives are quick to note, the election of Bill Clinton contributed to this open atmosphere. Though many homosexuals feel let down by his waffling on the military ban

they give him credit for being the first president to acknowledge gays and lesbians, let alone promote them. Last month former San Francisco supervisor Roberta Achtenberg became an assistant secretary of housing and urban development—and the first open homosexual ever confirmed by the U.S. Senate for political office. In the end, however, the new lesbian presence has as much to do with women power as gay power. "Sometimes I think it's like the year of the woman squared," says lesbian comic Kate Clinton (no relation to the president). "It's sort of like the year of the woman loving woman."

Yet lesbians are still struggling to define themselves politically and socially. "Are we the women's part of the gay movement or the lesbian part of the women's movement?" muses Torie Osborn, the head of the National Gay and Lesbian Task Force (NGLTF) in Washington. Obviously, they are both. Lesbian activists have toiled in behalf of issues—notably, AIDS and abortion—that are unlikely to affect them directly. "We have for years and years taken care of everybody but ourselves," says Ellen Carton of the Gay and Lesbian Alliance Against Defamation (GLAAD).

Now lesbians are determined to cast off their role as handmaidens to other activists and stake their own claims. It won't be easy. For all their new pride, lesbians face a lot of old prejudice. The emergence of openly lesbian couples—publicly affectionate or with their children—may test the limits of America's uneasy tolerance of homosexuality. Even many liberals who watched C-Span's unexpurgated coverage of the gay-rights march were offended by the spectacle of some women—albeit from the lesbian fringes—who were kissing or half naked. More mainstream lesbians themselves worry about the dangers of visibility. A look at some of the gains, goals and battles:

A Town Like No Other

Country-music fans gravitate to the Grand Ole Opry, painters dream of Provence and ski bums settle in Aspen. Lesbians have a mecca, too. It's Northampton, Mass., a.k.a. Lesbianville, U.S.A. In a profile of the town last year, the National Enquirer claimed that "10,000 cuddling, kissing lesbians call it home sweet home." While no one really knows how many of Northampton's 30,000 residents are homosexual women (the best guess is one in 10 women), lesbians are clearly an important and somewhat controversial presence. "It's more an issue of visibility than numbers," says Mayor Mary L. Ford, who is straight but has many lesbian supporters.

Every Monday night, the town's cable station telecasts "Out & About," a lesbian talk show. Lesbian tourists stay at bed and breakfasts just for women. Local bookstores sell lesbian erotica. There are five colleges nearby (including all-female Smith and Mount Holyoke); lesbians and academics are the town's major cultural influences. Lesbians run a summer festival that draws thousands of women from around the country. All year long, there are regular performances by lesbian singers and comics. "If you're looking for lesbians, they're every-

where," says Diane Morgan, codirector of the festival.

Northampton has been a lesbian haven since the late 1970s. Many of the pioneers were Smith and Mount Holyoke alumnae attracted by cheap living and a tolerant community. Friends followed, revitalizing the aging downtown with cafés and hip clubs. "I came because I wanted to meet other women like me," says Aliza Ansell, 34. In the early '80s, says Ansell, a codirector of the arts festival, the Zeitgeist was different: it was a "pretty radical, scary community." The politically correct uniform was flannel shirts and work boots.

That intensity survives in some parts of Northampton. One women's bookstore, Lunaria, still won't carry any books by men. But many lesbians say that there are so many of their own in Northampton that they now feel relaxed enough to dress any way they want and read anything they want. "In this town, you don't have to wear your sexuality like a flag," says Morgan, who wears her hair in a bob and uses lipstick. "You don't need the uniform to be able to spot each other in a crowd."

Motherhood was once taboo, but now, more and more Northampton lesbians

are having babies, usually through artificial insemination. There are parenting classes and a day-care center for children of lesbian mothers. One of the more famous residents, Lesléa Newman, wrote "Heather Has Two Mommies," the book that was used to bring down New York City Schools Chancellor Joseph Fernandez. Newman got the idea after a lesbian mother stopped her as she was walking past and asked her to write a book she could read to her daughters. "Only in Northampton," says Newman, "would a woman know who I was on the street and ask me a question like that."

Media 'hype': At Smith, the lesbian "invasion" has been a public-relations minefield. Although she supports the college's own lesbian community, Smith president Mary Maples Dunn has criticized the media for overemphasizing the lesbian presence on campus and in town. There have been numerous complaints from alumnae about more lurid stories, such as the Enquirer's, but Smith officials say contributions are down only slightly. They deny the drop is related to publicity about lesbians. At the same time, they say, applications are at a record high.

Some residents say lesbians

have become too visible. "You can see them making love almost anyplace," says Caroline Brandt, 71, registrar of the local Daughters of the American Revolution chapter. "I was walking down the street the other day and I saw an open parked car. Two of them were going to town in there."

Northampton isn't utopia for all lesbians, either. It's mostly a white community, with few minorities. "I'm waiting to go to Berkeley or New York," says one black Amherst College student who wears her hair in dreadlocks and is studying to be a percussionist in an Afrofunk band.

But most of Northampton's lesbian residents feel at home and accepted by their neighbors. "It is a good minority of the population, but it doesn't bother me," says Mark Brumberg, owner of The Globe, Northampton's main literary bookstore. "This is an open community." At the North Star, a restaurant and nightclub owned by lesbians, gays dance next to straight couples. "After living here for a couple of years," says Diane Morgan, "you begin to forget what it's like in the real world." But she's sure of one thing: the real world is nothing like Northampton.

Barbara Kantrowitz and
Danzy Senna in Northampton

ACTIVISM

"I'm a little amused at this renewed interest in lesbians," says Urvashi Vaid, former executive director of NGLTF. Vaid, who is writing a book about the gay-rights movement, notes that lesbians have played a prominent role in many social fights, from abolition and temperance to civil rights. Like gays generally, they are better educated than the overall population. But they have operated, by and large, from the closet. And when some of them tried to come out, it was their straight sisters who slammed the door shut. During the 1970s, the NOW (National Organization for Women) leadership purged open lesbians, lest their presence somehow taint the movement. They still worked

for the cause—often under the nom de guerre "radical feminists"—but the rebuff caused a good deal of bitterness. Today lesbians can take some measure of vindication from the appointment of Patricia Ireland, who has both a husband and a woman lover, as NOW president.

The '80s brought the devastation of AIDS, and with it a partial healing of an old rift between male and female homosexuals. For many lesbians, the bottom line about gays has always been that they are men, and often sexist to boot. "Straight men at least have an incentive to pretend they respect women," jokes Hillary Rosen, vice president of the Recording Industry of America and a member of the board of directors of the Human Rights Campaign Fund, a lobbying group. Yet many gay men now recognize the debt they owe lesbians, who embraced the cause of AIDS as their own. Lesbians, many of whom belonged to such "caring" professions as nursing and social work, helped start health-care networks. They lobbied for policy change and protested when it didn't happen fast enough. "AIDS did knit us into family," says Vaid. "Before, we existed in parallel worlds."

New fissures, however, have begun to show. While few lesbians would argue that it was wrong to rally round the AIDS fight, there have been rumblings about the need to refocus their energies. Lesbians consider themselves victims of both homophobia and sexism. Some issues now on the table, like the military ban, speak to the homosexuality of lesbians. Others are women's issues, such as pay equity, day care and the ERA. Some overlap, becoming in the process uniquely theirs. "Take reproductive freedom," says New York state legislator Deborah Glick, a lesbian. "It brings up areas of family law that haven't been dealt with, like artificial insemination." Lesbians have also begun demanding more money for research on breast cancer—a worry for all women but, because of its increased risk with childlessness, a particular concern among homosexuals.

But questions about how to reach their goals, and who will lead, continue to bedevil lesbian activists. Like the gay-rights movement generally, the lesbian ranks embody people of different colors, class, education and culture; their issues aren't always the same. Should lesbians pour money into mainstream lobbying groups, or take to the streets with the Lesbian Avengers, a protest outfit formed to attract media attention to lesbian causes? And what about those men, who still dominate gay leadership positions? "When a lesbian walks into a room of gay men, it's the same as when she walks into a room of heterosexual men," says one activist. "You're listened to and then politely ignored." That, politically active lesbians agree, is one thing that must change. "We're not going to be invisible anymore," says Lesbian Avenger Ann Northrop. "We are going to be prominent and have power and be part of all decision making."

YOUTHQUAKE

Coming of age sexually is always a rocky rite of passage; for homosexuals, even more so. But young lesbians seem less and less conflicted about their identity. Girls who "are growing up lesbian today," says Carton, 35, of GLAAD, "watch 'Roseanne,' and they see a main character played by Sandra Bernhard, who's a lesbian, and it's accepted on the show. That's the difference between me growing up in the '60s and seeing 'The Children's Hour' with Shirley MacLaine. She finds out she's a lesbian and she kills herself." Growing up in a small, Southern town, Ashley Herrin (who appears on NEWSWEEK's cover with her partner Catherine Angiel) turned to alcohol to deaden her feelings of sexual differentness. Today she's sober and is studying to become a therapist for homosexuals. Not all young lesbians believe they can tell their parents about their sexual orientation even now, but pioneers from the feminist trenches

GLOSSARY

FEMME Traditionally, the "feminine" partner; young women are now redefining the role as less submissive

BUTCH Wears suit, motorcycle jacket or other "manly" gear

LIPSTICK LESBIAN Part of the Madonna esthetic. Dolls up, has long nails, wears makeup and skirts.

SEX-POSITIVE Flaunts female-to-female eroticism, no-guilt, feel-good sex

VANILLA Likes kissing, holding hands, no rough stuff

detect a refreshing new sense of self-acceptance. "When I was 21, I was terrified," says Dorothy Allison, lesbian author of the best-selling novel "Bastard Out of Carolina." "These young lesbians aren't scared in the same way. They're living their lives instead of explaining their lives."

On a few campuses around the country, straights have found themselves on the defensive. "Once in a while you'll hear a first-year student slightly upset about being called a breeder or something," says Robin Russell, a recent graduate of Oberlin College in Ohio, considered to be a gay mecca by many young homosexuals. The annual Lesbutante Ball is a command performance for lesbian couples in their butch and femme finery. Earlier this year, at the University of Washington in Seattle, the student government sponsored its first Dyke Visibility Day. The catalogs of some 45 schools contain courses on the homosexual experience.

One common experience that doesn't appear in the course offerings is that of the "four-year lesbian." In today's politically correct atmosphere, say many students, it's become the in thing to experiment sexually. For some, that has meant lesbian relations. Feminist scholar Catharine Stimpson, dean of the graduate school at Rutgers University, says her students consider themselves to be a bisexual "Third Wave." "They're quite condescending about dividing humanity into heterosexual and homosexual," says Stimpson. The "LUG," or "lesbian until graduation" phenomenon, however, has alienated many people—not only straight alumni but lesbians, who suggest that it trivializes their long and difficult journey. "It's funny," says black lesbian author Jacqueline Woodson, 30. "When you go to college, you date all these baby dykes. Then you graduate, and you're still a lesbian, but they've gotten married and secure."

POP CULTURE

On March 10, an article about lesbian comedian Lea DeLaria appeared in the Los Angeles Times, saying, " 'The Tonight Show' is off-limits. 'Late Night' won't touch her." Arsenio Hall, DeLaria recalls, figured that if the other shows didn't want her, she was probably right for him. She passed her audition only to encounter resistance from Arsenio's lawyers. They didn't want her to use the word dyke, which, says DeLaria, "was basically my entire act. Arsenio himself walked in and said, 'If she wants to call herself a dyke, then it's not our business'." So there she was, some three weeks later, in a man's suit, beaming out to America: "It's great to be here because it's the 1990s, and it's hip to be queer and I'm a *big* dyke."

The appearance of an openly gay comic on national television was a rare event, indeed. Though everybody knows the arts are full of gays and lesbians, the entertainment industry has done its best to keep them in the closet. In the course of working on her forthcoming book on Hollywood, "But Wait a Second, We Haven't Finished Lunch," author Julia Phillips found that lesbians were particularly fearful about coming out. "It seems to me they're like where the guys were 30 years ago," says Phillips. "Hollywood is not really a brave kind of place anyway . . . and lesbians are right at the bottom of the list in terms of power structure."

The entertainment industry's treatment of gay and lesbian themes has been a mixed performance. TV has become somewhat more willing to project what lesbians consider to be a realistic image of their lives. Lesbians salute recent episodes of "Roseanne" and "Seinfeld," which portray them as normal people. The movies have a more troubling track record. Male fantasy, lesbians say, drove the sinister portrayal in "Basic Instinct." "I don't know any lesbian icepick killers," says Ellen Carton. "Do you?" The film "Fried Green Tomatoes" left the nature of the relationship between its two heroines ambiguous; the novella on which it was based left no doubt that they were lovers.

Some of Hollywood's reticence comes from an assumption that mainstream America isn't ready for gay and lesbian themes. But a number of lesbian authors have demonstrated their crossover appeal. Little, Brown has published hardcover editions of Sandra Scoppettone's mysteries, which include homosexual love scenes. Novelist Allison was even a little surprised by the success of her earlier, lesbian-oriented books among the public. "Eighty percent of the people at my readings are straight," she says. "It bothered me at first because I wasn't sure if I was being understood. But they read me the way I want to be read, which makes me hopeful."

SEX AND SOCIETY

Legend has it that Queen Victoria asked her ministers, "What do lesbians do?" Many straights still don't get it, but, says psychotherapist JoAnne Loulan, the Dr. Ruth of lesbian sex, "it is such a simple concept." For good or ill, lesbians have found it easy to "pass" because society accepts affectionate relations between women without assuming that they're sexual. Some straight men find the notion of two women together titillating. Others tend not to feel threatened by lesbians because "they can't imagine women having sex without [their] aid," says San Francisco psychology professor John De Cecco.

In fact, the desire to sleep with other women is perhaps the only common denominator in today's extraordinarily diverse lesbian culture. The pluralism is relatively new: in the '70s, the prevailing outlook was separatist and even prudish. Nine years ago, Debra Sundahl and Nan Kinney started On Our Backs, a lesbian magazine intended as a rebuke to feminist orthodoxy. "Women were denying themselves sexual pleasure because of politics," says Sundahl. "If it was male-identified, they decided not to do it." Now, says Carol Queen, an owner of a sexual paraphernalia store in San Francisco called Good Vibrations, "the lesbian community has a somewhat different take on sexual adventuring." There is a vital "sex-positive" scene, with nightly dancing at places like the Clit Club in New York and San Francisco's twice-a-month sex clubs.

Others don't have the energy to party—they're the "vanilla lesbians," home with their kids. There have always been lesbian parents, but in previous decades they tended to be women who discovered their sexuality some time after marriage and motherhood. Increasingly, there are lesbian couples who are becoming mothers together. Eileen Rakower, 33, and her partner each had a child by artificial insemination from the same unknown donor. "We have created a family this way, as out lesbians," says Rakower, a lawyer. Interestingly some of the deepest resistance the two women encountered came from older homosexuals. "What we saw," she says, "was a real self-doubting, self-hatred. We don't get that anymore from people who know us and know our kids," now 4 years old and 20 months old.

Lesbians are well aware that their new prominence brings with it the risk of backlash. Polls about gays suggest that Americans are most tolerant of sexual differences when they don't have to confront them. Many lesbians worry they'll become scapegoats for ultraconservatives—a fear exacerbated by North Carolina Sen. Jesse Helm's reported attacks on Achtenberg as a "damn lesbian." "The abortion issue has been lost. Now they're looking for a new target," says Dr. Dee Mosbacher, daughter of George Bush's secretary of commerce and a lesbian psychiatrist in San Francisco. "We fit the bill." Such concerns have long kept lesbians in the closet. But since the first salvo of the gay revolution in 1969, homosexuals have stressed the importance of coming out, and visibility remains the most pressing item on today's lesbian agenda. "More and more of us are starting to feel we have no choice," says Washington lobbyist Rosen, "and probably nothing to lose." At the very least, lesbians can claim some of the attention they say has so long, and so unfairly, eluded them.

Eloise Salholz with Daniel Glick in Washington, Lucille Beachy and Carey Monserrate in New York, Patricia King in San Francisco, Jeanne Gordon in Los Angeles and Todd Barrett in Chicago

69

Sex and the Brain

IN THE SUMMER OF 1991, NEUROBIOLOGIST SIMON LEVAY PUBLISHED A SMALL STUDY ON A MINUTE PART OF THE HUMAN BRAIN. LITTLE DID HE REALIZE IT WOULD CATAPULT HIM FROM HIS SCIENTIFIC IVORY TOWER INTO THE HEATED FRAY OF HOMOSEXUAL POLITICS.

David Nimmons

David Nimmons has written about science and health for more than a decade. He is the author of numerous books and articles on subjects ranging from microcomputers to immune-system-boosting nutrition. His most recent book, Ethics on Call, *addresses the protection of our rights in the health-care system. Despite the fact that Nimmons was formerly an associate editor at* Playboy, *he suspects that he has a teensy-weensy INAH3.*

You might say that Simon LeVay rose to fame though a venerable locker-room tradition: sizing up the sexual anatomy of males. In his case, though, the body part in question was a speck in the brain's spongy underbelly—to be precise, a tiny cell cluster known as the third interstitial nucleus of the anterior hypothalamus, or INAH3. "There's strong evidence," notes LeVay, "that this part of the hypothalamus is deeply involved in regulating male-typical sex behavior."

Two and a half years ago LeVay, then a neurobiologist at the Salk Institute in La Jolla, California, caused a sensation by reporting a minute but measurable difference in this brain area between homosexual and heterosexual men. You could almost hear millions of nervous guys breathe a sigh of relief: yes, on average, INAH3 *is* bigger in straight men than in gay men (though at its most virile, the tiny nucleus wouldn't even fill the "o" in *macho*). The gay men's cell clusters were in the same size range as women's.

Yet small as the difference was, it suggested an enormous idea. If you could spot a difference between gay and straight men in a key sexual center of the brain, that would imply sexual orientation was influenced by—or at least reflected in—anatomy. If that was true, being gay would be less a life-style choice, as the rhetoric of the far right would have it, than the result of a natural configuration in some people's brains. LeVay's research had provided a tantalizing clue that in the realm of sexual attraction and behavior, biology—at least to some extent—might be destiny.

It also made the unassuming LeVay one of the most misunderstood men in America. "It's important to stress what I *didn't* find," he points out with the courtly patience of someone who long ago got used to waiting for the rest of the world to catch up. "I did not prove that homosexuality is genetic, or find a genetic cause for being gay. I didn't show that gay men are 'born that way,' the most common mistake people make in interpreting my work. Nor did I locate a gay center in the brain—INAH3 is less likely to be the sole gay nucleus of the brain than part of a chain of nuclei engaged in men and women's sexual behavior. My work is just a hint in that direction—a spur, I hope, to future work."

Decades of scientific rigor have made caution a habit with LeVay. "Since I looked at adult brains," he says, "we don't know if the differences I found were there at birth or if they appeared later. Although most psychiatrists now agree that sexual orientation is a stable attribute of human personality, my work doesn't address whether it's established before birth. The differences I found could have developed after a person was born—a sort of 'use it or lose it' phenomenon—though I doubt it. The experiment one would love to do," he adds, "is to scan newborn children's brains, measure the size of the cell group, and wait 25 years to see how they turn out. But there's no technology right now to image structures as small as INAH3."

Yet what LeVay *did* say was plenty controversial enough: "I am saying that gay men have a woman's INAH3—they've got a woman's brain in that particular part. In a brain region regulating sexual attraction, it would make sense that what you see in gay men is like what you see in heterosexual women. But people get nervous, as if I'm painting gay men as women in disguise."

LEVAY HARDLY SEEMS THE SORT TO

inspire controversy. A soft-spoken, self-effacing man, he stands 5 foot 9, egg-bald except for a short fringe of graying hair that betrays his 50 years. He still has the trim body of a competitive bicyclist, which he was for three decades. Dressed, as usual, in jeans and an open-necked shirt, his appearance might be described as a precarious equilibrium between natty and rumpled. You wonder what made this quiet, unthreatening academic venture into "such a touchy subject," as he calls it.

LeVay was by no means the first to find sex-related anatomical differences in the brain. Neuroanatomists have documented such sexual dimorphism in brains since the early 1980s. "The corpus callosum—the nerve bundle connecting the two brain hemispheres—is relatively larger in females," LeVay points out. "So is the anterior commissure, another nerve pathway between the brain's two halves." (It was recently shown that the anterior commissure is larger in gay men too.) "On the other hand, part of the amygdala—an almond-shaped area near the hypothalamus that plays a role in sexual arousal—is larger in males than in females."

What most influenced LeVay, though, was a 1989 finding by Roger Gorski and Laura Allen, a UCLA team that had studied male-female brain differences in rats for years. "Laura showed that the INAH3 area in humans was, on average, more than twice as large in men as in women," explains LeVay. "Now, INAH3 is in a part of the hypothalamus known to be involved in directing typical male sex behavior, such as attraction to females. So I thought it reasonable to speculate about dimorphism by sexual *orientation* as well as gender." Would the difference that showed up between men and women, he wanted to know, also show up between straight and gay men?

Since the area can't be studied in the living, the work had to be done posthumously. Altogether LeVay autopsied the brains of 41 people—19 homosexual men, 16 heterosexual men, and 6 women—painstakingly dissecting, staining, and measuring their INAH3 clusters. It was no mean feat: at its largest, the human INAH3 constitutes approximately .000009 percent of the brain's mass. To avoid biasing the results, the study was done blind—that is, each brain sample was numerically coded to conceal whether its donor was straight or gay. After nine months of peering through his laboratory microscope, LeVay sat down one morning to break the first blind codes. "Once I'd decoded the first third of the sample, I saw what the data were telling me," he says, excitement edging into his usually soft voice. His hunch had apparently paid off. According to his lab notebooks, gay and straight men did differ in a key area controlling sexual behavior. The largest INAH3 clusters tended to belong to straight men, the smallest to gay men; in fact, on average, straight men had clusters twice the size of gay men's. "I was almost in a state of shock," LeVay recalls. "I took a

walk by myself on the cliffs over the ocean. I sat for half an hour just thinking what this might mean."

When the study was published in August 1991, it attracted immediate attention—no doubt partly because it was reported in a journal with *Science*'s prestige by a neuroscientist with LeVay's credentials. LeVay—raised in London, the son of a physician and a psychiatrist—has a master's degree in natural sciences from Cambridge and a doctorate in neuroanatomy from Göttingen University in Germany. In 1971 he moved to Harvard, joining the team of David Hubel and Torsten Wiesel, who won a Nobel Prize in 1981 for their work on the brain's visual system. In 1984 LeVay moved to the West Coast to head his own vision laboratory at the Salk Institute. "Until 1990 all my work was very basic, fundamental vision research," he recalls. "I studied how the brain integrates the input of our two eyes to give us a single, three-dimensional view of the world. It was a bit ivory-towerish, really."

His study on sexual orientation was something of an anomaly. Not that he hadn't thought about it in the past. "I've known I was gay since I was about 13," he says, his tanned face breaking

"As a gay man, I had the motivation to do this work. If I didn't, nobody else was in a hurry to do it. And as a scientist, I knew it was research I was qualified to do."

into a grin. "As a gay man, I had the motivation to do this work. If I didn't, nobody else was in a hurry to do it. And as a scientist, I knew it was research I was qualified to do. I was already working on structure and function in one part of the brain, so working on the sexual part of the brain wasn't a big switch."

What ultimately changed the direction of his research, though, was a deeply personal crisis. In 1990 LeVay's partner, Richard, an emergency room physician, died after a four-year struggle with AIDS. "Richard and I had spent 21 years together," he recalls, his voice still catching at the memory. "It was while looking after him that I decided I wanted to do something different with my life. You realize life is short, and you have to think about what is important to you and what isn't. I had an emotional need to do something more personal, something connected with my gay identity."

With the publication of his paper, LeVay's 15 minutes of fame exploded with a vengeance. In just a week he was rocketed from the hushed halls of the Salk Institute to the glare of *MacNeil/Lehrer, Oprah,* and *Donahue.* His work, career, and life were dissected on *Nightline* and in *Newsweek.* "It was quite a shock," he recalls. "I wasn't prepared to talk about the private aspects of my life; I never had talked about them, especially about my lover, in public. I found it very off-putting."

LeVay was pelted with questions. Because his gay subjects had died of AIDS, some critics questioned whether the AIDS virus could have skewed his results. LeVay thinks that "highly unlikely." He'd also included in his study six heterosexuals who'd died of AIDS and saw no difference in INAH3 size patterns between these patients and those who had died of other causes. (Nevertheless, to assuage his curiosity, LeVay later examined the brain of an HIV-negative gay man who had died of lung cancer: "I was very, very nervous when I decoded that sample," he admits. "I'd have lost a lot of faith in my data if that case had contradicted it." Yet that brain, too, fell into the gay-typical range.)

> "I remember
> floating on my
> back at
> night, looking up at
> all the stars. I
> felt I was floating
> out there in
> the universe. For me,
> looking at the
> brain is somewhat
> similar."

Anne Fausto-Sterling, a developmental geneticist at Brown University and one of LeVay's chief academic critics, was among those who questioned the way he interpreted his data. "He claimed a wide variation in the size of these brain nuclei in gay and straight men," she says, "but there was still a broad overlap between straight and gay. What he actually found was a distributional difference, with a few larger-than-average nuclei at one end, a few smaller-than-average nuclei at the other, and the vast majority falling in between. Even if we could say most people at one extreme were straight, and most at the other extreme were gay, that tells us little about the majority in the middle where the ranges overlap. If LeVay picked a nucleus size in the middle, he couldn't tell if it was heterosexual or homosexual."

Fausto-Sterling also took issue with LeVay for reducing the many subtle shades of human sexuality to a gay-straight dichotomy. "There are many gradations in sexual orientation.

What do you call men who have sex with their wives while fantasizing about men? Or guys who are mostly straight who pick up male prostitutes, or transsexuals, or serial bisexuals who may switch between exclusively gay and exclusively straight relationships? How do you count sexual behavior that changes over time in different circumstances?" She described LeVay's research as part of "a reification of sexualities into a binary scheme. It maps very poorly onto reality and makes thinking about the biology very tricky."

"That's a valid criticism, one I totally accept," says LeVay. "One just has to start somewhere, with simplifying assumptions." He also regrets excluding lesbians from his study. "One tragic result of the AIDS epidemic is that it's much easier to obtain brain samples of men known to be gay. Sexual orientation is far less likely to be noted on the medical charts of women who are lesbians."

The public's response to LeVay's study was equally spirited. "Some of it was loony stuff," LeVay says with a smile. "Wild theories that it's all due to diet. Then there were the letters from religious zealots, flatly stating that being gay is a sinful choice, as it says in the Bible." In the gay community some people branded LeVay a biological bigot and called his work an expression of internalized homophobia. "One critic said I wanted to prove that it's not my fault I'm gay," says LeVay, clearly pained. "I thought his charging I was a conflicted gay man was a bit off-color; I've been open about being gay since I was a teenager." LeVay also rejects another criticism: "Some say my work means gay men are simply 'straight men with a hole in their hypothalamus,' that it pathologizes gay men. I don't buy it. To say that, you'd have to consider it pathologizing to say that gay men have something femalelike, which I don't see as true. I don't think there's anything pathological about being a woman."

But the more typical response was enthusiasm. Letters poured in from gay men and their families. "Many gay men sent my study to their parents, particularly if they were somewhat estranged from them. And parents, in turn, wrote to say the study helped them understand their kids." It's obvious that LeVay takes pleasure in knowing that many people have found his labors useful.

"Some parents think of me as the person who took them off the hook," LeVay says, smiling. "They tend to see my work as proof that being gay is genetic. It's a mistake I am sympathetic with, because I happen to think gay people quite likely *are* born gay. Since I consider my work moving in that direction," he adds wryly, "I am not totally uncomfortable with that reaction."

In fact, LeVay has long suspected that homosexuality runs in families and has an inherited component—a suspicion reinforced by recent twin studies by psychologist Michael Bailey of Northwestern University and psychiatrist Richard Pillard of Boston University. The studies show that identical twins—who share the same genes—are about twice as likely to both be gay or lesbian as are fraternal twins, who share only half their genes. They are also five times more likely to both be gay than are adopted brothers who share an upbringing but no genes. "That clearly suggests that genetics accounts for a substantial fraction of the total causation," says LeVay. As anecdotal evidence, he shows off a family snapshot of himself and his four brothers: "Two and a half of us are gay," he says. (One brother is bisexual.) "You know, my father has never been comfortable that I'm gay. He doesn't approve. Since all the kids from his second marriage are straight, he insists it's all inherited from our mother's side of the family."

LeVay's disapproving father may yet be vindicated. Last July, LeVay points out, Dean Hamer's team at the National Institutes of Health located a region on the X chromosome of gay brothers that may turn out to carry a gay gene or genes; the X chromosome is, after all, always the mother's genetic contribution to her sons. Just how a gene in this area might make someone gay remains anyone's guess: maybe it influences how sex-related structures are formed in the hypothalamus. When it comes to sexual attraction and behavior, LeVay suspects, humans are largely shaped in utero. "Something different is happening when the gay brain organizes itself in fetal life," he says. "If I put my money anywhere, it's on the interaction of sex hormones and the brain. There may be genetic differences in how the fetus's brain cell receptors respond to sex hormones such as testosterone."

LeVay thinks that over the next five years the genetic influence on sexuality will become much clearer. And if Hamer turns out to be right, of course, the human libido would be pretty much set at the factory. Though upsetting to some, the notion jibes with accumulating evidence from biologists and ethologists that evolution has preserved diverse sexual orientations. Homosexuality has now been documented in dozens of species, from primates and elephants to sea gulls and fruit flies. But that raises a profound question: Why?

"It seems paradoxical, doesn't it?" says LeVay. "At first sight homosexuality seems not to favor reproduction, so why does it persist?" LeVay can only speculate on the phenomenon. Being gay might somehow foster the survival of one's relatives, who in turn pass along part of one's genetic heritage. But then you would expect homosexual animals to spend their time taking care of infants or getting food, and there's no real evidence that they do. Alternatively, perhaps genes linked to homosexuality confer some other benefit that's selected for, and homosexuality just persists as a by-product. "But there's an awfully big reproductive cost for homosexuality," says LeVay, "so whatever characteristic goes along with it must be highly advantageous, like, say, creativity." Another theory posits that homosexuality may be part of a selection for reduced aggression—what LeVay terms "the fights-break-out-at-football-matches-but-not-at-the-opera theory." "Frankly, none of these theories seems very satisfactory to me," says LeVay. If nature has some grand design for the *homo* in *Homo sapiens,* he admits, "it remains a mystery for now."

THESE DAYS LEVAY LIVES IN A MODEST

West Hollywood apartment that reflects an artist's life more than it does a scientist's. The walls of the small kitchen are papered with exquisitely detailed pencil and ink sketches LeVay has made of his father, his deceased lover, a pensive woman in a café. On the facing wall hangs a gay rainbow flag LeVay painted in fluorescent acrylics. A jumble of dusty cycling trophies and medals adorns the tops of the bookcases in the living room. The shelves spill over with some 1,200 books, an intellectual smorgasbord running from Montaigne to Bertrand Russell to paperbacks on vegetarian cooking.

The lone clue to LeVay's profession is a framed photograph. At first glance it could be mistaken for a lightning bolt in iridescent yellow and orange, or perhaps a river viewed from a great height. In fact it's a micrograph LeVay took of a single neuron meandering through the miasma of the visual cortex. "You've no idea how beautiful the brain is," he says. "I love

looking at it through the microscope. You can choose a small patch of cells out of the millions of neuronal cells in the visual cortex, staining them yellow with a dye. And as you focus down through them, it's like going through this incredible forest of neurons. You see all the little bumps—the synapses, where the connecting points between neurons are. If you use an electron microscope, you can even see thousands of vesicles containing the transmitters that shuttle messages across the gap between the synapses. You see it all. As you focus your way through layer

> *"Science alone can only go so far in rolling back prejudice, because prejudice is based in irrationality and can't always be approached with rational arguments."*

after layer of cells, you feel like you're walking through a cathedral filled with tracery and filigree and delicate architecture.

"I remember once swimming in Walden Pond, floating on my back at night, looking up at all the stars. I felt I was actually floating out there in the universe. For me, looking at the brain is somewhat similar: you feel as if you're really inside it, with the same sense of spaciousness." LeVay cheerfully admits to "spending hours looking at the beauty of it all, not really looking *for* anything. You can explore it forever and never exhaust all the beauty and complexity that's in there."

But he is keenly aware that there is danger as well as beauty in research like his. "Historically, there has been terrible homophobia in medical research. Farcical science—like the explanation that in gay men the nerves of the penis were misrouted to the anus, transferring the erotic response there. People were given electroshock and aversion therapy to change their sexuality. It's an ugly history of scientific and medical oppression of gay people."

Does LeVay worry about his own research being misused? "If scientists find a gay gene, and I think they will, it opens the possibility—even a probability—of misuse," he answers. The dangers he foresees include discriminatory employment tests and fetal tests followed by abortions of potentially gay children. That doesn't mean the search to understand sexual orientation should be given up, argues LeVay. "You avoid misuse by helping along the process of society accepting gay people. I would be very unhappy if mothers aborted fetuses more likely to be gay, but you don't prevent that by inhibiting research, or by prohibiting testing or abortion. You do it by education, by helping people understand that it's okay to have gay kids."

Although science is the bedrock of the educational process, LeVay has become convinced that it's not enough. "Science alone can only go so far in rolling back prejudice, because prejudice is based in irrationality and can't always be approached with rational arguments. There's a human dimension to it that also needs to be addressed. Besides," he continues, "on a purely moral level, there's no justification for discrimination against homosexuality, regardless of its causation. Even if homosexuality were not biological—even if it were a conscious choice—there would *still* be grounds to respect gay people, because of our beliefs about people's right to privacy and freedom of action and because of the contributions gays and lesbians make to society."

THAT REALIZATION LED LEVAY TO HIS

next decision. Less than a year after his *Science* paper appeared, this world-class scientist did the unheard-of: he resigned his academic positions, returned a half-million-dollar research grant to the National Institutes of Health, and quit his life in the lab. By then, he admits, the lab had lost some of its allure. "At a certain stage you become an administrator, raising money to pay for research and bringing in others to do the work you'd like to do yourself," he explains. "And I realized, when I'd come to the end of my life, I wanted to feel I'd done something to give me personal satisfaction. It's not entirely rational, but a lot of gay men are propelled into activism as a result of their experiences with AIDS. Richard and I were a couple, a hardworking doctor and a scientist, but not really involved in the gay community. His illness changed that."

In the spring of 1992, LeVay left Salk to help found a very different kind of institute: the West Hollywood Institute of Gay & Lesbian Education. The idea was born on a summer's bike ride taken by LeVay and a friend, Chris Patrouch. "Most gays and lesbians miss out on learning about their own culture and history. We aren't brought up by gay families, teachers don't tell us much, there's a huge gap in our knowledge about ourselves." Over several more bike rides, LeVay and Patrouch forged the idea for an extension college for adults, taught by gay and lesbian academics on nights and weekends. With another co-founder, Lauren Jardine, they persuaded the city of West Hollywood to provide classroom space. At first glance, it seems a typically dowdy classroom, right down to the American flag at the front of the room, until a closer look reveals the remnants of a gay Spanish lesson on the blackboard. The school—which is open to all—offers courses on topics such as sexual orientation and the law, homosexuality and religion, and literary sources of contemporary gay and lesbian identity. LeVay hopes that by better knowing themselves, students will become better ambassadors for the gay and lesbian community in the world at large. (The model student of the institute may be LeVay himself. "Last semester," he says happily, "I went to a different class each night.")

Meanwhile, the notion of a biological basis for homosexuality—the notion LeVay helped generate—has taken root in the most unlikely places. Posted on one of the institute's walls is a flier from a rural Tennessee town; it announces a "Christian fellowship breakfast for people who happen to have been born gay or lesbian in affectional orientation." In Phoenix, William Cheshire,

a staunchly conservative columnist for the *Arizona Republic,* wrote a startling editorial in June 1992 endorsing an ordinance to protect homosexuals against discrimination. "My moral perception came out of my religious background," Cheshire later said in an interview on British television, "but when I read the scientific evidence, I became persuaded that it was not something voluntary. . . . If it is the way you were born, then it ceases to be a sin, and one's whole theological and moral perspective shifts."

Now LeVay's work is moving from the lab bench to the judicial bench. Last year, in a precedent-setting decision, the Hawaii Supreme Court ruled that denying gay couples marriage licenses appeared to violate the state constitution; in a concurring opinion one of the justices cited research that homosexuality is "biologically fated." "Research suggesting that sexual orientation is deeply rooted or even has a biological component helps courts see why gay men and lesbians should be protected from discrimination," says Evan Wolfson, an attorney in that case. In the coming year, the debate over gays in the military will probably set the work of LeVay, Hamer, Pillard, and others before the nation's Supreme Court. "As in all equal-protection cases, biological evidence will play a role," comments Kevin Cathcart, executive director of the Lambda Legal Defense Fund, the lesbian and gay legal-advocacy organization. "Biology is an element the courts have traditionally used as a marker for the immutability of a characteristic, such as race, gender, or—now—sexual orientation." The "immutability" argument is also being used to combat antigay initiatives, such as the one in Colorado that was overturned in December.

Asked what role he now sees for himself, LeVay looks amused. "I sometimes block on those little forms at the bank, where you have to state your occupation. I used to write *scientist;* now I put *writer* or *teacher.*" Other than that, he has scarcely looked back since he closed the lab door behind him. "Sure," he says, "there are times I'd like to do some experiment. I'm interested in the work that Hamer and Cassandra Smith at Berkeley are doing on androgen-receptor gene expression. That's when I have to remind myself I don't have my lab anymore. Sometimes I feel a little like I deserted an area where there is so much to do. But I don't expect to make further contributions in neuroanatomy—others can do it. I'd rather concentrate on education."

The institute is one part of that educational effort. In addition, to help people catch up with recent work on sexual orientation, LeVay published a book last year called *The Sexual Brain.* He is now writing a much more ambitious book, *Queer Science,* a history of the study of homosexuality from Plato to the present day. (He is also writing a primer on lesbian and gay culture with lesbian novelist Elisabeth Nonas.)

LeVay believes that as a society we all stand to benefit from understanding homosexuality as part of the spectrum of human behavior. "Knowledge about ourselves as humans is the most basic knowledge we can acquire, and our sexuality is a big part of that. True, this kind of knowledge can be misused, but the only way around that problem," he insists, "is to keep expanding what we know rather than having just snippets.

"In the long run, expanding our knowledge is the only way to avoid fostering oppression. Just because there's been crazy science and wrong thinking in the past doesn't mean we should give up doing science on the subject. We should do better science. After all, isn't that the point of it all—bringing us closer to the truth?"

Hearts and Minefields

A son's admission of his homosexuality to his Marine father adds poignancy to the debate about how open gays can be in the military

JILL SMOLOWE

SCOTT PECK FELT THE FIRST STIRrings when he was just six years old. While his first-grade classmates in Odenton, Maryland, near Annapolis, wrestled with their ABC's, Scott grappled with a bewildering attraction to men. "I thought it was a phase I'd grow out of," he recalls. As the years passed, Scott fought his feelings. He dated girls and even slept with a woman in an attempt to disavow his inclination. Though he says it was "torture" trying to be a heterosexual, Scott fought on, at one point coming "dangerously close to getting married." Finally, Scott gave up the battle. "A year ago," he says, "I pretty well concluded that I was gay." Like many other homosexuals, Scott hugged that realization close, fearful of what might happen if his father, Marine Colonel Fred Peck, found out. "So many of my friends have lost their families," he says. "That's what I thought was going to happen."

But last week Scott's closet door blew wide open in front of a Senate panel probing the legitimacy of the military ban on gays. For Scott, the feeling was bittersweet as Colonel Peck strove before the

he feared disaster. During the past year, while studying journalism at the University of Maryland, he had written several articles for a student publication, the *Retriever*, that, he says, "left no doubt that I was gay." Scott was afraid that gay activists "would 'out' me to the media" in a bid to discredit his father's testimony. Pre-emptively, Scott phoned his stepmother, Marine Major Joanne Schilling, and asked her to inform his father about his homosexuality.

Four days later, the colonel called from his home in San Diego, and the father and son had an emotional two-hour conversation that swept away years of obfuscations and lies. "My dad found no moral problems with my being gay," says Scott. "He believes, as I do, it is a genetic factor, unchangeable, and not a matter for moral condemnation." By the time they hung up, their relationship, which had been shaky ever since Peck and Scott's mother divorced in the 1970s, was stronger than ever before. "I've been dealing with some stereotypes about Marines," Scott admits. "After hearing his response, I wish I'd talked to him 10 years ago."

seemed far less disturbed, however, by the prospect of a breakdown of military discipline so thorough that a soldier's life might be endangered by deliberate friendly fire. "I'm not saying that that's right or wrong. I'm telling you that's the way it is," he said. "Fratricide is something that exists out there."

Peck's personalizing of the debate was a touching surprise in what many critics saw as an orchestrated compromise on the gay-ban issue conducted by committee chairman Sam Nunn. "It's Nunn's dog-and-pony show," says Lieut. (j.g.) Tracy Thorne, a "Top Gun" navy bombardier who is being removed from active duty because of his homosexuality. "He's got the witness list totally skewed against those who want to lift the ban." When the Senate panel toured the Norfolk (Virginia) Naval Base last week to hear from the rank and file, 15 of the 17 witnesses supported the ban. Thorne claims that several straight officers and enlisted personnel had volunteered to testify in favor of lifting the ban but were screened out by base officials working with Nunn's staff. The Campaign for Military Service, a coalition of

"I love him as much as I do any of my sons... But he should not serve."

committee to reconcile his unwavering love for his homosexual son with his steadfast support of the ban. For the millions of viewers watching the televised hearing, the colonel's poignant struggle humanized a search for a compromise solution that has become shrill and riddled with stereotypes.

The drama was set in motion by a seemingly innocuous message, sent to Washington from Mogadishu. Colonel Peck had taken a break from his duties as chief spokesman for the U.S. military forces in Somalia to write the Senate Armed Services Committee with a request to testify in favor of the military ban on gays. When Scott learned of the pending appearance,

The next day the colonel faced the Senate committee, armed with knowledge of his son's homosexuality, a fact that both Peck men agreed should be made public. His fingers laced tightly and wearing what Scott calls "his nervous face," the colonel testified, "My son Scott is a homosexual, and I don't think there's any place for him in the military." In a single breath, he added, "I love him as much as I do any of my sons. I respect him. I think he's a fine person. But he should not serve."

The father's pain was evident as he expressed a personal concern for his son's safety. "He'd be in grave risk," he said. "I would be very fearful that his life would be in jeopardy from his own troops." Peck

groups opposed to the ban, also collected affidavits from more than 100 gays and lesbians at Norfolk who were willing to testify, provided they would not be fired. Nunn's staff turned them down.

During the tour, Thorne was particularly taken aback when Senator Strom Thurmond of South Carolina publicly lectured him about his homosexuality. "Your lifestyle is not normal," Thurmond said as the audience at the base applauded wildly. "It's not normal for a man to want to be with a man or a woman with a woman." Thurmond then asked if Thorne had ever sought help from "medical or psychiatric aids."

Back in Washington, Nunn brought in a military luminary to dim all others. "In every case that I'm familiar with," said retired General H. Norman Schwarzkopf of Desert Storm fame, "when it became known in a unit that someone was openly homosexual, polarization occurred, violence sometimes followed, morale broke down, and unit effectiveness suffered."

to question the fairness of the proceedings. "Nunn's already made up his mind," says a Navy admiral, voicing a view that has echoed through Washington corridors in recent days. Last week in an interview with the Washington *Post*, Nunn maintained, "We've had as fair a hearing as I

President Clinton by July 15, runs more toward "Don't ask, don't shout." This would place restraints on conduct that draws attention to a person's homosexuality. But, says a Defense official, the policy would strive to halt witch-hunts and protect homosexuals "from somebody shining a flashlight through the keyhole."

Like many other homosexuals, Scott Peck doubts that whatever policy Clinton eventually embraces will accelerate the number of gay disclosures. "The same constraints that incline most gays and lesbians to stay in the closet in civilian society apply to the military as well," he says. For Scott, such fears are no longer an issue. His candid conversation with his father and his many interviews with TIME and other media last week left few bases untouched. His father now knows that he plans to marry his lover Bobby if and when Maryland laws change. According to Scott, his father's "only stipulation was that he wouldn't give me away at my wedding."

"It's Nunn's dog-and-pony show," says Tracy Thorne. "He's got the witness list totally skewed."

Schwarzkopf argued that the military had its hands full with deep defense cuts, troop reductions and base closures. He also offered a graphic description of how military leaders would respond to any order to integrate gays into the forces: "They will be just like many of the Iraqi troops who sat in the deserts of Kuwait forced to execute orders they didn't believe in."

Committee members peppered Schwarzkopf and other witnesses with questions that seemed designed to depict gays as a greater risk to "unit cohesion" than women and blacks, two other groups that initially met with resistance before being successfully integrated into the military. When officers responded with sweeping generalizations that painted homosexuals as HIV infected, flamboyant and sexually predatory, they were not pressed for specifics.

While gay activists charge that the Senate hearings fall far short of the fair review promised by Nunn, some straight members of the military have also begun

know how to put forth." He seemed to undercut his own argument when he added with irritation, "Is everyone in this town supposed to be partial but me?"

Although there are more hearings to come, the Senate committee is rapidly moving toward the compromise that Nunn describes as "Don't ask, don't tell." In effect, it would make permanent the interim order issued by the White House in January that put a halt to asking new recruits their sexuality but still kicked out those whose orientation became known. Gay groups see that as no compromise at all. "It's based on the flawed assumption that people are proclaiming their sexual orientation, but the fact is that the majority are discharged because of rumor, innuendo, harassment, investigations," says Thomas Stoddard, executive director of Campaign for Military Service. "Gays and lesbians will continue to serve in fear of having their careers destroyed."

The thinking at the Pentagon, which is also formulating a new policy to present to

In arguing against gays in the trenches, Colonel Peck suggested to the Senators that they try to imagine the disruptions that would ensue "if you took someone of a different sexual orientation to live in your home and how it would affect the way you carry out your daily life." He seemed not to connect that he had done just that when Scott went to live with him at age 16—and that instead it was Scott's life that was miserable, the result of being closeted about his gay feelings. While the colonel remains convinced that gays can't make a home in the military, Scott says, "I have more faith in the Marines than my father does." —*Reported by Bruce van Voorst/Washington*

Lifting the Gay Ban

Charles L. Davis

Charles L. Davis is associate professor of political science at the University of Kentucky in Lexington. He is author of Political Control and Working Class Political Mobilization in Mexico and Venezuela. *He has published various articles on mass political behavior in Latin America and on political participation of soldiers in the U. S. Army.*

Marine Colonel Fred Peck, who served as the military spokesman for the operation in Somalia, captured public attention recently in testimony before the Senate Arms Services Committee investigating the ban on homosexuals in the armed forces. Colonel Peck, a staunch foe of lifting the ban, revealed that one of his sons was a homosexual and that he would counsel all his sons to stay out of the military if the ban were lifted. He expressed particular concern for his homosexual son, whose life, the Colonel believed, would be in jeopardy were he to enter military service (*The New York Times*, May 12, 1993).

Underlying Colonel Peck's attitude toward the gay ban is a particular view of U.S. military community and its culture that seems to be widely shared by proponents of the gay ban. The military community is presumed to be less tolerant of social and cultural diversity than is civilian society. Intolerance is presumed to be rooted in both the institutional needs of the military and its social composition. Group cohesion and unity are paramount institutional needs for maintaining "discipline, good order, and morale." Cohesion and unity cannot be achieved if the boundaries of social diversity are extended to include "outgroups"—those whose values and behavior patterns conflict with those of the larger military community. Furthermore, the boundaries of acceptable behavior and values are more narrowly drawn in the military than in civilian society because of the social composition of the military.

The military is presumed to attract a relatively homogeneous group in terms of cultural values and perspectives. The social and political outlooks of the military community are characterized as narrow, parochial, conservative, and conventional. The boundaries of what is socially acceptable in military communities, therefore, is more narrowly drawn than in civilian society. The proponents of the gay ban, therefore, argue that the military cannot be "a laboratory for social experimentation" unless one were willing to sacrifice its group cohesion and unity and, thus, its effectiveness. Perhaps, Colonel Peck goes to the extreme in arguing that violence would result, but he shares the view that the military community will not accept declared homosexuals. That assumption is central to the thinking of proponents of the ban.

Even those who, like Senator Sam Nunn and other senators, favor the "Don't ask, Don't tell" policy hold this view. This policy means that the military no longer asks recruits about their sexual orientation nor will it conduct investigations to identify homosexuals. However, gay men and women could not be open about their sexuality at the risk of being discharged from the

From *Society*, November/December 1993, pp. 24-28. © 1993 by Transaction Publishers. Reprinted by permission.

military. Also a strict code of conduct would be imposed on overt behavior—same-sex dancing and the like would be prohibited. The underlying assumption is the same, open homosexuality is outside the norms of acceptable behavior in military communities. To protect legally the right to such behavior or even the right to declare one's sexual orientation would disrupt group cohesion and prevent the emotional bonding upon which the military so vitally depends for its effectiveness.

Such views are reflected in the Department of Defense policy that bans homosexuals from military service. According to the current department directive, as revised on February 12, 1986:

> Homosexuality is incompatible with military service...The presence of such members adversely affects the ability of the Military Services to maintain discipline, good order, and morale; to foster mutual trust and confidence among service-members; to ensure the integrity of the system of rank and command; to facilitate assignment of worldwide deployment of service members who frequently must live and work under close conditions affording minimal privacy; to recruit and retain members of the Military Services; to maintain public acceptability of military services; and to prevent breaches of security.

While issues such as national security and privacy are invoked, the exclusionary policy is justified primarily in terms of the unacceptability of homosexuality to the military community and the general populace. Persuasive opinion data can be marshalled in support of this view. For example, one poll, completed in December 1992, found that 45 percent of the soldiers at two Texas Army bases indicated that they would resign if forced to serve with openly gay soldiers (*Lexington Herald-Leader*, April 30, 1993).

Other polls have also found widespread opposition within the military to lifting the ban. Within the general population, polls show the public has become more tolerant of gays, but even though, there is still substantial support for restricting the rights and opportunities of homosexuals. These data can be used to support the argument that recruitment, group cohesion, public support for the military, and so on would suffer as a consequence of lifting the ban.

An implicit assumption in this argument favoring the ban is that negative attitudes toward gays are not likely to change in the military community. Indeed, this assumption is central to much of the argument for retaining the ban. If it is granted that negative attitudes

and stereotypes of gays could change, then one would have to grant that many of the dire consequences that are predicted need not occur. If the military community were to become tolerant of open gays in the ranks, there would be no threat to the "discipline, good order, and morale" of the military. The central issue is whether the larger military community is capable of the attitude change needed to facilitate the integration of declared gays into the military service. My argument is that the military services may be far better able to adapt to such a policy change than proponents of the current ban claim.

Homophobic attitudes are deeply rooted in the military and in the general American culture.

No one can argue that attitude change on the gay issue is easily achieved. Homophobic attitudes are deeply rooted in the military culture as well as in the general American culture. Furthermore, negative attitudes toward gays tend to be more deeply rooted in emotions than for other "out-groups" in American society, as a recent empirical study has shown. Yet, attitude change in the military on the gay issue may not be so difficult as proponents of the ban suggest.

It would be unrealistic to expect homophobic elements in the military (or in civilian life) to condone homosexuality. But homophobic attitudes toward behavior need not change for attitudes to change about the rights of gay men and women. One need not like or approve of homosexuality in order to accept the premise that rights of consenting adults to privacy in their sexual conduct and to be free from discrimination based on sexual orientation ought to be respected. If such rights are accorded and respected, it is difficult to see why gay men and women would not be accepted in the work world of the military without disruption to "discipline, good order, and morale." The issue is not acceptance of homosexual behavior, as General Colin Powell and other proponents of the gay ban argue, but acceptance of gay rights in accordance with American liberal culture.

But would acceptance of gay rights lead military personnel to accept gays in their ranks as colleagues? The nature of contact experiences would be partly determinative. Positive experiences would contribute to reduction of prejudice and negative stereotyping, while negative experiences would reinforce existing prejudices and stereotypes. The nature of the work environment would seem to dictate what types of experiences would most likely occur. Positive experiences would seem more likely if harassment and intimidation of gays were not tolerated and existing norms about fraternization and intimacy in the military workplace respected. There is no reason to believe that such norms would be less respected by the entry of gays into the military. Allport's classic study of prejudice reduction suggests that close contact involving cooperative interdependence in the workplace helps to reduce prejudice and negative stereotyping of "out-groups"—not to increase hostility and conflict as suggested by proponents of the gay ban.

Individuals from diverse backgrounds must learn to interact and live together.

Racial integration of the military provides an instructive example. As Charles Moskos has made clear, conflict between black and white troops was common in the segregated armed forces. However, racial hostility disappeared among white and black troops who fought together in the Battle of the Bulge in 1944 in what was to be the first experiment with a racially integrated fighting force in American history. In "From Citizens' Army to Social Laboratory," (*The Wilson Quarterly*, Winter 1993) Moskos writes, "The soldiers who stepped forward performed exceptionally well in battle, gaining the respect of the white soldiers they fought next to and the high regard of the white officers under whom they served." The military has since become a model institution of racial harmony, Moskos notes. This case fully supports Allport's theory; it is not clear why integration of declared gays into the military would not also lead to prejudice reduction rather than to conflict.

The case of racial integration—and more than simply integration, the high degree of racial harmony that Moskos notes—illustrates that attitudes toward "out-groups" can and do change in the military community. What is not clear is why a similar attitude change toward gays in the military could not also occur. Those who view the military community as incapable of integrating gays may be overlooking the highly diverse character of the military and its demonstrated capacity to integrate individuals from highly diverse social and cultural backgrounds.

The military imposes a high degree of unity and uniformity on its personnel through its hierarchical structure of authority. But at the same time it recruits from a very broad base of American society, though perhaps less so since compulsory military service has ended. Individuals from diverse social, religious, cultural, and regional backgrounds are placed in a close working situation of cooperative interdependence in which they must learn to interact with each other and, in many cases, live together.

Furthermore, military personnel frequently move to different places all over the world. With manpower cutbacks, the military has increasingly been able to recruit a more educated force (though not as educated as during compulsory military service) and it utilizes various incentives to encourage further education of its members once they are inducted into the services. In short, the contemporary U.S. military is comprised of individuals who have experienced considerable social and cultural diversity, who have traveled widely, and who tend to be relatively well educated. In many ways, the United States military is already a laboratory in social and cultural diversity by virtue of the fact that it draws recruits from all strata of an extremely diverse society. The American soldier may thus be better prepared to deal with the lifting of the gay ban than many expect.

Moskos recognizes that the era of compulsory universal military service promoted cultural and social diversity: "It brought together millions of Americans who otherwise would have lived their lives in relative social and geographic isolation. No other institution has accomplished such an intermingling of diverse classes, races, and ethnic groups."

My own experience with the military leads me to believe that an usual degree of cultural and social diversity still exists in the post-draft military. What I encountered was a social and cultural diversity that was far greater than in other institutions, including institutions of higher learning. I was a college professor at the University of Kentucky Center at Fort Knox from 1977 to 1989 rather than a recruit or draftee. When I began teaching full-time at Fort Knox in the fall of 1977, I brought with me the full baggage of stereotypes about the United States military. I was not sure whether I would find an excessively deferential type of student or the narrow-minded, authoritarian type. I was also concerned about soldiers pulling rank in class discussions and the overall atmosphere of academic freedom. In short, I was afraid of pressures, both direct and subtle, to tow the line.

I do not wish to suggest that the University of Kentucky Center at Fort Knox was an academician's mecca. Our program was a very low priority with both the military and the University of Kentucky administration in Lexington. We were housed in an old WPA school building from the 1930s along with several other institutions of higher learning that offered programs at Fort Knox. Little of the elaborate and sophisticated equipment or modern facilities, used for military training, were available to us. Before the University of Kentucky program was pulled from Fort Knox, our offices were even shifted to an unused, run-down army barracks.

Whatever my reservations about the facilities and the priority of our program may have been, I soon began questioning my own negative stereotypes about the military community. Indeed, my experience is further confirmation of Allport's theory of prejudice reduction via social contact. Admittedly the student body at the Fort Knox Center was not a representative cross-section of the Fort Knox community, but I suspect that the social diversity of students reflected the diverse military community from which most students came. (It should be pointed out that students included civilian employees and spouses of military personnel as well as soldiers. Most students were connected to the military base at Fort Knox, even if not on active duty in the U.S. Army.) In any case, the diversity was far greater than what I have even experienced in conventional institutions of higher learning.

Not surprisingly, a significant number of students came form ethnic and racial minority groups, among them African-Americans, Koreans, and Hispanics. Minority groups were probably not proportionately represented in the student body, but their number was significantly greater than in more conventional institutions of higher learning. There was also a large number of students who did not come from the middle and upper-middle classes as do so many traditional college students. Many students represented the first generation in their families that attended college. In short, there was a higher degree of social and cultural diversity than one typically finds on most college or university campuses. Surprising too was the high degree of ideological diversity among the students—from one enlisted soldier who had joined a Democratic Socialist branch in nearby Louisville to a major who considered Milton Friedman too liberal.

What was particularly striking was the ability of these students to get along and to respect each other despite differences in social, cultural, or racial background, military rank, and even ideological orientation. Indeed, I suspect that informal norms that stress tolerance and mutual respect in the face of diversity were operative in this military community. Such norms may be vital for achieving the degree of cohesion and unity that the U.S. military needs to carry out its mission and may be the glue that holds military communities together.

My impressions of one military community are consistent with various sociological studies of the military with which I am familiar. While the available systematic research on the social and political attitudes of military personnel is still limited and not conclusive, there is nothing in that research to suggest that military personnel are more intolerant of "out-groups" or anti-democratic than their civilian counterparts.

Using a panel design for a larger study of political socialization of American youths, M. Kent Jennings and Gregory B. Markus compared attitude changes among respondents who had served in the military with those who had not. The panel consisted of a national probability sample of high school seniors, male and female, interviewed in 1965 and then reinterviewed in 1973 (N = 674 male respondents in the panel). These researchers found no evidence that prior military service results in a failure to acquire participatory skills and motivations, in spite of a time lag before many veterans become active voters. Nor did they uncover any evidence that military service is associated with heightened political intolerance. These findings are consistent with other research that shows that military service actually reduces authoritarian tendencies, as measured on Adorno's F-scale.

It might be objected that these findings are based on samples of inductees who served only briefly in the military and never acquired a syndrome of attitudes and beliefs more typical of the non-conscripted military. Furthermore, most respondents in the Jennings-Markus study had been reintegrated into civilian life. To account for these possibilities, Ronald D. Taylor and I conducted a study of students enrolled at the University of Kentucky Center at Fort Knox during the 1984/85 academic year (N=116). The military sub-sample included non-conscripted soldiers currently serving in the U.S. Army, most of whom intended to remain in the service for an extended period of time. This sub-sample of active-duty soldiers was found to be more interested in politics, better informed about politics, and more politically tolerant than either the veteran or civilian sub-samples. These findings suggest that active military service might result in more democratic and tolerant behavior than proponents of the gay ban would lead one to believe.

It would be rash to conclude that, because of its social diversity, the U. S. military provides an ideal laboratory of social experimentation for integrating gays into the mainstream of American life. Homophobic attitudes are entrenched in military communities as elsewhere in American society. Certainly there are elements in the military that are not likely to change long-held beliefs about homosexuals, and there are no assurances that events like the murder of the gay sailor, Allen R. Schindler, in 1992 will not happen again. Nevertheless, there are reasons to believe that the United States military is much better able to manage the task without significant disruption of "discipline, good order, and morale" than proponents of the ban would grant.

It seems that successful integration of declared gay men and women into the military depends on leadership more than anything else. If the military leadership continues to project their own homophobic fears and to manipulate popular stereotypes about the U.S. military, homophobic attitudes are not likely to change in military communities. Indeed, the cues that are now emanating from some of the leaders suggest that to be pro-gay rights is to be anti-military. An implicit linkage to President Clinton and the views on the military he expressed during the Vietnam era is also being made. Some military leaders seem intent on creating a self-fulfilling prophecy that negative attitudes and stereotypes regarding gays are not going to change in military communities.

The official Department of Defense policy of excluding homosexuals might also reinforce and justify negative attitudes and stereotypes regarding gays. Similarly, any policy that does not recognize and protect the rights of gays to privacy and to non-discrimination because of sexual orientation is likely to reinforce and justify existing attitudes and stereotypes as well as to create an environment of distrust and suspicion toward gays in the military.

To accord less than full rights to gays who serve in the military, as the "Don't ask, Don't tell" policy does, is to continue to stigmatize the gay community and to justify continued distrust and suspicion. If attitude change is to occur within the heterosexual community in the military, it is essential that the official policy unambiguously protect the rights of gay military personnel and that the leadership be fully committed to implementation of those rights.

I grew up in a southern community in the 1950s where it was frequently asserted that "the southern way of life" would never change. Racial mores and attitudes were presumed to be too deeply ingrained to permit peaceful integration. As with Colonel Peck, the fear of violence was used to justify the status quo. It was amazing how peacefully and quickly racial integration came once federal and state civil rights laws were passed and the political leadership endorsed racial equality.

Integrating declared gays into the military may not follow as smooth a course, but the posture of the military leadership and the nature of the official policy will certainly make a difference. The basic problem facing the military is not that rank-and-file soldiers or sailors are inherently incapable of handling social and cultural diversity and change.

READINGS SUGGESTED BY THE AUTHOR:

Davis, Charles L. and Ronald D. Taylor. "The Effects of Military Service on Political Participation: The Case of Long-Term Soldiers." *Journal of Political and Military Sociology*, 15 (Spring 1987): 89-103.

Gays: In or Out? The U.S. Military and Homosexuals; A Source Book. Washington, D. C.: Macmillan, 1993.

Jennings, M. Kent and Gregory B. Markus. "Political Participation and Vietnam War Veterans." In Nancy L. Goldman and David R. Segal (eds.), *The Social Psychology of Military Service.* Beverly Hills: Sage Publications, 1976: 175-200.

Jennings, M. Kent and Gregory B. Markus. "The Effects of Military Service on Political Attitudes: A Panel Study." *American Political Science Review*, LXXI, 1 (March 1977): 131- 147.

Moskos, Charles. "From Citizens' Army to Social Laboratory," *The Wilson Quarterly* (Winter, 1993).

Riggle, Ellen D. and Alan L. Ellis. "Political Tolerance of Homosexuals: The Role of Group Attitudes and Legal Principles." Forthcoming in the *Journal of Homosexuality*.

Interpersonal Relationships

- **Establishing Sexual Relationships (Articles 23 and 24)**

- **Responsible Quality Relationships (Articles 25–27)**

Most people are familiar with the term "sexual relationship." It denotes an important dimension of sexuality—interpersonal sexuality, or sexual interactions occurring between two (and sometimes more) individuals. This unit focuses attention on these types of relationships.

No woman is an island. No man is an island. Interpersonal contact forms the basis for self-esteem and meaningful living; conversely, isolation results in loneliness and depression for most human beings. People seek and cultivate friendships for the warmth, affection, supportiveness, and sense of trust and loyalty that such relationships can provide.

Long-term friendships may develop into intimate relationships. The qualifying word in the previous sentence is "may." Today many people, single, as well as married, yearn for close or intimate interpersonal relationships but fail to find them. Discovering how and where to find potential friends, partners, lovers, and soul mates is reported to be more difficult today than in times past. Fear of rejection causes some to avoid interpersonal relationships, others to present a false front or illusory self that they think is more acceptable or socially desirable. This sets the stage for a game of intimacy that is counterproductive to genuine intimacy. For others a major dilemma may exist—the problem of balancing closeness with the preservation of individual identity in a manner that at once satisfies the need for personal and interpersonal growth and integrity. In either case, partners in a relationship should be advised that the development of interpersonal awareness (the mutual recognition and knowledge of others as they really are) rests upon trust and self-disclosure—letting the other person know who you really are and how you truly feel. In American society this has never been easy, and today some fear it may be more difficult than ever.

The above considerations in regard to interpersonal relationships apply equally well to achieving meaningful and satisfying sexual relationships. Three basic ingredients lay the foundation for quality sexual interaction: self-awareness, understanding and acceptance of the partner's needs and desires, and mutual effort to accommodate both partners' needs and desires. Without these, misunderstandings may arise, bringing anxiety, frustration, dissatisfaction, and/or resentment into the relationship. There may also be a heightened risk of contracting AIDS or another STD, experiencing an unplanned pregnancy, or exhibiting sexual dysfunction by one or both partners. These basic ingredients, taken together, contribute to sexual responsibility. Clearly, no one person is completely responsible for quality sexual relationships.

As might already be apparent, there is much more to quality sexual relationships than our popular culture recognizes. Such relationships are not established based on correct sexual techniques or beautiful/handsome features. Rather, it is the quality of the interaction that makes sex a celebration of our sexuality. A person-oriented (as opposed to genitally oriented) sexual awareness coupled with a leisurely, whole-body/mind sensuality and an open attitude toward exploration make for quality sexuality.

The subsection *Establishing Sexual Relationships* opens with "The Lessons of Love," an article detailing the relatively new study of love in its various forms. The second article, "Motivating the Opposite Sex," tackles the confusion, common conflicts, and potential rewards of learning to more effectively communicate with the opposite sex, especially your relationship partner.

In the subsection *Responsible Quality Relationships*, the examination of sexual and intimate relationships continues through a blending of articles based on research, experience, and advice-giving. The first one, "Soulmates," explores our deep-seated human needs for attachment, nurturing, and nurturance. The next article addresses

issues of fidelity and nonfidelity in thought, emotion, and behavior. "Forecast for Couples" looks at intimate relationships through a systems approach involving "recurring cycles of promise and betrayal."

This unit allows readers to explore their own expectations and feelings about relationships. The articles provide a backdrop of experiences with which to compare their own.

Looking Ahead: Challenge Questions

What do you see as the greatest barriers to attaining satisfying intimate relationships? Are some people destined to fail at establishing and/or maintaining them? Explain who and why.

List 5 to 10 answers to the question, "What is love?" Are these things you have heard from others? Believe yourself? Experienced yourself?

What are some "lessons about love" that you believe you could pass on to others in order to help them find more satisfying, intimate relationships?

What are some characteristics of your gender that make communication with the opposite sex difficult? What are some characteristics of the opposite sex that inhibit or frustrate your efforts to communicate with them?

Have you ever imagined what your soul mate would be like? Describe your perfect soul mate. How important to you is finding such a person?

Do you think fantasies about others are harmful to relationships? Would you want to know if your partner fantasizes about others, flirts with others, or is sexually intimate with others? Why, or why not?

Do you feel that disappointment and conflict are part of the couple development process? If so, how can they be handled and resolved so as to increase the bond in the relationship?

THE LESSONS OF LOVE

Yes, we've learned a few things. We now know that it is the insecure rather than the confident who fall in love most readily. And men fall faster than women. And who ever said sex had anything to do with it?

Beth Livermore

As winter thaws, so too do icicles on cold hearts. For with spring, the sap rises—and resistance to love wanes. And though the flame will burn more of us than it warms, we will return to the fire—over and over again.

Indeed, love holds central in everybody's everyday. We spend years, sometimes lifetimes pursuing it, preparing for it, longing for it. Some of us even die for love. Still, only poets and songwriters, philosophers and playwrights have traditionally been granted license to sift this hallowed preserve. Until recently. Over the last decade and a half, scientists have finally taken on this most elusive entity. They have begun to parse out the intangibles, the *je ne sais quoi* of love. The word so far is—little we were sure of is proving to be true.

OUT OF THE LAB, INTO THE FIRE

True early greats, like Sigmund Freud and Carl Rogers, acknowledged love as important to the human experience. But not till the 1970s did anyone attempt to define it—and only now is it considered a respectable topic of study.

One reason for this hesitation has been public resistance. "Some people are afraid that if they look too close they will lose the mask," says Arthur Aron, Ph.D., professor of psychology at the University of California, Santa Cruz. "Others believe we know all that we need to know." But mostly, to systematically study love has been thought impossible, and therefore a waste of time and money.

No one did more to propagate this false notion than former United States Senator William Proxmire of Wisconsin, who in 1974 launched a very public campaign against the study of love. As a member of the Senate Finance Committee, he took it upon himself to ferret out waste in government spending. One of the first places he looked was the National Science Foundation, a federal body that both funds research and promotes scientific progress.

Upon inspection, Proxmire found that Ellen Berscheid, Ph.D., a psychologist at the University of Minnesota who had already broken new ground scrutinizing the social power of physical attractiveness, had secured an $84,000 federal grant to study relationships. The proposal mentioned romantic love. Proxmire loudly denounced such work as frivolous—tax dollars ill spent.

The publicity that was given Proxmire's pronouncements not only cast a pall over all behavioral science research, it set off an international firestorm around Berscheid that lasted the next two years. Colleagues were fired. Her office was swamped with hate mail. She even received death threats. But in the long run, the strategy backfired, much to Proxmire's chagrin. It generated increased scientific interest in the study of love, propelling it forward, and identified Berscheid as the keeper of the flame. Scholars and individuals from Alaska to then-darkest Cold War Albania sent her requests for information, along with letters of support.

Berscheid jettisoned her plans for very early retirement, buttoned up the country house, and, as she says, "became a clearinghouse" for North American love research. "It became eminently clear that there were people who really did want to learn more about love. And I had tenure."

PUTTING THE SOCIAL INTO PSYCHOLOGY

This incident was perfectly timed. For during the early 1970s, the field of social psychology was undergoing a revolution of sorts—a revolution that made the study of love newly possible.

For decades behaviorism, the school of psychology founded by John B. Watson, dominated the field. Watson argued that only overt actions capable of direct observation and measurement were worthy of study. However, by the early seventies, dissenters were openly calling this approach far too narrow. It excluded unobservable mental events such as ideas and emotions. Thus rose cognitive science, the study of the mind, or perception, thought, and memory.

Now psychologists were encouraged to ask human subjects what they thought and how they felt about things. Self-report questionnaires emerged as a legitimate research tool. Psychologists were encouraged to escape laboratory confines—to study real people in the real world. Once out there, they discovered that there was plenty to mine.

Throughout the seventies, soaring divorce rates, loneliness, and isolation began to dominate the emotional landscape of America. By the end of that decade, love had become a pathology. No longer was the question "What is love?" thought to be trivial. "People in our culture dissolve unions when love disappears, which has a lasting effect on society," says Berscheid. Besides, "we already understood the mating habits of the stickleback fish." It was time to turn to a new species.

Today there are hundreds of research papers on love. Topics range from romantic ideals to attachment styles of the young and unmarried. "There were maybe a half dozen when I wrote my dissertation on romantic attraction in 1969," reports Aron. These days, a national association and an international society bring "close relationship" researchers close together annually. Together or apart they are busy producing and sharing new theories, new questionnaires to use as research instruments, and new findings. Their unabashed aim: to improve the human condition by helping us to understand, to repair, and to perfect our love relationships.

SO WHAT *IS* LOVE?

"If there is anything that we have learned about love it is its variegated nature," says Clyde Hendrick, Ph.D., of Texas Tech University in Lubbock. "No one volume or theory or research program can capture love and transform it into a controlled bit of knowledge."

Instead, scholars are tackling specific questions about love in the hopes of nailing down a few facets at a time. The expectation is that every finding will be a building block in the base of knowledge, elevating understanding.

Elaine Hatfield, Ph.D., now of the University of Hawaii, has carved out the territory of passionate love. Along with Berscheid, Hatfield was at the University of Minnesota in 1964 when Stanley Schacter, formerly a professor there and still a great presence, proposed a new theory of emotion. It said that any emotional state requires two conditions: both physiological arousal and relevant situational cues. Already studying close relationships, Hatfield and Berscheid were intrigued. Could the theory help to explain the turbulent, all-consuming experience of passionate love?

Hatfield has spent a good chunk of her professional life examining passionate love, "a state of intense longing for union with another." In 1986, along with sociologist Susan Sprecher, she devised the Passionate Love Scale (PLS), a questionnaire that measures thoughts and feelings she previously identified as distinctive of this "emotional" state.

Lovers rate the applicability of a variety of descriptive statements. To be passionately in love is to be preoccupied with thoughts of your partner much of the time. Also, you likely idealize your partner. So those of you who are passionately in love would, for example, give "I yearn to know all about—" a score somewhere between "moderately true" and "definitely true" on the PLS.

True erotic love is intense and involves taking risks. It seems to demand a strong sense of self.

The quiz also asks subjects if they find themselves trying to determine the other's feelings, trying to please their lover, or making up excuses to be close to him or her—all hallmarks of passionate, erotic love. It canvasses for both positive and negative feelings. "Passionate lovers," explains Hatfield, "experience a roller coaster of feelings: euphoria, happiness, calm, tranquility, vulnerability, anxiety, panic, despair."

For a full 10 percent of lovers, previous romantic relationships proved so painful that they hope they will never love again.

Passionate love, she maintains, is kindled by "a sprinkle of hope and a large dollop of loneliness, mourning, jealousy, and terror." It is, in other words, fueled by a juxtaposition of pain and pleasure. According to psychologist Dorothy Tennov, who interviewed some 500 lovers, most of them expect their romantic experiences to be bittersweet. For a full 10 percent of them, previous romantic relationships proved so painful that they hope never to love again.

Contrary to myths that hold women responsible for romance, Hatfield finds that both males and females love with equal passion. But men fall in love faster. They are, thus, more romantic. Women are more apt to mix pragmatic concerns with their passion.

And people of all ages, even four-year-old children, are capable of "falling passionately in love." So are people of any ethnic group and socioeconomic stratum capable of passionate love.

Hatfield's most recent study, of love in three very different cultures, shows that romantic love is not simply a product of the Western mind. It exists among diverse cultures worldwide.

Taken together, Hatfield's findings support the idea that passionate love is an evolutionary adaptation. In this scheme, passionate love works as a bonding mechanism, a necessary kind of interpersonal glue that has existed since the start of the human race. It assures that procreation will take place, that the human species will be perpetuated.

UP FROM THE SWAMP

Recent anthropological work also supports this notion. In 1991, William Jankowiak, Ph.D., of the University of Nevada in Las Vegas, and Edward Fischer, Ph.D., of Tulane University published the first study systematically comparing romantic love across 166 cultures.

They looked at folklore, indigenous advice about love, tales about lovers, love potion recipes—anything related. They found "clear evidence" that romantic love is known in 147, or 89 percent, of cultures. Further, Jankowiak suspects that the lack of proof in the remaining 19 cultures is due more to field workers' oversights than to the absence of romance.

Unless prompted, few anthropologists recognize romantic love in the populations that they study, explains Jankowiak. Mostly because romance takes different shapes in different cultures, they do not know what to look for. They tend to recognize romance only in the form it takes in American culture—a progressive phenomenon leading from flirtation to marriage. Elsewhere, it may be a more fleeting fancy. Still, reports Jankowiak, "when I ask them specific questions about behavior, like 'Did couples run away from camp together?', almost all of them have a positive response."

For all that, there is a sizable claque of scholars who insist that romantic love is a cultural invention of the last 200 years or so. They point out that few cultures outside the West embrace romantic love with the vigor that we do. Fewer still build marriage, traditionally a social and economic institution, on the individualistic pillar of romance.

Romantic love, this thinking holds, consists of a learned set of behaviors; the phenomenon is culturally transmitted from one generation to the next by example, stories, imitation, and direct instruc-

---

LOVE ME TENDER

How To Make Love to a Man (what men like, in order of importance)	**How To Make Love to a Woman** (what women like, in order of importance)
taking walks together	taking walks together
kissing	flowers
candle-lit dinners	kissing
cuddling	candle-lit dinners
hugging	cuddling
flowers	declaring "I love you"
holding hands	love letters
making love	slow dancing
love letters	hugging
sitting by the fireplace	giving surprise gifts

---

tion. Therefore, it did not rise from the swamps with us, but rather evolved with culture.

THE ANXIOUS ARE ITS PREY

Regardless whether passionate, romantic love is universal or unique to us, there is considerable evidence that what renders people particularly vulnerable to it is anxiety. It whips up the wherewithal to love. And anxiety is not alone; in fact, there are a number of predictable precursors to love.

To test the idea that emotions such as fear, which produces anxiety, can amplify attraction, Santa Cruz's Arthur Aron recorded the responses of two sets of men to an attractive woman. But one group first had to cross a narrow 450-foot-long bridge that swayed in the wind over a 230-foot drop—a pure prescription for anxiety. The other group tromped confidently across a seemingly safe bridge. Both groups encountered Miss Lovely, a decoy, as they stepped back onto terra firm.

Aron's attractive confederate stopped each young man to explain that she was doing a class project and asked if he would complete a questionnaire. Once he finished, she handed him her telephone number, saying that she would be happy to explain her project in greater detail.

Who called? Nine of the 33 men on the suspension bridge telephoned, while only two of the men on the safe bridge called. It is not impossible that the callers simply wanted details on the project, but Aron suspects instead that a combustible mix of excitement and anxiety prompted the men to become interested in their attractive interviewee.

Along similar if less treacherous lines, Aron has most recently looked at eleven possible precursors to love. He compiled the list by conducting a comprehensive literature search for candidate items. If you have a lot in common with or live and work close to someone you find attractive, your chances of falling in love are good, the literature suggests.

Other general factors proposed at one time or another as good predictors include being liked by the other, a partner's positive social status, a partner's ability to fill your needs, your readiness for entering a relationship, your isolation from others, mystery, and exciting surroundings or circumstances. Then there are specific cues, like hair color, eye expression, and face shape.

Love depends as much on the perception of being liked as on the presence of a desirable partner. Love isn't possible without it.

To test the viability and relative importance of these eleven putative factors, Aron asked three different groups of people to give real-life accounts of falling in love. Predictably, desirable characteristics, such as good looks and personality, made the top of the list. But proximity, readiness to develop a relationship, and exciting surroundings and circumstances ranked close behind.

The big surprise: reciprocity. Love is at heart a two-way event. The perception of being liked ranked just as high as the presence of desirable characteristics in

the partner. "The combination of the two appears to be very important," says Aron. In fact, love just may not be possible without it.

Sprecher and his colleagues got much the same results in a very recent cross-cultural survey. They and their colleagues interviewed 1,667 men and women in the U.S., Russia, and Japan. They asked the people to think about the last time they had fallen in love or been infatuated. Then they asked about the circumstance that surrounded the love experience.

Surprisingly, the rank ordering of the factors was quite similar in all three cultures. In all three, men and women consider reciprocal liking, personality, and physical appearance to be especially important. A partner's social status and the approval of family and friends are way down the list. The cross-cultural validation of predisposing influences suggests that reciprocal liking, desirable personality and physical features may be universal elements of love, among the *sine qua non* of love, part of its heart and soul.

FRIENDSHIP OVER PASSION

Another tack to the intangible of love is the "prototype" approach. This is the study of our conceptions of love, what we "think" love is.

In 1988, Beverly Fehr, Ph.D., of the University of Winnipeg in Canada conducted a series of six studies designed to determine what "love" and "commitment" have in common. Assorted theories suggested they could be anything from mutually inclusive to completely separate. Fehr asked subjects to list characteristics of love and to list features of commitment. Then she asked them to determine which qualities were central and which more peripheral to each.

People's concepts of the two were to some degree overlapping. Such elements as trust, caring, respect, honesty, devotion, sacrifice, and contentment were deemed attributes of both love and commitment. But such other factors as intimacy, happiness, and a desire to be with the other proved unique to love (while commitment alone demanded perseverance, mutual agreement, obligation, and even a feeling of being trapped).

The findings of Fehr's set of studies, as well as others', defy many expectations. Most subjects said they consider caring, trust, respect, and honesty central to love—while passion-related events like touching, sexual passion, and physical attraction are only peripheral. "They are not very central to our concept of love," Fehr shrugs.

Recently, Fehr explored gender differences in views of love—and found remarkably few. Both men and women put forth friendship as primary to love. Only in a second study, which asked subjects to match their personal ideal of love to various descriptions, did any differences show up. More so than women, men tended to rate erotic, romantic love closer to their personal conception of love.

Both men and women deem romance and passion far less important than support and warm fuzzies . . .

Still, Fehr is fair. On the whole, she says, "the essence, the core meaning of love differs little." Both genders deem romance and passion far less important than support and warm fuzzies. As even Nadine Crenshaw, creator of steamy romance novels, has remarked, "love gets you to the bathroom when you're sick."

LOVE ME TENDER

Since the intangible essence of love cannot be measured directly, many researchers settle for its reflection in what people do. They examine the behavior of lovers.

Clifford Swensen, Ph.D., professor of psychology at Purdue University, pioneered this approach by developing a scale with which to measure lovers' behavior. He produced it from statements people made when asked what they did for, said to, or felt about people they loved . . . and how these people behaved towards them.

Being supportive and providing encouragement are important behaviors to all love relationships—whether with a friend or mate, Swensen and colleagues found. Subjects also gave high ratings to self-disclosure, or talking about personal matters, and a sense of agreement on important topics.

But two categories of behaviors stood out as unique to romantic relationships.

Lovers said that they expressed feelings of love verbally; they talked about how they enjoyed being together, how they missed one another when apart, and other such murmurings. They also showed their affection through physical acts like hugging and kissing.

Elaborating on the verbal and physical demonstrations of love, psychologist Raymond Tucker, Ph.D., of Bowling Green State University in Ohio probed 149 women and 48 men to determine "What constitutes a romantic act?" He asked subjects, average age of 21, to name common examples. There was little disagreement between the genders.

Both men and women most often cited "taking walks" together. For women, "sending or receiving flowers" and "kissing" followed close on its heels, then "candle-lit dinners" and "cuddling." Outright declarations of "I love you came in a distant sixth. (Advisory to men: The florists were right all along. Say it with flowers instead.)

. . . as one romance novelist confides, "love gets you to the bathroom when you're sick."

For men, kissing and "candle-lit dinners" came in second and third. If women preferred demonstrations of love to outright declarations of it, men did even more so; "hearing and saying 'I love you didn't even show up among their top ten preferences. Nor did "slow dancing or giving or receiving surprise gifts," although all three were on the women's top-ten list. Men likewise listed three kinds of activity women didn't even mention: "holding hands," "making love"—and "sitting by the fireplace." For both sexes, love is more tender than most of us imagined.

All in all, says Tucker, lovers consistently engage in a specific array of actions. "I see these items show up over and over and over again." They may very well be the bedrock behaviors of romantic love.

SIX COLORS OF LOVE

That is not to say that once in love we all behave alike. We do not. Each of us

has a set of attitudes toward love that colors what we do. While yours need not match your mate's, you best understand your partner's approach. It underlies how your partner is likely to treat you.

There are six basic orientations toward love, Canadian sociologist John Allen Lee first suggested in 1973. They emerged from a series of studies in which subjects matched story cards, which contain statements projecting attitudes, to their own personal relationships. In 1990 Texas Tech's Clyde Hendrick, along with wife/colleague Susan Hendrick, Ph.D., produced a Love Attitude Scale to measure all six styles. You may embody more than one of these styles. You are also likely to change style with time and circumstance.

Both men and women prefer demonstrations of love to outright declarations of it.

You may, for example, have spent your freewheeling college years as an Eros lover, passionate and quick to get involved, setting store on physical attraction and sexual satisfaction. Yet today you may find yourself happy as a Storge lover, valuing friendship-based love, preferring a secure, trusting relationship with a partner of like values.

There are Ludus lovers, game-players who like to have several partners at one time. Their partners may be very different from one another, as Ludus does not act on romantic ideals. Mania-type lovers, by contrast, experience great emotional highs and lows. They are very possessive—and often jealous. They spend a lot of their time doubting their partner's sincerity.

Pragma lovers are, well, pragmatic. They get involved only with the "right" guy or gal—someone who fills their needs or meets other specifications. This group is happy to trade drama and excitement for a partner they can build a life with. In contrast, Agape, or altruistic, lovers form relationships because of what they may be able to give to their partner. Even sex is not an urgent concern of theirs. "Agape functions on a more spiritual level," Hendrick says.

The Hendricks have found some gender difference among love styles. In general, men are more ludic, or game-playing. Women tend to be more storgic,

THE COLORS OF LOVE

How do I love thee? At least six are the ways.

There is no one type of love; there are many equally valid ways of loving. Researchers have consistently identified six attitudes or styles of love that, to one degree or another, encompass our conceptions of love and color our romantic relationships. They reflect both fixed personality traits and more malleable attitudes. Your relative standing on these dimensions may vary over time—being in love NOW will intensify your responses in some dimensions. Nevertheless, studies show that for most people, one dimension of love predominates.

Answering the questions below will help you identify your own love style, one of several important factors contributing to the satisfaction you feel in relationships. You may wish to rate yourself on a separate sheet of paper. There are no right or wrong answers, nor is there any scoring system. The test is designed to help you examine your own feelings and to help you understand your own romantic experiences.

After you take the test, if you are currently in a relationship, you may want to ask your partner to take the test and then compare your responses. Better yet, try to predict your partner's love attitudes before giving the test to him or her.

Studies show that most partners are well-correlated in the areas of love passion and intensity (Eros), companionate or friendship love (Storge), dependency (Mania), and all-giving or selfless love (Agape). If you and your partner aren't a perfect match, don't worry. Knowing your styles can help you manage your relationship.

Directions: Listed below are several statements that reflect different attitudes about love. For each statement, fill in the response on an answer sheet that indicates how much you agree or disagree with that statement. The items refer to a specific love relationship. Whenever possible, answer the questions with your current partner in mind. If you are not currently dating anyone, answer the questions with your most recent partner in mind. If you have never been in love, answer in terms of what you think your responses would most likely be.

FOR EACH STATEMENT:
A = Strongly agree with the statement
B = Moderately agree with the statement
C = Neutral, neither agree nor disagree
D = Moderately disagree with the statement
E = Strongly disagree with the statement

Eros
Measures passionate love as well as intimacy and commitment. It is directly and strongly correlated with satisfaction in a relationship, a major ingredient in relationship success. Eros gives fully, intensely, and takes risks in love; it requires substantial ego strength. Probably reflects secure attachment style.

1. My partner and I were attracted to each other immediately after we first met.

2. My partner and I have the right physical "chemistry" between us.

3. Our lovemaking is very intense and satisfying.

4. I feel that my partner and I were meant for each other.

5. My partner and I became emotionally involved rather quickly.

6. My partner and I really understand each other.

7. My partner fits my ideal standards of physical beauty/handsomeness.

Ludus
Measures love as an interaction game to be played out with diverse partners. Relationships do not have great depth of feeling. Ludus is wary of emotional intensity from others, and has a manipulative or cynical quality to it. Ludus is negatively related to satisfaction in relationships. May reflect avoidant attachment style.

8. I try to keep my partner a little uncertain about my commitment to him/her.

9. I believe that what my partner doesn't know about me won't hurt him/her.

10. I have sometimes had to keep my partner from finding out about other partners.

11. I could get over my affair with my partner pretty easily and quickly.

12. My partner would get upset if he/she knew of some of the things I've done with other people.

13. When my partner gets too dependent on me, I want to back off a little.

14. I enjoy playing the "game of love" with my partner and a number of other partners.

Storge
Reflects an inclination to merge love and friendship. Storgic love is solid, down to earth, presumably enduring. It is evolutionary, not revolutionary, and may take time to develop. It is related to satisfaction in long-term relationships.

15. It is hard for me to say exactly when our friendship turned to love.

16. To be genuine, our love first required caring for a while.

17. I expect to always be friends with my partner.

18. Our love is the best kind because it grew out of a long friendship.

19. Our friendship merged gradually into love over time.

20. Our love is really a deep friendship, not a mysterious, mystical emotion.

21. Our love relationship is the most satisfying because it developed from a good friendship.

Pragma
Reflects logical, "shopping list" love, rational calculation with a focus on desired attributes of a lover. Suited to computer-matched dating. Related to satisfaction in long-term relationships.

22. I considered what my partner was going to become in life before I committed myself to him/her.

23. I tried to plan my life carefully before choosing my partner.

24. In choosing my partner, I believed it was best to love someone with a similar background.

25. A main consideration in choosing my partner was how he/she would reflect on my family.

26. An important factor in choosing my partner was whether or not he/she would be a good parent.

27. One consideration in choosing my partner was how he/she would reflect on my career.

28. Before getting very involved with my partner, I tried to figure out how compatible his/her hereditary background would be with mine in case we ever had children.

Mania
Measures possessive, dependent love. Associated with high emotional expressiveness and disclosure, but low self-esteem; reflects uncertainty of self in the relationship. Negatively associated with relationship satisfaction. May reflect anxious/ambivalent attachment style.

29. When things aren't right with my partner and me, my stomach gets upset.

30. If my partner and I break up, I would get so depressed that I would even think of suicide.

31. Sometimes I get so excited about being in love with my partner that I can't sleep.

32. When my partner doesn't pay attention to me, I feel sick all over.

33. Since I've been in love with my partner, I've had trouble concentrating on anything else.

34. I cannot relax if I suspect that my partner is with someone else.

35. If my partner ignores me for a while, I sometimes do stupid things to try to get his/her attention back.

Agape
Reflects all-giving, selfless, nondemanding love. Associated with altruistic, committed, sexually idealistic love. Like Eros, tends to flare up with "being in love now."

36. I try to always help my partner through difficult times.

37. I would rather suffer myself than let my partner suffer.

38. I cannot be happy unless I place my partner's happiness before my own.

39. I am usually willing to sacrifice my own wishes to let my partner achieve his/hers.

40. Whatever I won is my partner's to use as he/she chooses.

41. When my partner gets angry with me, I still love him/her fully and unconditionally.

42. I would endure all things for the sake of my partner.

Adapted from Hendrick, Love Attitudes Scale

more pragmatic—and more manic. However, men and women seem to be equally passionate and altruistic in their relationships. On the whole, say the Hendricks, the sexes are more similar than different in style.

Personality traits, at least one personality trait, is strongly correlated to love style, the Hendricks have discovered. People with high self-esteem are more apt to endorse eros, but less likely to endorse mania than other groups. "This finding fits with the image of a secure, confident eros lover who moves intensely but with mutuality into a new relationship," they maintain.

When they turned their attention to ongoing relationships, the Hendricks' found that couples who stayed together over the course of their months-long study were more passionate and less game-playing than couples who broke up. "A substantial amount of passionate love" and "a low dose of game-playing" love are key to the development of satisfying relationships—at least among the college kids studied.

YOUR MOTHER MADE YOU DO IT

The love style you embrace, how you treat your partner, may reflect the very first human relationship you ever had—probably with Mom. There is growing evidence supporting "attachment theory," which holds that the rhythms of response by a child's primary care giver affect the development of personality and influence later attachment processes, including adult love relationships.

First put forth by British psychiatrist John Bowlby in the 1960s and elaborated by American psychologist Mary Ainsworth, attachment theory is the culmination of years of painstaking observation of infants and their adult caregivers—and those separated from them—in both natural and experimental situations. Essentially it suggests that there are three major patterns of attachment; they develop within the first year of life and

stick with us, all the while reflecting the responsiveness of the caregiver to our needs as helpless infants.

Those whose mothers, or caregivers, were unavailable or unresponsive may grow up to be detached and nonresponsive to others. Their behavior is Avoidant in relationships. A second group takes a more Anxious-Ambivalent approach to relationships, a response set in motion by having mothers they may not have been able to count on—sometimes responsive, other times not. The lucky among us are Secure in attachment, trusting and stable in relationships, probably the result of having had consistently responsive care.

While attachment theory is now driving a great deal of research on children's social, emotional, and cognitive development, University of Denver psychologists Cindy Hazan and Philip Shaver set out not long ago to investigate the possible effect of childhood relationships on adult attachments. First, they developed descriptive statements that reflect each of the three attachment styles. Then they asked people in their community, along with college kids, which statements best describe how they relate to others. They asked, for example, about trust and jealousy, about closeness and desire for reciprocation, about emotional extremes.

The distribution of the three attachment styles has proved to be about the same in grown-ups as in infants, the same among collegians as the fully fledged. More than half of adult respondents call themselves Secure; the rest are split between Avoidant and Ambivalent. Further, their adult attachment patterns predictably reflect the relationship they report with their parents. Secure people generally describe their parents as having been warm and supportive. What's more, these adults predictably differ in success at romantic love. Secure people reported happy, long-lasting relationships. Avoidants rarely found love.

Secure adults are more trusting of their romantic partners and more confident of a partner's love, report Australian psychologists Judith Feeney and Patricia Noller of the University of

Queensland. The two surveyed nearly 400 college undergraduates with a questionnaire on family background and love relationships, along with items designed to reveal their personality and related traits.

In contrast to the Secure, Avoidants indicated an aversion to intimacy. The Anxious-Ambivalent participants were characterized by dependency and what Feeney and Noller describe as "a hunger" for commitment. Their approach resembles the Mania style of love. Each of the three groups reported differences in early childhood experience that could account for their adult approach to relationships. Avoidants, for example, were most likely to tell of separations from their mother.

It may be, Hazan and Shaver suggest, that the world's greatest love affairs are conducted by the Ambitious-Ambivalents—people desperately searching for a kind of security they never had.

THE MAGIC NEVER DIES

Not quite two decades into the look at love, it appears as though love will not always mystify us. For already we are beginning to define what we think about it, how it makes us feel, and what we do when we are in love. We now know that it is the insecure, rather than the confident, who fall in love more readily. We know that outside stimuli that alter our emotional state can affect our susceptibility to romance; it is not just the person. We now know that to a certain extent your love style is set by the parenting you received. And, oh yes, men are more quickly romantic than women.

The best news may well be that when it comes to love, men and women are more similar than different. In the face of continuing gender wars, it is comforting to think that men and women share an important, and peaceful, spot of turf. It is also clear that no matter how hard we look at love, we will always be amazed and mesmerized by it.

Motivating the Opposite Sex

A practical guide to improving communication and getting what you want in your relationship.

John Gray, Ph.D.

Imagine that men are from Mars and women are from Venus. When we meet, fall in love, and have happy relationships together, it is because we respect each other's differences and accept the fact that we are from different planets.

Without such awareness, men and women remain at odds with each other. We become easily angered or frustrated because we expect the opposite sex to be more like ourselves—to want what we want and feel the way we feel. As a result, our relationships are often filled with friction and conflict. The mistake is to assume that if our partners love us, they will react and behave in certain ways—the same ways we react and behave when we are in love with someone. This attitude sets us up to be disappointed again and again, and ultimately prevents us from taking the time to communicate lovingly about our differences.

The most frequently expressed complaint women have about men is that men don't listen. Either a man completely ignores her when she speaks to him, or he listens for a few beats, assesses what is bothering her, and then proudly puts on his Mr. Fix-It cap and offers her a solution to make her feel better.

He is confused when she doesn't appreciate this gesture of love. No matter how many times she tells him that he's not listening, he just doesn't get it and keeps on doing the same thing. She wants empathy, but he thinks she wants solutions.

On the other hand, the most frequently expressed complaint men have about women is that women are always trying to change them somehow. When a woman loves a man she sometimes feels responsible to help him improve the way he does things. She may form a sort of home-improvement committee, making him her primary focus.

No matter how much he may resist her help, she persists—waiting for an opportunity to help. She thinks she's being nurturing, but he still feels he's being controlled. These two problems can finally be solved by first understanding why it is that men offer solutions and women seek to improve.

Men value power, competency, efficiency, and achievement. They are always doing things to prove themselves and develop their skills. Their sense of self is defined through their ability to achieve results. They experience fulfillment primarily through success and accomplishment. And for a man to feel good about himself, he must achieve these goals alone. Someone else can't achieve them for him. Autonomy is key.

Recognizing this characteristic can help women understand why men so strongly resist being corrected or being

Motivation:

Men want to feel *needed*, women need to feel *cherished*. With this awareness you can support your partner as well as get the support you need from them.

told what to do. To offer a man unsolicited advice is to presume that he doesn't know what to do or that he can't do it on his own. Needless to say, men are very touchy about this, because the issue of competence is of vital importance to them.

Task for Men: Learn to Listen

Because he is handling his problems on his own, a man rarely talks about them—unless he feels he needs some expert advice. He reasons: "Why involve someone else when I can do it by myself?" Asking for help is perceived as a sign of weakness.

On the other hand, if he truly does need help, then it is a sign of *wisdom* for him to go out and get it. In this case, he will find someone he respects and then talk about his problem—usually with another man, who feels honored by the opportunity to help. Automatically, *he* then puts on his Mr. Fix-It hat, listens for a while, and offers some jewels of advice.

This custom is one of the reasons men instinctively offer solutions when women talk about their problems. When a woman innocently shares her upset feelings or explores out loud the problems of her day, for instance, a man mistakenly assumes she is looking for some expert advice. This is his way of showing love and trying to help.

He wants to help her feel better by solving her problems. He wants to be useful to her. He feels he can be valued and thus worthy of her love when his abilities to help are used. Once he has offered a solution, however, and she continues to be upset, it becomes increasingly difficult for him to listen. He feels that his solution is being rejected, and that he is increasingly useless to her in this matter.

In fact, he has no idea that by just listening with empathy and interest, he can be supportive. He does not know that, for women, talking about problems is not an invitation to offer a solution. So many times a woman just wants to share her feelings, and her husband or boyfriend, thinking he is helping, interrupts her by offering her a steady flow of solutions. He has no idea why she isn't pleased.

Task for Women: Give up Giving Advice

Because constantly proving one's competence is not as important to a woman, offering help is thusly not as offensive. And needing help is not considered a sign of weakness.

Just as a man may feel offended when a woman seems to ignore his advice and urges him instead to simply listen, he may also take offense when a woman *offers him* her advice, because he feels she doesn't trust his ability to solve a problem on his own. Offering help to

Digest Synopsis: Men and women are motivated in different ways. By communicating clearly your needs and limits—without blame or assumption—you can create the relationship you want.

a man when he feels he doesn't need it can make him feel incompetent, weak, and even unloved.

Generally speaking, when a woman offers unsolicited advice or tries to help a man, she has no idea of how critical and unloving she may sound to him. Even though her intentions are to help, her suggestions will most likely offend and hurt. His reaction may be strong, especially if he felt criticized as a child or if he experienced his father being criticized by his mother.

Task for Both: Timing Is Everything

In pointing out these two major misperceptions I do not mean that everything is wrong with the Mr. Fix-It approach, nor with a woman trying to help out the man she is in love with. These are both very positive attributes; the mistakes are only in the timing and approach.

A woman greatly appreciates Mr. Fix-It, as long as he doesn't come out when she is upset. Men need to remember that when women talk about problems is not always the best time to offer solutions. Instead, she may simply need to be heard, and gradually she will feel better on her own. She does not necessarily need to be fixed.

Similarly, a man may greatly appreciate a woman's help on certain matters—as long as it is requested. Women need to remember that unsolicited advice or criticism—especially if he has made a mistake—make a man feel unloved and controlled. He needs her acceptance more than her advice in order to learn from his mistakes on his own. When a man feels that a woman is not trying to improve him, he is ironically much more likely to ask for her feedback.

Understanding these differences makes it easier to respect our partner's sensitivities and be more supportive. In addition, we recognize that when our partner resists us, it is probably because we have simply made a mistake in our timing or approach—we have assumed that they needed our help when, in fact, a sympathetic ear may have been more beneficial.

When a Man Loves a Woman

A surprising fact is that most men are not only hungry to give love—they are starving for it. Their biggest problem is that they don't know what they're missing. They rarely saw their fathers succeed in fulfilling their mothers. As a result they do not know that a major source of fulfillment for a man can come through giving.

When his relationships fail, he finds himself depressed and stuck in his "cave."

Give and take:

Quite often, when one partner makes a positive change, the other changes as well. When she decides to voice her needs, he wants to give her more.

He stops caring and doesn't know why he is so depressed.

At such times he withdraws from relationships or intimacy. He asks himself what it is all for and why he should bother. He doesn't know that he has stopped caring because he doesn't feel *needed*. He does not realize that by finding someone who needs him, he can shake off his depression and be motivated again.

When a man doesn't feel he is making a positive difference in someone else's life, it is hard for him to continue caring and feeling motivated about his relationships. To become motivated again he needs to feel appreciated, trusted, and accepted. Not to be needed is a slow death for a man.

When a Woman Loves a Man

Similarly, many men have little awareness of how important it is for a woman to feel supported by someone who cares. When a woman is upset, over-whelmed, confused, exhausted, or hopeless, what she needs most is companionship. She needs to feel she is not alone, that she is loved and cherished.

Empathy, understanding, validation, and compassion go a long way to assist her in becoming more receptive and appreciative of his support. Men don't realize this because their instincts tell them that it's best to be alone when they are upset. When she is upset, out of respect he will leave her alone, or if he stays he makes matters worse by trying to solve her problems. He does not instinctively realize how very important closeness, intimacy, and sharing are to her. What she needs most is just someone to listen.

By sharing her feelings with someone she can begin to feel that her emotional needs will be fulfilled. Doubt and mistrust begin to melt away, and her tendency to be compulsive relaxes as she remembers that she is worthy of love. She doesn't have to earn it; she can relax, give less, and receive more.

Giving up Blame

Yet when a woman feels she has been giving too much in her relationship, she will blame her partner for their unhappiness. She feels the injustice of not receiving what she deserved. Similarly, a man who *gives* less should not blame a woman for being negative or unreceptive to him.

In both cases, blaming does not work. Understanding, trust, compassion, acceptance, and support are the only possible solutions. Instead of blaming his partner for being resentful, a man can be compassionate and offer his support—even if she doesn't ask for it. He can listen to her even if at first it sounds like blame, and help her to trust and open up to him by doing little things for her to show that he cares.

Likewise, instead of blaming a man for giving less, a woman can accept and forgive her partner's imperfections. She can trust that he wants to give more even when he doesn't offer his support, and encourage him by appreciating what he does give and continuing to ask specifically for his support.

Let's look at an example. Jim was 39 and his wife, Susan, was 41 when they came for counseling. Susan wanted a divorce. She complained that she had been giving more than he had for 12 years and could not take it any more. She blamed Jim for being lethargic, selfish, controlling, and unromantic. She said she had nothing left to give and was ready to leave. He convinced her to come to therapy, but she was doubtful. In a six-month period they were able to move through the three steps for healing a relationship.

Step 1: Motivation

I explained to Jim that if he wanted to save his marriage and motivate his wife to work on it, he would have to do a lot of listening. For the first six sessions, I encouraged Susan to share her negative feelings and helped Jim patiently to understand them. This was the hardest part of their healing process. As he began to really hear her unfulfilled needs, he became increasingly confident that he could make the changes necessary to have a loving relationship.

Step 2: Responsibility

Jim needed to take responsibility for not supporting his wife, while Susan needed to take responsibility for not setting boundaries. Jim apologized for the ways he had hurt her. Susan realized that just as he had treated her disrespectfully (by yelling, grumbling, resisting requests, and invalidating feelings), she had not clearly set her boundaries. As she gradually acknowledged some responsibility for their problems, she was able to be more forgiving.

Step 3: Practice

Both Jim and Susan needed to learn how to express their feelings in a respectful way. They agreed to practice setting limits, knowing that at times they would make mistakes and allowing each other a safety net while they practiced. Some examples include:

• Susan practiced saying, "Please stop yelling or I will leave the room." After leaving the room a few times, she didn't need to do it anymore.

• When Jim made requests that she would later resent doing, she practiced saying, "No, I need to relax" or "No, I'm too busy today." She discovered that he was more attentive to her because he understood how busy or tired she was.

• Susan told Jim that she wanted to go on a vacation and when he said he was too busy she said that she would go alone. Suddenly he shifted his schedule and wanted to go.

• Susan's most difficult task was to practice asking for what she wanted: "Why should I have to ask, after all I have done for him?" But making him responsible for knowing her wants was not only unrealistic but a big part of her problem. She needed to be responsible for getting her needs fulfilled.

• Jim's most difficult challenge was to not expect Susan to be the same accommodating partner he originally married. He recognized that it was as difficult for her to set limits as it was for him to adjust to them.

As a man experiences limits, he is automatically motivated to question the effectiveness of his behavior and to start making changes. When a woman real-

More for less:

You don't necessarily have to give more to have a better relationship. Ironically, your partner may actually give you more when and if you begin to give them *less*.

izes that in order to receive she needs to set limits, then she automatically begins to forgive her partner and explore new ways of asking for and receiving support. When a woman sets such limits, she gradually learns to relax and receive more.

Learning to Receive

Setting limits and receiving are very scary for a woman. She is commonly afraid of needing too much and then being rejected, judged, or abandoned—a fear most painful because deep inside her unconscious she holds the incorrect belief that she is unworthy of receiving more.

A woman is particularly vulnerable to the incorrect belief that she doesn't deserve to be loved. Hidden in the unconscious, this feeling of unworthiness generates the fear of needing others. A part of her imagines that she will not be supported, so she unknowingly pushes away the support she needs. Her mistrust transforms her needs into a desperate expression of neediness and communicates to a man the message that she doesn't trust him to support her. Ironically, while men are primarily motivated by being *needed*, they are turned off by *neediness*.

The distinction is an important one: "Needing" is openly reaching out and asking for support from a man in a trusting manner, one that assumes he will do his best to try and fulfill it. "Neediness," however, is desperately needing support because you don't trust you will get it. It pushes men away and makes them feel rejected and unappreciated.

Feeling Worthy

When a woman realizes that she truly deserves to be loved, she is opening the door for a man to give to her. But, for example, when it takes her 10 years of overgiving to realize this, she feels like closing the door and not giving him the chance. She may feel something like this: "I have given to you and you have ignored me. You had your chance. I have nothing left to give. I deserve better. I can't trust you, and I will not let you hurt me again."

Repeatedly, when this is the case, I have assured women that they don't have

to give more to have a better relationship. Their partner will actually give them more if they give *less*. When a man has been ignoring her needs, it is as though they have both been asleep. When she wakes up and remembers her needs, he wakes up and wants to give her more.

It also works the other way around. Usually when a man realizes that he is unhappy and wants more romance and love in his life, his wife will suddenly begin to open up and love him again. The walls of resentment begin to melt, and love comes back to life. If there has been a lot of neglect, it may take a while to heal all the accumulated resentments, but it is possible.

Successful Relationships

Many men did not have successful role models while they were growing up. For them, staying in love, getting married, and having a family is as difficult as flying a jumbo jet without any training. While he may be able to take off, he feels he is almost certain to crash. And it is difficult to continue flying once you have crashed the plane a few times, or if you witnessed your father crash.

Good communication requires participation on both sides. A man needs to work at remembering that complaining about problems does not equal blaming, and that when a woman complains she is generally just letting go of her frustrations by talking about them. A woman can work at letting him know that although she appears to be complaining, she also appreciates him.

Remember that a woman does not have to suppress her feelings or even change them to support her partner. She does, however, need to express them in a way that doesn't make him feel attacked, accused, or blamed. Making a few small changes can actually make a big difference.

Without a good training manual, it is easy to understand why many men and women just give up.

The process of learning about relationships requires not only hearing and applying the new ideas in this essay, but also forgetting and then remembering them again. Give yourself (and your partner) permission to keep making mistakes. It takes time to work with these insights and integrate them into your life. Integrating this new wisdom of having loving relationships is a new challenge. You are traveling in new territory. Expect to be lost sometimes. Expect your partner to be lost. Use this guide as a map to lead you through uncharted lands again and again.

Relationships thrive when communication reflects a ready acceptance and respect of each individual's innate differences. When misunderstandings arise, remember that we speak different languages; take the time necessary to translate what your partner really means or wants to say. This definitely takes practice, but it is well worth it. I have witnessed a transformation in thousands of couples.

Not only do we need to hear these lessons 200 times, but we also need to unlearn what we have learned in the past—from parents, culture, and our own past experiences.

Next time you are frustrated with the opposite sex, remember men and women are different from each other. Even if you don't remember anything else, remembering that we are supposed to be different will help you to be more loving. By gradually releasing your judgments and blame and persistently asking for what you want, you can create the loving relationships you want, need, and deserve.

Soul Mates

With all of their inherent difficulties, relationships of all kinds enrich our lives and help fulfill the needs of the soul.

Thomas Moore

Thomas Moore, Ph.D., is a psychotherapist and writer. His books include The Planets Within, Rituals of the Imagination, Dark Eros, *and* Care of the Soul *(HarperCollins). As a young man, he lived as a monk in a Catholic religious order for 12 years. He lives with his wife and two children in western Massachusetts.*

When we consider the soul of relationship, unexpected factors come into view. In its deepest nature, for example, the soul involves itself in the stuff of this world, both people and objects. It loves attachment of all kinds—to places, ideas, times, historical figures and periods, things, words, sounds, and settings—and if we are going to examine relationship in the soul, we have to take into account the wide range of its loves and inclinations.

Yet even though the soul sinks luxuriantly into its attachments, something in it also moves in a different direction. Something valid and necessary takes flight when it senses deep attachment, and this flight also seems so deeply rooted as to be an honest expression of soul. Our ultimate goal is to find ways to embrace both attachment and resistance to attachment, and the only way to that reconciliation of opposites is to dig deeply into the nature of each. As with all matters of soul, it is in honoring its impulses that we find our way best into its mysteries.

ATTACHMENT

The soul manifests its innate tendency toward attachment in many ways. One way is a penchant for the past and a resistance to change. A particularly soulful person might turn down a good job offer, for example, because he doesn't want to move away from his hometown. The soulfulness of this decision is fairly clear: ties to friends, family, buildings, and a familiar landscape come from the heart, and honoring them may be more important for a

soulful life than following exciting ideas and possibilities that are rooted in some other part of our nature.

By definition, the soul is attached to life in all its particulars. It prefers relatedness to distancing. From the point of view of the soul, meaningfulness and value rise directly out of experience, or from the images and memories that issue modestly and immediately out of ordinary life. The soul's intelligence may not arrive through rational analysis but through a long period of rumination, and its goal may not be brilliant understanding and unassailable truth, but rather profound insight and abiding wisdom.

This penchant of the soul for the complications of life plays a role in personal relationships. Relatedness means staying in life, even when it becomes complicated and when meaning and clarity are elusive. It means living with the particular individuals who come into our lives, and not only with our ideals and images of the perfect mate or the perfect family. On the other hand, honoring the particular in our lives also means making the separations, divorces, and endings that the soul requires. The soul is always attached to what is actually happening, not necessarily to what could be or will be.

Rather than come up with new understandings and new and improved ways of doing things, the soul prefers to get what it can gradually, taking its nourishment from what is already present. Soul-work, therefore, demands patience and loyalty, virtues not in vogue in our fast-changing times. The soul asks that we live through our attachments rather than try to make swift, clean breaks. It may seem wise, at the end of a divorce or when we've been fired from a job, to "get the past behind us" and "start a new life." But the soul may need more reflection on that painful past, and there may be untouched fertile materials in past events.

It is possible to see our complaints about feeling stuck, or of not being able to get past the latest trauma, as the work of the soul binding us to our given existence. The soul doesn't propel, like spirit; it feels the impact of events. It is easily stung and disturbed. The spirited side enjoys power, strength, well-being, and superiority. The soul, given to the pleasures of earthly existence, suffers its intimacies to the extent that attachment often feels like bondage.

Parents may like the emotional closeness they feel with their children, but they are also, sometimes frustratingly, tied to them. We may go to great extremes in order to have a solid romantic relationship with another person, but then we are also caught in an emotional bond and may begin to feel a contrary desire for freedom to relate to others.

The feeling of longing, the ache of desire for a familiar place or thing, the urgency to visit old friends and places, are all expressions of the soul. The soul wants these things fiercely, as though its well-being required them, even if the demands of life make fulfilling these needs seem impractical.

Attachment to people, things, and places can feel like a burden. It's a nuisance to carry useless things around with us as we move from state to state and house to house. It takes care, attention, and time to write the letters and make the phone calls that sustain attachments. Care of the soul can be demanding, requiring a decision that the needs of the soul are as important as the more future-oriented things that claim our attention.

'The intimacy in sex is never only physical. In a sexual relationship we may discover who we are in ways otherwise unavailable to us, and at the same time we allow our partner to see and know that individual. As we unveil our bodies, we also disclose our persons.'

Every day we feel the soul's minor or major discomforts, but because we habitually overlook these signals of soul pain, we may fail to respond. Just as some people can't perceive colors or musical tones, so we may be soul-blind and soul-deaf. The soul's yearnings simply don't get through to consciousness; or if they do, we try to numb ourselves to them with medications, frenzied activities, or other palliatives. The resulting alienation within our very hearts bears its own painful melancholic loneliness.

A first step, then, in tending to the soul in regard to our relationships is to understand and honor its particular mode of being. It may help to realize that there are two pulls in us: one upward toward transcendence, ambition, success, progress, intellectual clarity, and cosmic consciousness; and another downward, into individual, vernacular life. As we work through difficult family relationships, struggle with the demands of marriage, apply ourselves to the job we're doing, become settled into the geographic region fate has chosen for us, and continually sort through the personality issues that never

seem to change or improve—in all these areas we are gathering the stuff of the soul. The soul wants to be attached, involved, and even stuck, because it is through such intimacy that it is nourished, initiated, and deepened.

NEAR AND FAR

We can apply these principles of attachment and freedom to our relationships, discovering that our involvement with people may be most soulful when we can live fully amid the tension of these two inclinations. If we have strong desires to have a family, live with another person, or join a community, but find, after these desires have been satisfied, that we are drawn in exactly the opposite direction, then we might remember that this complexity is simply the way of the soul. We may have to look for concrete ways to give life to both sides of the spectrum, enjoying both our intimacies and our solitude.

Sometimes the matter presents itself as a questioning of our own natures: Am I the kind of person who should get married, or do I need to live alone? Should I get a job in a large corporation, or should I be self-employed? The best answer to questions like these is intellectually and emotionally to hold both sides at once. Out of the tension may come a way of being attached and separate at the same time.

In everyday life there are always opportunities to honor both separateness and togetherness. Often one person in a relationship feels one emotion more than the other. In his essay on marriage, Carl Jung describes one partner as the "contained" and the other as the "container." Maybe the best way to tend these two needs is to notice where the anxiety is. A person in a marriage who is longing for freedom, finding marriage too confining, might best avoid the temptation to flee and instead work at reimagining marriage and partnership.

Many people seem to live the pain of togetherness and fantasize the joys of separateness; or, vice versa, they live a life of solitude and fill their heads with alluring images of intimacy. Bouncing back and forth between these two valid claims on the heart can be an endless struggle that never bears fruit and never settles down. In the end, the only answer is a polytheistic one. Honor both gods. Pursue and run away. Be lustful and chaste. Wholeheartedly link up with someone else but just as passionately find your own way.

For some of us, a strong dose of individuality can be the best quality to bring to a relationship. That nymph in your heart who runs away at the first sign of love, sex, and commitment might be doing an important service to the soul, which needs flight as much as it needs embrace. On the other hand, the proud spirit that rushes into relationships is also important to the soul. Without impetuous desire, there may be no intimacy.

All we can do is follow the lead of our emotions and images. An abstract comprehensive understanding is both impossible and undesirable. In matters of the heart, we may have no choice but to allow other forces beyond our intentional selves to work out the debates, the incongruities, and the contradictions, as we bring hope and desire to new love and affection.

SEX AND IMAGINATION

Sex is a great mystery of life that resists our many attempts to explain and control it. Along with money and death, it represents one of the few elements left in life that virtually pulsates with divinity, easily overwhelms our feelings and thoughts, and sometimes leads to profound compulsions.

'In matters of the heart, we may have no choice but to allow other forces beyond our intentional selves to work out the debates.'

Emotional compulsion is often regarded negatively as a failure of control or a sign of irrationality. We might see it rather as the soul yearning for expression and trying to thrust itself into life. Sexual compulsion may show us where and to what extent we have neglected this particular need. Compulsion asks for a response from us, but we might be careful lest we simply react to the felt need. Some respond by advocating "free love," as though the best way to deal with the compulsion were to give in to it literally.

This is the way of compensation, which doesn't solve the problem but only places us at the other end of it. The soulful way is to bring imagination to sex, so that by fulfilling the need at a deep level, the compulsion is brought to term.

We may try to keep the power of sex at bay through many clever maneuvers. Our moralism, for example, helps keep us clean of the mess sex can make of an otherwise ordered life. Sex education tries to teach us to avoid disease by placing sex under the light of science. Yet in spite of all our efforts, sexual compulsion interferes with marriages, draws people into strange liaisons, and continues to offend propriety, morality, and religion. Its dynamic is too big to fit into the cages we make for it.

We are in a difficult position in relation to sex: We believe it's important to have a healthy sex life, yet we also believe that the tendency of sex to spread easily into unwanted areas—pornography, extramarital affairs—is a sign of cultural decadence or moral and religious breakdown. We want sex to be robust, but not too robust.

Sex asks something of us—that we live more fully and manifest ourselves more transparently. This demand is so central and powerful that our resistances to it are also strong—our moralism, indirection, rationalization, and

acting out. It would help if we would stop thinking of sex as in the slightest way medical or biological. The whole sphere of sex—emotion, body, fantasy, and relationship—falls within the domain of the soul.

PORNOGRAPHY

It sometimes happens that one person in a relationship shows an interest in pornography while the other is offended or at least disturbed by it. A wife might think that if her husband is turning to pornography for sexual stimulation, there must be something lacking in her. A husband might say, "I guess I'm not what my wife is looking for in a man. She's interested in other men's bodies."

It's difficult to sort out issues surrounding pornography because in our culture response to pornography often divides into two extremes—compulsion and moral indignation. This split suggests that for us pornography is a problem rather than an element integrated into everyday life. When we respond to anything with compulsion and moralism, we can assume that we haven't yet found the soul in it.

An interest in pornography clearly shows the desire for some kind of increase in erotic life and an intensification and broadening of the sexual imagination. When we find this interest blooming in ourselves or in someone close to us, rather than move quickly into judgment, we might ask what it is doing there. Could this sexual interest be serving some purpose? The pornographic imagination doesn't have to be justified, but it might ease our minds if we could find a context for it.

SEX AND INTIMACY

Thinking about sex, we sometimes take either the position that it is entirely physiological or that it is primarily interpersonal. In either of these viewpoints, the soul of sex can be overlooked. Its soul is to be found in the imagination through which we experience sex, whether individually, interpersonally, or even societally. Each of us has a sexual history, persons who figure prominently for good or ill.

We may also have strong sexual hopes and longings. We might regard all these images as creations of the soul and be aware that each may resonate on many levels. The memory of a pleasurable experience may carry longings about pleasure in life itself, or a painful memory may epitomize a more general disillusionment and hopelessness about joy, pleasure, and initimacy. The image of oneself as a lover, as beautiful or capable, may be wrapped up in these memories. Deeper still may lie fears of exposure or the old dynamics of family relationships.

The intimacy in sex, while always attached to the body, is never only physical. Sex always evokes pieces of stories and fragments of characters, and so the desire and willingness to be sexually transparent is truly an exposure of the soul. In sex we may discover who we are in ways otherwise unavailable to us, and at the same time we allow our partner to see and know that individual. As we unveil our bodies, we also disclose our persons.

It makes sense that vulnerability requires inhibitions of all kinds. Part of sexual intimacy is protection of the other's inhibition, for that reserve is as much an expression of soul as is the apparent willingness to be exposed. It makes no difference whether the inhibition seems neurotic: It must be honored if soulful intimacy is to be maintained. It is not "abnormal" for a person to feel unusually reticent about physical and emotional exposure. Nor is it abnormal for a person to enjoy the exhibition of their sexuality.

Sexual intimacy begins with acknowledgment of and respect for the mystery and madness of the other's sexuality, for it is only in mystery and madness that soul is revealed. I'm referring to platonic madness, of course—the soul's natural expression that almost always appears deviant to normal society. At times we may have to protect ourselves from another's sexual confusion and acting out, but if we want an intimate relationship, we will have to create a place for the other's sexual fantasy.

To find sexual intimacy, we may also have to acknowledge that sex is often wounded. The soul of sexuality often enters through an opening made by sexual wounding. We can learn to see that the places of our sexual punctures and violations are areas of potential intimacy, even though on the surface they may seem to be precisely the areas of mistrust. All of us have sexual wounds. It does no good either to wallow in them or to deny them a place.

While sex is tender and sensitive to invasion, it is also profoundly involved with the soul. Sex is the soul's limpid mirror, its litmus, and its gesture. We can exploit sex, manipulate others with it, use it with fierce aggression, hide from it, misread it, and indulge excessively in it. These are the means of struggling with its potential soulfulness.

The soul of sex has the power to evoke relationship, to sustain it, and to make it worthwhile. As with all things of soul, we are asked to stand out of the way and be affected by its power to quicken life and to transform us from practical survivors into erotic poets of our own lives.

ADULTERY

OF THE HEART

*Is flirting good for your marriage, or
the ultimate betrayal?*

Lynn Peters

There's nothing like a little harmless flirting, is there? You look up and he's watching you. He holds your glance a fraction longer than he needs to. He smiles and tells you how great you look. And you forget that your hair needs washing, your skirt is too tight, and your youngest child is coming down with measles. Suddenly you feel terrific.

I was saying all this to my friend Suzanne the other day. I'd been working with an achingly attractive man—tall, dark-eyed, narrow-hipped, a cross between James Dean and a young Clint Eastwood—and I was telling her how much fun flirting was. I didn't even notice I was getting a pretty frosty reception until she cut me off. "You do realize," she said, "that you're talking about adultery."

You could have knocked me down with the froth from our cappuccinos. "I'm not

sleeping with him," I stammered, suddenly defensive and, quite frankly, astonished. "It isn't that sort of relationship. It isn't any sort of relationship."

She's overreacting, I thought. Adultery implies having sex, not just eye contact. You can't commit adultery just by thinking about it—otherwise you'd be guilty every time you fantasized about a night in the arms of Mel Gibson. Adultery is all about mutual lust and consuming passion, not shared jokes or a couple of harmless compliments.

I explained all this to Suzanne, but she was unimpressed. "Haven't you heard of adultery of the heart?" she said. "You don't have to actually sleep with someone to commit adultery. Just *lusting* after other men is a kind of betrayal."

As it happened, I hadn't heard this before. I thought she'd made it up just to make me feel bad. But then I started to think about it. There *is* a big shift in a relationship from those first lingering looks to going to bed with a man. Maybe adultery of the heart sums up pretty well what's going on in between. But at what stage do you become guilty? And could adultery of the heart really include the innocent, blameless, and entirely enjoyable act of flirting?

Surely not. A flirtation may make you feel sexy, desirable, and about ten years younger, but that isn't the same thing as wanting carnal knowledge. Just think of that queen of coquettes Scarlett O'Hara. Her dalliances had about as much to do with sex as with skydiving. Their purpose was simply to gain a man's admiration. If

I've rushed in to the office after a hectic morning packing the kids off to school, feeling terrible and looking worse, why shouldn't I engage in a few minutes of casual conversation with a male colleague who wants to tell me how wonderful I look? He thinks I'm attractive, and suddenly I am attractive. If I respond with a smile that looks like encouragement (and I always do), it's because I want to encourage him to go on making me feel this way. My morale gets a boost, and already the day looks brighter. Flirting is a way of forgetting the daily grind and keeping the memory of romance alive; of making a man acknowledge that you're a woman. It's about asserting your own femininity.

In fact, it's because sex and intimacy aren't ever going to be involved that this situation is so appealing. This man will never see you waxing your legs, nor will you ever wake to find him lying next to you, unshaven. It's romance movie-style: You get only the good bits.

But if flirting is innocent because you're not thinking about sex, where does this leave fantasy (when you are thinking about it)? Personally, I have a hard time rationalizing fantasy. It just doesn't seem right to be thinking of someone else while my husband makes love to me. This isn't to say I don't ever do it, but I do feel bad about it. Not that I should. According to sex therapists, fantasy is a good thing and virtually compulsory for a healthy sex life.

Perhaps the answer is that fantasy is acceptable if the situation is entirely imaginary and the man involved resembles no one you know (or are ever likely to know, like Richard Gere, sadly). It's not okay if he looks like that sexy man who smiled at you in the parking lot, or your neighbor who always squeezes your shoulders when he helps you on with your coat. On the face of it, there should be no difference between one kind of fantasy and the other, since no one knows about either. And weaving wonderful imaginings around a man doesn't imply an intention to carry them out. But once you've imagined yourself in a given situation, it suddenly becomes a lot easier to realize it.

As my friend Clare remarked, "We all have fantasies, however good the relationship. But fantasizing about someone real is dangerous because you can make it happen." Which is not to say that fantasy, any more than flirting, is going to land you in divorce court. Yet maybe it can prepare the groundwork. You embark on what seems like an innocent liaison, a casual daydream about someone you're attracted to, and gradually you're swept up into something you hadn't planned.

The problem with flirting is that it sometimes carries the same risks. You're employing the same courtship cues you used when you were single—eye contact, provocative remarks, and a recognition of each other's sexuality—and maybe you won't know where to stop. One day you're just enjoying a few laughs, doing nothing you couldn't tell your husband about; the next, it's all secret trysts and a need for discretion. That's the danger zone: where the risk of "trying on" a passionate attraction stops being a game and turns into the real thing.

I wandered into the danger zone once. I'd returned to work after several years at home with the kids (when my only male contact, aside from my husband, had been store clerks and my friends' husbands—in the company of their wives), so it was exciting to work with a boss with whom I had an instant rapport. He was attractive and fun, and he made me feel like my own person again, not just somebody's mother.

Sometimes we had lunch together, though there was nothing odd about that. We talked about the future of the company, how he saw my role developing. Then he started telling me about his personal problems and the affair he was having. I should have read the warning signals. But I was flattered to be taken into his confidence. I made a few jokes about this being another "my wife doesn't understand me" scenario—only more so because "in your case, your girlfriend doesn't understand you either." He laughed. We were always laughing.

I thought we had the perfect working relationship, with our unstated mutual attraction as the icing on the cake. That lasted until he dropped in to my office and pushed a brochure across the desk. It was for a hotel he'd booked us into for the weekend. I still remember how my knees shook. I felt so stupid. I'd thought that being attracted to each other was an end in itself. It didn't have to lead anywhere.

I learned the hard way that you have to be careful. The unfortunate truth is that some men think that if you flirt with them, you want sex. This can leave even the most harmless dalliance open to misinterpretation. You think you're being playful, acting a part, having fun. He thinks you're giving him a green light.

Sadly, the danger zones are many and various. I have a terrific working relationship with an all-male team, but if I have to work with just one of them, I sense a change in the atmosphere. It's as if you move from being two people who work together to being *a man and woman*. These days, in such situations, I avoid eye contact and become efficient and businesslike.

The boundary between flirting harmlessly and flirting with intent is easily crossed, and the borders aren't marked. Besides, they can vary for each of us. A poll of my friends isolated a few things that, with hindsight, we'd consider warning bells. Watch out if, despite your growing attraction, you ignore your instincts and try to convince yourself that men and women really can be just good friends. Think twice if you tell yourself that because you haven't touched, kissed, or been on a date, nothing is going on—if there's really nothing going on, the question wouldn't occur to you. Finally, if you're feeling guilty or secretive about any aspect of the relationship, then reconsider your position.

If adultery is all about sex, then adultery of the heart is all about deception. You might not have broken your marriage vows—yet. But the betrayal of trust can be just as damaging to a marriage as having sex with another man. As my friend Linda puts it, "Sex is only one aspect of adultery. If you're going behind your husband's back and you confide in someone other than your husband, then you're having an affair, no doubt about it."

In my own situation, it was the sudden need for deception that marked the line between flirting and adultery. Once my boss was discussing things I couldn't tell my husband, that had to be the end of the friendship. Until then, my intentions had made it innocent—in my own eyes anyway. And even if we'd done no more than gone on eating lunches together, there'd have been an undercurrent in that relationship, one I'd have to keep to myself.

We each have our own opinion of what's innocent and what's harmful, and the important thing is to know our own boundaries and stick to them. Which, as far as I'm concerned, means if any dark-eyed Adonis (or anyone else, for that matter) wants to put a smile on my face by telling me how terrific I am, it's okay with me. And incidentally, with my husband, too. I asked him, and he said, "Go ahead. What's wrong with a little flirtation?"

I smiled, thought about it for a minute, then began to worry. It sounds to me like he could be doing it himself. Just don't let me catch him!

FORECAST FOR
Couples

Painful and confusing as they may be, intimate relationships today actually follow particular dynamic patterns; they evolve through recurring cycles of promise and betrayal. Herewith, a map of the territory.

Barry Dym and Michael Glenn, M.D.

For both men and women, intimate relationships have come to assume an importance that is perhaps unprecedented. And while the sexes are having a devilishly hard time getting together in these days of rapid role change, they are clearly struggling to make things work in a way that satisfies both partners. What is so surprising is that the struggles have been taking place almost entirely in the absence of a general cultural understanding about the nature of relationships. In occasional articles over the past 10 issues, PSYCHOLOGY TODAY has sought to relay what family therapists know—that relationships have rules of their own. Each is a system, something larger and different from each partner individually. In "The Reinvention of Marriage [Jan/Feb 1992]," for example, PT introduced a developmental perspective to relationships, explaining how they naturally develop over time. In this article, two noted family therapists add another dimension: Relationships progress not in a straight line, but through endless cycles of advance and retreat.—The Editors

Not so long ago, a simple story stated that a couple began when a man and a woman fell in love. They would then marry and form a family. The woman would take care of the home and children; the man would support them by toiling in the heartless world. They would both sacrifice their individual goals to the greater good of the family. Their romance would gradually melt into affection and partnership. The man would be the acknowledged leader, following law and custom, but the woman would rule in domestic matters.

Not every couple followed this prescription—far from it. Forms of coupling varied from couple to couple and from community to community. But each couple, whatever they did, had to contend with this story, this cultural narrative. Some adopted it with relative ease; some twisted and changed themselves in order to accommodate; others were defiant, but their very defiance proved the story's continued vitality. Anyone could invoke it as an authority against a partner who failed to play the assigned role. The same is true today, albeit in response to a different cultural narrative.

The contemporary couple is changing rapidly, responding to shifts in where and how people live, in the economics of employment, in the different kinds of power women and men wield, in beliefs about how things are supposed to be between the sexes, and in the nature of the family. As couples change, so does the cultural narrative about them. One result of the rapid changes is that both men and women tend to overestimate the power the *other* sex wields in intimate relations today. Both feel like victims in the war between the sexes.

Fascination with couples fills today's media and shapes our popular imagination. The romantically engaged couple is

From *Psychology Today*, July/August 1993, pp. 54-57, 78-79, 81-83, 86. Excerpted from *Couples: Exploring and Understanding the Cycles of Intimate Relationships* by Barry Dym and Michael Glenn, M.D. © 1993 by Barry Dym and Michael Glenn, M.D. Reprinted by permission of HarperCollins Publishers, Inc.

the icon of our time, a major focus of movies, television, books, and music. Most people devote tremendous energy to trying to find the perfect partner. And yet the couple is an isolated and fragile form, caught between great expectations and declining resources. It is supposed to be the cure for all that ails you. In fact, our commitment to the inner life of relationships has grown as our commitment to the larger society recedes. But the couple falls apart almost as easily as it comes together: half of all marriages end in divorce; early love often fades into domestic boredom. Contemporary couples must develop in the shadow of their potential demise.

There have always been many different kinds of couples: "just living together" couples, gay and lesbian couples, childless couples, interracial couples, post-divorce

Contemporary couples must develop in the shadow of their potential demise. As they struggle to avoid breaking up, they often distort the very relationships they are trying to preserve.

couples, couples of vastly different age, and so on. The life course of real couples varies widely; few march in a straight line past every predictable milepost, from the first romantic attachment to the birth of children to the empty-nest syndrome, and finally into retirement together. But *certain* stories regularly prevail. Against them, social diversity continues to build, often in unexpected ways (as by the impact of new immigrant families).

People—psychotherapists included—often participate in, theorize about, and try to fix ailing couples without a clear sense of what a couple is or an understanding of how it has gotten that way. This is like trying to treat the heart without knowing something about its normal functioning. Intimate couple relationships, painful and confusing as they may be, follow particular patterns; yet couples today have only the most rudimentary map of the territory through which life takes them. They are in a psychological and moral wilderness. Self-help books and psychotherapists try to

help but often fail. What is needed is the creation of a living narrative, new language, new concepts, and new metaphors—a map of couples in our time.

As family therapists, we began our thinking with a simple observation: so many people seem disappointed in their relationships. What is the disappointment all about? Psychotherapists look for the roots of disappointment in unresolved childhood conflicts; philosophers and psychologists note its origins in our attachments to specific goals and material comfort. But the more we thought about it, the more a simpler answer emerged: relationships are disappointing because they do not seem to fulfill their early promise.

Our culture asks so much of couple relationships—romance and passion, partnership, friendship, and nurturance—that disappointment is inevitable. The expansive promise of new beginnings often comes to seem like a youthful illusion at best, a cruel hoax at worst. The implicit contracts people make with each other—which are based more on potential than on past performance—come tumbling down. Partners break promises; individuals break their own resolutions. Husbands and wives are forever noting, "This is not the person I thought I had married" and "If I had known then what I know today, I never would have married her." These statements are not simply sour grapes or the distorted complaints of dissatisfied individuals. They reflect the truth of broken promises.

CONTRADICTIONS

This is a revolutionary time in male and female relationships and therefore in the lives of couples. In times of change, contradictions sharpen. This process marks the lives of contemporary couples, making both partners tense and excited. We can point out three basic conflicts with which couples today must cope.

1. The clash between great expectations and limited resources.

According to our cultural narrative, the romantically engaged couple is an answer for everything. We want more from our partners, but we're less and less able to give of ourselves. Our partners must be passionate lovers as well as loyal confidantes, willing to join us intensely when we want, but leaving us alone when we need "private space." We ask for romance in our quiet moments, but want a sturdy partner to help raise children, maintain a household, and coordinate schedules. These activities

interfere with one another, and our expectations don't mix.

The couple is supposed to be a stable haven in a cool, hostile, unpredictable world. In the past, women had the role of maintaining domestic relationships, but now that two incomes are required to get by, more and more couples are made up of two working partners. Many couples, even those without children, return home each day exhausted. No one stands at the threshold to welcome them and soothe their return.

The couple is supposed to be a stable haven in a cool, hostile unpredictable world.

At the same time, couples are more than ever isolated from the resources that used to sustain them, such as extended families and communities. We all have friends, but fewer of us live close to our families. Who can we depend on, no questions asked, to take care of the kids when we are in a pinch? Who will support us and offer us wisdom through the hard times? Most couples are jammed for time, for emotional energy, and for patience. "I just need a minute to myself" has become our modern litany. Our partner's company sometimes drains us more than it enhances us. We probably do more for one another these days, but we expect so much that we're still often disappointed.

2. The clash between the individual and the couple.

We always marvel at those selfless individuals who place others' needs and comforts first. In an age such as ours, individual pleasures, development, and fulfillment often come first. The contemporary concern with self intensifies the basic tension between our allegiance to the relationship and allegiance to ourselves.

In couple relationships this tension is often polarized by gender: women have tended to stand for the relationship, connection, and mutual dependence; men for individualism and independence. Such polarization, where it exists, exaggerates and distorts and leads to dramatic confrontations such as those in which women feel abandoned while men feel controlled. This is probably the most common dilemma presented to couple therapists today, and can be seen as the archetypal struggle of the modern couple.

But there is a growing trend to dissolve this simple division by gender. Women are also concerned with their own development, with being independent, respected partners, capable of pursuing their goals outside of the relationship. The question then arises: just *who* in the couple is committed to the relationship?

In other eras, romantic love centered on the partner. "What can I do to win you?" was a burning question. These days we look for partners who can bring out the best in ourselves. "What can you do for *me?*" we ask. The ideal partner today is a cross between a psychotherapist and a good parent. Even generosity, we are told, proceeds best from self-fulfillment: only if we feel good about ourselves will we be good to our partners. But when we feel bad about ourselves, and our partners are not filling our needs, we may soon lose our commitment to the relationship. We and our partner then become two islands in an unfriendly sea.

3. The clash between staying together and splitting up, marriage and divorce.

Many relationships last a short time. We discard our partners—or they discard us—and we move on. Even longer relationships have a way of fizzling out after a year or so: they just don't seem right any more; nasty arguments turn us sour; our involvement fades away. Even those relationships that lead to marriage have trouble holding fast. And yet we keep starting relationships again, hoping each time we'll find the right partner—or at least take a more realistic attitude towards them.

We seem less angry, less disillusioned with relationships than with ourselves or our current partner. As difficulties in a relationship mount, we often persist because we have so much "invested" in it; but eventually we wonder if it makes sense to put any more into such a losing relationship.

Most of us become less willing to accept a stale relationship. As breakup and divorce have become easier, so has our dream of the good partner. We imagine anew that someone out there will save us from loneliness, redeem us as individuals, and help us avoid the problems that destroyed our last relationship.

We're vividly aware that breakup and divorce are possible. Such awareness can take the edge off our own commitment: it is an escape clause, a skepticism built into contemporary relationships. We react to this skepticism by nervously maintaining

a safer distance, withholding a part of ourselves, and trying to let go of some of our romantic intensity. As we struggle to avoid breaking up, we often distort the very relationships we are trying to preserve.

In trying to understand the disappointment of couples, we began asking couples about their original promises. What was it they had originally pledged to one another, what contract had they tacitly made? And how did this contract affect the dissolution or reconciliation that followed their sense of betrayal? Further, how did couples move *beyond* their outrage? How did the resolution of their disappointment affect how they subsequently thought of themselves—both as individuals and as a couple? Out of the answers and our observations of hundreds of couples arose our notion that couples continually move through a three-stage cycle of promise, betrayal, and resolution. It was surprisingly simple. But the more we turned it over and measured it against our experience, the more it seemed to fit.

Our basic idea was that couples initially pass through three recognizable stages: Expansion and Promise; Contraction and Betrayal; and Resolution. The early expansiveness of relationships expresses our desire for romance, our yearnings to burst through the walls of our isolation and alienation to connect with another person, and our longings to be more than insignificant beings on this "little" planet.

Later in relationships we contract and pull back into our skin. This contraction demonstrates our pessimism, our cynicism, our capacity to see ourselves as victims, and our lack of vision and enduring discipline. It expresses our belief that men and women are not natural allies but naturally at war, and our conviction that we were fools for believing in romance.

When in our lives we bring these two opposing currents together, when we struggle past our pessimism with a sense of perspective and compromise, there is a period of resolution, a time of apparent stability. But new challenges, like the birth of a child or one partner's press towards self-fulfillment and growth, often threaten and topple these stable places. No couple can stay at a point of resolution forever; they must always adjust. The character of couples is thus constantly evolving.

COUPLE DEVELOPMENT

In order for a couple to endure, the partners must resolve the problems that emerge in their relationship. No couple does this by moving in a straight line.

Instead all pass through series after series of endlessly spiraling three-stage cycles of Expansion and Promise, Contraction and Betrayal, and Resolution.

Couples first move through times of positive hopes and experiences, then through times of trouble and disappointment—perhaps the positive experiences were not deep enough, perhaps they did not last long enough. Then they move into some middle ground between the two opposing conditions. Each cycle reflects their effort to recognize and reconcile a conflict: the freedom and the promise of the early relationship versus the crushing defeat that invariably follows.

Initially, two people come together enough to form a lasting relationship. This is the task of the first Expansive Stage. According to today's cultural narrative, couples should begin in a burst of romance, exploration, and sexual attraction. But not every couple, and not every partner, falls in love. Instead, couples commonly begin with a shared experience of expansiveness and promise, which may include romantic love, but may also arise from a warm and respectful friendship.

In this stage, individuals feel somehow larger, more witty and charming, stronger yet more vulnerable—in short, closer to their ideal selves than ever before. The developmental trajectories of men and women converge for a moment, so that men take time to talk and understand, while women appear more independent. Each partner's appreciation spurs the other to expand his or her capacities. Early relationships lack the constricting patterns that eventually emerge. They are spacious instead, encouraging both exploration and experimentation.

The Expansive Stage is one of the few times when we tell our whole story to another person, who bears witness to it and helps shape it further. The two individual narratives are then woven into a couple narrative, which takes on a life, an identity, of its own. People will say, "This is how we do things" and "That is just how we are." Individual identity becomes inextricably bound to the character of the couple.

But couples must also find a way to include the fears and insecurities, the ineptness and even the cruelty that figures prominently in their lives. Introducing this material into the relationship is the task of the Contraction and Betrayal Stage.

This second stage begins when one partner pulls back to routine ways. The withdrawal may be neutral, not angry; but the person who is left feels abandoned and betrayed. When she (it is almost always the woman who stays connected longer) objects, he may feel controlled and withdraw further; she may then be both frightened and furious, insistently asking that the person she had gotten to know reemerge. In response, he may build his shell thicker, and so the sequence grows.

This nightmarish cycle makes caricatures of the two partners. The great potential of the Expansive Stage, when men and women shared "male" and "female" attributes, dissolves into cruel stereotypes. Each partner feels trapped and betrayed—not only by the other but also by himself or herself. More than anything, people wish to remain the person they were in the Expansive Stage, the person they had striven to be through years of dreaming and preparing. Now they feel immensely let down by their own failures. They blame both self and other, and a mood of accusation permeates the relationship.

Just as the Expansive Stage brings us closer to our ego ideal, so the Contraction Stage confronts us with our greatest fears and our poorest self-image. During this stage, distinctive, repetitive struggles form and consolidate. They seem to define the whole relationship. The struggles are so distressing that the couple may draw someone, like a child or parent, or something, like alcohol or excessive work, into the relationship to buffer the conflict. These patterns become integral parts of the couple's moments together—and recur throughout the life of the couple. They become as familiar and distinctive as the implicit promises of expansion. Couples grow very accustomed to the predictable experiences of contraction.

Even though it is a difficult stage, contraction is essential. Unless partners can bring their wounds and uncertainties into the relationship, they will feel neither real nor whole, and the vigilance required to protect themselves will make them guarded and superficial. In contraction, critical themes from the partners' past enter the couple's experience, further deepening their character. Contraction, then, is not a "negative" stage; it is as necessary as the others. We confront ourselves honestly in contraction's harsh light, telling the truth about our limitations and those of our partner. The insights must be folded into the relationship. Couples who endure contraction will look back on it as a time when they were tested and triumphed.

RESOLUTION

To survive, couples must climb out of the Stage of Contraction without entirely excluding its messages. They must at least partially reconcile the first two stages. This is the task of the third stage, the Stage of Resolution.

This is a stage of compromise, negotiation, accommodation, and integration. The partners struggle to be reasonable and maintain perspective, to affirm complexity and to handle difficult situations with competence and maturity. In contrast to the intense, narrow focus on one another that characterized the first two stages, the couple now opens up more to family and community. Having a child, for example, may serve as a bridge of common concern to repair long-strained relationships with parents; it may become a rite of passage into a more durable adulthood.

The early desire for fusion in the Expansive Stage gives way to close, bitter struggles in the Stage of Contraction. Paradoxically, the blaming and rejection may eventually lead to a sense of perspective. For example, a statement uttered in close, angry combat, like "I'm not at all like you," may usher in a realization of genuine difference: "We really are different." With this realization comes alienation, then at least tolerance and possibly acceptance, followed by a flood of relief.

For a moment the struggle seems over. What had seemed mean in one's partner now seems tolerable. Relief follows, and renewed optimism often comes in its wake. At this point the couple frequently moves forward into another Expansive Stage; but

Conflict is not an aberration that can be ignored or cured in couple's lives.

just as quickly, they can be thrown back into contraction, with each partner feeling disappointed, as if the whole experience had been an illusion.

This moment of increased perspective represents a foray into resolution. The accumulation of these moments of realization, from contraction into resolution, put the couple past a threshold that consolidates their growth. The forays overwhelm the experience of contraction—which comes to seem like a crabby, limited view. The couple moves forward.

Couples try to hold onto their new perspective and the optimism that follows, but they invariably fail. The progress of expansion, contraction, and resolution is a spiral through time: stages cascade one after the other. The character of the couple, as distinguished from the character of the individual partners, is shaped more by the overall cycles than by any single stage. Cycles can be precipitated by a wide number of crises and events.

At first, the promise of the Expansive Stage and the fears of the Stage of Contraction remain relatively separate; but with each turn of the cycle, they become more integrated. Each revolution brings new information into the couple's domain. One partner's terrible and characteristic rages, for example, which show up in other domains, may suddenly emerge in the relationship after years of life together, and eventually become acknowledged and worked into their ways of being together. So, too, with many positive traits, such as capacities that emerge only in response to dangerous situations, such as courage in the face of danger.

For those couples who survive many turnings of the cycle, the Stage of Resolution tends to broaden in content and lengthen in time. Couples spend more and more time in it, and its qualities of tolerance and accommodation increasingly come to define their character.

The character of couples is shaped as much by the rhythm of the cycles as by the content of their stages. In this, couples vary greatly. Some couples, for example, move through wild swings: everything's great, then everything's awful; then there is a brief moment of reconciliation, after which everything's better (or worse) than ever. For others, the stages pass more subtly and their cycles are relatively smooth. Some couples move slowly out of one stage into another; others seem to cycle all the time.

Every couple has a Home Base, a stage in which they generally reside. This habitual stage represents both its public persona and its evolved self-image, but not its full character. Those who reside in contraction, for instance, think of themselves as conflicted and troubled, even though they have moments in expansion and resolution. Once a couple has settled into a stage as its Home Base, its cycles will tend to begin and end there. The couple in contraction might climb out through one compromise or another, relax momentarily in resolution, which feels good enough to revive some old romantic feelings reminiscent of expansion. But with its first minor disappointment, fall back to their familiar Home Base in contraction.

After the first few cycles the stages in each couple's repertoire become more like different states of being. The couple can enter them, know them as familiar, and then move on. In this sense the stages become a relatively constant, autonomous reality in the relationship.

But it is a couple's first turn through the cycle that imparts a distinctive style that will tend to endure. We develop our characteristic ways of loving and being loved, of being warm and affectionate, in our first time through expansion. Subsequent expansive moments will usually bring back the memory and flavor of these patterns. Similarly, the fights we had in our first cycle usually recur over and over again through our relationship. No new fight seems all that new, but looks like a variation on the old one. Later, in our first passage through resolution, we develop our characteristic ways of solving problems—our distinctive ways of talking, negotiating, tolerating, and accepting.

CONFLICT AND RESOLUTION

The character of couples is forged through regular cycles of conflict and resolution. Conflict is not an aberration that can be ignored or cured; it is inherent in couples' lives. It stems from real dilemmas that couples must acknowledge and resolve. In relationships, conflict often appears as a choice: individual versus collective good; women's rights versus male entitlement; one partner's style of upbringing versus the other's.

As they continue to cycle, couples struggle for a perspective that can embrace both the good and the bad and help them move ahead. But the perspectives they reach, and the solutions they attain, are always partial: they resolve enough so they can move on, but they rarely resolve disputes completely. Core conflicts hang around, serving as sources of new antagonisms.

Just as we feel we have resolved a conflict about sex, money, or children, our solution unravels or another problem appears. Partners need to negotiate everything, from how to structure child care to how and when to make love—and who should initiate it. Couples will be frustrated if they expect to solve their conflicts once and for all. But if they learn to recognize their cycles of conflict and resolution and adapt to them, they may survive the hard times, grow together, and thrive.

TURNING POINTS AND TRANSFORMATIONS

At some point, almost all couples find themselves in a profoundly disturbing and immovable impasse. No matter what they do, they cannot escape; there are no more areas of conversation to open up, no more strategies to try, no more activities to limit. They feel totally stuck. Many couples separate at this point. Many others, perhaps only through inertia or devotion to children or to the idea of marriage, stay together. Most couples simply endure, emerging diminished but essentially unchanged after their ordeal.

But some couples are transformed by these terrifying crises. Instead of simply enduring, the partners manage to give up their blaming and bitterness but remain in the relationship. They realize they cannot get what they want by demanding, by manipulating, or even by negotiating. In despair and exhaustion, they finally stop trying to change their partner, and stop trying to make themselves over as well. Giving up this fight has a paradoxical effect: for a moment, the partners may experience one another in a new, fresh, and undefined way.

This experience is so dramatic it often takes on a spiritual dimension. The partners feel enhanced—better known and accepted for who they are, joined anew. They feel as if they have awakened. Beyond the conflict—and their own selfish version of what's right—they can sense a deeper meaning of their relationship.

This awakening becomes a great divide in the history of their relationship, separating a time of truth from one of ignorance. The partners can then return emotionally to one another and share the wisdom and inner strength they've now gained.

Not every couple goes through this trying time of transformation. Nor can the experience be taken on willfully. It has to emerge through the difficulties of life. Still, there is something heroic about people who have the capacity to sustain crushing disappointment, undergo repeated tests of their relationship, yet feel enhanced by their commitment to each other.

We are strongly moved, deeply impressed by the energy and courage of couples who refuse their own dissolution and who seek instead to explore the potential for fulfillment in their relationship.

Reproduction

- **Birth Control (Articles 28–31)**

- **Pregnancy and Childbirth (Articles 32–34)**

While human reproduction is as old as humanity, many aspects of it are changing in today's society. Not only have new technologies of conception and childbirth affected the *how* of reproduction, but personal, social, and cultural forces have also affected the *who*, the *when*, and the *when not*. Abortion remains a fiercely debated topic, and legislative efforts for and against it abound. Unplanned pregnancies and parenthood in the United States and worldwide, however, present significant, sometimes devastating, problems for the parents, children, families, and society.

In light of the change of attitude toward sex for pleasure, only birth control has become a matter of prime importance. Even in our age of sexual enlightenment, some individuals, possibly in the height of passion, fail to correlate "having sex" with pregnancy. In addition, even in our age of astounding medical technology, there is no 100 percent effective, safe, or aesthetically acceptable method of birth control. Before sex can become safe as well as enjoyable, people must receive thorough and accurate information regarding conception and contraception, birth and birth control. They must make a mental and emotional commitment to the use of an effective method of their choice. Only this can make every child a planned and wanted one.

Despite the relative simplicity of the above assertion, abortion and birth control remain emotionally charged issues in American society. While opinion surveys indicate that most of the public supports family planning and abortion, at least in some circumstances, there are individuals and groups strongly opposed to some forms of birth control and to abortion. Within the past few years, voices for and against birth control and abortion have

Make a baby – make a lifetime commitment.

grown louder, and on a growing number of occasions have led to overt behaviors, including disobedience and violence. Some Supreme Court and legislative efforts have added restrictions to the right to abortion. Others have mandated freer access to abortion and reproductive choice and restricted the activities of antiabortion demonstrators. Voices on both sides are raised in emotional and political debate between those who feel that "we must never go back to the old days" (of illegal and unsafe back-alley abortions) and those who cry "the baby has no choice."

Many of the questions raised in this unit about the new technologies of reproduction and its control are likely to remain among the most hotly debated issues for the remainder of this century. It is likely that various religious and political groups will continue to posit and challenge basic definitions of human life, as well as the rights and responsibilities of women and men regarding sex, procreation, and abortion. The very foundations of our pluralistic society may be challenged. We will have to await the outcome.

The opening article in the *Birth Control* subsection, "Choosing a Contraceptive," integrates up-to-date information with other factors that go into decisions about this intimate, important issue, such as individual and couple preferences, lifestyle, and aesthetic factors. The next article provides information on one of the newer contraceptive choices: the female condom. The final two articles take a global view of reproduction, contraception, and family planning, and they explore several philosophical, population, gender-based, and humanitarian issues.

The first two articles in the *Pregnancy and Childbirth* subsection address some of the latest technological possibilities for human reproduction. Each raises questions about scientific advancements that not too long ago may have seemed more like science fiction. The final article raises some difficult questions about who should make decisions regarding unplanned pregnancies. The problems are illustrated by presenting the experiences of eight men whose partners made reproductive choices sometimes with, but often without, the father's input.

Looking Ahead: Challenge Questions

In your opinion, what are the most important characteristics of a contraceptive? Why?

What personal feelings or expectations make you more likely to regularly use contraception?

Under what circumstances might a person not use contraception and risk an unintentional pregnancy?

How do you feel that contraceptive responsibilities should be assigned or shared between men and women?

How have recent events in the right to choose arena affected you? Have they changed your beliefs and/or attitudes?

Have you found a fairly comfortable way to talk about contraception and/or pregnancy risk and prevention with a partner? If so, what is it? If not, what do you do?

In the situation of an unplanned pregnancy, what should be the role of the female and the male with respect to decision making? What if they do not agree?

Do you know of a couple who has experienced infertility? If so, what was it like for them? If you were unable to have a child, what treatments would you consider? Are there any you would not consider? Why? As a taxpayer, do you feel the expense of infertility treatments should be covered by insurance? Why, or why not?

CHOOSING A CONTRACEPTIVE

Merle S. Goldberg

Choosing a method of birth control is a highly personal decision, based on individual preferences, medical history, lifestyle, and other factors. Each method carries with it a number of risks and benefits of which the user should be aware.

Each method of birth control has a failure rate—an inability to prevent pregnancy over a one-year period. Sometimes the failure rate is due to the method and sometimes it is due to human error, such as incorrect use or not using it at all. Each method has possible side effects, some minor and some serious. Some methods require lifestyle modifications, such as remembering to use the method with each and every sexual intercourse. Some cannot be used by individuals with certain medical problems.

Spermicides Used Alone

Spermicides, which come in many forms—foams, jellies, gels, and suppositories—work by forming a physical and chemical barrier to sperm. They should be inserted into the vagina within an hour before intercourse. If intercourse is repeated, more spermicide should be inserted. The active ingredient in most spermicides is the chemical nonoxynol-9. The failure rate for spermicides in preventing pregnancy when used alone is from 20 to 30 percent.

Spermicides are available without a prescription. People who experience burning or irritation with these products should not use them.

Barrier Methods

There are five barrier methods of contraception: male condoms, female condoms, diaphragm, sponge, and cervical cap. In each instance, the method works

DISEASE PREVENTION

For many people, the prevention of sexually transmitted diseases (STDs), including HIV (human immunodeficiency virus), which leads to AIDS, is a factor in choosing a contraceptive. Only one form of birth control—the latex condom, worn by the man—is considered highly effective in helping protect against HIV and other STDs. Reality Female Condom, made from polyurethane, may give limited protection against STDs but has not been proven as effective as male latex condoms. People who use another form of birth control but who also want a highly effective way to reduce their STD risks, should also use a latex condom for every sex act, from start to finish.

In April 1993, FDA announced that birth control pills, Norplant, Depo-Provera, IUDs, and natural membrane condoms must carry labeling stating that these products are intended to prevent pregnancy but do not protect against HIV infection and other sexually transmitted diseases. In addition, natural membrane condom labeling must state that consumers should use a latex condom to help reduce the transmission of STDs. The labeling of latex condoms states that, if used properly, they will help reduce transmission of HIV and other diseases. ∎

From *FDA Consumer*, Vol. 27, No. 7, September 1993, pp. 18-25. Reprinted by permission.

MALE CONDOM

FEMALE CONDOM

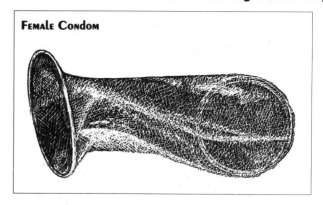

Only latex condoms have been shown to be highly effective in helping to prevent sexually transmitted diseases.

by keeping the sperm and egg apart. Usually, these methods have only minor side effects. The main possible side effect is an allergic reaction either to the material of the barrier or the spermicides that should be used with them. Using the methods correctly for each and every sexual intercourse gives the best protection.

Male Condom

A male condom is a sheath that covers the penis during sex. Condoms are made of either latex rubber or natural skin (also called "lambskin" but actually made from sheep intestines). Only latex condoms have been shown to be highly effective in helping to prevent STDs. Latex provides a good barrier to even small viruses such as human immunodeficiency virus and hepatitis B. Each condom can only be used once. Condoms have a birth control failure rate of about 15 percent. Most of the failures can be traced to improper use.

Some condoms have spermicide added. This may give some additional contraceptive protection. Vaginal spermicides may also be added before sexual intercourse.

Some condoms have lubricants added.

These do not improve birth control or STD protection. Non-oil-based lubricants can also be used with condoms. However, oil-based lubricants such as petroleum jelly (Vaseline) should not be used because they weaken the latex. Condoms are available without a prescription.

Female Condom

The Reality Female Condom was approved by FDA in April 1993. It consists of a lubricated polyurethane sheath with a flexible polyurethane ring on each end. One ring is inserted into the vagina much like a diaphragm, while the other remains outside, partially covering the labia. The female condom may offer some protection against STDs, but for highly effective protection, male latex condoms must be used.

FDA Commissioner David A. Kessler, M.D., in announcing the approval, said, "I have to stress that the male latex condom remains the best shield against AIDS and other sexually transmitted diseases. Couples should go on using the male latex condom."

In a six-month trial, the pregnancy rate for the Reality Female Condom was about 13 percent. The estimated yearly failure rate ranges from 21 to 26 percent. This means that about 1 in 4 women who use Reality may become pregnant during a year.

Sponge

The contraceptive sponge, approved by FDA in 1983, is made of white polyurethane foam. The sponge, shaped like a

Barrier methods, which work by keeping the sperm and egg apart, usually have only minor side effects.

small doughnut, contains the spermicide nonoxynol-9. Like the diaphragm, it is inserted into the vagina to cover the cervix during and after intercourse. It does not require fitting by a health professional and is available without prescription. It is to be used only once and then discarded. The failure rate is between 18 and 28 percent. An extremely rare side effect is toxic shock syndrome (TSS), a potentially fatal infection caused by a strain of the bacterium *Staphylococcus aureus* and more commonly associated with tampon use.

Diaphragm

The diaphragm is a flexible rubber disk with a rigid rim. Diaphragms range in size from 2 to 4 inches in diameter and are designed to cover the cervix during and after intercourse so that sperm cannot reach the uterus. Spermicidal jelly or cream must be placed inside the diaphragm for it to be effective.

The diaphragm must be fitted by a health professional and the correct size prescribed to ensure a snug seal with the vaginal wall. If intercourse is repeated, additional spermicide should be added with

BIRTH CONTROL GUIDE

Efficacy rates given in this chart are estimates based on a number of different studies. They should be understood as yearly estimates, with those dependent on conscientious use subject to a greater chance of human error and reduced effectiveness. For comparison, 60 to 85 percent of sexually active women using no contraception would be expected to become pregnant in a year. This chart should not be used alone, but only as a summary of information in the accompanying article.

Type	Male Condom	Female Condom	Spermicides Used Alone	Sponge	Diaphragm with Spermicide	Cervical Cap with Spermicide
Estimated Effectiveness	About 85%	An estimated 74–79%	70–80%	72–82%	82–94%	At least 82%
Risks	Rarely, irritation and allergic reactions	Rarely, irritation and allergic reactions	Rarely, irritation and allergic reactions	Rarely, irritation and allergic reactions; difficulty in removal; very rarely, toxic shock syndrome	Rarely, irritation and allergic reactions; bladder infection; very rarely, toxic shock syndrome	Abnormal Pap test; vaginal or cervical infections; very rarely, toxic shock syndrome
STD Protection	Latex condoms help protect against sexually transmitted diseases, including herpes and AIDS	May give some protection against sexually transmitted diseases, including herpes and AIDS; not as effective as male latex condom	Unknown	None	None	None
Convenience	Applied immediately before intercourse	Applied immediately before intercourse; used only once and discarded	Applied no more than one hour before intercourse	Can be inserted hours before intercourse and left in place up to 24 hours; used only once and discarded	Inserted before intercourse; can be left in place 24 hours, but additional spermicide must be inserted if intercourse is repeated	Can remain in place for 48 hours; not necessary to reapply spermicide upon repeated intercourse; may be difficult to insert
Availability	Nonprescription	Nonprescription	Nonprescription	Nonprescription	Rx	Rx

ls	Implant (Norplant)	Injection (Depo-Provera)	IUD	Periodic Abstinence (NFP)	Surgical Sterilization
97%–99%	99%	99%	95–96%	Very variable, perhaps 53–86%	Over 99%
Blood clots, heart attacks and strokes, gallbladder disease, liver tumors, water retention, hypertension, mood changes, dizziness and nausea; not for smokers	Menstrual cycle irregularity; headaches, nervousness, depression, nausea, dizziness, change of appetite, breast tenderness, weight gain, enlargement of ovaries and/or fallopian tubes, excessive growth of body and facial hair; may subside after first year	Amenorrhea, weight gain, and other side effects similar to those with Norplant	Cramps, bleeding, pelvic inflammatory disease, infertility; rarely, perforation of the uterus	None	Pain, infection, and, for female tubal ligation, possible surgical complications
None	None	None	None	None	None
Pill must be taken on daily schedule, regardless of the frequency of intercourse	Effective 24 hours after implantation for approximately 5 years; can be removed by physician at any time	One injection every three months	After insertion, stays in place until physician removes it	Requires frequent monitoring of body functions and periods of abstinence	Vasectomy is a one-time procedure usually performed in a doctor's office; tubal ligation is a one-time procedure performed in an operating room
Rx	Rx; minor outpatient surgical procedure	Rx	Rx	Instructions from physician or clinic	Surgery

DiaphRagm

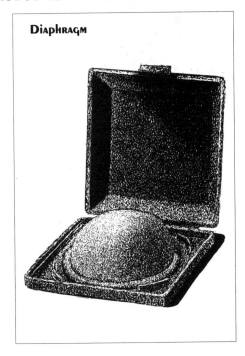

BiRth ControL PiLLs

the diaphragm still in place. The diaphragm should be left in place for at least six hours after intercourse. The diaphragm used with spermicide has a failure rate of from 6 to 18 percent.

In addition to the possible allergic reactions or irritation common to all barrier methods, there have been some reports of bladder infections with this method. As with the contraceptive sponge, TSS is an extremely rare side effect.

Cervical Cap

The cervical cap, approved for contraceptive use in the United States in 1988, is a dome-shaped rubber cap in various sizes that fits snugly over the cervix. Like the diaphragm, it is used with a spermicide and must be fitted by a health professional. It is more difficult to insert than the diaphragm, but may be left in place for up to 48 hours. In addition to the allergic reactions that can occur with any barrier method, 5.2 to 27 percent of users in various studies have reported an unpleasant odor and/or discharge. There also appears to be an increased incidence of irregular Pap tests in the first six months of using the cap, and TSS is an extremely rare side effect. The cap has a failure rate of about 18 percent.

Hormonal Contraception

Hormonal contraception involves ways of delivering forms of two female

Methods of hormonal contraception, when used properly, are extremely effective.

reproductive hormones—estrogen and progestogen—that help regulate ovulation (release of an egg), the condition of the uterine lining, and other parts of the menstrual cycle. Unlike barrier methods, hormones are not inert, do interact with the body, and have the potential for serious side effects, though this is rare. When properly used, hormonal methods are also extremely effective. Hormonal methods are available only by prescription.

Birth Control Pills

There are two types of birth control pills: combination pills, which contain both estrogen and a progestin (a natural or synthetic progesterone), and "mini-pills," which contain only progestin. The combination pill prevents ovulation, while the mini-pill reduces cervical mucus and causes it to thicken. This prevents the sperm from reaching the egg. Also, progestins keep the endometrium (uterine lining) from thickening. This prevents the fertilized egg from implanting in the uterus. The failure rate for the mini-pill is

1 to 3 percent; for the combination pill it is 1 to 2 percent.

Combination oral contraceptives offer significant protection against ovarian cancer, endometrial cancer, iron-deficiency anemia, pelvic inflammatory disease (PID), and fibrocystic breast disease. Women who take combination pills have a lower risk of functional ovarian cysts.

The decision about whether to take an oral contraceptive should be made only after consultation with a health professional. Smokers and women with certain medical conditions should not take the pill. These conditions include: a history of blood clots in the legs, eyes, or deep veins of the legs; heart attacks, strokes, or angina; cancer of the breast, vagina, cervix, or uterus; any undiagnosed, abnormal vaginal bleeding; liver tumors; or jaundice due to pregnancy or use of birth control pills.

Women with the following conditions should discuss with a health professional whether the benefits of the pill outweigh its risks for them:
- high blood pressure
- heart, kidney or gallbladder disease
- a family history of heart attack or stroke
- severe headaches or depression
- elevated cholesterol or triglycerides
- epilepsy
- diabetes.

Serious side effects of the pill include blood clots that can lead to stroke, heart attack, pulmonary embolism, or death. A

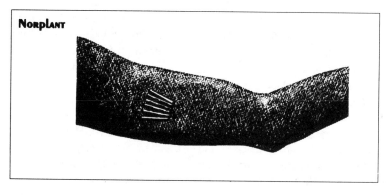

Norplant

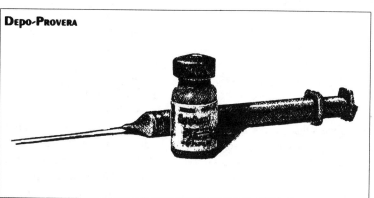

Depo-Provera

Intrauterine Devices

clot may, on rare occasions, occur in the blood vessel of the eye, causing impaired vision or even blindness. The pills may also cause high blood pressure that returns to normal after oral contraceptives are stopped. Minor side effects, which usually subside after a few months' use, include: nausea, headaches, breast swelling, fluid retention, weight gain, irregular bleeding, and depression. Sometimes taking a pill with a lower dose of hormones can reduce these effects.

The effectiveness of birth control pills may be reduced by a few other medications, including some antibiotics, barbiturates, and antifungal medications. On the other hand, birth control pills may prolong the effects of theophylline and caffeine. They also may prolong the effects of benzodiazepines such as Librium (chlordiazepoxide), Valium (diazepam), and Xanax (alprazolam). Because of the variety of these drug interactions, women should always tell their health professionals when they are taking birth control pills.

Norplant

Norplant—the first contraceptive implant—was approved by FDA in 1990. In a minor surgical procedure, six matchstick-sized rubber capsules containing progestin are placed just underneath the skin of the upper arm. The implant is effective within 24 hours and provides progestin for up to five years or until it is removed. Both the insertion and the removal must be performed by a qualified professional.

Because contraception is automatic and does not depend on the user, the failure rate for Norplant is less than 1 percent for women who weigh less than 150 pounds. Women who weigh more have a higher pregnancy rate after the first two years.

Women who cannot take birth control pills for medical reasons should not consider Norplant a contraceptive option. The potential side effects of the implant include: irregular menstrual bleeding, headaches, nervousness, depression, nausea, dizziness, skin rash, acne, change of appetite, breast tenderness, weight gain, enlargement of the ovaries or fallopian tubes, and excessive growth of body and facial hair. These side effects may subside after the first year.

Depo-Provera

Depo-Provera is an injectable form of a progestin. It was approved by FDA in

Only two IUDs are presently marketed in the United States; both have a 4 to 5 percent failure rate.

1992 for contraceptive use. Previously, it was approved for treating endometrial and renal cancers. Depo-Provera has a failure rate of only 1 percent. Each injection provides contraceptive protection for 14 weeks. It is injected every three months into a muscle in the buttocks or arm by a trained professional. The side effects are the same as those for Norplant and progestin-only pills. In addition, there may be irregular bleeding and spotting during the first months followed by periods of amenorrhea (no menstrual period). About 50 percent of the women who use Depo-Provera for one year or longer report amenorrhea. Other side effects, such as weight gain and others described for Norplant, may occur.

Intrauterine Devices

IUDs are small, plastic, flexible devices that are inserted into the uterus through the cervix by a trained clinician. Only two IUDs are presently marketed in the United States: ParaGard T380A, a T-shaped device partially covered by copper and effective for eight years; and Progestasert, which is also T-shaped but contains a progestin released over a one-year period. After that time, the IUD should be replaced. Both IUDs have a 4 to 5 percent failure rate.

It is not known exactly how IUDs work. At one time it was thought that the IUD affected the uterus so that it would be inhospitable to implantation. New evidence, however, suggests that uterine and tubal fluids are altered, particularly in the case of copper-bearing IUDs, inhibiting the transport of sperm through the cervical mucus and uterus.

The risk of PID with IUD use is highest in those with multiple sex partners or with a history of previous PID. Therefore, the IUD is recommended primarily for women in mutually monogamous relationships.

In addition to PID, other complications include perforation of the uterus (usually at the time of insertion), septic abortion, or ectopic (tubal) pregnancy. Women may also experience some short-term side effects—cramping and dizziness at the time of insertion; bleeding, cramps and backache that may continue for a few days after the insertion; spotting between periods; and longer and heavier menstruation during the first few periods after insertion.

Periodic Abstinence

Periodic abstinence entails not having sexual intercourse during the woman's fertile period. Sometimes this method is called natural family planning (NFP) or "rhythm." Using periodic abstinence is dependent on the ability to identify the approximately 10 days in each menstrual cycle that a woman is fertile. Methods to help determine this include:

• **The basal body temperature method** is based on the knowledge that just before ovulation a woman's basal body temperature drops several tenths of a degree and after ovulation it returns to normal. The method requires that the woman take her temperature each morning before she gets out of bed.

• **The cervical mucus method,** also called the Billings method, depends on a woman recognizing the changes in cervical mucus that indicate ovulation is occurring or has occurred. There are now electronic thermometers with memories and electrical resistance meters that can more accurately pinpoint a woman's fertile period. The method has a failure rate of 14 to 47 percent.

Periodic abstinence has none of the side effects of artificial methods of contraception.

Surgical Sterilization

Surgical sterilization must be considered permanent. Tubal ligation seals a woman's fallopian tubes so that an egg cannot travel to the uterus. Vasectomy involves closing off a man's vas deferens so that sperm will not be carried to the penis.

Vasectomy is considered safer than female sterilization. It is a minor surgical procedure, most often performed in a doctor's office under local anesthesia. The procedure usually takes less than 30 minutes. Minor post-surgical complications may occur.

Tubal ligation is an operating-room procedure performed under general anesthesia. The fallopian tubes can be reached by a number of surgical techniques, and, depending on the technique, the operation is sometimes an outpatient procedure or requires only an overnight stay. In a minilaparotomy, a 2-inch incision is made in the abdomen. The surgeon, using special instruments, lifts the fallopian tubes and, using clips, a plastic ring, or an electric current, seals the tubes. Another method, laparoscopy, involves making a small incision above the navel, and distending the abdominal cavity so that the intestine separates from the uterus and fallopian tubes. Then a laparoscope—a miniaturized, flexible telescope—is used to visualize the fallopian tubes while closing them off.

Both of these methods are replacing the traditional laparotomy.

Major complications, which are rare in female sterilization, include: infection, hemorrhage, and problems associated with the use of general anesthesia. It is estimated that major complications occur in 1.7 percent of the cases, while the overall complication rate has been reported to be between 0.1 and 15.3 percent.

The failure rate of laparoscopy and minilaparotomy procedures, as well as vasectomy, is less than 1 percent. Although there has been some success in reopening the fallopian tubes or the vas deferens, the success rate is low, and sterilization should be considered irreversible.

Merle S. Goldberg, a writer in Washington, D.C., has also been involved in contraceptive services for women, both in the United States and developing countries, for the last 25 years.

The Female Condom

Reality is all about women protecting themselves

....

BETH BAKER

t was really weird," says Deborah Keaton, of Phoenix, Arizona, recalling her initial reaction to the new female condom, Reality. "It was like . . . BIG. I showed it to my friends, and they couldn't believe it."

"Hilarious!" says Felicia Bembower, of Virginia Beach, Virginia, who also participated in the trial study for the new device. "It made for a lot of laughs."

But Dr. Mary Ann Leeper, senior vice president at Wisconsin Pharmacal, isn't laughing. She's responsible for developing the female condom for the United States market, with women's safety in mind. Reality has two flexible rings, one on either end of a six-inch polyurethane sheath. The sheath is wider than the male condom, but not longer. To use the condom, a woman must squeeze the ring at the closed end of the sheath and insert it into her vagina (similar to fitting a diaphragm). The other ring, at the open mouth of the sheath, extends about an inch beyond the vaginal opening. During intercourse, the prelubricated sheath fills the vagina while the outer ring lies flat against the labia, thus shielding the partners from skin-to-skin contact. Reality requires no prescription and may be used only once. One size fits all.

According to Dr. Leeper, the condom can be used in any coital position (except standing up) and, ideally, won't be felt by either partner during intercourse. The key is the proper amount of lubricant. Eighty percent of the women in the study said they were unaware of the condom during intercourse and some even said it actually increased their pleasure. Overall, 71 percent of the women liked Reality.

Then there's the other 29 percent: "It made me feel like an alien," says Michelle Smith, of Chesapeake, Virginia. "I tried to put it in in advance and the plastic swished when I walked. It's like having a plastic Baggie stuck in you." Others complained that the condom occasionally can become twisted or slip, and that the lubricant makes it messy. Some men said that they were more aware of the sheath than they are of the male condom.

If the Food and Drug Administration (FDA) gives the new device the go-ahead as expected, Reality, to be sold over the counter, will be in general distribution this summer. Each condom costs $2.50 and will be available in packets of three, with a tube of extra lubricant and a detailed instructional leaflet.

The price—nearly three times that of the male condom—reflects the higher cost of polyurethane compared to the latex used in most male condoms. (Perhaps the high price is also a result of the $7 million spent by Pharmacal over the past four years for research and testing to meet FDA requirements.)

Despite this higher cost, Reality does have advantages over the male condom. Polyurethane is a stronger yet thinner material that is a better conductor of heat than latex. Because it is not dependent on a male erection, a woman can insert the device ahead of time. But the most significant factor in its favor is that in covering the labia and the base of the penis, the female condom has the potential to offer the greatest protection against sexually transmitted diseases (STDs), including HIV/AIDS and herpes. As a result, women's health advocates and AIDS organizations have joined forces to put

Reality on a fast track for FDA approval.

Last December, despite concerns about insufficient data verifying Reality's effectiveness against STDs, the FDA advisory panel recommended approval of the device, citing the "moral imperative" of HIV prevention. To ensure maximum protection against HIV, some health professionals suggest using a spermicide with the condom; Reality has a 15 percent failure rate. Although some may be tempted to use male and female condoms simultaneously, Dr. Leeper says it can't be done and not to try it.

Reality's biggest selling point is that it will be the first protection against disease—short of abstinence—that women can control themselves. The issue of control extends to its proper use. "With a male condom, I might not know if my partner has put it on properly," says a nurse who participated in the trial study in Virginia. "But with the female condom, I'd know right away if it were misplaced. I'd feel the ring inside me."

Assuming that the female condom is a reliable way to prevent pregnancy and the spread of disease, the big unknown remains public acceptance. Unfortunately, the product's targeted market was not included in the trials. Wisconsin Pharmacal wanted to test the product among women with multiple partners or among couples in which one partner is HIV-positive, but the FDA said no. "We were told, 'It's just not done,' " says Dr. Leeper. Instead, the FDA insisted that the trial study be conducted with monogamous, disease-free couples, whom the agency felt would be more likely to follow the test protocol.

As a result, a valuable opportunity to see how the new device would be accepted by the women most at risk was lost. The research was conducted among married couples, who presumably feel at ease with each other and can more readily deal with the woman emerging from the bathroom with her new appendage. But will young single women have enough self-confidence to use the condom? If her partner is convulsed with laughter, or if his ardor is cooled by her appearance, or if he just plain refuses, will she have the gumption to insist on using it? And will she be able to afford it?

Dr. Denese Shervington, a psychiatrist with Louisiana State University Medical Center, is optimistic. She conducted focus groups among low-income African American women in New Orleans and reports that the women knew the cost, and were still enthusiastic. Wisconsin Pharmacal, the distributor of Reality in the U.S., Mexico, and Canada, has agreed to sell the condom at a discount to public health providers in the U.S. A similar stance was taken by the primary international distributor as well.
Beth Baker is a writer living in Takoma Park, Maryland.

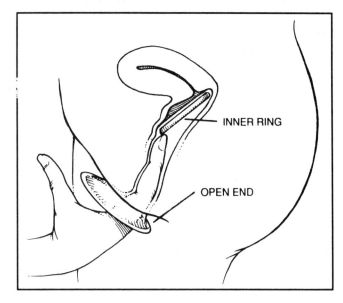

INNER RING

OPEN END

The Femidom In Europe

The female condom is marketed under the trade name Femidom in Europe. It is currently available in Austria, Holland, Switzerland, and the United Kingdom, but by the end of 1993, should be available in most of Western Europe. Femidom sells for about 30 to 45 cents less than Reality. Manufactured by the British firm Chartex International, Femidom is distributed through grocers, drugstores, pharmacies, and supermarkets.

Still new to women, Femidom has sparked an array of responses; initial reactions reflect a mixture of anxiety and naïveté. Women have described Femidom as "gross," "disgusting," "ridiculous," "huge," and "big enough for an elephant or rhinoceros"—responses not unlike their initial responses to other barrier methods.

On first use, women report that Femidom is slippery and sometimes hard to insert. Some find the lubricant too much and others say not enough. Some women complain that the outer ring rubs on the labia and clitoris, while others don't notice the ring at all. Then too there are reports that Femidom does not stay in place during intercourse.

Aesthetics are another consideration: many women do not like the way the device

Our Bodies, Ourselves

hangs out of the vagina and cite that as inhibiting foreplay. Some point out that it also can be noisy.

Reported advantages are that it virtually never breaks, women can insert it before lovemaking, and some men like this method better. Everyone agrees it takes some getting used to—at least three or four tries before couples feel comfortable and competent. Those who like Femidom best have had problems with other methods of birth control.

—The Boston Women's Health Book Collective

The Philosopher's Stone

Contraception and Family Planning

M. Potts and M. Campbell

Malcolm Potts is the Bixby Professor of Population and Family Planning at the University of California at Berkeley. Martha Campbell is a Visiting Scholar in the School of Public Health at the University of California at Berkeley.

In his opening statement at the 1992 Earth Summit, Secretary-General Maurice Strong warned, "Population must be stabilized, and rapidly. If we do not do it, nature will, and much more brutally." The urgency of the population problem is now widely recognized, but there is still unnecessary confusion about how population growth is to be stabilized. Data show that over the past three decades, family planning has failed, not because people are averse to using it, but because family planning services have not kept pace with demand.

Many people throughout the world want smaller families. This fact is not yet widely understood. Social surveys show that 50 to 80 percent of married women in developing countries want to limit or space future births. Where appropriate, services have been provided and fertility has fallen two to five times more rapidly than in the West's comparable stage of demographic transition. But women suffering from botched abortions lie two to a bed in many Third World hospitals. These women did not want to be pregnant but were unable to get the contraceptives they needed.

The empirical evidence suggests that family size is heavily dependent on the options people have. When given the chance, women take advantage of family planning methods. Fifteen years ago in Bangladesh, women wanted to have five children; today they want 2.9 children. Family planning services have resulted in a desired family size 30 percent lower than the most ambitious population target envisioned by the government. Recent surveys have demonstrated similar patterns in a number of other developing countries.

The fundamental challenge to family planning policy is to remove the barriers that separate the options people want and the technologies they need. In developing countries, over 120 million couples desire family planning but lack access to it. The growth of this number through-

out the 1980s demonstrates the failure of recent policies. Since almost half the population in many developing countries is below the age of marriage, the number of women needing contraception a decade from now will increase by over 30 percent. Unless family planning access expands rapidly, more women will die during this decade from complications in pregnancy, childbirth and abortion than in any other decade of human history.

SOCIO-ECONOMIC MISCONCEPTIONS

Much attention has been focused upon the correlation between family size and socio-economic status. Wealth and education certainly make it easier to surmount the barriers that society erects to prevent family planning; however, compelling evidence now suggests that these goals, while they clearly have their own merit, are not prerequisites for fertility decline.

Bangladesh, a country the size of North Carolina with a population of 114 million people (growing by 2.7 million per year), is afflicted with endemic poverty and accords very low status to women. Nevertheless, birth rates have begun to drop rapidly—the result of a family planning policy which offers a range of choices, including at least partial access to safe and early abortions. Certainly, family planning services could be greatly improved, but they are excellent when compared to those available in Pakistan. Pakistan is a richer and more urbanized country, but its high fertility rate has only changed slightly since the 1960s because its citizens have little access to family planning resources.

The belief that socio-economic change is a prerequisite for fertility decline is dangerously distorting population policy objectives. A recent World Bank "population" program in Malawi included funding for bio-gas energy systems. Though no doubt a good idea in their own right, bio-gas plants do not help women control their fertility. Instead, they drain resources from family planning programs—the simplest, cheapest and most essential element of policies aimed at fertility decline.

World Bank/Curt Carnemark

Bridging the information gap is essential for successful family planning.

VATICAN AND TRADITIONAL INFLUENCES

The Philippines (65 million people, increasing by 1.5 million a year) is three and a half times as rich as Bangladesh and has a substantially higher literacy rate. Pressure from the Catholic Church, however, has undermined the country's attempts to restrain runaway population growth. As a result, fewer women in the Philippines use family planning than in Bangladesh. From Argentina to Zambia, governments have bowed to Vatican pressure and limited the options necessary for women to manage their own fertility.

Studies show that few people reject family planning out of religious conviction. Italy and Spain, the countries with the lowest birth rates in the world, are both predominately Catholic. Limits placed on the services available to individuals, the real impact of the Vatican's "pelvic theology," are indirect but destructive. Two-thirds of the health centers in desperately overpopulated Rwanda are run by the Catholic Church and do not offer modern contraceptive methods. Argentine women's heavy reliance on illegal abortions and Brazilian women's high sterilization rates for "medical" reasons are partly consequences of Vatican influence on government policies.

It is time to regard religious stands that serve as obstacles to reproductive choices—from any religion—as public policy to be openly debated, rather than as sensitive and unassailable beliefs. We can no longer afford to do otherwise.

Traditional life patterns and expectations have long served to maintain order in families, communities and nations and should be treated with respect. The positive aspects of tradition can be seen in most pre-literate societies, where low birth rates are prevalent. Furthermore, established patterns of breast feeding are a significant restraint on fertility in Africa and parts of Asia. Some family planning programs have overlooked these values of tradition at a great loss.

Too often, however, tradition serves as a stranglehold on women's rights and opportunities. Islamic conventions as interpreted in traditional countries such as Jordan, Iran, Saudi Arabia and Pakistan suppress women's options, bolster their economic dependence on males, and greatly reduce their reproductive choices. In India, parts of Africa and much of the Middle East, men have traditionally been accorded greater value than women. In these countries, women's lives are characterized by economic privation, limited access to health care, and high fertility rates. Of all the traditional values, the preference for male babies, and the greater investment in boys than in girls, does the most damage by reducing women's options and encouraging higher fertility.

We need to be asking hard questions about the relationships between the order and discipline found in many traditional cultures and the cultural biases that provide men with economic advantages and greater political participation. We need to analyze critically what different traditions mean in terms of both women's lives and population growth. Fortunately, there are innovative communication programs in Mexico, Kenya and India that are enabling women to make reproductive decisions for themselves and their families. Access to family planning is often the first step in raising the status of women. At the same time, however, there is a synergism between the two; increased female education and other aspects of socio-economic development facilitate the use of family planning.

THE FLAWED MARKET

Lawrence Summers, a former chief economist of the World Bank, has asked why the market has not responded to the unmet need for family planning. Does an unmet need for family planning actually exist? The demand is indeed real, but several factors skew the market. Many people are too poor to pay for modern contraceptives—even condoms must be subsidized in Bangladesh. The cost of voluntary sterilization, though low when amortized over a life span, presents an exorbitant one-time capital investment for a poor couple.

More significantly, deep-seated societal values distort the family planning marketplace. In theory, people's family planning needs could be met by the provision of simple abortion equipment to every primary health care center of the world. There is little doubt that individuals of almost all economic backgrounds could afford the minimal cost of an abortion. In many countries, however, this practice is illegal, and in most countries, frequent abortion is regarded as an objectionable means of controlling fertility.

Medical barriers to family planning often distort the market for contraception even more than religious barriers. Family planning should be seen as a service provided for consumers, not a treatment for the sick. Many health care providers, however, ignore this basic difference in philosophy, and still contrive to make family planning a treatment for disease. For example, sterilization may often be permitted only to those of a certain age or to those who have a given number of children. Human reproductive behavior cannot be sensibly reduced to such simple equations. Injectable contraceptives have never been offered on a large scale in India, although there is little doubt that they would be widely used. These contraceptives would save many women from death in childbirth or abortion. In addition, oral contraceptives could be made available without prescription. Finally, confusing preventive medicine with family planning has made screening tests, like pap smears, a prerequisite for receiving oral contraceptives. Such tests give no information related to prescribing contraceptive pills; they are a good idea, but can stand as a barrier to family planning.

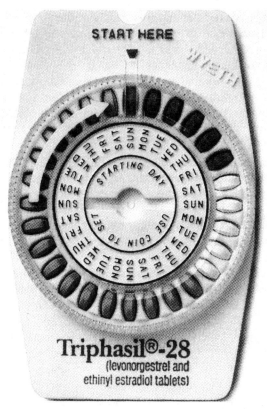

Is the pill the philosopher's stone of this century?

POORLY DESIGNED PROGRAMS

Government-run, health-related family planning programs consume a great deal of money and effort. However, family planning clinics can play only a limited role in a population strategy. Family planning programs must go beyond clinics. Fifty percent of the people attending a health clinic in the Third World live within a two mile radius of the facility, but clearly it is impossible to place clinics every four miles throughout the developing world. Furthermore, while clinics can be useful for training personnel and as a base for outreach programs, they risk imposing a medical bias onto family planning. This bias is inappropriate and commonly acts as a deterrent to potential users. Finally, many women find clinic staff members insensitive to their needs, the clinic hours or locations inconvenient, and telephone appointments impossible to make. Despite the discomforts involved, however, millions seek out existing clinics and demonstrate the determination of women to manage their own fertility. Abuses have occurred in state-supported programs, but they are less common than the failure to extend family planning choices to all couples who need them.

Undoubtedly, no method meets everyone's needs. The needs of most people change during their fertile lives. Successful family planning programs must make a wide variety of methods available through a broad number of distribution channels while remaining sensitive to the needs of particular cultures. Furthermore, since all methods have disadvantages as well as advantages, the consumer deserves access to objective information in order to make informed choices.

With the notable exception of Indonesia, most government programs are less efficient and less amenable to users than those of the private sector. Free programs that employ armies of poorly supervised field workers, such as those in India and Pakistan, are particularly inefficient. "Community based distribution" (CBD) systems are often superior. CBD programs train people such as village shopkeepers or headmen's wives to distribute condoms and birth control pills. They charge the consumer a small amount and make a small profit. CBD systems developed by the Population and Development Association of Thailand and the Mexican Federation of Private Associations for Health and Community Development have successfully reached many people without wasting resources. Payment for these services may not cover all costs, but it gives the consumer a means for quality assurance. Partial payment also guarantees freedom of choice, particularly for sterilization. People, especially the poor, rarely pay for what they do not want.

Perhaps the most pragmatic and successful family planning program in the world has been that of South Korea. The government subsidized the private sector to provide family planning options such as the IUD and voluntary sterilization; consumers paid what they could and the government made up the difference. As a result, family size in South Korea has fallen from 6 to 1.6 in the last 30 years. While economic progress has made family planning easier, it is also true that effective family planning has helped propel Korea's remarkable economic development.

THE INFORMATION GAP

In a subject as intimate as family planning, myths are sometimes more influential than facts. All over the world, women believe that the pill causes cancer or infertility and can damage a baby. Additionally, surveys show that the majority of women believe that taking the pill is more dangerous than childbirth. In reality, the advantages of hormonal methods such as pills, injections, and implants greatly outweigh their risks. Unfortunately, elite groups attempting to control women by reducing their contraceptive choices sometimes actively promote rumors about pills, IUDs and the safety of abortion. For example, Roman Catholic priests in the San Joaquin Valley of California are currently telling the young brides of immigrant agricultural workers that the pill causes cancer.

Ironically, by focusing on past mistakes of family planning programs, organized groups of women have promoted the false impression that free-standing family planning programs are harmful to women. The first generation of high dose pills (which contained almost as much hormone in one tablet as a woman receives in an entire month from contemporary varieties) raised the risk of heart attack, stroke and thrombotic diseases. But these risks have virtually disappeared with the new, low dose pills. Furthermore, oral (and probably injectable) contraceptive use has a marked *protective* effect against uterine and ovarian cancer, a fact surveys show to be known only by a very small minority of women. Overall, the pill has neither adverse nor beneficial effects on breast cancer, although for some sub-groups there may be small changes which epidemiologists are still attempting to unravel. After 30 years of use and detailed follow-up, we can be confident that for nearly all women the benefits of the pill, even independent of pregnancy protection, significantly outweigh the risks. Only women over 40 who smoke more than 15 cigarettes a day would be better advised to use some other method. The pill is a unique product in the pharmacopoeia: its use by younger

---

The pill is a unique product in the pharmacopoeia: its use by younger women, on average, actually extends life expectancies. It is the philosopher's stone of the second half of the 20th century.

---

women, on average, actually extends life expectancies. It is the philosopher's stone of the second half of the 20th century.

THE ALLOCATION OF RESOURCES

Resources are needed to subsidize contraception for the poor in the developing world, if the unmet demand for family planning is to be satisfied. With this reality in mind, those working in family planning need to devote more attention to designing cost-effective programs. The cost per couple-year of protection (CYP) is an accurate measure of the cost effectiveness of any program. It assumes that a woman uses 13 packages of pills or 150 condoms, or calculates the mean age of voluntary surgical contraception. The most efficient programs, such as those in Ethiopia, Bangladesh, India and Cameroon, usually include "social marketing," the simplest form of CBD. Such programs utilize existing retail outlets and established marketing techniques to distribute subsidized contraceptives. The successful Bangladesh social marketing program costs approximately US$7 per CYP. Some clinic based programs cost up to US$50 per CYP, and one of the early World Bank sponsored programs in Africa had a larger CYP than the per capita income of the targeted country. Nonsense like this gives family planning a bad name.

Perhaps a day will dawn when contraceptives will be freely available at low cost, informed consumers will be able to buy what they need, and health professionals will provide a full range of family planning services and early abortion without imposing arbitrary rules. But for the present, we must do the best we can. With so many young people in the world, global population will continue to grow for most of the next century, no matter how rapidly fertility falls. Unless family planning becomes a higher priority, many women and children will die unnecessarily. Fortunately, immediate action can have an important impact on the level of population at which the world will eventually stabilize. If we meet the growing demand for family planning, population could stabilize at

---

A recent summit meeting of scientific academies, including the United States' National Academy of Sciences, felt that global population could easily exceed the planet's capacity to support it. Fortunately, the planet has a choice. It is time to trust women and to stop treating them like children.

---

well under 10 billion people. To meet this goal it will be necessary to reach well over 100 million new users of family planning within the next decade. As a result of an annual increase of 18 million couples of reproductive age, keeping pace with this growing demand will mean providing services to close to 900 million couples in the year 2015, almost twice the number now served. Such a level of contraceptive use would mean far lower fertility (an average of 2.5 children per woman) and place us well on the path to a stable world population.

The cost of family planning is met by consumers, national governments and international donors such as the US Agency for International Development. Currently,

only one percent of the relatively small amount of money that goes into foreign aid from the OECD countries is earmarked for family planning. In the past, the role of family planning may have been exaggerated, but it certainly warrants more than one percent of development financing. With a focus on large-scale, cost-effective programs such as social marketing and maximum cost recovery from consumers, an allocation of perhaps three to four percent of the OECD development budget could ensure a virtual universal availability of family planning by the end of the decade.

The sums of money are small for a world used to spending a million dollars a minute on armaments, or for a country such as the United States, which spends over $600 million a year on costumes and candies for its children on Halloween. We are not suggesting that children should not enjoy themselves, but that large numbers need to be set in perspective. Because people want smaller families, for a penny per day per Western citizen, we can ensure that our children and grandchildren will inherit a world with fewer than twice as many people instead of three times as many as currently inhabit it.

A recent summit meeting of scientific academies, including the United States' National Academy of Sciences, felt that global population could easily exceed the planet's capacity to support it. Fortunately, the planet has a choice. It is time to trust women and to stop treating them like children. It is also time to offer all adults a full range of reproductive choices through as many channels as possible. As Adrienne Germain of the International Women's Health Coalition has written, "Women can and will make rational decisions about their fertility and sexuality if appropriate information and services are available."

The sane policy is to listen to what women want, not to tell them what to do. It is inexcusable to deny people access to family planning choices, or to coerce them into using methods that they do not want to use. Access to family planning saves lives: one woman a minute dies from pregnancy, childbirth or abortion. Unlocking the gates that now constrain women's options will enable them to make choices that will benefit both today's women and tomorrow's children.

Men, Sex, *and* Parenthood *in an* Overpopulating World

Because women bear the primary responsibility for childrearing and family life in every country, they are also presumed to bear the primary responsibility for excess population growth. But family planning is unlikely to succeed—and population is unlikely to stabilize—until men share fully in those responsibilities.

Aaron Sachs

Aaron Sachs is a staff researcher at the Worldwatch Institute.

In almost all mammalian species, the male lives the life of a philanderer. From pandas to pumas, mammalian fathers tend to abandon their mate right after conception, leaving to the mother the entire burden of childrearing. The very classification "mammal" refers to a mother's independent capacity to nurse her babies: it's always the female bear that people see feeding, training, and protecting the cubs.

But human males are different. From the beginning, they have tended to stay with their mates and their children, and today many anthropologists and biologists believe that men's participation in the family played a critical role in the evolution of *homo sapiens'* most distinctive features, especially our capacity for psychosocial development. The children of very few other species, over the millennia, have been lucky enough to receive the attention of two caring adults.

Unfortunately, as human culture continues to evolve, more and more men are breaking with tradition and shirking their childrearing responsibilities. And the world's women and children are bearing the costs of this neglect. According to Judith Bruce, a senior associate at the Population Council in New York, the amount of time contributed by mothers to childcare is commonly seven times greater than that contributed by fathers, and the mothers' share only seems to be increasing. While important social revolutions in the industrialized world have begun to free women from an imposed dependence on men, some husbands and fathers are using this broadening of women's opportunities as an excuse to contribute less time and money to their families. By 1980, for instance, American men aged 20 to 49 were spending almost 50 percent less time living with their young children than they were in 1960. In less developed countries, even when there is a long tradition of male financial contributions to the family, men often abandon their wives and children because of increasing economic pressures: fewer and fewer are able to succeed as breadwinners. A recent Chilean study of low-income adolescent couples and their first-born children found that, by the children's sixth birthday, 42 percent of the fathers were providing no child support whatsoever.

Male sexual behavior, too, puts a strain on society: besides the indirect stresses caused by men's failure to avoid fathering children they might not be able to support later, their higher fertility levels contribute disproportionately to population growth. Because men stay fertile much longer than women do, and because they tend to be more promiscuous, the average man, by the end of his lifetime, is responsible for more children than the average woman. In the 18th century, a Moroccan emperor had reportedly fathered more than 1,000 children by the time he turned 50. Though childrearing is becoming more expensive and parents are finding themselves with fewer resources to pass on to their children (whether in the form of cash or land), many men have continued to have large families. In some sub-Saharan African countries, the average man wants to have more than 10

From *World Watch*, March/Arpil 1994, pp. 12-19. © 1994 by the Worldwatch Institute. Reprinted by permission.

Of 333 fathers with eight-year-old children, only 22 percent were still living with their child.

children, in part because large families serve as cultural symbols of a man's virility and wealth. Consequently, under male-dominated social systems that tend not to hold fathers accountable for the well-being of their children, the women of the Third World are increasingly finding themselves doing hard labor for food as well as walking several miles every day for water and fuelwood—all with babies on their backs or at their breasts.

Society has long expected women to take ultimate responsibility for the duties of raising a family. Currently in the United States, fathers head only one of every 40 single-parent households: men just aren't expected to juggle childcare and a job. Single women often end up simply raising their children by themselves, whether or not they have access to resources. In all parts of the world, both women and children would no doubt be better off if women faced fewer barriers to economic independence—and if men fulfilled their familial obligations. According to a recent study in Barbados, of 333 fathers with eight-year-old children, only 22 percent were still living with their child, and the children of the fathers who stayed were doing significantly better in school than all the others. And in the Chilean study, children's diets and nutrition levels tended to be much healthier when their fathers were living at home.

Men's failure to embrace their familial responsibilities begins with a failure to acknowledge that families get started through sex. A growing body of sociological research suggests that a family's eventual size and welfare depend largely on how the father and mother interact in bed—that men who are attentive to their partner's concerns tend later to be attentive to their family's concerns. Unfortunately, many men continue to see sex not as a shared experience but as their prerogative, as simply an opportunity to fulfill their desires. When interviewed by the demographer Alex Chika Ezeh, men in Ghana explained bluntly that their large families reflected, most of all, their desire to assert their culturally sanctioned sexual dominance over their wives. "The woman has no right to choose the number [of children] she prefers," said one man, "since it is you, the man, who decides when to have sex with her."

Over the past decade, then, many advocates for women's and children's welfare have turned to family planning as a way of addressing men's irresponsibility. And many family planning organizations, in turn, have recognized a need to supplement their efforts to provide women with safe, appropriate contraception with efforts to educate men. In the mid-1980s, for instance, the poster campaigns of many national-level affiliates of the International Planned Parenthood Association (IPPF) targeted men's sexual attitudes quite explicitly. They attempted to make men empathize with women, to help them understand that, though they themselves do not get pregnant, they do have a role in reproduction.

Family planners reason that if men take full responsibility for their potential to procreate by participating in family planning, then each of the children they do father will be both expected and wanted—and presumably they will father only the number of children for whom they are able to provide. No culture directly encourages men not to care about their families, after all. Emphasizing male responsibility in family planning, therefore, is a key to getting men both to fulfill their broader responsibilities as husbands and fathers and to contribute their fair share to population stabilization.

THE HIGHER FERTILITY OF MEN

Of course, family planning is still, at heart, a women's issue. The development of the birth control pill, the IUD, and safe methods of female sterilization have remained the most important and revolutionary innovations in the history of family planning, because they finally gave a significant number of women control over their own fertility. After all, as Margaret Sanger, America's family planning pioneer of the early 20th century, frequently noted, it is the woman who risks her life in childbirth. Even at the end of the 20th century, maternal mortality rates remain high in the developing world. In Afghanistan and Sierra Leone, for instance, according to the World Health Organization (WHO), one mother dies for every 100 live births—a rate 250 times higher than that of some European countries. And many maternal deaths in developing countries are attributed by WHO to excessive childbearing.

The focus of family planning policies and programs, then, should not be shifted away from women, but rather broadened to include men as well. Though the importance of female methods of birth control seems to lie in their very independence from male influence, and though many women would not be using contraception were it not for private, female-only clinics, the exclusion of men from family planning has also had some negative consequences for women that were not foreseen by many activists. "Putting all the responsibility onto women," says Gill Gordon of IPPF's AIDS prevention unit, "has the effect of marginalizing men and making them *less* likely to behave responsibly." In many places where female birth control methods predominate, the connection between sexuality and reproduction has disappeared in the minds of many men, and they simply haven't had to confront or even consider the very serious reasons women might have for wanting to limit their childbearing. Though giving all women control over their fertility would be a significant accomplishment, it would not insure their well-being, or the well-being of any children they might eventually want to have.

The reality in many developing countries is that if a man's wife resists childbearing, he will often simply withdraw his financial support and marry another woman. Even worse, many men have resorted to violence in order to keep their wives from using contraception. One recent study showed that more than 50 percent of Mexican women using state-sponsored birth control services do so secretly, for fear of being physically abused by their husbands. A woman's ability to regulate her own fertility is often contingent upon her partner's recognition of her right to do so—which means that family planners need to work that much harder to make men empathize with women and understand their own responsibilities.

Changing men's sexual attitudes in a patriarchal world is delicate, time-consuming, expensive work, and the cost-effectiveness of education campaigns aimed at men is always difficult to measure, since progress is inevitably so slow. It would be a mistake, then, to let male-focused policies and programs take away any of the already limited resources currently devoted to women and family planning. But changing men's attitudes about familial decision-making is still crucial, especially since men currently tend to be responsible for more children than do women. All around the developing world, the population pressures caused by high fertility are contributing at least indirectly to problems as varied as wood and water shortages, joblessness, inadequate sanitation, the spread of infectious diseases, and the accumulation of waste—all of which have a direct impact on families. And, if current demographic trends continue, the globe's current population of almost 5.6 billion will probably have risen to about 8.4 billion by 2025. Ninety-five percent of those new babies will be born in the Third World.

Traditionally, population programs and policies have held women responsible for high fertility, at least implicitly. For years, national censuses and surveys did not even consider men's fertility. A country's fertility rate—the target of most programs and policies—is always measured as the average *female* fertility rate, because women are the ones who actu-

MEN HAVE MORE CHILDREN

Average Number of Living Children of Men and Women over 50, Selected Countries in Sub-Saharan Africa.

COUNTRY	MEN	WOMEN	PERCENTAGE BY WHICH MALE RATE IS HIGHER
CAMEROON	8.1	4.8	69
NIGER	6.7	4.9	37
KENYA	9.6	7.9	22
GHANA	8.5	7.4	15

Source: Demographic and Health Surveys

ally have children. Over the last decade, however, as demographers have begun to provide more relevant data, population policies guided solely by analyses of women's fertility have begun to seem less appropriate. Especially in societies where polygyny is common, family planning programs would do better to focus on men, since most of the excess childbearing in such societies can be traced to sexual pairings of older men—who might be able to provide child support for only a few more years—with much younger women. In Kenya, Ghana, and Cameroon, for instance, married men over the age of 50, who might continue to father children until their death, tend to have between eight and 10 living children. Married women at the end of their reproductive years report having five to eight.

THE POLITICS OF CONTRACEPTION

Since so many men in the developing world are so strongly predisposed to reject family planning, and since progress in changing their attitudes is so hard to measure in the short term, Third World development experts have tended to focus their family-planning efforts on couples who are already interested in limiting childbearing. Most development funders like to support programs that aspire to deliver a certain number of contraceptives to a certain number of people and achieve a measurable decline in fertility. And, without question, expanding access to birth control devices is crucial in the struggle both to improve women's and children's health and welfare and to help stabilize the world's burgeoning population. A 1992 study by Population Action International (then called the Population Crisis Committee) found 22 countries in which men and women still have no access, in effect, to birth control information or services. The contraceptive prevalence rate—or percentage of married women of reproductive age (15 to 49) using birth control—has surpassed 50 percent in a few countries in Latin America and Asia, but in sub-Saharan Africa, for example, it averages only 14 percent.

Simply flooding developing nations with contraceptives will go only so far, however. To make a significant contribution to population stabilization on a global scale, family planning programs will have to change people's attitudes, and especially men's attitudes, about the number of children they want to have. Unfortunately, in addition to the broad social and cultural factors that discourage men from participating in family planning, there are several more intimate factors about which men tend to express concern. Some men worry, for instance, that their wives would become promiscuous if provided with the means of preventing pregnancy. More generally, many men fear—probably with good reason—that, whether or not their wives ended up using birth control for extramarital affairs, the simple fact that it would allow them to assert a new form of control over sex and their bodies would probably change the power dynamics of the marriage. And men often have genuine concerns about the threats to their partner's health that many contraceptive devices are reputed to pose. Some of their fears—about pelvic inflammatory disease from IUDs, and nausea and headaches from the pill—are valid, while others—that the pill causes arthritis and sterility—are myths perpetuated by failings in information and education systems.

Men usually have even stronger negative feelings about the three birth control methods commonly thought of as male-initiated—withdrawal, the condom, and vasectomy. Withdrawal and the condom represent an unreasonable sacrifice of sexual pleasure to many men. Family planning field workers commonly report that suggestions of condom use are most often greeted with smiles and quickly composed maxims, such as "You can't wash your feet with your socks on," or "That would be like eating a sweet with the wrapper still on it." Vasectomies are even less acceptable in many parts of the developing world, because it seems highly unnatural to many men to have surgery on their sexual organ, or because they don't understand exactly what the operation entails. In the Sudan, 34 percent of male participants in a recent study thought that getting a vasectomy was equivalent to being castrated.

Many of these concerns could be easily overcome, though, since they stem from simple gaps in information or services. Family planning programs that cater to the specific concerns of men, and that offer a wider selection of contraceptive options, with complete explanations of their risks and how they are to be used, could make converts of millions. Already, more men than ever before are at least considering the use of family planning, if only, in many cases, for spacing their children further apart.

In the early 1970s, surveys of men in sub-Saharan Africa showed consistently that more than half fervently disapproved of birth control. In the 1990s, though, outright rejection of contraception is rare even in this region. Approval ratings are still low in some countries, such as Mali, where only 17 percent of men aged 20 to 55 support family planning; but in Burundi, for instance, male approval has soared to 94 percent. In 10 other recent Third World surveys cited in a paper written by Cynthia Green for WHO, countries reported contraceptive approval rates among men of between 56 percent and 96 percent. Of course, a positive survey response hardly guarantees that a man will practice contraception, but it is a first step. Some men have even begun to express a more philosophical attitude about so sensitive an issue as female promiscuity. If a woman "wants to go out," noted a member of a 1989 focus group in Burkina Faso, "whether she takes the pill or not, she can go out." And a young telephone operator in Quito, Ecuador, went so far as to connect family planning with shared parental responsibility: "Even if you have enough money to ensure the children have a good education, they probably suffer from lack of attention if there are too many. And men here never help the women at home—she has to do everything. These kinds of decisions must be taken together by the man and the wife."

JUST FOR MEN

One way for a man to begin sharing the burden of planning and caring for a family is to offer to use a male method of birth control. Unfortunately, though, because contraceptive research has always been guided by the assumption that contraception is woman's work, men's options remain limited. While women theoretically have access to several modern, semi-permanent but fully reversible methods, ranging from the pill and the IUD to Norplant and injectables such as Depo-Provera, research on modern methods for men seems to have stopped at vasectomy. The IPPF's *Medical Bulletin* estimates that "only approximately 8 percent of the world contraceptive budget is spent on the development of male methods." It is true that certain chemical methods just aren't well suited to male physiology: developing a "male pill," for instance, would mean finding a way of blocking the ongoing production of millions of sperm without blocking the production of male hormones, a task much more daunting than chemically blocking the production of one egg every month. "Physically," however, as Elaine Lissner, the director of the Male Contraception Information Project in Santa Cruz, points out, "it's easier to stop millions of sperm than one egg. The sperm all travel through the vas deferens, a small, easily accessed tube, where they can be incapacitated or blocked." In any case, family planning researchers have hardly even begun to develop the potential range of useful contraceptive services for men.

Meanwhile, about one quarter of the world's couples who are currently using contraception rely on male methods. Withdrawal is perhaps the most dubious birth control method, with a failure rate of about 18 percent. But it has a long and notable history. Withdrawl was especially important in the 19th century during Europe's massive demographic transition to replacement-level fertility (when each man and woman have, on average, just two surviving children). The men of the Victorian era, perhaps aided by a pervasive cultural prudery, present the ultimate example of male responsibility, remembering their duty to their family even at the height of passion. Today, withdrawal still provides a free, safe method of birth control for about 15 million couples in the developing world who perhaps have no other options.

Vasectomy remains an important birth control method for men who don't want any more children. Because so many births are accidental, and because sterilization is almost 100 percent successful as a birth control method, the average vasectomy in the developing world is thought to prevent about two births. More reproductive health clinics are expanding their services and offering comprehensive vasectomy programs. PRO-PATER, in Sao

MEN *WANT* MORE CHILDREN

Average Number of Desired Children of Men and Women, Selected Countries in Sub-Saharan Africa.

COUNTRY	MEN	WOMEN	PERCENTAGE BY WHICH MALE RATE IS HIGHER
CAMEROON	11.2	7.3	53
NIGER	12.6	8.5	48
GHANA	7.6	5.3	43
BURUNDI	5.5	5.5	0
KENYA	4.8	4.8	0

Source: Demographic and Health Surveys

Of 204 published references on the Latin American family, only two discussed the role of fathers.

Paulo, Brazil, has been particularly successful in attracting men, thanks to a carefully planned, high-profile outreach program. Its staffers go to workplaces to talk about family planning with men in settings where they feel at ease. The clinic also runs a series of television advertisements that describe vasectomy as "an act of love" and reassure men that it does not affect sexual functioning—a key strategy with male sterilization. Nick Danforth, men's programs advisor for the Association of Voluntary Surgical Contraception in New York, likes to point out that although vasectomy—increasingly performed without a scalpel—is technically simpler, safer, and quicker than female sterilization, it is still used only a third as often.

Overall, condom use is probably the most significant male method, because it is not only cheap, easy, highly effective, and free of side effects, but it is also the one contraceptive additionally capable of preventing the spread of sexually transmitted diseases (STDs), including AIDS. Unfortunately, the condom's association with disease makes it that much more controversial as a birth control device. Many men and women, especially in regions where STDs have become widespread, take suggestions of condom use as insults: the person making the suggestion is either admitting that he or she might have a disease or expressing the fear that his or her partner might have a disease. In both cases, the implication is that someone has been unfaithful. For this reason, many couples feel uncomfortable about even acquiring condoms. "The condom is not seen as a contraceptive like, for example, the pill," explains a 50-year-old man in Burkina Faso. "It has come with AIDS. . . . If you want a condom, then that means you want to have an affair. So you have to get it via a third person. You cannot go yourself." Obtaining condoms may be even more problematic for women, because of the double standard operating in so many cultures. Men are expected to be discreet if they want to be promiscuous, but women are simply not expected to be promiscuous. Many women, intimidated by such strong stigmatization and by their male-dominated societies, end up risking pregnancy and disease rather than risking their partner's wrath by asking him to use a condom.

As with all male methods, condoms leave the woman in a particularly vulnerable situation: she must depend on her partner to use them, and use them correctly. But AIDS is making condoms increasingly important to women's health in the developing world. HIV is passed much more easily from a man to a woman than from a woman to a man, and it has already infected a significant portion of the adult, heterosexual population in Africa and Asia, where prostitution and male promiscuity are common. For now, women have to rely on male condoms for their safety, and while the female condom might give women slightly more control, using it will still probably entail complicated sexual negotiations. It is essential, then, that men acknowledge the sensitivity of the situation and take the lead in encouraging condom use. Perhaps family planners and AIDS activists can join forces to produce education campaigns that will help to inform couples about the specifics of sexually transmitted diseases and their consequences, and help to dissipate sexual tensions by allowing partners to anticipate and understand each other's anxieties.

In the end, a willingness to participate in sexual and familial decisions as a concerned, forthcoming, equal partner is the real key to male responsibility. More than being willing to use a male method of birth control, men have to be willing to listen—to learn how to be sensitive to their partners' health, welfare, and desires. As Mary Daly, a leader of the modern feminist movement, has remarked, true responsibility is defined by an ability to be responsive.

NOT-SO-GREAT EXPECTATIONS

In almost all matters of policy, the family is defined as the mother-child unit: policymakers and program directors forget about gender dynamics, or simply don't expect men to take part. All too often, well-intentioned representatives of industrialized countries simply press packages of pills into the outstretched palms of Third World women, "as if women alone," in the words of the Population Council's Judith Bruce, "could bring about fertility decline, and as if their sexual and parental roles were determined autonomously." The United Nations Educational, Scientific, and Cultural Organization (UNESCO) recently asked a sociologist to do a review of the current literature on the Latin American family. Of the 204 documents she examined, only two mention fatherhood or the situation of men.

In the 1990s, men's family planning and parenting responsibilities need to be explicitly defined. A logical starting point would be prioritizing the goal of establishing paternity and enforcing child support payments—as leaders have in Nigeria, where, according to the new national population policy,

children have a legal claim on their father's time and money. Even in so "advanced" a country as the United States, where most of the so-called "deadbeat dads"—fathers who have abandoned their partner and child to the welfare system—could actually afford to pay child support, only about 18 percent do.

Changes in men's roles will not emerge quickly or with anything resembling ease. In some places, as economies modernize, the direct costs of child-rearing—from medicines and nutritious foods to schooling fees—are increasing, and familial resources are getting tight. Instead of having smaller families, though, many fathers simply shift the financial burden to the mother or the older children. And even when men genuinely want to act more responsibly, they sometimes believe they are unable to because of certain social and economic factors that continue to be neglected by policymakers. Both fathers and mothers, for instance, feel in many cases that children provide them with their only means of achieving economic and social security. And many fathers insist that they would have fewer children if they could be sure that more of them would survive: a study by the World Bank revealed that, on average, the prevention of 10 infant deaths results in one to five fewer births. But fathers in sub-Saharan Africa, where the infant mortality rate has remained as deplorably high as 10 percent—compared to one percent in the industrialized world—feel that they cannot afford to take chances with their fertility. And some fathers are contributing no financial resources to their children simply because they have none to give. Often they are desperately searching for work, perhaps in a far-off city.

YOU REAP WHAT YOU SOW

Still, educational efforts—ideally in tandem with pointed policy initiatives that force men to take up some of the economic burden of raising children—have considerable potential. If more field workers sought out men and provided them with better information, they would surely have more influence over men's family planning decisions. Good strategies for increasing male responsibility range from integrating family planning into community development programs to integrating sex and gender education into primary school systems. A recent IPPF report stated that, in general, field workers have had the most success changing men's attitudes and behavior through peer counseling: when men felt they were being advised by people who really identified with their concerns, whether sexual or financial, they were much more likely to respond favorably to suggestions of taking on more familial responsibility.

4. REPRODUCTION: Birth Control

In Colombia, men started turning out in droves at vasectomy clinics modeled after Sao Paulo's PRO-PATER when male clinicians began offering more reproductive health services, including urological exams, infertility treatment, and sexuality counseling. Between 1985 and 1987 the number of vasectomies being performed quadrupled in Bogota and increased tenfold in Medellin.

The National Family Planning Council of Zimbabwe ran an intensive media campaign in 1989 designed specifically to increase men's responsibility in family planning and encourage joint decision making among couples. Male educators gave a series of 80 informational and motivational talks, and an entertaining serial drama about the consequences of irresponsible sexual and familial behavior was broadcast over the radio twice a week for six months, reaching about 40 percent of the country's men. By the end of the campaign, 61 percent of the men who had tuned in to "Akarumwa Nechekuchera"—variously translated as "Man is his own worst enemy" or "You reap what you sow"—reported a change in their attitudes about their families, and 17 percent of the men who had attended at least one talk reported that they actually started using a family planning method. Most importantly, the number of men saying that family planning decisions ought to be made jointly by husband and wife had risen by 40 percent: the council's educational programs were getting men and women to talk.

Some fatalists argue that because of undeniable evolutionary and physiological differences between men and women, men aren't likely ever to take much responsibility as parents: they are no better than all the other mammalian males. But such arguments overlook thousands of years of male contributions to family welfare—from big-game hunting to protection, wage earning, counseling, mentoring, and even nurturing. Men have the potential to participate fully in planning and raising a family. It is only because they have society's implicit permission that some men still limit their participation to the act of sex.

Reproductive Revolution Is Jolting Old Views

Gina Kolata

Suppose that Leonardo da Vinci were suddenly transported to the United States in 1994, says Dr. Arthur Caplan, an ethicist at the University of Minnesota. What would you show him that might surprise him?

Dr. Caplan has an answer. "I'd show him a reproductive clinic," he said. "I'd tell him, 'We make babies in this dish and give them to other women to give birth,' " And that, Dr. Caplan predicted, "would be more surprising than seeing an airplane or even the space shuttle."

It was only 15 years ago that the world's first baby was born through the use of in vitro fertilization, the method of combining sperm and egg outside the body and implanting the embryo in the uterus. That step ushered in a new era of reproductive technology that has moved so far, so fast that ethicists and many members of the public say they are shaken and often shocked by the changes being wrought.

Although its aims are laudable—helping infertile couples to have children—the new reproductive science is raising piercing challenges to longstanding concepts of parenthood, family and personal identity.

It is now possible for a woman to give birth to her own grandchild—and some women have. It is possible for women to have babies after menopause—and some have. There may soon be a way for a couple to have identical twins born years apart. It may also become feasible for a woman to have an ovary transplanted from an aborted fetus, making the fetus the biological mother of a child.

These events are frightening, Dr. Caplan said. "I never thought that technology would throw the American public into a kind of philosophical angst, but that's what's going on here," he said.

Dr. Mark Siegler, director of the clinical ethics program at the University of Chicago, said that it does not matter so much whether large numbers of people use the new technologies. Their very existence throws long-held values into deep confusion. They introduce, he said, "the idea that making babies can be seen as a technological rather than a biological process and that you can manipulate the most fundamental, ordinary human process—having children."

In the most recent stunning development, a scientist at Edinburgh University said last week that he was working on transplanting the ovaries of a fetus into infertile women, adding that he can do this already in mice. The scientist, Dr. Roger Gosden, said that a 10-week-old human female fetus has six million to eight million eggs. He estimated that it might take a year for a newly transplanted fetal ovary to grow and start producing mature eggs. Several ethicists pointed out that an ovary transplant could lead to a bizarre situation: women who donated their fetus's ovaries might become grandmothers without ever being mothers.

Dr. Gosden said he also expected to be able to help women undergoing chemotherapy, which can destroy the ovaries, by freezing strips of a patient's own ovary and then putting them back after the treatment was over. He has perfected this method in sheep, he said. In principle, both of these ovary transplant methods could also allow women to avoid menopause altogether, remaining potentially fertile until the end of their days.

A few months ago, researchers at George Washington University said they had cloned human embryos, splitting embryos into identical twins or triplets. The method could enable couples to have identical twins born years apart.

But ovary transplants and clones are in the future. Already here are other methods that were unimaginable just a short while ago. For example, doctors routinely freeze extra human embryos that are produced by in vitro fertilization, storing them indefinitely or until the couple asks for them again. Thousands of embryos rest in this frozen limbo in freezers around the nation.

THE MEANING OF 'MOTHER'

Using donated eggs, women can now have babies after menopause. And egg donors are enabling women to give birth to babies to whom they bear no genetic relationship.

Each new development gives rise to new questions of personal identity, experts say. For example, several ethicists said they were repelled by the idea of using eggs from a fetus to enable an infertile woman to become pregnant. They asked, for example, how a child would feel upon discovering its genetic mother was a dead fetus.

The cloning experiment elicited questions of what it says about the uniqueness of individuals if embryos can be split into identical twins or triplets. Just as copying a work of art devalues it, might copying humans devalue them?

Egg donors raise the question of what it means to be a biological mother. Is the mother the woman who donated her egg or is it the woman who carried the baby to term? At least one ethicist and lawyer, George Annas of Boston University, argues that the only logical answer is that both are the mother. This means, he added, that for the first time in history, children can have two mothers.

Pregnancy after menopause threatens the ancient concept of a human life cycle. Until now, there was a time when a woman's reproductive life came to an end. Now, she can be fertile indefinitely. "It makes the life course incoherent," Mr. Annas said.

The growing hordes of frozen embryos call into question the status of these microscopic cell clusters. Do they deserve some consideration as potential humans or is it acceptable to simply discard them if they go unclaimed? Are they potential brothers and sisters of children already born, or are these just spare cells, not much different from blood in blood banks?

"It really is a brave new world," said Jay Katz, a law professor at Yale University.

TROUBLED BY TECHNOLOGY

Yet, said Dr. Susan Sherwin, a professor of philosophy and women's studies at Dalhousie University in Nova Scotia, "the profound question is whether we treat these developments as profound or take them for granted." Although, she said, "our technologically oriented society is fairly good at adapting quickly," the new reproductive technologies give her pause.

For example, Dr. Sherwin said, the possibility of pregnancy after menopause means that there no longer is a point when an infertile couple must give up their quest for a child. If women can have ovarian transplants, will it be even less acceptable for them to grow old without fighting it through medical intervention?

"An enormous industry has grown up in recent years to postpone or prevent menopause through hormone replacement therapy; now reproductive life can also be prolonged," Dr. Sherwin said. She added, "There are questions of what we value in women."

Making babies can now be seen as a technological, not a biological, process.

Mr. Annas said he hopes that people in the next century will look back on these reproductive technologies and find them "as strange as can be." He added: "We have a couple of billion more people on this planet than we need. What are we doing trying to figure out new ways to let couples have more babies? On a societal level, we have to ask, 'What's driving this?'"

But others said they thought the new technologies are heralding a future so astonishing as to be almost unbelievable.

"We're starting to see hints of 21st century reproductive technology," Dr. Caplan said. "We're getting early sight-ings and we can start to talk about them."

DEATH AND BIRTH

Dr. Siegler predicted that the technologies would change views of the start of life just as profoundly as the developments in the past quarter century changed views of life's end.

A generation ago, Dr. Siegler said, "death was not optional," adding, "When people reached the natural end of their lives thorough a failure of their heart or liver or kidneys or lungs, they died." But then researchers discovered kidney dialysis, machines that could take over kidneys and allow people to live even when their kidneys had failed. And they developed respirators that allowed people to keep breathing when they no longer could draw a breath on their own. Those machines, Dr. Siegler said, "opened a new rang of options about life and death."

"By what process do people decide to use them?" he asked. "Who is in control? When do you start? When do you stop?"

As a consequence of these technologies, Dr. Siegler added, "the first 25 years of medical ethics has been devoted heavily to death and dying and informed consent."

How Far Should We Push

Mother Nature?

*Making Babies: Technology is evolving faster than our ability
to weigh the cost and ethics*

The news came bursting out of Europe and rattled bedrooms around the world. First, a 59-year-old British businesswoman gave birth to twins, using donated eggs implanted in her uterus at a fertility clinic in Rome. Her coup was quickly eclipsed by the news that a 62-year-old Italian woman, who visited the same clinic, will deliver a baby in June. Next came the word that a black woman in Italy had recently given birth to a white baby using donor eggs; she and her Caucasian husband said they wanted to give their child "a better future." Then came an even bigger bombshell: press reports from Scotland said researchers had delivered baby mice using the ovaries of aborted mouse fetuses. There was talk that the process might someday be duplicated in humans, raising the freakish prospect of creating babies whose genetic mothers had never been born.

Things used to be so simple. A father provided sperm, a mother provided the egg and if something went wrong or if either partner was too old, that was just tough luck. But the Brave New World of reproductive technology, and particularly in-vitro fertilization (IVF), has changed all that forever. It is now technologically possible for a single infant to have five contributing parents: sperm donor, egg donor, surrogate mother, in addition to the mom and pop who raise him. The news from Europe showed that once again, technology was pushing the boundaries of the possible, raising questions society isn't prepared to answer or even debate in a cogent way. Is there no upper limit on the age at which women can bear children? (And what's wrong with that, if men can be fathers in their 70s and get ribbed by admiring buddies?) "In the future, people may wait till they retire to have kids—flip the whole life course," mused Arthur Caplan, director of the Center for Biomedical Ethics at the University of Minnesota. Beyond timing when to have their children, should couples be able to select their race? If the Scottish researchers continue their work, could a woman someday abort her daughter and give birth to her own grandchildren? (Talk about skip-generation families.)

To the millions of American couples on the emotional front lines of infertility, the ethical hypotheticals paled against the excitement of new possibilities. "Five years ago, this would have never happened to me," says Charline Pacourek, 45, who subjected herself to seven years of hormone injections, ovulation stimulation, artificial insemination, egg retrieval and embryo transfers. In November she learned that she is finally pregnant, thanks to eggs donated by a friend. Pacourek calls her baby a "miracle—it's fantastic! I would recommend this for anyone."

In Europe, however, government ministers were racing to curtail the high-tech options. French officials proposed banning IVF for women past menopause. Italy announced plans to limit artificial pregnancies at clinics like Dr. Severino Antinori's, where the 59-year-old and 62-year-old women got pregnant. Alarmed that the British woman had gone to Italy after being denied IVF at home, British Health Secretary Virginia Bottomley said she would seek uniform rules across Europe to prevent what some called "procreative tourism." But it's doubtful that the EC could ever agree on such touchy issues. "They have enough problems deciding what sort of cheese should be sold," said Oxford philosophy teacher Jonathan Glover. Germany, still chastened by the legacy of the Nazi experiments, prohibits fertilization by donated sperm or eggs, or any genetic manipulation of embryos.

In the United States, too, there were some calls to stop pushing the frontier of reproductive technology, or at least pause to consider where it is going. "We need to start to define those lines in society that we will not cross," said Dr. Thomas Raffin, codirector of the Stanford University Center for Biomedical Ethics. European-style laws are unlikely here, however. There are no federal rules or guidelines governing the estimated 300 assisted-fertility clinics operating nationwide, which generate some $2 billion in business a year. Starting this fall, a new law sponsored by Rep. Ron Wyden of Oregon will require clinics to report their success rates uniformly, so that consumers can sort out their wildly competing claims. But there are no rules specifying who clinics can or can't treat by age, marital status or any other factor.

> *'In the future, people may wait till they retire to have kids—flip the whole life course.'*

Nor are there rules requiring fertility clinics to match donors and recipients according to characteristics like race and religion. In that sense, the era of "designer babies" is already here. Sperm-bank customers can flip through catalogs listing the height, hair color, eye color, ancestry—sometimes even the IQ—of potential donors. Many donated eggs come from friends or family members; Maryann Fiore's sister provided the eggs for her triplets, born when she was 44. But some programs also have descriptions of potential egg donors from which couples can choose. Debbie Karnell, a nurse at a West Coast fertility clinic, decided to try IVF with donor eggs when she saw the caliber of the women who volunteered. At first, Karnell says she was attracted to the prettiest ones. But in the end, she chose a donor who was young and had already proved her fertility. It worked for Karnell too: she had a baby five months ago, at the age of 46.

Long odds: Biotech gadfly Jeremy Rifkin worries that selecting racial and genetic characteristics is a dangerous step toward eugenics, and thinks that donor eggs should be outlawed. But to many ethicists, the only thing more frightening than unfettered reproductive technology would be Congress playing God and imposing limits. "This is an individual matter, an ethical and moral choice, not the business of government or call-in talk shows," says University of Southern California law professor Susan Estrich. (She also thinks that if society is going to get upset about who's having babies, "we ought to worry more about children having children than a few wealthy middle-aged women with enough resources to do this.") Most couples pursuing IVF technology are indeed affluent; each attempt with donor eggs can cost $10,000 to $20,000, and some women undergo repeated efforts before succeeding or giving up. Only a few states require insurance companies to fund IVF procedures. And because of the expense and long odds, it is one of the few technologies specifically excluded under Bill Clinton's health-reform proposal.

Bluntly put, that leaves rich people free to pursue baby-making technology, and others out of luck. But some ethicists see no problem in that standard: as Caplan views it, society can't stop you from having a child, but it doesn't owe you one by any means. He also says the debate over a double standard for older men and women ignores the simple fact that older men can produce sperm naturally, while older women need help. "No one is talking about devoting a lot of

technology to getting impotent old men to have babies," Caplan says.

Dr. Geoffrey Sher, medical director of the Pacific Fertility Medical Center in San Francisco, says he had misgivings the first time a woman in her 50s came into his office seeking to become pregnant. "I thought, 'Why should we get into this? We don't need this controversy'." But the woman's husband, who was 40 years old, challenged Sher's prejudices by asking if he'd have qualms if their ages were reversed. Sher had to admit he wouldn't, and after that, he decided to resolve every case on an individual basis. His clinic, with one of the largest donor-egg programs in the

Rich people can now take extreme measures to make their own babies, but other people can't.

country, has treated more than 100 women over 40, and a handful past 50. He claims that 56 percent give birth on the first try, regardless of their age, as long as the donor is under 35 and the recipient has a healthy uterus.

Midnight feedings: Older mothers face some greater risks to their own health from pregnancy. But most IVF programs, like Sher's, carefully screen out candidates who are not in excellent condition. Using donor eggs from younger women eliminates the increased risk of genetic and other problems in an older woman's own eggs. Most doctors are more concerned that fiftysomething mothers won't have the physical stamina to put up with midnight feedings or chase after toddlers. But experts on aging pooh-pooh such fears, noting that scores of grandmothers are energetically raising grandchildren by default these days. "A woman of 59 or 61 on average is pretty healthy today," says Dr. Marcia Ory of the National Institute on Aging. Couples with the financial means to pursue IVF can probably afford a nanny, she notes, and may be better equipped emotionally as well. "Mature mothers make good mothers, especially in contrast to a child-parent of 15."

But isn't it cruel for parents to bear a child when they might not live to see him

or her reach puberty or college? "It's not a very nice prospect for a child of 10 or 12 to go to sleep every night, praying that his or her mother will live as long as he needs her," says Gail Sheehy, author of "Passages" and "The Silent Passage: Menopause." Georgette Bennett thought about that a lot when she decided to try IVF two years ago, when she was 45 and her husband was 21 years older. She got pregnant on the first attempt using her own eggs and sperm her husband had frozen years earlier. The nine months she carried her son was "the world's easiest pregnancy. I never stopped working, never took a single nap." Sadly, her husband died seven weeks before his son was born. Still, Bennett, 47, calls 16-month-old Joshua-Marc "a great monument to my husband." She also says she appointed guardians, and "very consciously set about peopling my son's life with a wide diversity of folk of all ages."

Do the new methods offer real hope, or just more pressure to keep trying at any cost?

For older parents who already have grown kids, the new technology can complicate family relationships. Jonie Mosby Mitchell, a country singer and nightclub owner, had four children with ease in her first marriage: "Boom. Boom. Boom. Boom," she says. She remarried 17 years ago and adopted a baby girl in 1988. She was planning to adopt again when she read an article about postmenopausal pregnancies and decided to try it. She was 52 when she gave birth to Morgan, now 21 months old. One of her older daughters was pregnant the same time she was. Another is pregnant now, and Mitchell has three grandchildren who are older than their uncle. Her new kids call her first husband "grampa." She says her older offspring are a little uncomfortable with all this. (Her oldest daughter said, "Mom, if you've got extra time, spend it with *my* kids.") Having young children in her 50s "is not an easy job," Mitchell admits. "They fight and they argue and they fuss and they want. It poops me out." But overall, she thinks she is a better mother this time than when she was younger and worked on the road.

In truth, IVF clinics see very few 50-something women hoping to start second families. Far more of their patients are women in their 40s who delayed marriage and childbearing, then were surprised to discover how difficult it was to conceive, and how desperately they wanted to. Author Anne Taylor Fleming, now 44, struggled for 10 years to get pregnant before abandoning the attempt, an odyssey she describes in her forthcoming book, "Motherhood Deferred: A Woman's Journey." She says a whole generation of women have been caught in the boomerang of changing attitudes toward motherhood: they were born in the family-focused 1950s, came of age in the '60s era of contraception and free love, and then followed the feminist advice of the '70s to "make money, be equal to men, don't get caught." When they realized that wanting children might be part of feminism too, Fleming says, many were unprepared, as she was. Despite her career, happy marriage and four stepsons, Fleming says, "I was startled by the strong emotion of both wanting a baby and the inability to have one—just knocked sideways."

Like Fleming, many infertile couples eventually have to come to terms with reproductive failure and reconcile themselves to adoption—if they can find an agency that will accept them—or being childless. Does the news that a few 50- and 60-year-old women are having babies really offer more hope—or more long-odds promises to chase? "With so many new techniques at their disposal, it's harder for doctors to say, 'We've gone as far as we can go.' And the couples themselves have an even harder time saying 'Enough is enough'," Ronny Diamond, a New York social worker who counsels infertile couples. Fleming agrees: "It is sort of bitter joy that something else dangles out there." But she says that going through fertility attempts "humbles you about making choices for other women."

For all the startling headlines and new hopes, IVF is "still a horrible, expensive, stressful, emotionally trying crisis in a couple's life and no one would put themselves through it on purpose," says Carole Lieber-Wilkins, a therapist who counsels couples in West Los Angeles. Even if doctors can slow down the biological clock for some women, that doesn't mean that younger women can take late-life pregnancy for granted, or that retirement communities will be setting up day-care centers. Someday scientists may be able to hormonally manipulate men to carry fetuses, or grow human embryos in animal surrogates. (Could your mother, as well as your forefathers, be a chimpanzee?) But marching hand in hand with reproductive breakthroughs is the idea that society has to set priorities, and accept some limits, in an era of scarce medical resources. It will be up to many of these high-tech babies in the future to try to balance all those competing needs.

MELINDA BECK *with* MARY HAGER *and* PAT WINGERT *in Washington,* PATRICIA KING *in San Francisco,* JEANNE GORDON *in Los Angeles,* STANLEY HOLMES *in Chicago and* SUSAN MILLER *in New York*

ABORTION, ADOPTION OR A BABY?

Does a woman's right to choose leave men with no rights at all?

James Sturz

James Sturz is a freelance writer based in New York City.

There are more than 3.6 million unplanned pregnancies in America every year—each one of them a crisis, a challenge or a godsend. The dilemma of what to do next is left, by law, to women. Some men know this better than they'd like. Here are voices of men who did not get to choose.

DANIEL,* 29, human-resources manager, Oakland, California When I was a senior in college, my mother treated our family to ten days on a dude ranch at Christmas. I'd just begun seeing a woman at school, and for the first time in my life I was sexually active. I found myself saying, "Wow, this sex thing is really great!" The ranch was pretty much paradise. There was a big party on New Year's Eve, and I ended up spending the night with a woman I met there. We started making love, the two of us in this plush fantasy world. But right when I told her I was going to come, she said, "It's okay, it's okay." So I figured it was either the right time in her cycle, or she was

*Names and other identifying characteristics have been changed to protect privacy.

on the Pill. And the next day my plane left. I was 21 at the time.

Then a month before I was going to graduate, I got a call—I hadn't heard from this woman since that night—and she said, "I'm really confused. I'm really scared. But I'm pregnant, and I know you're the father." This was close to the six-month point of no return. I went into complete shock. I was still seeing the woman I'd been dating on campus. I couldn't tell her. I couldn't tell a soul. But I wrote this woman letters, saying, "You can't have this child. There's no way you can deny me the right of choice." Still, it was very clear from our conversations on the phone that she didn't want an abortion. I tried to push her, and we got into arguments. It turned out she'd had an abortion before. She said it had been an awful experience for her and she wouldn't go through it again. I couldn't relate to what that experience was like. I could only imagine it had to be really horrible. And so I agreed.

It killed me that when we slept together she had told me so casually, "It's okay." And it infuriated me that she'd had an abortion before but wasn't going to have one this time. This was not the way I wanted to bring my first child into the world. "You have the ability to have more children, so why now? Why me?" I asked. "I'm not going to force you to do anything

to your body you don't want, but you've got to understand that this is killing me." I thought, "You're just destroying my life. It as our choice to be together, and I'll take as much responsibility as you do. But I should have as much say as you do about whether this child is born." She denied me that choice. I felt ripped off.

My son was about 18 months old before I could bring myself to tell my girlfriend. She was in her first year of law school by then, and we were living together, planning to get married. One night we had a heart-to-heart. She said, "This relationship really isn't going anywhere." For obvious reasons—I had a huge part of me I wasn't telling her about. She said to me, "I need to tell you I was seeing someone for a summer when we were apart." And then she said, "You don't seem to be bothered by that." I said to myself, "That doesn't compare." I told her about my child, and we broke up after that.

It was another year before I told anyone else in my life that my son existed. He was 2½, and I'd never seen him. Then a counselor told me, "You need to tell your parents, you need to tell *yourself*," and gradually I started telling people at work. One thing I did to change my life was change jobs. I felt so awkward saying, "Oh, by the way, did I tell you I had a son?" So when I started at a new company,

I put a picture of my son on my desk. Now he has turned out to be one of the greatest things in my life. I try only to look at the positives now, because I want to be a loving force for him.

ROGER, 29, student, New York, New York I made a short film at New York University a year ago. I showed a guy going to play basketball and a woman walking into Planned Parenthood. I cut back and forth from the guy shooting hoops to the front doors of the clinic. I made the film to work through feelings I had about my ex-girlfriend's two abortions.

The first abortion wasn't so bad, but the second one was very different. I was older then, and we were living together. I thought we might get married someday. I was always pro-choice, but I never felt good about abortions. I said, "We should get married." And she said, "I don't want that." But I realized it wasn't my choice. It didn't matter what I thought. It wasn't like we could argue and the one with the better points would win. After the second abortion, she was pretty pissed off at me. For getting her pregnant, and for disagreeing with her. I was angry too. Because she was having the abortion, and because I felt powerless about it. We weren't getting along well. We weren't caring about each other. It was never tender. It was, "How dare you tell me what to do!"

In the movie, the camera and the audience do not go into the building. The movie is really about the guy. At the end of the movie, he's just sitting on the pavement against the fence, holding the ball between his legs. Then he lets the ball go, and it rolls away from him. And he gets up and walks out of the playground, without the ball. he meets the girlfriend outside the playground, and they walk off together. But we see that he's been left out of the whole thing.

I was really embarrassed about the abortions. I didn't tell any of my friends or family, and I didn't get any support. It took making the film to be open about it. Nobody knew anything. Then a guy on my crew asked why I was making this.

TREVOR, 36, civil engineer, San Jose, California Six years ago I was dating a woman, and she decided to have a kid without my permission. I told her, "No, I don't want to have a kid, I'm not ready." And not only did she have the child against my will, I have to pay child support. I haven't had a lot of contact with my daughter. But I didn't want to be a father to begin with, and I found myself having to make a choice about caving in.

We went out for about six months. I was starting to get to the point where I didn't like her that much, but I just didn't have the heart to break up with her. Then one day she said she was pregnant. My first reaction was not as frightened as I should have been, given what I know now. Right away, I told her I didn't want to be a father. I also told her that I had been wanting to break up with her. I felt bad about the timing, but I didn't want to give her any illusions about our future relationship. That was a dreadful day. We went for a long walk, where we could talk about things without having to look each other in the eye. I said I would stand by her, but I made it very clear my support was going to be friendly, not romantic. I encouraged her to arrange an adoption. We went to see a lawyer who specialized in adoptions. A couple took us to dinner.

When I saw her belly start to swell, I felt weird. Here I was the father, but I still didn't want to be a father. We went to childbirth classes. I was not a proud father. I was an embarrassed father. We were in a car on the way to a party celebrating the end of the class when she told me she was going to keep the child.

My resentment about her decision has been terrible for my daughter—I keep away and have seen her less than a dozen times and not in over a year.

Women have a tough time feeling compassion for men who are forced into fatherhood. I pay a fourth or a fifth of my after-tax income in child support, because I don't want to be viewed as a deadbeat dad. But I still feel like a second-class citizen.

Recently I got married, and now I am a stepfather. This time I got to choose fatherhood. I just took my stepson on a big outing with his school. I love him, and I tell him that. In a way, I love my daughter, too, but I'm filled with pain about the whole situation.

JASON, 38, attorney, Seattle, Washington My story's a lot like other guys' stories—because they're all basically the same. A woman decides she wants to have a child. The stock story is the woman says, "Don't worry, I'm on the Pill," and then the next thing you hear is, "Whoops, I'm pregnant. I want child support."

I have a daughter who's now a teenager. Her mother and I had gone together, off and on, for a long time. She just didn't bother to tell me she'd stopped taking the Pill. Then she wanted to get married. I said no. My feeling, then *and*

now, is I wasn't going to get involved in a marriage with someone who would deceive me. That's like asking it to fail. So she said, "Okay, don't marry me. I'll just force you to pay child support." And that's the way it went. I had to sue to get visitation rights. There were years at a time when I couldn't see my daughter at all.

Unfortunately, under the law, pro-choice means *women's* choice. I truly believed we were behaving responsibly. But people look at me as a happy-go-lucky, do-anything-you-want guy. I've never been that way. I have no other children.

There are a lot of people who won't even associate with me. I've fought job discrimination because of this. I am a father who never married, and automatically people see me as a deadbeat. I'm paying all this support, doing the right thing, and yet people condemn me.

PETER, 24, graduate student, St. Louis, Missouri When I was a senior in college, my girlfriend of nine months thought she was pregnant. I was shocked because we had been careful. She was in tears. We went to Planned Parenthood, and they asked her if she had any doubts about who the father was. I said no, accepting responsibility. At that point in our relationship, I was more than willing to get married and have the child. But she wanted to schedule an abortion. She was so distraught, there was no point discussing it.

There was a two-week waiting period, and by that time I was committed to the decision because being pregnant was such a painful experience for her. When she came out after the abortion, my whole concern was for her. We drove in the car but didn't say a word to each other. She just kept her hand on my arm while I drove, and all through the night she cried.

She didn't want anybody to know, so I took the full emotional brunt. But one day I became suspicious. The doctor had told us when the child was conceived, and I knew she'd been home for Thanksgiving break then and had seen her old boyfriend within that time period. I asked her about it and she pretty much denied it. Then, eventually, she wrote me a letter explaining what she couldn't say to my face.

I found all this out about three months after the abortion. I felt betrayed. I had gone through such overwhelming trauma and guilt. Every time I was with her after that I felt angry. I'd sit at my desk in a silent rage. I felt like a fool, too. One time, we drove home and we were in the garage, and she just started crying when I brought the subject up. I grabbed her and said, "You're not leaving the car until we finish this." I remember exploding. She couldn't even respond. She got out of the car and went into the apartment, and that was the beginning of the end of our relationship.

WILLIAM, 25, events coordinator, New York, New York My parents were married sooner than they had planned, after my mother got pregnant. I used to think my father was sad that he didn't have the opportunity to chase his life's dreams, but they went through with the pregnancy, and here I am. The first thing my folks told me as I got older was, "Don't go getting any girls pregnant."

Then I did, when I was 18. I was seeing a French woman. I think she wanted a green card, and she offered me money to marry her. I told her, "Under no circumstances am I going to marry you." Then she came back and said she was pregnant. I said, "I like you and I want to be with you, but if you have this child, I'm telling you, honestly, I'll buy a plane ticket to Hong Kong." And I would have done it, too. I got on the phone to Continental Airlines. She got the picture. When she saw she couldn't trap me, she had an abortion.

We had been using condoms, but there were times when she'd tell me, "It's okay, it's not the time of the month when I can get pregnant." I listened. It was a stupid thing, and then I did it again a year later.

The woman I was with then had a polyp on her cervix, and sometimes it would bleed. We mistook it for her period, so we thought she wouldn't get pregnant if we didn't use anything. Then we got one of those drugstore pregnancy tests. It says it'll normally take two minutes. This one turned blue in about fifteen seconds. I was so scared. I was shaking. She'd had an abortion before and felt bad about it, and she didn't want to have another one now. I think I used the Hong Kong thing again, but now I was just bluffing. She was scared she wouldn't be able to have kids again. It took a lot of coaxing, but we got an abortion. She's married now and has a child. I keep thinking it could have been my kid. In the same situation, my parents went through with it. And they had me. So even if the most overwhelming feeling is relief, I still have a sense of loss.

ROBERT, 38, student, Madison, Wisconsin When I came back from studying in Korea, I got together with an old girlfriend. It was just a hot, romantic get-together a few times, and then she got pregnant.

When she told me, I was angry. And I was disappointed in myself—and a little bit disappointed in her. I'm somewhat of a religious person, but I crash and burn every once in a while. I had understood that she was using birth control or had a knowledge of her cycle. This responsibility was not what I wanted.

We started talking about our options. I didn't want to influence her either way, but, still, I think human life is sacred and I didn't like the idea of an abortion. She'd already had one in the past and didn't want to have another. So she said, "I always wanted to have your baby anyway. I don't care if you marry me or not."

I asked her if she'd consider giving it up for adoption. But when she was about three or four months pregnant, she said she wouldn't even consider it. I didn't feel too attached right away, but toward the last few months, I accepted the reality that this baby was my child, whether I married her or not.

The baby was born just two weeks ago. It's a beautiful baby, a little girl. She came over last night with the baby. I cooked dinner. Now I'm thinking about marrying her. But I just didn't plan on coming back to the U.S. to do that. I came home to go to school. I'm stubborn and don't like being manipulated, and I don't like feeling out of control.

I think I've surrendered one level at a time. I've surrendered to the fact that I have a child, that I'm responsible for it and that I'm going to love it. That's a surrender to reality. The second surrender I'm still working on. That's a commitment to being a good husband and a good father, living together in a home.

NICHOLAS, 33, attorney, St. Cloud, Minnesota I was a college sophomore involved with a freshman. She got pregnant. I was in love. Although the pregnancy was not what I'd planned or wanted right then, I really wasn't disappointed. I was even kind of happy after the initial shock.

Abortion never crossed my mind, but she said that was what she wanted. I thought I'd be able to convince her other-

---

WHERE MEN STAND

Nearly 1.6 million women in the U.S. choose abortions each year. Twenty years ago, *Roe* v. *Wade* secured a woman's unimpeded right to first-trimester abortion. *Planned Parenthood* v. *Danforth,* three years later, struck down the requirement of spousal consent. Last year, the Supreme Court ruled in *Planned Parenthood* v. *Casey* that even spousal *notification* was more of a hindrance than the American constitution could allow. The pro-choice movement is reviled as the "pro-abortion movement" by Operation Rescue, but it's called the "*women's*-choice movement" by still another significant set: the men scattered across the country who have struggled to have a say of their own. Some have sought injunctions to block abortions, only to be left mourning when the law leaves them without permanent recourse. Others, who would have chosen adoption or abortion, have discovered a different kind of power-lessness, retreating into detachment, ignominy or neglect as styles of fatherhood.

While James Bopp Jr., the general counsel for the National Right to Life Committee, acknowledges that the *Casey* decision has closed the issue of seeking stays, the New York City–based National Center for Men will file a class-action suit in U.S. district court later this year, arguing that equal protection under the law necessitates giving men the right during the first trimester to relinquish all future financial responsibility to a child. The thinking goes: If women have the right to bring a child into the world without considering men's wishes, men should have the right to waive the related responsibility. Support for this legal position has come from unlikely places. Karen DeCrow, a former president of the National Organization for Women, has argued that "autonomous women making independent decisions about their lives should not expect men to finance their choice." But while changes in law may free a man's checkbook, the ties of kinship continue to be forged against his will. —*J S*

wise, but soon it became clear I couldn't. Then I remembered that Iowans for Life had an office in town, and I went there. I asked, "Is there any information I can give my girlfriend to convince her not to have an abortion?" The woman there told me the laws were completely on my girlfriend's side but suggested I contact Fathers for Equal Rights. That next day, I went to their office, and they wrote up a petition and headed to the courthouse. We got to the Iowa Supreme Court just before closing. The judge said he'd hold a hearing the next week.

I went back to the dorm. My girlfriend called me that night and wanted to talk. I said, "Can you come down? I've got a lot to tell you, and you're probably going to hate me for what I've been doing all day." I felt she had to be warned that she was going to be served papers and that she would have to go to a hearing. We talked till four o'clock that morning. She had spoken with a number of women whose names had been given to me—they had all gone through abortions and wished they hadn't. She said she appreciated talking to them but was very disturbed about telling her parents. I should have made her call her dad right then. But I just didn't have the energy to argue anymore. The next morning, she had the abortion.

For a couple of years afterward, an hour didn't pass that I didn't think about it. I was a typical college idiot. We weren't using birth control. I went through a lot of guilt. I created a life only

for it to be destroyed out of my own stupidity. This was worse than when my brother and father died, even though this was not even a baby I could hold. My father and brother weren't my responsibility, people I had to take care of. The baby was something that was taken away from me.

Now I'm married and have a child. If any woman I was with told me she was having an abortion, I'd be gone. I couldn't go through that again.

STEPHEN, 40, graphic designer, Los Angeles, California We had two abortions. The first one was before we were married. When her doctor told her she was pregnant, we wondered, "How can we handle this?" We were just out of school. Our apartment was about the size of the *Apollo* capsule. Moreover, her father was coming from across the country to be here for the wedding. She told me, "I cannot walk down the aisle with my father and be five months pregnant."

It was a hard decision, and I'm still not comfortable with it. The second pregnancy happened the following year. This time, she'd gone in to have a chest X ray as part of a medical exam for her new job—and we found out we were pregnant. But she'd just been irradiated. So this went back and forth in our heads: "Are we ready to be parents now? We're in a very small apartment. We have no money. The kid has just been irradiated." But again it boiled down to a question of

convenience. I had a say, but I did not exercise it the way I could have. If she'd wanted to keep the child, I'd have agreed, because that was what was in my heart. So there's a part of me that took the coward's way out.

Today, we have a daughter, and she was fully planned. She has this charming little face. I never thought that seven and a half pounds could make me so happy. My daughter is in diapers now, but some day she's going to be 19. And I've decided that if she says to me, "Dad, I'm pregnant, what should I do?" I will extend her an option—"If you want to drop out of school and carry this kid to term and put the child up for adoption, that is no problem here."

Sometimes I'll get depressed and this will surface. It's very unnerving. I don't know how to make peace with this question, and I don't think confessing it helps. None of my friends know. My family doesn't know. My friends would shrug their shoulders and say, "It happens." Simple words for such a big question.

I believe in God. I wonder if I'm going to go to hell over it. My wife is Catholic, but she says she doesn't think about the abortions. Once she said: "Sometimes I worry about myself. It was such a matter-of-fact decision for me, and I've never thought twice about it. When I talk to women who struggle with it, I wonder what I've done wrong."

I say, "I'm not sure you've done anything wrong. I would say your position is somewhat enviable."

Sexuality through the Life Cycle

- **Youth and Their Sexuality (Articles 35–37)**

- **Sexuality in the Adult Years (Articles 38–43)**

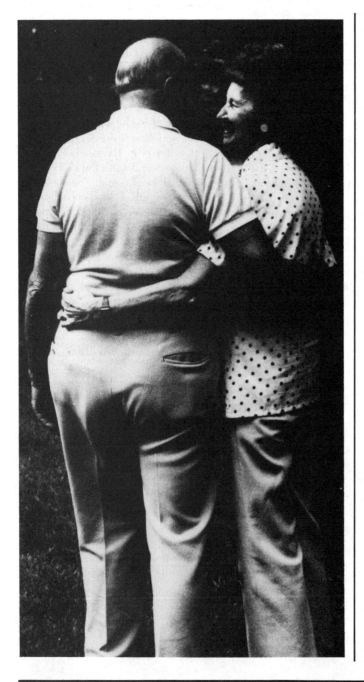

Individual sexual development is a lifelong process that begins at birth and terminates at death. Contrary to popular notions of this process, there are no latent periods during which the individual is nonsexual or noncognizant of sexuality. The growing process of a sexual being does, however, reveal qualitative differences through various life stages. This section devotes attention to these stages of the life cycle and their relation to sexuality.

As children gain self-awareness, they naturally explore their own bodies, masturbate, display curiosity for the bodies of the opposite sex, and show interest in the bodies of mature individuals such as their parents. Exploration and curiosity are important and healthy aspects of human development. Yet it is often difficult for adults (who live in a society that is not comfortable with sexuality in general) to avoid making their children feel ashamed of being sexual or showing interest in sexuality. When adults impose their ambivalence upon a child's innocuous explorations into sexuality, fail to communicate with children about this real and important aspect of human life, or behave toward children in sexually inappropriate ways, distortion of an indispensable and formative stage of development occurs. This often leaves profound emotional scars that hinder full acceptance of self and sexuality later in the child's life.

Adolescence, the social status accompanying puberty and the transition to adulthood, proves to be a very stressful period of life for many individuals as they attempt to develop an adult identity and forge relationships with others. Because of the physiological capacity of adolescents for reproduction, sexuality tends to be heavily censured by parents and society at this stage of life. Yet individual and societal attitudes place tremendous emphasis on sexual attractiveness—especially for females—and sexual competency—especially for males. These physical, emotional, and cultural pressures combine to create confusion and anxiety in adolescents and young adults about whether they are okay or normal. Information and assurances from adults can alleviate these stresses and facilitate positive and responsible sexual maturity if there is mutual trust and willingness in both generations.

Sexuality finally becomes socially acceptable in adulthood, at least within marriage. Yet routine, boredom, stress, pressures, the pace of life, extramarital sexual activity, and/or lack of communication can exact heavy tolls on the quantity and quality of sexual interaction. Sexual misinformation, myths, and unanswered questions, especially about emotional and/or physiological changes in sexual arousal/response or functioning, can also undermine or hinder intimacy and sexual interaction in the middle years.

Sexuality in the later years of life is also socially and culturally stigmatized because of the prevailing misconception that sex is for young, attractive, and married adults. Such an attitude is primarily responsible for the apparent decline in sexual interest and activity as one grows older. Physiological changes in the aging process are not, in and of themselves, detrimental to sexual expression. A life history of experiences, health, and growth can make sexual expression in the later years a most rewarding and fulfilling experience.

The three articles chosen for the *Youth and Sexuality* subsection address several difficult and somewhat controversial issues related to sexuality, society, and children. "How Should We Teach Our Children about Sex?" acknowledges the many, powerful, and mixed messages today's children receive about sex. Its examination of issues related to the initiation of sexual activity, the risk of AIDS/HIV, teenage childbearing, and sex education efforts leaves us with an important reminder: failure to teach children about sex harms all of society. Next, "What Do Girls See?" raises questions and concerns about gender role socialization and allows readers into the world of today's preteen and teenaged women. Finally, "Coming Out in Care" explains why Pride Place, a United Kingdom residential living option for children who are wards of the state and coming to terms with their gay, lesbian, or bisexual orientation, is a needed adjunct to more traditional community care.

Sexuality in the Adult Years deals with a variety of issues for individuals and couples who are "twentysomething," "thirtysomething," "ninetysomething," and older. "Let the Games Begin: Sex and the *Not*-Thirtysomethings" looks at 30-year-olds who are caught between their conservative safe-sex upbringing and the explicit MTV generation. Their sexual and biological clocks encourage them to "get it while you can; you are not getting any younger." The next two articles combine information of experts with some unabashedly straightforward suggestions for keep-

ing relations hot, fun, and sexy through the years, children, and changes. The third article, "Do Men Go Through Menopause?" responds to questions men and women have about midlife health and sexuality.

The final two articles focus on sexuality in what can be viewed as the sunset years. The first presents what the author, a doctor who lists his age as the late 70s, asserts doctors and others need to know about human sexuality and aging. In the process, he does a lot of myth-busting and normalizing of sexuality as a lifelong human dimension. The final article, "Sexuality and Aging: What It Means to Be Sixty or Seventy or Eighty in the '90s," is a special edition of the Mayo Clinic newsletter written for senior citizens and anyone who cares about them. It provides a wealth of information and explores the human side of the issue by including some personal experiences of people in their 60s, 70s, and beyond.

Looking Ahead: Challenge Questions

Do you remember trying to get answers about your body, sex, or similar topics as a young child? How did your parents respond? How did you feel?

As an adolescent, where did you get answers to your questions about sex? Are you still embarrassed at any lack of information you have? Why, or why not?

Would you like to be a junior high school–aged young person today? Why, or why not? In what ways is being a young teen easier than when you were that age? How is it harder? In what ways is it different being a young male? A young female? A gay or lesbian adolescent?

How do you view sex and sexuality at your age? In what ways is it different than 5 to 10 years ago? Are there things you feel you have missed? What are they?

Close your eyes and imagine a couple having a pleasurable sexual interlude. When you are done, open your eyes. How old were they? If they were younger than middle age, can you replay your vision with middle-aged or older people? Why, or why not? How does this relate to your expectations regarding your own romantic and/or sexual life a few decades from now?

What do you know about the aging process and how it affects sexuality? Do you worry about growing older and losing sexual desire or sexual attractiveness? Why, or why not?

How Should We Teach Our Children About SEX?

Bombarded by mixed messages about values, students are more sexually active than ever, and more confused

Nancy Gibbs

SOME INGREDIENTS IN THE STEAMING HORMONAL STEW THAT IS American adolescence:

For Prom Night last week, senior class officers at Benicia High School in California assembled some party favors—a gift-wrapped condom, a Planned Parenthood pamphlet advocating abstinence and a piece of candy. "We know Prom Night is a big night for a lot of people, sexually," senior Lisa Puryear told the San Jose *Mercury News.* "We were trying to spread a little responsible behavior." But administrators confiscated the 375 condoms, arguing that the school-sponsored event is no place for sex education.

Fifty students in Nashville, Tennessee, stand in front of a gathering of Baptist ministers to make a pledge: "Believing that true love waits, I make a commitment to God, myself, my family, those I date, my future mate and my future children to be sexually pure until the day I enter a covenant marriage relationship."

Tonya, 17, began having sex when she was 12, but rarely uses a condom. "I know a lot of people who have died of AIDS," she says, "but I'm not that worried." Every six months she gets an AIDS test. "The only time I'm worried is right before I get the results back."

Last Wednesday the student leaders at Bremerton High in Seattle voted that no openly gay student could serve in their school government. The goal, they stated, was "to preserve the integrity and high moral standards that BHS is built upon."

Teenagers in York County, Pennsylvania, celebrate the Great Sex-Out, a sex-free day to reflect on abstinence. Among activities suggested as alternatives to sex are baking cookies and taking moonlit walks. Since the event was held on a Monday, it wasn't much of a problem. But Friday, said one student, "that would be harder."

Owen, 19, of Kill Devil Hills, North Carolina, carries a key chain bearing the inscription, A TISKET, A TASKET, A CONDOM OR A CASKET.

Just Do It. Just Say No. Just Wear a Condom. When it comes to sex, the message to America's kids is confused and confusing. The moral standards society once generally accepted, or at least paid lip service to, fell victim to a sexual revolution and a medical tragedy. A decade marked by fear of AIDS and furor over society's values made it hard to agree on the ethical issues and emotional context that used to be part of learning about sex. Those on the right reacted to condom giveaways and gay curriculums and throbbing MTV videos as signs of moral breakdown. Those on the left dismissed such concerns as the rantings of religious zealots and shunned almost any discussion of sexual restraint as being reactionary or, worse yet, unsophisticated. "Family values" became a polarizing phrase.

Now, however, the children of the sexual revolution are beginning to grapple with how to teach their own children about sex. Faced with evidence that their kids are suffering while they bicker, parents and educators are seeking some common ground about what works and what doesn't. It is becoming possible to discuss the need for responsibility and commitment without being cast as a religious fanatic and to accept the need for safe-sex instruction without being considered an amoral pragmatist.

In one sense, the arrival of AIDS in the American psyche a decade ago ended the debate over sex education. Health experts were clear about the crisis: By the time they are 20, three-quarters of young Americans have had sex; one-fourth of teens contract some venereal disease each year. About 20% of all AIDS patients are under 30, but because the incubation period is eight years or more, the CDC believes a large proportion were infected with HIV as teenagers.

In such a climate of fear, moral debate seemed like a luxury. Get them the information, give them protection, we can talk about morality later. There is a fishbowl full of condoms in the nurse's office, help yourself. While only three states mandated sex ed in 1980, today 47 states formally require or recommend it; all 50 support AIDS education.

But as parents and educators watch the fallout from nearly a decade of lessons geared to disaster prevention—here is a diagram of female anatomy, this is how you put on a condom—

there are signs that this bloodless approach to learning about sex doesn't work. Kids are continuing to try sex at an ever more tender age: more than a third of 15-year-old boys have had sexual intercourse, as have 27% of 15-year-old girls—up from 19% in 1982. Among sexually active teenage girls, 61% have had multiple partners, up from 38% in 1971. Among boys, incidents like the score-keeping Spur Posse gang in California and the sexual-assault convictions of the Glen Ridge, New Jersey, jock stars suggest that whatever is being taught, responsible sexuality isn't being learned.

Beyond what studies and headlines can convey, it is the kids who best express their confusion and distress. Audrey Lee, 15, has taken a sex-education class at San Leandro High School in California, but, she asserts, "there's no real discussion about emotional issues and people's opinions." The program consists mostly of films and slides with information on sex and birth control. It lacks any give-and-take on issues like date rape and how to say no to sexual pressure. "The school doesn't emphasize anything," she says. "If you have a question, you go to your friends, but they don't have all the answers." As for her family, "sex is not mentioned."

Adults have one foot in the Victorian era while kids are in the middle of a world-wide pandemic," complains pediatrician Karen Hein, of Albert Einstein College of Medicine in New York City, who has seen too many teens infected with HIV and other sexually transmitted diseases come through her hospital. She laments the fact that sex ed is only "about vaginas, ovaries and abstinence—not about intimacy and expressing feelings." Kids, she says, "don't know what they're supposed to be doing, and adults are really not helping them much."

America has long wrestled with the tension between its Puritan and pioneer heritages, and its attitude toward sex has often seemed muddled. Victorian parents, fearful of their children's sexuality, would try to delay the onset of puberty by underfeeding their children. By 1910 exploding rates of syphilis drove the crusade for sex education in much the way AIDS does today. In 1940 the U.S. Public Health Service argued the urgent need for schools to get involved, and within a few years the first standardized programs rolled into classrooms. But by the 1960s came the backlash from the John Birch Society, Mothers Organized for Moral Stability and other groups. By the early '70s they had persuaded at least 20 state legislatures to either restrict or abolish sex education.

"There's something wrong," sex educator Sol Gordon once said, "with a country that says, 'Sex is dirty, save it for someone you love.'" But families at least agreed on a social standard that preached, if not practiced, the virtues of restraint and of linking sex to emotional commitment and marriage. "It used to be easy to say it's just wrong to have sex before marriage. You could expect churches to say that, adults from many walks of life to somehow communicate that," notes Peter Benson, president of Minneapolis-based Search Institute, a research organization specializing in child and adolescent issues. "We went through a sexual revolution since the '60s that poked a major hole in that. And nothing has come along to replace it. What's responsible sexuality now? Does it mean no sex unless you're in love? No sex unless you're 21? No sex unless it's protected?

Nothing approaching a consensus has emerged to guide kids in their decisions. A TIME/CNN poll of 500 U.S. teenagers found that 71% had been told by their parents to wait until they were older before having sex: more than half had been told not to have sex until they were married. The teens were almost evenly split between those who say it is O.K. for kids ages 16 and under to have sex and those who say they should be 18 or older.

Some social scientists argue that there is nothing wrong with increased sexual expression among teens. "Feeling, thinking and being sexual is an endemic part of being a teenager," says UCLA psychologist Paul Abramson. "Let's say a couple has paired off, wants to be monogamous and uses condoms. I'd say that's a legitimate part of their sexual expression as a couple in the '90s."

There are many factors, besides increased permissiveness, that make the trend toward increased casual sex among kids seem almost inevitable. Since the turn of the century, better health and nutrition have lowered the average age of sexual maturity. The onset of menstruation in girls has dropped three months each decade, so the urges that once landed at 14 may now hit at 12. At the same time, the years of premarital sexual maturity are much greater than a generation ago. The typical age of a first marriage has jumped to 25, from 21 in the 1950s.

School cutbacks and working parents have left teens with a looser after-school life. Many use that time for afternoon jobs, but less to pay for college than for a car, for freedom and the chance to socialize more with peers, who may pressure each other into ever greater sexual exploration. Sandra, 17, in Des Moines, Iowa, pregnant and due in November, says she has slept with 33 boys. She keeps count and doesn't think her behavior is all that unusual. "A lot of girls do the same. They think if they don't have sex with a person, that person will not want to talk to them anymore."

In the inner cities the scarcity of jobs and hope for the future invites kids to seek pleasure with little thought for the fallout. "You'd think AIDS would be a deterrent, but it's not," says Marie Bronshvag, a health teacher at West Side High School in upper Manhattan. Their lives are empty, she observes, and their view of the future fatalistic. "I believe in God," says student Mark Schaefer, 19. "If he wants something bad to happen to me, it will happen. Anyway, by the time I get AIDS I think they'll have a cure."

Nor is fear of pregnancy any more compelling. "The kids feel," says Margaret Pruitt Clark, executive director of the Center for Population Options, "that the streets are so violent that they are either gonna be dead or in jail in their 20s, so why not have a kid." Most striking, she adds, is the calculation that young women in the inner cities are making. "They feel that if the number of men who will be available to them as the years go on will be less and less, the girls might as well have a child when they can, no matter how young they are."

Finally, there is the force that is easiest to blame and hardest to measure: the saturation of American popular culture with sexual messages, themes, images, exhortations. Teenagers typically watch five hours of television a day—which in a year means they have seen nearly 14,000 sexual encounters, according to the Center for Population Options. "Kids are seeing a

How often did you use birth control when you had sex?*

Every time	61%
Sometimes	26%
Never	13%

*Asked only of teens who said they have had sexual intercourse.

Where have you learned the most about sex?

13-15	**AGE 16-17**
Parents	
30%	22%
Friends	
26%	37%
School	
26%	15%
Entertainment	
15%	18%

From a telephone poll of 500 American teenagers (age 13 to 17) taken for TIME/CNN on April 13-14 by Yankelovich Partners Inc. Sampling error is ± 4.5%.

Have you ever had sexual intercourse?

YES

Age 13-15	19%
Age 16-17	55%

How old were you when you first had sex?*

Under 14	23%
14	24%
16	20%
17	6%

How many different people have you had sex with?*

1	42%
2 to 3	29%
4	6%
5 or more	15%

*Asked only of those 151 teens who said they had had sexual intercourse.
Sampling error ± 8%.

What are the reasons kids you know have sex?**

GIRLS	**BOYS**
They were curious and wanted to experiment	
80%	76%
They wanted to be more popular or impress their friends	
58%	58%
They were in love	
65%	50%
They were under pressure from those they were dating	
65%	35%

**Asked only of those 373 teens who know another teen who has had sexual intercourse. Sampling error is ± 5%.

world in which everything is sensual and physical," says Dr. Richard Ratner, who this week takes office as president of the American Society for Adolescent Psychiatry. "Even in this era of feminism, rap songs preach, 'Take this bitch and ——— her.' Everything is more explicit. It's the difference between wearing a bathing suit and walking around nude."

The content of popular culture has been a favorite target among politicians caught up in the culture wars, but kids themselves have their own criticisms of what they see. Many recoil at the sexual pressures they feel from Calvin Klein ads, MTV, heavy-breathing movies, all the icy, staged or oddball sex they see in books by Madonna and rock videos. "If you turn on TV, there's a woman taking off her clothes," says Marcela Avila, a senior at Santa Monica High, who was among a group of students who sat down with TIME's Jim Willwerth to discuss the sexual landscape they face. "It makes you doubt yourself. Am I O.K.? You put yourself down—I'll never be able to satisfy a guy." Her classmate Elizabeth Young agrees. "The media doesn't make it seem like it's really about love," she says. "Nowadays sexuality is the way you look, the way you wear your hair. It's all physical, not what's inside you."

Many kids, who can be lethal critics of the sexual mores of their parents' generation, say they are offended that adults have so little faith in them. "Not all teenagers have sex. They're not all going to do it just because everyone else is," says Kristen Thomas, 17, of Plymouth, Minnesota. "They kind of have a lack of faith in us—parents and general society."

Traditionally, it's been the role of parents to convey the messages about love and intimacy that kids seem to be missing in their education about sex. Although today's parents are the veterans of the decade that came after free love and before safe sex, that doesn't automatically make them any more able to *talk* about sex with their children; if anything, the reverse may be true. Hypocrisy is a burden they carry. "Do as I say," they instruct their teenagers, "not as I did."

As for those who sat out the sexual revolution, they may be too embarrassed or intimidated to talk to teens—or afraid of giving the wrong information. Phyllis Shea, director of teen programs for the Worcester, Massachusetts, affiliate of Girls Inc. (formerly Girls Clubs of America), recently ran a sex-education workshop for 12 girls and their mothers. In many cases, she says, mothers lag far behind their daughters in knowledge. Five of the mothers had never seen a condom. A mother who had been completely unwilling to discuss sex with her daughter told the group that she had been molested as a child. On the way home, she and her daughter drove around for two hours, deep in conversation.

O f all the mixed messages that teenagers absorb, the most confused have to do with gender roles. The stereotypes of male and female behavior have crumbled so quickly over the past generation that parents are at a loss. According to the TIME/CNN poll, 60% of parents tell their daughters to remain chaste until marriage, but less than half tell their sons the same thing. Kids reflect the double standard: more than two-thirds agree that a boy who has sex sees his reputation enhanced, while a girl who has sex watches hers suffer.

That is not stopping girls from acting as sexual aggressors, however. Teenagers in TIME's survey say girls are just as interested in sex as boys are—an opinion confirmed by recent research. "My friends and I are a lot less inhibited about saying what we want to do," says Rebecca Tuynman of Santa Monica High. "A lot of the change is admitting that we like it." Tuynman says that while she was taught that boys don't like girls who come on too strong, her brother set her straight. "He said he'd like it if girls came after him. I'll always be grateful to him for saying that." Her classmate Tammy Weisberger notes that like so many boy jocks, girls on her soccer team brag about whom they've slept with—but with a difference. "The guys say how many girls they did it with. With the girls, it's *who* they did it with."

For all the aggressive girl talk, some experts are worried that what the sexual revolution has really done for teenage girls is push them into doing things they may not really want to do. "The irony is that the sexual revolution pressured girls into accepting sex on boys' terms," argues Myriam Miedzian, author of *Boys Will Be Boys: Breaking the Link Between Masculinity and Violence.* "If they don't engage in sex, they're not cool. At least under the old morality, girls had some protection. They could say their parents would kill them if they had sex."

As for boys, researchers are finding that among parents, the fear that their son will grow up to be aggressively promiscuous is nothing compared with the fear he will turn out to be gay. Manhattan social worker Joy Fallek has seen boys who fear that they might be gay if they haven't had sex with a girl by age 16. Parents have told Miedzian that they will not let their boys watch TV's Mr. Rogers because of his gentle demeanor. "This is a major barrier to parents' raising their sons to be caring and sensitive people," she contends. "Other parents have told me that they're afraid not to have their sons play with guns because they'll grow up gay. And yet there's not the slightest shred of evidence for this."

Schools are attempting to fill in where parents have failed. But it has been hard for educators over these past few years to know what to teach when society itself cannot agree on a direction. Absent any agreement over what is "proper" sexual conduct, teachers can be left reciting, word for word, the approved text on homosexuality or abortion or masturbation. The typical sex-ed curriculum is remarkably minimalist. Most secondary schools offer somewhere between 6 and 20 hours of sex education a year. The standard curriculum now consists of one or two days in fifth grade dealing with puberty; two weeks in an eighth-grade health class dealing with anatomy, reproduction and AIDS prevention, and perhaps a 12th-grade elective course on current issues in sexuality.

Joycelyn Elders, President Clinton's nominee for Surgeon General, is leading the fight for a more comprehensive approach from kindergarten through 12th grade. As head of the Arkansas health department, she was one of the country's most outspoken advocates of wide-ranging sex education. "We've spent all our time fighting each other about whose values we should be teaching our kids," she complains. "We've [been]

allowed the right to make decisions about our children for the last 100 years, and all it has bought us is the highest abortion rate, the highest nonmarital birth rate and the highest pregnancy rate in the industrialized world." But Elders is no advocate of values-free instruction. "Proper sex education would be teaching kids to develop relationships and about the consequences of their behavior. Kids can't say no if they don't first learn how to feel good about themselves."

But the issue of teaching kids about sex remains politically explosive. This week the results are expected to be announced in an unusually bitter election for New York City community school boards in which the religious right joined with the Catholic Church to try to elect more tradition-minded representatives. Earlier this year, the system's highly regarded Chancellor Joseph Fernandez was ousted largely because of his effort to expand condom distribution and teach children about gay lifestyles. The New York City Board of Education last week chose as its new president a conservative Queens mother who had cast the deciding vote against the chancellor.

If there is one point of agreement among all parties in the debate, it is that sex education has to be about more than sex. The anatomy lesson must come in a larger context of building relationships based on dignity and respect. The message these programs have in common: learn everything you want and need to know, and then carefully consider waiting.

Some of the most innovative and successful efforts have been launched by private religious and social-service organizations. Girls Inc., with 165 chapters nationwide, launched Preventing Adolescent Pregnancy (PAP) in 1985 to help low-income teens avoid cycles of early pregnancy, poverty and hopelessness. The first section, called Growing Together, invites girls ages 12 to 14 to talk over issues of sexuality with their mothers. The second section, Will Power/Won't Power, is designed to help girls develop strategies for postponing sexual activity and preventing pregnancy. "It's our experience that kids this age really know it's too early to be having sex," says Heather Johnston Nicholson, director of the National Resource Center for Girls Inc., in Indianapolis. "But when you're that age, you don't want to be considered a complete dweeb. We're establishing a peer group that says it's O.K. not to be sexually active."

In the third segment, Taking Care of Business, 15- to 17-year-olds are encouraged to focus on their goals. The final step, Health Bridge, helps older teens establish ties with a community clinic to ensure that they will have continued access to affordable reproductive health care. "It gives kids an opportunity to think through the reasons for not becoming sexually active," says Nicholson. But she cautions that "this is not a Just Say No program. When kids ask questions, they get straight answers. While we're focusing on postponement, we're not doing it in a context of fear and scare tactics."

That approach distinguishes PAP from the more hard-line abstinence programs that are gaining ground all across the country (*see box*). While both types of programs are designed to help teens make healthy decisions, there remains a fault line over whether to include detailed information on contraception or to focus on abstinence in a way that assumes that no lessons on applying condoms will be necessary.

Making the Case for Abstinence

By Philip Elmer-Dewitt

AMID ALL THE ANGUISH, CONFUSION AND MIXED SIGNALS surrounding teenage sexuality, the simplicity of one group's message is striking: sex outside marriage is just plain wrong. To instruct children in the mechanics of birth control or abortion, it argues, is to lead them down the path of self-destruction. That's the philosophy of the abstinence-only movement, a coalition of conservative parents, teachers and religious groups that, in the absence of any national sex-education consensus, has been remarkably successful in having its approach adopted as the official curriculum in schools across the U.S.

But is it the best approach? Its adherents claim the message is both morally correct and demonstrably effective. Opponents argue that in an age in which most teenagers are already sexually active, preaching the case for chastity without teaching the case for condoms is dangerously naive. "All the parents I know are absolutely in favor of abstinence," says Carole Chervin, senior staff attorney for the Planned Parenthood Federation. "It's the abstinence *only* approach that's bothersome. We believe sex education should be comprehensive."

The fight has moved into the courts. In what could become a landmark case, Planned Parenthood of Northeast Florida and 21 citizens in Duval County, Florida, have sued the local school board for rejecting a broad-based sex-education curriculum developed by the board's staff in favor of a controversial abstinence-only program from Teen-Aid, Inc. of Spokane, Washington. Planned Parenthood complains that the material in the text is biased, sensationalist and, at times, misleading. Some school-board members argue that the real issue is whether the local community has the right to choose the sex-education curriculum it wants, however flawed.

Late last week a similar case in Shreveport, Louisiana, went against the abstinence-only movement when a district judge ruled that a prochastity text called "Sex Respect" was biased and inaccurate and ordered it pulled from the Caddo-Parish junior high schools. The court is scheduled to rule this week on the fate of the abstinence-only text still being used in the high schools.

Abstinence is hardly a new idea, but the organized abstinence-only movement dates back to a Reagan-era program that set aside $2 million a year for the development of classroom materials to teach adolescents to say no to sex. Today there are more than a dozen competing curriculums on the market, each offering lesson plans, activities and workbook exercises designed to encourage abstinence among teenagers.

"Sex Respect," developed by Project Respect in Golf, Illinois, is one of the most widely used, having been adopted by a couple of thousand schools nationwide. Class activities include listing ways humans are different from animals, making bumper stickers that read CONTROL YOUR URGIN'/ BE A VIRGIN, and answering multiple-choice test questions about what kinds of situations put pressure on teens to have sex. The teacher's manual features a section on sexual messages in the media, a list of suggested alternatives to sex when on dates (bicycling, dinner parties, playing Monopoly) and a chapter on "secondary virginity"—the decision to stop having sex until marriage, even after one is sexually experienced.

Missing from the Sex Respect curriculum is the standard discussion of the comparative effectiveness of various birth-control methods found in most sex-education courses. Furthermore, it fails to offer any follow-up programs, outside counseling or guidance for teens who might become pregnant or contract a sexually transmitted disease. Kathleen Sullivan, director of Project Respect, defends her program: "We give the students a ton of information," she says. "We point out, for example, the tremendous failure rate of condoms."

One argument put forward for abstinence-only programs is that they work. Sullivan cites a study conducted by Project Respect showing that pregnancy rates among students who have taken the course are 45% lower than among those who have not. But critics say none of these studies have been reviewed by outside scientists and wonder whether any will bear close scrutiny. The San Diego *Union* looked into one of the most widely reported success stories—that the Teen-Aid program lowered the rate of pregnancy at a San Marcos, California, high school from 147 to only 20 in two years—and reported that while the 147 figure was well documented, the number 20 had apparently been made up.

The argument most often used against abstinence-only programs is that they are a thinly disguised effort to impose fundamentalist religious values on public-school students and thus violate the constitutional separation of church and state. Some of the texts started out as religious documents and were rewritten to replace references to God and Jesus with nonsectarian words like goodness and decency. Still, it makes little sense to criticize the programs simply because they originate from a religious perspective; what matters is not where the courses came from but what they say.

That's the real issue with the Teen-Aid text at the center of the Florida lawsuit. In making the case for chastity, Teen-Aid has asserted, among other things, that "the only way to avoid pregnancy is to abstain from genital contact" and that the "correct use of condoms does not prevent HIV infection but only delays it." Most teens don't need a school course to know that neither of those statements is correct. How are they going to believe in abstinence if those who preach don't have their facts straight?

—Reported by Lisa H. Towle/Raleigh

At least a dozen abstinence-based curriculums are on the market; one of the largest, Sex Respect, is used in about 2,000 schools around the country. What Sex Respect does not include is standard information about birth control, which prompts some critics to charge that purely abstinence-based programs are inadequate. Michael Carrera, who eight years ago founded a highly successful teen-pregnancy-prevention program in Harlem, deplores the "ungenerous, unforgiving" nature of some abstinence programs. "The way you make a safe, responsible abstinent decision is if you're informed, not if you're dumb." Carrera attributes the success of his program to this more comprehensive approach: in a part of Manhattan with a 50% dropout rate, 96% of Carrera's kids are still in school.

Trust Dr. Ruth Westheimer, the high priestess of pleasure, to provide parents and teens with a middle ground. She has just published *Dr. Ruth Talks to Kids,* in which she writes for ages 8 through 14. Her thesis: teach kids everything, and then encourage them to wait. "Make sure even the first kiss is a memorable experience, is what I tell kids," she says. "I don't think kids should be engaging in sex too early, not even necking and petting. I generally think age 14 and 15 is too early, in spite of the fact that by then girls are menstruating and boys may have nocturnal emissions."

Above all, she says, kids need to have their questions addressed. Learning and talking about sex do not have to mean giving permission, she insists. "On the contrary, I think that a child knowing about his or her body will be able to deal with the pressure to have sex. This child can say no, I'll wait." In fact, Westheimer is a big advocate of waiting. "I say to teenagers, What's the rush?"

—Reported by Wendy Cole, Margaret Emery and Janice M. Horowitz/New York, Lisa H. Towle/Raleigh and Marc Hequet/St. Paul

What Do Girls See?

Kristen Golden

Kristen Golden, founder of Golden Touch Productions, is an independent film producer.

*a*t last count, there were 10 million adolescent girls in the United States. Too often teachers ignore them, boys and men harass them, women lie to them, and society downplays their needs as well as the challenges they face. What if, even for a day, everyone dropped whatever they were doing and focused on girls? Take Our Daughters to Work (TODTW)—the Ms. Foundation for Women's public education campaign to make girls "visible, valued, and heard"—captured the imagination of the country with this simple, compelling concept. As project manager coordinating the first TODTW campaign, I experienced firsthand the roller coaster of responses to making girls the center of attention. Girls were thrilled, women energized, fathers proud, employers welcoming, teachers appreciative, and the media fascinated. Those were the good days. Other times, mothers of sons were furious, fathers indifferent, employers rigid, columnists reactive, boys hostile, and teachers too overwhelmed to hear us out. The most disheartening reaction was the outcry, "What about the boys?"

The pervasive sexism that keeps attention rooted on boys and men is the foundation of many of the barriers and challenges facing young women. Adolescence is the critical point when they start reflecting on their chances as adults. "What girls see is a very powerful force in motivating and shaping their behavior," says Ruby Takanishi, executive director of the Carnegie Council on Adolescent Development.

What *do* girls see? Less opportunity in the workplace for women than for men and greater responsibility in the home, the degradation of women in the media, an absence of girls and women in school curricula, conflicting messages about female sexuality, the prevalence of racism and violence, and adults enforcing gender roles. At this juncture, girls—as documented originally by Carol Gilligan and Harvard University's project on women and girls—tend to lose their self-esteem.

According to "Reflections of Risk: Growing Up Female in Minnesota," a survey of 36,000 girls and boys issued by the Minnesota Women's Fund, adolescent girls "appear to be under more stress than boys, and to deal with the problems they face by turning them inward." While girls are often spirited and determined to survive the unique pressures of female adolescence, many emerge as adults with damaged self-confidence and low expectations. We are losing girls, quietly. But if we listen

POVERTY

More than one and a half million adolescent girls live in poverty, which creates a formidable barrier to overcome in developing effective programs. Marya Grambs, cofounder of the Girls After School Academy (GASA), is all too aware of the problems this poses. GASA is an after-school and weekend multidisciplinary program that teaches Afrocentric, woman-centered academics, economic development, and culture to young women in San Francisco's Sunnydale housing project. Grambs says: "We're in a public housing development, and while I'm sure that some of these girls are losing their self-esteem and are not good in math, those aren't the only issues. The girls that we're working with are living in a gun-ridden neighborhood, where there's a body found once a week. There are no grocery stores, movie theaters, or banks. There are not many role models who look like them and have productive and fulfilling lives. Yet despite their surroundings, these girls are vibrant, funny, energetic, and loving. It's wonderful to be among them."

Women organizing on behalf of girls living in poverty have to be especially tenacious and creative. For girls, family responsibilities often take precedence over a program that benefits only them, making consistent attendance difficult. (Studies indicate that girls are seven times more likely than boys to drop out of school for family reasons, such as needing to care for siblings, older relatives, or their own children.) To attract girls who are juggling so many constraints, programming must be concise and compelling.

Space for programming and activities is often difficult to secure. In 1992, Kathy Thurber, while vice president of the Park and Recreation Board, had to fight for prime time on Minneapolis' public basketball courts for girls in low-income areas. Once she had the space and did "extensive outreach to get lots of girls," Thurber says she had "to fight to make sure the girls weren't harassed for taking up space. There was an improvement in staff sensitivity over time but the guys were still howling outside." Despite the resistance she encountered, Thurber encourages women and girls in other cities to take public space. "When women and girls are absent, public space becomes a men's club."

The organizers of GASA also had to conduct a series of negotiations with men in the neighborhood who had taken control of the community center. "We had to win their respect and approval in order to use the space," says Grambs. "They asked us to get a GED program going for the adults of Sunnydale and we did. So now our administrative offices are in the community center." —K.G.

---

closely, we can hear them calling out to women to help them navigate the rocky waters of adolescence.

The good news is that women can make a fundamental difference. That message came across loud and clear when I talked to girls for this report. Those who seemed self-confident each had a strong, confiding relationship with a woman who talked with her openly and listened to her respectfully. But girls whose responses to my queries were painfully inaudible or simply "I don't know" tended to have little support from the adults in their lives.

While few of us are in a position to single-handedly stop the violence or change the media, each of us can give girls some of the things they want—information, autonomy, and support. But for women to impart critical information requires tremendous courage. We must be willing to tell sometimes painful truths about the realities of our lives, to speak openly and honestly about everyday forms of sexism, and how we do and do not challenge them. By preparing girls for what they are likely to encounter and affirming their capabilities, we equip them to better understand sexism, to recognize that it is not a result of their failures or worthlessness, and to develop strategies to address it.

The best news is that an exciting new girls' movement is taking shape, based on the premise that by learning to resist limiting social messages, girls can become strong, healthy young women. Fostering this movement is clearly feminist work. By listening to what girls say about their lives and becoming familiar with the terrain, we can begin to leverage resources and ensure that girls have access to the full range of life's options.

SEXUAL HARASSMENT

"I don't want to make sweeping generalizations, but the wolf-pack mentality is very important. Guys act in groups, and everyone goes along when they make fun of girls. One kid is not going to stop and say, 'Hey, guys, we're out of control.'"
—Lizzie Francis, 16, Washington, D.C.

Girls are no strangers to sexual harassment, and the perpetrators are both boys and men. In the streets, malls, movie theaters, and on a daily basis at school, girls are harassed. "Sexual harassment is a well-known secret that takes place in public every day in schools across the country," according to "Secrets in Public," the first national study of sexual harassment in schools. This joint 1993 report (by the Center for Research on Women at Wellesley College and the NOW Legal Defense and Education Fund) found sexual harassment in public and private schools a more serious problem than previously believed: 89 percent of girls said they had received sexual comments, gestures, or looks, and 83 percent reported being touched, pinched, or grabbed. Almost two thirds of the girls told their harassers to stop, and over one third resisted with physical force. Most disturbing to many is that other people were present in over two thirds of the reported incidents.

For some girls, sexual harassment may be their first foray into the thorny field of gender politics. Lizzie Francis attends the National Cathedral School, a private all-girls school in Washington, D.C. A sexual harassment prevention advocate, she ran into hostility from the boys at their brother school, St. Alban's, when she organized a joint assembly on the subject. "They were like, 'This is ridiculous. Why should we bend over backward to worry about what we say to you?'"

Lizzie thinks different tactics are needed: "If you say 'sexual harassment,' guys *and* girls will get defensive. Although it's serious, you need to approach it in a more relaxed manner. High school is too late to educate young people about the issue. We have to start in the lower grades, before girls start hanging out with guys. If you learn to deal with it when you're younger, you'll feel much stronger in later life."

VIOLENCE

"Girls got it hard. Boys don't go through the things girls go through. They don't get pregnant, they don't get raped, as most girls do. And I worry about getting killed one day, because of drugs and stuff." —Ebony Black, 14, Chicago

Violence and abuse are an integral part of daily life for many girls, giving them matter-of-fact knowledge beyond their years. In "Programmed Neglect: Not Seen, Not Heard," the Ms. Foundation report on girls' programs in the U.S., researcher and author Martha Garcia found that although girls reported high levels of violence in their lives, this ugly reality receives little programmatic attention. "Most girls have experienced gender violence," says Garcia, "but the introduction to violence has not been with their peers. Violence has been introduced in their families. Violence in families is physical, verbal, psychological and sexual abuse, and neglect."

Adults who work with girls say that sexual abuse is widespread and its impact on a girl's sense of self is devastating. But victims receive little institutional or social support. The daily struggle to survive in these situations is arduous. As Mariana Romo-Carmona, program coordinator at Project Reach, a multiracial youth program in New York City, points out: "It's exhausting for young women to function at the same time that they have to deal with continuing sexual abuse, the trauma of past sexual abuse, and maybe even preventing future abuse of younger siblings. As they are trying to find a way out for themselves, they are keenly aware that younger siblings may be abused."

Too often the situation is exacerbated by the fact that sexual abuse victims are not believed. Some family members, including mothers, consciously or unconsciously collude with the perpetrator in order to keep the family "intact." The pressure on girls who are victims of sexual abuse to remain silent is enormous. Notes Laura Watkins, executive director of the Patriots' Trail Girl Scout Council in Boston: "When sexual abuse is in the home, the consequences of reporting it are worse than enduring it. It's a really hard decision because a girl knows that if she tells, everyone will be mad at her, her family will blame her, she'll be taken out of her home, and she won't be at her school anymore."

"Verbal violence leads one thing to another. Then comes the physical part. The bruises will go away, but the emotional stuff will not. There's so much hatred and violence out there. It scares me." —Audrey Lee, 17, San Leandro, California

Girls talk about living with violence at home, at school, and on the streets. Many express rage at the pervasive influence of "gangsta" rap and its glorification of the abuse of women. The intense pressure on teenagers to be in a relationship, the prevalence of violence in the home and in our society, and the sexual stereotypes rampant in popular culture all contribute to teenage dating violence. (Studies indicate that at least 28 percent of adolescents say they have experienced physical violence in a dating relationship.) The law provides little help—only a handful of states will issue an order of protection to a female under the age of 18.

"A lot of girls don't know the meaning of date rape and violence against women. They don't know they have rights. Girls believe they did something wrong," says 17-year-old Audrey Lee, a member of the San Leandro, California, Girls Incorporated affiliate. Girls Inc., whose mission is to "make every girl strong, smart, and bold," offers innovative programs through its national network of affiliates.

Monica Watkins, 18, who also belongs to the San Leandro group, says: "When I started going to Girls Inc., I was insecure about myself. When I got beat up by my boyfriend, I thought it was O.K. Now he is out of my life. I feel powerful inside. I feel good about myself, I feel educated. I have people around me who can help me."

In New York City, Anna Toro, 18, conducts discussions on violence at young women's group meetings at Project Reach. She weaves personal stories with statistics and poses "What if?" scenarios. Toro enables the young women's opinions and experiences to flow freely, while gently guiding them toward a fuller understanding of the issue. "If you do know somebody in a battering situation, don't give up on the woman," she tells them. "Be there for her, talk to her, don't give up on her."

RACISM and SEXISM

"My mother is Vietnamese, and my father is African American. People have stereotypes about me. They think, she's Asian: she's smart, she doesn't need help. Or she's a black girl: she's likely to get pregnant."
—Monica Watkins, 18, San Leandro, California

The impact of racism and sexism is very much on the minds of young women. Page Erickson, 11, of Bradenton, Florida, says: "Our biggest problem is racism. I don't really know what to do about it because you can't change what someone thinks." Her sister, Erin, 14, agrees: "Part of it is the way you were raised and what your parents told you about race and religion. If my parents said, 'Don't like black people' or 'Only like Catholics,' I wouldn't have half the friends I have now."

Just as they are keenly aware of how racism damages individuals and society, many girls are also absolutely certain that they're not treated the same as boys, and a lot of them are resigned to the fact that boys have it easier. Boys agree. A study of elementary, middle, and high school students, conducted by the Michigan State Board of Education, showed that both girls and boys believed that males have more inherent value, and that females are expected to place highest priority on their appearance. Asked if they ever wanted to be the opposite sex, 98 percent of boys said no.

Michelle Fine, a professor of social psychology at the City University of New York (CUNY) Graduate Center, notes that "increasingly girls are asking for all-girls groups in which to try to make sense of race and gender politics." In New York City at Project Reach, single-sex groups meet once a week to work through issues of gender, race, and sexual difference: "It's explicit that the purpose of the men's group is to challenge each other on sexism, and the purpose of the women's group is to support each other," asserts Romo-Carmona.

SEXUALITY

"Parents need to understand that no matter how much they tell them no, kids will go out and experiment."
—Jessica O'Loughlin, 18, Melrose, Massachusetts

Women and girls are constantly sexualized by the media, by the law, and by men. Whether through abortion laws, sexual abuse, the threat of violence, or social constraint, our sexual agency is limited. We do not have complete control of our bodies.

"Girls shoulder the responsibility for not getting pregnant, the blame for getting pregnant, the guilt for having an abortion, and the pressure to give the child up for adoption," writes Garcia in "Programmed Neglect." The pejorative way girls' sexuality is framed may discourage them from seeking reproductive health services, even if they're sexually active, placing them at risk for pregnancy, HIV/AIDS, and other sexually transmitted diseases.

All girls need a safe space to learn about their bodies, understand their rights, and openly discuss sexuality and sexual pleasure. But the issues become even more complex for certain communities. Young lesbians have little access to accurate information about their sexuality, and what they gather from popular culture is hateful. They rarely have a confidante with whom they can compare notes, share crushes, and discuss insecurities. Often they do not reveal their sexual orientation to anyone during adolescence, because they fear the consequences in this homophobic society. The opportunities for girls with disabilities to develop healthy attitudes toward sex are even more limited. The ignorance and insensitivity of nondisabled people fuels the widespread denial of the sexuality of people with disabilities, which results in, among other things, their common omission from sex education materials and the scarcity of media images of people with disabilities in sexual contexts.

"Even though we spend most of our time in school, they are just touching bases about sex," says Monica Watkins. "Get down to it! Show us and teach us what our rights are. Young people need to understand how you can get pregnant, and about AIDS." But parents tend to be uncomfortable discussing sex with inquisitive young people, and too many don't promote sex education in schools. On average, secondary schools offer only six and a half hours a year on sex education, less than two of them on contraception and prevention of STDs. This de-spite the fact that by 1988, 27 percent of unmarried 15-year-old girls reported having had intercourse, up from 19 percent in 1982, and one in five sexually active girls use no contraception.

EDUCATION

"The teachers are constantly watching boys, so if they raise their hands, they get called on. It makes me mad."
—Jasmine Victoria, 12, New York City

Sitting in the same classroom, reading the same textbook, listening to the same teacher, boys and girls receive very different educations," write Myra and David Sadker in *Failing at Fairness: How America's Schools Cheat Girls* (Scribner's). Based on more than 25 years of research, their book reveals the unwitting bias of teachers and the steady decline of girls' potential as they advance through the educational system. In classrooms across the country, girls are encouraged to speak quietly, defer to boys, avoid math and science classes, and value neatness over participation and appearance over intelligence. As a result, says Myra Sadker, "a girl knows that she has to find the exact middle ground. She will say she got a B when she got an A—a B or a B minus is safe territory, not too brainy, not too bimbo."

In an effort to better develop girls' academic potential, the concept of all-girls classes is catching on, particularly in math and science. "Girls who are in all-girls classes say it allows them to be themselves," explains Myra Sadker. "The environment is markedly different. Girls ask a barrage of questions. When they don't get something, they

MEDIA

Girls are furious about the way women and girls are portrayed by the media. "It makes me so mad every time they say a female like First Lady Hillary Clinton is bossy," fumes Nayamka Ward, 14, of Chicago. "Women are supposed to shut up and be bimbos. That's what TV shows. They don't show female athletes."

Like many of her peers, New York City's Jasmine Victoria, 12, deplores the fact that the media rarely portray independent young women or place them at the center of attention. She scoffingly says, "Old Prince Charming is going to save the princess. In horror movies, when they're running away from the guy, women always fall. We're portrayed as weak and helpless."

Rarely visible in children's cartoons, movies, and video games, girls don't even appear on the pop culture scene until they hit puberty and become the love interests of boys and men. Then the beauty myth comes into play with waif-like models and blond women actors as belle ideal.

Most young women have very little direct access to the media. "Girls are frustrated with how they are silenced. They want a chance to tell their side without being reinterpreted by the media or adults," says the Girl Scouts' Laura Watkins. To that end a partnership between a Boston cable station and the Girl Scouts produces a totally youth-run television show, where the girls create their own media images.

One of the few places in TV land where girls can travel safely is Nickelodeon's *Nick News*. The syndicated news show, produced by award-winning journalist Linda Ellerbee, is aimed at children between the ages of 8 and 13. Says Ellerbee, "At *Nick News*, we're in a place to be a real champion for girls. We are not only showing girls doing unstereotypical things, but we are also showing girls as the norm."

—K.G.

ask for an explanation. Sometimes the classes may move more slowly, but if they're excited to learn, it's worth it."

The Marin Academy in northern California was one of the first schools to initiate an all-girls algebra class. Evelyn Flory, the associate headmaster at the private academy, told the New York *Times*: "It may not be the solution to the world's problems, but it seems to be serving our young women." Although its legality in public schools has yet to be determined, Isabel Stewart, national executive director of Girls Inc., says: "I'm thoroughly in favor of providing the option of all-girls classes. I'm a product of an all-girls high school and college, and for ten years I lived at Spelman College." Marie C. Wilson, president of the Ms. Foundation, concurs: "All-girls classes are the way to go. Think of the stages of people moving through oppression. People need their own caucus first to figure out who they are, and then they come together with others."

But CUNY professor Michelle Fine believes the notion of all-girls classes avoids the key issue. She says: "Maybe girls have the opportunity to learn more, but where is the male accountability? It's as if we all believe that male public social violence can't be controlled." And Myra Sadker cautions: "Girls also need to be more responsible for their own empowerment. They need to know that getting a good grade, sitting quietly in the back, doesn't do it. Girls need to learn to express themselves, which is mostly what you do out in the real world."

HEALTH

"It's easy for someone to say don't starve yourself. But why not? Your friends are skinny. If guys are like, 'she's a cow,' why not? If the images from modeling are adult women in baby-doll dresses wearing Mary Jane shoes, why not? My school is rampant with eating disorders." —Lizzie Francis

Good health, both physical and psychological, is fundamental to girls' ability to meet all their other challenges. Social and economic issues, changing health needs, lack of information, low self-esteem, and few resources targeting health create a number of enormous hurdles. And so many of the factors that stand in the way of girls' good health—poverty and violence, racism and sexism—point directly to the need for major social and economic reforms, all of which require women's action. In addition to our political action, women can assist girls greatly by talking openly with them about their bodies, setting an example by living healthily ourselves, and guiding them through the maze of the medical community.

As they hit puberty, girls encounter a whole host of new health needs. They often feel betrayed by their bodies. At a time when they are internalizing messages to be thin, lean, and angular, their bodies are gaining fat and acquiring curves. It is at this point that they are often discouraged from playing sports and eating heartily. Small wonder that they are twice as likely as boys to experience depression, which is often linked to dissatisfaction with their appearance. "Reflections of Risk: Growing Up Fe-

male in Minnesota" found that girls were more than twice as likely as boys to have a negative body image. This tyranny of slenderness drives many young women to abuse their bodies in a variety of ways: constant dieting or fasting, use of stimulants or diet pills, and smoking.

Drug use among teens is rampant, and girls' low self-esteem plays a critical role in their vulnerability to addiction. Research shows that they are likely to be introduced to illicit drugs by guys, usually within the context of dating, and few use drugs when they're alone. Girls Inc. has the only national substance abuse prevention program that addresses the specific needs of girls. It teaches 12- to 14-year-olds about the dangers of substance abuse as well as how to walk away from precarious situations and still maintain their cool. They are then certified to teach younger girls. "At an age when girls are feeling they want to belong, it's a powerful experience for them to go into a classroom where the little kids are wide-eyed and adoring," says Isabel Stewart of Girls Inc. This helps strengthen the older girls' resolve to avoid drug and alcohol abuse.

The rate of teen pregnancy in the U.S. is nearly the highest in the industrialized world. Each year more than one million teenagers become pregnant, and 50 percent of those pregnancies result in births. Teen pregnancy programs are the most funded type of girls' programs. That nearly all messages about the issue are directed at girls only reinforces the double standard that places reproductive responsibility solely on women's shoulders. And this approach fails to adequately address the fact that adolescent pregnancy is due not just to a lack of information about sex or birth control. It is also a result of poverty, minimal options, and gender oppression. Any serious attempt to curb teenage pregnancy has to focus on the full range of issues and conditions that contribute to the problem. As Martha Garcia points out, "It's too simplistic an answer to say, 'Let's just teach them not to get pregnant.'"

The fact that teenagers make up the fastest growing population of new AIDS cases only intensifies the burdens. Says Garcia: "Girls talk about AIDS, think about AIDS. Girls who are dating are afraid. They know that guys sleep around. And girls are into exploring their sexuality. They want to try it, but they don't want to die."

More than anything, says Jessica O'Loughlin, 18, from Melrose, Massachusetts, "kids need a confidential place, to be able to ask questions and get answers." Jessica, a Girl Scout who achieved her gold award for a project in AIDS education, believes strongly that high schools should make condoms available and set up on-site teen health centers.

JOIN THE MOVEMENT

The status of girls in this country is extremely precarious. They struggle to survive in a society that openly discriminates against them and offers them little institutional support. Less than 8 percent of all programs provide services to girls between the critical ages of 9 and 15; even fewer provide separate, safe space. Too many projects and services tend to have a single-issue focus, requiring girls to check their other concerns at the door, while too few address the issues that face girls of color, girls with disabilities, or young lesbians. Project Reach in New York City is one that has a space for lesbian and gay youth and integrates antiracism, antihomophobia and anti-ableism training into its curriculum. On a national level, the YWCA has developed a range of programs that reflect its mission to eliminate racism.

Yet, despite the obstacles that surround them, many girls remain resilient and optimistic. What shores them up? The Ms. Foundation hopes to find out—and thereby discover the key to physical and psychological health for all girls. "We need to think of resilient girls as girls who hold onto their voices," says president Marie Wilson. "They develop a sense of authority and learn to assess the situations where they can bring it out. They learn to become strategic. They learn how to survive."

What strategies and interventions make meaningful changes in girls' lives? Girls and the adults who work with them agree that developing skills and competence can provide the courage and confidence missing from their socialization. Like many girls who have been involved with groups that offer skills-building, Jessica O'Loughlin is clear about the benefits. She says: "Girl Scouts makes me more of a well-rounded person. It gives me the self-confidence to say no to peer pressure, and gives me the power to make well-thought-out decisions."

Advocacy work, particularly within their own communities, enables girls to develop self-reliance and learn innumerable skills. But girls also need a safe space where they can be themselves and have a confiding relationship with an adult who is willing to tell them the truth. For example, Picture This, a popular Chicago-based project that pairs girls with professional women photographers, is cited more for the relational than technical experiences it provides. Fourteen-year-old Nayamka Ward says: "We can talk to the coaches about things. I like not only talking about photography but girl stuff like pregnancy, sex, money, and jobs."

As Girls Inc. director Isabel Stewart says, "If a girl can have someone she trusts telling her the truth about the options and pitfalls she faces, she feels more confident to face the world." Women aren't the only adults needed for this work. Judy Patrick, the director of Girls Count, an advocacy group in Colorado, also urges fathers to get involved. "A father encouraging his daughter to learn skills rather than helplessness will impact all her relationships with men."

Working with girls is exhausting. They demand high energy, long hours, and no bullshit. And if they think you're not really listening, they'll shut down on you in a minute. "When I led a group on my own, it blew away all my concepts of teenagers even though I was one," explains Cindy Monheim, 20, an intern working at a Girls Inc. affiliate in Rapid City, South Dakota. "I thought the girls would be interested in what I had to say, and that we would stick to the half-hour slots that I planned. I stunk. It was a horrible feeling. I didn't know what I did wrong. After the second day, I gave up the security of schedules and plans. I realized that everybody needs to have a say in what we do, and we have to go with whatever happens. I'm now a hands-off leader."

Developing trust and strong bonds between girls and women is critically important—and especially challenging because of the messages that say that women are not trustworthy and that pit women against one another. Girls want to connect with women but often think they're gutsier than the women in their lives. "Women have to show girls what women can do," says Lizzie Francis. "Demonstrate that the women's movement isn't over. Show us women who are happy with their lives."

Women and men who care about girls must work to create a better future for girls by making their safety our primary goal. Without that, all other freedoms become irrelevant. We need to show girls that we value them for what they think and do, not how they look. We have to vastly increase the resources, programs, and opportunities available to girls.

Girls ask that women act with personal courage. All the time. For all our rhetoric of equality, girls see what we do, more than what we say, as a cue to women's possibilities. As you go through your day, remember: girls are watching you. What are they learning about being a woman?

Coming Out in Care

The first independent care home in Birmingham, Pride Place, offers young lesbian and gay people a safe and supportive home.

Sarah Knibbs

Coming out as a gay person is hard. But for young people in care it can be almost intolerable. They often face bullying from their peers while adults tell them they are just going through a phase. But Pride Place, a new project in Birmingham [U.K.], aims to offer supportive residential care to young people who identify themselves as lesbian or gay.

Pride Place is a six-bedroomed home offering residential and respite care including preparation for fostering or independent living. Standing in a leafy suburban street, the house has been decorated to look as different as possible from the sort of institution young people in care are used to.

Service manager James Finnegan is keen that it looks and feels like 'just another house in the community'. The staff at Pride Place argue that for lesbians and gay men the care system is permeated with fear.

Terry Beavington, one of the project's service managers, says: 'The majority are not out because they feel unsafe.' And this fear also affects people who work in the system. 'You feel you have to choose your career or choose yourself,' says team leader Gerry Want. Beavington adds: 'Staff function better as people and professionals when they haven't got to hide.'

Pride Place's mixed staff team includes people who can emphathise and act as role models. 'We are here and we are out and in authority,' says Beavington, 'and that is what is mainly lacking in the statutory and voluntary sectors.'

The victimisation of young lesbians and gay men is an all too common experience in the care system. Homophobic insults are often tolerated by staff. One person had 'AIDS boy' scrawled on his door. Others have found broken glass or excrement in their beds. One young man said he ran away because he felt safer on the streets than he did in care.

Beavington argues: 'On the street they may get involved in risky situations because it is the only way to express themselves sexually or have contact with the commercial gay scene and, also, it is a means of survival.'

By the time a young person arrives at Pride Place they are likely to have experienced many changes. There may be a history of failed foster placements, absconding or living in appropriate specialist care institutions. According to Want: 'By the time the young people reach us, they arrive with a sorry attitude about themselves and society.'

'By the time the young people reach us, they arrive with a sorry attitude about themselves and society'

Social services departments send clients with objectives they want to see fulfilled, but the client's own priorities are also addressed from the assessment stage onwards.

Day-to-day decisions are also made through negotiation and their dignity is respected in ways that are sometimes lacking in institutions—individual's bedrooms, for example, are not entered without permission.

The staff feel that with the young person's sexual identity no longer a major issue, they have more chance of helping them cope with the reasons for them ending up in care in the first place.

Preparation for leaving the care system is an important part of the project's work. Beavington says: 'It is not just about teaching them the usual things like how to pay a bill, it is about knowing what is safe and unsafe.'

The project has a system of mentors who can help support a young person, add to their social education, and act as an advocate if necessary.

As the first independent care home in Birmingham, Pride Place is working in partnership with the SSD. Its registration is currently being completed and some interested SSDs are waiting to make referrals.

Local authorities may be nervous of falling foul of section 28, which says they must not 'actively promote' homosexuality. But the notorious and vaguely worded section will not affect Pride Place's work, since it deals with people who identify themselves as lesbian or gay and is not encouraging people to do anything other than to live safely and within the law.

Political nervousness surrounds attitudes to adolescent sexuality. And as the recent age of consent debate for gay men reflected, it is difficult for adults to accept young people they know are gay or lesbian. But the Children Act, which does mention young lesbian and gay people in care, specifies professionals should listen to what young people say about themselves.

If social work professionals acknowledge they have lesbian or gay clients, Pride Place would like them to acknowledge that they need specialist support to meet their needs.

Pride Place is run by Triangles Courses and Resources. [Mailing address: Suite 1, Waverly Court, 28 Wake Green Rd., Birmingham, United Kingdom B13 9PA. Telephone: 44-021-350-0526. ED]

Let the Games Begin

Sex and the <u>not</u>-thirtysomethings

SIMON SEBAG MONTEFIORE

*I*n sending out special correspondent Simon Sebag Montefiore to research and report on sex among the thirtysomething set, we realized there existed a new non-sequitur in the language. The term "thirtysomething"—thanks to a moribund and not-quite-defunct TV show (thanks to syndicated reruns)—continues to refer to those lovable, suspender-wearing whiners of the 1980s.

What we needed to do was redefine the term: the "<u>not</u>-thirtysomethings" or, as we refer to them, the "thirtynothings." We don't mean that derogatorically. Rather, that since the focus has shifted with the aging baby boomers, who are now fortysomething, those in their early thirties suddenly find themselves out of the limelight to a certain extent—caught, for the moment at least, in media limbo.

Nevertheless, they are alive and well and living in paradise—enjoying an age of acquisition, feeling their oats and not shy about sowing them.—The Editors

When you begin reading this article, imagine you can hear a clock ticking, like a time bomb. The decade from 30 to 40 years old is the period when everyone is suddenly aware that time is passing faster and faster. I spoke to many people in their thirties about their sexuality, and I don't think there was a single person who did not mention time.

Thirty is the age that dares not speak its name. If sex is a war between male and female, power and trust, orgasm and death, commitment and adventure, then today's early thirtynothings may be living in a kind of no-man's land on the battlefield of sex: Teenagers are in the trenches, twentysomethings are the cavalry, and people in their forties and older are far behind the lines at headquarters. But the young thirties are something of a forgotten race—unsure whether to return to their lines, ride with the cavalry, or simply wait for the war to end.

Unfairly, the sexes are perceived very differently if they are unmarried in their thirties: single men are envied as strutting predatorial bachelors without the slightest pressure to get hitched, while single women are simply "left-on-the-shelf" products

whom everyone tries to introduce to any single man they know.

In America, the country that invented feminism, there is an "age-ism"—which is really sexism—that implies that real beauty rests in teenage looks. (Ironically, in Europe, the traditional home of chauvinism, there has always been a cult of the earthy, knowing, sensual, and utterly attractive thirtynothing woman, which alters the way men and women of that age are treated in real life.) But it turns out that—despite the media images of youth as "Adonis culture" (hard waists; big breasts and biceps), the risk of AIDS, the miseries of divorce, and the fear of being "on the shelf"—today's thirtynothings, especially women, are enjoying a concealed festival of sexuality. While the MTV culture condemns them to grim silence (relegated to "soft-rock" radio stations and VH1), the thirtynothings are having the time of their sexual lives.

*M*y mission was to discover whether thirtynothing sex was different from twentysomething sex. In addition, to answer these important questions: Does marriage improve sex, end it, or lead to extramarital affairs? Has AIDS affected the love life of the thirtynothings in the same way it has the twentysomethings? Are the thirties the woman's decade? Do divorcées in their thirties face celibate loneliness or the ultimate liberation? For this I canvassed a random sampling of 30 to 40 people from around the country, in different careers and from different backgrounds, married and single, religious and not.

"It's far too late to start that!" was the usual response from men, as if safe sex was like a healthy diet.

Roberta is an attractive pediatrician from Philadelphia, 34, who loves her career, works very hard, possesses a bustling cheerful energy that is as sexy as it is wholesome. She finished an eight-year relationship with an older man two years ago and laughs when I ask if she wishes she were married.

Roberta: "Not exactly. You want to know the truth about sex in the thirties? It's the best. I dreaded the end with Eric. I mourned for weeks. Of course I'd have married him. I was *dying* to get married. I yearn to get married now. But I have my own career. I don't need a man in the traditional way. But lately, I've been dating the most *in*-appropriate guys. It's my right—guys without jobs, younger guys, even really dumb buys with great bodies who were 21 years old. I mean I haven't had sex like that since *I* was 21! It's difficult to suddenly go back to a nice marriageable guy of my age after that. I guess folks in their thirties just say: Let the games begin! And boy, they do!"

Scott, 37, a New York advertising executive who got married three years ago, puts it another way: "I know what I like now. That makes the sex you have in your thirties the best, whether you're married or not. And women my age know what they like. *That's* sexy. It's as if there's no hanging around anymore—they're less inhibited than at any other age. But this goes for both sexes; we're all scared of time ticking, so why beat around the bush? Sex now is the best. This is the icing on the cake."

More Sex, Less Safe

Do thirtynothings practice safe sex in "this day and age"—that euphemism for the AIDS era that I discovered in my previous article on sex amongst the twentysomethings? Since they are older and (supposedly) more responsible, I expected to find that singles in their thirties practice safer sex than any other group. While the twentysomethings are a generation formed by fear, who feel deeply guilty when they do not use condoms (which is often), the thirtynothings are even more oblivious to the danger. The twentysomethings at least have the shame (if we can call it that) to lie to their parents, lovers, and friends about condom use; the thirtynothings apparently do not lie at all.

"It's far too late to start *that*!" was the usual response from men, as if safe sex was like a healthy diet. The women were even less aware of it. Their general response was: "I hate those things. Besides, he was younger." As if their lover's youth were some sort of shield. If their boyfriend was divorced, the general comment was: "Look, Jim's fine. He's been married for five of the last ten years!" If they are divorced themselves, the women answer: "After what I've been through, don't expect me to live in a nunnery."

The whole culture which came of adolescence in the '70s and '80s was built around promiscuity, from James Bond to the Rolling Stones, from Jack Kennedy to Warren Beatty. It is difficult to change in midstream, and the thirtynothings were just getting a taste for the apple when it rotted in their hands.

This attitude is partly the result of the fact that the safe-sex campaign is aimed at teenagers and twentysomethings, presuming (wrongly, as it turns out) that thirtynothings are more responsible and less promiscuous. On the contrary, thirtynothings (single ones) told me that they have far more sex now than they did as teenagers. Why?

I talked to Jane, 37, a consumer-affairs reporter in Chicago, who divorced her husband, Ron, in 1992: "I guess we're more desperate. I could kid you with stuff about women's later sexual peak—I know that's true. But I think it's just because time is ticking and I've got to take advantage of it while I've got it. I don't have one relationship at the moment. I've done that and I'm having a great time, better than ever before."

Jane's answer to the condom question? "I usually insist but the guys never want to."

Martin, 39, is a graphic designer in Miami who has never been married, always has a girlfriend, and thinks it may be time to get married ("I'd like kids"): "Look, I should probably use a condom, but it's just too late now. I'm not even sure I could do it with a condom. I'm stuck in a time warp—I was at Studio 54, I had a wild time in the '80s and I figure, if I've got it, I've got it; and if I *do* have it, I don't even want to know!"

Of course, the ones who are most afraid of AIDS and are fully aware of the importance of safe sex are those who are least at risk—the happily married couples who are faithful and sit tight in the warm castle of marriage, which they imagine is surrounded by all manner of threats, seducers, and deadly diseases. Josh, 36, an investment banker, cuddles his pregnant wife and shivers as he looks back at his single days: "I'm so glad I'm married and safe. I was scared of getting AIDS when I was single because I enjoyed the scene, the bars. One thing terrified me more than anything—not the actual dying, but the thought of dying foolishly from an unsatisfying, silly encounter with a woman whom I hated the next morning."

Only the Good Look Young

Three traditions are increasingly extinct amongst the thirtynothings: dating, foreplay, and the outdated need to marry in order to have children. "I don't date," says Martin. "Everyone's so obsessed with diet, weight, what health club you're a member of, whether you eat red meat, and whether you've seen the latest TV show. Thirtynothings just end up telling each other how young they are. It makes me sick."

Most of the single thirtynothings I interviewed had given up the good old all-American date—that familiar tradition designed for two people to investigate one another before going further. The date has died of the "youth pantomime," which is the sad and comical result of the Adonis cult and is practiced by many segments of our society; although the thirtynothings appear to be its most avid experts.

Roberta: "So many women in their thirties have been so intimidated by advertising that they are desperate to look and sound young. That's why I gave up dates. What's the point of sitting there with one person saying, 'I'm young,' and then the other one saying, 'I'm young, too.' It's humiliating."

As for motherhood, Jennifer, 38, sums up her feelings: "What women in their thirties need these days is a kid, not a man. I've had what you might call an active love life since I was 15, and I still do. I know who the father is, but I'm with a different guy now, so why should I parade around his name as if I'm scared without it? I'd have given my right hand to fall in love and marry a guy and have kids, but it didn't happen and I'm almost 40 so I got pregnant. It's the best thing I ever did."

Sex and Marriage

The majority of people in their thirties are married or have been married, but since divorce is more common than ever before, there are more single thirtynothings today than ever before. Many of the married couples I spoke to have fantastic sex lives—even if none of them have sex as much as they did when they were single—and are blissfully happy. Amongst married couples, the biggest lie I found, passed man to man and woman to woman, is that they are all having lots of sex. Several married couples admitted that they imply to their friends that they have far more sex than they actually do.

Brent and Lisa, both 31, have been married for four years, have a daughter, and live in Detroit. He works in the auto industry and she works in hotels. Brent: "When you're married, there's no pressure to do it when you don't want to or are tired. We have great fun when we do. When I go out, sure, I look, but it's great not having to chase girls anymore."

Lisa: "When we were living together, we had sex every night. Now it varies, but usually it's a treat on Sunday, once a week. We know each other so well it's always great. I don't lie to my friends about it, but I do sort of imply that we do it a bit more than we do. I don't know why, because we're probably all lying to one another.

The big question is: Can a marriage be truly happy without sex?

Stephanie, a 34-year-old public-relations powerhouse who is itching to get married (the guys always seem to run away), sees boring sex as the price of happy marriage: "If I'm going out with a guy, I won't stand for bad sex. If the guy needs guidance, it's curtains. The only circumstance in which I'd put up with bad sex is

in a relationship that'll end in marriage. If I was married, I'd get used to bad sex."

Pat, who married at 23 and is still happily married 10 years later, is an investment banker, outgoing, a sportsman, who has always hinted at his vigorous sex life with his wife, Kelly. Pat does not usually confide about sex, but when I told him I was writing this article, he dropped this bombshell: "You won't believe this, but we simply don't have sex anymore. On holidays we do, but really only to convince each other. I mean, we *talk* as if we had good sex. I guess we're happy, but it suddenly occurred to me that a chunk of my life that used to be real important to me is dead. Maybe it's the cost of being happy."

Kelly: "After about five years, we stopped doing it. Maybe we're just not sexual people. Some people are, some people aren't; but I feel I could be more. We go skiing in Vail every year and share a house with our best friends. The walls there are paper thin and, as we lie there, we can hear them making love—real noisy, shouting and grunting. If we're at home, Pat is as quiet as a mouse when we make love. Not a whisper. But when we're in Vail, he grunts and screams which is great. I guess it turns him on hearing them. Or else he's into the competition thing."

The Fornication Express

The blonde does not look like a married woman. That is the first rule of being married, being in your 30s, and living in the '90s: never *look* married. Married is dull even if marriage is healthy. Linda, 35 (but looks 28) is a tanned Californian visiting New York City.

Brad, 31, single, met her at an Irish bar with a group of friends from work. He persuaded her to go dancing. At the end of the evening, outside his apartment, they kissed on the stairwell.

Linda: "I haven't kissed anyone since I was married, two years ago. We fooled around. I let him touch me because I figured that's okay. That's not sex. Then I went home. But he made me promise to have tea with him at home next day. I guess I shouldn't have gone."

Brad: "Why else would she agree to come unless she wanted to have sex? The moment she arrived we started fooling around, and spent the whole day in bed. We did everything *but*. She was very cute, and it was a big turn-on that she belonged to another man, that it was illicit. She really believed she had not been unfaithful."

Linda: "I really want the marriage to work, but we were having financial problems and job problems and I just had to

get away, so a month in New York was good for me. Brad helped a lot. I don't know if the marriage will last but, you know, I didn't give myself a hundred percent. I mean, not really. So I didn't have to lie to my husband."

The story is typical of the infidelities of a thirtynothing couple because it contains: a) a rocky marriage haunted by money worries, job worries, and angst about aging; b) a transcontinental trip to think things through that has become the staple of the '90s relationship (one married woman told me rather proudly that she called the flight from L.A. to New York "The Fornication Express"); c) condoms were not even mentioned; and d) Linda denied the affair had really happened, while shamelessly enjoying its benefits.

A Thousand Days of Desire

Barbet Schroeder, the film director, said that, even in marriage, sexual attraction only lasts a thousand days, but that love can last forever. Of course, the figure is absurd, but, whatever the life span of desire, it often ends in the 30s. What happens when it ends?

When I visited an upscale strip bar in New York, in which thirtynothing men provide the overwhelming percentage of the clientele, I discovered there are harmless, if extremely bland, ways to find some fun without breaking the marital vows. I talked to Kevin, an attorney with a small firm, who is about 35 years old and happily married. His wife knows he goes to strip joints after work: "She thinks it's a boys' thing. For me, it's a relaxing way to have a beer, and the girls are cute as hell. She knows we guys need some entertainment every now and then. Even if I could, I wouldn't touch 'em."

The clubs exist on the premise that nothing illicit happens there. Hence, the very '90s concept of "lap-dancing," wherein a stripper sits in a man's lap and shakes her breasts in his face, while he enjoys the gyrations without touching. Yet while the implant-enhanced women appeared quite bizarre and borderline attractive, the bigger and more unnatural the breasts appeared, the louder the men shout and yahoo.

Ladies, Start Your Engines

The biggest difference in sexual practices between the twenties and thirties lies in the behavior of the women, not the men. Partly, I believe this is the result of the sexual revolution that made it completely acceptable for women to pursue their own desires.

The thirties is the decade when the office becomes a major component in the lives of most women and men these days, especially if they are married. Often the marriage itself becomes a threesome: husband, wife, office. Of course, the office has always provided a wealth of secret opportunities for men, hence that very thirtynothing alibi for infidelity—"working late at the office." Ironically, many men and women (who would never truly be unfaithful) become "married to the office" (another thirtynothing cliché), because they have no great desire to return home to their spouses.

The change in the '90s is not that sex is happening in the office, but that nowadays it is *women* in positions of power who are acting as the predators. This is the first decade where there are scores of women in the top echelons of most companies. Like men, the women begin to reach senior positions in their thirties, offering plenty of opportunities for a new sexual formula. (How long before a man brings a case of sexual harassment against his female boss?)

Geoff is a 27-year-old associate in a big Wall Street law firm. His boss, Kim, is a tall, forbidding 35-year-old, a cruel taskmaster engaged to a partner in his forties. Geoff always enjoyed following her along the corridors in her tight-fitting, short-skirted business suits, but was terrified of her too.

Geoff: "At the party the senior associates give for the first years, we went dancing and she didn't dance with anyone except me. I barely dared speak because she's the terror of the firm. Finally, she just says, 'Let's go somewhere else!' So we go to another club and dance until we're sweaty and drunk. Then she pulls me over and says, 'Kiss me.' So I'm wondering if she's gonna fire me if I try to go any further. I decide it's better not to so she makes every move. She makes me take her home. She gives all the orders. We make love for hours. She says she has to be hard at work because she's determined to be a partner and a woman has to be that much better than a man to make it. But, she joshes, I am her reward, her prerogative. Next day, she says hello with a nice smile, but it's all business. We never mentioned it again."

Shelly, 38, is a fit, long-legged real estate broker with an eternal tan who loves

The sound of passing time is so deafening to the thirtynothings that they are more afraid of age than they are of death from AIDS.

her husband and children. She relays a common frustration among women: "I can't believe how long I spent being a little lady, waiting for guys to hit on me, never doing a thing until we'd had at least four dates. I was like that until I turned 30 and thought, why shouldn't I live like men always live? It takes you until you're thirtyish to be free about what you want."

But there is a balance between the sudden celebration of sexual jubilation of the Kims and the Shellys of this world and the miserable, lonely feeling of creeping age coupled with a culture that so elevates every part of young erotic energy. The books of Madonna, the videos on MTV, the photos of Cindy Crawford and models in *Vogue* and on television have all taken their toll.

Cornelia, 39, talked to me the week her divorce from her husband, Harry, came through about what she calls "the erotic dictatorship." She learned suddenly that he had a young girlfriend and was leaving her for this nubile: "My nightmare rival came to life in the young girls in "Beverly Hills 90210." I was jealous of her. I knew she was 25 and I just felt and still feel so inadequate, so…*old*. It's so unfair. How can I compete? I hate all these videos. They make watching television agony."

Tick…Tick…Tick…

The other difficult part of the thirtynothing experience is finding out who you really are before it is too late. Again, everyone I spoke to mentioned a sense of time ticking. Just as the women I've quoted discovered their true sexual calling, so Julia recently discovered her husband's calling was towards his own sex.

Julia's husband, Ted, is the most conventionally straight guy imaginable. At the time they were married, it never occurred to her that Ted was gay. Maybe it never occurred to Ted either. He says simply: "I'd always had feelings, but my parents wanted me to marry, my colleagues at the firm expected me to marry, and I wanted to marry too, to have kids. In fact, I wanted to stay married. But as my thirties went on, I felt that it wasn't the real me and that I was wasting my youth on a false premise. I couldn't tell Julia but I really wanted her to know."

Julia: "I felt de-womanized by his leaving me for another man. So here I am, married for life, but now suddenly single with a big problem: I just don't know how to trust men after Ted. I can't really forgive him. I'm 38 and I don't want to be alone."

Time is still ticking. Time is passing. The sound of passing time is so deafening to the thirtynothings that they are more afraid of age than they are of death from AIDS. Hence, they will be the last generation who play on, condomless, at their game of sexual roulette while younger generations fear death itself. But the thirtynothings, especially women, are also the first generation to really enjoy the benefits of the feminist and sexual revolutions together, so they can climb up corporate ladders, hunt in the office, have marital affairs—just as men always have. But if this piece has a theme, it is that despite the Adonis cult that dominates U. S. culture today, the 30s is the golden age of sexuality, the feast at which both sexes—having learned the mistakes of the past and knowing what pleases them now—collect the glittering prizes before they are gone forever. Or as Roberta puts in biblically, "It's the *knowing* that's sexy about being in your thirties. We're like Adam and Eve—we've eaten of the fruit of the knowledge of good and evil, and we like both."

25 ways to make your
MARRIAGE SEXIER

What does it take to keep a relationship exciting and passionate? We asked top marriage and sex experts—including America's sexiest wives, who answered LHJ's own survey. Here's their advice.

Lynn Harris

Call to say "I love you." Just one quick romantic phone call during the day, even a message on his voice mail, is "all it takes to keep your sex life simmering," says Judy Seifer, Ph.D., R.N., a sex educator and therapist, and spokesperson for the Chicago-based American Association of Sex Educators, Counselors and Therapists. "If you connect like that during the day, you don't feel disconnected when you get home together," she says. "Those little things can go a long way to make our whole lives sexier."

Listen to one another. You may be an expert at the fine art of lovemaking, but the most important skill is the ability to *listen* to your partner. "Everything else is secondary," says Andrew Stanway, M.D., a psychosexual and marital physician, and author of the just-published book *The Art of Sexual Intimacy* (Carroll & Graf). "If you are able to truly listen to each other—really putting yourself aside and listening with your heart—great sex will follow."

Take bubble baths—together. You don't need a heart-shaped bathtub in a honeymoon suite in order to share some suds. According to psychologist Dr. Joyce Brothers, a bubble bath may be a new, exciting experience for your husband no matter where you take the plunge. "He may have been parasailing and skydiving, but he's probably never taken a bubble bath," she says. "Women tend to associate bubble baths with pampering, relaxation and taking care of themselves. Our society doesn't really give men permission to do these things—but a bubble bath does. It gives men a chance to express something that's not ordinarily in their lexicon." And besides, what could be sexier—and more fun—than the two of you in the tub?

Take a walk down memory lane. Remember how hot and heavy your love life used to be? If you bring back some of the things you used to do, your relationship can be steamy once again. "Think back to all your flirtatious, impulsive courtship behavior, and return to what worked for you before," says Helen Singer Kaplan, M.D., Ph.D., director of the Human Sexuality Program at New York Hospital–Cornell Medical Center. If you still live in the same area, seduce each other at an old haunt, or steam up the car windows while parking on the old lovers' lane. You'll find all those sparks are still smoldering—and you may kindle some new ones.

Be mischievous. There's nothing wrong with sex as usual, but why not try something different every so often? "Create an exotic world for yourselves now and then," suggests Pepper Schwartz, Ph.D., president of the Society for the Scientific Study of Sex and professor of sociology at the University of Washington, in Seattle. But that doesn't mean you have to pack your bags and head off to the tropics. For busy couples, "exotic" may simply mean a few hours away from work, kids and telephones. "Allow yourself to be mischievous," Schwartz advises. Take a long lunch and meet your husband for a quickie, or borrow the keys to a friend's cabin for an afternoon of romance. Trying these kinds of sexy escapades every now and then will add adventure to your at-home lovemaking.

Indulge in fantasy. "A lot of women don't realize that fantasizing about or during sex is perfectly okay," says Janet Reibstein, Ph.D., a psychotherapist and co-author of the soon-to-be-published *Sexual Arrangements* (Scribners). Fantasizing doesn't mean that something is wrong with your sex life. On the contrary, "It's having a sense of freedom in your relationship that allows fantasy to awaken," she says. "You can use it to introduce novelty into your sex life"—and that's often what keeps things steamy. There's no need for complex plots—"a fantasy can be nothing more than a fleeting idea," says Reibstein. "Simply let your imagination run free. If you decide to share your fantasy with your partner, you'll find that just talking about it can be a turn-on." Be sure to give him the chance to tell you about one of his fantasies, too.

Try a new technique. Just like experimenting with when or where you make love, experimenting with *how* you do it can rescue your sex life from the routine. "Have sex in a position you've never tried before," suggests sex therapist Dr. Ruth Westheimer. "Thinking of new positions together means that you're thinking about one another's pleasure, and that you're taking responsibility for making sex as sexy as it can be." You can't go wrong: While you might discover that variety is the spice of your sex life, you may also rediscover how much you enjoy it the old way.

Make love with your eyes open. You're supposed to close your eyes when you're transported by passion, right? Not necessarily. Keeping your eyes open during sex creates an intense connection between you and your partner, according to David Schnarch, Ph.D., sex therapist and author of *Constructing the Sexual Crucible: An Integration of Sex and Marital Therapy* (Norton, 1991). "Opening your eyes gives you a real jolt—you'll realize that sex can be more intimate than you ever thought."

Remember that getting there is more than half the fun. "Many people think of sex like a staircase, with

know how to say it, tell him that you don't know how—and then say it anyway. He'd rather have your guidance than worry about looking inept." While you're at it, ask him what *he* likes. Even if you've asked each other this question before, ask again. Sexual tastes can change with your mood, the time of day, even the weather. "Check it out with each other constantly," recommends Young.

Be playful. "Just have lots of fun together," says Bernie Zilbergeld, Ph.D., sex and marriage therapist and author of *The New Male Sexuality: The Truth About Men, Sex and Pleasure* (Bantam, 1992). Sheer enjoyment is what gives you the energy that fuels hot sex. Dancing is a great way to generate some of that kind of electricity. Says Zilbergeld, "It's not that far from the dance floor to the bedroom floor."

Talk to each other during lovemaking. Your sex life may be active, but is it all action and no talk? "Many people say, 'Was it good?' or 'All done? Okay, thanks,' but there's so much more to be said," says Samuel Janus, Ph.D., co-author with his wife, Cynthia Janus, M.D., of the recently released *The Janus Report on Sexual Behavior* (Wiley). Instead, try a little body language: "During sex, describe what you're about to do, what you're doing, what you'd like your partner to do, how good it feels." This openness, says Janus, "can add an extra dimension of sharing and satisfaction to your sex life."

Take him by **surprise.**

Maintaining a spirit of surprise and inventiveness is the key to sensational sex, says Brenda Venus, author of the just-published *Secrets of Seduction: How to Be the Best Lover Your Woman Ever Had* (Dutton). Her favorite surprise scenario: "Show up at his desk, whisper that you're not wearing any underwear, kiss him passionately, say, 'See you tonight,' and leave." He'll definitely be ready for love when he comes home—or maybe you'll both end up taking the rest of the day off! Outrageous, perhaps, but, says Venus, "You can never go too far with the one you love."

Reverse your roles. Does one of you usually take charge during lovemaking? If so, then try doing things the other way around, suggests New York clinical psychologist and sex therapist Janet Wolfe, Ph.D., author of *What to Do When He Has a Headache* (Penguin, 1993). "Changing roles expands your repertoire," she says. So if you tend to be more passive, here's your chance to initiate sex, decide on positions and discover new ways of arousing your partner. If you're usually the aggressive one, allow yourself to relax and let go. Chances are, both of you will find the switch exciting—and erotic.

Take your time. As you initiate lovemaking, take a few extra minutes to wind down from your day—and to wind up for each other. When you make that transition slowly, "You have a chance to relax and start thinking sexy thoughts," says Maggie Scarf, author of *Intimate Partners: Patterns in Love and Marriage* (Ballantine, 1988). "Otherwise, you're still worrying about getting that report done and reminding yourself to call the window washer," she says. What should the two of you do during that transition time? "Forget about genitals for a while—practice the art of the tender caress," says Scarf. "Remember that every inch of our skin is erotic."

each step leading to the next. But unfortunately, they're unhappy if they don't reach the top, and then they forget about all the other steps along the way," says Beverly Whipple, Ph.D., R.N., a sex researcher and co-author of *Safe Encounters* (McGraw-Hill, 1989), and *The G-Spot* (Holt, 1982). "How about thinking of it as a circle, where each point along the circumference is an end in itself?" she suggests. That way, kissing, cuddling and other foreplay will feel just as important as intercourse.

Stop worrying about your flaws. "What gets in the way of good sex is that we're so hung up on our bodies, we're busy trying to hide instead of turning each other on," says Patti Putnicki, author of the forthcoming *101 Things Not to Say During Sex* (Warner). "Kiss his bald spot, touch his potbelly—celebrate the very things that he probably thinks are his worst flaws." Transforming trouble spots into erogenous zones will make you more comfortable and able to focus on pleasing one another.

Don't expect him to read your mind—or to read his. "There's not a man born who knows how to touch a woman until she tells him how," says Bill Young, director of the Masters & Johnson Institute, in St. Louis. "If you don't

Give yourself pleasure. Touching yourself will light up lovemaking for both of you, says Susan Crain Bakos, author of *Sexual Pleasures* (St. Martin's, 1992) and *What Men Really Want* (St. Martin's, 1990). Your own pleasure will skyrocket—and what could be sexier than this expression of total freedom and intimacy? He'll be turned on, too: "There's nothing more exciting for a man than an aroused woman," says Bakos.

Build anticipation. When you were first together, the thrill of anticipating sex practically outdid the act itself. That passion is something you need never outgrow. "Prolong [lovemaking] as long as possible," says Shirley Zussman, Ed.D., a sex and marital therapist in New York City. "You can start arousing yourself even before he's there." Take a warm bath, put on some perfume, conjure up your favorite fantasy. When he joins you, don't take things too fast. Instead, build up to lovemaking: Undress one another garment by garment, indulge in some slow, luxurious foreplay. Then, says Zussman, "when you feel you're nearing orgasm, slow down and bring yourself back again to where you were to prolong the pleasurable experience."

Advice from America's sexiest wives

. . . when we published the results of our landmark survey "The love life of the American wife," the response was tremendous. Suddenly everyone from Jay Leno on the *Tonight Show* to morning talk-show hosts all over the country were commenting on our survey results.

What we found was that women today are more honest and adventurous in the bedroom than ever before. And through in-depth statistical analysis and cross-tabulation, we discovered a group of highly eroticized wives who reported making love more often and with greater skill than our other respondents. We decided to look more closely at this group to try to find out what their secrets are. Below, the characteristics they share and what we can all learn from them:

Be affectionate. Our respondents report that their marriages are still romantic, and that sexuality is not something they save only for the bedroom. Instead, they eroticize their lives with affection. To let their husband know how much they love him, the sexiest wives cook his favorite foods, call him during the day to tell him they love him and write him love notes. Happily, husbands reciprocate with romantic gestures of their own: They bring their wife flowers, call her to say "I love you" and write her love letters. In fact, according to our findings, men are getting *more* romantic today. In our previous sex survey ten years ago, just 35 percent of women reported that their husband sent them flowers and wrote them love notes; today, 56 percent do. These gestures make both partners feel loved and loving, and keep the spark in their marriage. Says one wife, "Because we are kind and thoughtful of each other at all times, it spills over to make our lovemaking indescribably beautiful."

Every couple can benefit from this kind of nurturing, according to Evelyn Moschetta, D.S.W., a marriage counselor in New York City. "Sex begins *outside* the bedroom," she says. "Physical and verbal affection, helping each other out, coming through for each other—that's what activates the warm, close, loving feelings you take into the bedroom." Telling him how much you love him is especially important, adds New York–based family therapist Bonnie Eaker Weil, Ph.D., author of the forthcoming book, *Adultery: The Forgivable Sin* (Birch Lane Press). "You and your partner should say loving and endearing things to one another for at least thirty seconds twice a day, once right when you wake up and again before you go to sleep," she says.

Make time for love. Busy as they may be, sexy wives make lovemaking a top priority in their relationships. "We put each other first and foremost," says one wife. She, like our other respondents, knows that lovemaking is a habit: The more you do it, the more you like it, and the more you like it, the more you do it. And like it they do: These wives make love with their husbands an average of three to five times a week.

How can you increase the frequency of lovemaking? Schedule time for [it], says Lonnie Barbach, Ph.D., co-author of *Going the Distance: Finding and Keeping Lifelong Love* (Plume, 1993). "Set aside one whole evening a week that's yours alone; don't let anything get in the way. Find a baby-sitter, dress up, go out to eat or get take-out, flirt with each other—even try candles, lingerie, exotic videos—whatever will make it a wonderful event for both of you to look forward to."

Be good to each other in bed. Erotic wives are self-confident— and that's one of the greatest sexual turn-ons. If a woman thinks she's good in bed, then she *is* good in bed. She also knows that it's important to be just as loving to her partner, telling him he's sexy and exciting. And chances are, he is. Our respondents rate themselves and their husbands as good or excellent lovers. "Making love is a special gift we give to each other," says one very satisfied wife who's been married for

seventeen years. "We're just positive that we've got a corner on the market and no one in the world could possibly make love like we do!"

Try a little spontaneity. Sexy wives break the rules. Instead of making love only at night after the kids are in bed, they seduce their husbands (or let him seduce them) when the urge strikes. Some women say they've called in late for work so they can spend a passionate morning with their partners; others have left a party early to go home and make love. These sexy couples know that the thrill of giving in to desire—when they should be at work or at a social function—keeps their relationship fresh and passionate.

"Where is it written that sex happens *after* dinner and a movie?" asks psychologist Carol Cassell, Ph.D., author of the about-to-be-published *Tender Bargaining: Negotiating an Equal Partnership with the Man You Love* (Lowell House). "What about right now, when you're feeling what you're feeling, and what about right there on the kitchen counter?" She says couples should ask themselves: What patterns have we established? What can we do to jolt them? Explore changes—even small ones—that both of you feel comfortable with.

Be adventurous. The bedroom isn't the only place where the most erotic wives rendezvous with their husbands. In fact, they've learned that getting out of the bedroom is one of the ways married couples can be more innovative. Instead of safe sex behind a locked bedroom door, they enjoy being daring and making love in unexpected places: the tub or shower, the living room, outdoors, even in the car.

"For many of us, the naughtiest and most thrilling sex there is is sex that flirts with public discovery," says sex therapist Dagmar O'Connor, author of *How to Put the Love Back into Making Love* (Doubleday, 1989) and *How to Make Love to the Same Person for the Rest of Your Life* (Bantam, 1986). "It's the secretiveness that makes these public games exciting and that can make us feel closer to one another." She suggests starting with something tame, like a public kiss. If you're ready for something a little more risqué, try advanced under-the-table footsie—the more formal the dinner affair, the better!

Be willing to experiment. The sexiest couples are open-minded. They don't censor sexual experiences or tell each other what they should and shouldn't like. The sexiest wives in our study report using erotic materials—videos, sex toys and sexy magazines—with their husbands. And 54 percent report that *both* partners find it exciting.

Learn what pleases you the most. Sexy wives almost always reach orgasm—usually through intercourse or oral sex. What's the key? They're familiar with their bodies, they know what pleases them, and they focus on their own sensuality. And when a wife gets turned on, so does her husband. The more excited she gets, the more excited he gets and the more exciting their relationship is. "We both want to please each other," says one wife. "And our sex life just keeps getting better than ever!"

Sex How to Keep It Hot After Kids Come Along

Samuel L. Pauker, M.D., and Miriam Arond

Samuel L. Pauker, M.D., is a clinical associate professor of psychiatry at New York Hospital/ Cornell University Medical College and practices in New York City. Miriam Arond is articles editor at Child. *They are co-authors of* The First Year of Marriage: What to Expect, What to Accept, and What You Can Change for a Lasting Relationship. *They are married and have two children.*

BEFORE WE HAD kids we had sex three times during a typical weekend. Now we're lucky if we have sex three times a month," says Wendy Lintner,* a 36-year-old Los Angeles mother of two preschoolers. "When we finally find the time for sex, it's still great—that is, if we're not interrupted by one of the kids calling out for a drink of water or wandering into our bedroom after having a bad dream."

If the secret to good sex is rooted half in the mind and half in the body, then the mental and physical changes that you inevitably go through as you journey into and through parenthood help explain why your sex life may go through major somersaults and turnarounds.

For some couples, parenthood brings a change only in sexual frequency, but for others there's a change in sexual quality as well. Being prepared for these changes—and having a sense of what's normal and what's not—can prevent unnecessary disappointment and panic. And while keeping the lustful aspect of

your love life alive is definitely a challenge, sex is also a wonderful release from, and balance to, all of the work and responsibility of childrearing. Here's a guide to the sexual stages you can anticipate as parents, plus ideas for how you can recharge your relationship with intimacy, excitement, and fun.

*Some parents' and kids' names have been changed

The Sexual Stages of Parenthood

To sexually survive—and thrive during—the ups and downs of parenthood, it helps to be prepped for what to expect.

THE PREGNANCY PICTURE A nine-month roller coaster of hormonal fluctuation, pregnancy invigorates a woman's sex drive in some cases and in others, calls it to an abrupt halt. Male response also varies. Some husbands regard pregnancy as a spectacular sexual adventure, filled with experimentation and free of contraceptive paraphernalia and fears. Others find it difficult to keep raw sexual desire growing along with their wife's increasingly maternal figure. If you both react to pregnancy differently—perhaps one of you is excited and the other is turned off—it can lead to sexual tensions.

Survival Tip: Be sensitive to each other as you acknowledge how the physical transformations of pregnancy or discomfort may be affecting your sex life. To ease you through this vulnerable transition period, make a special effort to express your love and caring in nonsexual ways, such as by hugging, holding hands, and being extra considerate.

LABOR AND LIBIDO Childbirth can give another jolt to a couple's sex life. For some husbands, being present in the delivery room can temporarily lessen their libido. As Kirk Appell of Portland, Oregon, the father of a 1-year-old, put it: "For the first few months after we had our baby, I kept picturing my wife 'pushing' in the delivery room every time we had sex. It was *not* a turn-on." For other husbands, however, the joy of sharing the childbirth experience can cement a close bond with their wives that translates into even greater physical affection.

Survival Tip: Share your feelings about what went on in the delivery room. Even if your labor experience wasn't what you'd hoped, by talking you'll overcome the disappointment and move on.

POST-BIRTH PITFALLS The standard advice from obstetricians is that new mothers can engage in sexual intercourse after their six-week, post-delivery checkup. The reality: The exhaustion, anxiety, and preoccupation experienced by new moms often make them less than eager to resume an active sex life. Some also experience physical pain, perhaps due to a Caesarean incision or a tear in the vaginal area during childbirth.

If you're a husband who's trying to make love to such a sexually disinterested wife, it can feel like insult is being added to injury. Not only is your newborn the cherished focus of your wife's attention, but now you no longer have the physical affirmation of her love. Or, perhaps, you both find it hard to merge your new parental roles and responsibilities with the fun, carefree feeling that was once synonymous with your sex life.

Survival Tip: Recognize that you both may be feeling new pressures and need affirmation in different ways. At this stage, bringing home a takeout dinner for two, splitting weekend shifts of babycare, or renting a video just to let you both relax may help a partner feel more appreciated than a night of lovemaking.

THE TIME TRAP Once you're ready to resume your sex life, you may find it's tough to fit it in when you're balancing parenting and work. Maybe your spouse is a "lark," you're a "night owl," and you never seem to go to bed at the same time. Or maybe you both say that it's hard to find time for sex but sense that it's really just an excuse to avoid being intimate. Perhaps you're having sex on a regular basis, but it's not the same now that you're parents. And you may find with the arrival of a second or third child, time as a couple becomes even more precious.

Survival Tip: Be alert to the sources of—as well as the obstacles to—your sexual satisfaction. Is sex best when you've first had time just to be alone together and talk? Is your resentment about other marital issues, such as who does what around the house, interfering with your sex life? Are you too inhibited to share your fantasies and let your partner know what you'd really like? Remember, only by getting in touch with what you find sexually satisfying can you help your spouse be attuned to your desires and needs.

Smart Sex Sense

The trick in dealing effectively with these sexual passages is to recognize that sex is multilayered. What happens in the bedroom reflects and affects what's going on in the rest of your relationship. It also is impacted by many hidden emotional messages from your childhood.

The following are questions to ask yourselves to help pinpoint possible obstacles to your sexual satisfaction:

1. *Now that you're a parent, do you feel*

MARRIAGE WORKSHOP
The Sensual Connection

This exercise, often prescribed to spouses in couples or sex therapy, begins with nonsexual touching and moves slowly toward the sensual and sexual. Its aim is to help you communicate and become more sexually comfortable with yourselves and each other.

First week. Pick a night when neither of you is tired. Decide which partner will give the first massage. The "receiving" partner should lie on the bed, on a towel, wearing underwear, to emphasize the nonsexual aspect of the exercise. The spouse who is giving the massage should stroke the front and back of her partner's body—about 15 minutes on each side. Set aside a few minutes for the head, scalp, and feet. Use oils and lotions if desired. Reverse roles.

When receiving the massage, be aware of anything that makes it hard to relax. Are you having angry feelings about a recent fight or about your partner not putting enough effort into the massage? These thoughts may mirror difficulties in other areas of your relationship.

When you're giving the massage, be attuned to any thoughts that intrude on your concentration. Perhaps you are worried about your ability to be satisfying to your partner.

After the massage, give each other feedback. The recipient should list three things that were good about the massage and two things that would have caused greater satisfaction.

Second week. The goal is to have genital stimulation without intercourse. After orgasm the "receiving partner" should be given a few minutes to relax, then the roles are reversed. Again, acknowledge three things that your partner did well and two things that could be improved next time. Do this step at least twice to allow for some experimentation and variation. This will improve your comfort with, and attunement to, each other.

Third week. In this step, genital stimulation includes penetration. The "giving" partner tries to accommodate the other partner's desire. The receiving partner should focus on what sexual position is most pleasurable. By this time you should be sensitive to how your thoughts add to, or subtract from, your satisfaction. Give each other feedback, being open to what each of you enjoys. Again, list three positives and two ways to improve the experience.

guilty about having sex with your spouse? Guilt is the biggest hindrance to good sex. Growing up, you may have felt guilty about sex because you sensed your parents' disapproval. Now you may consciously or unconsciously feel guilty about sex because it's allowing you to have pleasure away from your children—and that goes against your view of what a self-sacrificing parent should do. It's vital to realize that there's no better gift that you can give your child than providing him with a role model of a close loving relationship.

2. *What's your MSP (marital sex perception)?* Each one of us brings to marriage conscious and unconscious expectations about sex. Often these are based on what we observed in our parents' marriage. If we saw them being physically affectionate, we associate such intimacy with marriage and parenting. If we never saw our parents kissing or sensed their physical attraction, it may be difficult for us to integrate sexuality with parenthood.

Consider the sexual relationship modeled by your parents and how that's affecting your ability to connect parenthood and sexual desire. Visualize the benefits that your child and your marriage can potentially reap from your having good sex with your spouse as well as fun raising your children—and work on living up to that ideal.

3. *Have you adjusted your sexual expectations to parenthood?* If you had sex three times per weekend pre-kids and expect to keep up that pace post-kids, you're probably setting yourself up for disappointment. Review your schedules and consider what's *realistic*. Are weekends the best time for you to get together? Will a once-a-month weekend getaway—with the grandparents babysitting—assure you and your spouse the time you need together? Talk about frequency and what feels right for each of you.

4. *Do you communicate about sex?* Before you had children you might have gotten away with dealing with sex nonverbally—that's when spontaneous sex was an option and before you had to cope with pregnancy, sleepless nights, hormonal turmoil, and parental stresses like a baby running a high fever, a temperamental toddler running you ragged, or increased financial pressures.

With so much happening in your lives,

it's risky to assume that you understand what each other wants and thinks. If your spouse says he's "too tired" for sex that may be true—or it may be a "cover-up" for anger or frustration.

Talk about how you feel about the balance of parenting and marital intimacy in your lives and how you see yourself and each other in sexual terms since becoming parents. You may discover that your partner is feeling less sexy and desirable, in which case a surprise gift of lingerie or a guest appearance in the shower may be just what is needed.

5. *Has sex begun to feel dull and less passionate?* What might have started as a lustful relationship may feel like anything but lustful after facing the daily routines of parenthood. Coming to terms with the changing nature of love needs to be balanced with the attempt to keep some sexual excitement burning.

Remember that part of being turned on "downstairs" is being turned on "upstairs"—in your head. Is boredom in your sex life a reflection of boredom with your lives together? If you've fallen into the pattern of talking only about the kids, make plans to get out for one night a week to see a movie, play tennis, or visit with friends. Sometimes just seeing each other in a different environment—and sharing interests *other* than the kids—can start the sparks flying all over again.

Or maybe you've let yourselves fall into a rut, always having sex at the same time, in the same position, with the same pacing. Approach your sex life now the way you did when you were courting—imaginatively. Let your fantasies energize and inspire you to be adventurous. And don't resist the temptation to splurge on some aromatic body or massage lotions or rent an adult film to perk things up.

6. *Are you feeling less attractive or attracted?* Along with pregnancy weight gain, stretch marks, and breastfeeding comes a change in a woman's body image—which can boost or bust her sex life. Men are not immune to physical transformations either. Some husbands gain weight in "sympathy" with their pregnant wives, others find they have less time for sports or the health club now that fatherhood responsibilities call.

If you're not feeling good about your body, you'll have a hard time being an

enthusiastic sex partner. If your self-image is suffering, think about what you can do to feel good about yourself. It may mean arranging a half-hour to exercise daily, taking 15 minutes at night for a pampering bath routine, or bothering to put on makeup even though most days you're just hanging out with the baby and won't be seeing many adults. If you feel attractive, chances are your partner will also find you attractive.

If you are finding your spouse less appealing since becoming parents, rather than complaining about weight gain, make it a point to keep in shape together by joining a health club or supporting each other in athletic pursuits. Compliment your partner when he takes the effort to look his best.

7. *Are you taking your partner's sexual attitude too personally?* Perhaps you are annoyed and hurt by your spouse's disinterest in sex, when actually your partner is not disinterested but exhausted because of work responsibilities or the seemingly endless demands of childrearing. Don't personalize every sexual "no" or assume that it's a predictor of a lifetime of sexual disinterest or rejection.

Also recognize that at certain stages, you and your spouse may have different needs for sex. If masturbating is what you need to do to stay sexually fit while your partner is going through a less sexually interested phase, then so be it. Just be sure to let your spouse know that you do want to boost your sexual frequency—and you're ready when he or she is.

8. *Can you feel satisfied with "good enough" sex?* Sex can be satisfying in many ways. Sometimes it's raw and passionate. Other times it's more friendly and playful. One of the joys of a long-term relationship is being able to experience these different nuances as a couple. "I finally realized that sex doesn't always have to be amazing," one mom recently confided to us. "Sometimes we're too tired to be energetic and imaginative. But it can still be good just being together."

Be realistic about sex. Sometimes the earth may shake, other times it might be just a tremor. The main thing is not to neglect the sexual aspect of your marriage. Good sexuality is an important component of adult happiness—and happy couples make good parents.

DO MEN GO THROUGH MENOPAUSE?

Some doctors say that boosting older men's sex-hormone levels can restore virility. Here are the facts.

A deep, masculine voice opened a recent ABC News Special with these dramatic words: "Losing interest in life or love? It could be male menopause. And that can be treated." The Today Show, 20-20, Vanity Fair, and Reader's Digest have all chimed in during the past year with similar features on the hormonal crisis that supposedly strikes most middle-aged men.

In Europe, enterprising physicians have launched "viropause" clinics that claim to rejuvenate aging men by injecting their patients with testosterone. One prominent member of Parliament has even suggested that England's National Health Service should make such testosterone therapy available to all older men.

The notion of "male menopause" is catching on in the U.S., too, where prescriptions for injectable testosterone nearly doubled between 1987 and 1992. Close to a dozen drug companies are working on new testosterone formulations, including a skin patch that would make the treatment more appealing to the millions of potential users—up to half of all men over age 65, according to the president of one pharmaceutical firm.

But this rush to cash in on so-called male menopause is not only premature but possibly dangerous as well, because testosterone may fuel cancerous growth of the prostate gland. Indeed, doctors often treat prostate cancer with drugs that block production of the hormone.

Fortunately, there are a variety of cheaper, safer, and better validated ways for men to maintain their vitality than by getting shot full of testosterone. Here's what you should know.

Sex hormones in older men

The research on testosterone and aging is still sketchy. But at least one clear finding has emerged: The changes that middle-aged and older men go through bear only the faintest resemblance to the changes that can accompany female menopause (see box). Blood levels of estrogen, the main female hormone, plummet in women at some point in their late 40s or early 50s, precipitating dramatic symptoms and physiological changes over the next few years, including hot flashes, rapid bone loss, and pain during intercourse due to thinning and dryness of the vaginal lining.

Nothing comparable happens in men, whose sex hormones do not drop precipitously. Instead, biologically active testosterone—the portion that's actually free to interact with the tissues—declines slowly and steadily in healthy men after age 40 or 50, falling by an estimated average total of perhaps 30 percent by age 70.

That decline seems to leave most older men with testosterone levels near the lower limit for what

From *Consumer Reports on Health,* October 1993, pp. 105-108. © 1993 by Consumers Union of U.S., Inc., Yonkers, NY 10703-1057. Reprinted by permission.

would be normal in a younger man. A small percentage of older men—no one knows exactly how many—fall somewhat below that limit.

Proponents of hormone replacement therapy for men argue that even those gradual, moderate declines can cause significant physical and emotional problems. It's true that younger men with extremely low testosterone levels—usually due to glandular dis-

Testosterone treatment raises blood levels of a protein that may reflect cancerous growth of the prostate.

ease—have smaller muscles, thinner bones, a higher incidence of depression, less sex drive, and a greater risk of impotence than other men. And older men do tend to develop several similar problems:

■ On average, men lose 12 to 20 pounds of muscle between ages 40 and 70.

■ Men lose about 15 percent of their trabecular bone tissue—the dense tissue that provides most of the skeleton's strength—during those years. (While men's bones thin more slowly than women's, one-sixth of all men in their 80s have suffered a hip fracture.)

Sexual desire wanes with age, and impotence becomes more common, affecting about 20 percent of men by age 55, 30 percent by age 65, and more than 50 percent by age 75.

However, major bouts of depression do not become increasingly common as men get older. A study from the National Institutes of Mental Health, which evaluated nearly 4000 men of all ages, found that the incidence of depression unrelated to disability or physical disease actually declined steadily with advancing age. That finding belies the popular notion that men often suffer an emotionally devastating "midlife crisis"—a notion that has fed the belief in male menopause.

And the other problems—loss of bone, muscle, and sexual ability—may be linked only coincidentally with ebbing testosterone levels in older men. That gradual decline may have far different effects than an abrupt hormonal plunge in a young person, which usually results from illness or injury.

Dubious benefits, possible dangers

Most research so far has failed to demonstrate that falling testosterone levels in older men contribute significantly to any major problem, or that adding testosterone could be helpful. One study of some 1300 older men, for example, found no correlation between testosterone levels and impotence. (While declining testosterone levels may contribute to the gradual waning of the sex drive itself, clinical experience suggests that depression or loss of interest in one's sexual partner plays a greater role than hormones do.)

The one trial of testosterone treatment that measured bone density in older men failed to find any significant benefit. While supplementary testosterone builds some muscle even in men with normal testosterone levels, actual strength has not increased substantially in the few studies done thus far. And there's virtually no evidence that testosterone treatment reduces depression in older men.

Even if further research eventually proves that such hormone treatment has significant benefits for older men, the therapy might well be too risky for most of them. Testosterone can worsen existing cases of benign prostate enlargement and possibly of prostate cancer as well. Of course, men with diagnosed cases of either condition could simply avoid going on testosterone therapy. But prostate cancer often goes undetected: An estimated 30 percent of all men over the age of 50, and 60 to 70 percent of those over age 75, may have the disease, usually a small, undiagnosed tumor.

In addition, many researchers worry that raising testosterone levels may trigger the development of prostate enlargement or cancer in men who were initially free of those problems. Indeed, one study of men with no apparent prostate problems found that testosterone therapy substantially raises blood levels of a protein called prostate-specific antigen (PSA), which may reflect either benign or malignant growth of the gland (see CRH, 4/92).

Men who consistently have difficulty getting an erection should be thoroughly checked for underlying physical disorders, including diseases of the testicles and pituitary gland, which can severely deplete testosterone levels. But Consumers Union's medical consultants believe that the currently available evidence does not support using testosterone to treat impotence—or loss of muscle or bone—when levels of the hormone are still in the normal or nearly normal range.

Fortunately, there are other less risky, more reliable steps you can take to help prevent or treat each of those problems.

Protect your bones

Both men and women can fight osteoporosis in these three ways:

■ **Get enough calcium.** According to one survey, most men consume considerably less than the currently recommended 1000 mg of calcium per day. And several studies have found that consuming too little calcium at virtually any age raises the risk of osteoporosis and fractures, while boosting intake of the mineral reduces the risk.

Good sources of calcium include yogurt (about 415 to 450 mg per cup); milk (about 300 mg per cup); cheese (150 to 270 mg per ounce); sardines (350 mg per small can) or salmon (210 mg per small can), both with bones; firm tofu (about 515 mg per cup); regular tofu (260 mg per cup); and blackstrap molasses (about 135 mg per tablespoon). People who can't get enough calcium from their diet should consider taking a modest supplement.

■ **Get enough vitamin D.** Without vitamin D, the body cannot absorb calcium. There are two sources of the vitamin: diet and sunlight, which stimulates the skin to synthesize the nutrient. People can get an adequate annual supply of the vitamin just by going outdoors a few times a week during the warmer months. Older Miami residents with fair skin, for example, need only two to three minutes of exposure; older, dark-skinned Minneapolis residents may need about 30 minutes.

Alternatively, a small serving of fish typically supplies more than 200 international units (IU) of the vitamin, the recommended daily intake, and two glasses of fortified milk provide the recommended amount. Older people who can't get outdoors and don't eat foods containing vitamin D may need a daily supplement containing no more than 200 IU.

■ **Get enough exercise.** Bone deteriorates when it's not stimulated by exercise. (People confined to bed, for example, lose bone 25 times faster than normal.) And most older people get too little exercise. On the other hand, getting regular weight-bearing exercise—such as weight lifting, jogging, aerobic dance, or brisk walking—can reduce or even prevent bone loss in older people.

Stay strong

Regular exercise can also prevent or even reverse the physical frailty that afflicts many older people. One study showed that lifelong weight lifters are stronger at age 70 than the average 20-year-old who doesn't lift weights. Another found that male runners older than age 50 lose no muscle in their legs over the course of a decade—despite their presumably declining testosterone levels. And one group of people in their 80s and 90s nearly tripled their leg strength in just two months by lifting weights.

When treatment fails to correct the problem, men can try a number of mechanical ways to create an erection.

Both men and women can preserve their upper-body muscles by doing strengthening exercises once or twice a week, using weights, machines, or elastic bands (see CRH, 5/92). Doing regular aerobic exercise will generally preserve adequate leg strength.

TRUE MENOPAUSE VERSUS "MALE MENOPAUSE"

While testosterone levels do decline with age, men do not experience anything resembling menopause. The table below lists the key differences in the hormone-related changes that aging men and women experience.

	Women	Men
Sex hormones	Blood levels of estrogen, the main female hormone, plummet during menopause, to very low levels.	Testosterone levels decline gradually after age 40 or 50, and generally do not fall much below normal.
Fertility	The ovaries stop producing eggs at menopause, which begins at some time between ages 45 and 55.	The testicles continue to manufacture viable sperm throughout life, although sperm counts may decline with age.
Major symptoms	Hot flashes, and discomfort during intercourse due to thinning and dryness of the vaginal tissues.	No symptoms linked to gradually declining sex hormones, although surgically castrated men, who abruptly lose all their testosterone, may experience hot flashes.
Bone loss	Bone density drops by roughly 25 percent between ages 40 and 70, with rapid bone loss during the five to seven years after menopause.	Bone density falls steadily by roughly 15 percent, between ages 40 and 70.
Muscle loss	Women typically lose 7 to 11 pounds of muscle between ages 40 and 70.	Men typically lose 12 to 20 pounds of muscle between ages 40 and 70.
Sex drive	Sexual appetite stays pretty much the same throughout life. Testosterone and other male hormones, not estrogen, fuel the sex drive, and women maintain roughly the same small amount of male hormones throughout life.	Sexual appetite declines gradually after young adulthood.

Help for impotence

While relatively low testosterone levels theoretically may contribute to impotence in older men, other age-related causes usually predominate:

■ **Impaired circulation.** Most cases of impotence stem from reduced blood flow to, or excessive blood flow from, the penis. Lowering elevated cholesterol levels or controlling diabetes may help prevent or even reverse clogging of those arteries. Giving up cigarettes, which constrict the arteries, can also help. In some cases, surgery can restore adequate circulation to the penis.

■ **Weakened nerve signals.** Several factors, including diseases like diabetes or multiple sclerosis, spinal-cord injury, prostate surgery, and aging itself, can weaken the nerve impulses needed to activate the penis. Unfortunately, normal nerve function generally cannot be restored.

■ **Drugs.** A host of medications that affect either the circulation or the nerves can cause impotence. Common offenders include blood-pressure drugs, antidepressants, antihistamines, antipsychotics, antispasmodics, tranquilizers, and ulcer medications. Reducing the dosage or switching to an alternative drug may eliminate the problem.

Note that the most common potency-destroying drug is alcohol, which eventually damages the nerves that trigger an erection. Of course, even a few drinks may temporarily interfere with sexual function. (For more information on drugs that impair sexual ability, see CRH, 8/93.)

■ **Psychological problems.** Stress or depression can contribute to impotence. Anxiety over occasional failures to achieve an erection can compound the problem, creating a vicious cycle of growing anxiety and increasingly frequent failure. Counseling by a sex therapist or treatment for the depression may help some men.

When treatment fails to correct the underlying problem, men can try a number of mechanical techniques for creating an erection. Those include injecting a drug directly into the base of the penis; using a vacuum pump to draw blood into the penis; and surgically implanting a rigid or inflatable device. Of course, none of those methods restores the spontaneity of a natural erection, and some of them can cause discomfort.

More common than total impotence in older men is waning sexual energy and increased difficulty getting or sustaining an erection, or ejaculating. Those men can compensate by fantasizing or using erotic materials; asking their partner for more direct tactile stimulation of the penis; or trying new positions or new surroundings. A gradual increase in the time needed to reach orgasm may even have certain benefits, enabling older men to prolong the pleasure for themselves and their partner.

What Doctors and Others Need to Know

Six Facts on Human Sexuality and Aging

Richard J. Cross, MD

Certified Specialist in Internal Medicine, Professor Emeritus at the Robert Wood Johnson Medical School, NJ

Most of us find that our definition of old age changes as we mature. To a child, anyone over forty seems ancient. Sixty-five and older is the common governmental definition of a senior citizen, and it is the definition that I will follow here, although the author (who is in his late 70s) long ago began to find it hard to accept. There is, of course, no specific turning point, but rather a series of gradual physical and emotional changes, some in response to societal rules about retirement and entitlement to particular benefits.

Demographically, the elderly are a rapidly growing segment of the population. In 1900, there were about three million older Americans; by the year 2000, there will be close to 31 million older Americans. Because of high male mortality rates, older women outnumber men 1.5 to 1, and since most are paired off, single women outnumber single men by about 4 to 1. By definition, the elderly were born in the pre–World War I era. Most were thoroughly indoctrinated in the restrictive attitudes toward sex that characterized these times.

In my opinion, the care of the elderly could be significantly improved if doctors and other health workers would remember the following six, simple facts.

Fact #1: All Older People Are Sexual

Older people are not all sexually active, as is also true of the young, but they all have sexual beliefs, values, memories, and feelings. To deny this sexuality is to exclude a significant part of the lives of older people. In recent decades, this simple truth has been repeatedly stated by almost every authority who has written about sexuality, but somehow the myth persists that the elderly have lost all competence, desire, and interest in sexuality, and that those who remain sexual, particularly if sexually active, are regarded as abnormal and, by some, even perverted. This myth would seem to have at least three components. First,

it is a carryover of the victorian belief that sex is dangerous and evil, though necessary for reproduction, and that sex for recreational purposes is improper and disgusting. Second is what Mary S. Calderone, SIECUS co-founder, has called a tendency for society to castrate its dependent members: to deny the sexuality of the disabled, of prisoners, and of the elderly. This perhaps reflects a subconscious desire to dehumanize those who we believe to be less fortunate than ourselves in order to assuage our guilt feelings. Third, Freud and many others have pointed out that most of us have a hard time thinking of our parents as being sexually active, and we tend to identify all older people with our parents and grandparents.

For whatever reason, it is unfortunate that young people so often deny the sexuality of those who are older. It is even more tragic when older people themselves believe the myth and then are tortured by guilt when they experience normal, healthy sexual feelings. Doctors and other health workers need to identify and alleviate such feelings of guilt.

How many people are sexually active? It is generally agreed upon by experts that the proportion of both males and females who are sexually active declines, decade by decade, ranging according to one study from 98% of married men in their 50s to 50% for unmarried women aged 70 and over.[1] At each decade, there are also some people who are inactive. It is important to accept abstinence as a valid lifestyle as well—at any age—as long as it is freely chosen.

Fact #2: Many Older People Have a Need for a Good Sexual Relationship

To a varying extent, the elderly experience and must adapt to gradual physical and mental changes. They may find themselves no longer easily able to do the enjoyable things they used to do; their future may seem fearful; retirement and an "empty nest" may leave many with reduced incomes and no clear goals in life; friends and/or a lifetime partner may move away, become ill, or die; and the threat of loneliness may be a major concern. Fortunately, many older people are not infirm, frustrated, fearful, bored, or lonely; nonetheless, some of these elements may be affecting their lives. An excellent antidote for all this is the warmth, intimacy, and security of a good sexual relationship.

Fact #3: Sexual Physiology Changes with Age

In general, physiological changes are gradual and are easily compensated for, if one knows how. But when they sneak up on an unsuspecting, unknowledgeable individual, they can be disastrous. Health workers need to be familiar with these changes and with how they can help patients adapt to them.

Older men commonly find that their erections are less frequent, take longer to achieve, are less firm, and are more easily lost. Ejaculation takes longer, is less forceful, and produces a smaller amount of semen. The refractory period (the interval between ejaculation and another erection) is often prolonged to many hours or even days. The slowing down of the sexual response cycle can be compensated for simply by taking more time, a step usually gratifying to one's partner, especially if he or she is elderly. But in our society many men grow up believing that their manliness, their power, and their competence depend on their ability to "get it up, keep it up, and get it off." For such an individual, slowing of the cycle may induce performance anxiety, complete impotence, and panic. Good counseling about the many advantages of a leisurely approach can make a world of difference for such an individual.

The prolonged refractory period may prevent a man from having sexual relations as often as he formerly did, but only if he requires that the sexual act build up to his ejaculation. If he can learn that good, soul-satisfying sexual activity is possible without male ejaculation, then he can participate as often as he and his partner wish. Finally, men (and sometimes their partners) need to learn that wonderful sex is possible without an erect penis. Tongues, fingers, vibrators, and many other gadgets can make wonderful stimulators and can alleviate performance anxiety.

Some women find the arrival of menopause disturbing; others feel liberated. If one has grown up in a society that believes that the major role for women is bearing children, then the loss of that ability may make one feel no longer a "real woman." The most common sexual problem of older women, however, is vaginal dryness which can make sexual intercourse painful, particularly if her partner is wearing an unlubricated condom. The obvious solution is to use one of the many water-soluble lubricants available in drug stores. Saliva is a fairly good lubricant and it does have four advantages over commercial products: 1) it is readily available wherever one may be; 2) it is free; 3) it is at the right temperature; and 4) its application is more intimate than something from a tube.

An alternative approach attacks the root of the problem. Vaginal drying results from a decrease in estrogen and can be reversed with estrogen replacement which also prevents other consequences of menopause like hot flashes and loss of calcium from the skeleton. But estrogen administration may increase the risk of uterine cancer; therefore, each woman and her doctor will need to balance out the risks and benefits in her particular situation.

Aging inevitably changes physical appearance and, in our youth-oriented culture, this can have a profound impact on sexuality. It is not easy to reverse the influence of many decades of advertisements for cosmetics and clothes, but doctors can at least try to avoid adding to the problem. Many medical procedures—particularly mastectomy, amputations, chemotherapy, and ostomies—have a profound impact on body image. It is of utmost importance to discuss this impact before surgery and to be fully aware of the patient's need to readjust during the postoperative period. When possible, involvement of the patient's sexual partner in these discussions can be very helpful.

Fact #4: Social Attitudes Are Often Frustrating

As indicated above, society tends to deny the sexuality of the aged, and in so doing creates complications in their already difficult lives. Laws and customs restrict the sexual behavior of older people in many ways. This is particularly true for women, since they have traditionally enjoyed less freedom and because, demographically, there are fewer potential partners for heterosexual, single women, and many of the few men that are available are pursuing women half their age.

Some professionals have suggested that women explore sexual behaviors with other women. However, we know that sexual orientation, although potentially fluid throughout a life-span, is more complicated than the suggestion implies. While some women discover lesbian sexuality at an older age, it is rarely the result of a decrease in the availability of male partners. When doctors see an older woman as a patient, they can, at least, inquire into sexual satisfaction. If sexual frustration is expressed, they can be understanding. Some women can be encouraged to try masturbating, and some will find a vibrator a delightful way to achieve orgasm.

Older people are living in a variety of retirement communities and nursing homes. This brings potential sexual partners together, but tends to exaggerate the gender imbalance. In retirement homes, single women often outnumber single men, eight or ten to one. Furthermore, rules, customs, and lack of privacy severely inhibit the establishment of intimate relationships at these sites. Administrators of such homes are often blamed for this phenomenon. Some are, indeed, unsympathetic, but we must also consider the attitudes of the trustees, the neighbors, and the legislators who oversee the operation, and particularly the attitudes of the family members. If two residents establish a sexual relationship, it is often followed by a son or daughter pounding the administrator's desk and angrily shouting, "That's not what I put Mom (Dad) here for!"

Fact #5: Use It Or Lose It

Sexual activity is not a commodity that can be stored and saved for a rainy day. Rather, it is a physiologic function that tends to deteriorate if not exercised, and it is particularly fragile in the elderly. If interrupted, it may be difficult (though not impossible) to reinvigorate. Doctors should work with the patient and partner on reestablishing the ability if desired.

Research Note

Andrew Greeley, priest, author, and sociologist at the University of Chicago analyzed national-poll data of 6,000 respondents and found that sexual activity is plentiful, even after the age of 60. He reported in 1992 that 37 percent of married people over 60 have sexual relations at least once a week—and one in six respondents had sexual relations more often. Greeley concluded that sexually active married men are happier with their spouses at 60 than 20-year-old single males who have many sexual partners. His report, "Sex After Sixty: A Report," based on surveys by the Gallup Organization and the National Opinion Research Center included the following results:

Married Men and Women:		
	in their 20s	in their 60s
Who have sexual relations outdoors	55%	20%
Who have sexual relations once a week	80%	37%
Who undress each other	70%	27%

Fact #6: Older Folks Do It Better

This may seem like an arrogant statement to some, but much depends on what is meant by "better." If the basis is how hard the penis is, how moist the vagina, how many strokes per minute, then the young will win out, but if the measure is satisfaction achieved, the elderly can enjoy several advantages. First, they have usually had considerable experience, not necessarily with many different partners. One can become very experienced with a single partner. Second, they often have more time, and a good sexual relationship takes a lot of time. The young are often pressured by studies, jobs, hobbies, etc., and squeeze their sexual activities into a very full schedule. Older folks can be more leisurely and relaxed. Finally, attitudes often improve with aging. The young are frequently insecure, playing games, and acting out traditional roles because they have not explored other options. Some older folks have mellowed and learned to roll with the punches. They no longer need to prove themselves and can settle down to relating with their partner and meeting his or her needs. Obviously one does not have to be old to gain experience, to set aside time, or to develop sound attitudes. Perhaps the next generation of Americans will discover how to learn these simple things without wasting thirty or forty years of their lives playing silly games. One hopes so.

Conclusion

In summary, older people are sexual, often urgently need sexual contact, and yet encounter many obstacles to enjoying its pleasures, some medical, most societal. Doctors and other healthcare providers need to be aware of these problems and need to help those who are aging cope with them.

Dr. Richard J. Cross originally wrote this article for the SIECUS Report in 1988.

Author's References

1. Brecher EM. *Love, Sex, and Aging.* New York: Little, Brown and Company, 1984

Sexuality and Aging

What it means to be sixty or seventy or eighty in the '90s

"It's the awfulness of it, " Harry said when asked how he was getting along after his wife died. It was the way he said the "awe"—with a stunned sound, as if he hadn't expected the blow to be so crushing.

Pounder of pianos, designer of great, black locomotives, father of five, this new fragility was a surprise. But it wasn't his last surprise.

After a year of bridge parties with old friends, Harry and his new fiancée turned up at a family dinner.

Their only worry was that the children would think Martha too young for him. She was 69. He was 78.

When they left for their honeymoon, the family still had questions. No one, including Harry and Martha, knew quite what to expect.

Three trends, longer life expectancy, early retirement and better health, are stretching the time between retirement and old age. These trends are redefining our image of aging for the 31 million Americans older than age 65. If you are in your 60s or 70s, you are probably more active and healthy than your parents were at a similar age. Many people are retiring earlier. This opens a whole new segment of your life.

Like everyone of every age, you prob-ably want to continue sharing your life with others in fulfilling relationships. And, you may want to include sex in an intimate relationship with someone you love.

WHAT IS SEXUALITY?

The sexual drive draws humans to-gether for biological reproduction, but it goes beyond this. Your sexuality influences your behavior, speech, appearance; indeed, many aspects of your life.

You might express your sexuality by buying an attractive blouse, playing a particular song or holding hands. Some people express their sexuality through shared interests and companionship. A more physical expression of sexuality is intimate contact, such as sexual inter-course.

Sexuality brings people together to give and receive physical affection. Al-though it's an important form of inti-macy, sexual intimacy isn't the only one. For many people, sexual intimacy isn't an available or desired form of closeness. A close friendship or a loving grand-parent-grandchild relationship, for exam-ple, can provide rewarding opportunities for non-sexual intimacy.

For some older people, though, sexual intimacy remains important. Despite this importance, sexuality in people after age 60 or 70 is not openly acknowledged.

MYTHS AND REALITIES

The widespread perception in Amer-ica is that older people are not sexually active. Try to remember the last time the media portrayed two seniors in a passio-nate embrace. In America, sex is consid-ered the exclusive territory of the young.

Comedian Sam Levinson expressed it well when he quipped, "My parents would never do such a thing; well, my father—maybe. But my mother—NEVER!"

This is a myth.

Realities
The reality is that many older people enjoy an active sex life that often is better than their sex life in early adulthood. The idea that your sexual drive dissolves sometime after middle age is nonsense. It's comparable to thinking your ability to enjoy good food or beautiful scenery would also disappear at a certain point.

In now famous studies, Dr. Alfred C. Kinsey collected information on sexual behavior in the 1940s. Drs. W. B. Mas-ters and V. E. Johnson continued this research in the 1970s. Little of their research looked at people over 60. But in the last decade, a few telling studies

From *Mayo Clinic Health Letter,* February 1993, pp. 1-8. Reprinted by permission of the Mayo Foundation for Medical Education and Research, Rochester, MN 55905.

show the stark difference between myth and reality.

In a 1992 University of Chicago study, Father Andrew Greeley, author and professor of sociology, released "Sex After Sixty: A Report." According to Greeley, "The happiest men and women in America are married people who continue to have sex frequently after they are 60. They are also most likely to report that they are living exciting lives."

Greeley's report, an analysis of two previous surveys involving 5,738 people, showed 37 percent of married people over 60 have sex once a week or more, and 16 percent have sex several times a week.

A survey of 4,245 seniors done by Consumers Union (*Love, Sex, and Aging*, 1984), concludes that, "The panorama of love, sex and aging is far richer and more diverse than the stereotype of life after 50. Both the quality and quantity of sexual activity reported can be properly defined as astonishing."

These surveys are helping today's seniors feel more comfortable acknowledging their sexuality. A 67-year-old consultant to the Consumers Union report wrote:

"Having successfully pretended for decades that we are nonsexual, my generation is now having second thoughts. We are increasingly realizing that denying our sexuality means denying an essential aspect of our common humanity. It cuts us off from communication with our children, our grandchildren and our peers on a subject of great interest to us all—sexuality."

SEX AFTER SIXTY: WHAT CAN YOU EXPECT?

Once you've reshaped your idea of what society should expect of you, you're faced with the sometimes more worrisome obstacle of what you can expect of yourself. Sex, something you've taken for granted most of your life, may suddenly be "iffy" at sixty.

Changes in women

Many women experience changes in sexual function in the years immediately before and after menopause. Contrary to myth, though, menopause does not mark the end of sexuality.

Generally, if you were interested in sex and enjoyed it as a younger woman, you probably will feel the same way after

---

Health and sexuality

Sex, like walking, doesn't require the stamina of a marathoner. It does require reasonably good health. Here are some guidelines:

■ *Use it or lose it* — Though the reason is unclear, prolonged abstinence from sex can cause impotence. Women who are sexually active after menopause have better vaginal lubrication and elasticity of vaginal tissues.

■ *Eat healthfully* — Follow a balanced, low-fat diet and exercise regularly. Fitness enhances your self-image.

■ *Don't smoke* — Men who smoke heavily are more likely to be impotent than men who don't smoke. Smokers are at an increased risk of hardening of the arteries, which can cause impotence (see page 172). Similar studies for women are needed.

■ *Control your weight* — Moderate weight loss can sometimes reverse impotence.

■ *Limit alcohol* — Chronic alcohol and drug abuse causes psychological and neurological problems related to impotence.

■ *Moderate coffee drinking may keep sex perking* — A recent study reported that elderly people who drank at least one cup of coffee a day were more likely to be sexually active than those who didn't. The reason for this association is unknown; further studies are needed.

■ *Protect against AIDS and other STDs* — The best protection against AIDS and other sexually transmitted diseases (STDs) is a long-standing, monogamous relationship. Next best: Use a condom.

---

menopause. Yet menopause does bring changes:

• *Desire*—The effects of age on your sexual desire are the most variable of your sexual responses. Although your sex drive is largely determined by emotional and social factors, hormones like estrogen and testosterone do play a role.

Estrogen is made in your ovaries; testosterone, in your adrenal glands. Surprisingly, sexual desire is affected mainly by testosterone, not estrogen. At menopause, your ovaries stop producing estrogen, but most women produce enough testosterone to preserve their interest in sex.

• *Vaginal changes*—After menopause, estrogen deficiency may lead to changes in the appearance of your genitals and how you respond sexually.

The folds of skin that cover your genital region shrink and become thinner, exposing more of the clitoris. This increased exposure may reduce your sensitivity or cause an unpleasant tingling or prickling sensation when touched.

The opening to your vagina becomes narrower, particularly if you are not sexually active. Natural swelling and lubrication of your vagina occur more slowly during arousal. Even when you feel excited, your vagina may stay somewhat tight and dry. These factors can lead to difficult or painful intercourse (dyspareunia = DYS - pa - ROO - nee - ah).

• *Orgasm*—Because sexual arousal begins in your brain, you can have an orgasm during sexual stimulation throughout your life. You may have diminished or slower response. Women in their 60s and 70s have a greater incidence of painful uterine contractions during orgasm.

Changes in men

Physical changes in a middle-aged man's sexual response parallel those seen in a postmenopausal woman.

• *Desire*—Although feelings of desire originate in your brain, you need a minimum amount of the hormone testosterone to put these feelings into action. The great majority of aging men produce well above the minimum amount of testosterone needed to maintain interest in sex into advanced age.

• *Excitement*—By age 60, you may require more stimulation to get and maintain an erection, and the erection will be less firm. Yet a man with good blood circulation to the penis can attain erections adequate for intercourse until the end of life.

• *Orgasm*—Aging increases the length of time that must pass after an ejaculation and before stimulation to another climax. This interval may lengthen from just a few minutes at the age of 17, to as much as 48 hours by age 70.

Changes due to illness or disability

Whether you're healthy, ill or disabled, you have your own sexual identity and desires for sexual expression. Yet illness or disability can interfere with how you respond sexually to another person. Here's a closer look at how some medical problems can affect sexual expression:

• *Heart attack*—Chest pain, shortness of breath or the fear of a recurring heart attack can have an impact on your sexual behavior. But a heart attack will rarely turn you into a "cardiac cripple." If you were sexually active before your heart attack, you can probably be again. If you have symptoms of angina, your doctor may recommend nitroglycerine before intercourse. Most people who have heart disease are capable of a full, active sex life (see "Sex after a heart attack: Is it safe?").

Even though pulse rates, respiratory rates and blood pressure rise during intercourse, after intercourse they return to normal within minutes. Sudden death during sex is rare.

• *Prostate surgery*—For a benign condition, such as an enlarged prostate, surgery rarely causes impotence. Prostate surgery for cancer causes impotence 50 to 60 percent of the time. However, this type of impotence can be treated (see next page).

• *Hysterectomy*—This is surgery to remove the uterus and cervix, and in some cases, the fallopian tubes, ovaries and lymph nodes. A hysterectomy, by itself, doesn't interfere with your physical ability to have intercourse or experience orgasm once you've recovered from the surgery. Removing the ovaries, however, creates an instant menopause and accelerates the physical and emotional aspects of the natural condition.

When cancer is not involved, be sure you understand why you need a hysterectomy and how it will help your symptoms. Ask your doctor what you can expect after the operation. Reassure yourself that a hysterectomy generally doesn't affect sexual pleasure and that

Sex and illness

Changes in your body due to illness or surgery can affect your physical response to sex. They also can affect your self-image and ultimately limit your interest in sex. Here are tips to help you maintain confidence in your sexuality:

■ *Know what to expect* — Talk to your doctor about the usual effects your treatment has on sexual function.

■ *Talk about sex* — If you feel weak or tired and want your partner to take a more active role, say so. If some part of your body is sore, guide your mate's caresses to create pleasure and avoid pain.

■ *Plan for sex* — Find a time when you're rested and relaxed. Taking a warm bath first or having sex in the morning may help. If you take a pain reliever, such as for arthritis, time the dose so that its effect will occur during sexual activity.

■ *Prepare with exercise* — If you have arthritis or another disability, ask your doctor or therapist for range-of-motion exercises to help relax your joints before sex.

■ *Find pleasure in touch* — It's a good alternative to sexual intercourse. Touching can simply mean holding each other. Men and women can sometimes reach orgasm with the right kind of touching.

If you have no partner, touching yourself for sexual pleasure may help you reaffirm your own sexuality. It can also help you make the transition to intercourse after an illness or surgery.

hormone therapy should prevent physical and emotional changes from interfering.

• *Drugs*—Some commonly used medicines can interfere with sexual function. Drugs that control high blood pressure, such as thiazide diuretics and beta blockers, can reduce desire and impair erection in men and lubrication in women. In contrast, calcium channel blockers and angiotensin converting enzyme (ACE) inhibitors have little known effect on sexual function.

Other drugs that affect sexual function include antihistamines, drugs used to treat depression and drugs that block secretion of stomach acid. If you take one of these drugs and are experiencing side effects, ask your doctor if there is an equally effective medication that doesn't cause the side effects. Alcohol also may adversely affect sexual function.

• *Hardening of the arteries and heart disease*—About half of all impotence in men past age 50 is caused by damage to nerves or blood vessels to the penis. Hardening of the arteries (atherosclerosis) can damage small vessels and restrict blood flow to the genitals. This can interfere with erection in men and swelling of vaginal tissues in women.

• *Diabetes*—Diabetes can increase the collection of fatty deposits (plaque) in blood vessels. Such deposits restrict the flow of blood to the penis. About half of men with diabetes become impotent. Their risk of impotence increases with age. Men who've had diabetes for many years and who also have nerve damage are more likely to become impotent.

If you are a woman with diabetes, you may suffer dryness and painful intercourse that reduce the frequency of orgasm. You may have more frequent vaginal and urinary tract infections.

• *Arthritis*—Although arthritis does not affect your sex organs, the pain and stiffness of osteoarthritis or rheumatoid arthritis can make sex difficult to enjoy. If you have arthritis, discuss your capabilities and your desires openly with your partner. As long as you and your partner keep communications open, you can have a satisfying sexual relationship.

• *Cancer*—Some forms of cancer cause anemia, loss of appetite, muscle wasting or neurologic impairment that leads to weakness. Surgery can alter your physical appearance. These problems can decrease your sexual desire or pleasure.

Cancer may also cause direct damage to your sexual organs or to their nerve and blood supplies; treatment can produce side effects that may interfere with sexual function, desire or pleasure. Discuss possible effects of your treatment with your doctor. If cancer has disrupted your usual sexual activity, seek other ways of expression. Sometimes cuddling or self-stimulation can be enough.

TO REMAIN SEXUALLY ACTIVE, WHAT CAN A WOMAN DO?

Long-term estrogen replacement therapy (ERT) can not only prevent osteoporosis (bone thinning) and heart disease, it can help prevent changes in vaginal tissue, lubrication and desire as well.

Testosterone enhances sexual desire in women. But, it also can produce unwanted, sometimes irreversible side effects such as deepening of the voice and increased facial hair.

Your doctor may prescribe estrogen cream which, applied to your genital area, can prevent dryness and thinning of

---

Sex after a heart attack: Is it safe?

If you can climb a flight of stairs without symptoms, you can usually resume sexual activity. Ask your doctor for specific advice. Here are some guidelines:

■ *Wait after eating* — Wait three or four hours after eating a large meal or drinking alcohol before intercourse. Digestion puts extra demands on your heart.

■ *Rest* — Make sure you are well rested before you have intercourse, and rest after.

■ *Find comfortable positions* — Positions such as side-by-side, or your partner on top, are less strenuous.

---

vaginal tissue. You can also use over-the-counter lubricants just before sexual activity. It's best to use a water-based lubricant, such as K-Y jelly, rather than oil-based mineral oil or petroleum jelly.

If you have problems reaching orgasm, talk to your physician. Your doctor might adjust your medications or offer other options, including counseling, if the problem is non-medical; or, your doctor may refer you to a specialist.

What can a man do?

Only a few years ago doctors generally thought that about 90 percent of impotence was psychological. Now they realize that 50 to 75 percent of impotence is caused by physical problems. There is a wide range of treatments. Keep in mind that the success of any treatment depends, in part, on open communication between partners in a close, supportive relationship. Here are some treatment options:

• *Psychological therapy*—Many impotence problems can be solved simply

---

After age 60, intercourse may require some planning

Problems	Solutions	
Decreased desire	■ Use mood enhancers (candlelight, music, romantic thoughts). ■ Hormone replacement therapy (estrogen or testosterone).	■ Treatment for depression. ■ Treatment for drug abuse (alcohol). ■ Behavioral counseling.
Vaginal dryness; Vagina expands less in length and width	■ Use a lubricant. ■ Consider estrogen replacement therapy.	■ Have intercourse regularly. ■ Pelvic exercises prescribed by your doctor.
Softer erections; More physical and mental stimulation to get and maintain erection	■ Use a position that makes it easy to insert the penis into the vagina. ■ Accept softer erections as a normal part of aging.	■ Don't use a condom if disease transmission is not possible. ■ Tell your partner what is most stimulating to you.
Erection lost more quickly; Takes longer to get another	■ Have intercourse less frequently. ■ Emphasize quality, not quantity.	■ Emphasize comfortable sexual activities that don't require an erection.

by you and your partner understanding the normal changes of aging and adapting to them. For help in this process, your doctor may recommend counseling by a qualified psychiatrist, psychologist or therapist who specializes in the treatment of sexual problems.

• *Hormone adjustment*—Is testosterone a magic potion for impotence? No. Although testosterone supplementation is used in rare instances, its effectiveness for aging men experiencing a normal, gradual decline in testosterone is doubtful.

• *Vascular surgery*—Doctors sometimes can surgically correct impotence caused by an obstruction of blood flow to the penis. However, this bypass procedure is appropriate in only a small number, less than 2 percent, of young men who have impotence problems. The long-term success of this surgery is too often disappointing.

• *Vacuum device*—Currently one of the most common treatments for impotence, this device consists of a hollow, plastic cylinder that fits over your flaccid penis. With the device in place, you attach a hand pump to draw air out of the cylinder. The vacuum created draws blood into your penis, creating an erection.

Once your penis erect, you slip an elastic ring over the cylinder onto the base of your penis. For intercourse, you remove the cylinder from your penis. The ring maintains your erection by reducing blood flow out of your penis. Because side effects of improper use can damage the penis, you should use this device under your doctor's care.

• *Self-injection*—Penile injection therapy is another option. It involves injecting a medication directly into your penis. One or more drugs (papaverine, phentolamine and prostaglandin-E1) are used. The injection is nearly painless and produces a more natural erection than a vacuum device or an implant.

• *Penile implants*—If other treatments fail or are unsatisfactory, a surgical implant is an alternative. Implants consist of one or two silicone or polyurethane cylinders that are surgically placed inside your penis. Implants are not the perfect solution. Mayo experts say there is a 10 to 15 percent chance an implant will malfunction within five years, but the problem almost always can be corrected. Many men still find the procedure worthwhile.

There are two major types of implants: one uses malleable rods and the other uses inflatable cylinders. Malleable rods remain erect, although they can be bent close to your body for concealment. Because there are no working parts, malfunctions are rare.

Inflatable devices consist of one or two inflatable cylinders, a finger-activated pump and an internal reservoir, which stores the fluid used to inflate the tubes. All components—the cylinders, pump and reservoir—are implanted within your penis, scrotum and lower abdomen. These devices produce more "natural" erections.

• *Medications*—Neurotransmitters are chemicals in your brain and nerves that help relay messages. Nitric oxide is now recognized as one of the most important of these chemicals for stimulating an erection. Unfortunately, there is as yet no practical way to administer nitric oxide for treatment of impotence. Other drugs have not proven effective.

SEX IN SYNC

You might wonder how sex can survive amidst tubes, pumps and lubes that can make you feel more like a mechanic than a romantic.

Actually, many people discover that late-life sexuality survives in an increased diversity of expression, sometimes slow, tender and affectionate, and sometimes more intense and spontaneous.

In some ways, middle- and late-life sex are better than the more frantic pace of your younger years. Biology finally puts sex in sync. As a young man, you were probably more driven by hormones and societal pressure . You may find that now desire, arousal and orgasm take longer and aren't always a sure thing. You may find setting and mood more important. Touch and extended foreplay may become as satisfying as more urgent needs for arousal and release.

As a woman, you were probably more dependent on setting and mood when you were younger. You may feel more relaxed and less inhibited in later life. You may be more confident to assert your sexual desires openly.

COMMUNICATION

It can be difficult to talk to another person about sex—doctor, counselor or even a lifetime lover. But, good communication is essential in adapting your sex life to changes caused by aging. Here are three cornerstones of good communication:

• *Be informed*—To start the process, know the facts. Gather as much reliable information as you can about sex and aging and share the facts with your partner.

• *Be open*—If there are unresolved problems in your relationship, sex won't solve them. Be sensitive to the views and feelings of your partner. Work out the differences that are inevitable - before you go to bed. Appropriate sexual counseling can help you and your partner work out problems and enhance your relationship.

• *Be warned*—Most likely, your physician will be willing to discuss questions concerning sexuality with you, but it would be unusual if he or she were a specialist in treating sexual problems. Ask your doctor to refer you to a specialist in this area.

ADAPTING TO CHANGES

As your sexual function changes, you may need to adapt not only to physical changes but to emotional changes as well, perhaps even to changes in your living arrangements.

Lovemaking can lose its spontaneity. Adapting may mean finding the courage to experiment with new styles of making love with the same partner. It may mean trying alternatives to intercourse. You may feel self-conscious about suggesting new ways to find pleasure. But, by changing the focus of sex, you minimize occasional erectile failures that occur.

And, adapting may mean having the flexibility to seek a new partner if you're single. Because women outlive men an average of seven years, women past 50 outnumber unmarried men almost three to one. Older women have less opportunity to remarry.

Families also need to be flexible. Children may need to deal with issues such as inheritance and acceptance of the new spouse.

Another factor that often limits sexual activity is the status of your living arrangements. If you live in a nursing home, you may face an additional problem. Although there are a few nursing homes that offer the privacy of apartment-style living, most do not. Fortunately, this problem is becoming more widely recognized. In the future, nursing homes may offer more privacy.

If you live independently, getting out and around may be a chore. Yet, many older men and women do find new partners. And, they report the rewards of sharing your life with someone you care for may be well-worth the extra effort.

THE NEED FOR INTIMACY IS AGELESS

It takes determination to resist the "over-the-hill" mentality espoused by society today. Age brings changes at 70 just as it does at 17. But you never outgrow your need for intimate love and affection. Whether you seek intimacy through non-sexual touching and companionship or through sexual activity, you and your partner can overcome obstacles. The keys are caring, adapting and communicating.

Old/New Sexual Concerns

- Sexual Hygiene (Articles 44–48)

- Sexual Abuse and Violence (Articles 49–53)

- Males/Females—War and Peace (Articles 54–59)

This final unit deals with several topics that are of interest or concern for different reasons. In one respect, however, these topics have a common denominator—they have all recently emerged in the public's awareness as social issues. Unfortunately, public awareness of issues is often a fertile ground for misinformation and misconceptions. In recognition of this, it is the overall goals of this section to provide some objective insights into pressing sexual concerns.

Health consciousness has increased through the 1980s and 1990s. In the past decade, the term wellness has been coined to represent healthiness encompassing physical and emotional factors. Sexual health or wellness is often incorporated into this sought-after ideal. In order to accomplish sexual health, we must learn about sexual hygiene, normative sexual processes, and the effects of diseases on our sexual functioning. Of particular concern in this area are diseases misappropriately labeled "social diseases." This stigmatization may reflect a still-prevalent negative aura that surrounds sexuality. We can achieve sexual health only when we can learn about and be responsible for our sexual selves in a positive and accepting way.

The Sexual Hygiene subsection of this unit strives to help readers achieve sexual health by providing articles on sexually transmitted diseases, including both those presently getting media coverage and public attention (such as HIV/AIDS) and others that receive less attention, but should be of concern to sexually active persons (such as chlamydia, syphilis, gonorrhea, genital warts, and herpes). Each of the five articles in this subsection provides fact-filled objectivity with strong words of warning designed to get readers to sit up and take notice. Several of the articles confront people's failure to discuss disease-prevention methods with partners as a big part of the problem. "The HIV Dating Game" explores the far-reaching effects an HIV-positive status has on a person's life.

Sexual abuse and violence are especially pernicious when the abuser is an acquaintance, family member, or someone who has some kind of power over the victim (or potential victim), such as an employer, professor, or landlord. In all of these abuse scenarios, victims feel their trust has been violated and their self-concept may be damaged beyond repair. The healing process may take many years.

Another kind of sexual abuse or misuse has been gathering increasing media attention: sexual harassment. Like other kinds of sexual abuse and violence, sexual harassment has existed for some time prior to gaining media attention. Initially fueled by the media event involving the televising of Professor Anita Hill's sexual harassment allegations against then–Supreme Court nominee Clarence Thomas, sexual harassment has become the sexual abuse topic of the 1990s.

The five articles in the Sexual Abuse and Violence subsection strive to address these timely and high-charged issues with a dual purpose crucial to positive and healthy sexuality. First, they seek to put an end to myths, misinformation, and tendencies to "blame the victim." Secondly, they provide for all readers the kind of practical information and guidance that will empower and assist them in distinguishing abusive or harassing sexual (mis)conduct from positive and self- or relationship-enhancing conduct.

The final subsection, Males/Females—War and Peace, focuses on the age-old battle of the sexes, which many today report is taking on a more overt, adversarial, and louder tone. While examining the likelihood that biological, genetic, and brain differences contribute to male and female similarities and differences, the articles also illustrate the social, interpersonal, and cultural factors involved in gender roles, behaviors, and conflicts. It is likely that some of the articles will kindle a fire, or at least an emotional response, in many readers of both genders. It is hoped, however, that they also provide insights, strategies, and impetus for ending the battle between the sexes. For only by seeing through our differences, recognizing our similarities, and stopping the blame game can we truly find the intimacy for which we yearn.

Looking Ahead: Challenge Questions

How knowledgeable are you about sexual health issues and sexually transmitted diseases? What keeps you from being more informed and involved in your own sexual wellness?

How concerned are your classmates and friends about contracting AIDS? Are you more or less concerned than they? Why?

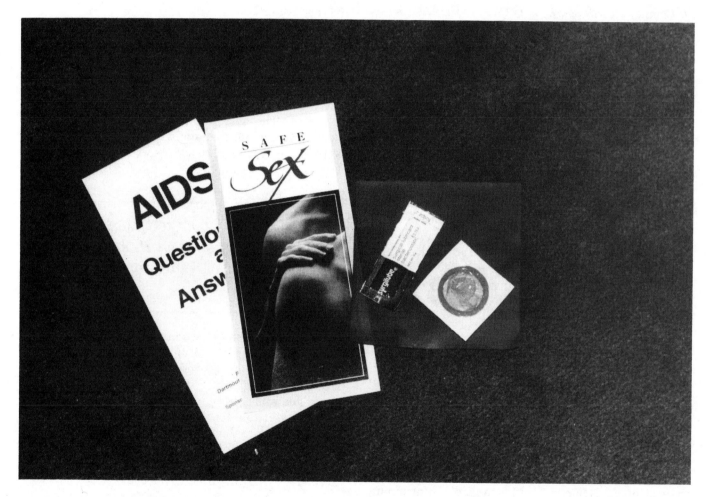

What does your college/university do with respect to HIV/AIDS? Do you support HIV/AIDS education efforts? Condom distribution? Have you considered the likelihood that there are HIV-positive (and possibly full-blown AIDS) students in some of your classes? What do you feel and think about your and your school's role in the HIV/AIDS crisis?

Is date or acquaintance rape a problem on your campus or in your town? What do you see as the most promising ways to prevent it?

Have you or someone close to you been affected by rape? What was your response and how has it affected you and your actions?

Have you overheard or participated in formal or informal discussions about potential or real sexual harassment at your job or your school? How do you, your coworkers, or your classmates feel about it? How would you rate your employer or school as far as their awareness, prevention programming, and response? Explain.

How do you feel about male/female differences? Have you ever wished that the opposite sex could be more like you? When and why?

THE FUTURE OF AIDS

Dr. William A. Haseltine

William A. Haseltine, Ph.D., is Chief of the Division of Human Retrovirology, Dana-Farber Cancer Institute; Professor, Department of Pathology Harvard Medical School; and Professor, Department of Cancer Biology, Harvard School of Public Health.

AIDS is caused by infection with the human immunodeficiency virus. It is estimated that ten to twenty million people are now infected. In the absence of an effective vaccine or other effective means to control the spread of the disease, a reasonable estimate is that 100 million people will be infected with the virus by the year 2000, given the explosive growth of the epidemic in Sub-Saharan Africa, in the Indian subcontinent, in South America and in Asia. In Bombay, the number of people infected rose from a few hundred to more than half a million over the past five years. In northern Thailand, the fraction of 18-year-old men inducted into the army infected by the AIDS virus rose from an almost undetectable level to about 20 percent in the same period.

New epidemics will also arise from the ever expanding population of patients with depleted immune function. The population of people with AIDS serves as a reservoir and breeding ground for deadly diseases. For example, the new worldwide epidemic of tuberculosis arises directly from the population of people with AIDS. Unlike AIDS, some of these diseases will not require sexual contact for transmission. As the number of immune suppressed people grows, it is likely that the world population will suffer multiple, concurrent, lethal epidemics consequent to the AIDS epidemic.

The future of AIDS is indeed the future of humanity.

SCIENTIFIC AND MEDICAL PROGRESS

The collective ability of humans to analyze and to comprehend natural phenomena is formidable. Our

This article contains excerpts from a speech Dr. Haseltine delivered to the French Academy of Science in Paris, November 16, 1992. [Priorities] invites responses to this provocative text.

power to rearrange nature to our own liking is limited. The AIDS epidemic illustrates human strengths and weaknesses.

AIDS was first identified as a new, progressive disease of the immune system in 1981. By the end of 1982, it was known that the AIDS virus was caused by an infectious agent that could be transmitted by sexual contact and by blood. The AIDS virus was first observed in 1983. In 1984, a test for the AIDS virus was developed. The test permits identification of those people who are infected and who are capable of transmitting the infection to others. This is remarkable progress by any standard.

Given what we know today, it cannot be predicted when, or even if, effective treatments and vaccines for AIDS will be developed.

AIDS research has grown into a formidable scientific and medical endeavor world-wide. AIDS research is at the cutting edge of discovery in many fields, including structural biology, drug design and vaccine development. The effort is characterized by close, collaborative, collegial relations.

Why then, does the future look so bleak? The answer, simply put, is that given what we know today, it cannot be predicted when, or even if, effective treatments and vaccines for AIDS will be developed.

TREATMENT

Medical interventions can be designed either to cure or to treat a disease. The intent of curative therapy is to eliminate the cause of the disease. Alternatively, treatment aims to control disease without necessarily eliminating the underlying cause.

The nature of the AIDS virus demands that medical intervention be designed to treat rather than to cure the disease. Upon infection, the genetic information of

From *Priorities*, Winter 1993, pp. 30-32. © 1993 by Dr. William A. Haseltine. Reprinted by permission.

the AIDS virus is inserted into the genetic material—the DNA—of the host. Infection by AIDS involves most of the major organ systems including blood, lymph nodes, bone marrow, brain, skin, intestines, liver and heart. Infection cannot be eliminated from these tissues or organs without destroying the infected cells. In many of these tissues the viral information remains silent, undetectable by any means for months or years. Eradication of the infection is beyond our present comprehension. For this reason, work is directed toward discovery of a treatment, not a cure.

The collective ability of humans to analyze and to comprehend natural phenomena is formidable.

Our power to rearrange nature to our own liking is limited.

The AIDS epidemic illustrates human strengths and weaknesses.

A consequence of life-long infection by the AIDS virus is the requirement for lifelong therapy. Therefore, the cumulative effects of treatment over months and years must be non-toxic.

Drugs have been developed that slow the progress of the virus. Typically, such drugs inhibit the function of critical components of the virus. To date such drugs have had, at best, only limited effect on the disease for two reasons—virus resistance to the drugs develops, and the drugs are toxic. New methods of treatment are now being developed, specifically immune therapy—a treatment that alters the ability of the immune system to respond to the virus after infection and gene therapy—the insertion of novel genes into normal cells to decrease growth of the virus. Unfortunately, it is likely that the AIDS virus will also develop resistance to both new types of treatment.

Progress toward developing an effective treatment is also slowed by the lengthy course of the disease. A minimum of two to three years is required to evaluate the effectiveness of each new treatment. The treatments now being developed are both labor intensive and expensive. Such treatments will not be available to most infected people for both economic and social reasons.

For these reasons, an AIDS cure is unlikely. Moreover, it cannot be predicted when, or even if, effective AIDS treatment will be developed in the foreseeable future.

VACCINES

The greatest hope for a medical solution to the AIDS epidemic is an effective vaccine. Vaccines educate the immune system and prevent or limit the consequences of infection. There are multiple obstacles for the creation of an effective AIDS vaccine. The AIDS virus changes as it grows. The rate of change is so great that no one virus is identical to any other. Vaccines rely on prior recognition of similarity. The development of a single or even a limited set of vaccines that prevent infection by the virus is not likely.

Most vaccines work by preparing the immune system for early elimination of the virus once infection is initiated. Such vaccines will probably not work for AIDS. Once infection is established, the AIDS virus is not naturally eliminated by the immune system. Central features of the lifestyle of the AIDS virus, including the ability of the virus to change within a single individual, its ability to establish a silent state of infection that is invisible to the immune system and its ability to infect immunologically privileged organs such as lymph node and brain, permit the virus to evade immune surveillance.

For these reasons, it is likely that to be effective, an AIDS vaccine must prevent the establishment of primary infection altogether, a requirement not met by any existing vaccine.

To be effective, an AIDS vaccine must prevent the establishment of primary infection altogether, a requirement not met by any existing vaccine.

The most common route of infection, exposure of sexual membranes to virus and virus infected cells in seminal and vaginal fluid, poses an additional difficulty for vaccine development. Immune cells at the surface of mucous membranes can be infected by the AIDS virus. These cells naturally migrate from the surface to the interior of the body where they come in contact with other cells of the immune system. By this means the virus infection spreads from the initial point of contact at the surface of the mucous membrane throughout the body. It has proved difficult to induce long lasting immune protection at the surface of mucous membranes to any microorganism.

For these reasons, it is not possible at present to predict when, or even if, a vaccine will be developed.

Consideration of the difficulties inherent in the discovery of an AIDS cure and AIDS vaccine does not mean that the efforts should be abandoned. To the contrary, the peril to human existence of the AIDS epidemic is so great the efforts to discover both a cure and a vaccine must be redoubled.

INDIVIDUAL AND COLLECTIVE BEHAVIOR

Society cannot rely on a medical miracle—a cure or vaccine—for salvation from the AIDS epidemic. Despite our best efforts such a miracle may never occur. Scientists around the world are working night and day in an unprecedented effort to control this disease. Each day there is a new hope. On a weekly basis, the scientific and lay press describe new insights regarding the AIDS virus, progress towards treatment and progress in vaccine development. This cumulative, intense effort may bring about the hoped for miracle, but society should not count on it. If such a miracle does occur it may be too late for many millions of people. Until that day, it is the responsibility of individuals, singly and collectively, to save themselves.

There is very little evidence to suggest that sexual behavior in any part of the world has changed significantly in response to the AIDS epidemic. The changes in sexual behavior that have been reported to have occurred in some groups have proved, for the most part, to be transient. For example, bath houses and sex clubs in many cities have either reopened or were never closed. The incidence of other sexually transmitted diseases such as syphilis and gonorrhea, as well as the incidence of unwanted pregnancies, both indirect measures of risky sexual behavior, have not declined significantly. In some parts of the world the incidence of sexually transmitted diseases has risen sharply over the past five years.

The dance of sex and death is not new. The lessons of the past, most recently the experience in the nineteenth century with syphilis, are not comforting. Until individuals recognize the risk to themselves and to their families of unprotected sex with multiple partners, and until they learn to modify their behavior accordingly, the AIDS epidemic will continue.

It is our collective responsibility to provide education to all so that each person has clear, unambiguous knowledge of how to avoid infection.

There are two known means to reduce the risk of infection in addition to abstinence and limiting the number of sexual partners. Condoms have been shown to reduce the risk of infection by about 90 percent. For this reason, condoms should be available to everyone world-wide, at a cost that is affordable. Although condoms do not provide absolute protection from infection, universal use of condoms would dramatically slow the progress of the epidemic.

The risk of infection can also be reduced by testing a potential partner for evidence of infection by the AIDS virus. The AIDS test detects more than 95 percent of those infected. The current AIDS test fails to detect infection for only a very brief period, the first four to six weeks immediately following primary exposure. Simple, reliable tests that require only five to ten minutes to complete, that are easy to use, that require no equipment and that require only a drop of blood or a spot of saliva are now available. Such AIDS tests should be made widely available at affordable cost. Prior testing of each new sexual partner substantially reduces the risk of infection. If used routinely, such tests could dramatically slow the progress of the epidemic.

Richer countries should provide resources to poorer countries for education, condom distribution and AIDS testing. Richer countries should also provide medical treatment for highly infectious diseases that arise from the AIDS infected population, including tuberculosis. The world is truly united by this global epidemic. The health of all nations is intertwined.

This epidemic makes it clear that we are all our brother's keeper. We must be compassionate for those who are ill; we must provide care and support for those afflicted; and we must work together to find both social and medical solutions.

Campuses Confront AIDS:

Tapping the Vitality of Caring and Community

Richard P. Keeling, M.D.

Richard P. Keeling, M.D., is director of the University of Wisconsin-Madison Health Center.

The Human Immunodeficiency Virus (HIV) causes a chronic, progressive immunodeficiency disorder called HIV disease, which is manifest in a spectrum of conditions that occur in a sequence of phases; AIDS is the most advanced phase of HIV disease. HIV is responsible for significant premature mortality among both male and female adolescents and young adults in the United States.[1] Many college and university communities are now all too familiar with the enormous cost of the epidemic in human terms: the losses of potential, creativity, contributions, physical and psychological health, and life itself. In response to the needs created by the epidemic, higher education institutions have struggled to develop or redesign effective policies and services and to promote behavioral changes that can help prevent the spread of this disease.

Epidemiology of HIV on campus

After three years of nationwide studies on a variety of campuses, the American College Health Association (ACHA) and the Centers for Disease Control and Prevention (CDC) estimate that approximately 0.2 percent of college and university students (25,000–30,000 individuals) have HIV.[2] The frequency of infection is higher at colleges located in metropolitan areas with a greater prevalence of AIDS; on some such campuses, as many as 0.9 to 1.0 percent of students have HIV.[3] The collective campus experience is that the overwhelming majority of students with HIV acquired their infection through unprotected sexual intercourse. Research observations also confirm that the majority of students with HIV disease in any of its stages are men who have sex with men. The number of women on campus with HIV has been considerably smaller, but with shifts in the patterns of HIV transmission, it is likely that in the future, college communities will have to address the needs of more HIV-positive women.

Future trends in the tempo and extent of the HIV epidemic on campus are difficult to predict. One major influence will be the patterns of sexual and needle-sharing behavior among students. The existence of a reservoir of HIV among students (and among their partners off campus) makes it likely that unprotected intercourse will continue to spread HIV gradually in student communities. Another important factor is the increasing occurrence of HIV disease among adolescents: especially among disadvantaged teenagers, HIV has become a critical health problem.[4] Whereas higher education institutions have been concerned chiefly with the possibility that students would become infected with HIV while on campus, it is likely that in the future, urban and commuter colleges will admit more students who already have HIV.

Teenagers have been more likely than college students to contact HIV through heterosexual contact,[5] but heterosexual transmission of HIV is becoming more common in all age groups;[6] at the same time, the proportion of cases of AIDS resulting from unprotected intercourse between men has been declining.[7] Thus, to the extent that campus trends reflect national patterns, in coming years it is less likely that the average student with HIV will be a gay or bisexual man. Currently, however, there are no reliable longitudinal studies with which to define year-to-year trends and variations in the frequency or patterns of HIV transmission among students. A balanced view is that campuses will witness a progressive but gradual expansion of the population of students with HIV and that many, but not all, students who need care and services in the next five years will be gay or bisexual men.

Responding to HIV in campus communities

Reacting to the AIDS Issue
College and university communities shared an unusual early experience with HIV disease: campuses initially reacted to possibilities, rather than to actual occurrences. Concern about HIV first appeared less often in the context of caring for people who were sick than as a reaction to risks — the possibility that someday the campus would have to deal with someone who had HIV, or that behavior in the community (usually assumed to be exclusively, or at least especially, among students) might result in someone s acquiring HIV. Thus, for many schools, HIV and AIDS were theoretical concerns; AIDS was an issue, not a person.

Early AIDS policies were administratively protective: salvaging the institution's reputation, preventing legal liability, rendering

enrollment safe and healthy, and providing safety for persons who interacted with someone with HIV. Many of these policies affirmed the institution s commitment to avoid discriminating against people with HIV or AIDS in its academic, recreational, and residential programs, but most did not construct mechanisms of investigation or redress to employ in the event of discrimination. Although some policies recognized the need to provide care and assistance for students or employees who already had HIV, few

More than ten years into the HIV epidemic, HIV remains a theoretical problem on a great many campuses; the fear of what might happen still drives discussions and molds policy.

specifically assigned responsibility for services or defined the nature and extent of the care to be offered. Similarly, while many policies addressed the value and importance of educational programs in preventing HIV infection, only a few required specific kinds of activities or demanded assessments and evaluations to guide those programs.

Services and education: informal networks
Effective responses to HIV and AIDS as educational or humane concerns for a campus community typically resulted from highly per-

sonal events and connections: students, faculty, or staff knew someone who had HIV. HIV was no longer just an issue or an external hazard, but a personal challenge that created real-life problems. Fearing that disclosing the existence or identity of a student or employee with HIV might result in protest, violence, embarrassment, or sanctions, people who knew of the presence or needs of persons with HIV frequently remained officially silent. Simple, unstructured referral networks emerged on hundreds of campuses; it was not unusual for employees or students to provide support or services in a quiet, private way (often unknown, in detail, to campus administrators). In many ways, this careful though informal system evolved not only because of the social stigmas and fears associated with HIV, but also because of the connection between HIV and gay men. Because support for gay, lesbian, or bisexual students, faculty, and staff was (and, unfortunately, sometimes still is) hard to sustain in the official policies, procedures, programs, and agencies of many higher education institutions, informal service and education networks already existed around campus gay communities. It was almost inevitable that similar structures, commonly developed by the same people, arose to deal with HIV.

Health promotion and education programs designed to reduce the risk of HIV infection initially evolved informally, as well. Worried clinicians, counselors, and educators whose personal experience with HIV (or with other health issues associated with sexual behavior on campus) organized to write brochures, conduct programs, and begin training peer educators. Details of the methods and content of educational activities were commonly protected from ordinary administrative oversight; educators often felt that their superiors might restrict the kind of programming they could provide and thereby limit its efficacy. Controversies over the appropriateness of distributing condoms, talking explicitly about sexual acts, or developing specific prevention programs for gay students embroiled educators and administrators in disputes that commonly became vividly public.

Evolution of campus responses

Interestingly, the development of an official administrative process and the rise of an informal network of services and education often proceeded in tandem and even shared some people and resources, though the two typically operated with different assumptions and values. The breadth and depth of the difference between them varied, depending on the particular community s values and attitudes. On some campuses, the influence of exemplary leadership and a spirit of caring and community has served to merge the informal network into the official system without damaging the humane qualities of the former. But on other campuses, only the presence of a few committed individuals preserves reasonable educational programs or effective services. In some places, attitudes remain so negative and fear so strong that students concerned about HIV seek services off campus. More than ten years into the HIV epidemic, HIV remains a theoretical problem on a great many campuses; the fear of what might happen still drives discussions and molds policy.

An effective campus response

Policies

Many campus AIDS policies are now obsolete; few institutions have used, reviewed, or revised them. More recent policies and revisions reflect the enlightened institution's

humane desire to make affirmative statements about its recognition of the importance of HIV disease as a campus concern; its knowledge of the contributions people with HIV have made, and will make, to the life of its community; its commitment to developing effective educational programs; and its intent to care gently and reasonably for people with HIV disease. On campuses where fear and moralism still reign, such affirmative statements may have both particular preciousness and tremendous potential to generate controversy and dismay. On any campus, writing down in the language of policy the basics of what the institution believes about HIV and how it wants to relate to people with HIV remains helpful in clarifying values and creating a humane atmosphere.

One area currently demanding attention in institutional policies and procedures is occupational risk. The CDC and the Occupational Safety and Health Administration (OSHA) have issued guidelines and rules for reducing the likelihood of HIV transmission in the workplace, and especially in health care settings.[8] These guidelines and standards also apply to teaching and training sites; likewise, they apply to athletic training rooms, physical therapy units, and teaching and research laboratories. Wise and ethical occupational health practices for both students and employees require that institutions adopt, monitor, and enforce policies and procedures that enhance safety in accordance with these agency mandates.

Services

The spectrum of services required by students with HIV is determined by the medical and psychological history of HIV disease, the age of the student population, the institution's commitment to student services, and the availability

and accessibility of care in the community. Because of the prolonged asymptomatic phase of HIV disease, people who have symptomatic or advanced disease are likely to be older than traditional undergraduates – graduate and professional students, nontraditional or returning learners, and members of the faculty or staff. Comprehensive universities and urban or commuter campuses are, accordingly, more likely to encounter students with symptoms, and therefore may need to provide (or refer for) more complex or specialized services.

Most students with HIV, though, have relatively early-stage disease, and many are unaware of their infection. Available and accessible HIV antibody testing programs; counseling services for students concerned about risks of HIV; psychological support (including employee assistance programs) for people who are trying to manage having HIV; and clinical evaluation and management of early-stage disease are, therefore, appropriate interventions for a campus community. The success of currently available medical therapies in improving both the quality and length of life for people with HIV disease demands that everyone who thinks they might have HIV have barrier-free access to counseling and antibody testing programs, and that individuals shown to have HIV be referred for competent, comprehensive medical case management. Being a college student should not be a barrier to safe testing or to receiving appropriate medical and psychological services for established HIV disease.

Different institutions have developed different patterns of providing, or referring for, those services; in general, the level of care an institution offers students with HIV should be parallel to the level of services it provides for students with other chronic illnesses. The presence (or absence) of a dedicated student health service does not of itself determine an institution's need (or capacity) to respond; for example, every college and university should know where to refer students for safe, accessible HIV antibody testing. Some institutions have integrated HIV-related services effectively into their counseling and health programs; health services on some campuses provide exemplary primary care for students with HIV; and many college counseling services have developed special programs to address the individual and group needs of students who have HIV, feel concerned about the possibility of HIV, or are dealing with a loved one's HIV disease. Providing effective medical and psychological services for people with HIV often requires professional development programs for clinicians and counselors. Because many people with HIV are gay or bisexual men, it is essential that providers of medical or psychological services be knowledgeable, competent, and comfortable in understanding and addressing the concerns of this population.

Education and prevention

The greatest challenge on most campuses is to imagine, design, and implement effective prevention programs: strategies that will reliably and durably help students change risky behavior. Both qualitative and quantitative research studies repeatedly confirm what campus educators and clinicians regularly observe in their work: while students have learned a lot about HIV, they continue to put themselves at

risk.[9] Because HIV is a particularly serious health issue, and because what we are learning about behavior in regard to HIV is deeply relevant to risks of other sexually transmitted diseases, unwanted pregnancies, sexual assault, regretted intercourse, and substance abuse, addressing the inconsistencies of knowledge and behavior is critically important.

The evolution of college and university HIV prevention programs away from information-based strategies and toward a more holistic recognition of the multiple determinants of behavior reflects the synthesis of developmental theory with educational practice.[10] The resulting second generation of activities designed to promote sexual health in higher education is diverse in character and content, but the activities do share certain consistent key features:

• **A clear, comprehensive focus on behavior, rather than on information.** The most important strategy in most programs is skills building. Since skills in decision making, intimacy, communication, and assertiveness are adaptable to a great many other health decisions, HIV prevention programs are now closely integrated with activities dealing with other sexual health issues, campus violence, and substance abuse. Decisions about alcohol, for example, are often closely connected to choices (or the abrogation of choices) about sex. Thus, interventions that enhance the possibility of coherent decision making about alcohol also reduce the probability of unwanted pregnancy and HIV infection.

• **Highly specific, targeted programs for each student's needs.** Using peer education as a dominant model, campuses now use diverse approaches in addressing the specific needs of different constituencies (such as people of color; women; gay, lesbian, and bisexual students; athletes; and faculty and staff). Programs now reflect different learning styles and can be adapted to different patterns of campus life and different levels of presence and involvement in activities.

• **Comprehensive inclusion of students.** Involving students at all levels of decision making (from planning to evaluation) has helped college and university health promotion programs to be more effective and more respectful of students in their content, format, and tone; in respectful programs, health education messages do not preach, demean, belittle, frighten, blame, or infantilize students.

• **A focus on self, identity, and competency as deep determinants of behavior.** New strategies recognize the critical influence of the sense of self on motivation, competency, and resistance — all fundamental factors in making and sustaining changes in behavior. Confronting the enormous problems of self-esteem, identity, and meaning among college and university students is the major challenge of health promotion; through exciting interdisciplinary programs, campus clinicians, counselors, and educators have begun to test and evaluate innovative strategies that help students regain a centered, self-conscious approach to understanding risks, making choices, and assuming responsibility for themselves.

Understanding and addressing social and cultural norms. Community standards, values, and norms have enormous power to shape the context within which individual decisions about health behavior are made.[11] Managing individual risks and decisions therefore requires understanding and managing the social and cultural context that both mirrors and determines them. Changing the social norms that influence behavior is, of course, a gargantuan task in a complex culture; the conflicting messages of media, advertising, music, and entertainment create a seductive, visual environment in which the advice and precautions of health promotion may seem sterile and uninteresting. In the future, health educators at all levels will be agents of deep community change, and the highest and best use of peer educators probably will be to exert a kind of growth pressure on community values.

Building caring and community. Experienced as a sense of caring and connectedness, the spirit of community on campus promotes safety and health among students.[12] A broader and deeper sense of community on campus transcends health promotion, but is absolutely integral to the success of such programs. For example, a spirit of community promotes both a broad sense of justice and respect for difference and a specific commitment to caring about the consequences of unprotected intercourse. This high-level

work is just beginning on many campuses; it represents only the latest in a series of cycles by which the wisdom of a community is incorporated into the community's systems.

Conclusion

The experience of responding to HIV in campus communities has taught us much. As students, faculty, and staff, we have come to understand human differences more deeply and to appreciate the richness of our communities in a more authentic way. We have confronted uncertainty, dealt with fear, and found new dimensions in love and caring. In the harsh clarity fostered by this epidemic, we have come to a more lively, but more careful, understanding of sexuality, intimacy, risk, and the influence of social and cultural forces on human behavior. We have felt the power and vitality of caring and community. Campus communities have found ways to be more caring toward people with HIV and more responsive to their needs. Thus, in becoming more connected to their experience, we have, in fact, strengthened the spirit of community that unites us all.

Notes

[1] Buehler, J.W., O.J. Devine, R.L. Berkelman, and F.M. Chevarley. "Impact of the Human Immunodeficiency Virus Epidemic on Mortality Trends in Young Men," *American Journal of Public Health*, 80: 1080-1086; Chu, S.Y., J.W. Buehler, and R.L. Berkelman. "Impact of the Human Immunodeficiency Virus Epidemic on Mortality in Women of Reproductive Age," *JAMA: The Journal of the American Medical Association*, 264: 225–229.

[2] Gayle, H.D., R.P. Keeling, M. Garcia-Tunon, et al. "Prevalence of HIV Infection Among College

and University Students," *New England Journal of Medicine*, 393: 1526–1531.

[3] Brian Edlin and Richard P. Keeling, Principal Investigators, personal communication.

[4] St. Louis, M.E., G.A. Conway, C.R. Hayman, et al. "Human Immunodeficiency Virus Infection in Disadvantaged Adolescents. Findings from the U.S. Job Corps," *JAMA: The Journal of the American Medical Association*, 266: 2387–2391.

[5] Ibid.

[6] Centers for Disease Control. "HIV/AIDS Surveillance – United States. AIDS Cases Reported Through December, 1991." Washington, DC: U.S. Department of Health and Human Services, 1992; Holmes, K.K., J.M. Karon, and J. Kreiss. "The Increasing Frequency of Heterosexually Acquired AIDS in the United States," *American Journal of Public Health*, 80: 858–863.

[7] Brookmeyer, R. "Reconstruction and Future Trends of the AIDS Epidemic in the United States," *Science*, 253: 37–42.

[8] Centers for Disease Control. "Recommendations for Prevention of HIV Transmission in Health Care Settings," *Morbidity and Mortality Weekly Report*, 36(suppl 2): 1S–18S.

[9] Carroll, L. "Gender, Knowledge About AIDS, Reported Sexual Behavioral Change, and the Sexual Behavior of College Students," *Journal of American College Health*, 40: 5–12; Fennell, R. "Knowledge, Attitudes, and Beliefs of Students Regarding AIDS: A Review," *Health Education*, 21: 260–267; Keeling, R.P. "Time to Move Forward: An Agenda for Campus Sexual Health Promotion in the Next Decade," *Journal of American College Health*, 40: 51–55.

[10] Gould, J. and R.P. Keeling. "Principles of Effective Sexual Health Promotion: Theory to

Practice," in Richard P. Keeling, M.D., ed., *Effective AIDS Education on Campus*. San Francisco: Jossey-Bass, 1992.

[11] Ekstrand, M.L. and T.J. Coates, "Maintenance of Safer Sexual Behaviors and Predictors of Risky Sex: The San Francisco Men's Health Study," *American Journal of Public Health*, 80: 973–977; Fisher, J.D., "Possible Effects of Reference-Group Based Social Influence on AIDS Risk Behavior and AIDS Prevention", *American Psychologist*, 43: 914–920; Keeling, R.P. and E.L. Engstrom, "Building Community for Effective Health Promotion," in Keeling, R.P., ed., *Effective AIDS Education on Campus*. San Francisco: Jossey-Bass, 1992.

[12] Burns, W.D. and M. Klawunn. "The Web of Caring: An Approach to Accountability in Alcohol Policy." Unpublished manuscript. Office of the Assistant Vice President for Student Life Policy and Services, Rutgers, the State University of New Jersey, New Brunswick; Keeling and Engstrom, ibid.

The HIV Dating Game

Men and women who carry the AIDS virus must
make tough choices when they become intimate

Like many men his age, Brad Wojcoski, 34, is looking for love. "I didn't want to be single," says Wojcoski, an administrative assistant to the chairman of Home Box Office in New York. "I had hoped that by this juncture in my life I would be more settled. I'd much rather be going home to a lover and cooking dinner. But the heinous thing about AIDS is that it infects everything. It's omnipresent. It doesn't make anything easier, from my finances to my social life to my love life to my sex life. Your chances of being in communion with someone are rare, and then to have to inject a sense of mortality into a casual encounter—it doesn't make it casual anymore. It's always very serious, heavy duty."

The dating scene has always been a roller-coaster ride, but it's an especially bumpy one for the thousands of Americans like Wojcoski who carry the AIDS virus. When the epidemic began a decade ago, people got sick so fast that romance was low on their list of priorities. Now, with earlier diagnosis and better drugs to prevent and treat symptoms, men and women who are HIV-positive may live for many years with the virus, often looking good and feeling fine. Whether they are homosexual or heterosexual, they frequently go through a period of celibacy while adjusting to their diagnosis, but eventually recognize the need for companionship and intimacy. Faced with an uncertain future, they are unwilling to accept a present bereft of relationships.

Linda Luschei found out she was HIV-positive just a few days after her husband died seven years ago. They had been married only five months, and although he had suffered from chronic fatigue and other symptoms, he was not tested for AIDS until the day before he died. "We used to say to each other, 'Thank God we found each other just in time because this AIDS business is so scary'," says Luschei. A widow at 27, she moved back to Los Angeles from New York—and gave up on love. But she was terribly lonely, and finally decided to try dating again.

Like many HIV-positive men and women, Luschei insisted on telling the engineer she began dating about her status before they became physically intimate. To her surprise, instead of running away, he went out and bought a book about AIDS. She had no objections to his using a condom, but he also insisted on wearing rubber gloves during intercourse—and immediately afterward, he would jump out of bed and into the shower. "It would leave me in tears," says Luschei, "but I didn't feel I had any rights. I knew all along that it was not an emotionally correct relationship for me, but I thought it was all I could have."

Wondering if she might feel more comfortable with someone who was also infected, Luschei joined Friends for Life, a Los Angeles social and support group for HIV-positive men and women. "But I was scared to death," she says. "I'd already lost a husband. Do I want to care deeply for someone who may die also?" She thought about other ways to reveal her HIV status if a man she liked were negative. "What I pictured was, I'd meet somebody, go out with him a lot, a lot, a lot of times until he was hopelessly in love with me, and then tell him—and hope he was so enamored of me that he wouldn't run the other way," she says.

When that scenario failed to materialize, Luschei took out an ad in the L.A. Weekly, mentioning her HIV status. To her amazement, she received 72 replies. She went out with 10 of the men, and slept with two. Negotiating intimacy, she says, was far easier than it had been before. Now she feels confident enough to tell any man she likes of her status early in the game—and she's eager to get on with her search. "I don't think I'll feel complete or fulfilled unless I have another shot at a really good relationship," she says. "Doesn't it make sense that somebody confronted with the possibility of an earlier death would want to grasp life all the more?"

In all HIV-positive relationships, the issue of what to tell when inevitably arises. Wojcoski, who is gay and finds he usually gets involved with men who are HIV-negative, believes in full and prompt disclosure. "Sometimes I talk about AIDS too much," he says, "as though I want to test people to see if they're going to run. If they are, I want them to run soon, not hurt me more when it matters later on."

For others who are HIV-positive, the fear of rejection can be so intense that it obliterates honesty. Pat Griffin, a trustee for the National Community AIDS Partnership, was infected with the AIDS virus in the mid-1980s. But she has only recently decided to tell the dozen or so men she has slept with that she is HIV-positive. Acknowledging that it was wrong not to tell them sooner, she rationalizes the omission. "Being involved with men who are married helps," she says. "They aren't being honest; why should I be honest with them?"

Candor and caution are especially difficult to instill in young people, who may resist linking sex with death. "If you're smart, you assume everyone's infected," says Scott Walker, codeveloper of Bay Area Youth Positives, a San Francisco support group for HIV-positive people in their late teens and 20s. "That's a big jump to ask a young person [to make]." Bill Hunt, who has been HIV-positive since 1985 and oversees the counseling service of the AIDS Resource Center in Dallas, worries about teenagers. "I think about how scary it is for them to start dating in the middle of all this," he says. "I've had a happy life. I'm 37; I had my fun. For a 20-year-old to get AIDS, it's a tragedy."

No judgments: Some HIV-positive men and women find great relief in socializing with others who carry the virus. In New York, Blood Brothers night at the Comeback Club in the West Village draws 200 HIV-positive men every Thursday. "For a person with AIDS, it feels like returning to the mainstream," says founder Will Leonard, 27, who learned last year that he carries the virus. "It's wonderful," says Wojcoski. "You don't have to go through the whole goddam issue of discussing what you are. I can't tell you how refreshing it was just not to have to bother for once."

Kevin Dimmick, a 35-year-old California computer programmer who says he acquired the AIDS virus 12 years ago, believes that most of the major AIDS organizations have neglected the needs of heterosexuals who are affected by the disease. So last March he organized an Infected and Affected Straight Folks Party—followed by five more. People feel safe at these gatherings, says Dimmick. "Everybody understands without a word spoken. Nobody is going to cast judgment on you for having the virus." He is currently dating an HIV-positive woman, Cyndi Angenette, 40.

If there is a small silver lining to the tragedy of AIDS, it is that the looming threat posed by the virus has made many people think hard about what's important in a relationship—about finding joy and expressing tenderness before time runs out. "Someone who dates me has to be a little transcendent," says Wojcoski. "They have to rise to the occasion. They can't be weak. They can't be fearful. They have to take a lot. I don't mean to sound silly, but I feel I'm capable of a rich relationship. AIDS can pull people apart. It complicates people being together. I made love to someone a couple of weeks ago for the first time in a while, and I had forgotten what it felt like to be loved physically. I was very quiet the next day because I was not used to being loved or being made love to or being touched in a fond way. I want that so badly, and I don't get it very often right now."

JEAN SELIGMANN *with* MARC N. PEYSER
in Los Angeles, LUCILLE BEACHY *in New York,*
BINNIE FISHER *in Dallas and* DOGEN HANNAH
and ANTHONY DUIGNAN-CABRERA
in San Francisco

AIDS Update:

Women

over 50

SUSAN BUTTENWIESER

Susan Buttenwieser is the research director at "Ms."

A decade ago women were practically invisible in the AIDS epidemic. By 1989, the number of women diagnosed with HIV/AIDS was sky-rocketing. And now, in addition to the growing incidence among adolescent girls, we are seeing an ever-increasing number of women over the age of 50 with HIV/AIDS.

Of the 357,916 reported AIDS cases in the U.S., 36,225 are people age 50 and older, and approximately 100,000 additional people over 50 are believed to be HIV-positive. Women make up approximately 11 percent of the reported AIDS cases in this age group, and the number of cases among midlife and older women has been steadily increasing. (European Americans compose 46 percent of AIDS cases in women over 50, African Americans 37 percent, Latinas 15 percent, Asian Americans 1.2 percent, and Native Americans .18 percent). Until recently, blood transfusions have been the major source of transmission of HIV in adults 50 and over; researchers are now predicting that in the future sex will be the main route of transmission.

Yet midlife and older women are among those least likely to practice safer sex and to get tested. "Of the women that we have seen, condom use among older women and their partners is virtually zero," says Judith Cohen, director of the Association of Women's AIDS Research and Education (AWARE) in the San Francisco Bay area—a pattern confirmed by researchers in other cities. Public misconceptions and delusions of safety continue to put midlife and older women at risk.

Anyone who is sexually active can be at risk. Yet the majority of safer-sex education and outreach programs have largely overlooked women over 50, focusing instead on women in their twenties and thirties. And safer-sex information, when available, sometimes fails to counter dangerous misconceptions. For example, many women still erroneously assume that warnings about "multiple partners" apply only to a person who is sexually active with several people over the same period of time. But precautions also must also be taken by women who have been in short-term sequential relationships ("serial monogamy"). Others may make the mistake of assuming that because they're monogamous, their partner is as well. In addition, woman-to-woman transmission of HIV

Doctors, assuming there's "nothing going on," may overlook the possibility of HIV/AIDS.

is seldom addressed. Although there is still little information, no news—as AIDS has consistently proven—is by no means good news. There needs to be a concerted effort to educate and encourage safer sex for all women in this age group, regardless of sexual orientation.

Certain biological changes that accompany aging make midlife and older women particularly vulnerable to HIV transmission. During menopause, the vaginal wall becomes thinner and more likely to tear. As women age, decreased acidity in the vagina, which can facilitate urinary tract infections, and changes in the immune system also contribute to increased vulnerability to HIV.

As can happen with women of all ages, health care providers often fail to ask women over 50 about their sexual histories or current practices, let alone about risky behavior. The problem is compounded for older women because ageist biases still abound: doctors, assuming there's "nothing going on," may overlook the possibility of HIV/AIDS, and therefore not test for it even when signs indicate that testing may be warranted. As a result, AIDS is often discovered only in its later stages in women over 50. Even though the revised definition of AIDS now recognizes many woman-specific symptoms, signs of the disease are still missed in women of all ages. The situation can be particularly acute for older women because many of the symptoms—fatigue, muscle weakness, rashes, coughs, forgetfulness, and dementia—mimic those of some aging-related diseases. According to "AIDS and Aging: What People over 50 Need To Know," a curriculum designed by Health Care Education Associates in California, some older persons have been diagnosed as having dementia or Alzheimer's disease when they actually have AIDS.

Researchers and advocates find that when doctors do discuss HIV/AIDS with their older patients, they sometimes give dangerous advice. Sylvie Drew Ivie, head of the To Help Everyone Clinic, which provides services for low-income women with AIDS in Los Angeles, tells of a woman who came to her clinic because she suspected that she might be HIV-positive. Her doctor had refused to test her, saying he had known her for so long, he knew she wasn't "that" kind of person. But not being "that" kind of woman didn't stop her from testing positive.

Once older women are diagnosed with HIV or AIDS, they face a whole new set of problems in getting the care they need. Many are caregivers for family members and are reluctant to take time out to care for themselves.

The World Health Organization (WHO) estimates that in the 13 years since AIDS was first identified, upward of three million people have developed the disease, and more than 14 million adults and about one million children have been infected with HIV. In 1993 alone, more than one million women worldwide became infected with HIV. The WHO predicts that by the year 2000, more than 13 million women will have been infected with HIV, and about four million of them will have died.

In the United States there are 357,916 reported AIDS cases to date, 43,999 of whom are adult women. And of the estimated one million people in the U.S. infected with HIV, more than 160,000 are women. As is true for women throughout the world, heterosexual intercourse is now the leading cause of HIV transmission to women in the U.S.

Low-income women may be especially unable to seek medical attention or get adequate services. People with AIDS (PWAs) who need elder care face discrimination in many facilities. According to Stephen Crystal in *AIDS in an Aging Society* (Springer Publishing), "efforts at placement in nursing homes have often met with resistance," either by other patients and their relatives or by management. As a result, older PWAs must rely, for the most part, on in-home care—an option that may not be feasible for many women.

Clearly there is a need for more extensive research. "AIDS has consistently exploited what we know the least about," says Ron Stall of the Center for AIDS Prevention Studies at the University of California, San Francisco; he points out that a major problem is the lack of information on patterns of sexual behavior among midlife and older people. But there is some hope. Last November, the American Association of Retired Persons and the Center for Women Policy Studies organized the first-ever conference on HIV/AIDS and midlife and older women. And finally, a four-year national study sponsored by the National Institutes of Health will be looking at women of all ages and HIV. Although this is coming very late in the game, it should provide vital and lifesaving information. In the meantime we need to advocate safer sex practices for *all* sexually active women.

Preventing STDs

This article is part of a series with important health information for teenagers. Unlike previous articles, however, it contains sexually explicit material in an effort to reduce the incidence of STDs among teens. Parents and teachers may want to review the article before giving it to teenagers.

Judith Levine Willis

Judith Levine Willis is editor of FDA Consumer.

It's important to read the information printed on the package to make sure a condom's made of latex and labeled for disease prevention. The label may also give an expiration date and tell you if there is added spermicide or lubricant.

You don't have to be a genius to figure out that the only sure way to avoid getting sexually transmitted diseases (STDs) is to not have sex.

But in today's age of AIDS, it's smart to also know ways to lower the risk of getting STDs, including HIV, the virus that causes AIDS.

Infection with HIV, which stands for human immunodeficiency virus, is spreading among teenagers. From 1990 to 1992, the number of teens diagnosed with AIDS nearly doubled, according to the national Centers for Disease Control and Prevention. Today, people in their 20s account for 1 out of every 5 AIDS cases in the United States. Because HIV infection can take many years to develop into AIDS, many of these people were infected when they were teenagers.

You may have heard that birth control can also help prevent AIDS and other STDs. This is only partly true. The whole story is that *only one form of birth control—latex condoms* (thin rubber sheaths used to cover the penis)—is highly effective in reducing the transmission (spread) of HIV and many other STDs.

(When this *FDA Consumer* went to press, the Food and Drug Administration was preparing to approve Reality Female Condom, a form of birth control made of polyurethane. It may give limited protection against STDs, but it is not as effective as male latex condoms.)

So people who use other kinds of birth control, such as the pill, sponge, diaphragm, Norplant, Depo-Provera, cervical cap, or IUD, also need to use condoms to help prevent STDs.

Here's why: Latex condoms work against STDs by keeping blood, a man's semen, and a woman's vaginal fluids—all of which can carry bacteria and viruses—from passing from one person to another. For many years, scientists have known that male condoms (also called safes, rubbers, or prophylactics) can help prevent STDs transmitted by bacteria, such as syphilis and gonorrhea, because the bacteria can't get through the condom. More recently, researchers discovered that latex condoms can also reduce

From *FDA Consumer,* June 1993, pp. 33-35. Reprinted by permission.

If a condom is sticking to itself, as is the one on the left, it's damaged and should not be used. The one on the right is undamaged and okay to use.

the risk of getting STDs caused by viruses, such as HIV, herpes, and hepatitis B, even though viruses are much smaller than bacteria or sperm.

After this discovery, FDA, which regulates condoms as medical devices, worked with manufacturers to develop labeling for latex condoms. The labeling tells consumers that although latex condoms cannot entirely eliminate the risk of STDs, when used properly and consistently they are highly effective in preventing STDs. FDA also provided a sample set of instructions and requested that all condoms include adequate instructions.

Make Sure It's Latex

Male condoms sold in the United States are made either of latex (rubber) or natural membrane, commonly called "lambskin" (but actually made of sheep intestine). Scientists found that natural skin condoms are not as effective as latex condoms in reducing the risk of STDs because natural skin condoms have naturally occurring tiny holes or pores that viruses may be able to get through. Only latex condoms labeled for protection against STDs should be used for disease protection.

Some condoms have lubricants added and some have spermicide (a chemical that kills sperm) added. The package labeling tells whether either of these has been added to the condom.

Lubricants may help prevent condoms from breaking and may help prevent irritation. But lubricants do not give any added disease protection. If an unlubricated condom is used, a water-based lubricant

New Information on Labels

Information about whether a birth control product also helps protect against sexually transmitted diseases (STDs), including HIV infection, is being given added emphasis on the labeling of these products.

"In spite of educational efforts, many adolescents and young adults, in particular, are continuing to engage in high-risk sexual behavior," said FDA Commissioner David A. Kessler, M.D., in announcing the label strengthening last April. "A product that is highly effective in preventing pregnancy will not necessarily protect against sexually transmitted diseases."

Labels on birth control pills, implants such as Norplant, injectable contraceptives such as Depo Provera, intrauterine devices (IUDs), and natural skin condoms will state that the products are intended to prevent pregnancy and do not protect against STDs, including HIV infection (which leads to AIDS). Labeling of natural skin condoms will also state that consumers should use a latex condom to help reduce risk of many STDs, including HIV infection.

Labeling for latex condoms, the only product currently allowed to make a claim of effectiveness against STDs, will state that if used properly, latex condoms help reduce risk of HIV transmission and many other STDs. This statement, a modification from previous labeling, will now appear on individual condom wrappers, on the box, and in consumer information.

Besides highlighting statements concerning sexually transmitted diseases and AIDS on the consumer packaging, manufacturers will add a similar statement to patient and physician leaflets provided with the products.

Consumers can expect to see the new labels by next fall. Some products already include this information in their labeling voluntarily. FDA may take action against any products that don't carry the new information.

FDA is currently reviewing whether similar action is necessary for the labeling of spermicide, cervical caps, diaphragms, and the Today brand contraceptive sponge.

Looking at a Condom Label

Like other drugs and medical devices, FDA requires condom packages to contain certain labeling information. When buying condoms, look on the package label to make sure the condoms are:
• made of latex
• labeled for disease prevention
• not past their expiration date (EXP followed by the date).

(such as K-Y Jelly), available over-the-counter (without prescription) in drugstores, can be used but is not required for the proper use of the condom. Do *not* use petroleum-based jelly (such as Vaseline), baby oil, lotions, cooking oils, or cold creams because these products can weaken latex and cause the condom to tear easily.

Condoms with added spermicide give added birth control protection. An active chemical in spermicides, nonoxynol-9, kills sperm. Although it has not been scientifically proven, it's possible that spermicides may reduce the transmission of HIV and other STDs. But spermicides alone (as sold in creams and jellies over-the-counter in drugstores) and spermicides used with the diaphragm or cervical cap do not give adequate protection against AIDS and other STDs. For the best disease protection, a latex condom should be used from start to finish every time a person has sex.

FDA requires condoms with spermicide to be labeled with an expiration date. Some condoms have an expiration date even though they don't contain spermicide. Condoms should not be used after the expiration date, usually abbreviated EXP and followed by the date.

Condoms are available in almost all drugstores, many supermarkets, and other stores. They are also available from vending machines. When purchasing condoms from vending machines, as from any source, be sure they are latex, labeled for disease prevention, and are not past their expiration date. Don't buy a condom from a vending machine located where it may be exposed to extreme heat or cold or to direct sunlight.

Condoms should be stored in a cool, dry place out of direct sunlight. Closets and drawers usually make good storage places. Because of possible exposure to extreme heat and cold, glove compartments of cars are *not* a good place to store condoms. For the same reason, condoms shouldn't be kept in a pocket, wallet or purse for more than a few hours at a time.

How to Use a Condom

• Use a new condom for every act of vaginal, anal and oral (penis-mouth contact) sex. Do not unroll the condom before placing it on the penis.

STD Facts

• Sexually transmitted diseases affect more than 12 million Americans each year, many of whom are teenagers or young adults.
• Using drugs and alcohol increases your chances of getting STDs because these substances can interfere with your judgment and your ability to use a condom properly.
• Intravenous drug use puts a person at higher risk for HIV and hepatitis B because IV drug users usually share needles.
• The more partners you have, the higher your chance of being exposed to HIV or other STDs. This is because it is difficult to know whether a person is infected, or has had sex with people who are more likely to be infected due to intravenous drug use or other risk factors.
• Sometimes, early in infection, there may be no symptoms, or symptoms may be confused with other illnesses.
• You cannot tell by looking at someone whether he or she is infected with HIV or another STD.

STDs can cause:
• pelvic inflammatory disease (PID), which can damage a woman's fallopian tubes and result in pelvic pain and sterility
• tubal pregnancies (where the fetus grows in the fallopian tube instead of the womb), sometimes fatal to the mother and always fatal to the fetus
• cancer of the cervix in women
• sterility—the inability to have children—in both men and women
• damage to major organs, such as the heart, kidney and brain, if STDs go untreated
• death, especially with HIV infection.

See a doctor if you have any of these STD symptoms:
• discharge from vagina, penis or rectum
• pain or burning during urination or intercourse
• pain in the abdomen (women), testicles (men), or buttocks and legs (both)
• blisters, open sores, warts, rash, or swelling in the genital or anal areas or mouth
• persistent flu-like symptoms—including fever, headache, aching muscles, or swollen glands—which may precede STD symptoms.

• Put the condom on after the penis is erect and before *any* contact is made between the penis and any part of the partner's body.

• If the condom does not have a reservoir top, pinch the tip enough to leave a half-inch space for semen to collect. Always make sure to eliminate any air in the tip to help keep the condom from breaking.

• Holding the condom rim (and pinching a half inch space if necessary), place the condom on the top of the penis. Then, continuing to hold it by the rim, unroll it all the way to the base of the penis. If you are also using water-based lubricant, you can put more on the outside of the condom.

• If you feel the condom break, stop immediately, withdraw, and put on a new condom.

• After ejaculation and before the penis gets soft, grip the rim of the condom and carefully withdraw.

• To remove the condom, gently pull it off the penis, being careful that semen doesn't spill out.

• Wrap the condom in a tissue and throw it in the trash where others won't handle it. (Don't flush condoms down the toilet because they may cause sewer problems.) Afterwards, wash your hands with soap and water.

Latex condoms are the only form of contraception now available that human studies have shown to be highly effective in protecting against the transmission of HIV and other STDs. They give good disease protection for vaginal sex and should also reduce the risk of disease transmission in oral and anal sex. But latex condoms may not be 100 percent effective, and a lot depends on knowing the right way to buy, store and use them.

BREAKING
THE
SILENCE

When these rape victims went public with their real names, they risked shame.
What they discovered, however, profoundly changed their lives.

Megan Rosenfeld

Megan Rosenfeld is a reporter for *The Washington Post*.

Four years ago last fall, two young women in Boone, North Carolina, were kidnapped and raped by the same man, Daniel Lee, 23. The first, Jeni Gray, a 27-year-old employee at Appalachian State University, was missing for five days when Leigh Cooper, a 20-year-old college student and champion runner, was abducted at gunpoint during an early evening jog.

Lee took Cooper into the mountains and repeatedly raped and threatened her. At one point he held a gun before her eyes and promised to shoot if she didn't say "I love you" convincingly enough. He had killed Jeni Gray, he confided, and described where he'd left the body. Between bouts of sobbing and hysteria, Cooper tried to convince him that no one would notice her absence, in the hope that he wouldn't kill her. Her lie bought her some time; Lee said he'd take her home and kill her later.

Then Lee asked if she was hungry. she said yes but refused the cold cheeseburger he had in the back of his car, telling him it was too fatty. When he offered to take her back to his house for pizza, she said cheese made her sick. "Well," he said, "I have to stop for gas. I'll get you some-

thing there." When another man drove up while he was in the gas station's convenience store, she ran to safety.

A few days later the local newspaper ran a graphic account of the attack—including that Lee had raped his victim orally, anally, and vaginally—but didn't print Leigh Cooper's name. Eighty-five miles away, however, *The Winston-Salem Journal* published a much shorter, less detailed version but included her name, obtained from police reports.

It wasn't hard for Boone residents to piece together the two accounts. "The prosecutor told me my case might make the papers," she says today. "It didn't bother me because I knew I didn't do anything wrong." What did surprise her was the enormous show of support: Friends and strangers alike sent flowers and cards; others wrote letters to the papers lauding her courage. "People thought I was a hero because I caught Jeni Gray's murderer," she says. What *was* painful, she says, was that her grandmother and younger sister read specifics in the paper that she had tried to spare them.

While television stations and other newspapers withheld Cooper's name during the rape trial, once Lee was sentenced to death Cooper was asked if she would talk on the record. At first her boyfriend, Chris Wallace (to whom she is now married; the couple have a two-year-old son), was distressed about the idea because he was so shaken by the attack in the first place. "I was disgusted with people," he

says. "I didn't trust anybody, any men, even my friends, to be around her. I didn't want her to go out in public. I was scared."

But encouraged by the positive earlier reaction she had gotten from her community, Cooper decided to let her name be used. She has no regrets. Each September she speaks at a safety-awareness rally held by the university for incoming students. She's gratified to be helping young women protect themselves.

The Journal's managing editor, Joe Goodman, defends the paper's policy of publishing rape victims' names, arguing that Leigh Cooper's positive experience proves him right. But Cooper wonders if her case is an exception. "I had a very strong family and a lot of support," she says. "Other people might have a different experience."

Should rape victims' names continue to be kept secret? The debate, which reflects society's complicated attitudes about rape itself, is controversial and volatile.

Before the 1970s, when rape was considered a crime that never befell a "nice" woman, many newspapers printed a victim's name, and even her address. The information is easily available; when a rape victim reports the crime to the police, it becomes public record. The choice not to publish names has been driven purely by chivalry or chauvinism; there is no law that's been upheld in court to prevent news organizations from publishing these names.

Then the debate became politicized. Victims and their advocates argued that subjecting a woman to public exposure was a double violation and left her vulnerable to more threats. Also, they said, a promise of privacy would encourage more victims to come forward. By the mid-seventies, due to both pressure and persuasion, most newspapers and television stations followed an unwritten rule of withholding a rape victim's name.

Over the last few years, however, this policy has been questioned anew and fiercely argued—not just in newsrooms but in living rooms. In 1989 Geneva Overholser, editor of *The Des Moines Register,* wrote a fiery editorial urging women to go public with their names, to destroy the stigma against rape. "Editors do not hesitate to name the victim of a murder attempt," she wrote. "Does not our very delicacy in dealing with rape victims subscribe to the idea that rape is a crime of sex rather than the crime of brutal violence that it really is? . . . Rape is an American shame. Our society needs to . . . attend to it, not hide it or hush it up."

A 29-year-old Iowa wife and mother, Nancy Ziegenmeyer was already angry about the many legal maneuvers that delayed bringing her own rapist to trial when she read the Overholser editorial. Galvanized, she came forward and told the story of her rape and the subsequent

---

> "The prosecutor told me my case might make the papers. It didn't bother me because I knew I didn't do anything wrong."
>
> **—Leigh Cooper**

---

trial and conviction of her attacker, Bobby Lee Smith, allowing both her name and picture to be used. The five-part series was published in February 1990 and won a Pulitzer prize. Although other women's real names had been used in newspapers before, it was the story about Ziegenmeyer that sparked a nationwide debate among journalists. Ziegenmeyer became a sought-after guest on talk shows, wrote a book, and was the subject of a television movie.

Today Ziegenmeyer works as a waitress and volunteer to survivor groups in her hometown of Grinnell, Iowa. Her life with her husband and three children has mostly returned to normal. She found some of her TV appearances bruising (one talk show host actually asked her twice whether she would choose to be raped if she had to do it over again), but in the end she's glad she spoke on the record.

"My greatest reward is the mail I've gotten," she says of the thousands of letters of support she's received. "It's up to those of us who can speak out to do so for the people who can't. I'll be a victim, advocate, survivor, for the rest of my life."

THE PRICE OF GOING PUBLIC

The women in two subsequent high-profile cases did not fare as well: Patricia Bowman, who charged, in 1991, that med student William Kennedy Smith took her to his beachfront family home and sexually assaulted her, and college freshman Desiree Washington, who, later the same year, accused boxing champ Mike Tyson of date rape. (Smith was acquitted; Tyson was found guilty and is serving six years.)

Washington went public with her name and gave *People* magazine permission to use her photo and name on the cover; she also granted Barbara Walters an interview on *20/20*. As a result, she endured widespread character assassination. Many accused her of, at best, naivete for having gone back to Tyson's hotel alone in the early morning hours; at worst, she was called a liar, out to cash in on Tyson's fortune. She has recently declined to give interviews.

Bowman was vilified by some in the press, described as promiscuous and a possible drug user with a troubled past and an illegitimate child. Once the Florida-based tabloid *The Globe* broke with convention and printed her name in a cover story, NBC's *Nightly News* and *The New York Times* followed suit, sparking a worldwide media frenzy that, Bowman says today, "ruined my life. My child is having to grow up knowing what rape is. People come up to me in grocery stores and start telling me terrible stories," she continues. "I believe in the First Amendment, but not as a weapon against crime victims."

Bowman talks movingly about the unrelenting circus that followed the NBC broadcast: Reporters staked out her house day and night, peering through her windows and ringing her phone. Finally, she eluded the press by smuggling herself (and her then-one-year-old) out of her house and into the trunk of a car to hide at a friend's place.

It was in self-defense, Bowman says, that she finally agreed to give interviews but only to journalists she felt had shown sensitivity to crime victims. On *Prime Time Live* she told Diane Sawyer, "I'm a human being. I have nothing to be ashamed of."

Today Bowman says she has deliber-

> "I'm glad I went public. It was an opportunity to turn a bad experience into a way to help other people."
>
> **—Donna Drejza**

---

ately gained 30 pounds and cut her hair to keep from being recognized. She can be reached only through a post office box. Nonetheless, she has received thousands of supportive letters mostly from women. And when she speaks to media groups she angrily drives home her message: Don't use a victim's name unless she agrees to it, and if she doesn't, don't try to hound her into changing her mind. Violating a victim's privacy, she feels, has serious repercussions; her own treatment, she believes discouraged other women from reporting rapes. "I don't want another victim to think that if she reports the crime," says Bowman, "she'll have a satellite dish in her backyard."

A MATTER OF PRIDE

Portia Douglas, a bankruptcy lawyer in Indianapolis, was brutally raped in her apartment two years ago by a fellow resident, who followed her to her door asking to borrow some salt. The assailant, Rodney Lee Cook, 22, shot Douglas in the chest, dragged her to her dressing room, and raped her. When he left the room briefly, she tried to crouch out of view in the bathtub. But he returned and shot her once more, hitting her in the arm and forehead. She survived; the damage to her arm was serious, but the head wound was superficial.

The first newspaper reports of the horrendous attack did not include her name. Btu when a prosecutor asked if she would talk on the record to a local reporter, she readily agreed. She also later allowed the television program *Rescue 911* to reenact the crime. Later still, her name appeared in a *New York Times* story about the April 1992 sentencing hearing, when Cook got 80 years.

"I was not embarrassed," says Douglas, 34, about the exposure her case got. "This guy shot me and tried to kill me. I wanted to say to other rape victims, 'I am not ashamed of this, and you shouldn't be either.' I also wanted to pass along the fact that you can't trust everybody like I did. I really feel women have a moral obligation to report a crime. otherwise he'll just go out and do it again to someone else." What's more, she says, women who don't talk freely about their attacks, often because they feel humiliated about the sexual nature of a rape, will not fully recover emotionally. "Verbalizing the experience is part of healing," she says.

Donna Drejza, a Washington, D.C., real estate marketing manager, was moved to speak publicly about her rape too, despite being advised by nearly everyone close to her not to do so. In 1987, when she was 26, she had briefly dated Jeffrey Darrell Smith, 36, the son of an administrative law judge. One night Smith called to say he needed to talk. They spent time at her apartment talking. She then fell asleep and awoke to find him assaulting her. She fought back; he held his hand over her face so tightly the blood vessels burst in her eyes. After years of hounding police, she finally saw Smith brought to trial. He pleaded guilty to one count of sodomy, and was sentenced to not less than two and half years and not more than seven and a half.

After Smith was behind bars, Drejza got a call from a *Washington Post* reporter doing a story about acquaintance rape. (The reporter got her name and number from the rape crisis center where Drejza had gone after her attack; she had told counselors she'd review requests for interviews on a case by case basis.) But she allowed the paper to use only her first name.

"I had just started a new job, and people warned me that I would get strange phone calls, and that everyone would think I was weird," Drejza says. "But I felt bad about not using my whole name. It was like admitting shame, which I did not feel." So a year later when the *Post* reporter called back for a follow-up, Drejza decided to go public—and wrote the story herself. She later went on the CBS *Evening News* and *Good Morning America*. "Then I stopped agreeing to these things—I didn't want to always be the Rape Victim.

"Most people close to me thought I was courageous to speak out," Drejza continues. "I got only one strange phone call, and that was from someone who said I'd better get my phone number unlisted." But a few of the men she's dated have been a little nervous about being intimate. "One—a lawyer, of course—was sort of joking, but sort of serious. He said, 'You *are* consenting, right?' Still, I'm glad I went public. It was an opportunity to turn a bad experience into a way to help other people."

THE RIGHT TO CHOOSE
Some observers are concerned that all rape victims will now feel pressure to go public, and be criticized if they don't. "Do I admire women who allow their names to be used? Yes," says Alice Vachss, a former Queens, New York, district attorney who spent nearly a

decade prosecuting rapists and wrote about it in her book *Sex Crimes*. "But how much can you expect from people who have already had all the courage in the world just to come forward and report the crime?"

Linda Fairstein, head of the New York City Sex Crimes Prosecution Unit and author of *Sexual Violence: Our War Against Rape*, is also cautious. She applauds the women who choose to go public because "until we put names and faces to these stories, there will continue to be a stigma." But, she says, "Going public is not for everyone because, sadly, our society has not come tremendously far in removing that stigma." In other words, the women who are the first to come forward will bear the brunt of the prejudice.

Without exception, the women interviewed here agree that public

---

"This guy shot me and tried to kill me. I wanted to say to other rape victims, 'I am not ashamed of this, and you shouldn't be either.' "

—Portia Douglas

---

exposure should be the victim's choice. Publishing a woman's name without her permission only increases her trauma. Consider the case of Ellen Webb Halbert of Austin, Texas, who was the victim of a horrendous crime in 1986. A man dressed in a ninja costume attacked her in her home. During the hour and a half she was held hostage, the assailant, Troy Wigley, 19, raped her, stabbed her four times, beat her, and hammered a knife into her head. He left her for dead, but Halbert, then 43, survived and phoned the police. When Wigley arrived at Halbert's bank to cash a check he had forced her to write, police were waiting for him.

In the hospital Halbert was in such pain (she needed 600 stitches) that when she was asked to let the technicians take "rape test" samples, she asked them to wait; the tests were never done. Although Halbert testified about the rape two months later, the lack of physical evidence partly contributed to Wigley's being charged with only aggravated burglary. He was sentenced to 60 years, which in Texas at the time meant he had to serve at least 20.

It was then that a reporter for a small community paper—one that, it turned

out, had never covered a rape before and hadn't set a policy—printed Halbert's name. She complained, and the paper's editor apologized, but the damage was already done. "I was devastated," she says. "I truly felt as though everyone knew who I was. People were too scared to talk to me. They didn't know what to say. And they felt that if it could happen to me, it could happen to them."

It took Halbert a long time to heal, physically and emotionally. Nine months after the attack her marriage fell apart. "My husband couldn't deal with it," she says. "Some men just want it not to have happened. They just want you to be like you were before." She was aided enormously, she says, by the Austin Rape Crisis Center and the support of her parents, her children, and her stepchildren.

A year and a half after the attack, Halbert spoke at a rally on the steps of the state capitol in honor of National Crime Victim's Rights Week. It was covered extensively by the local media, and for the first time she agreed to use her name. She found the experience cathartic. She joined a group for victims and their families, and through it met Joel Halbert, an electrical engineer, who became her third husband. Today she is a full-time volunteer for victims' rights; in 1991 she was appointed to the Texas Board of Criminal Justice, a citizen's commission that oversees the state prisons' probation and parole systems.

Even after having taken charge of her life in all these ways, Halbert says she still has bouts of stress-related illnesses, especially around the anniversary of the attack. She cannot say that going public is right for every woman. "There will be a stigma about rape for a long, long time."

RAPE VICTIM BACKLASH
Women who choose to speak publicly about being raped cite many different motivations. Some say it's important to give other women a survivor role model, or to educate people about safety or the criminal justice system, or to dispel the stereotypes about women who get raped. But even when

---

"I've sensed a backlash against women who charge men with rape. If you even talk about rape, you're accused of male bashing."

---

the motivation is clear and strong, speaking out is never an easy decision.

Many victim counselors actually advise their clients *not* to talk to the press, at least not soon after the attack. While it can be empowering, too many women seem to think the interviews will take the place of therapy, warns Lynn Thompson-Haas, executive director of the Austin Rape Crisis Center.

Even if a victim chooses to go public, Thompson-Haas says she's concerned about new hostility directed at these women. "In the past few years I've sensed a backlash against women who charge men with rape. It's as though if you even talk about rape, you're accused of male bashing." Much of this hostility springs from the controversy over date rape cases. Some critics say women charge rape in a spasm of morning-after regret. This is why, they argue, a man's name should be kept private too, until—and only if—he is found guilty.

"I am neither blind nor cold to that argument," says Fairstein. "It's a great injustice to be falsely accused. But our

> *"People were too scared to talk to me. They didn't know what to say. And they felt that if it could happen to me, it could happen to them."*

law has built-in protections—there has to be probable cause before an arrest, and someone has to examine a case before a charge is made."

Vachss, on tour recently to publicize her book, says hardly a day went by that she didn't get an abusive phone call, some charging that women cry rape whenever they want to get back at a man. And Pat Foley, community educator at the Plymouth County Rape Crisis Center, says that nearly every time she appears to testify before a committee, the first thing she is asked about are inci-

dents of false reporting, as if, she says, there were a conspiracy against men.

The shame attached to rape victims is a cultural taboo left over from the days when a woman was considered the possession of her father or husband, and her worth was measured by her virginity. And the myths about rape—that the woman must have provoked it or ought to have known how to avoid it—still linger in people's minds.

Marlene Young, executive director of the National Organization for Victim Assistance, believes the stigma is still strong even among victims. She recently gave a speech to the staff of a rape crisis center, where she had been told that 75 percent of the staff were rape survivors themselves. But when she asked the group how many of them had been raped, not one woman raised her hand, and this in the sheltered, enlightened environment of a roomful of trained counselors.

"There has been positive change in the way the media handles this issue," says Young. "But I'm not sure there has been as much progress in society."

Six cases to challenge your moral gyroscope

IS *THIS* SEXUAL HARASSMENT?

Robin Warshaw

Sexual harassment? Not you. You're the new breed of male, sensitive to the age-old gender stereotypes women have had to battle as they gain the equality and respect rightfully theirs in a male-dominated business world. As far as you're concerned, bartering promotions for sexual favors is inappropriate office conduct of the worst sort—the kind of behavior that not only demeans co-workers but also tarnishes your own character and diminishes managerial effectiveness.

No. In this matter your conscience is as shiny and clean as Sir Galahad's shield.

So throughout the long media blizzard precipitated by Anita Hill, Clarence Thomas and the Senate judiciary peanut gallery, you sat snug and cozy, hands warming by the fire of your own morally appropriate behavior. But when the storm subsided, you may have found a new America waiting to challenge your conduct.

It is an America in which women, overcoming their fear of reprisal and disbelief, are bringing their grievances to court in record numbers. In the first half of 1992 alone, reports of harassment made to the Equal Employment Opportunity Commission increased more than 50 percent over the previous year.

It is also an America that is finally ready to take these grievances seriously. And while you may applaud this trend that's finally packing muscle onto what was formerly a pleasant but ineffective civil rights sentiment, the bottom line is that you may get caught in the crossfire.

The problem faced by men in this new environment is twofold: First, while most media-worthy cases of sexual harassment involve spectacularly colorful instances of inappropriate behavior, the majority of unheralded arguments currently being heard in the nation's courts don't fit so neatly into the public's perceptions of right and wrong. Harassment sometimes is in the eye of the beholder, and what may be one man's clumsy attempt at friendship or even honest romance may be one woman's sheer hell.

From *Exec*, Summer 1993, pp. 62-65. © 1993 by Robin Warshaw. Reprinted by permission.

Complicating the whole matter are the hazy boundaries of the law. Except in cases of actual assault, there's still no steadfast uniformity regarding the type of behavior the courts and mediating agencies should judge to be harassing.

The following cases have all been culled from legal battles and disputes brought before public hearing examiners. Each has been chosen because it explores in some fashion the gray areas that lie just outside the realm of obviously inoffensive and threatening behavior. As you read them, ask yourself: Are the women involved simply too sensitive? Or are these in fact bona fide cases of harassment? Before you read the verdict, make your own judgment and see whether your behavioral gyroscope is guiding you straight and true—or wobbling dangerously.

CASE #1

Is Sex Between Consenting Adults Harassment?

THE SECURITIES AND EXCHANGE Commission office was a sociable place to work—sociable, that is, if you were one of several employees, including supervisors, having romantic affairs with each other, holding frequent parties and leaving the office during the day to go drinking.

But one female attorney who did not participate in the carousing found her co-workers' behavior repulsive. She claimed she was harassed by the environment in which she had to work. Moreover, she said, women who had affairs with male supervisors were rewarded with bonuses and promotions. The woman conceded that no one had pressured her for sex or denied her any promotions because she wasn't one of the crowd.

Was she being too touchy?

THE DECISION: Although the woman wasn't harassed on a quid pro quo (give something to get something) basis, a judge ruled that the "pervasive" behavior in the SEC office had created an offensive work environment. She was awarded back pay, a promotion and her choice of two jobs. The SEC also agreed to an outside review of its personnel practices.

THE EXPERT ANALYSIS: "That's a hostile work environment—no question about it," says Thomas A. McGinn, a human-resources consultant in Charlottesville,

Virginia, and co-author (with Nancy Dodd McCann) of *Harassed: 100 Women Define Inappropriate Behavior in the Workplace* (Business One Irwin).

Socializing at work has its limits, and those limits certainly were crossed in the Roman Empire–type revels at that SEC office. Federal guidelines warn specifically that an employer who gives benefits to anyone in exchange for sex may be held liable for discriminating against other workers. But any affairs within an office— even among peers—can raise the potential for unequal treatment of nonparticipants.

CASE #2:

That's Entertainment?

FEW THINGS ARE AS BORING AS MOST corporate meetings. In an attempt to liven up the presentations, an oil company brought a barely clad woman on a motorcycle to a regional meeting, according to a sexual-harassment complaint filed by a female supervisor for the company.

Moreover, she charged, when the corporation held a sales meeting at a restaurant, the entertainment was provided by strippers. And at a slide show held for employees, one slide featured the female supervisor's clothed rear end.

Was the woman harassed?

THE DECISION: The federal judge presiding over this case noted that the incidents were without question inappropriate but weren't "sufficiently severe or pervasive to constitute a hostile environment." That noted, he found that no harassment had taken place.

THE EXPERT ANALYSIS: Surely there are other ways to entertain and inform employees, suggests Anthony M. Micolo, a human-resources representative with Eastman Kodak in New York City. As for the incidents in the case: "I would probably feel myself, as a man, uncomfortable with this stuff," he says.

More to the point is that while a "hostile environment" charge often needs more than one or two incidents to substantiate it, other judges might find episodes such as the preceding sufficient to establish a pervasive climate of harassment. Micolo points out that corporations need to consider what conduct will be deemed acceptable. "Above and beyond sales goals and operational goals, there have to be people goals," he says. "You have to view the work environment as one that's productive to employees, not oppressive to them."

CASE #3

Just a Friendly Ride

A MIDWINTER SNOWSTORM HIT SO hard that one Virginia corporation sent its workers home early. A female word-processing technician needed a ride, which was readily offered by a male engineer for whom she had done some work. He assured her that his four-wheel drive vehicle would have no trouble navigating the storm.

Indeed, it didn't. When they arrived, he entered her apartment. He says he only kissed her. She says he tried to kiss and fondle her, despite her protestations. When she complained to their employer, the man was reprimanded and warned he would be fired if he committed another such act.

Was he simply a clumsy guy looking for companionship or a threatening menace?

WHAT HAPPENED: The woman's lawyers showed in court that the corporation had received previous complaints from other women about the man's behavior. After a ruling determined that the company had a legal responsibility to prevent the incident, the employer made an out-of-court settlement.

THE EXPERT ANALYSIS: According to Louise Fitzgerald, a psychologist and researcher on sexual harassment at the University of Illinois at Champaign, such a scenario is common but not innocuous. "This is unwanted sexual attention of a predatory nature and is a violation of someone's right to bodily integrity." In research Fitzgerald conducted among working women, 15 percent had been victims at work of undesired attempts at touching, fondling, grabbing or kissing.

CASE #4

The Chummy Boss

THE NEW SECRETARY THOUGHT IT strange that her boss walked her to her car every night, but she believed it was to offer security. She couldn't explain why he walked her to the bathroom, hovered over her desk, left her personal notes about her appearance or bought her gifts. She complained about this to her friends, but not to management.

She hoped that by letting her boss know she was happily married, the unwanted attention would stop. Instead, when she was hospitalized for back surgery, he

199

called frequently, visited, sent notes and brought flowers. When she returned to work, he tried to give her back rubs whenever he noticed her stretching. She told him to stop. Finally, she spoke to a supervisor, who told her to talk to her boss again. Ultimately, she quit the job after her boss accused her of having an affair with a male co-worker and threatened to withhold a promised raise if it was true.

Was the boss anything more than an annoying pest?

WHAT HAPPENED: A local human-relations commission ruled in the woman's favor and the company offered a $6,700 settlement. She declined the settlement and went to court.

Then a federal judge asserted that no harassment had taken place. He ruled that the boss's conduct "would not have interfered with a reasonable person's work performance or created an intimidating, hostile or offensive working environment." He added that the woman's protests to her boss "were not delivered with any sense of urgency, sincerity or force." Legal experts say such cases will now more often be decided by juries, with verdicts increasingly likely to favor complainants.

THE EXPERT ANALYSIS: Some argue that in order to dispel any hint of sexual harassment in an office, all friendly interactions would have to stop. However, Jonathan A. Segal, a management attorney in Philadelphia who advises companies on sexual harassment issues, disputes that dour view. "An occasional compliment is not harassment," he says, "but an excessive interest in an employee's private life is."

Segal spends most of his time providing employers with preventive education on how to avoid situations such as the one above. "Any thorough training program would make clear that what this individual did was wrong," he says. Moreover, he adds, complaints should never be handled by the individuals charged with harassment.

CASE #5

The Writing on the Wall

A WOMAN LEARNED THAT OBSCENE cartoons about her had been posted in the men's room of her office building. The graffiti sketches depicted various sex acts and mentioned her name.

The lewd illustrations remained on display in the public bathroom for a week, even after the company's chief executive had seen them. It was only after he

WHAT MAY BE ONE MAN'S CLUMSY ATTEMPT AT FRIENDSHIP OR EVEN HONEST ROMANCE MAY BE ONE WOMAN'S SHEER HELL.

learned the woman was upset about the cartoons that they were removed.

Was the office worker sexually harassed or was she just the target of crude, yet childish, pranksters?

WHAT HAPPENED: The court sided with the woman, determining that the cartoons were "highly offensive to a woman who seeks to deal with her fellow employees and clients with professional dignity." The employer agreed to pay her full salary and psychiatric bills until she found new employment.

In a similar case, a federal judge in Jacksonville, Florida, determined that pinup calendars and posters of women's genitals that were displayed at a shipyard were a "visual assault on the sensibilities of female workers," constituted sexual harassment and kept women out of jobs there.

THE EXPERT ANALYSIS: Where certain men might feel flattered or amused to have their names attached to sexually explicit cartoons, most women would likely feel shame and humiliation. Joan Lester, director of the Equity Institute, an Emeryville, California, consultancy in multicultural issues, points out that for a woman to be chosen for such treatment is "chilling and intimidating." It's also potentially dangerous: "The cartoons could be an incitement to sexual violence." For the targeted woman, that fear—coupled with the ridicule—could quickly destroy her work world.

It would have been far better if a male co-worker had taken the pictures down immediately, but such allies for women are often rare in work settings. "There's the fear [for a male co-worker] of breaking rank, that his masculinity will be ques-

tioned," says Lester. The situation was worsened by the company president's knowledge of the drawings. "It shows he didn't have an understanding of the human consequences and the legal issues," Lester adds.

CASE #6

What Is Reasonable

T WO OFFICE EMPLOYEES, FEMALE and male, worked at desks just a few yards away from each other. One day they went to lunch together.

When the man later asked the woman out for yet another lunch (and perhaps a drink), she turned him down. After that rebuff, he began sending her love letters, including one that was three pages long and single-spaced. The woman became increasingly frightened about the unwanted attention and filed a sexual harassment complaint.

Was the man just doing some harmless, old-fashioned courting?

WHAT HAPPENED: The woman's case was dismissed at first by a judge who called the man's behavior "trivial," but an appellate court, in a precedent-setting decision, found that sexual harassment should be viewed as a "reasonable woman" might experience it and remanded it back to the lower court. More and more future cases will be decided using this "reasonable woman" standard.

THE EXPERT ANALYSIS: In a society in which sexual assault is not uncommon, such persistent, unwelcome advances from a man are frightening. "Physical size and physical well-being have a lot to do with it," says San Francisco labor attorney Cliff Palefsky, who represents plaintiffs in sexual harassment cases. That's why, Palefsky explains, if a man is subjected to excessive staring by a woman, he might think, "So what?" But when the situation is reversed, "it's enough to give a woman the creeps." Most men, he adds, have never experienced such scary intrusiveness.

Because of men's and women's disparate views, the evaluation of sexual harassment charges is now moving away from the legal tradition of using a "reasonable man's" (or "reasonable person's") interpretation of an incident to judgments based on how a "reasonable woman" might view an event. Palefsky says the concept has received quick acceptance. "This isn't paternalistic protection for women," he says. "It's a reality. There's such a huge difference in perspective."

THE **PAIN** OF SEXUAL HARASSMENT AFTER 50

Why older women are vulnerable . . . and how they should fight back

Deborah Mason

DEBORAH MASON is a critic and essayist whose work appears often in the NEW YORK TIMES. A contributing editor to NEW CHOICES, she writes the Up Front column in the magazine.

"She told me there was this one guy in the office—maybe 19, 20—who was always making suggestive remarks to her. She couldn't figure out what was going on. At first she thought it must be something she was doing. So she stopped wearing V-necked blouses. She pulled her hair back into a bun. And she started wearing a jacket to cover herself up. Things didn't change. As a matter of fact, they got a lot worse. One day he walked over to her and said, 'Valerie, you're just so fantastic—see what you made me do?' He opened up his hand. What he'd done was to fill it with white hand lotion as if it were semen."

This story, told to the leader of a sexual-harassment workshop, has a footnote that would probably surprise most people. Valerie is 58.

The Navy's Tailhook scandal and the Clarence Thomas–Anita Hill hearings may have finally dragged the dirty secret of sexual harassment out into the daylight, but one dark corner remains: the sexual harassment of women 50 and older. Most Americans don't know it even exists; many of those who do know shy away from talking about it. Among those who stay silent are the women themselves—office workers, executives and housewives who often have a hard time recognizing and acknowledging the sexual harassment, let alone doing something about it.

For this article, some of these women agreed to break their silence and tell *NEW CHOICES* their stories. The picture that emerged was unsettling. Though their harassment was sometimes less blatant than that of younger women, its effects were usually more devastating. The reason: 50-plus women have a built-in set of vulnerabilities that may intensify sexual harassment's already terrible toll.

There is one trait many older women share with the rest of the culture: a mix of misunderstanding and denial when the topic is raised at all. "Oh, come on! Who would want to look at me? I'm 59 years old!" snapped Roberta, the owner of my local coffee shop, when I mentioned my article. Like most people, she took it as a given that sexual harassment happens as a result of simple physical attraction or some special mix of youth and beauty. Therefore, this reasoning goes, once a woman is no longer young and curvaceous, once time inscribes a few lines on her face, the problem evaporates.

Roberta—and most Americans—don't know the truth. "It's an out-and-out myth that sexual harassment is about attraction or attractiveness," says Susan Webb, whose Seattle-based management consulting firm runs workshops nationwide on how to prevent harassment in the workplace—and the person to whom Valerie (not her real name) told her story. "What really drives harassment is power, someone's need to assert power over another person by intimidation, to 'keep them in their place.'"

When a man harasses a woman, experts say, the message underlying his actions is: "You may think you're a big deal, but I'm here to remind you—by brushing up against your body every time we pass in the hall, or making comments about your sex life, by hanging a pornographic picture on my wall—that in the end, you're just a woman. And don't you forget it."

What matters most of all to the harasser is the woman's gender. Sexual harassment is an equal-opportunity tormentor, targeting

What drives sexual harassment is power—someone's need to 'keep [other people] in their place' —Susan Webb

women of all ages. Indeed, the full report of the Tailhook investigation revealed that one of the harassment victims was a woman in her mid-60s.

"It's out there, all right: Sexual harassment of older women is not only in the workplace—it's in hospitals, in their apartment houses, even in nursing homes," says Sandy Warshaw, president of the Greater New York chapter of the Older Women's League, a national advocacy group for midlife and older women. "When I speak about it in public and give examples of the forms it takes, women always come up and say, 'That's what happened to me.'" Among those forms are the straying hands of the hospital orderly as he helps a patient out of bed, the snide sexual comments of the nursing-home aide the woman depends on for her breakfast tray, the apartment super who corners

the female tenant in her own kitchen. But society's routine dismissal of the older woman, its general uneasiness about connecting her with anything sexual—and the way she herself buys into both biases—contribute to the reluctance to recognize what is going on.

The official statistics? "As far as I know, those numbers just don't exist," says Webb. "People don't think much about older women."

Data that does exist suggests why 50-plus women are particularly susceptible. "Sure, sexual harassment occurs more at younger ages," says Webb. "But I also know that there is data that it happens more to widowed, divorced, separated or single women—women without men, women whose husbands are not going to beat the living daylights out of the guy. Harassers pick people with whom they think they can get away with it." And by those yardsticks, older women are frequent targets.

Sometimes the harassers are the men whom widows and divorcees depend upon most of all—their therapists, lawyers and doctors. Indeed, a recent rash of such cases has pushed the American Bar Association, among other professional groups, to issue its first formal opinion on sexual ethics.

Seattle psychologist Shirley Feldman-Summers, Ph.D., points out that the sexual harassment in these "fiduciary relationships" is particularly insidious because their cornerstone is trust—the woman's trust that her best interest will be paramount to the professional. She assumes he will understand that she may be at one of the most emotionally vulnerable times of her life—suffering through the end of a long marriage, coping with the death of her husband, contending with fears about her health.

Feldman-Summers has encountered the case of a 49-year-old teacher whose harassment occurred after an abusive childhood and a 30-year marriage in which her husband battered her and denigrated her as ugly and stupid.

"She came to her gynecologist feeling unloved, unwanted and mistreated, open to flattery and his professions of caring," says

Feldman-Summers, who wrote about the case in her chapter of *Sexual Exploitation in Professional Relationships* (edited by Glen Gabbard). During an exam, he made sexual advances that she found difficult to resist and that ultimately led to intercourse.

"The older woman is at risk—more than other women in some sense—because we put such a premium on youth," Feldman-Summers told NEW CHOICES. "In your 40s and 50s, you're more likely to start questioning your desirability—you're more vulnerable."

Additionally, a 50-plus woman in our society has been raised with a view of doctors and lawyers as deities. She sees their wisdom and power as infinite. What she doesn't see is that this attitude can prevent her questioning the appropriateness of their actions or facing up to their betrayal of her trust.

"First of all, it was the dirty jokes. There wasn't a clean word that came out of that man's mouth. And they were constant. If you say you don't like it, that doesn't stop it. Then you get snide comments implying that at the age of 50 a woman has no sex life left—like 'You must really need it' or 'I guess you don't want it anymore.' In my mind, that's just as demeaning as being touched.

"Then there was the crowding. As he would tell these dirty jokes, he would kind of crowd into me—one day, he even crowded me against the office bulletin board where the Equal Employment Opportunity Commission laws against sexual harassment were listed."

Sandy Warshaw, now 59, endured this type of sexual harassment, known legally as "hostile work environment," while contract manager at one of New York's city agencies. Only when she was getting ready to take early retirement, her pension of 24 years secure, did she feel safe in confronting her harasser. "He looked at me blankly and said, 'You know, you're the only woman in the office who doesn't like my jokes.' I said to him, 'The other women in the office really need their paychecks.'"

In a job market that is bleak no matter what your age, it is even bleaker for the 50-plus woman. "I think that for every Anita Hill, there is an Anita Hill Senior out there," says Warshaw, "an older woman who makes no noise, because if she loses this job, she can't just move on to another one the way a younger woman would."

He said: 'You're the only woman who doesn't like my jokes.' I said: 'The others need their paychecks' —Sandy Warshaw

For this type of woman, the workplace can be a prison where her daily dose of sexual harassment is as routine as the coffee break. Susan Webb tells about a woman close to retirement, a secretary in a government forestry agency in the West. Every man who worked in the forest would go past her desk each morning and, in a much too familiar way, say "Hi, Babe" or "Hi, Honey." "What they don't understand when they do it," she told Webb, "is that I hear a million comments like that a day! And I hate it. I dread seeing them come through that door." "But if she had complained," says Webb, "there'd be the fear that she'd be fired!"

Middle-aged women who have worked their way up to a position of power can also be at risk—when male colleagues see them as a threat and target them to be "taken down a peg." The men often do it by using sexual intimidation. And women know all too well that to blow the whistle may jeopardize careers they've spent years training for and building, step by step.

Stanford University neurosurgeon Frances Conley, M.D., 53, experienced repeated incidents of harassment, which included a male colleague commenting on the size of her breasts and another putting his hand on her leg at a luncheon. She finally resigned her 16-year teaching post when the man whom she felt had fostered the sexist environment in the department was nominated to be chairman of neurosurgery. She agreed to return after his nomination was canceled and the medical school instituted a program requiring staff members to undergo gender-sensitivity training.

Conley chose to fight back—and won. Other women find it difficult to take that first step. Over and over, 50-plus women have told *NEW CHOICES* they felt confusion, self-doubt and quiet pain before they decided what, if anything, to do about their harassment. "When it happens, it's much more devastating for an older woman," says Isabelle Pinzler, head of the American Civil Liberties Union's Women's Rights Project. "Because the phenomenon is not well recognized, you have a smaller support system—or none at all." That makes it harder to bounce back, harder to even think of talking about it.

"When these women do try to talk about their harassment," says Judith Avner, director of New York State's Division for Women, "the messages they get back are 'You should be happy you have a job,' and 'You should be thrilled someone is paying attention to you!'— both of which reinforce their own feelings and those old myths about what it means to be a woman."

It also doesn't help to have been raised at a time when the cardinal rule of womanhood was to never make waves, to always "make nice." Such early training often kicks in when the 50-plus woman is harassed. It encourages her to remain a smiling, super-efficient, oh-so-conscientious employee— and one in full denial that there is anything wrong with submitting to a back rub from her boss.

This woman does not recognize, or does not want to recognize, what is really going on. "If you fear growing older, you are not going to look at these things," says Warshaw. Or you're going to try to deflect them with a joke. When she talks to some older women, Warshaw adds, "They say, 'Oh, if only I could be harassed!' "

Another efficient escape route particularly favored by the 50-plus "good girl" is to simply, neatly blame it on herself. "It must be something I've done" goes the refrain she knows by heart. All she has to do is to stop wearing V-necked blouses, like Valerie, and the problem will be solved without "ruffling anyone's feathers."

But denial has its costs; feelings of powerlessness, unconscious though they may be, create problems. These women may go home and eat too much or drink too much. Or snap at their families. Or wake up in the middle of the night grinding their teeth. Mornings, they may have a lot of trouble getting out of bed. At work, they may lose their focus or dedication.

Fortunately, women are beginning to learn that they must confront the reality. Talking about it with their family and colleagues is a first step many take. "I think the whole issue is just dawning on these women who have been working in a sexually charged, hostile atmosphere for 25 years," says the ACLU's Pinzler. "They always knew that something was wrong with it, but there wasn't a word for it, and they thought there was nothing they could do about it." Now they're learning that the suffering that they thought of as "the name of the game" affects 40 to 60 percent of working women and that *now* it is against the law.

For many 50-plus women, the impetus of the women's movement paired with the clarity and assertiveness often called "postmenopausal zest" may generate new, more straightforward ways of handling harassment. "I see them saying, 'What? Do you want me to slap you into tomorrow?' " says Susan Webb with relish.

At the same time, Webb says she still sees enormous reluctance to report incidents because, most women tell her, "No one around here is going to pay attention to what I say." In the elevator, at the coffee machine, in the ladies' room, they hear about the punishing consequences of reporting sexual harassment. "The way it stands now, there are no rewards for telling the truth," says Bernice Friedlander, di-

How You Should Fight Back

What to do if you are sexually harassed by your lawyer, doctor or therapist: "First, seek out a counselor to talk about possible options," says Seattle psychologist Shirley Feldman-Summers. "Then if you decide to pursue it legally, talk to a couple of lawyers to find out what's involved. Reporting the incident to the appropriate professional association and licensing board is an arduous procedure: Find a professional who'll be your advocate. It's good to have someone on your side."

What to do if you are sexually harassed on the job:

1. Deal with the harassment directly when it occurs, or prepare by practicing in case it happens again, by saying, "I'm not interested" or "I prefer that you do not touch me when we talk." Say it firmly, without smiling or apologizing, making it clear the behavior is inappropriate.

2. Keep a diary or log of what is happening to you, in a bound book to which sheets of paper cannot be added. Take accurate notes of what is said or done, including dates, times, places. Include direct quotes. Save any letters, notes or materials sent to you. Keep everything in a secure place, preferably at home—not in your desk or locker at work.

3. Talk to your co-workers about the incident to learn if anyone witnessed it or if anyone else has been harassed. Witnesses and documentation provide proof of harassment. Otherwise, the only evidence may be your word against the harasser's.

4. If the harasser persists, you may state in writing that you object to this behavior. This will allow you to organize and communicate your feelings without being interrupted. If the letter does not get the harasser to stop, send a copy to a supervisor. Keep a copy for your files. The letter can later be used in support of a formal complaint or lawsuit, if needed.

5. Use formal complaint procedures at work. Report the harassment to the designated human-resources representative or to your supervisor. If you are being harassed by your supervisor, report the harassment to that person's supervisor.

Where to go for legal help: Your state's Department of Human Rights and the U.S. Equal Employment Opportunity Commission, 1801 L Street NW, Washington, DC 20507 (800/669-4000). The EEOC has offices around the country. Check your telephone book under "U.S. Government." (EEOC regulations do not cover employers with fewer than 15 workers. You must file within 300 days of the alleged violation.)

The work-related guidelines were drawn up by Women Employed, a national women's advocacy group based in Chicago (312/782-3902). Another resource: the National Hotline of 9 to 5 (800-522-0925), one of the largest legislative advocacy groups for working women.

---

rector of public affairs for the Department of Labor's Women's Bureau. "If you even make a move toward filing a complaint, you're marked as a troublemaker and no one will want to hire you."

In other words, you're someone who doesn't act the way a woman —and especially an "older" woman —should. Someone who won't avert her eyes or just leave quietly. Someone like Betty Hall from Franklin Lakes, New Jersey, who has taken a company to court.

"It was 3 o'clock on a Friday afternoon, and about 60 of us in the office had gathered for a party for a young man who was getting married. It was sponsored by my supervisor, Bob Ulrich, and Bob Prieto, a man in his late 30s who had taken over as director of corporate development at my company, Parsons Brinckerhoff Quade & Douglas, an international engineering and transportation design firm in downtown Manhattan.

"First of all, gifts were presented to the guest of honor. He opened them to find condoms, 'horny pills,' and worst of all, a plastic life-sized model of a woman's genitals.

"The cake was in the shape of a woman's body with big breasts topped by chocolate candy nipples. Three balloons had been placed in the genital area to represent a penis and testes. The bulletin board was covered with sexually oriented postcards and posters.

"I found the whole thing so degrading—I was so outraged—that I finally decided to tell the chairman of the board, Henry Michel, for whom I'd done a lot of work. I pointed out to him that I was no prude, but that I'd found the party very offensive. I also said I was concerned that it could damage the company's reputation."

Betty Hall, now 65, is a veteran public-relations woman who was employed by Parsons Brinckerhoff for 10 years as their chief business writer, editing 10 annual reports and collaborating on numerous proposals that helped the company win lucrative contracts. The allegations in her pending lawsuit, which she summarized for *NEW CHOICES* above, also extend into the weeks and months following the party:

After her meeting with the company chairman, she also delivered to human resources her confidential report on the incident—carefully following the procedures in the employee manual. She was the only employee who did.

"I was supposed to have a written report back in 10 days. The people responsible were supposed to have been disciplined," Hall told *NEW CHOICES*. "There should have been a company-wide announcement by the president or the chairman of the board that this was not appropriate. Instead, I was the one who suffered."

Ten days after reporting the incident, Hall had her annual review. Until then, she had scored "outstanding" and "above average" in most areas. Now she was downgraded to "average" and given no raise. In the months that followed, according to her complaint, she lost her window office, and the terms and conditions of her employment changed for the worse.

Hall protested her treatment by filing a complaint with the Equal Employment Opportunity Commission. The EEOC investigation lasted nearly a year, leaving Hall feeling isolated and insecure. "I had everything taken away from me. No one cared, no one protected me. The company just let me twist in the wind. I felt despondent. I couldn't sleep. I gained weight." In May 1991, one year after the party (and shortly after Hall had completed the annual report), she was fired. The official reason? She was laid off as part of a force reduction.

The whole ordeal was so anguishing, so humiliating, Hall says, that it took a long time before she could talk to anyone outside her family about it. The turning point came when she went to a workshop on sexual harassment, several months after the Anita Hill hearings. "Every speaker emphasized: Don't keep it inside—it will kill you. From then on, I started talking about it."

Still waiting for the ruling on her first case, Hall filed a second complaint with the EEOC, charging retaliation. Several months later, after what her lawyer, Arlene Boop, of Alterman & Boop, describes as "a perfunctory investigation," the EEOC issued "no probable cause" rulings on both charges. (Such a ruling is not considered to be a conclusive determination of the legal merits of a case.) Hall was issued a "right to sue" letter for each complaint. On December 24, 1991, she filed a civil suit in federal court, charging Parsons Brinckerhoff with sexual harassment, age and gender discrimination, and retaliation. "I think they figured I was just some little old lady who wouldn't have the nerve to do anything about it," she says.

Parsons Brinckerhoff responded by denying most of the allegations in Betty Hall's complaint as well as any wrongdoing. Contacted by *NEW CHOICES*, spokeswoman Marcia Earle said that the company could not comment in any detail because the matter was still in court. The case is now in the process of deposition—the pertinent people on both sides testifying before the lawyers as to what they did and why.

With women like Betty Hall, Sandy Warshaw and Frances Conley, the tragic silence about the sexual harassment of 50-plus women is finally ending. Indeed, their wrenching testimony and that of other older women at recent New York state and city hearings pushed the Governor's Task Force on Sexual Harassment, chaired by Judith Avner, to take a groundbreaking step: the first full-scale survey of sexual harassment's impact on women 55 and older. The results will be released this month.

"Yes, these last couple of years have been traumatic," Betty Hall told *NEW CHOICES*. "But it would have been worse not to fight it, not to do anything about it. Now that I have, I don't feel like a victim. Now, maybe my daughter and my granddaughter will never have to fight this terrible battle." Nor anyone's granddaughter, mother or grandmother, ever again.

When "No" Isn't Enough:
How to Handle Sexual Harassment

If you think that none of your workers are being sexually harassed, think again.

"Sexual harassment is going on in almost every company in the country," says Freada Klein of Klein Associates, a management consulting firm in Cambridge, Mass. "Our data suggests that 15 percent of women and 5 percent of men encounter behavior they define as sexual harassment every year they're on the job."

Compounding the problem is the fact that the majority of victims do not come forward with any complaints. But whether or not companies are aware of complaints, says Klein, "sexual harassment is costing them money: It's disruptive to morale and productivity, and is directly related to high turnover."

Factor in the ever-increasing number of large judgments that courts are awarding victims of sexual harassment—many in six figures—not to mention the toll on human dignity that such harassment takes, and it's clear that all employers ignore the issue of sexual harassment at their own peril.

To protect employees and employers itself from problems involving sexual harassment, there are a number of steps that should be taken.

You can start, says Klein, by letting employees know how you feel about sexual harassment. "Raise the issue," she advises. "State, 'This behavior is prohibited. We don't tolerate it.'"

Of course, that alone will not keep sexual harassment from occurring. To help prevent problems—and offer a measure of legal protection if complaints are made—you need to develop a comprehensive program that defines what constitutes sexual harassment, provides for employee training on the issue, and creates a special grievance and discipline procedure.

Because sexual harassment can take so many forms, Barbara Otto—director of program and public affairs for 9 to 5, the National Association of Working Women—suggests involving your employees from the earliest stage of policy development.

When people are given the opportunity to ask questions and contribute to the policy, they understand it better, she notes, "and they then have a much better understanding of how to interact with one another."

Additional tips for developing a strong policy on sexual harassment:

• Personalize the policy.

To be effective, Klein says, a policy needs to be tailored to the kinds of behaviors that may arise in your specific business.

• Give examples.

"You want to have a good working definition that is fairly easy for people to understand and not cluttered with 'legalese,'" says attorney Ellen Wagner, president of Creative Solutions Inc., a New Jersey-based firm that specializes in legal issues of human resources.

Offering examples is critical, Otto believes, because it helps employees distinguish between acceptable behavior and behavior that is unwelcome, offensive or abusive.

• Avoid stereotypes.

When most people think about sexual harassment, the image that comes to mind is one of a woman being victimized by her male boss. But men can be the victims too, emphasizes Pamela J. Thomason, regional attorney for the Los Angeles District Office of the United States Equal Employment Opportunity Commission.

Nor does harassment depend on two people of the opposite sex being involved. "Sexual harassment can occur from any conduct of a sexual nature, including men against men or women against women," Thomason says.

• Include nonemployees.

Your employees need to know that harassment can include inappropriate behavior that takes place off-site with nonemployees, says Klein. "It isn't just what happens within the walls of the office."

To help prevent this type of harassment, Klein recommends including a clause in your agreements with clients, specifying that this type of behavior will not be tolerated and will be grounds for terminating the business arrangement.

Training the troops

Once you've developed a written policy on sexual harassment—and have posted it, or, better yet, distributed copies to all employees—the next step is to provide employee training on the issue.

Even if you cannot afford to hire professional consultants to offer training on the issue, you can provide your employees with an informal, in-house training program.

"Just take your opportunities where you would naturally find them, like during orientation sessions," suggests Wagner. "If you are replacing your policy manual or handbook, take that opportunity to include sexual harassment in them. Or if you have a management meeting, don't forget to include the issue of sexual harassment."

Employee reviews and departmental meetings are two other times when it may be appropriate to broach the subject of harassment, says Klein.

Paying attention

Another crucial element in any comprehensive program to combat sexual harassment is some sort of monitoring effort. "Since we're talking about behavior that for the most part starts subtly or ambiguously and then escalates," notes Klein, "your goal must be to surface it early and get it to stop."

Are there certain problem departments? Problem functions in the organization? Is there confusion about how the policy and complaint channels work? "Gathering this type of information can be done most systematically through surveys," she

From *Human Rights*, Spring 1993, pp. 12-13. © 1993 by Anne Blakey. Reprinted by permission of the author.

notes, "but it also can be accomplished by committees, task forces, and other means of pulse-taking among the employee population."

Just being aware of how people interact can tip you off to potential problems, adds Otto. "You can tell when someone is uncomfortable. Or when you have an employee who is avoiding someone else in the office, or an employee who is consistently calling in sick when he or she has to work with a certain individual."

You must try to recognize signs of sexual harassment even before there is a claim or report filed, she stresses. If you don't catch a problem early on, the victimized employee may very well resign and claim "constructive discharge" along with harassment.

Handling complaints

Because sexual harassment is such an emotionally charged issue, says Klein, company policies must incorporate flexible and understanding grievance procedures if they hope to encourage employees to report problems.

"You need to help employees handle situations in a way that not only is calculated to end the sexual harassment, but that also protects their careers and privacy."

Everybody involved is going to have rights, and those rights frequently conflict, Wagner points out. "The issues of confidentiality, non-retaliation, and disclosure have to be gone over carefully and clearly with every individual who is being interviewed," she says.

Klein's suggestion? Include informal problem-solving meetings along with more formal investigations, and allow employees to chose where they feel most comfortable entering the process.

"Even then," adds Wagner, "they may not report sexual harassment if the company's internal complaint mechanism is not viewed as credible or effective. That's why any good policy should not ask people to take their complaint back to their supervisor."

Otto agrees: "As an employer, you need to set up an alternative grievance procedure, separate from your regular procedure, because nine times out of ten the harasser is a direct supervisor."

She suggests directing employees to a female in a power position with whom women would feel comfortable talking about their complaint.

Despite the delicacy of these situations, companies have a legal duty to investigate claims of sexual harassment. "That investigation has to be prompt and thorough," Wagner says, "but it also needs to minimize the amount of discussion in the workplace, because when sexual harassment is claimed, the possibility of defaming someone who may be innocent is not far behind."

Taking action

What kind of discipline? Otto recommends that a company's policy specify possible disciplinary measures— everything from, say, a three-day suspension without pay to outright termination in some cases.

Disciplinary action ought to match the behavior in terms of severity and be consistent with how other serious policy violations are handled.

It should also be applied consistently, "regardless of the value of the perpetrator to the company," says Klein.

As complicated and difficult as this issue may be, companies must not be afraid to act. Concludes Wagner: "Unfortunately, the issue of sexual harassment in the workplace is not going to go away. If you want to minimize the legal risk to your business, you'd better do everything possible to protect your employees from being harassed."

— Anne Blakey
Anne Blakey is a Los Angeles-based editor and writer.

SEXUAL Correctness

Has it gone too far?

SARAH CRICHTON

THE WOMEN AT BROWN UNIversity play hardball. Three years ago, fed up with an administration that wasn't hopping into action, they scrawled the names of alleged rapists on the bathroom stalls. Brown woke up, revamped its disciplinary system and instituted mandatory sexual-assault education for freshmen. But that really hasn't calmed the siege mentality. This fall, Alan S., class of '94, returned to Brown after a one-year suspension for "non-consensual physical contact of a sexual nature," the first student to come back after such disciplinary action. And two weeks ago, all over Brown—on the doors of dorms, on bulletin boards, by the mailroom in Faunce House—posters cropped up. Under a mug shot cut from a class book, it read, "These are the facts: [Alan S.] was convicted of 'sexual misconduct' by the UDC, was sentenced to a one-year suspension; he has served his term and is back on campus." It was signed "rosemary and time." As these posters go, it was low-key. But that doesn't matter. Alan S. had been publicly branded as an "assaulter."

No big deal, said senior Jennifer Rothblatt, hanging out in the Blue Room, a campus snack bar. "As a protest against the system, it's valid and necessary," she said, brushing her long, golden-brown hair off

Watch what you say, watch what you do. Will the new rules of feminist politics set women free—or set them back?

her face. Besides, she added, the posters simply state the facts.

Well, wait. What are the facts? Who is the victimizer here and who is the victim? In the ever-morphing world of Thou Shalt Not Abuse Women it's getting mighty confusing. Crimes that hurt women are bad; we know that. But just as opportunities keep expanding for women, the list of what hurts them seems to grow, too. A Penn State professor claims Goya's luscious "The Naked Maja," a print of which hangs in her classroom, hurts her ability to teach; it sexually harasses her. A Northwestern University law professor is trying to make street remarks—your basic "hey baby" stuff—legally punishable as assaultive behavior that limits a woman's liberty. Verbal

coercion can now constitute rape. But what is verbal coercion—"Do me or die"? Or, "C'mon, Tiffany, if you won't, I'm gonna go off with Heather." If the woman didn't want it, it's sexual assault. And thanks to nature, he's got the deadly weapon.

Feminist politics have now homed in like missiles on the twin issues of date rape and sexual harassment, and the once broad-based women's movement is splintering over the new sexual correctness. "The Morning After: Sex, Fear and Feminism on Campus," a controversial new book by Katie Roiphe, argues that issues like date rape reduce women to helpless victims in need of protective codes of behavior. The much-publicized rules governing sexual intimacy at Antioch College seem to stultify relations between men and women on the cusp of adulthood. Like political correctness on campuses, there's pitifully little room for debate or diverse points of view. For expressing her ideas, Roiphe has received threats. A NEWSWEEK photographer at Antioch—a woman who had permission to photograph—was attacked by a mob of students and, yes, sexually harassed by several who exposed themselves.

The workplace, the campuses and the courts are the new testing grounds of sexual correctness. Complaints of harassment on the job have ballooned in the last three years as men and women try to sort out when they can and cannot flirt, flatter, offer a friendly pat. Too many rules? Maybe. The obsession with correct codes of behavior seems to portray women not as thriving on their hard-won independence but as victims who can't take care of themselves. Will the new rules set women free? Or will they set them back?

Young men and women used to be sent off to college with a clear sense of how it would be. Back in the dark ages, when guys still wielded mighty swords and girls still protected their virtue (which is to say, the mid-1960s), in a military school overlooking the Tennessee River, a colonel gathered his graduating cadets for the everything-you-need-to-know-about-sex lecture.

"Gentlemen," he drawled, "soon you'll go off and get married and before you do, you need to understand the differences between men and women."

He began to draw a chart on the blackboard. At the top of one column he wrote MEN, at the top of another, WOMEN. It looked like this:

MEN	WOMEN
love	LOVE
SEX	sex

"That's what men and women believe in," he said, and then went on to describe a typical wedding night. When the bride finally climbs into bed and sees the groom, he warned, "chances are she'll scream and probably throw up. Don't worry: this is perfectly natural."

Bette Midler had a name for a night like that. Back in the early '70s, she sang of romantic disappointment in a little ditty called "Bad Sex." Everyone had bad sex back then and, to hear them tell, survived just fine. Now feminists on campus quote Andrea Dworkin: "The hurting of women is . . . basic to the sexual pleasure of men."

Rape and sexual harassment are real. But between crime and sexual bliss are some cloudy waters. To maneuver past the shoals, corporations and universities try a two-pronged approach: re-education and regulations. Some rules make sense: "It is unacceptable to have sex with a person if he/she is unconscious." Others seem silly. After attending mandatory sexual-harassment seminars at Geffen Records where she works, Bryn Bridenthal is rethinking every move she makes. "Everybody is looking for anything to be misinterpreted." Bridenthal used to quite innocently stroke the arm of a man who had a penchant for wearing luxuriously soft cashmere sweaters. "I never thought anything about it, but through the seminars I realized that I shouldn't do that," she says. "It's not worth doing anything that might be construed by anyone as sexual harassment."

If it's chilly in the workplace, it's downright freezing on campus. No school has concocted guidelines quite as specific as Antioch College's. Deep among the cornfields and pig farms of central Ohio in the town of Yellow Springs. Antioch prides itself on being "A Laboratory for Democracy." The dress code is grunge and black; multiple nose rings are *de rigueur,* and green and blue hair are preferred (if you have hair). Seventy percent of the student body are womyn (for the uninitiated, that's women—without the dreaded m-e-n). And the purpose of the Sexual Offense Policy is to empower these students to become equal partners when it comes time to mate with males. The goal is 100 percent consensual sex, and it works like this: it isn't enough to ask someone if she'd like to have sex, as an Antioch women's center advocate told a group of incoming freshmen this fall. You must obtain consent every step of the way. "If you want to take her blouse off, you have to ask. If you want to touch her breast you have to ask. If you want to move your hand down to her genitals, you have to ask. If you want to put your finger inside her, you have to ask." Well, Molly Bloom would do fine.

How silly this all seems; how sad. It criminalizes the delicious unexpectedness of sex—a hand suddenly moves to here, a mouth to there. What is the purpose of sex if not to lose control? (To be unconscious, no.) The advocates of sexual correctness are trying to take the danger out of sex, but sex is inherently dangerous. It leaves one exposed to everything from euphoria to crashing disappointment. That's its great unpredictability. But of course, that's sort of what we said when we were all made to wear seat belts.

What is implicit in the new sex guidelines is that it's the male who does the initiating and the woman who at any moment may bolt. Some young women rankle at that. "I think it encourages wimpy behavior by women and [the idea] that women need to be handled with kid gloves," says Hope Segal, 22, a fourth-year Antioch student. Beware those boys with their swords, made deaf by testosterone and, usually, blinded by drink.

Drink—the abuse of it, the abuses that occur because of it—is key. In up to 70 percent of acquaintance rapes, alcohol plays a role, says Manhattan sex-crimes prosecutor Linda Fairstein, author of "Sexual Violence: Our War Against Rape." And because alcohol poses such a powerful problem, it is the rule at almost every school (and the law in most states) that "consent is not meaningful" if given while under the influence of alcohol, drugs or prescription medication. If she's drunk, she's not mentally there, and her consent counts for zip. If the man is just as drunk as the woman, that's no excuse. Mary P. Koss is a professor of psychology at the University of Arizona and the author of a highly regarded, if controversial, survey of rape and college-age students. "The Scope of Rape" indicates that one in four college-age students has been the victim of a rape or an attempted rape. In those numbers Koss includes women who have been coerced into having sex while intoxicated. "The law punishes the drunk driver who kills a pedestrian," she argues. "And likewise, the law needs to be there to protect the drunk woman from the driver of the penis."

"Men and women just think differently," Antioch president Alan Guskin says, "and we've got to help the students understand the differences." It's a policy, he says, designed to create a "safe" campus environment. But for all the attempts to make them

---

A lot of young college women today just feel like sitting ducks

---

feel secure, a lot of young college women just feel like sitting ducks. "As a potential survivor . . ." a Barnard student said to a visiting reporter. As a *what?* Potential survivor equals an inevitable victim. Every Wednesday night at Dartmouth, a group of undergraduate women gather to warn one another about potential date rapists. At the University of Michigan, and several other schools as well, when sorority women attend frat parties, a designated "sober" monitor stands guard over her friends. "Whenever people start going upstairs, you go up to them right away," says Marcy Myers. "You ask, 'Do you know this guy? You're drunk, do you want to go home? You can call him tomorrow'." "My friends won't go to parties at Dartmouth without other women," says Abby Ross, and before they leave the dorm, they check each other's outfits, too. No one wears short skirts. "You should be able to wear whatever you want. But the reality is that you're not dealing with people who have the same set of values," says Ross.

This defensive mind-set is at the heart of the escalating battle over date rape. Critics charge feminists with hyping the statistics and so broadening the definition of rape that sex roles are becoming positively Victorian. Women are passive vessels with no responsibility for what happens; men are domineering brutes with just one thing on their minds. "People have asked me if I have ever been date-raped," writes Katie Roiphe in "The Morning After." "And thinking back on complicated nights, on too many glasses of wine, on strange and familiar beds, I would have to say yes. With such a sweeping definition of rape, I wonder how many people there are, male or female, who haven't been date-raped at one point or another... If verbal coercion constitutes rape, then the word 'rape' itself expands to include any kind of sex a woman experiences as negative."

Roiphe, 25, a Harvard graduate and now a doctoral candidate at Princeton, argues that a hysteria has gripped college campuses, fomented by "rape-crisis feminists." "The image that emerges from feminist preoccupations with rape and sexual harassment is that of women as victims, offended by a professor's dirty joke, verbally pressured into sex by peers. This image of a delicate woman bears a striking resemblance to that '50s ideal my mother and the other women of her generation fought so hard to get away from. They didn't like her passivity . . . her excessive need for protection . . . But here she is again, with her pure intentions and her wide eyes. Only this time it is the feminists themselves who are breathing new life into her."

ROIPHE IS GETTING WHOMPED FOR her provocative, though too-loosely documented, book. A "traitor," says Gail Dines, a professor of sociology and women's studies at Wheelock College, who lectures about rape and pornography. She calls Roiphe the "Clarence Thomas of women," just trying to suck up to the "white-male patriarchy." She thinks Roiphe will get her comeuppance. Warns Dines, in a most unsisterly fashion: "[When] she walks down the street, she's one more woman."

So how much of a threat is rape? What are women facing on dates with acquaintances or on the streets with strangers? Throughout her book, Roiphe wrestles with Koss's one-in-four statistic. "If I was really standing in the middle of an epidemic, a crisis," she asks, "if 25 percent of my female friends were really being raped, wouldn't I know about it?"

Heresy! Denial! Backlash! In an essay in The New Yorker, Katha Pollitt fired back: "As an experiment, I applied Roiphe's anecdotal method myself, and wrote down what I knew about my own circle of acquaintance: eight rapes by strangers (including one on a college campus), two sexual assaults (one Central Park, one Prospect Park), one abduction (woman walking down street forced into car full of men), one date rape involving a Mickey Finn, which resulted in pregnancy and abortion, and two stalkings (one ex-lover, one deranged fan); plus one brutal beating by a boyfriend, three incidents of childhood incest (none involving therapist-aided "recovered memories"), and one bizarre incident in which a friend went to a man's apartment after meeting him at a party and was forced by him to spend the night under the shower, naked, while he debated whether to kill her, rape her, or let her go."

Holy moly. Pollitt is one of the wisest essayists around; a fine poet, too. And far be it for us to question her list. So what does the list prove? Well, that even wise feminists fall precisely into the same trap as Roiphe: you can't extrapolate from your circle of acquaintance; friends don't constitute a statistical average. What's more, Pollitt is almost 20 years older than Roiphe; her friends presumably have lived more years, too. Still, Pollitt's litany is shocking. It's punch-my-victim-card time: How full's yours.

"When one woman is raped on campus, all women are afraid to go to the library and finish their chemistry homework," Pat Reuss, a senior policy analyst with the NOW Legal Defense Fund, told a workshop at the NOW National Convention this summer. Today, college students are handed, as part of their orientation programs, pamphlets that spell out the threat and, over and over, the same dire figures appear: As Penn State's Sexual Assault Awareness pamphlet reads, in can't-miss-it type: "FBI statistics indicate that one in three women in our society will be raped during her lifetime."

Except there are no such FBI figures. The figures the FBI does have to offer are both out-of-date and so conservative that most people dismiss them. The FBI recognizes rape only as involving forcible penetration of the vagina with a penis. Oral sex, anal sex, penetration with an object—these do not officially constitute rape. It doesn't matter to the FBI if a woman was made incapacitated by alcohol or drugs, and the agency certainly isn't interested in verbal coercion. Rape is as narrowly defined by the FBI as could be imagined.

So, in the rape-crisis mentality, the numbers keep being bloated. Which is crazy, considering the fact that even the most conservative numbers are horrifying. College students are a high-risk group. The No. 1 group to be sexually assaulted in this country are 16- to 19-year-olds. The second largest group hit are the 20- to 24-year-old age bracket. Women are four times more likely to be assaulted during these years than at any other time in their lives. Forty-five percent of all rapists arrested are under 25. And as for the most conservative, yet trustworthy, numbers: according to the National Victim Center survey last year—a survey that did not include intoxication—13 percent of adult women are victims of forcible rape. That's one in seven.

THAT'S A LOT. BUT IT DOESN'T mean all women are victims—or survivors, as we are supposed to call them. And it sure doesn't mean all "suffering" warrants attention or retribution—or even much sympathy. When New York state Assemblyman Harvey Weisenberg misspoke during a speech and said "sex" instead of "six," he covered up his error by looking at Assemblywoman Earlene Hill (Democrat of Hempstead) and joked, "Whenever I think of Earlene, I think of sex." Another brutish colleague wouldn't move his legs so she could get to her seat and made her climb over him. Sexual harassment, she cried, saying: "If I don't speak up, then they won't realize it's wrong and there will be a new victim." Oh, please. A student at the University of Virginia told The New York Times that she favored a ban on all student/faculty dating because "One of my professors asked me out and it made me really uncomfortable." So tell him to bug off. Artist Sue Williams plopped a six-feet-in-diameter piece of plastic vomit on the floor of the Whitney Museum as her protest against the male-dominated beauty-obsessed culture that makes women stick fingers down their throats. Tell them to get some therapy and cut it out. You want to talk victimization? Talk to the mothers all over America whose children have been slaughtered in urban cross-fire.

"I'm sick of women wallowing in the victim state," says Betty Friedan. "We have empowered ourselves. We are able to blow the whistle on rape. I am not as concerned with that as I am with violence in our whole society."

It does seem ironic that the very movement created to encourage women to stand up and fight their own battles has taken this strange detour, and instead is making them feel vulnerable and in need of protection. From the grade schools to the workplace, women are asking that everything be codified: How to act; what to say. Who to date; how to date; when to mate. They're huddling in packs, insisting on a plethora of rules on which to rely, and turning to authority figures to complain when anything goes wrong. We're not creating a society of Angry Young Women. These are Scared Little Girls.

If she's drunk, she's not mentally there, and her consent counts for zip

---

For all the major advances in the status of women in the last 25 years, the shifts in attitudes don't seem to have percolated down to our kids. Parents still raise girls to become wives, and sons to be sons. "I think to some extent we're dealing with a cultural lag," says Janet Hansche, a clinical psychologist and director of the Counseling and Testing Center at Tulane University. "Society still trains women to be pliant, to be nice, to try to avoid saying no, and my guess is that that's most everywhere."

And we're not doing any better raising boys. Obviously something's still screwy in this society. Boys are still being brought up to believe it's the height of cool to score—as if ejaculation were a notable achievement for an adolescent male. Young men still "get tremendous status from aggressiveness," says Debra Haffner, executive director of S[I]ECUS (the Sex Information and Education Council of the U.S.). "But no one teaches them how to live in the real world." It is a weird real world when "nice" boys in a "nice" community, good students, good athletes, good family, rape a mentally handicapped girl with a broomstick handle and a plastic baseball bat, and try to claim it was consensual. "Aren't they virile specimens?" Don Belman boasted to a New York Times reporter about his three Spur Posse sons, one of whom was awaiting trial for allegedly trying to run over several girls with a pickup truck while another had been arrested on sexual charges.

All right. Not all boys turn into Glen Ridge, Spur Posse, Tailhook-grabbing beings. But when it comes to human sexuality, the messages that are being sent to kids—male and female—remain cloaked in myth. In 1993, girls who want sex are still sluts, those who don't are still teases. And those who finally make it to college are completely befuddled.

Which is why it's time for everyone who doesn't have a serious problem to pipe down.

What is happening on the campuses is scary, because it is polarizing men and women. Rather than encouraging them to work together, to trust one another, to understand one another, it is intensifying suspicion. Brown sophomore David Danon complains, "Women have all the power here on sexual conduct . . . It's very dangerous for us." If women are so profoundly distrustful of men, how will they raise boys? And if men are so defensive about women, how will they raise little girls? The most pressing problem the majority of American women face isn't rape or sexual harassment. It's the fact that, in addition to holding down full-time work, they still are burdened with the lion's share of parenting and housework responsibility. Add it up, says sociologist Arlie Hochschild, and it comes to a full month's worth of 24-hour days. Line up the 100 most involved fathers

you know and ask one question: what size shoes do your children wear?

Real life is messy, rife with misunderstandings and contradictions. There's no eight-page guide on how to handle it. There are no panels of mediators out there to turn to unless it gets truly bad. Those who are growing up in environments where they don't have to figure out what the rules should be, but need only follow what's been prescribed, are being robbed of the most important lesson there is to learn. And that's how to live.

With DEBRA ROSENBERG *in Providence,* STANLEY HOLMES *in Yellow Springs, Ohio,* MARTHA BRANT *in New York,* DONNA FOOTE *in Los Angeles,* NINA BIDDLE *in New Orleans and bureau reports*

Why Don't We Act Like The
Opposite Sex?

The new field of sociobiology prompts arguments as to whether different behavior by men and women is inherited or learned.

Anthony Layng

Dr. Layng is professor of anthropology, Elmira (N.Y.) College

Social scientists long have been aware of the distinctive sex roles characteristic of tribal societies around the world, but many are reluctant to conclude that this is anything other than learned behavior. Most American cultural an-

thropologists have assumed that sex roles are largely arbitrary. This is illustrated by citing examples characteristic of males in one population and females in another—as in the American Southwest, where Navajo weavers are women and Hopi weavers are men.

To suggest that female roles are determined to any significant degree by biological factors invites an implication that the lower social status of

women found in most societies also might be attributed to innate differences between the sexes, that "anatomy is destiny." American anthropologists have been influenced by social liberalism to such an extent that any scholarly proponent of biological determinism (racism, sexism, etc.) is likely to be challenged immediately. Their arguments against racism have pointed out that there is no reliable correlation

ability of sex roles from one society to another, there are certain behavior patterns and attitudes that appear to be the same in both traditional and modern societies. For example:

* Women generally prefer older men as mates, while most males prefer younger females.
* In courtship and mating behavior, most men are more sexually aggressive and most women are more coy.
* Males are more inclined to delay marriage.
* Men are more likely to seek a variety of mates.
* Women tend to be more tolerant of adulterous mates.
* Females are more likely to be domestic and nurturing.

In some societies, women prefer men who are considerably older than themselves; in others, the age discrepancy is slight. What is constant is that, on average, the male in each couple is older. Unlike bands of apes, where females are the usual initiators of copulation, "presenting" themselves to males, it is far more common for men to initiate sex, while women are more likely to take a relatively passive role beyond flirtation. Nearly everywhere, shyness or coquettishness is associated strongly with female sexual behavior.

Although some males may have to sell the idea of marriage to their mates, it is far more usual for women to be in the position of favoring such a binding relationship and men to be reluctant to commit themselves. However, males are less reticent about participating in purely sexual relationships, often doing so with more than one partner concurrently. Females seem far more inclined to restrict themselves to one mate, or at least to one at a time. These behavioral differences often are reflected in the "double standard"—the attitude that female infidelity is a far more serious moral breech than male unfaithfulness. Typically, both men and women are more inclined to condemn the adultress. This is not to say that wives do not disapprove strongly of spouses who cheat on them. The point is that a woman far more often will put up with such a husband. Men, on the other hand, are more likely to leave,

between race and social behavior; people of the same race may have sharply contrasting cultures; and a given population can alter its culture dramatically without, presumably, altering its genes. For instance, the Aztecs and Apache were of the same race, but the former evolved a complex state civilization while the latter remained primitive nomads. The post–World War II Japanese have shown us how much a homogeneous racial population can change its culture in a very short time.

When it comes to sexism—the belief that the distinctive behavior of females and males is influenced significantly by their differing physiology—ethnographic challenges are less convincing. One major difficulty is the fact that there are no societies where men and women act alike. Even where conscious attempts have been made to eliminate behavioral differences between the sexes, distinctions remain. A study of American communes in the 1970s found that none have "come anywhere near succeeding in abolishing sex-role distinctions, although a number . . . have made this their highest ideological priority."

Another reason why cross-cultural comparisons have been relatively ineffectual in undermining sexist thinking is that, regardless of the great vari-

severely beat, or even kill an unfaithful mate.

Finally, men are far less inclined toward "nesting" and nurturing. It is the women in all societies who are the most domestic and more adept at nursing the sick and comforting those who are troubled. Both sexes generally agree that it is a woman's nature that makes her so well suited to these activities.

If women and men naturally are inclined to view each other in programmed ways regardless of their class or culture and naturally are predisposed to act toward each other in similarly uniform ways, it might seem reasonable to conclude that female human nature is clearly distinct from that of males and that an Equal Rights Amendment goes against nature. As an active proponent of the ERA and an opponent to all sexism, I am troubled by such a conclusion, but unable simply to dismiss it.

In light of such global uniformity in behavior and attitudes, it is difficult to account for these patterns solely in terms of socialization. Cultures differ dramatically from one to another, and religious beliefs, kinship systems, social structures, political traditions, and subsistence systems vary. So why do men in such contrasting societies all behave so aggressively in the pursuit of sex? Why do male hunters, farmers, and warriors tend to show such interest in seducing new sex partners? Why do Latin American and Asian women put up with adulterous husbands? Why do females in primitive tribes and industrial societies usually prefer older men? Why do peasant women and debutantes tend to want marriage before their male counterparts do? Why are both American and African men relatively disinterested in domestic chores? If it is all a matter of learning, of cultural conditioning, why are there not some societies where most men and women do not conform to these patterns?

Are these traits determined to some extent by the biological peculiarities of the different sexes? If so, it is distressing to consider the social and political implications of such a finding. If human nature (and not only nurture) leads females to behave in a distinctive way, is it therefore not suitable that they be treated in a discriminating fashion? If chasing women only is doing what comes naturally to men, then promiscuous females should have less excuse for their infidelities. Should husbands, even of working wives, be excused from house cleaning and child care? Clearly, one need not be a militant feminist to be made very uncomfortable by such questions.

It is further disturbing to liberals to learn about the findings of sociobiology, a new discipline which suggests some rather startling explanations for behavior traits such as those cited above. According to many sociobiologists, mating practices are the result of an evolutionary process favoring genes that most successfully replicate themselves. This theory states that those most successful in this regard give rise to behavior and attitudes maximizing reproductive success.

Supposedly, genetically inherited behavior that causes people to have the most offspring eventually results, through natural selection, in such action becoming more and more common. Genes which induce people to behave otherwise, by the same selective process, are weeded out since people who behave this way have fewer children—that is, they do not produce as many carriers of their genes. Over time, as the result of this process, genes which most successfully cause men and women to produce carriers of these genes become more and more prevalent.

The most convincing illustrations of sociobiological explanations have been provided by studies of animal populations. For example, when a male langur monkey takes over a harem from an older male, he proceeds to kill all the infants of nursing mothers in the troop. From the perspective of Darwin's Theory of Evolution (survival of the fittest), this makes no sense at all, for it destroys healthy and fit infants as well as any others. From a sociobiological perspective, however, this wholesale infanticide is a sound reproductive strategy because it ensures that the genes of this newly dominant male soon will be replicated and in maximum numbers. Were he to wait until each female weaned her infant and ceased to lactate—a prerequisite to coming back into heat—it would be that much longer before he could impregnate them. By killing all the infants carrying some other male's genes, he speeds up the process whereby his genes begin to predominate. Also, he does not waste any energy protecting infants not carrying his genes.

The females of any species, goes this theory, are likely to develop very different kinds of reproductive strategies given the fact that they produce fewer offspring than do males. The genes of males, in competition with those of other males, induce behavior that results in the greatest number of offspring. Females, who are not able to produce nearly as many offspring as are males, compete for quality, rather than quantity, behaving so as to ensure that each child produced will be likely to survive and reproduce. In these ways, males and females alike are directed by their genes to see to it that they reproduce them as successfully as possible.

REPRODUCTIVE STRATEGIES

Among human beings, the fact that men prefer younger wives is fully consistent with their desire to have children since young women are highly fertile and the most likely to bear full-term healthy offspring. A young wife may devote her entire reproductive potential to producing children fathered by her husband. Since the reproductive strategy of women stresses *quality* of offspring, they are inclined to seek established and mature men as providers and protectors of their children. Male sexual aggressiveness serves to spread male genes. Female coyness helps to assure a potential mate that pregnancy has not occurred already. Her fidelity helps to convince him to stay around to protect what he therefore can assume to be his own offspring. (The sexual aggressiveness of female apes would be inappropriate in a human population, but not for them since male apes are not providers. Given the human sexual division of labor, men and women are economically dependent on each other; apes are not.)

By delaying marriage, a man is free to impregnate more women who will bear his children (his genes) without obligating him to care for them. A woman seeks marriage to monopolize not a man's sexuality, but, rather, his political and economic resources, to ensure that her children (her genes) will be well provided for. She may worry about her husband's infidelities, but only because this can siphon off resources she wants for her children. He, on the other hand, is far more concerned about sexually monopolizing her. He wants assurance that he is the father of any child she gives birth to; otherwise, he will be providing for those who do not carry his genes. Moreover, if she becomes pregnant by another man, it will be many months before she can produce a fetus carrying her husband's genes. With or without her husband's faithfulness, she can get pregnant and produce the maximum number of children carrying her genes. Thus, a wife's affair is less tolerable to her husband for, according to the sociobiological perspective, it threatens to diminish the number of offspring he can produce by her.

The domesticity of women and the wanderings of men also are consistent with the differential reproductive strategies each sex has evolved. In stressing the quality of her offspring, since she can have relatively few, a woman provides a comfortable domicile for her children and stays home to nurture them, to better ensure their survivability so they are most likely to mature and further reproduce her genes. Meanwhile, the man is off chasing women, producing as many children as possible and being far less concerned with sticking around to guarantee their welfare. If he were to limit himself sexually to one woman, he greatly would diminish the number of children he potentially could propagate. In short, from a sociobiological perspective, she "succeeds" by being faithful to her husband since this helps to ensure that he will provide for her children; he does so not only by monopolizing her as a producer of his offspring, but by having children with other women as well.

By this point, you probably are thinking of people who exemplify sociobiologically sound traits of lecherous males and the women who put up with them. Certainly, we all are familiar with this behavior. Even though it often runs counter to accepted moral standards, we frequently hear people say, "That's the way men (or women)

are." Sociobiologists seem to be offering theoretical confirmation of this folk wisdom.

Is human social behavior influenced by our genes? Whether further research will confirm or refute sociobiological theory as it applies to human behavior, we shall have to wait until far more information is available. No matter what the effect on our behavior, we should keep in mind that learning plays an important role. Consequently, social policy should not be based on any assumption that biological determinants of human behavior and attitudes are more instrumental than learning, for cultural factors can counteract human genetic predispositions. Our early ancestors were subject to natural selection. Since the time of the Neanderthals, though, human populations have adapted to environmental change almost entirely by altering their learned behavior and attitudes—their culture, not their genes. There are individuals whose behavior conforms to sociobiological generalizations, but, especially among the educated, one finds many contrasting examples—men who do not chase young women, females who are sexually aggressive and/or disinterested in marriage, and couples who choose to have no children at all.

If traditional social inequality be-

tween men and women somewhat is perpetuated by genetically determined and sexually specific reproductive strategies, why are contraceptives and abortions so popular in modern society? Even most modern women may seem to conform to sociobiologically correct behavior (being attracted to older men, tolerating unfaithful spouses, accepting primary responsibility for domestic duties, etc.). Since most males still earn more than females do and since society continues to socialize boys and girls quite differently (encouraging girls to play with infant dolls, rewarding boys for being physically aggressive, etc.), the continuation of such behavior may be more a matter of cultural inertia than genetic compulsion.

So, even if inborn factors influence male and female human sexual behavior, the extent to which they do so clearly is limited and subordinate to learning and conditioning. Consequently, we neither need fear intellectually the findings of sociobiologists nor allow them significantly to influence interpersonal behavior and social attitudes regarding gender-specific behavior. If men and women continue to behave differently (and it seems there is no clear trend away from this pattern), we may yet learn just why we do not act like the opposite sex.

men, women & computers

Cyberspace, it turns out, isn't much of an Eden after all. It's marred by just as many sexist ruts and gender conflicts as the Real World.

B A R B A R A   K A N T R O W I T Z

AS A LONGTIME "STAR TREK" devotee, Janis Cortese was eager to be part of the Trekkie discussion group on the Internet. But when she first logged on, Cortese noticed that these fans of the final frontier devoted megabytes to such profound topics as whether Troi or Crusher had bigger breasts. In other words, the purveyors of this "Trek" dreck were all *guys*. Undeterred, Cortese, a physicist at California's Loma Linda University, figured she'd add perspective to the electronic gathering place with her own momentous questions. Why was the male cast racially diverse while almost all the females were young, white and skinny? Then, she tossed in a few lustful thoughts about the male crew members.

After those seemingly innocuous observations, "I was chased off the net by rabid hounds," recalls Cortese. Before she could say "Fire phasers," the Trekkies had flooded her electronic mailbox with nasty messages—a practice called "flaming." Cortese retreated into her own galaxy by starting the all-female Starfleet Ladies Auxiliary and Embroidery/Baking Society. The private electronic forum, based in Houston, now has more than 40 members, including psychologists, physicians, students and secretaries. They started with Trektalk, but often chose to beam down and go where no man had ever wandered before—into the personal mode. When Julia Kosatka, a Houston computer scientist, got pregnant last year, she shared her thoughts with the group on weight gain, sex while expecting and everything else on her mind. Says Kosatka: "I'm part of one of the longest-running slumber parties in history."

From the Internet to Silicon Valley to the PC sitting in the family room, men and women often seem like two chips that pass in the night. Sure, there are women who spout techno-speak in their sleep and plenty of men who think a hard drive means four hours on the freeway. But in general, computer culture is created, defined and controlled by men. Women often feel about as welcome as a system crash.

About a third of American families have at least one computer, but most of those are purchased and used by males. It may be new technology, but the old rules still apply. In part, it's that male-machine bonding thing, reincarnated in the digital age. "Men tend to be seduced by the technology itself," says Oliver Strimpel, executive director of The Computer Museum in Boston. "They tend to get into the fast-race-car syndrome," bragging about the size of their discs or the speed of their microprocessors. To the truly besotted, computers are a virtual religion, complete with icons (on-screen graphics), relics (obsolete programs and machines) and prophets (Micro-soft's Bill Gates, outlaw hackers). This is not something to be trifled with by mere . . .females, who seem to think that machines were meant to be *used,* like the microwave oven or the dishwasher. Interesting and convenient on the job but not worthy of obsession. Esther Dyson, editor of Release 1.0, an influential software-industry newsletter, has been following the computer field for two decades. Yet when she looks at her own computer, Dyson says she still doesn't "really care about its innards. I just want it to work."

Blame (a) culture (b) family (c) schools (d)

> 'Men tend to be seduced by the technology. They get into the faster-race-car syndrome,' bragging about the speed of their microprocessors.

> Women are much more practical, much more interested in the machine's utility. 'I don't really care about its innards. I just want to do the job.'

all of the above. Little boys are expected to roll around in the dirt and explore. Perfect training for learning to use computers, which often requires hours in front of the screen trying to figure out the messy arcanum of a particular program. Girls get subtle messages—from society if not from their parents—that they should keep their hands clean and play with their dolls. Too often, they're discouraged from taking science and math—not just by their schools but by parents as well (how many mothers have patted their daughters on the head and reassured them: "Oh, I wasn't good at math, either").

The gender gap is real and takes many forms.

Barbie vs. Nintendo

GIRLS' TECHNOPHOBIA BEGINS EARLY. Last summer, Sarah Douglas, a University of Oregon computer-science professor, took part in a job fair for teenage girls that was supposed to introduce them to nontraditional occupations. With great expectations, she set up her computer and loaded it with interesting programs. Not a single girl stopped by. When she asked why, the girls "told me computers were something their dads and their brothers used," Douglas sadly recalls. "Computer science is a very male profession . . . When girls get involved in that male world, they are pushed away and belittled. Pretty soon, the girls get frustrated and drop out."

Computer games usually involve lots of shooting and dying. Boy stuff. What's out there for girls? "If you walk down the street and look in the computer store, you will see primarily male people as sales staff and as customers," says Jo Sanders, director of the gender-equity program at the Center for Advanced Study in Education at the City University of New York Graduate Center.

Boys and girls are equally interested in computers until about the fifth grade, says University of Minnesota sociologist Ronald Anderson, who coauthored the recent report "Computers in American Schools." At that point, boys' use rises significantly and girls' use drops, Anderson says, probably because sex-role identification really kicks in. Many girls quickly put computers on the list of not-quite-feminine topics, like car engines and baseball batting averages. It didn't have to be this way. The very first computer programmer was a woman, Ada Lovelace, who worked with Charles Babbage on his mechanical computing machines in the mid-1800s. If she had become a role model, maybe hundreds of thousands of girls would have spent their teenage years locked in their bedrooms staring at screens. Instead, too many are doing their nails or worrying about their hair, says Marcelline Barron, an administrator at the Illinois Mathematics and Science Academy, a publicly funded coed boarding school for gifted students. "You're not thinking about calculus or physics when you're thinking about that," says Barron. "We have these kinds of expectations for young girls. They must be neat, they must be clean, they must be quiet."

Despite great strides by women in other formerly male fields, such as law and medicine, women are turning away from the computer industry. Men earning computer-science degrees outnumber women 3 to 1 and the gap is growing, according to the National Science Foundation. Fifteen years ago, when computers were still new in schools, they hadn't yet been defined as so exclusively male. But now girls have gotten the message. It's not just the technical and cultural barrier. Sherry Turkle, a Massachusetts Institute of Technology sociologist who teaches a course on women and computers, says that computers have come to stand for "a world without emotion," an image that seems to scare off girls more than boys.

In the past decade, videogames have become a gateway to technology for many boys, but game manufacturers say few girls are attracted to these small-screen shoot-'em-ups. It's not surprising that the vast majority of videogame designers are men. They don't call it Game *Boy* for nothing. Now some manufacturers are trying to lure girls. In the next few months, Sega plans to introduce "Berenstein Bears," which will offer players a choice of boy or girl characters. A second game, "Crystal's Pony Tale," involves coloring (there's lots of pink in the background). Neither game requires players to "die," a common videogame device that researchers say girls dislike. Girls also tend to prefer nonlinear games, where there is more than one way to proceed. "There's a whole issue with speaking girls' language," says Michealene Cristini Risley, group director of licensing and character development for Sega. The company would like to hook girls at the age of 4, before they've developed fears of technology.

Girls need freedom to explore and make mistakes. Betsy Zeller, a 37-year-old engineering manager at Silicon Graphics, says that when she discovered computers in college, "I swear I thought I'd seen the face of God." Yet she had to fend off guys who would come into the lab and want to help her work through problems or, worse yet, do them for her. "I would tell them to get lost," she says. "I wanted to do it myself." Most women either asked for or accepted proffered help, just as they are more likely to ask for directions when lost in a strange city. That may be the best way to avoid driving in circles for hours, but it's not the best way to learn technical subjects.

Schools are trying a number of approaches to interest girls in computers. Douglas and her colleagues are participating in a mentorship program where undergraduate girls spend a summer working with female computer scientists. Studies have shown that girls are more attracted to technology if they can work in groups; some schools are experimenting with team projects that require computers but are focused on putting out a product, like a newspaper or pamphlet. At the middle-and high-school level, girls-only computer classes are increasingly popular. Two months ago Roosevelt Middle School in Eugene, Ore., set up girls-only hours at the computer lab. Games were prohibited and artists were brought in to teach girls how to be more creative with the computer. Students are also learning to use e-mail, which many girls love. Says Debbie Nehl, the computer-lab supervisor: "They see it as high-tech note-passing."

Power Networks

AS A RELATIVELY NEW INDUSTRY, THE leadership of computerdom might be expected to be more gender-diverse. Wrong; few women have advanced beyond middle-management ranks. According to a study conducted last year by The San Jose Mercury News, there are no women CEOs running major computer-manufacturing firms and only a handful running software companies. Even women who have succeeded say they are acutely conscious of the differences between them and their male co-workers. "I don't talk the same as men," says Paula Hawthorn, an executive at Montage Software, in Oakland, Calif. "I don't get the same credibility." The difference, she says, "is with you all the time."

Women who work in very technical areas, such as programming, are often the loneliest. Anita Borg, a computer-systems researcher, remembers attending a 1987 conference where there were so few women that the only time they ran into each other was in the restroom. Their main topic of discussion: why there were so few women at the conference. That bathroom cabal grew into Systers, an on-line network for women with technical careers. There are now 1,740 women members from 19 countries representing 200 colleges and universities and 150 companies. Systers is part mentoring and part consciousness-raising. One graduate student, for example, talked about how uncomfortable she felt sitting in her shared office when a male graduate student and a professor put a picture of a nude woman on a computer. The problem was resolved when a couple of female faculty members, also on the Systers network, told their offending colleagues that the image was not acceptable.

Women have been more successful in developing software, especially when their focus is products used by children. Jan Davidson, a former teacher, started Davidson & Associates, in Torrance, Calif., with three programs in 1982. Now it's one of the country's biggest developers of kids' software, with 350 employees and $58.6 million in revenues. Multimedia will bring new opportunities for women. The technology is so specialized that it requires a team—animators, producers, scriptwriters, 3-D modelers—to create state-of-the-art products. It's a far cry from

> Many men on the net aren't out to win sensitivity contests. 'In the computer world, it's "Listen, baby, if you don't like it, drop dead".'

> 'What really annoys women is the flaming and the people boasting—the things that annoy women are things that men do all the time.'

the stereotype of the solitary male programmer, laboring long into the night with only takeout Chinese food for company. At Mary Cron's Rymel Design Group in Palos Verdes, Calif., most of the software artists and designers are women, Cron says. "It's like a giant puzzle," she adds. "We like stuff we can work on together."

As more women develop software, they may also help create products that will attract women consumers—a huge untapped market. Heidi Roizen, a college English major, cofounded T/Maker Co. in Mountain View, Calif., a decade ago. She says that because women are often in charge of the family's budget, they are potential consumers of personal-finance programs. Women are also the most likely buyers of education and family-entertainment products, a fast-growing segment of the industry. "Women are more typically the household shopper," Roizen says. "They have tremendous buying power."

Wired Women

THE INFOBAHN—A.K.A. THE INFORMA-tion Superhighway—may be the most hyped phenomenon in history—or it could be the road to the future. In any case, women want to get on. But the sign over the access road says CAUTION. MEN WORKING. WOMEN BEWARE. Despite hundreds of thousands of new users in the last year, men still dominate the Internet and commercial services such as Prodigy or CompuServe. The typical male conversation on line turns off many women. "A lot of time, to be crude, it's a pissing contest," says Lisa Kimball, a partner in the Meta Network, a Washington, D.C., on-line service that is 40 percent female. Put-downs are an art form. When one woman complained recently in an Internet forum that she didn't like participating because she didn't have time to answer all her e-mail, she was swamped with angry responses, including this one (from a man): "Would you like some cheese with your whine?"

Some men say the on-line hostility comes from resentment over women's slowly entering what has been an almost exclusively male domain. Many male techno-jocks "feel women are intruding into their inner sanctum," says André Bacard, a Silicon Valley, Calif., technology writer. They're not out to win sensitivity contests. "In the computer world, it's 'Listen, baby, if you don't like it, drop dead'," says Bacard. "It's the way men talk to guys. Women aren't used to that."

Even under more civilized circumstances, men and women have different conversational styles, says Susan Herring, a University of Texas at Arlington professor who has studied women's participation on computer networks. Herring found that violations of long-established net etiquette—asking too many basic questions, for example—angered men. "The women were much

> Men typically imagine devices that could help them conquer the universe. Men think of machines as an extension of their physical power.

> Women want machines that meet people's needs, the perfect mother. And one who can be turned on and off at the flick of a switch.

> The vast majority of videogame designers are men; they make games they want to play. Why do you think it's called Game Boy?

> Girls tend to prefer nonlinear games, where there's more than one way to win. Some even dislike having characters die on screen.

Toys and Tools

IN ONE INTRIGUING STUDY BY THE CENter for Children and Technology, a New York think tank, men and women in technical fields were asked to dream up machines of the future. Men typically imagined devices that could help them "conquer the universe," says Jan Hawkins, director of the center. She says women wanted machines that met people's needs, "the perfect mother."

Someday, gender-blind education and socialization may render those differences obsolete. But in the meantime, researchers say both visions are useful. If everyone approached technology the way women do now, "we wouldn't be pushing envelopes," says Cornelia Bruner, associate director of the center. "Most women, even those who are technologically sophisticated, think of machines as a means to an end." Men think of the machines as an extension of their own power, as a way to "transcend physical limitations." That may be why they are more likely to come up with great leaps in technology, researchers say. Without that vision, the computer and its attendant industry would not exist.

Ironically, gender differences could help women. "We're at a cultural turning point," says MIT's Turkle. "There's an opportunity to remake the culture around the machine." Practicality is now as valued as invention. If the computer industry wants to put machines in the hands of the masses, that means women—along with the great many men who have no interest in hot-rod computing. An ad campaign for Compaq's popular Presario line emphasizes the machine's utility. After kissing her child good night, the mother in the ad sits down at her Presario to work. As people start to view their machines as creative tools, someday women may be just as comfortable with computers as men are.

With DEBRA ROSENBERG *in Boston*, PATRICIA KING *in San Francisco and* KAREN SPRINGEN *in Chicago*

more tolerant of people who didn't know what they were doing," Herring says. "What really annoyed women was the flaming and people boasting. The things that annoy women are things men do all the time."

Like hitting on women. Women have learned to tread their keyboards carefully in chat forums because they often have to fend off sexual advances that would make Bob Packwood blush. When subscribers to America Online enter one of the service's forums, their computer names appear at the top of the screen as a kind of welcome. If they've chosen an obviously female name, chances are they'll soon be bombarded with private messages seeking detailed descriptions of their appearance or sexual preferences. "I couldn't believe it," recalls 55-year-old Eva S. "I said, 'Come on, I'm a grandmother'."

More and more women are signing on to networks that are either coed and run by women, or are exclusively for women. Stacy Horn started ECHO (for East Coast Hang Out) four years ago because she was frustrated with the hostility on line. About 60 percent of ECHO's 2,000 subscribers are men; among ECHO's 50 forums, only two are strictly for women. "Flaming is nonexistent on ECHO," Horn says. "New women get on line and they see that. And then they're much more likely to jump in." Women's Wire in San Francisco, started in January, has 850 subscribers, only 10 percent of them men—the reverse of most on-line services. "We wanted to design a system in which women would help shape the community and the rules of that community from the floor up," says cofounder Ellen Pack. The official policy is that there is no such thing as a dumb question—and no flaming.

Male subscribers say Women's Wire has been a learning experience for them, too. Maxwell Hoffmann, a 41-year-old computer-company manager, says that many men think that only women are overly emotional. But men lose it, too. A typical on-line fight starts with two guys sending "emotionally charged flames going back and forth" through cyberspace (not on Women's Wire). Then it expands and "everybody starts flaming the guy. They scream at each other and they're not listening."

If only men weren't so *emotional*, so *irrational*, could we all get along on the net?

WOMEN & MEN

Can we get along? Should we even try?

Lawrence Wright

Texas Monthly

On top of the intense racial and economic tensions that plague American life today, it seems that animosity between men and women has hit a boiling point once again. Less obvious than in the early '70s, when the emerging women's movement challenged and forever changed relationships between the sexes, the gender war is now being played out more subtly against a series of public events that have inspired heated debates in the workplace, on the park bench, and in the bedroom. The tensions started a year or so ago, when it was possible to watch both the Clarence Thomas hearings and the William Kennedy Smith trial on television during the day, then go see Thelma and Louise *after dinner, and curl up with either Robert Bly's* Iron John *or Susan Faludi's* Backlash *before bed. Add to this backdrop more recent events like the Navy's Tailhook incident and Dan Quayle's attack on Murphy Brown, and it should come as no surprise that men and women are having a hard time getting along at all.*

In his early studies on the origins of neurosis, Sigmund Freud came to a damning conclusion about men. So many of his patients had revealed stories about sexual experiences in infancy or childhood that Freud decided the "seduction" of children must be the root of all neurotic behavior. When his own sister began to exhibit signs of neurosis, Freud declared: "In every case the father, not excluding my own, had to be blamed as a pervert."

I consider this statement as I stroke my daughter's hair. Caroline is 10 years old. Her eyes are closed, and her head is in my lap. This should be a tender, innocent scene, but we no longer live in a time when anyone believes in innocence. Blame and suspicion color the atmosphere. As a man and a father, I feel besieged and accused. I am appallingly aware of the trust I hold, in the form of my daughter's sleeping body. The line between affection and abuse is in the front of my mind. I feel like a German coming to grips with Nazi guilt. Yes, some men are perverts—but all men? Am I?

Freud later rejected his early hypothesis after his own father died. He suspected that many of the stories his patients had related were fantasized. But now there are those who say in effect that Freud was closer to the truth the first time.

"Men are pigs and they like it that way," an angry writer stated in the op-ed section of the *New York Times.* At a 1991 women's political symposium, Texas governor Ann Richards' ethics adviser, Barbara Jordan, decreed: "I believe that women have a capacity for understanding and compassion which a man structurally does not have, does not have it because he cannot have it. He's just incapable of it." At the same meeting, Houston mayor Kathy Whitmire said that men are less intelligent than women. If these female chauvinists had been speaking of any constituency other than men, they would be run out of public life. But men feel too guilty to defend themselves.

Contempt for men pervades the most obscure strata of our society. A magazine called *House Rabbit Journal* devoted a recent issue to the failings of men as nurturers. "We assume that women perform the primary care-giving role with the house rabbit (as with the kids), and they form the strongest bonds with the bunny," wrote one author. The magazine advised wom-

I'm mad at men too, but I'm also mad at being the object of slanders.

en rabbit owners who want their men to share in their rabbit pleasures to avoid talking about the warm, fuzzy, cuddly aspects of the animal and instead emphasize its traits of integrity, fortitude, and spirit. "I have found, in my relationship with my husband, that having large numbers of animals living with us has put a strain on our relationship," admitted the writer. "With each piece of furniture that has been destroyed, each time we had to avoid the urine puddles in our bed at night, each time we've spent 300 dollars at the vet for a rabbit I picked up at the pound, there has been some initial resentment on the part of my husband. But ultimately he, too, has learned the value of caring."

There is plenty of evidence of the damage men do. Look at the battered women in the shelters. Every year about 20,000 women in Texas alone seek refuge in the shelters from physical abuse in their homes, but the shelters are able to accommodate *fewer* than half of them. In 1990 more than 100,000 women were reported raped in America, the highest total in history and an increase of 12.6 percent over the number of reported rapes per capita in 1980. A prosecutor I know works in the Family Justice Division of the Travis County, Texas, district attorney's office. In the '70s, that office prosecuted only a handful of child-abuse cases a year. Now, Frank Bryan says, he has more than 200 indictments on his desk and a backlog of cases he doesn't want to discuss. "Generally, my impression of men has plummeted," he told me. "I tell all my friends with children never to hire a male baby-sitter. The things these guys do . . ."

But my 15-year-old son is a baby-sitter. That's how Gordon earns his pocket money. It saddens me that he would be shunned because he's a male and therefore a candidate for perversion. On the other hand, I might not hire a male to watch Caroline. Her safety and self-esteem are too important to place in jeopardy.

"Come over and sit in my lap," a grandfatherly preacher friend of mine said out of a lifetime of habit to a little girl he knew. He was at a gathering of friends and family. Suddenly, the room went dead quiet and every woman turned to stare daggers at him. In that moment, the preacher realized that he would never ask a little girl to sit in his lap again. His presumption of innocence had been revoked—not because of his past behavior, which had been exemplary, but simply because he is a man. He has suffered a loss, and so has the little girl. She is being held apart from the love and comfort he has to offer. And at some level she must have understood the subliminal message that hung in the air: Don't trust men.

Is it possible that of the two genders nature created, one is nearly perfect and the other is badly flawed? Well, yes, say the psychobiologists. Unlike women, who carry two X chromosomes, men have an X and a Y. The latter has relatively little genetic information except for the gene that makes us men. A woman who has a recessive gene on one X chromosome might have a countering dominant gene on the other. That's not true for men, who are therefore more vulnerable to biological and environmental insults, as well as more prone to certain behavioral tendencies that may be genetically predetermined. Although male hormones (called androgens) don't cause violent criminal or sexual behavior, they apparently create an inclination in that direction. A low level of arousability—that is to say, a lack of responsiveness to external stimuli—is more common in men than in women. It is reflected in the greater number of male children who die of sudden infant death

syndrome and the much larger proportion of boys who are hyperactive and require far more excitement than most children to keep from becoming bored. In adults, this biological need for extra stimulation seems to be connected to higher rates of criminality. Androgens are associated with a number of other male traits (in humans as well as animals), including assertive sexual behavior, status-related aggression, spatial reasoning, territoriality, pain tolerance, tenacity, transient bonding, sensation seeking, and predatory behavior. Obviously, this list posts many of the most common female complaints about men, and yet androgens make a man a man; one can't separate maleness from characteristic male traits.

"Why have any men at all?" wrote Sally Miller Gearhart in a 1982 manifesto titled "The Future—If There Is One—Is Female." Gearhart is an advocate of ovular merging, a process that involves the mating of two eggs, which has been successfully accomplished with mice. Only female offspring are produced. I've always worried that one day women would figure out how to get along without us and they would be able to reproduce unilaterally, like sponges. It's not genocide, exactly. It's more like job attrition, the way employers cut back positions without actually firing anyone. "A 75 percent female to 25 percent male ratio could be achieved in one generation if one half of a population reproduced heterosexually and one half by ovular merging," according to Gearhart. "Such a prospect is attractive to women who feel that if they bear sons, no amount of love and care and non-sexist training will save those sons from a culture where male violence is institutionalized and revered. These women are saying, 'No more sons. We will not spend 20 years of our lives raising a potential rapist, a potential batterer, a potential Big Man.' "

Every man is a "potential" rapist; the only way to eliminate the potential is to get rid of potency. During the Clarence Thomas hearings, Tom Brokaw asked a female legal expert about the lack of a pattern of sexual harassment in Thomas' behavior. "He's not dead yet," she snapped.

I'm mad at men too. I am disgusted by the rise in child-abuse cases and reported rapes. I deplore sexual

Contempt for men pervades even the most obscure strata of our society.

harassment. I'm grateful for the ascendancy of women in business and politics, which may yet advance the humanity of those callings. I have to issue these disclaimers because I'm a man writing on the subject. But I'm also mad at being the object of slanders such as that men are incapable of compassion. Anyone looking at men today should be able to see that they are confused and full of despair. It's not just our place in society or the family that we are struggling for; we're fighting against our own natures. We didn't create the instincts that make us aggressive, that make us value action over consensus, that make us more inclined toward strength than sympathy. Nature and human history have rewarded those qualities and in turn have created the kind of people men are. Moreover, these competitive qualities have been necessary for the survival of the species, and despite the debate over masculinity, they are still valued today. Some trial lawyers now include their levels of testosterone, the most abundant of the androgens, on their résumés.

A couple of weeks ago I went to pick Caroline up at her after-school day-care center at the neighborhood Presbyterian church. She had a new teacher, a man, in fact. I made a point of going over to introduce myself and making him feel welcome. The new man was out on the playground with a walkie-talkie. "I'm Caroline's dad," I said, but before I could get around to my welcoming speech, he said, "I'm sorry, but I'm going to have to ask you for a picture ID." As Caroline's father, I appreciated the security, but as a man, I took offense at having to prove that I was not a pervert. True, women are also asked to show identification, but I suspect that it is done in the spirit of fairness. Everybody assumes it is men who are the problem.

Advocacy groups have been using hugely inflated statistics to bludgeon the public into believing that men are waging a war against women and children. "One out of four men is a rapist" is an anecdotal statistic I've heard on several occasions that is not tied to any real survey that I can find.

The real statistics are bad enough. According to Department of Justice victimization studies, the actual chance that a woman will experience a rape or an attempted rape during her lifetime is 8 percent (1 out of 12). Yet a recent study by Neil Gilbert, a professor of social welfare at the University of California at Berkeley, showed that the incidence of date rape, though still far too high, has actually declined substantially since 1980.

Figures about child abuse and domestic violence have been similarly inflated and biased against men. I've read that one out of four females, and one in six males, will be molested or raped by the time they are 18. Most of these scary figures are conjectures based on reports of abuse received by police and child-abuse hotlines. More than a million such reports are filed every year. About 60 percent of them turn out to be unfounded. More than half of the cases that are categorized as neglect or abuse are actually "deprivation of necessities," such as poor medical care, inadequate clothing or shelter, malnutrition—problems of poverty, in other words. Only about 5 percent involve serious physical battering of the sort that we think of as child abuse, and about the same amount turns out to be actual sexual abuse.

Many women dismiss female violence in the home either as innocuous and different in nature from male violence or as self-defense, but Suzanne Steinmetz, a sociology professor at Indiana University, found that some men become targets of abuse when they attempt to protect their children from the mother's violence—the reverse of the stereotype. Other studies have concluded that women typically are just as assaultive as their husbands. Although the men characteristically cause more injuries, wives strike the first blow in 48 percent of the cases, according to one study. The effect of using inflated and, in some cases, falsified statistics to make rape, child abuse, and wife beating seem more prevalent than they actually are—to make them seem, in some dreadful manner, the norm—is to slander the character of men, who are presumed to be the perpetrators of domestic violence, which is not an exclusive feature of male character.

Women also have power that they sometimes discredit. Most men I know feel overwhelmed by women—and by their own need for women. Therefore the rage women feel at men can be terrifying and sexually daunting. Lately I hear women complaining about wimps, about men being uninterested and emotionally withdrawn and sexually unavailable. The ancient stereotype of the frigid woman is being replaced by that of the impotent male. It's not just a fear of intimacy that causes men to founder sexually, nor the dread of AIDS. Men are discovering what women have always known: Sex is a dangerous theater. When women felt powerless, they were sexually passive. Increasingly, now it's the men who are passive and for the same reasons women were in the past. They're afraid. They're afraid of being punished, of being engulfed by women's anger. They feel paralyzed by changes in the social fabric that leave them confused about how to behave around women or even how to talk to them. They sense that the relations between the sexes have become politicized and legalized as never before. Men are going to have to learn how to come to terms with powerful women, how to get used to women with muscles and anger and sexual demands. At the same time, women are going to have to find a way of celebrating manliness without putting it down.

My wife has 15 children in her kindergarten class, and it's rare that she has more than two with a father at home. Sometimes when I visit Roberta's class, the children stare at me as if I were another species. Until a male art teacher arrived last year, I was the only man many of these children would see all day. "You look like Superman in those glasses," a 5-year-old boy told me. He meant Clark Kent. I'm an average-sized man, but to children who rarely see men except from a distance or on television, all men look alike—huge and forbidding and hiding explosive, supernatural strength. This is just one of the harmful effects of the absence of men in children's lives: We've become mythologized.

Here in public school you can see the appalling truth that the traditional family is dead. The men have gone; in many cases, they were never there in the first place. Christine Williams and Debra Umberson, sociologists at the University of Texas, undertook a study of why men disengaged from their children. "We wanted to interview 50 divorced men who did not have custody of their children," says Umberson. "It took us a year to find 43. The reason is it was too painful for them to talk about. When you finally reach them, you hear a lot of complaints about the system, how they are treated as 'just a pocket,' a source of money. They're not invited to be a part of the family, and they don't feel the system

---

The majority of children sexually abused by men are girls; the majority of children battered and killed by women are boys.

Women earn about 30 percent less than men; 20 men are killed on the job for each woman who is fatally injured at work.

Most of these statistics come from U.S. Statistical Abstracts. For specific citations, see the reference section of the book Knights Without Armor (Jeremy P. Tarcher, Inc., 1991) by Aaron R. Kipnis and Backlash (Doubleday, 1991) by Susan Faludi.

appreciates the effort they do make to take care of their kids."

"Was there anything about this study that surprised you?" I asked Umberson.

"Well, yes," she said. "It was that some of these men were so involved with their children—their kids were really incredibly important to them. That surprised me, because when you read the literature, you get the picture that men just don't care."

It's true that traditional male roles have been compromised or usurped. "The feeling men had that

Figures about child abuse and domestic violence have been inflated and biased against men.

their home is their castle can't be sustained any longer when more than 50 percent of married women work outside the home," said Williams. "Men don't get their authority handed to them on a platter anymore. Women demand to be listened to now. It's no wonder that men feel under siege and that the sense of gratification in being a man is being taken away from them. And who better to blame than women?"

But blame is not the point, for men or women. The point is that families without men are more likely to be poor, and children without fathers are more likely to be deprived—not just of the material comforts but of the sense of the mutuality of the sexes.

Somehow men have got to find a place for themselves again in the family. We're only beginning to see some of the consequences of fatherlessness, especially where boys are concerned. My personal fear is that fatherlessness will have unanticipated political and spiritual consequences, such as a longing for authoritarianism and a further lack of attachment between the sexes. The rise in gangs seems to be connected to the absence of male role models. There is a well-established connection between children of broken homes (a term that seems quaint these days) and the likelihood of committing serious criminal offenses. In any case, children who grow up not knowing who men are pay a price as well. I'm not saying that single mothers—or single fathers—can't do a good job of raising children. But a society of children who don't understand men produces men who don't understand themselves.

I lift up Caroline and take her to bed. Nothing in the world means more to me than our love for each other. I love the difference between us, her femaleness and my maleness. It is a powerful and curious experience to see parts of myself manifested in little-girl form; she is a sort of mirror for me, across time and gender.

I'm afraid of what life has to offer her. I'm worried that the family idea is finished and that the sexes have pulled so far apart that some radical and soulless bureaucratic arrangement is in the process of replacing it. I want Caroline to find love and to experience the joy that I have in being her parent. I want her to find a man who will love her as deeply as I do, who will take care of her and nurture her and stay with her the rest of her life. But I think the chances of that happening are small.

I know that her relationships with men will depend, in large measure, on what she gets from me. That is the most important thing I can give her, a sense of being with a man, trace memories of having me tickle her and toss her in the air, of my taking her temperature when she's sick and rubbing her face with a cool cloth, of her dancing on my shoes. She will remember these things in some almost unrememberable way: They will be a part of her character; she will be the kind of person these things happened to. Therefore she will probably be more trusting of men. That may be a mistake. Who knows what kind of men she is going to meet?

But perhaps her generation will come to a different conclusion. They may decide that the sexes have something special to offer each other, and they'll be able to look at the very things that separate men and women and appreciate them, even savor them. In that case, the language they will learn to speak to each other will be that of love, not blame.

It's a jungle out there, so get used to it!

Women need to realize that men are testosterone-driven animals

Camille Paglia

Rape is an outrage that cannot be tolerated in civilized society. Yet feminism, which has waged a crusade for rape to be taken more seriously, has put young women in danger by hiding the truth about sex from them.

In dramatizing the pervasiveness of rape, feminists have told young women that before they have sex with a man, they must give consent as explicit as a legal contract's. In this way, young women have been convinced that they have been the victims of rape. On elite campuses in the Northeast and on the West Coast, they have held consciousness-raising sessions, petitioned administrations, demanded inquests. At Brown University, outraged, panicky "victims" have scrawled the names of alleged attackers on the walls of women's rest rooms. What marital rape was to the '70s, "date rape" is to the '90s.

The incidence and seriousness of rape do not require this kind of exaggeration. Real acquaintance rape is nothing new. It has been a horrible problem for women for all of recorded history. Once fathers and brothers protected women from rape. Once the penalty for rape was death. I come from a fierce Italian tradition where, not so long ago in the motherland, a rapist would end up knifed, castrated, and hung out to dry.

But the old clans and small rural communities have broken down. In our cities, on our campuses far from home, young women are vulnerable and defenseless. Feminism has not prepared them for this. Feminism keeps saying the sexes are the same. It keeps telling women they can do anything, go anywhere, say anything, wear anything. No, they can't. Women will always be in sexual danger.

One of my male students recently slept overnight with a friend in a passageway of the Great Pyramid in Egypt. He described the moon and sand, the ancient silence and eerie echoes. I will never experience that. I am a woman. I am not stupid enough to believe I could ever be safe there. There is a world of solitary adventure I will never have. Women have always known these

Women will always be in sexual danger.

somber truths. But feminism, with its pie-in-the-sky fantasies about the perfect world, keeps young women from seeing life as it is.

We must remedy social injustice whenever we can. But there are some things we cannot change. There are sexual differences that are based in biology. Academic feminism is lost in a fog of social constructionism. It believes we are totally the product of our environment. This idea was invented by Rousseau. He was wrong. Emboldened by dumb French language theory, academic feminists repeat the same hollow slogans over and over to each other. Their view of sex is naive and prudish. Leaving sex to the feminists is like letting your dog vacation at the taxidermist's.

The sexes are at war. Men must struggle for identity against the overwhelming power of their mothers. Women have menstruation to tell them they are women. Men must do or risk something to be men. Men become masculine only when other men say they are. Having sex with a woman is one way a boy becomes a man.

College men are at their hormonal peak. They have just left their mothers and are questing for their male identity. In groups, they are dangerous. A woman going to a fraternity party is walking into Testosterone Flats, full of prickly cacti and blazing guns. If she goes, she should be armed with resolute alertness. She should arrive with girlfriends and leave with them. A girl who lets herself get dead drunk at a fraternity party is a fool.

A girl who goes upstairs alone with a brother at a fraternity party is an idiot. Feminists call this "blaming the victim." I call it common sense.

For a decade, feminists have drilled their disciples to say, "Rape is a crime of violence but not of sex." This sugar-coated Shirley Temple nonsense has exposed young women to disaster. Misled by feminism, they do not expect rape from the nice boys from good homes who sit next to them in class.

Aggression and eroticism are deeply intertwined. Hunt, pursuit, and capture are biologically programmed into male sexuality. Generation after generation, men must be educated, refined, and ethically persuaded away from their tendency toward anarchy and brutishness. Society is not the enemy, as feminism ignorantly claims. Society is woman's protection against rape. Feminism, with its solemn Carry Nation repressiveness, does not see what is for men the eroticism or fun element in rape, especially the wild, infectious delirium of gang rape. Women who do not understand rape cannot defend themselves against it.

The date-rape controversy shows feminism hitting the wall of its own broken promises. The women of my '60s generation were the first respectable girls in history to swear like sailors, get drunk, stay out all night—in short, to act like men. We sought total sexual freedom and equality. But as time passed, we woke up to cold reality. The old double standard protected women. When anything goes, it's women who lose.

Today's young women don't know what they want. They see that feminism has not brought sexual happiness. The theatrics of public rage over date rape are their way of restoring the old sexual rules that were shattered by my generation. Because nothing about the sexes has really changed. The comic film *Where the Boys Are* (1960), the ultimate expression of '50s man-chasing, still speaks directly to our time. It shows smart, lively women skillfully anticipating and fending off the dozens of strategies with which horny men try to get them into bed. The agonizing date-rape subplot and climax are brilliantly done. The victim, Yvette Mimieux, makes mistake after mistake, obvious to the other girls. She allows herself to be lured away from her girlfriends and into isolation with boys whose character and intentions she misreads. *Where the Boys Are* tells the truth. It shows courtship as a dangerous game in which the signals are not verbal but subliminal.

Neither militant feminism, which is obsessed with politically correct language, nor academic feminism, which believes that knowledge and experience are "constituted by" language, can understand pre-verbal or non-verbal communication. Feminism, focusing on sexual politics, cannot see that sex exists in and through the body. Sexual desire and arousal cannot be fully translated into verbal terms. This is why men and women misunderstand each other.

Trying to remake the future, feminism cut itself off from sexual history. It discarded and suppressed the sexual myths of literature, art, and religion. Those myths show us the turbulence, the mysteries and passions of sex. In mythology we see men's sexual anxiety, their fear of women's dominance. Much sexual violence

Girls have lower self-esteem and attempt suicide more frequently than boys; five times more boys than girls successfully commit suicide.

Breast cancer kills more than 40,000 women annually; prostate cancer kills more than 30,000 men.

is rooted in men's sense of psychological weakness toward women. It takes many men to deal with one woman. Woman's voracity is a persistent motif. Clara Bow, it was rumored, took on the USC football team on weekends. Marilyn Monroe, singing "Diamonds Are a Girl's Best Friend," rules a conga line of men in tuxes. Half-clad Cher, in the video for "If I Could Turn Back Time," deranges a battleship of screaming sailors and straddles a pink-lit cannon. Feminism, coveting social power, is blind to woman's cosmic sexual power.

To understand rape, you must study the past. There never was and never will be sexual harmony. Every woman must take personal responsibility for her sexuality, which is nature's red flame. She must be prudent and cautious about where she goes and with whom. When she makes a mistake, she must accept the consequences and, through self-criticism, resolve never to make that mistake again. Running to Mommy and Daddy on the campus grievance committee is unworthy of strong women. Posting lists of guilty men in the toilet is cowardly, infantile stuff.

The Italian philosophy of life espouses high-energy confrontation. A male student makes a vulgar remark about your breasts? Don't slink off to whimper and simper with the campus shrinking violets. Deal with it. On the spot. Say, "Shut up, you jerk! And crawl back to the barnyard where you belong!" In general, women who project this take-charge attitude toward life get harassed less often. I see too many dopey, immature, self-pitying women walking around like melting sticks of butter. It's the Yvette Mimieux syndrome: Make me happy. And listen to me weep when I'm not.

The date-rape debate is already smothering in propaganda churned out by the expensive Northeastern colleges and universities, with their overconcentration of boring, uptight academic feminists and spoiled, affluent students. Beware of the deep manipulativeness of rich students who were neglected by their parents. They love to turn the campus into hysterical psychodramas of sexual transgression, followed by assertions of parental authority and concern. And don't look for sexual enlightenment from academe, which spews out mountains of books but never looks at life directly.

As a fan of football and rock music, I see in the simple, swaggering masculinity of the jock and in the noisy posturing of the heavy-metal guitarist certain fundamental, unchanging truths about sex. Masculinity is aggressive, unstable, combustible. It is also the most creative cultural force in history. Women must reorient themselves toward the elemental powers of sex, which can strengthen or destroy.

The only solution to date rape is female self-awareness and self-control. A woman's number one line of defense is herself. When a real rape occurs, she should report it to the police. Complaining to college committees because the courts "take too long" is ridiculous. College administrations are not a branch of the judiciary. They are not equipped or trained for legal inquiry. Colleges must alert incoming students to the problems and dangers of adulthood. Then colleges must stand back and get out of the sex game.

The blame game

The cause of equality will not be served by pointing fingers

SAM KEEN

Any man who hasn't spent the past 25 years watching Rambo movies or lobbying for the NRA has noticed by now that feminism has profoundly changed our cultural climate. Feminism isn't a passing storm; it is a permanent shift in the weather patterns. A generation of men has been deluged by feminist analysis, rhetoric, demands, and political programs. The women we most admire, fear, and struggle with are feminists. Many men were intimidated by feminism and chose to ignore its challenge. Others passively acquiesced to it, or uncritically accepted it, surviving on a spoon-fed diet of blame and guilt. What the majority of men has not done is confront the feminist analysis and worldview and sort out the healing treasures from the toxic trash. It is time to do it.

"Feminism" is a label describing a kaleidoscope, the many-faceted responses of a multitude of women wrestling with the question of self-definition and seeking social changes that will give greater justice, power, and dignity to women. But we need to make a rough and ready distinction between the best and worst of feminism, between feminism as a prophetic protest and feminism as an ideology.

Prophetic feminism is a model for the changes men are beginning to experience.

Ideological feminism is a continuation of a pattern of general enmity and scapegoating that men have traditionally practiced against women.

As a prophetic movement, feminism has been a cry of the agony of women, a vision of what women may become, and a celebration of the feminine. For more than 20 years, a powerful community of feminist activists has worked to secure economic and legal justice for women. And feminist theorists have revisioned history, philosophy, language, and the arts in an effort to recover women's contribution to the intellectual life of Western culture. Because it was born out of a painful awareness of the indignities and political disenfranchisement of women, prophetic feminism has remained aware of the wounding nature of our social and economic system itself—wounding to both men and women.

Ideological feminism, by contrast, is animated by a spirit of resentment, the tactic of blame, and the desire for vindictive triumph over men that comes out of the dogmatic assumption that women are the innocent victims of a male conspiracy. Perhaps the best rule of thumb to use in detecting ideological feminism is to pay close attention to the ideas, moral sentiments, arguments, and mythic history that cluster around the notion of "patriarchy." All of the great agonies of our time are attributed to the great Satan of patriarchy. The rule of men is solely responsible for poverty, injustice, violence, warfare, technomania, pollution, and the exploitation of the Third World.

This type of demonic theory of history renders men responsible for all of the ills of society, and women innocent. If there is warfare it is because men are naturally hostile and warlike, not because when tribes and peoples come into conflict it is the males who have historically been conditioned, trained, and expected to fulfill the role of warrior. If there is environmental pollution it is not because it is the inevitable result of the urban-technological-industrial life-style that modern people have chosen, but because of patriarchal technology. And if there is injustice in society it is not because some men and some women are insensitive to the

From *Utne Reader,* January/February 1993, pp. 65-68. Excerpted from *Fire in the Belly: On Being a Man* by Sam Keen. © 1991 by Sam Keen. Reprinted by permission of Bantam Books, a division of Bantam Doubleday Dell Publishing Group, Inc.

Just friends

─────

Can men and women do it—without doing it?

WHY IS IT OFTEN SO DIFFICULT FOR MEN AND women who like each other to keep sex from muddying the waters of friendship?

Friendship itself is ambiguous, and the ambiguities of male/female friendships are even stronger. There's no set standard and precious little discussion about the terms for friendships across gender lines. If you've slept together, does that rule out friendship? If you're attracted to one another but don't consummate the relationship, are you "friends" or merely flirts?

Part of the problem may be a lack of role models depicting men and women as friends. With the exception of Huck Finn and Becky Thatcher, what other characters from books or films or the tube are strictly platonic friends? Harry and Sally ended up in bed; Sam and Diane thought things were through but, in fact, they weren't; *Moonlighting* went off the air as soon as Maddy and David started fooling around; and we all know what happened to Annie Hall.

The instinctive (and typically female) tendency toward self-blame can also be a factor, causing a woman to feel guilty and confused if a man starts blurring the line between friendship and romance. The question of who's sent what signals to whom can get awfully complicated when two hormonally equipped parties are involved. In all fairness, I know plenty of women who, having been attracted to men who just wanted to "be friends" (whatever their definition may be), were disappointed when their more romantic hopes weren't reciprocated. Still, I have never met a woman who ended a friendship because the man refused to hop into bed.

"There are many different ways to express intimacy," says Carla Golden, associate professor of psychology at Ithaca College. "There's

sexual expressiveness and then there's just plain talking. I think women are far more versed in expressing themselves intimately without being sexual."

So what do women get from friendships with men? One very basic thing is safety. Traveling with a man is a completely different experience from traveling alone or with another woman. Even walking down the street takes on a different meaning when I'm with a man—there are no whistles, no catcalls, no horns honking.

But that's not all there is to it. My relationships with men are also important to me because they provide a respite from introspection. As Golden puts it, "Sometimes women want a sense of difference, an edge. While many women enjoy talking about personal things [with other women], sometimes it gets to be too much."

There's also the much bigger—and murkier—issue of self-acceptance and self-worth. Since men possess the bulk of the world's power and status, it's no wonder women value their attention so much. I hate to admit it, but I feel a lot more connected to the rest of the world when I'm out with a man, even if he is just a pal.

And then there's just a basic fascination with an often alien world. In grade school I envied the boys because they always seemed to have more fun than we girls. Theirs was a world filled with vigorous activities like sports, while the female world was filled with Barbie dolls, cooking sets, and talk. By the same token, I resented those boys because they really didn't seem to care if we girls were there. They were perfectly content to toss a football around without us.

Later, in high school and college, the guys did invite us to

participate in their games, but by that time touch football had a completely different meaning. Of course, that was part of the fun—tackling someone was perfectly legitimate, a safe way to release pent-up sexual aggression.

It's that same sexual energy that's so alluring—and frustrating—about cross-gender friendships. The inevitable flirtations and sexual tensions add spice to the relationship, an excitement that often can't be found in same-sex friendships. Because, if the truth be told, there's usually some sort of attraction between any two people who become friends, and if you're straight, it's that much more intense with people of the opposite sex. Whether you choose to act on the attraction is something else, but the issue is bound to pop up at some point. (My gay male friends, by the way, have said that they encounter the same problems establishing "just friends" relationships with other gay males.)

In the best of friendships, both parties address these issues and try to overcome them, either by acknowledging the sexual tension but refusing to act on it or by acting on it and getting it out of the way. Pointedly ignoring the sexual vibes rarely works, for ultimately it's too hard to pretend nothing's going on when you know something is.

—Abby Ellin
Boston Phoenix

Excerpted with permission from Alternet News Service. *First published in* Boston Phoenix *(June 19, 1992). Subscriptions: $41.50/yr. (52 issues) from 126 Brookline Av., Boston, MA 02215. Back issues available from the same address.*

sufferings of others, but because white male oppressors dominate all women and people of color. Should a Margaret Thatcher, Indira Gandhi, or Imelda Marcos exhibit signs of the pathology of power, an ideological feminist will hasten to explain that she has been colonized by patriarchal attitudes.

Early on, many feminists borrowed the categories oppressed minorities and colonial peoples used in their fight against racism and imperialism to press their case against "the patriarchy." All men, by definition, became guilty of sexism and all women, by definition, were victims. Including all women in the same oppressed "class" seated Marie Antoinette and Rosa Parks side by side in the back of the same bus.

The notion that women are a class or a repressed minority like migrant workers, blacks, Indians in America, or Jews in Germany trivializes the pain involved in class structure and the systematic abuse suffered by ethnic minorities. The injustices that go with class and race are too severe to be confused with the gender problem. All upper classes are composed of equal numbers of men and women. The fruits of exploitation are enjoyed equally by men, women, and children of the upper classes. The outrages of exploitation are borne equally by men and women and children of the lower classes. Both class and ethnic minorities suffer real oppression. It is an insult to the oppressed of the world to have rich and powerful women included within the congregation of the downtrodden merely because they are female.

Ever since Adam, men have been blaming their problems on women. Women have been systematically accused of being temptresses, seducers, powerful contaminants. And if they were viewed as the weaker sex, they were nevertheless blamed whenever a scapegoat was needed.

But the cause of reclaiming female dignity and achieving greater economic justice for women will not be well served by a switch in the dialectics of blame from women to men. This only keeps the old game alive and ensures that the battle between the sexes will continue. We need to find new ways of thinking about men and women, and about the painful and marvelous ways in which we have related and may relate to each other.

Feminists of all sorts are right to be outraged by the dehumanization, destruction, and desecration caused by the modern corporate-industrial-warfare system. They are also right to indict men for their role in creating and maintaining this system, and right to insist on masculine guilt. They, however, are disastrously wrong in excusing women from responsibility

for the destructive aspects of a cultural system that can only be created and perpetuated by consensual interaction of men and women (especially the men and women of the elite, powerful, privileged, and ruling classes).

Men are angry at women because they resent being blamed for everything that has gone wrong since Adam ate the apple. Yes, we felt guilty because we went to useless wars (but what right do women who were in no danger of draft or combat have to criticize?). Yes, we feel guilty because we created technologies that proved to be destructive (but didn't women, the poor, and the underdeveloped nations crave all those new cars and labor-saving devices?). Yes, we feel guilty because we were born white, middle-class, and on the fast track to power and prestige (but haven't the women we married encouraged us to succeed and provide?).

It's easy enough to scoff at men's new awareness of wounds and feelings of victimhood, to suspect them of crocodile tears. But I suggest something far more interesting than hypocrisy is happening when men begin to feel the pain and poverty of their positions. When the powerful begin to feel their impotence, when the masters begin to feel their captivity, we have reached a point where we are finally becoming conscious that the social system we have all conspired to create is victimizing us all. At the moment, sensitive women and men are both somewhat depressed by the overwhelming complexity and seeming intractability of the techno-economic-gender system that is oppressing our psyches and destroying our ecosphere. But our depression can turn into a sense of empowerment when we begin to look carefully at the way men and women interact in a codependent way to maintain the system.

The world is dangerous, threatened, and wounding. There can be no question but that the historical humiliation of women is a fact. But men's suffering from gender roles and the social system is also a fact. The healing of the relationship between the sexes will not begin until men and women cease to use their suffering as a justification for their hostility. It serves no useful purpose to argue about who suffers most. Before we can begin again together, we must repent separately. In the beginning we need simply to listen to each other's stories, the histories of wounds.

Then we must examine the social-economic-political system that has turned the mystery of man and woman into the alienation between the genders. And, finally, we must grieve together. Only repentance, mourning, and forgiveness will open our hearts to each other and give us the power to begin again.

Ending the battle between the sexes

First separate, then communicate

Aaron R. Kipnis & Elizabeth Herron

SPECIAL TO *UTNE READER*

Aaron R. Kipnis, Ph.D., *is a consultant to numerous organizations concerned with gender issues and lectures for many clinical training institutes. He is author of the critically acclaimed book* Knights Without Armor: A Practical Guide for Men in Quest of Masculine Soul, *(Jeremy Tarcher, 1991, Putnam, 1992).*

Elizabeth Herron, M.A., *specializes in women's empowerment and gender reconciliation. She is co-director of the Santa Barbara Institute for Gender Studies and is co-author of* Gender War/Gender Peace; The Quest for Love and Justice Between Women and Men *(Feb. 1994, Morrow).*

H ave you noticed that American men and women seem angrier at one another than ever? Belligerent superpowers have buried the hatchet, but the war between the sexes continues unabated. On every television talk show, women and men trade increasingly bitter accusations. We feel the tension in our homes, in our workplaces, and in our universities.

The Clarence Thomas-Anita Hill controversy and the incidents at the Navy's Tailhook convention brought the question of sexual harassment into the foreground of national awareness, but it now appears that these flaps have merely fueled male-female resentment instead of sparking a productive dialogue that might enhance understanding between the sexes.

Relations between women and men are rapidly changing. Often, however, these changes are seen to benefit one sex at the expense of the other, and the mistrust that results creates resentment. Most men and women seem unable to entertain the idea that the two sexes' differing perspectives on many issues can be equally valid. So polarization grows instead of reconciliation, as many women and men fire ever bigger and better-aimed missiles across the gender gap. On both sides there's a dearth of compassion about the predicaments of the other sex.

For example:
• Women feel sexually harassed; men feel their courting behavior is often misunderstood.

• Women fear men's power to wound them physically; men fear women's power to wound them emotionally.

• Women say men aren't sensitive enough; men say women are too emotional.

• Women feel men don't do their fair share of housework and child care; men feel that women don't feel as much pressure to provide the family's income and do home maintenance.

• Many women feel morally superior to men; many men feel that they are more logical and just than women.

• Women say men have destroyed the environment; men say the women's movement has destroyed the traditional family.

• Men are often afraid to speak about the times that they feel victimized and powerless; women frequently deny their real power.

• Women feel that men don't listen; men feel that women talk too much.

• Women resent being paid less than men; men are concerned about the occupational hazards and stress that lead to their significantly shorter life spans.

• Men are concerned about unfairness in custody and visitation rights; women are concerned about fathers who shirk their child support payments.

It is very difficult to accept the idea that so many conflicting perspectives could all have intrinsic value. Many of us fear that listening to the story of another will somehow weaken our own voice, our own initiative, even our own identity. The fear keeps us locked in adversarial thinking and patterns of blame and alienation. In this frightened absence of empathy, devaluation of the other sex grows.

In an attempt to address some of the discord between the sexes, we have been conducting gender workshops around the country. We invite men and women to spend some time in all-male and all-female groups, talking about the opposite sex. Then we bring the two groups into an encounter with one another. In one of our mixed groups this spring, Susan, a 35-year-old advertising executive, told the men, "Most men these days are insensitive jerks. When are men going to get it that we are coming to work to make a living, not

From *Utne Reader,* January/February 1993, pp. 69-76. © 1993 by Aaron R. Kipnis, Ph.D., and Elizabeth Herron, M.A. Reprinted by permission.

to get laid? Anita Hill was obviously telling the truth. Most of the women I work with have been harassed as well."

Michael, her co-worker, replied, "Then why didn't she tell him ten years ago that what he was doing was offensive? How are we supposed to know where your boundaries are if you laugh at our jokes, smile when you're angry, and never confront us in the direct way a man would? How am I supposed to learn what's not OK with you, if the first time I hear about it is at a grievance hearing?"

We've heard many permutations of this same conversation:

"I just can't listen to women's issues anymore while passively watching so many men go down the tubes."

Gina, a 32-year-old school teacher in Washington, D.C., asks, "Why don't men ever take *no* for an answer?"

Arthur, a 40-year-old construction foreman, re-

His-and-hers politics

A woman explains her unease about the men's movement

I'm in the habit of noticing the symbols on rest room doors because I believe they are cultural icons. Not long ago in a restaurant, I noted that the "Men's" symbol was the routine international stick figure: one head, two arms, two legs, the sort of thing that could be beamed into deep space to show alien life forms what we look like here on Earth. The "Women's," on the other hand, showed a silhouette of someone wearing a beehive hairdo and applying lipstick. I observed: These things are not equivalent.

My daughter often brings home work sheets from preschool that remind me how we all acquire this habit of looking for matching pairs. Draw a circle around the things that go together. Salt and pepper. Cup and saucer. Left and right. Romeo and Juliet. His and Hers. When I try to understand the collection of ideas and goals that has come to be called the men's movement, what disturbs me is that it generally stands as an "other half" to the women's movement, and in my mind it doesn't belong there. It is not an equivalent. Women are fighting for their lives, and men are looking for some peace of mind.

I do believe that men face some cultural problems that come to them solely on the basis of gender: They are so strictly trained to be providers that many other areas of their lives are neither cultivated nor validated. They usually have to

grow up without the benefit of close bonding with a same-sex parent. They struggle with guilt and doubts associated with a history of privilege.

Women struggle with the fact that they are statistically likely to be impoverished, worked to the bone, and raped.

If there is kindness in us, we will not belittle another's pain, regardless of its size. When a friend calls me to moan that she's just gotten a terrible haircut, I'll give her some sympathy. But I will give her a lot more if she calls to say she's gotten ovarian cancer. Let's keep some perspective. The men's movement and the women's movement aren't salt and pepper; they are hangnail and hand grenade.

I met a friend for lunch today, in a restaurant I'm fond of for its rest room iconography and other reasons. The co-owners, a gay man and woman, are the parents of a child whose family also includes their gay and lesbian partners. Once when my own daughter asked me if every child needed to have a mom and a dad, I pointed to this family to widen her range. I told her that in a world where people didn't hurt each other for reasons of color or gender, families could look all kinds of different ways, and they could be happy. We're still waiting for that world, obviously, but in the meantime I like the restaurant: The service is friendly and the vegetables are pesticide-free. The bathroom has nothing at all on the door, because there is only one. It serves one customer at a time, fairly and well, regardless of gender.

I had come to the restaurant to meet a friend, and while I waited

my mind ran from rest rooms to Iron John, so that when she arrived and sat down I asked abruptly, "What do you think of the men's movement?"

My friend blinked a couple of times and said, "I think it's a case of people thinking that feminism is only for women, and if there's a 'Hers' there has to be a 'His,' too."

That's it, exactly. The tragedy is that the formation of a men's movement to "respond" to feminism creates antipathy in place of cooperation. The women's movement is called by that name because women are its heartiest proponents—of necessity, because of lives on the line—but what it asks is simply for all humans to be treated fairly and well, regardless of gender. If its goals could be met, those of the men's movement would be moot points: When women and men are partners in the workplace and the home, sons will be nurtured by fathers; the burden of breadwinning will be shared; the burdens of privilege, if there are any, will surely be erased when power comes up as evenly as grass.

To reach this place, we don't need a "His" and "Hers." What we need is for both sides, the beehive hairdos and the creatures of planet Earth, to claim the goal of equal rights as "Ours."

—*Barbara Kingsolver*

plies that in his experience, "some women *do* in fact say no when they mean yes. Women seem to believe that men should do all the pursuing in the mating dance. But then if we don't read her silent signals right, we're the bad guys. If we get it right, though, then we're heroes."

Many men agree that they are in a double bind. They are labeled aggressive jerks if they come on strong, but are rejected as wimps if they don't. Women feel a similar double bind. They are accused of being teases if they make themselves attractive but reject the advances of men. Paradoxically, however, as Donna, a fortyish divorcée, reports, "When I am up front about my desires, men often head for the hills."

As Deborah Tannen, author of the best-seller about male-female language styles *You Just Don't Understand*, has observed, men and women often have entirely different styles of communication. How many of us have jokingly speculated that men and women actually come from different planets? But miscommunication alone is not the source of all our sorrow.

Men have an ancient history of enmity toward women. For centuries, many believed women to be the cause of our legendary fall from God's grace. "How can he be clean that is born of woman?" asks the Bible. Martin Luther wrote that "God created Adam Lord of all living things, but Eve spoiled it all." The "enlightened" '60s brought us Abbie Hoffman, who said: "The only alliance I would make with the women's liberation movement is in bed." And from the religious right, Jerry Falwell still characterizes feminism as a "satanic attack" on the American family.

In turn, many feel the women's movement devalues the role of men. Marilyn French, author of *The Women's Room*, said, "All men are rapists and that's all they are." In response to the emerging men's movement, Betty Friedan commented, "Oh God, sick . . . I'd hoped by now men were strong enough to accept their vulnerability and to be authentic without aping Neanderthal cavemen."

This hostility to the men's movement is somewhat paradoxical. Those who are intimately involved with the movement say that it is primarily dedicated to ending war and racism, increasing environmental awareness, healing men's lives and reducing violence, promoting responsible fatherhood, and creating equal partnerships with women—all things with which feminism is ideologically aligned. Yet leaders of the men's movement often evoke indignant responses from women. A prominent woman attorney tells us, "I've been waiting 20 years for men to hear our message. Now instead of joining us at last, they're starting their *own* movement. And now they want us to hear that they're wounded too. It makes me sick."

On the other hand, a leader of the men's movement says, "I was a feminist for 15 years. Recently, I realized that all the men I know are struggling just as much as women. Also, I'm tired of all the male-bashing. I just can't listen to women's issues anymore while passively watching so many men go down the tubes."

Some of our gender conflict is an inevitable by-product of the positive growth that has occurred in our society over the last generation. The traditional gender roles of previous generations imprisoned many women and men in soul-killing routines. Women felt dependent and disenfranchised; men felt distanced from feelings, family, and their capacity for self-care.

Even in our own culture, women and men have traditionally had places to meet apart from members of the other sex.

With almost 70 percent of women now in the work force, calls from Barbara Bush and Marilyn Quayle for women to return to the home full time seem ludicrous, not to mention financially impossible. In addition, these calls for the traditional nuclear family ignore the fact that increasing numbers of men now want to downshift from full-time work in order to spend more time at home. So if we can't go back to the old heroic model of masculinity and the old domestic ideal of femininity, how then do we weave a new social fabric out of the broken strands of worn-out sexual stereotypes?

Numerous participants in the well-established women's movement, as well as numbers of men in the smaller but growing men's movement, have been discovering the strength, healing, power, and sense of security that come from being involved with a same-sex group. Women and men have different social, psychological, and biological realities and receive different behavioral training from infancy through adulthood.

In most pre-technological societies, women and men both participate in same-sex social and ceremonial groups. The process of becoming a woman or a man usually begins with some form of ritual initiation. At the onset of puberty, young men and women are brought into the men's and women's lodges, where they gain a deep sense of gender identity.

Even in our own culture, women and men have traditionally had places to meet apart from members of the other sex. For generations, women have gathered over coffee or quilts; men have bonded at work and in taverns. But in our modern society, most heterosexuals believe that a member of the opposite sex is supposed to fulfill all their emotional and social needs. Most young people today are not taught to respect and honor the differences of the other gender, and they arrive at adulthood both mystified and distrustful, worried about the other sex's power to affect them. In fact, most cross-gender conflict is essentially *conflict between different cultures*. Looking at the gender war from this perspective may help us develop solutions to our dilemmas.

In recent decades, cultural anthropologists have come to believe that people are more productive members of society when they can retain their own cultural identity within the framework of the larger culture. As a consequence, the old American "melting pot" theory of cultural assimilation has evolved into a new theory of diversity, whose model might be the "tossed salad." In

Both men and women feel they are in a double bind.

this ideal, each subculture retains its essential identity, while coexisting within the same social container.

Applying this idea to men and women, we can see the problems with the trend of the past several decades toward a sex-role melting pot. In our quest for gender equality through sameness, we are losing both the beauty of our diversity and our tolerance for differences. Just as a monoculture is not as environmentally stable or rich as a diverse natural ecosystem, androgyny denies the fact that sexual differences are healthy.

In the past, perceived differences between men and women have been used to promote discrimination, devaluation, and subjugation. As a result, many "we're all the same" proponents—New Agers and humanistic social theorists, for example—are justifiably suspicious of discussions that seek to restore awareness of our differences. But pretending that differences do not exist is not the way to end discrimination toward either sex.

Our present challenge is to acknowledge the value of our differing experiences as men and women, and to find ways to reap this harvest in the spirit of true equality. Carol Tavris, in her book *The Mismeasure of Women*, suggests that instead of "regarding cultural and reproductive differences as problems to be eliminated, we should aim to eliminate *the unequal consequences that follow from them.*"

Some habits are hard to change, even with an egalitarian awareness. Who can draw the line between what is socially conditioned and what is natural? It may not be possible, or even desirable, to do so. What seems more important is that women and men start understanding each other's different cultures and granting one another greater freedom to experiment with whatever roles or lifestyles attract them.

Lisa, a 29-year-old social worker from New York participating in one of our gender workshops, told us, "Both Joel [her husband] and I work full time. But it always seems to be me who ends up having to change my schedule when Gabe, our son, has a doctor's appoint-

Who's on top?

A revisionist history of men and women

ROBERT GRAVES, THE POET AND HISTORIAN, SAYS, "The most important history of all for me is the changing relationship between men and women down the centuries."

For thousands of years there has been a tragic situation—the domination by men and the degradation of women. We are so used to it we do not notice it.

This was not always so. Now there is an underlying feeling that true equality is impossible because men and women are so different. We can never be like each other. But I disagree. We once were and we must again become noble equals.

Go back three thousand years to Asia Minor, the first civilization that was somewhat stable. In those happy and far-off days women were deeply respected and loved by men and had a kind of wise command over things. This was evidenced by the greatest queen of all time, perhaps, Semiramis of Assyria, a great wise and beneficent ruler. And she had another quality of women then—bravery, for she was also a great soldier. In fact that was what especially charmed her husband. She reigned 42 years.

There were not startling physical differences between men and women then. The statue of the Winged Victory of Samothrace had not knock-knees, poor musculature, nor enormously exaggerat-

ed breasts. There is a beautiful Greek statue of Orestes and Electra who were brother and sister, their arms over each other's shoulders. They are the same height, built identically alike with the same limber prowess and athletic beauty.

In Ancient Egypt, Diodorus Siculus tells us, the women ruled their husbands. There is no ambiguity about it; the wives were absolutely supreme. Herodotus said: "With them the women go to market, the men stay home and weave. The women discharged all kinds of public affairs. The men dealt with domestic affairs." In Sparta women were the dominant sex. They alone could own property. This was the case among the Iroquois, the Kamchadale people of Siberia, and countless others. "When women ruled in Kamchatka, the men not only did the cooking but all the housework, docilely doing everything assigned to them," according

ment or a teacher conference, is sick at home or has to be picked up after school. It's simply taken for granted that in most cases my time is less important than his. I know Joel tries really hard to be an engaged father. But the truth is that I feel I'm always on the front line when it comes to the responsibilities of parenting and keeping the home together. It's just not fair."

Joel responds by acknowledging that Lisa's complaint is justified; but he says, "I handle all the home maintenance, fix the cars, do all the banking and book-keeping and all the yard work as well. These things aren't hobbies. I also work more overtime than Lisa. Where am I supposed to find the time to equally co-parent too? Is Lisa going to start mowing the lawn or help me build the new bathroom? Not likely."

In many cases of male-female conflict, as with Lisa and Joel, there are two differing but *equally valid* points of view. Yet in books, the media, and in women's and men's groups, we only hear about most issues from a woman's point of view or from a man's. This is at the root of the escalating war between the sexes.

For us, the starting point in the quest for gender peace is for men and women to spend more time with members of the same sex. We have found that many men form intimate friendships in same-sex groups. In addition to supporting their well-being, these connections can take some of the pressure off their relationships with women. Men in close friendships no longer expect women to satisfy *all* their emotional needs. And when women meet in groups they support one another's need for connection and also for empowerment in the world. Women then no longer expect men to provide their sense of self-worth. So these same-sex groups can enhance not only the participants' individual lives, but their relationships with members of the other sex as well.

If men and women *remain* separated, however, we risk losing perspective and continuing the domination or scapegoating of the other sex. In women's groups, male-bashing has been running rampant for years. At a recent lecture we gave at a major university, a young male psychology student said, "This is the first time in three years on campus that I have heard anyone say a single positive thing about men or masculinity."

Many women voice the same complaint about their experiences in male-dominated workplaces. Gail, a middle management executive, says, "When I make proposals to the all-male board of directors, I catch the little condescending smirks and glances the men give one another. They don't pull that shit when my male colleagues speak. If they're that rude in front of me, I can only imagine how degrading their comments are when they meet in private."

There are few arenas today in which women and men can safely come together on common ground to frankly discuss our rapidly changing ideas about gender justice. Instead of more sniping from the sidelines, what is needed is for groups of women and men to communicate directly with one another. When we take this

---

to the historian C. Meiners. "Men are so domesticated that they greatly dislike being away from home for more than one day. Should a longer absence than this become necessary, they try to persuade their wives to accompany them, for they cannot get on without the women folk."

In Abyssinia, in Lapland, men did what seems to us women's work. Tacitus, describing the early Teutons, tells how women did all the work, the hunting, tilling the soil, while men idled and looked after the house, equivalent now to playing bridge and taking naps. The heirlooms in the family, a harnessed horse, a strong spear, a sword and shield passed on to the women. They were the fighters.

And so they were in Libya, in the Congo. In India under the Queens of Nepal only women soldiers were known. In Dahomey, the king had a bodyguard of war-rior women and these were braver than any of his men warriors. And physiologically, things were reversed: The women, more active and strenuous, became taller, stronger, tougher than the sedentary home-body men.

Now about women's current

One of the best ways to be a great man would be to be a true friend of women.

physical inferiority. To feel superior, men chose wives with low-grade physical prowess, unable to walk or run decently, with feeble feet, ruined knees, and, as at present, enormously exaggerated breasts. Their offspring, of course, dwindle and become inferior. And men chose such women, as Bertrand Russell said, "because it makes them feel so big and strong without incurring any real danger."

It seems to me one of the best ways to be a great man would be to be a true friend of women. How? Neither pamper nor exploit them. Love in women their greatness which is the same as it is in men. Insist on bravery, honor, grandeur, generosity in women.

I say this because I think there is a state of great unhappiness between us. If we can be true equals, we will be better friends, better lovers, better wives and husbands.
—*Brenda Ueland*

From the book Strength to Your Sword Arm: Selected Writings *by Brenda Ueland. Copyright © 1992 by The Estate of Brenda Ueland. Reprinted by permission of Holy Cow! Press. The book is available for $16.70 postpaid from Holy Cow! Press, Box 3170, Mt. Royal Station, Duluth, MN 55803; 218/724-1653.*

next step and make a commitment to spend time apart and then meet with each other, then we can begin to build a true social, political, and spiritual equality. This process also instills a greater appreciation for the unique gifts each sex has to contribute.

Husband-and-wife team James Sniechowski and Judith Sherven conduct gender reconciliation meetings—similar to the meetings we've been holding around the country—each month in Southern California. In a recent group of 25 people (11 women, 14 men), participants were invited to explore questions like: What did you learn about being a man/woman from your mother? From your father? Sniechowski reports that, "even though, for the most part, the men and women revealed their confusions, mistrust, heartbreaks, and bewilderments, the room quickly filled with a poignant beauty." As one woman said of the meeting, "When I listen to the burdens we suffer, it helps me soften my heart toward them." On another occasion a man said, "My image of women shifts as I realize they've been through some of the same stuff I have."

Discussions such as these give us an opportunity to really hear one another and, perhaps, discover that many of our disagreements come from equally valid, if different, points of view. What many women regard as intimacy feels suffocating and invasive to men. What many men regard as masculine strength feels isolating and distant to women. Through blame and condemnation, women and men shame one another. Through compassionate communication, however, we can help one another. This mutual empowerment is in the best interests of both sexes, because when one sex suffers, the other does too.

Toward the end of our meetings, men and women inevitably become more accountable for the ways in which they contribute to the problem. Gina said, "I've never really heard the men's point of view on all this before. I must admit that I rarely give men clear signals when they say or do something that offends me."

Arthur then said, "All my life I've been trained that my job as a man is to keep pursuing until 'no' is changed to 'yes, yes, yes.' But I hear it that when a woman says no, they want me to respect it. I get it now that what I thought was just a normal part of the dance is experienced as harassment by some women. But you know, it seems that if we're ever going to get together now, more women are going to have to start making the first moves."

After getting support from their same-sex groups and then listening to feedback from the whole group, Joel and Lisa realize that if they are both going to work full time they need to get outside help with family tasks, rather than continuing to blame and shame one another for not doing more.

Gender partnership based on strong, interactive, separate but equal gender identities can support the needs of both sexes. Becoming more affirming or supportive of our same sex doesn't have to lead to hostility toward the other sex. In fact, the acknowledgment that gender diversity is healthy may help all of us to become more tolerant toward other kinds of differences in our society.

Through gender reconciliation—both formal workshops and informal discussions—the sexes can support each other, instead of blaming one sex for not meeting the other's expectations. Men and women clearly have the capacity to move away from the sex-war rhetoric that is dividing us as well as the courage necessary to create forums for communication that can unite and heal us.

Boys and girls need regular opportunities in school to openly discuss their differing views on dating, sex, and gender roles. In universities, established women's studies courses could be complemented with men's studies, and classes in the two fields could be brought together from time to time to deepen students' understanding of both sexes. The informal discussion group is another useful format in which men and women everywhere can directly communicate with each other (see *Utne Reader* issue no. 44 [March/April 1991]). In the workplace the struggle for gender understanding needs to go beyond the simple setting up of guidelines about harassment; it is essential that women and men regularly discuss their differing views on gender issues. Outside help is often needed in structuring such discussions and getting them under way. Our organization, the Santa Barbara Institute for Gender Studies, trains and provides "reconciliation facilitators" for that purpose.

These forums must be fair. Discussions of women's wage equity must also include men's job safety. Discussions about reproductive rights, custody rights, or parental leave must consider the rights of both mothers and fathers—and the needs of the children. Affirmative action to balance the male-dominated political and economic leadership must also bring balance to the female-dominated primary-education and social-welfare systems.

We call for both sexes to come to the negotiating table from a new position of increased strength and self-esteem. Men and women do not need to become more like one another, merely more deeply themselves. But gender understanding is only a step on the long road that must ultimately lead to fundamental institutional change. We would hope, for example, that in the near future men and women will stop arguing about whether women should go into combat and concentrate instead on how to end war. The skills and basic attitudes that will lead to gender peace are the very ones we need in order to meet the other needs of our time—social, political, and environmental—with committed action.

Abnormal: Anything considered not to be normal, i.e., not conforming to the subjective standards a social group has established as the norm.

Abortifacients: Substances that cause termination of pregnancy.

Abortion: The termination of a pregnancy.

Acquaintance (date) rape: A sexual encounter forced by someone who is known to the victim.

Acquired immunodeficiency syndrome (AIDS): Fatal disease caused by a virus that is transmitted through the exchange of bodily fluids, primarily in sexual activity and intravenous drug use.

Activating effect: The direct influence some hormones can have on activating or deactivating sexual behavior.

Actual use failure rate: A measure of how often a birth control method can be expected to fail when human error and technical failure are considered.

Adolescence: Period of emotional, social, and physical transition from childhood to adulthood.

Adultery: Extramarital sex without the knowledge of the spouse.

Adultery toleration: Marriage partners extending the freedom to each other to have sex with others.

Affectional: Relating to feelings or emotions, such as romantic attachments.

Agenesis (absence) of the penis (ae-JEN-a-ses): A congenital condition in which the penis is undersized and nonfunctional.

AIDS: Acquired immunodeficiency syndrome.

Ambisexual: Alternate term for bisexual.

Amniocentesis: A process whereby medical problems with a fetus can be determined while it is still in the womb; a needle is inserted into the amniotic sac, amniotic fluid is withdrawn, and fetal cells are examined.

Anal intercourse: Insertion of the penis into the rectum of a partner.

Androgen: A male hormone, such as testosterone, that affects physical development, sexual desire, and behavior.

Androgynous: Possessing high frequencies of both masculine and feminine behaviors and traits.

Anejaculation: Lack of ejaculation at the time of orgasm.

Apgar test: An exam that determines the overall health of a newborn by testing his or her color, appearance, heart rate, reflex ability, and respiration.

Aphrodisiacs (af-ro-DEE-aks): Foods or chemicals purported to foster sexual arousal; they are believed to be more myth than fact.

Apoptosis: Programmed cell death that occurs naturally in living tissues. HIV may induce abnormal apoptosis in immune cells.

Apotemnophilia: A rare condition characterized by the desire to function sexually after having a leg amputated.

Areola (a-REE-a-la): Darkened, circular area of skin surrounding the nipple of the breast.

Artificial insemination: Injection of the sperm cells of a male into a woman's vagina, with the intention of conceiving a child.

Asceticism (a-SET-a-siz-um): Usually characterized by celibacy, this philosophy emphasizes spiritual purity through self-denial and self-discipline.

Asexuality: A condition characterized by a low interest in sex.

Autoerotic asphyxiation: Accidental death from pressure placed around the neck during masturbatory behavior.

Autofellatio (fe-LAY-she-o): A male providing oral stimulation to his own penis, an act most males do not have the physical agility to perform.

Autogynephilia: The tendency of some males to become sexually aroused by the thought or image of themselves with female attributes.

Bartholin's glands (BAR-tha-lenz): Small glands located in the opening through the minor lips that produce some secretion during sexual arousal.

Behavior therapy: Therapy that uses techniques to change patterns of behavior; often employed in sex therapy.

Berdache (bare-DAHSH): Anthropological term for cross-dressing in other cultures.

Bestiality (beest-ee-AL-i-tee): A human being having sexual contact with an animal.

Biological essentialists: Those who believe that sexual orientation is an inborn trait, resulting from biological factors during development.

Biphobia: Prejudice, negative attitudes, and misconceptions relating to bisexual people and their life-styles.

Bisexual: Refers to some degree of sexual activity with or attraction to members of both sexes.

Bond: The emotional link between parent and child created by cuddling, cooing, and physical and eye contact early in a newborn's life.

Bondage: Tying, restraining, or applying pressure to body parts as part of sexual arousal.

Brachioproctic activity (brake-ee-o-PRAHK-tik): Known in slang as "fisting"; a hand is inserted into the rectum of a partner.

Brothel: House of prostitution.

Bulbourethral glands: Also called Cowper's glands.

Call boys: Highly paid male prostitutes.

Call girls: Highly paid female prostitutes.

Case study: An in-depth analysis of a particular individual and how he or she might have been helped to solve a sexual or other problem.

Catharsis theory: A suggestion that viewing pornography will provide a release for sexual tension, thus preventing antisocial behavior.

Celibacy (SELL-a-ba-see): Choosing not to share sexual activity with others.

Cervical cap: A contraceptive device that is shaped like a large thimble and fits over the uterine cervix and blocks sperm from entering the uterus.

Cervical intraepithelial neoplasia (CIN): Abnormal, precancerous cells sometimes identified in a Pap smear.

Cervix (SERV-ix): Lower "neck" of the uterus that extends into the back part of the vagina.

Cesarean section: A surgical method of childbirth in which delivery occurs through an incision in the abdominal wall and uterus.

Chancroid (SHAN-kroyd): A STD caused by the bacterium *Hemophilus ducreyi* and characterized by sores on the genitals, which, if left untreated, could result in pain and rupture of the sores.

Child molesting: Sexual abuse of a child by an adult.

Chlamydia (klud-MID-ee-uh): Now known to be a common STD, this organism is a major cause of urethritis in males; in females it often presents no symptoms.

Circumcision: Of clitoris—surgical procedure that cuts the prepuce, exposing the clitoral shaft; in the male, surgical removal of the foreskin from the penis.

Climacteric: Mid-life period experienced by both men and women when there is greater emotional stress than usual and sometimes physical symptoms.

Climax: Another term for orgasm.

Clinical research: The study of the cause, treatment, or prevention of a disease or condition by testing large numbers of people.

Clitoridectomy: Surgical removal of the clitoris; practiced routinely in some cultures.

Clitoris (KLIT-a-rus): Sexually sensitive organ found in the female vulva; it becomes engorged with blood during arousal.

Clone: The genetic-duplicate organism produced by the cloning process.

Cloning: A process involving the transfer of a full complement of chromosomes from a body cell of an organism into an ovum from which the chromosomal material has been removed; if allowed to develop into a new organism, it is an exact genetic duplicate of the one from which the original body cell was taken; the process is not yet used for humans, but it has been performed in lower animal species.

Cohabitation: Living together and sharing sex without marrying.

Coitus: Heterosexual, penis-in-vagina intercourse.

Coitus interruptus (ko-EET-us *or* KO-ut-us): A method of birth control in which the penis is withdrawn from the vagina prior to ejaculation.

Comarital sex: One couple swapping sexual partners with another couple; also called mate swapping.

Combining of chromosomes: The process by which a sperm unites with an egg, normally joining 23 pairs of chromosomes to establish the genetic "blueprint" for a new individual. The sex chromosomes establish its sex: XX for female and XY for male.

Coming out: To acknowledge to oneself and others that one is a lesbian, a gay male, or bisexual.

Condom: A sheath worn over the penis during intercourse to collect semen and prevent conception or venereal disease.

Consensual adultery: Permission given to at least one partner within the marital relationship to participate in extramarital sexual activity.

Controlled experiment: Research in which the investigator examines what is happening to one variable while all other variables are kept constant.

Coprophilia: Sexual arousal connected with feces.

Core gender identity: A child's early inner sense of its maleness, femaleness, or ambivalence, established prior to puberty.

Corona: The ridge around the penile glans.

Corpus luteum: Cell cluster of the follicle that remains after the ovum is released, secreting hormones that help regulate the menstrual cycle.

Cowper's glands: Two small glands in the male that secrete an alkaline fluid into the urethra during sexual arousal.

Cross-genderists: Transgenderists.

Cryptorchidism (krip-TOR-ka-diz-um): Condition in which the testes have not descended into the scrotum prior to birth.

Cunnilingus (kun-a-LEAN-gus): Oral stimulation of the clitoris, vaginal opening, or other parts of the vulva.

Cystitis (sis-TITE-us): A nonsexually transmitted infection of the urinary bladder.

Deoxyribonucleic acid (DNA): The chemical in each cell that carries the genetic code.

Depo-Provera: An injectable form of progestin that can prevent pregnancy for 3 months; it was approved for use in the United States in 1992.

Deprivation homosexuality: Can occur when members of the opposite sex are unavailable.

Desire phase: Sex researcher and therapist Helen Singer Kaplan's term for the psychological interest in sex that precedes a physiological, sexual arousal.

Deviation: Term applied to behaviors or orientations that do not conform to a society's accepted norms; it often has negative connotations.

Diaphragm (DY-a-fram): A latex rubber cup, filled with spermicide, that is fitted to the cervix by a clinician; the woman must learn to insert it properly for full contraceptive effectiveness.

Diethylstilbestrol (DES): Synthetic estrogen compound once given to mothers whose pregnancies were at high risk of miscarrying.

Dilation: The gradual opening of the cervical opening of the uterus prior to and during labor.

Direct sperm injection: A technique involving the injection of a single sperm cell directly into an ovum. It is useful in cases where the male has a low sperm count.

Discrimination: The process by which an individual extinguishes a response to one stimulus while preserving it for other stimuli.

Dysfunction: Condition in which the body does not function as expected or desired during sex.

Dysmenorrhea (dis-men-a-REE-a): Painful menstruation.

Dyspareunia: Recurrent or persistent genital pain related to sexual activity.

E. Coli (Escherichia coli): Bacteria naturally living in the human colon, which often cause urinary tract infection.

Ectopic pregnancy (ek-TOP-ik): The implantation of a blastocyst somewhere other than in the uterus (usually in the fallopian tube).

Ejaculation: Muscular expulsion of semen from the penis.

Ejaculatory inevitability: The sensation in the male that ejaculation is imminent.

ELISA (enzyme-linked immunosorbent assay): The primary test used to determine the presence of HIV in humans.

Embryo (EM-bree-o): The term applied to the developing cells when, about a week after fertilization, the blastocyst implants itself in the uterine wall.

Endometrial hyperplasia (hy-per-PLAY-zhee-a): Excessive growth of the inner lining of the uterus (endometrium).

Endometriosis (en-doe-mee-tree-O-sus): Growth of the endometrium out of the uterus into surrounding organs.

Endometrium: Interior lining of the uterus, innermost of three layers.

Endorphins: A chemical produced by the brain in response to physical intimacy and sexual satisfaction.

Epidemiology (e-pe-dee-mee-A-la-jee): The branch of medical science that deals with the incidence, distribution, and control of disease in a population.

Epididymis (ep-a-DID-a-mus): Tubular structure on each test is in which sperm cells mature.

Epididymitis (ep-a-did-a-MITE-us): Inflammation of the epididymis of the testis.

Episiotomy (ee-piz-ee-OTT-a-mee): A surgical incision in the vaginal opening made by the clinician or obstetrician to prevent the baby from tearing the opening in the process of being born.

Epispadias (ep-a-SPADE-ee-as): Birth defect in which the urinary bladder empties through an abdominal opening and the urethra is malformed.

Erectile dysfunction: Difficulty achieving or maintaining penile erection (impotence).

Erection: Enlargement and stiffening of the penis as internal muscles relax and blood engorges the columns of spongy tissue.

Erogenous zone (a-RAJ-a-nus): Any area of the body that is sensitive to sexual arousal.

Erotica: Artistic representations of nudity or sexual activity.

Erotomania: A very rare form of mental illness characterized by a highly compulsive need for sex.

Erotophilia: Consistent positive responding to sexual cues.

Erotophobia: Consistent negative responding to sexual cues.

Estrogen (ES-tro-jen): Hormone produced abundantly by the ovaries; it plays an important role in the menstrual cycle.

Estrogen replacement therapy (ERT): Controversial treatment of the physical changes of menopause by administering dosages of the hormone estrogen.

Ethnocentricity: The tendency of the members of one culture to assume that their values and norms of behavior are the "right" ones in comparison to other cultures.

Ethnography: The anthropological study of other cultures.

Ethnosexual: Referring to data concerning the sexual beliefs and customs of other cultures.

Excitement: The arousal phase of sex researchers William Masters and Virginia Johnson's four-phase model of the sexual response cycle.

Exhibitionism: Exposing the genitals to others for sexual pleasure.

External values: The belief systems available from one's society and culture.

Extramarital sex: Married person having sexual intercourse with someone other than her or his spouse; adultery.

Fallopian tubes: Structures that are connected to the uterus and lead the ovum from an ovary to the inner cavity of the uterus.

Fellatio: Oral stimulation of the penis.

Female condom: A lubricated polyurethane pouch that is inserted into the vagina for intercourse to collect semen and help prevent disease transmission and pregnancy.

Female sexual arousal disorder: Difficulty for a woman in achieving sexual arousal.

Fetal alcohol syndrome (FAS): A condition in a fetus characterized by abnormal growth, neurological damage, and facial distortion caused by the mother's heavy alcohol consumption.

Fetishism (FET-a-shizm): Sexual arousal triggered by objects or materials not usually considered to be sexual.

Fetus: The term given to the embryo after 2 months of development in the womb.

Fibrous hymen: Condition in which the hymen is composed of unnaturally thick, tough tissue.

Follicles: Capsules of cells in which an ovum matures.

Follicle-stimulating hormone (FSH): Pituitary hormone that stimulates the ovaries or testes.

Foreplay: Sexual activities shared in early stages of sexual arousal, with the term implying that they are leading to a more intense, orgasm-oriented form of activity such as intercourse.

Foreskin: Fold of skin covering the penile glans; also called prepuce.

Frenulum (FREN-yu-lum): Thin, tightly-drawn fold of skin on the underside of the penile glans; it is highly sensitive.

Frotteurism: Gaining sexual gratification from anonymously pressing or rubbing one's genitals against others, usually in crowded settings.

G Spot: A vaginal area that some researchers feel is particularly sensitive to sexual stimulation.

Gamete intra-fallopian transfer (GIFT): Direct placement of ovum and concentrated sperm cells into the woman's fallopian tube to increase the chances of fertilization.

Gay: Refers to persons who have a predominantly same-gender sexual orientation and identity. More often applied to males.

Gender dysphoria (dis-FOR-ee-a): Some degree of discomfort with one's identity as male or female, and/or nonconformity to the norms considered appropriate for one's physical sex.

Gender identity: A person's inner experience of gender feelings of maleness, femaleness, or some ambivalent position between the two.

Gender identity disorder: The expression of gender identity in a way that is socially inconsistent with one's anatomical gender; may also be described as gender dysphoria.

Gender transportation: Gender dysphoria.

Gene Therapy: Treatment of genetically caused disorders by substitution of healthy genes.

General sexual dysfunction: Difficulty for a woman in achieving sexual arousal.

Generalization: Application of specific learned responses to other, similar situations or experiences.

Genetic engineering: The modification of the gene structure of cells to change cellular functioning.

Genital herpes (HER-peez): Viral STD characterized by painful sores on the sex organs.

Genital warts: Small lesions on genital skin caused by papilloma virus; this STD increases later risks of certain malignancies.

Glans: Sensitive head of the female clitoris, visible between the upper folds of the minor lips; in the male, the sensitive head of the penis.

Gonadotropin releasing hormone (GnRH) (go-nad-a-TRO-pen): Hormone from the hypothalamus that stimulates the release of FSH and LH by the pituitary.

Gonads: Sex and reproductive glands, either testes or ovaries, that produce hormones and, eventually, reproductive cells (sperm or eggs).

Gonorrhea (gon-uh-REE-uh): Bacterial STD causing urethral pain and discharge in males; often no initial symptoms in females.

Granuloma INGUINALE (gran-ya-LOW-ma in-gwa-NAL-ee *or* -NALE): STD characterized by ulcerations and granulations beginning in the groin and spreading to the buttocks and genitals.

Group marriage: Three or more people in a committed relationship who share sex with one another.

Hard-core pornography: Pornography that makes use of highly explicit depictions of sexual activity or shows lengthy scenes of genitals.

Hedonists: People who believe that pleasure is the highest good.

Hemophiliac (hee-mo-FIL-ee-ak): Someone with the hereditary blood defect hemophilia, primarily affecting males and characterized by difficulty in clotting.

Hepatitis B: Liver infection caused by a sexually transmitted virus (HBV).

Heterosexism: The biased and discriminatory assumption that people are, or should be, attracted to members of the other gender.

Heterosexual: Attractions or activities between males and females.

HIV: Human immunodeficiency virus.)

Homophobia (ho-mo-PHO-bee-a): Strongly held negative attitudes and irrational fears relating to gay men and/or lesbians and their lifestyles.

Homosexual: The term that is traditionally applied to romantic and sexual attractions and activities between members of the same gender.

Hookers: Street name for female prostitutes.

Hormone implants: Contraceptive method in which hormone-releasing plastic containers are surgically inserted under the skin.

Hormone pumping: A fertility-enhancing technique involving the injection of progesterone into a woman's system.

Hormone replacement therapy (HRT): Treatment of the physical changes of menopause by administering dosages of the hormones estrogen and progesterone.

Hot flash: A flushed, sweaty feeling in the skin caused by dilated blood vessels, often associated with menopause.

Human chorionic gonadotropin (HCG): A hormone detectable in the urine of a pregnant woman. Most home pregnancy tests work by detecting its presence in woman's urine.

Human immunodeficiency virus: The virus that initially attacks the human immune system, eventually causing AIDS.

Hustlers: Male street prostitutes.

H-Y antigen: A biochemical produced in an embryo when the Y chromosome is present; it causes fetal gonads to develop into testes.

Hymen: Membranous tissue that can cover part of the vaginal opening.

Hyperfemininity: A tendency to exaggerate characteristics typically associated with femininity.

Hypermasculinity: A tendency on the part of someone to exaggerate manly behaviors, sometimes called machismo.

Hypersexuality: Unusually high level of interest in and drive for sex.

Hypoactive sexual desire (HSD) disorder: Loss of interest and pleasure in what were formerly arousing sexual stimuli.

Hyposexuality: An especially low level of sexual interest and drive.

Hypospadias (hye-pa-SPADE-ee-as): Birth defect caused by incomplete closure of the urethra during fetal development.

Imperforate hymen: Lack of any openings in the hymen.

Impotence (IM-pa-tens): Difficulty achieving or maintaining erection of the penis.

In vitro fertilization (IVF): A process whereby the union of the sperm and egg occurs outside the mother's body.

Incest (IN-sest): Sexual activity between closely related family members.

Incest taboo: Cultural prohibitions against incest, typical of most societies.

Infertility: The inability to produce offspring.

Infibulation: Surgical procedure, performed in some cultures, that seals the opening of the vagina.

Informed consent: The consent given by research subjects, indicating their willingness to participate in a study, after they are informed about the purpose of the study and how they will be asked to participate.

Inhibited sexual desire (ISD): Loss of interest and pleasure in formerly arousing sexual stimuli.

Internal values: Intrinsic values.

Intersexuality: A combination of female and male anatomical structures, so that the individual cannot be clearly defined as male or female.

Interstitial-cell-stimulating hormone (ICSH): Pituitary hormone that stimulates the testes to secrete testosterone; known as luteinizing hormone (LH) in females.

Intrauterine devices (IUDs): Birth control method involving the insertion of a small plastic device into the uterus.

Intrinsic values: The individualized beliefs and attitudes that a person develops by sorting through external values and personal needs.

Introitus (in-TROID-us): The outer opening of the vagina.

Kiddie porn: Term used to describe the distribution and sale of photographs and films of children or young teenagers engaging in some form of sexual activity.

Kleptomania: Extreme form of fetishism in which sexual arousal is generated by stealing.

Labor: Uterine contractions in a pregnant woman; an indication that the birth process is beginning.

Lactation: Production of milk by the milk glands of the breasts.

Lamaze method (la-MAHZ): A birthing process based on relaxation techniques practiced by the expectant mother; her partner coaches her throughout the birth.

Laparoscopy: Simpler procedure for tubal ligation, involving the insertion of a small fiber optic scope into the abdomen, through which the surgeon can see the fallopian tubes and close them off.

Laparotomy: Operation to perform a tubal ligation, or female sterilization, involving an abdominal incision.

Latency period: A stage in human development characterized, in Freud's theory, by little interest in or awareness of sexual feelings; recent research tends to suggest that latency does not exist.

Lesbian (LEZ-bee-un): Refers to females who have a predominantly same-gender sexual orientation and identity.

Libido (la-BEED-o or LIB-a-do): A term first used by Freud to define human sexual longing or sex drive.

Lumpectomy: Surgical removal of a breast lump, along with a small amount of surrounding tissue.

Luteinizing hormone (LH): Pituitary hormone that triggers ovulation in the ovaries and stimulates sperm production in the testes.

Lymphogranuloma venereum (LGV) (lim-foe-gran-yu-LOW-ma-va-NEAR-ee-um): Contagious STD caused by several strains of *Chlamydia* and marked by swelling and ulceration of lymph nodes in the groin.

Major lips: Two outer folds of skin covering the minor lips, clitoris, urethral opening, and vaginal opening.

Male condom: A sheath worn over the penis during intercourse that collects semen and helps prevent disease transmission and conception.

Male erectile disorder: Difficulty achieving or maintaining penile erection (impotence).

Mammography: Sensitive X-ray technique used to discover small breast tumors.

Marital rape: A woman being forced by her husband to have sex.

Masochist: The individual in a sadomasochistic sexual relationship who takes the submissive role.

Massage parlors: A business that provides massage treatment; places where women can be hired to perform sexual acts in addition to or in lieu of a massage.

Mastectomy: Surgical removal of all or part of a breast.

Ménage à trois (may-NAZH-ah-TRWAH): Troilism.

Menarche (MEN-are-kee): Onset of menstruation at puberty.

Menopause (MEN-a-poz): Time in mid-life when menstruation ceases.

Menstrual cycle: The hormonal interactions that prepare a woman's body for possible pregnancy at roughly monthly intervals.

Menstruation (men-stru-AY-shun): Phase of menstrual cycle in which the inner uterine lining breaks down and sloughs off; the tissue, along with some blood, flows out through the vagina; also called the period.

Midwives: Medical professionals, both women and men, trained to assist with the birthing process.

Minor lips: Two inner folds of skin that join above the clitoris and extend along the sides of the vaginal and urethral openings.

Miscarriage: A natural termination of pregnancy.

Modeling theory: Suggests that people will copy behavior they view in pornography.

Molluscum contagiosum (ma-LUS-kum kan-taje-ee-O-sum): A skin disease transmitted by direct bodily contact, not necessarily sexual, that is characterized by eruptions on the skin that appear similar to whiteheads, with a hard seed-like core.

Monogamous: Sharing sexual relations with only one person.

Monorchidism (ma-NOR-ka-dizm): Presence of only one testis in the scrotum.

Mons: Cushion of fatty tissue located over the female's pubic bone.

Moral values: Beliefs associated with ethical issues, or rights and wrongs; they are often a part of sexual decision making.

Müllerian ducts (myul-EAR-ee-an): Embryonic structures that develop into female sexual and reproductive organs unless inhibited by male hormones.

Müllerian Inhibiting Substance: Hormone produced by fetal testes that prevents further development of female structures from the Müllerian ducts.

Multiplier effect: When biological and socioenvironmental factors build on one another more and more in the process of human development.

National Birth Control League: An organization founded in 1914 by Margaret Sanger to promote use of contraceptives.

Natural childbirth: A birthing process that encourages the mother to take control, thus minimizing medical intervention.

Necrophilia (nek-ro-FILL-ee-a): Having sexual activity with a dead body.

Nongonococcal urethritis (NGU) (non-gon-uh-KOK-ul yur-i-THRYT-us): Urethral infection or irritation in the male urethra caused by bacteria or local irritants.

Nonspecific uethritis (NSU) (yur-i-THRYT-us): Infection or irritation in the male urethra caused by bacteria or local irritants.

Normal: A subjective term used to describe sexual behaviors and orientations. Standards of normalcy are determined by social, cultural, and historical standards.

Normal asexuality: An absence or low level of sexual desire, considered normal for a particular person.

Normalization: Integration of mentally retarded persons into the social mainstream as much as possible.

Norplant implants: Contraceptive method in which hormone-releasing rubber cylinders are surgically inserted under the skin.

Nymphomania (nim-fa-MANE-ee-a): A term sometimes used to describe erotomania in women.

Obscenity: Depiction of sexual activity in a repulsive or disgusting manner.

Onanism (O-na-niz-um): A term sometimes used to describe masturbation, it comes from the biblical story of Onan, who practiced coitus interruptus and "spilled his seed on the ground."

Open-ended marriage: Marriage in which each partner in the primary relationship grants the other freedom to have emotional and sexual relationships with others.

Opportunistic infection: A disease resulting from lowered resistance of a weakened immune system.

Organizing effect: Manner in which hormones control patterns of early development in the body.

Orgasm (OR-gaz-em): A rush of pleasurable physical sensations and series of contractions associated with the release of sexual tension; usually accompanied by ejaculation in men.

Orgasmic release: Reversal of the vasocongestion and muscular tension of sexual arousal, triggered by orgasm.

Orgy (OR-jee): Group sex.

Osteoporosis(ah-stee-o-po-ROW-sus): Disease caused by loss of calcium from the bones in postmenopausal women, leading to brittle bones and stooped posture.

Ova: Egg cells produced in the ovary. One cell is an ovum; in reproduction, it is fertilized by a sperm cell.

Ovaries: Pair of female gonads, located in the abdominal cavity, that produce ova and female hormones.

Ovulation: Release of a mature ovum through the wall of an ovary.

Ovum Donation: Use of an egg from another woman for conception, with the fertilized ovum then being implanted in the uterus of the woman wanting to become pregnant.

Oxytocin: Pituitary hormone that plays a role in lactation and in uterine contractions; brain secretions that act as natural tranquilizers and pain relievers.

Pansexual: Lacking highly specific sexual orientations or preferences; open to a range of sexual activities.

Pap smear: Medical test that examines a smear of cervical cells to detect any cellular abnormalities.

Paraphilia (pair-a-FIL-ee-a): A newer term used to describe sexual orientations and behaviors that vary from the norm; it means "a love beside."

Paraphiliac: A person who is drawn to one or more of the paraphilias.

Partial Zone Dissection (PZD): A technique used to increase the chances of fertilization by making a microscopic incision in the zona pellucida of an ovum. This creates a passageway through which sperm may enter the egg more easily.

Pedophilia (peed-a-FIL-ee-a): Another term for child sexual abuse.

Pelvic inflammatory disease (PID): A chronic internal infection associated with certain types of IUDs.

Penile strain gauge: A device placed on the penis to measure even subtle changes in its size due to sexual arousal.

Penis: Male sexual organ that can become erect when stimulated; it leads urine and sperm to the outside of the body.

Perimetrium: Outer covering of the uterus.

Perinatal: A term used to describe things related to pregnancy, birth, or the period immediately following the birth.

Perineal area (pair-a-NEE-al): The sensitive skin between the genitals and the anus.

Peyronie's disease (pay-ra-NEEZ): Development of fibrous tissue in spongy erectile columns within the penis.

Phimosis (fye-MOE-sus): A condition in which an abnormally long, tight foreskin on the penis does not retract easily.

Pimps: Men who have female prostitutes working for them.

Placenta (pla-SENT-a): The organ that unites the fetus to the mother by bringing their blood vessels closer together; it provides nourishment and removes waste for the developing baby.

Plateau phase: The stable, leveled-off phase of sex researchers William Masters and Virginia Johnson's four-phase model of the sexual response cycle.

Plethysmograph: A laboratory measuring device that charts physiological changes over time. Attached to a penile strain gauge, it can chart changes in penis size. This is called penile plethysmography.

Polygamy: The practice, in some cultures, of being married to more than one spouse.

Pornography: Photographs, films, or literature intended to be sexually arousing through explicit depictions of sexual activity.

Potentiation: Establishment of stimuli early in life that form ranges of response for later in life.

Premature birth: A birth that takes place prior to the 36th week of pregnancy.

Premature ejaculation: Difficulty that some men experience in controlling the ejaculatory reflex, which results in rapid ejaculation.

Premenstrual syndrome (PMS): Symptoms of physical discomfort, moodiness, and emotional tensions that occur in some women for a few days prior to menstruation.

Preorgasmic: A term often applied to women who have not yet been able to reach orgasm during sexual response.

Prepuce (PREE-peus): In the female, tissue of the upper vulva that covers the clitoral shaft.

Priapism (pry-AE-pizm): Continual, undesired, and painful erection of the penis.

Primary dysfunction: A difficulty with sexual functioning that has always existed for a particular person.

Progesterone (pro-JES-ter-one): Ovarian hormone that causes the uterine lining to thicken.

Prolapse of the uterus: Weakening of the supportive ligaments of the uterus, causing it to protrude into the vagina.

Promiscuity (prah-mis-KIU-i-tee): Sharing casual sexual activity with many different partners.

Prostaglandin: Hormone-like chemical whose concentrations increase in a woman's body just prior to menstruation.

Prostaglandin or saline induced abortion: Used in the 16th–24th weeks of pregnancy, prostaglandins, salt solutions, or urea are injected into the amniotic sac, administered intravenously, or inserted into the vagina in suppository form, to induce contractions and fetal delivery.

Prostate: Gland located beneath the urinary bladder in the male; it produces some of the secretions in semen.

Prostatitis (pras-tuh-TITE-us): Inflammation of the prostate gland.

Pseudohermaphrodite: A person who possesses either testes or ovaries in combination with some external genitals of the other sex.

Pseudonecrophilia: A fantasy about having sex with the dead.

Psychosexual development: Complex interaction of factors that form a person's sexual feelings, orientations, and patterns of behavior.

Psychosocial development: The cultural and social influences that help shape human sexual identity.

Puberty: Time of life when reproductive capacity develops and secondary sex characteristics appear.

Pubic lice: Small insects that can infect skin in the pubic area, causing a rash and severe itching.

Pubococcygeus (PC) muscle (pyub-o-kox-a-JEE-us): Part of the supporting musculature of the vagina that is involved in orgasmic response and over which a woman can exert some control.

Pyromania: Sexual arousal generated by setting fires.

Random sample: A representative group of the larger population that is the focus of a scientific poll or study in which care is taken to select participants without a pattern that might sway research results.

Rape trauma syndrome: The predictable sequence of reactions that a victim experiences following a rape.

Recreational adultery: Extramarital sex with a low level of emotional commitment and performed for fun and variety.

Recreational marriage: Recreational adultery.

Refractory period: Time following orgasm during which a man cannot be restimulated to orgasm.

Reinforcement: In conditioning theory, any influence that helps shape future behavior as a punishment or reward stimulus.

Resolution phase: The term for the return of a body to its unexcited state following orgasm.

Retarded ejaculation: A male who has never been able to reach an orgasm.

Retrograde ejaculation: Abnormal passage of semen into the urinary bladder at the time of ejaculation.

Retrovirus (RE-tro-vi-rus): A class of viruses that reproduces with the aid of the enzyme reverse transcriptase, which allows the virus to integrate its genetic code into that of the host cell, thus establishing permanent infection.

Rh factor: A blood-clotting protein agent whose presence or absence in the blood signals an Rh+ or Rh- person.

Rh incompatibility: Condition in which a blood protein of the infant is not the same as the mother's; antibodies formed in the mother can destroy red blood cells in the fetus.

Rho GAM: Medication administered to a mother to prevent formation of antibodies when the baby is Rh positive and its mother Rh negative.

Rhythm method: A natural method of birth control that depends on an awareness of the woman's menstrual/fertility cycle.

RU 486: A French abortion drug; a progesterone antagonist used as a postcoital contraceptive.

Rubber dam: Small square sheet of latex, such as that used in dental work, placed over the vulva, vagina, or anus to help prevent transmission of HIV during sexual activity.

Sadist: The individual in a sadomasochistic sexual relationship who takes the dominant role.

Sadomasochism (sade-o-MASS-o-kiz-um): Refers to sexual themes or activities involving bondage, pain, domination, or humiliation of one partner by the other.

Sample: A representative group of a population that is the focus of a scientific poll or study.

Satyriasis (sate-a-RYE-a-sus): A term sometimes used to describe erotomania in men.

Scabies (SKAY-beez): A skin disease caused by a mite that burrows under the skin to lay its eggs, causing redness and itching; transmitted by bodily contact that may or may not be sexual.

Scrotum (SKROTE-um): Pouch of skin in which the testes are contained.

Secondary dysfunction: A difficulty with sexual functioning that develops after some period of normal sexual functioning.

Selective reduction: The use of abortion techniques to reduce the number of fetuses when there are more than three in a pregnancy, thus increasing the chances of survival for the remaining fetuses.

Self-gratification: Giving oneself pleasure, as in masturbation; a term typically used today instead of more negative descriptors.

Self-pleasuring: Self-gratification; masturbation.

Semen (SEE-men): Mixture of fluids and sperm cells that is ejaculated through the penis.

Seminal vesicle (SEM-un-al): Gland at the end of each vas deferens that secretes a chemical that helps sperm to become mobile.

Seminiferous tubules (sem-a-NIF-a-rus): Tightly coiled tubules in the testes in which sperm cells are formed.

Sensate focus: Early phase of sex therapy treatment, in which the partners pleasure each other without employing direct stimulation of sex organs.

Sex addiction: Inability to regulate sexual behavior.

Sex therapist: Professional trained in the treatment of sexual dysfunctions.

Sexual aversion disorder: Avoidance of or exaggerated fears toward forms of sexual expression (sexual phobia).

Sexual differentiation: The developmental processes—biological, social, and psychological—that lead to different sexes or genders.

Sexual dysfunctions: Difficulties people have in achieving sexual arousal and in other stages of sexual response.

Sexual harassment: Unwanted sexual advances or coercion that can occur in the workplace or academic settings.

Sexual individuality: The unique set of sexual needs, orientations, fantasies, feelings, and activities that develops in each human being.

Sexual orientation: A person's erotic and emotional attraction toward and interest in members of one or both genders.

Sexual revolution: The changes in thinking about sexuality and sexual behavior in society that occurred in the 1960s and 1970s.

Sexual surrogates: Paid partners used during sex therapy with clients lacking their own partners; only rarely used today.

Sexually transmitted diseases (STDs): Various diseases transmitted by direct sexual contact.

Shaft: In the female, the longer body of the clitoris, containing erectile tissue; in the male, cylindrical base of penis that contains three columns of spongy tissue: two corpora cavernosa and a corpus spongiosum.

Shunga: Ancient scrolls used in Japan to instruct couples in sexual practices through the use of paintings.

Situational homosexuality: Deprivation homosexuality.

Skene's glands: Secretory cells located inside the female urethra.

Smegma: Thick, oily substance that may accumulate under the prepuce of the clitoris or penis.

Social constructionists: Those who believe that same-gender sexual orientation is at least partly the result of social and environmental factors.

Social learning theory: Suggests that human learning is influenced by observation of and identification with other people.

Social scripts: A complex set of learned responses to a particular situation that is formed by social influences.

Sodomy laws: Laws that, in some states, prohibit a variety of sexual behaviors, often described as deviate sexual intercourse. These laws are often enforced discriminatorily against particular groups, such as gay males.

Sonograms: Ultrasonic rays used to project a picture of internal structures such as the fetus; often used in conjunction with amniocentesis or fetal surgery.

Spectatoring: Term used by sex researchers William Masters and Virginia Johnson to describe self-consciousness and self-observation during sex.

Sperm: Reproductive cells produced in the testes; in fertilization, one sperm unites with an ovum.

Sperm banks: Centers that store frozen sperm for the purpose of artificial insemination.

Spermatocytes (sper-MAT-o-sites): Cells lining the seminiferous tubules from which sperm cells are produced.

Spermicidal jelly (cream): Sperm-killing chemical in a gel base or cream, used with other contraceptives such as diaphragms.

Spermicides: Chemicals that kill sperm; available as foams, creams, jellies, or implants in sponges or suppositories.

Sponge: A thick polyurethane disk that holds a spermicide and fits over the cervix to prevent conception.

Spontaneous abortion: Another term for miscarriage.

Staphylococcus aureus (staf-a-low-KAK-us): The bacteria that can cause toxic shock syndrome.

Statutory rape: A legal term used to indicate sexual activity when one partner is under the age of consent; in most states that age is 18.

STDs: Sexually transmitted diseases.

Sterilization: Rendering a person incapable of conceiving, usually by interrupting passage of the egg or sperm.

Straight: Slang term for heterosexual.

Streetwalkers: Female prostitutes who work on the streets.

Suppositories: Contraceptive devices designed to distribute their spermicide by melting or foaming in the vagina.

Syndrome (SIN-drome): A group of signs or symptoms that occur together and characterize a given condition.

Syphilis (SIF-uh-lus): Sexually transmitted disease (STD) characterized by four stages, beginning with the appearance of a chancre.

Systematic desensitization: Step-by-step approaches to unlearning tension-producing behaviors and developing new behavior patterns.

Testes (TEST-ees): Pair of male gonads that produce sperm and male hormones.

Testicular cancer: Malignancy on the testis that may be detected by testicular self-examination.

Testicular failure: Lack of sperm and/or hormone production by the testes.

Testosterone (tes-TAS-ter-one): Major male hormone produced by the testes; it helps to produce male secondary sex characteristics.

Testosterone replacement therapy: Administering testosterone injections to increase sexual interest or potency in older men; not considered safe for routine use.

Theoretical failure rate: A measure of how often a birth control method can be expected to fail when used without error or technical problems.

Thrush: A disease caused by a fungus and characterized by white patches in the oral cavity.

Toucherism: Gaining sexual gratification from the touching of an unknown person's body, such as on the buttocks or breasts.

Toxic shock syndrome (TSS): An acute disease characterized by fever and sore throat, and caused by normal bacteria in the vagina that are activated if tampons or contraceptive devices such as diaphragms or sponges are left in for long periods of time.

Transgenderists: People who live in clothing and roles considered appropriate for the opposite sex for sustained periods of time.

Transsexuals: People who feel as though they should have the body of the opposite sex.

Transvestism: Dressing in clothes considered appropriate for the other gender.

Transvestite: An individual who dresses in clothing and adopts mannerisms considered appropriate for the opposite sex.

Trichomoniasis (trik-uh-ma-NEE-uh-sis): A vaginal infection caused by the *Trichomonas* organism.

Troilism (TROY-i-lizm): Sexual activity shared by three people.

True hermaphrodite: A person who has one testis and one ovary. External appearance may vary.

Tubal ligation: A surgical cutting and tying of the fallopian tubes to induce permanent female sterilization.

Umbilical cord: The tubelike tissues and blood vessels originating at the embryo's navel that connect it to the placenta.

Urethra (yu-REE-thrah): Tube that passes from the urinary bladder to the outside of the body.

Urethral opening: Opening through which urine passes to the outside of the body.

Urophilia: Sexual arousal connected with urine or urination.

Uterus (YUTE-a-rus): Muscular organ of the female reproductive system; a fertilized egg implants itself within the uterus.

Vacuum curettage (kyur-a-TAZH): A method of induced abortion performed with a suction pump.

Vagina (vu-JI-na): Muscular canal in the female that is responsive to sexual arousal; it receives semen during heterosexual intercourse for reproduction.

Vaginal atresia (a-TREE-zha): Birth defect in which the vagina is absent or closed.

Vaginal atrophy: Shrinking and deterioration of vaginal lining, usually the result of low estrogen levels during aging.

Vaginal fistulae (FISH-cha-lee or -lie): Abnormal channels that can develop between the vagina and other internal organs.

Vaginismus (vaj-uh-NIZ-mus): Involuntary spasm of the outer vaginal musculature, making penetration of the vagina difficult or impossible.

Vaginitis (vaj-uh-NITE-us): General term for inflammation of the vagina.

Values: System of beliefs with which people view life and make decisions, including their sexual decisions.

Variation: A less pejorative term to describe nonconformity to accepted norms.

Varicose veins: Overexpanded blood vessels; can occur in veins surrounding the vagina.

Vas deferens: Tube that leads sperm upward from each testis to the seminal vesicles.

Vasa efferentia: Larger tubes within the testes, into which sperm move after being produced in the seminiferous tubules.

Vasectomy (va-SEK-ta-mee or vay-ZEK-ta-mee): A surgical cutting and tying of the vas deferens to induce permanent male sterilization.

Villi: Fingerlike projections of the chorion; they form a major part of the placenta.

Viral hepatitis: Inflammation of the liver caused by a virus.

Voyeurism (VOYE-yu-rizm): Sexual gratification from viewing others who are nude or who are engaging in sexual activities.

Vulva: External sex organs of the female, including the mons, major and minor lips, clitoris, and opening of the vagina.

Vulvovaginitis: General term for inflammation of the vulva and/or vagina.

Western blot: The test used to verify the presence of HIV antibodies already detected by the ELISA.

Wolffian ducts (WOOL-fee-an): Embryonic structures that develop into male sexual and reproductive organs if male hormones are present.

Yeast infection: A type of vaginitis caused by an overgrowth of a fungus normally found in an inactive state in the vagina.

Zero population growth: The point at which the world's population would stabilize, and there would be no further increase in the number of people on Earth. Birthrate and death rate become essentially equal.

Zona pellucida (ZO-nah pe-LOO-sa-da): The transparent, outer membrane of an ovum.

Zoophilia (zoo-a-FILL-ee-a): Bestiality.

Zygote: An ovum that has been fertilized by a sperm.

SOURCES

Sexuality Today, Fourth Edition, 1994. The Dushkin Publishing Group, Guilford, CT 06437.

Pregnancy, Childbirth, and Parenting (Wellness,) 1992. The Dushkin Publishing Group, Guilford, CT 06437.

(1995–1996)

Credits/ Acknowledgments

Cover design by Charles Vitelli

1. Sexuality and Society

Facing overview—Photo courtesy of Sandra Nicholas.

2. Sexual Biology, Behavior, and Orientation

Facing overview—Photo by AP/Wide World Photos.

3. Interpersonal Relationships

Facing overview—The Dushkin Publishing Group, Inc., photo by Pamela Carley.

4. Reproduction

Facing overview—Photo courtesy of the North Carolina Coalition on Adolescent Pregnancy. 115-116—Photo and illustration courtesy of Wisconsin Pharmacal Company. 118—World Bank photo by Curt Carnemark. 119—Photo by Wyeth-Ayerst Laboratories.

5. Sexuality Through the Life Cycle

Facing overview—Photo courtesy of Marcuss Oslander. 160— Photo by Nick Vaccaro.

6. Old/New Sexual Concerns

Facing overview—The Dushkin Publishing Group, Inc., photo by Pamela Carley.

PHOTOCOPY THIS PAGE!!!*

ANNUAL EDITIONS ARTICLE REVIEW FORM

■ NAME: _____ DATE: _____

■ TITLE AND NUMBER OF ARTICLE: _____

■ BRIEFLY STATE THE MAIN IDEA OF THIS ARTICLE: _____

_____

_____

_____

_____

■ LIST THREE IMPORTANT FACTS THAT THE AUTHOR USES TO SUPPORT THE MAIN IDEA:

_____

_____

_____

_____

_____

_____

■ WHAT INFORMATION OR IDEAS DISCUSSED IN THIS ARTICLE ARE ALSO DISCUSSED IN YOUR
TEXTBOOK OR OTHER READING YOU HAVE DONE? LIST THE TEXTBOOK CHAPTERS AND PAGE
NUMBERS:

_____

_____

_____

_____

_____

_____

■ LIST ANY EXAMPLES OF BIAS OR FAULTY REASONING THAT YOU FOUND IN THE ARTICLE:

_____

_____

_____

_____

■ LIST ANY NEW TERMS/CONCEPTS THAT WERE DISCUSSED IN THE ARTICLE AND WRITE A
SHORT DEFINITION:

_____

_____

_____

_____

*Your instructor may require you to use this Annual Editions Article Review Form in any number of ways:
for articles that are assigned, for extra credit, as a tool to assist in developing assigned papers, or simply
for your own reference. Even if it is not required, we encourage you to photocopy and use this page;
you'll find that reflecting on the articles will greatly enhance the information from your text.

ANNUAL EDITIONS: HUMAN SEXUALITY 95/96
Article Rating Form

Here is an opportunity for you to have direct input into the next revision of this volume. We would like you to rate each of the 59 articles listed below, using the following scale:

1. **Excellent: should definitely be retained**
2. **Above average: should probably be retained**
3. **Below average: should probably be deleted**
4. **Poor: should definitely be deleted**

Your ratings will play a vital part in the next revision. So please mail this prepaid form to us just as soon as you complete it.
Thanks for your help!

Annual Editions revisions depend on two major opinion sources: one is our Advisory Board, listed in the front of this volume, which works with us in scanning the thousands of articles published in the public press each year; the other is you—the person actually using the book. Please help us and the users of the next edition by completing the prepaid article rating form on this page and returning it to us. Thank you.

Rating	Article	Rating	Article
	1. A Closer Look at Sexuality Education and Japanese Youth		31. Men, Sex, and Parenthood in an Overpopulating World
	2. The New Generation		32. Reproductive Revolution Is Jolting Old Views
	3. Late-Night Talk Show: Giving Listeners What They Want		33. How Far Should We Push Mother Nature?
	4. Who Should Wear the Apron?		34. Abortion, Adoption, or a Baby?
	5. Family, Work, and Gender Equality: A Policy Comparison of Scandinavia, the United States, and the Former Soviet Union		35. How Should We Teach Our Children about Sex?
			36. What Do Girls See?
	6. When Is a Woman Not a Woman?		37. Coming Out in Care
	7. A Fine Line		38. Let the Games Begin: Sex and the *Not*-Thirtysomethings
	8. Man Troubles: Making Sense of the Men's Movement		39. 25 Ways to Make Your Marriage Sexier
	9. Feminism at the Crossroads		40. Sex: How to Keep It Hot after Kids Come Along
	10. Sex in America: Faithfulness in Marriage Is Overwhelming		41. Do Men Go Through Menopause?
	11. The New Sexual Revolution: Liberation at Last? Or the Same Old Mess?		42. What Doctors and Others Need to Know: Six Facts on Human Sexuality and Aging
	12. Male Hormone Molds Women, Too, in Mind and Body		43. Sexuality and Aging: What It Means to Be Sixty or Seventy or Eighty in the '90s
	13. Premature Ejaculation: Is It Really Psychogenic?		44. The Future of AIDS
	14. Etiology and Treatment of Early Ejaculation		45. Campuses Confront AIDS: Tapping the Vitality of Caring and Community
	15. The Truth about Women and Sex		46. The HIV Dating Game
	16. Sexual Arousal of College Students in Relation to Sex Experiences		47. AIDS Update: Women over 50
			48. Preventing STDs
	17. Psychotrends: Taking Stock of Tomorrow's Family and Sexuality		49. Breaking the Silence
	18. Born Gay?		50. Is *This* Sexual Harassment?
	19. The Power and the Pride		51. The Pain of Sexual Harassment after 50
	20. Sex and the Brain		52. When "No" Isn't Enough: How to Handle Sexual Harassment
	21. Hearts and Minefields		53. Sexual Correctness: Has It Gone Too Far?
	22. Lifting the Gay Ban		
	23. The Lessons of Love		54. Why Don't We Act Like the Opposite Sex?
	24. Motivating the Opposite Sex		
	25. Soul Mates		55. Men, Women, and Computers
	26. Adultery of the Heart		56. Women and Men: Can We Get Along? Should We Even Try?
	27. Forecast for Couples		57. It's a Jungle Out There, So Get Used to It!
	28. Choosing a Contraceptive		
	29. The Female Condom		58. The Blame Game
	30. The Philosopher's Stone: Contraception and Family Planning		59. Ending the Battle between the Sexes

(Continued on next page)

ABOUT YOU

Name_____ Date_____

Are you a teacher? ☐ Or student? ☐

Your School Name _____

Department _____

Address _____

City _____ State _____ Zip _____

School Telephone # _____

YOUR COMMENTS ARE IMPORTANT TO US!

Please fill in the following information:

For which course did you use this book? _____

Did you use a text with this Annual Edition? ☐ yes ☐ no

The title of the text? _____

What are your general reactions to the Annual Editions concept?

Have you read any particular articles recently that you think should be included in the next edition?

Are there any articles you feel should be replaced in the next edition? Why?

Are there other areas that you feel would utilize an Annual Edition?

May we contact you for editorial input?

May we quote you from above?

ANNUAL EDITIONS: HUMAN SEXUALITY 95/96